Art, Cult and Commerce
Japanese Cinema Since 2000

Art, Cult and Commerce

Japanese Cinema Since 2000

by

Mark Schilling

Awai Books
New York and Tokyo

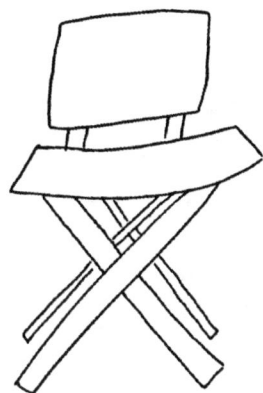

illustrations by Tomoki Watanabe

This book is dedicated to Lisa Schilling

for her help, support and always appreciated comments.

Published by Awai Books, an imprint of Awai LLC, New York. 1133 Broadway, Suite 708, New York, NY 10010

Book design by Aoi Ota

Paperback ISBN: 978-1-937220-09-9

An Awai Books Trade Paperback Original /// An Awai Books e-book Original.

First edition: November 2019

CONTENTS

INTRODUCTION

Introduction: why this book exists

This book is a serendipitous follow-up to "Contemporary Japanese Film," a 1999 collection of my reviews and interviews for "The Japan Times," as well as original essays on the state of the Japanese film industry. It covered an approximately ten-year period, from my start reviewing Japanese films in 1989.

The basic format – reviews, interviews and articles – is unchanged from "Contemporary Japanese Film," but this book covers about twice as much ground, the first two decades of the 21st century. Also proportions have shifted, with more interviews, fewer reviews per year. The new book focuses on the work of all the notable directors active in the current millennium, with the occasional omission. (I gave up trying to review every film released by the prolific Takashi Miike as they became more commercial and less interesting.)

The Japanese film industry is in some ways as unchanging as Mt. Fuji. So-called "production committees" – consortiums of film studios, TV networks and other media companies – continue to churn out films based on hit manga, bestselling novels and popular TV series in 2019, just as they did in 2009 and 1999 and 1989. And anime continues to regularly top the local box office, including series like "Doraemon" and "Pokemon" that have entertained kids for decades.

But today's industry is also quite different from the one of 2000. The number of Japanese films released grew from 282 in 2000 to 613 in 2018. Also, the total number of screens rose from 2,524 to 3,561 in the same period, while total box office increased from 170 billion yen to 222.5 billion yen. Finally, domestic films have taken a majority share of the box office every year since 2008.

These figures seem to point to a healthy and thriving market for Japanese films, but it's not that simple. Most of the money is made by a relatively small number of releases. And Toho, which produces, distributes and exhibits films — its theater chain is Japan's largest — claims the lion's share of the annual box office Best Ten year after year.

Meanwhile, the budgets of indie films, which make up the vast majority, have shrunk, as has the scale of their releases. To sum up, the rich are getting richer and the poor poorer.

Also, the film industry has become a follower rather a leader in Japan's pop culture hierarchy. For every Hayao Miyazaki, whose name lures millions to the theaters, dozens of directors-for-hire are cranking out commercial films that are last links in a media chain, for fans that know the original manga or bestseller, but rarely the makers of the film they happen to be watching. This is hardly a new development – Japanese movies began to lose their "king of entertainment" title with the broad diffusion of television in the early 1960s – but the number of Miyazaki-like auteurs known to the general public has grown hardly at all in the past two decades.

And the names of active Japanese directors well known outside Japan have changed little in that period: In addition to the indefatigable Miike, who became internationally notorious for his 1999 cult shocker "Audition," Hirokazu Koreeda, Naomi Kawase, Kiyoshi Kurosawa and Takeshi Kitano – the so-called "4K" group — made similar breakthroughs in the 1990s and have continued to represent Japanese cinema to the world to this day, while younger filmmakers struggle for recognition beyond Japan. Others, such one-time cyberpunk rebel Shinya Tsukamoto and veteran provocateur Sion Sono, have long had cult followings overseas though Tsukamoto, with his ventures into serious non-genre cinema, and Sono, with his successful segue to commercial filmmaking, no longer fit comfortably into the "cult director" box.

The lack of change in the "Japanese directors famous abroad" list is not due to the indifference of the 4K crowd – all have mentored the younger generation as a film school instructor (Kurosawa), the leader of a production company (Koreeda), the executive director of a film festival (Kawase) or the founder of a talent agency (Kitano). It also not true that younger filmmakers simply lack the talent of their elders: Directors such as Koji Fukada, Ryusuke Hamaguchi and Miwa Nishikawa have made some of the best Japanese films of the current millennium, while winning kudos abroad, if not yet the highest honors.

Instead blame can be apportioned to institutional inertia – festivals stick with certain favorites, even when their latest work is no longer quite up to snuff – and the tendency of foreign critics and fans to focus on a few familiar directorial names from an industry otherwise unfamiliar. Just as Akira Kurosawa, Yasujiro Ozu and Kenji Mizoguchi were once the sum and total of Japanese cinema to much of the outside world, the 4K group, together with Miike, Sono and Tsukamoto, have largely dominated overseas discussion of Japanese live-action films for decades.

In the world of anime the situation is somewhat different since foreign anime fans may rave about Miyazaki, but they also follow the work of such younger animators as Masaaki Yuasa, Mamoru Hosoda, Keiichi Hara and Makoto Shinkai, all of whom have moved to the industry forefront since 2000. When Shinkai's 2016 romantic fantasy "Your Name" became the highest-earning Japanese animation worldwide of all time, with a total gross of $358 million, even non-anime-fans abroad realized that one-time box office behemoth Miyazaki now had a rival.

But while foreign gatekeepers, with their coveted festival invitations and prizes, may still have clout – Koreeda's win of the Cannes Palm d'Or for his 2018 family drama "Shoplifters" propelled it to the box office stratosphere in Japan – young Japanese filmmakers now have other ways to grab attention, from crowd-funding campaigns to social media blitzes.

One is Shinichiro Ueda, director of "One Cut of the Dead," a comedy about a zombie film shoot that becomes "infected" by the real undead thing. Made for a budget of 3 million yen with the backing of Enbu Seminar, a school for aspiring actors and directors, "One Cut of the Dead" was cast with unknowns and had a publicity budget of zero. None of that mattered.

Following its international premiere at the Udine Far East Film Festival in April 2018, where the audience gave it a five-minute standing ovation, the film opened at two Tokyo theaters in June. Ueda, together with Enbu Seminar president Koji Ichihashi and members of the cast and crew, made frequent stage appearances and posted ceaselessly on social media. Celebrity endorsements, assiduously solicited by Ueda, also helped get the word out.

More importantly, the film was funny, heart-warming and, in its twist climax, inspiring. As rave followed rave on Twitter and screening after screening sold out, the film became news in the mass media – and a must-see event for ordinary filmgoers.

After mid-sized distributor Asmik Ace partnered with Enbu Seminar, which had first released the film, the number of screens quickly expanded, as did earnings. By the end of the year "One Cut of the Dead" had made over 3 billion yen – 1,000 times its budget – while demonstrating that proven properties, idol stars and big media ad spends are not needed to generate hits. Whether Ueda or anyone else can replicate this miracle is still a question mark, however.

Despite starvation incomes and uncertain futures, indie filmmakers like Ueda are turning out far more films now than they were at the millennium's start. And for all the negatives of micro budgets, such as limitations on story and theme (lots of coming-of-age films, not many historical dramas) they make it easier to recoup – or rather harder to disastrously fail. Ichihashi told this writer that "One Cut of the Dead" would have needed only 5,000 admissions to earn back its investment. (It finally exceeded the two million mark).

Meanwhile, streaming services such as Netflix and Amazon Prime have aggressively entered the Japanese market, but have yet to achieve a US-level of influence and impact. Instead Japan's five major networks, as well as big manga and book publishers, still exert more sway over the cultural conversation. And these networks and publishers still back the majority of films that lead the box office, year in and year out. By the same token, actors and their agencies may take pride in foreign film festival invitations and trophies, but they know that real fame and fortune comes from TV appearances be it in a sober-sided historical drama or a goofy variety show. The ultimate payoff, however, is the fat contract for serving as the face of a media ad campaign.

Also, the Japanese film industry is still highly insular by Western and even Asian standards, with most of its films aimed solely at the local audience, though since the turn of the millennium it has become more open to outside influences while more Japanese film investment and talent has flowed abroad.

Among internationally minded younger directors are Akio Fujimoto, who went to Myanmar to film his 2017 dysfunctional family drama "Passage of Life," Takeshi Fukunaga, who shot his 2015 migrant drama "Out of My Hand" in Liberia and New York, and Katsuya Tomita, who set his 2016 relationship drama "Bangkok Nites" in Thailand and Laos.

At home, Japanese film companies have been remaking more foreign and especially Asian films including "Sunny: Our Hearts Beat Together," Hitoshi One's reworking of a 2011 Korean female buddy movie, "You Are the Apple of My Eye," Yasuo Hasegawa's take on the 2011 Giddens Ko film about teen romance in Taiwan, and "Memoirs of a Murderer," Yu Irie's 2017 detective thriller based on the 2012 Korean hit "Confession of Murder."

Also, though not a remake, the 2018 "Ten Years Japan" was inspired by "Ten Years," a 2015 omnibus that speculated about the state of Hong Kong in ten years' time. Supervised by Hirokazu Koreeda, the film features segments by five young Japanese directors set in a near-future Japan.

Co-productions between Japanese and Asian partners have also been on the upswing. The biggest to date is "Legend of the Demon Cat," a historical fantasy directed by Chinese auteur Chen Kaige, but based on a novel by Mineo Yoneyama and starring Shota Sometani as the legendary monk Kukai. Backed by a consortium that included Kadokawa — the novel's publisher and the film's co-distributor – "Legend" earned $15 million in Japan following its February 2018 release, disappointing given its reported $200 budget.

This trend can only accelerate following the conclusion of a co-production treaty between Japan and China in May 2018. For Japanese filmmakers the treaty's big advantage is that co-produced films can avoid the quota China places on foreign film imports. But some Japanese films have both qualified for the quota and done excellent business in China, encouraging Japanese distributors to target the territory. The most spectacular example is Makoto Shinkai's "Your Name," which earned $81 million in China following its December 2016 release – an all-time record in the world's second largest film market.

Meanwhile, more non-Japanese actors, directors and producers are now working in the Japanese industry, while ascending its power structure. One is Welshman John Williams, who has been directing films in Japan for more twenty years, his most recent being his 2018 version of Kafka's "The Trial." Another is Canadian Jason Gray, who together with his wife Eiko Mizuno-Gray, produces cross-border films with name Japanese talents, including Kiyoshi Kurosawa for his set-in-Uzbekistan drama "To the Ends of the Earth." Still another is American actor Bryerly Long, who has worked with Koji Fukada on several films, most notably his 2015 dystopian sci-fi drama "Sayonara," starring as a dying woman being cared for by a robot in a dystopic near-future Japan.

All this ferment does not mean the Japanese film industry will ever open as widely to the world as Hollywood. Ultimately it exists to serve the domestic market first and foremost. And for reasons cultural and linguistic, native Japanese will always have significant advantages over non-Japanese in catering to that market.

But with freer exchanges of investment and talent come greater opportunities to not only make films that appeal beyond Japan's borders, but also for outsiders to work with their Japan counterparts, be it as a producer on an indie comedy or as a star in a commercial drama. And as Japan's population continues to age and decline, the local industry will continue to look for new ways to escape its demographic doom, with internationalization high on the list. The status quo is a recipe for senescence.

Still another trend signaling greater inclusion is the growth in the number of women directors since 2000. The pioneer was Naomi Kawase, who became a Cannes regular after winning the festival's Camera d'Or prize for new directors in 1997 for her debut fiction feature "Suzaku." A sui generis, stubbornly independent talent – she is based in her home prefecture of Nara, far the industry's power centers, while expressing her own aesthetic centered on nature and family – Kawase nonetheless opened the way for women filmmakers with a variety of outlooks and approaches.

At the top of the list is Miwa Nishikawa, who worked as an assistant director for Hirokazu Koreeda, but has since carved out her own directorial identity in taking aim at human duplicity ("Dear Doctor"), the elusiveness of truth ("Sway") and the potential for even serial liars to redeem themselves ("The Long Excuse"). She also has her own work style, starting with the writing of a novel, proceeding to a screenplay and finally to a film. Not surprisingly, the gaps between her films tend to be long.

More commercially minded, if equally individual, is Naoko Ogigami. After studying filmmaking at the University of Southern California, she targeted the domestic female audience with films about quirky heroines who discover their grooves in a foreign clime ("Kamome Diner"), an island resort ("Glasses") and by "renting" felines to strangers ("Rent-a-Cat"). But tiring of hearing that her hit films were a cinematic form of aromatherapy, she changed direction with "Close-Knit," a 2017 film about a transgender woman who dreams of raising her live-in boyfriend's neglected niece. The film garnered many overseas festival invitations and awards, including a Special Jury Prize at Berlin.

Despite this sort of critical and commercial success women are seldom hired to direct big commercial films. One reason: Many of their directors come from the world of TV drama, which is still largely a male preserve behind the camera, though the audience is mostly female. Also, TV drama has traditionally been a scriptwriter's medium – and many high-rated dramas have been scripted by women.

But not all films for mass audiences are directed by faceless journeymen from the TV ranks. Former "pink" (softcore porn) filmmaker Ryuichi Hiroki has become the industry's go-to director of romantic dramas, starting with his 2009 hit "April Story," while continuing to make much-praised indie films, such as the 2018 Fukushima-disaster-themed drama "Side Job." Meanwhile, one-time horror scripter ("Dark Water) Yoshihiro Nakamura has churned out commercial thrillers and mysteries, such "The Triumphant Return of General Rouge," while winning overseas fans for offbeat, ingeniously plotted films such as "Fish Story" (world-ending apocalypse averted by a punk rock song) and "See You Tomorrow, Everyone" (an agoraphobic guy pledges to spend his entire life in a housing project).

Also, Shinuke Sato has built his brand as a master of effects movies with such hits as "Gantz," "I Am a Hero" and "Inuyashiki." His latest film, "Kingdom," a period actioner filmed in China and Japan with all Japanese actors, is his first venture abroad. A more accepting (if highly competitive) destination for his talents, though, may be Hollywood.

Meanwhile, Kazuya Shiraishi has won acclaim for "Blood of Wolves," a gritty 2018 crime film starring Koji Yakusho as a roguish cop who works on both sides of the law. A major inspiration, according to Shiraishi himself, was Kinji Fukasaku, a maker of ground-breakingly realistic yakuza movies for Toei in the 1960s and 1970s.

Last year, Shiraishi also released "Dare to Stop Us," an affectionate, un-blinkered look at rebel filmmaker Koji Wakamatsu and his circle in his 1960s and 1970s heyday. A former assistant director to Wakamatsu, Shiraishi has inherited his mentor's scrappy, no-compromise mantle.

Similarly bringing his own style to commercial product is Hitoshi One, a TV director whose feature breakthrough was the 2011 "Moteki," a comedy about a nerdy guy (Mirai Moriyama) who suddenly and gloriously becomes attractive to women, celebrated in an exuberant song-and-dance number. In his subsequent films One has proven adept at combining laughs with sharp character portrayals and realistic details. For "Bakuman," a 2015 comedy about aspiring teenage manga artists, One and his crew meticulously recreated the famously cluttered office of "Shonen Jump" magazine, where much of the action is set.

The true king of comedy over the past two decades, however, is Shinobu Yaguchi, who started making films in the 1980s but had his first box office smash with "Waterboys," a 2001 comedy about a high school boy's synchro swim team. The film's zero-to-hero storyline became an industry template, but after directing "Swing Girls," a comedy about a high school girls' swing band, Yaguchi turned his fertile imagination to other themes. His 2016 "Survival Family," about an ordinary Tokyo family forced to live by their wits on the road during a worldwide power blackout, was funny, chilling and instructive.

While drama, action and comedy are flourishing genres domestically, horror has yet to produce successors to Kiyoshi Kurosawa ("Cure"), Hideo Nakata ("Ring") and Takashi Shimizu ("Ju-on: The Grudge"), all avatars for the worldwide J-horror boom of the late 1990s and early 2000s. Both Nakata and Shimizu went to Hollywood hoping to replicate their Japanese successes but have since returned home chastened, if still in demand. But neither has re-ascended to their respective professional peaks, now two decades or so the past.

Meanwhile, Kurosawa has continued to unsettle audiences with his unique atmospherics, which rely more on rustling curtains and ghostly figures in the background than CGI monsters. Also, he has diversified his themes and settings beyond J-horror genre limits, from the alien invasion of "Foreboding" to the Uzbekistanian backdrop of "To the Ends of the Earth." All this and more has found favor with foreign festival programmers, especially Cannes where Kurosawa has long been a regular.

His 4K colleagues have also enjoyed warm welcomes at the world's most prestigious festival though only Koreeda has won its biggest prize, the Palme d'Or, for his 2018 family drama "Shoplifters." Kurosawa received the Un Certain Regard Jury Prize for his 2008 dysfunctional family drama "Tokyo Sonata" and Kawase, the Cannes competition Jury Prize for her 2007 drama "The Mourning Forest." Only Kitano is still prize-less at Cannes: His 2010 gang actioner "Outrage" screened in competition, but left with only brutal reviews. He submitted his follow-up "Beyond Outrage" to the friendlier purviews of Venice.

Cannes has not totally neglected younger Japanese directors in its programs: Koji Fukada took the Un Certain Regard Jury prize for his 2016 dark family drama "Harmonium," while Ryosuke Hamaguchi's 2018 relationship drama "Asako I & II" screened in the Cannes competition to middling reviews. Even so, of the many non-4K filmmakers who have submitted their films to Cannes, relatively few have been chosen in the current millennium.

As frustrating as this may be for said filmmakers and their backers, they also have more ways to get their films out in the world than two decades ago. The Tokyo International Festival, Tokyo Filmex and the Yubari International Fantastic Film Festival have launched many local films by young directors on the international festival circuit. Meanwhile, the Udine Far East Film Festival in Udine, Italy, Nippon Connection in Frankfurt, Germany and the New York Asian Film Festival in New York are among the growing number of foreign festivals that have broadened their programming of Japanese films to the entire indie-to-commercial spectrum while welcoming young filmmakers.

These festivals – and the fans that flock to them – have encouraged DVD and theatrical distributors to expand their Japanese film lineups beyond a handful of big names or Asian Extreme cult items. The most proactive is Third Window Films, a UK-based DVD distributor that since 2005 has been releasing not only certified cult hits like "One Cut of the Dead," but also non-cultish comedies and dramas.

Company founder Adam Torel has branched out into producing, including "Lowlife Love," Eiji Uchida's 2015 black comedy set in the lower reaches of the Japanese film world, and "Love and Other Cults," Uchida's 2017 quirky coming-of-age movie starring Sairi Ito as a teenage "goddess" to a religious cult who evolves into a wised-up porn star. Both films traveled widely on the festival circuit and were released on DVD by Third Window.

But in January 2018, its sales agent shuttered its doors and Third Window faced a near-death crisis as distribution and cash flow slowed. Fortunately, together with fellow Asian film distributor Terracotta Distribution, the company signed a sales and distribution deal in March with the larger Arrow Films. Even so, the future of Third Window, as well as of all distributors of Japanese films on physical media, looks difficult if not yet hopelessly dim.

But whatever the fate of individual companies, Japanese films will no doubt continue to be seen abroad by a far wider audience than was thought possible when I started reviewing them for "The Japan Times" in 1989. Streaming, whether by legitimate rights holders or pirates of various sorts, will see to that.

Harder to predict is how the films themselves will change. Manga, bestseller and TV drama adaptations forever? Perhaps, since films have relied on other media for inspiration since their start. More films by members other disadvantaged groups, including LGBT filmmakers? Almost certainly yes, though Ryosuke Hashiguchi, an out gay director whose 2015 film "Three Stories of Love" won a shelfful of awards, is not just a stand-out but almost a stand-alone.

And will documentaries, which in Japan tend to play in tiny theaters for limited runs to coterie audiences, move closer to the mainstream, as they have in the West? Perhaps, but the signs are not encouraging. A crusading director with a sense of drama like Kazuo Hara, whose 2017 "Sennan Asbestos Disaster" was an incisive, in-depth look at a decades-long legal struggle by asbestos poisoning victims, bears comparison to Michael Moore, but Hara is not only working on smaller budgets but also facing higher barriers to the mass audience than his American counterpart. For one thing, the big Japanese distributors, fearful of controversy, hesitate to release Hara's sort of anti-establishment documentary.

They are, in fact, not fans of controversy in general — and neither is the industry as a whole. In everything from the Toho line-up to the nominees for the Japan Academy Prize – the local equivalent to the Oscars — films that aim to stir debate or inspire action are few, those that seek to simply entertain, many.

So it was somewhat of a surprise when Koreeda's "Shoplifters" did so well at the domestic box office in 2018, earning a splendiferous 4.6 billion yen – the fourth best total of the year for a Japanese film. "Shoplifters" was criticized for both its content — posters on rightist message boards complained that its focus on society's underbelly sullied Japan's image — and Koreeda's stance of distancing himself from the current government, exemplified by his rejection of an invitation from the culture minister following his Cannes win. Prime Minister Shinzo Abe returned the favor, issuing no public message of congratulations. But the thumbs down from Abe and others on the political right may have helped rather than hurt the film with moviegoers.

In any case, "Shoplifters" showed that controversy is not necessarily box office poison. The true test, however, will be when filmmakers whose name is not Koreeda try to follow in his footsteps with similarly challenging themes in otherwise mainstream films. Given the quickness of the industry to seize on a hit or trend, we will probably have less than a millennium to wait.

PART 1:
ESSAYS ON JAPANESE CINEMA

A quarter century of Japanese films in review

In 25 years of reviewing Japanese films and interviewing Japanese filmmakers for "The Japan Times," I've written 1 million words, give or take a few. This is clearly something no normal person would do, but for me it beats working. The idea that writing about movies could be as fun as watching them was first planted in my brain by Neal Gabler, a reviewer for my college newspaper. His verbally dexterous, madly cinephilic inspiration, famed critic for "The New Yorker" Pauline Kael, later became mine as well, but the possibility of doing what they did seemed vanishingly remote. I thus feel incredibly lucky to have had a chance to follow, however uncertainly, in their footsteps.

I filed my first film review for "The Japan Times" in July 1989, on "Bakayaro! 2: I Want to be Happy," a four-part omnibus comedy scripted by Yoshimitsu Morita. The choice was mine — I liked the films Morita had directed, and also liked the film's predecessor, "Bakayaro! I'm Plenty Mad," another four-part omnibus, made by four little-known young directors. One was Tetsuya Nakashima, who went on to direct the 2010 hit revenge drama "Confessions," selected as Japan's nominee for the best foreign film Oscar. Another was Yukihiko Tsutsumi, whose long list of hits includes "20th Century Boys," a 2008-9 sci-fi/fantasy trilogy.

Back then, however, few were hailing Nakashima, Tsutsumi and their fellow indie directors as future saviors of the Japanese film industry. The view shared by both industry insiders and reviewers of Japanese films for English-language publications was that Japanese cinema's best days were long behind it, and that the local film industry had little chance of beating back Hollywood.

I didn't disagree. Who was I — then a new reporter for a movie-trade magazine — to question the pessimism of veterans with decades of experience in the business? Also, my fellow reviewers, particularly the late Alan Booth, who wrote for "The Asahi Evening News," were gleefully (and, I was sure, rightly) skewering idol movies, monster epics and other films made from tired formulas by studio hacks. Shortly after I started, Booth finally threw in the towel, saying in a farewell column that he had enjoyed only a handful of the hundreds of films he had reviewed in the past decade.

As one of two reviewers for "The Japan Times" I wrote about foreign films, from "Jurassic Park" to "Farewell My Concubine," in addition to my Japanese film reviews. However, in the first half of the 1990s I shifted to reviewing only Japanese films. I was frustrated being the 1,000th reviewer to the latest Hollywood blockbuster or Cannes prize winner, usually months after their first release. I was also becoming more interested in the work of new Japanese directors.

First, a bit of background. In the '80s, Japan's bubble economy put more money in the pockets of young people, who used it to travel the world and otherwise indulge their curiosity in all things foreign, from food to films. This encouraged the rise of so-called mini theaters — art-house cinemas that screened the type of non-Hollywood foreign films ignored by major distributors. The Japanese film industry took notice of this trend and began developing a mini-theater sector for Japanese films.

One model was Art Theater Guild (ATG). Founded in 1961 with the backing of Toho, ATG became a producer, distributor and exhibitor of independent Japanese films, including those by New Wave auteurs such as Nagisa Oshima, Masahiro Shinoda and Yoshishige (later Kiju) Yoshida. At their peak during the '60s and '70s, ATG films were both daringly experimental and uncompromisingly uncommercial, but in the '80s the company backed young directors who provided the admixture of entertainment bubble-era audiences preferred. Yoshimitsu Morita's "The Family Game," from 1983, made a pointed critique of the Japanese middle-class family, but it was also a laugh-out-loud black comedy. ATG ceased production in 1986 and distribution in 1992.

Taking a more populist approach from the start was Argo Project, a company founded in 1990 by six independent producers. Argo produced, distributed and screened films in its two theaters in Tokyo and Osaka. But Argo directors also pushed boundaries of subject matter and treatment. One was Shun Nakahara, a former pink film (soft pornography) director whose first straight feature was the 1990 ensemble drama "The Cherry Orchard." Unfolding in real time in the two hours prior to the start of the titular Anton Chekhov play at a girls' high school, the film was both structurally bold and sharply observant, examining its four principal heroines without the usual seishun eiga (youth film) filters, including the ones for sexuality.

Audiences, unfortunately, did not come to these films in the numbers Argo hoped for (though I tried to do my bit for Argo films in "The Japan Times") and in 1993 Argo was restructured into a production and distribution company. When the Japanese economy stalled in the early '90s, other indie companies and producers — as well as the mini theaters that screened their films — faced an uncertain future as box-office revenues and production budgets declined.

Ironically, some of the most prominent new directors of the '90s, including Takeshi "Beat" Kitano, Takashi Miike, Hirokazu Koreeda and Kiyoshi Kurosawa, began with the support of major media companies, rather than struggling indie producers and distributors. Kitano distributed 1993's "Sonatine" — the blackly funny, starkly violent yakuza film that became his international breakthrough — through the Shochiku studio (and had a well-publicized falling out with its head of production, Kazuyoshi Okuyama, who thought the film was self-indulgent). Koreeda's feature debut "Maborosi" (Maboroshi no Hikari"), an elegiac drama of loss, mourning and recovery selected for the 1995 Venice Film Festival competition, was funded by TV Man Union, a large TV production house that employed the director.

Both Miike and Kurosawa launched their directorial careers via the V-Cinema line of straight-to-video genre films backed by Toei, another major producer and distributor. Coincidentally, V-Cinema is also celebrating its 25th anniversary this year. These directors initially flew under my radar since their early films were only given brief runs (if that) in theaters, though I did review Kurosawa's "Cure" — a 1997 thriller that made brilliant use of minimalistic atmospherics to impart a mood of creeping dread. I also praised Miike's "Gokudo Kuroshakai" ("Rainy Dog"), his 1998 action film about a Japanese hit man (Sho Aikawa) working for a Taiwanese gang. For all its coolly stylish violence, the film foregrounded the hero's feeling of isolation as well as a ungangsterlike tenderness toward a boy left by an ex-lover.

These and other talented directors who rose to prominence during the '90s — including Shunji Iwai, Jun Ichikawa, Makoto Shinozaki, Ryuichi Hiroki, Rokuro Mochizuki, Nobuhiro Suwa, Shinji Aoyama and Shinya Tsukamoto — convinced me that the doomsayers were wrong. Beginning with a 1994 essay for "Japan Quarterly" titled "New Signs of Life in Japanese Cinema," I wrote about what I called the New Wave of the 1990s. I wasn't the only one to notice this revival; British critic and programmer Tony Rayns was an early champion of Kitano, beginning with his 1989 debut "Violent Cop" ("Sono Otoko Kyobo ni Tsuki"). Even my mentor and friend Donald Richie, who had little good to say about Kitano and Miike, became a warm, early supporter of Koreeda, whom he regarded as a successor to the best traditions of Japanese humanist cinema.

But the annus mirabilis for Japanese films and the rising generation of filmmakers was 1997. Kitano won a Venice Golden Lion that year for his cop-on-a-mission drama "Hana-Bi." Also, Hayao Miyazaki, whose animations had regularly topped charts since his '89 hit "Kiki's Delivery Service," had a smash with "Princess Mononoke." Released in July by Toho, it became the most popular Japanese film of all time, with distributor revenues of ¥11.3 billion. Miyazaki ascended into a box-office stratosphere of his own, where he stayed to the end of his career. My praise for the film in "The Japan Times" (I called it a "highly individualized work of animation art") was but part of a large and swelling global chorus.

Also making a worldwide impact about the same time was the genre that came to be known as J-horror. The Japanese film industry had been making horror movies for decades, notably Nobuo Nakagawa's shockers of the '50s, which mixed elements of Western horror with local folklore about ghosts bent on revenge. Also, Kiyoshi Kurosawa was beginning to attract overseas attention for films that seemed to come from the director's own troubled psyche — or nightmares.

The true breakthrough, however, was "Ring" — Hideo Nakata's gripping psychological horror featuring a mysterious videotape that kills anyone who watches it. Released early in 1998, "Ring" was screened widely abroad and later remade in Hollywood, with Naomi Watts as a journalist trying to uncover the tape's deadly secret, a role played in the original by Nanako Matsushima. By the late '90s, the genres and directors that were to dominate overseas discussions of Japanese films through the first decade of the new millennium were already well established. Even today, surprisingly little has changed in everything from foreign fan adulation to serious critical opinion. This is similar to the once-frequent citing by foreign critics and journalists of Oshima and other New Wave directors as challengers to the Japanese film establishment, long after much of their work had taken a more commercial turn.

This was certainly true of Kitano, who lost his critically successful (i.e., box-office failure) reputation with the quirky period action film "Zatoichi" (2003). This entertaining reworking of an iconic series, featuring Kitano as a blind swordsman, earned a resounding ¥2.85 billion. Miike also evolved from a straight-to-video rebel to a reliable director of commercial hits, with his 2004 horror film "One Missed Call" being a crucial turning point. The films of both Kitano and Miike, however, were arguably more interesting when their budgets were smaller.

Since the turn of the millennium, the Japanese film world's biggest success story, at least in terms of international reputation, was Sion Sono. Once a maker of indie exercises in minimalism — see "The Room," from 1992, for a soporific example — Sono became a global cult sensation in the early 2000s with films that combined extreme violence, black humor, Christian imagery, Western classical music and other disparate elements in ways unpredictable and unique. His most entertaining film to date, 2008's "Love Exposure," took nearly four hours to tell its absurd story of an upskirt photographer who finds religion and romance. Sono's most bone-chilling is "Cold Fish," from 2010, which is mostly set in two tropical-fish stores, one run by a human piranha who preys on his weaker competitor. Directors, actors and other elements of most commercial releases in Japan are as interchangeable as Lego blocks, but it's hard to imagine anyone other than Sono conceiving and making these films.

Another big industry story of the current millennium is how those commercial films vanquished their Hollywood rivals in Japan, taking a majority market share for seven of the past eight years. The blockbuster films of Miyazaki are one big reason for this reversal of fortune. Another is the rise of franchises, usually based on a hit manga, novel or TV show, from which canny producers such as Fuji TV's Chihiro Kameyama have generated income through a variety of media streams. The so-called production committee system they developed, in which a consortium of companies share the risks and rewards, has been criticized as destructive to creativity but has also proven effective at drawing audiences.

More heartening to me is the emergence of a growing cohort of talented female directors over the past decade. Filmmakers such as Miwa Nishikawa, Mika Ninagawa, Yuki Tanada, Momoko Ando, Yong-hi Yang, Mipo Oh and Ayumi Sakamoto are not only finding a foothold in an industry that long marginalized women, but are also making some of Japan's most interesting films.

So, have the events of the past quarter-century proven the Japanese-films-are-dead crowd wrong? Not quite. Miyazaki's retirement from making feature films last September, as well as the lack of successors with anything approaching his box-office clout, left a market opening that has been brilliantly exploited by Disney's "Frozen," whose ¥25 billion gross makes it the third-highest earning film ever in Japan. Hollywood may yet re-establish the dominance it lost in Japan in the middle of the last decade.

Also, the newer directors who have received critical and popular acclaim in the past decade, including Nobuhiro Yamashita, Yoshihiro Nakamura and Mamoru Hosoda, have yet to attain the high international profile of directors such as Kitano or Miike. Instead, overseas attention has shifted to other regions and countries, such as Korea, whose bureaucrats and businessmen have made the export of Korean films and other popular culture a national priority in ways their Japanese counterparts are fumbling to duplicate. After all this time, I'm still curious to see how it plays out.

(September 3, 2014, "The Japan Times")

But will they spell my name right in the credits?

Hollywood and history have never gotten along very well. Hollywood makes entertainment and history has a tendency to be boringly complex, so accuracy and authenticity often get lost on the way to the multiplex. Some Hollywood filmmakers, however, are trying harder to get it right. One is Edward Zwick — the director of "Glory," "Legends of the Fall" and, as I learned by e-mail from Zwick himself in June 2002, "The Last Samurai." Zwick said he needed people in Japan — including me — to help him with the Japanese dialogue and the historical details. In short, to get as much as right as possible without sacrificing the drama.

He admitted to heavily fictionalizing the real-life rebellion, led by Saigo Takamori, that inspired the film. "I know full well that [the rebels] took up modern arms to overthrow the Tokugawa Shogunate, and that I've fudged the dates of conscription and the edicts," he wrote. "What I need is for you to highlight those descriptions, interactions, issues that will evoke giggles, if not outrage, from the Japanese audience."

This, he added was not just a commercial consideration, but "a personal and artistic one." "I honestly believe," he continued, "(and this is, perhaps, the greatest hubris of all) that I can present rounded, complex, heroic Japanese characters to an international audience; that 16-year-olds everywhere might just come away with an awakened sense that our history and that of Japan were intertwined long before Pearl Harbor; that words like honor and duty have resonance throughout history; and that the birth of the modern and such wrenching transitional moments have resonance and application to our present circumstance."

How could I not sign on? My first job was to send Zwick notes on the script. I picked a few nits, found a few howlers. One of the characters, a young samurai, was called Yoritomo, the name of a famous 12th-century warrior and statesman. It was, I wrote Zwick, like calling a character in a 19th-century British period drama "the Sheriff of Nottingham."

Zwick ditched the name. He also accepted several other of my suggestions, such as changing the martial art the samurai practice from karate — which was then known only in Okinawa — to jujitsu. Several others, however, he passed over in silence. In one scene, the rebel leader flings his sword end-over-end at an enemy. Couldn't happen, I said — samurai weren't knife throwers. But Zwick liked the image — and it stayed in.

More importantly, I found him a Japanese scriptwriter who could rewrite the Japanese-language script — a direct translation from the English that Zwick admitted was "horrible." Yo Takeyama is a period-drama veteran whose credits included the hit NHK drama "Hideyoshi" and the Kon Ichikawa film "Ka-chan." Meeting several times during the summer at a Tokyo ryokan hotel, we went over the script line by line. I had to make sure Takeyama's rewrites were reflected accurately in the English script. In several scenes, he not only corrected the Japanese, but added new dialogue, all of which had to be translated.

We also met with Zwick once in Tokyo. Late for our appointment in the lobby of the Imperial Hotel, I spotted a short, bearded, dark-haired man eyeing me through the crowd, rushed over to him and starting apologizing in Japanese.

It was Zwick. In my panic I had taken him for a vaguely Japanese-looking assistant — but he loved being mistaken for one of the natives. He also hit it off with Takeyama, a tall, lanky former actor who is an engaging raconteur and had the answers to his questions about Meiji court etiquette.

Early in September, Takeyama and I sent off our final batch of corrections. That October, we went to see the final day of shooting in Japan, which took place at a temple in Kyoto. When I got to the set, at around 7 in the morning, Zwick was preparing a simple scene — Tom Cruise walking up the temple steps with two foreign companions. Beaming, he introduced me to his star, who was being frantically fussed over by three women — one in charge of his Army officer costume, the other his makeup, the other his hair.

I had the odd feeling of stepping out of sleepy, early morning Japan and into a hyper-charged Hollywood moment. I noticed that Cruise had tiny crow's feet around his eyes, wore a retainer on his teeth and was looking straight at me with that trademark burning gaze. No surprise there; I had never expected Cruise to be laid back. I was even ready for the retainer, having read about it on an Internet gossip column.

What shocked me, first, however, was his height — I had thought it was about the same as mine. I later realized that his boots made him stand several centimeters taller.

Second, he really wanted to talk, asking me where I was from, how long I had been in Japan, and how I liked Tokyo. He was trying to put me at ease, but a normal conversation with Tom Cruise was my idea of the bizarre. Also, I had my own questions — but it wasn't the time or place to ask about Nicole.

That brief encounter, and a check, were two of my big rewards for being what Warner Brothers called a "Japanese script liaison." I also got several later revisions of our own revisions, considerately forwarded to me by Zwick's company, Samurai Pictures.

At least one of my ideas made it into the final version, as I recently saw at screening for the press: Samurai practicing jujitsu in the tall grass. In Hollywood, scriptwriters commonly get rewritten out of existence — I felt lucky to have, in some small way, survived.

(September 3, 2003, "The Japan Times")

Screen violence is in the eye of the beholder

Some people avoid violent films, while others watch little else. Professional movie reviewers, who may see hundreds of films annually, cannot afford to be so picky. If you are covering the Cannes Film Festival competition, as I did one year for the Screen International daily critics' poll, you cannot blow off a film on grounds of genre ("I hate action movies!"), sexual politics ("The director is a misogynist!") or body count ("A dozen dead in the trailer alone!"). In fact, the best films at Cannes or elsewhere often challenge, shock and disturb. If, as a critic, you can't handle that, you should find another line of work.

But as much as we claim to be hardened types who can take anything the screen throws at us, we critics are people too. We may not write about the death of our dogs or the breakup of our marriages or any other personal turmoil in our reviews, but there are inevitably echoes — or silences.

When I saw "Aku no Kyoten" ("Lesson of the Evil"), Takashi Miike's 2012 thriller about a psychotic teacher who takes a shotgun to his own class, it reminded me too uncomfortably of the then-recent mass slaying of teenagers in Norway by a lunatic who resembled Miike's hero in his deadly implacability. I wondered whether my anger about the real-life massacre might spill over into my review. Rather than raise my blood pressure, I simply skipped reviewing "Lesson of the Evil."

If I had been commissioned to cover the film at a festival, though, I would have reviewed it — while feeling that the 40-minute climax, in which the hero gleefully blasts frightened junior high kids into oblivion, one by one, was repulsive. Was Miike entirely to blame for that reaction? No, since it was influenced by an incident with no direct relationship to his film. Was he entirely innocent? No, since his obvious aim was exploitation.

That, I hoped, would be a rare case. After all, I had written a book on yakuza movies — not the most pacifistic of genres — and agreed with one of their makers, Kinji Fukasaku, when he told me that "Violence is a pillar of filmmaking." I did not want to head for the exits, mentally or physically, every time blood spilled on the screen.

And then my own blood spilled.

Walking to a hotel near Rome's Termini Station on the night of April 28, I was assaulted by two men. One second I was checking a building number, the next I was being punched in the face again and again, with relentless speed and force. The assailant, who had spiky blonde hair and was a head taller than me, gashed my forehead, broke my nose, broke or chipped five of my teeth and dislocated my jaw. His partner choked me unconscious, leaving a large hematoma on my throat, and grabbed my suitcase, computer bag and wallet, ripping my back pocket to shreds in the process.

But all I remember, after the punches began falling, is somehow breaking free and reeling down the street like a drunk, with blood streaming over my face, jacket and shirt. On the corner I found an outdoor cafe where the kind Middle-Eastern-looking manager swabbed my face with a towel and called the police. They arrived in less than five minutes, with an ambulance, but the assailants were gone.

Fortunately, I still had my passport, camera and cellphone, though nearly everything else of value had been stolen. After a three-hour wait in the emergency room of Rome's largest hospital, I had stitches put in my forehead, nose and scalp and then dozed in a chair until morning without further treatment. When my wife, who had just arrived from Japan, saw me in the ER, with my puffy, battered face and still wearing my blood-encrusted clothes, she looked as shocked as I had ever seen her — and I realized how badly I had been beaten. (The ER had no mirrors, even in the toilets.) I spent a total of six days in the hospital and, a month later, am recovering from my injuries, but at least know that I can still read, write and think.

So what do I think about violence in films now?

One friend jokingly compared my experience to a boxing match. It was nothing like a sport with gloves, a referee and a bell. It was a brutal assault with no rules or limits, save maybe murder. It was also like no movie that I had ever seen, though the police told me that the method — hit and grab — was not uncommon.

In the hospital I gained a new appreciation of Takeshi Kitano, who grew up in a tough Tokyo neighborhood and once told me that real-life street fights were brief. "One punch and it's over," he said. The many scenes in his films of one guy, usually played by Kitano himself, working over another now made more sense. I had once thought them stylized ego trips for their director; they now struck me as simple realism.

On the other hand, Iranian director Amir Naderi's Japan-made "Cut," whose masochistic hero (Hidetoshi Nishijima) allows himself to be hit in the face by gangsters for hours on end as a money-making ploy, now seemed like a puerile fantasy. When you're a kid, you might imagine yourself heroically taking blow after blow from a gang of foes, but for this adult a smashed-in face and a blacked-out mind were reality checks. I didn't spring back, ready for more; I just wanted it to stop.

Finally, researching this article, I found that nearly all the debate about violence in films revolves around whether on-screen mayhem encourages susceptible viewers to commit the real thing. What about the effect on the millions of victims of everything from domestic abuse to foreign wars? I suppose they're just expected to change the channel or buy a different theater ticket.

Can I, after a street mugging that half killed me, still stand to watch on-screen beatings of the realistic sort? The ultimate test will probably be the work of Quentin Tarantino, who has called violence in films "cool" but claims to hate it in real life. "When violence enters our world," he once told the Orlando Sentinel, "it kind of just rears its ugly head and we are not prepared for it." His example was a man slapping his wife in a restaurant, jolting the other customers including, I guess, Tarantino.

He might have made a more convincing case if he'd been a victim rather than a spectator, but I wouldn't wish my experience on him, not really. And I think I'll hold off renting "Django Unchained."

(June 7, 2013, "The Japan Times")

Takeshi Kitano: from manzai comic to giant of Japanese film

Many Japanese filmmakers try to promote their films and talents abroad but stumble more than they succeed: Either Cannes rejects their latest masterpiece or Hollywood turns down their J-horror script. By contrast, Takeshi Kitano, the country's most internationally celebrated director of the 1990s, began his rise almost by accident.

He also became a leader in what came to be called the Japanese New Wave of the 1990s — a movement of younger Japanese directors who rejected or subverted the conventions of their studio-trained forebears. Although some of these filmmakers — Jun Ichikawa, Shinji Somai, Sogo Ishii, Hitoshi Yazaki and Shinya Tsukamoto — began making films in the 1980s, it was in the Heisei Era that their careers and their visions truly began to take flight.

In the 1980s Kitano became a ubiquitous media presence, first as a member of the popular manzai (comic duo) act The Two Beats and then as a ferociously productive, fearlessly iconoclastic multitalent. As "Beat Takeshi," the stage name he adopted for his manzai career, he played the sharp-tongued wisecracker, be it as the emcee of a current affairs program or the titular host of "Takeshi's Castle," a wacky game show in which contestants competed in various challenges, with Kitano presiding as the mock castle's "count." The show aired from 1986 to 1989 on the TBS network and had a long afterlife through many international versions.

Alongside those roles, Kitano was acting on TV and launched his film career in earnest with a part as a brutal guard at a prisoner-of-war camp in Nagisa Oshima's "Merry Christmas, Mr. Lawrence" (1983).

"Whenever I appeared on screen, audiences would start laughing no matter what role I was in," Kitano told me in a 1998 interview. "It took about 15 years for audiences to regard me as something other than a comedian."

In 1989, producer Kazuyoshi Okuyama asked Kitano to direct "Violent Cop," a hard-boiled film veteran director Kinji Fukasaku had exited due to a scheduling conflict. Kitano accepted the offer, though he had never before sat in the director's chair." In the beginning I didn't know very much how to move the camera and so on," he commented in the same interview. "So ('Violent Cop') turned out looking like a souvenir snapshot."

But the critics raved about the film, which starred Kitano as a violence-prone, revenge-seeking cop, and he was awarded the best director prize at the Yokohama Film Festival. "Violent Cop" also earned ¥780 million at the box office — not bad for a first-time director, but perhaps a byproduct of Kitano's national celebrity.

In the films that followed, Kitano developed a distinctive style characterized by long takes, limited camera movement, dry humor, clipped dialogue and, in films featuring gangsters and cops, sudden outbursts of violence. Unlike the many Japanese directors who filmed tough guys rising phoenix-like after seemingly knockout blows in street fights or fatal wounds in gun battles, Kitano showed such characters falling like puppets whose strings had been cut.

This, Kitano once told me, was simple realism. Growing up in a tough Tokyo neighborhood, he said, he would often see yakuza fighting each other. "Usually it would be over in one punch," he added.

In his films, Kitano usually took the starring role, be it as the psychotic gangster in "Boiling Point" (1990) or the sardonic gang subboss in "Sonatine" (1993), and was usually the one delivering the blows. Call it directorial ego-tripping, but Kitano was a strong on-screen presence: cool but intense, stoic but volatile. After a 1994 scooter accident that nearly killed him, his damaged face served as a mask that could frighten or intimidate, though his puckish sense of humor never left him.

Abroad, however, Kitano and his films were largely unknown until "Sonatine" screened in the Un Certain Regard section of the 1993 Cannes Film Festival and in that year's London Film Festival.

Some viewers were unimpressed. French star Alain Delon complained that "(Kitano) is not an actor — he only has three facial expressions," while others praised Kitano's film about a gang war in Okinawa, which mixed comedy (gangsters sumo wrestling on a beach) and violence (Kitano's mad dog character taking out an entire banquet hall of gangsters with an assault rifle) in ways that were fresh and disturbing. Kitano acquired an enthusiastic overseas following, including director

Quentin Tarantino, who later released the film on his own DVD label.

At home, though, "Sonatine" was a flop, earning back less than one-fifth of its ¥500 million budget, although composer Joe Hisaishi, who would become a frequent Kitano collaborator, received a Japan Academy Prize for his minimalist score.

Kitano next released "Getting Any?" (1995), a goofball comedy about the quest of the halfwit hero, played by Kitano disciple Minoru Iizuka (better known as Dankan), to have sex by any means necessary, and "Kids Return" (1996), a poignant drama about two buddies who drop out of high school — one to become a boxer, the other a gangster — but are held back by their personal demons.

With his seventh film, "Hana-Bi," Kitano broke free of the "cult director" label and ascended to the upper echelon of international cinema. A spare, violent, elegiac drama about a cop (Kitano) who goes rogue after his partner (Ren Osugi) is half-paralyzed by a gangster's bullet, "Hana-Bi" won the Golden Lion prize at the 1997 Venice Film Festival.

This accolade, which had last been awarded to a Japanese film in 1958 (Hiroshi Inagaki's "Rickshaw Man"), made Kitano a globally celebrated auteur, while raising his critical stock at home. "Kinema Junpo" magazine's critics' poll named "Hana-Bi" the best Japanese film of 1998 and Akira Kurosawa included it in his list of 100 best films of all time — a symbolic passing of the torch from a giant of Japanese cinema's Golden Age to the Heisei Era's now-leading director.

Kitano's own assessment of the film was more modest. Comparing "Hana-Bi" to an entrance exam for a public university, he told me, "I think I scored an average of 60 points on all the subjects and passed."

That has since proven to be his highest score, at least as far as international awards go. Several of his later films were selected for Cannes and Venice, but none walked away with the biggest prizes.

Kitano finally hit the box-office jackpot with "The Blind Swordsman: Zatoichi," his 2003 take on the Zatoichi franchise about a wandering blind swordsman. With Kitano playing the blonde-haired lead, this quirky, action-packed film earned ¥2.85 billion — a career high and the fifth-best haul among domestic releases that year.

And though his one attempt at an "international" film — the 2001 yakuza-goes-to-LA actioner "Brother" — was a commercial disappointment, Kitano found more success with the "Outrage" trilogy about gang wars with high body counts. The final installment, 2017's "Outrage Coda," which starred Kitano as an old-school gangster who kills with all the emotion of a roach exterminator, made a respectable ¥1.59 billion.

It also recycled familiar tropes from earlier Kitano films, including the take-no-prisoners persona of its hero.

In recent years others have contested Kitano's crown as Japan's most eminent working director, with Hirokazu Koreeda arguably overtaking him by winning the Cannes Palme d'Or for his 2018 family drama, "Shoplifters."

"(Kitano) is still a filmmaker worth following," said Aaron Gerow, a Yale University professor and Japanese film scholar who wrote a 2008 book on the filmmaker. "But one doesn't see him leading Japanese cinema like he used to, and fewer young filmmakers appear who want to emulate his recent work. He is not radically questioning Japanese film like he did before, and thus his work doesn't speak on a meta-level like it used to."

In other words, don't expect a Palme d'Or to grace Kitano's trophy case anytime soon. But no one can take away that Golden Lion.

(March 13, 2019, "The Japan Times")

Sharing films with a master critic

Donald Richie was my friend and mentor for more than 20 years and my inspiration before that. When I was preparing to come to Japan for the first time in 1975, I read many books about the place, but Donald's masterpiece "The Inland Sea" was the one that entranced me. My first long trip after my arrival was to — where else? — the Inland Sea, with the woman who would become my wife.

I didn't meet Donald until 1991, however. I had been writing film reviews for "The Japan Times" for about two years, with him very much in mind, when he sent me a complimentary note about one — my first-ever fan letter. I was over the moon: My hero had validated me, though he was similarly generous with many other younger film writers and scholars, I was later to realize. Donald was hardly a saint, but territoriality and the competitiveness that goes with it were foreign to his makeup. (What did the writer of "The Films of Akira Kurosawa" and "Ozu: His Life and Films," as well as other seminal texts on Japanese cinema, have to fear from the latest successor to his old reviewing gig?)

Not long after, we shared a bullet train from Tokyo to Odawara: The then editor of "The Japan Times Weekly" had invited us to his apartment there for a contributors' party. The thought of boring the author of "The Inland Sea" on a long train ride terrified me, but Donald immediately put me at ease and I found, to my relief and delight, that we shared more than a thing for Kurosawa and Ozu (he rated the latter higher than the former; I at the time, the opposite). We were both from small-town Ohio (he Lima, me Zaneville), were both left-handed (though he had been "corrected" out of it as a child, to his regret) and, more importantly, could make each other laugh with wisecracks, though his came out sounding like epigrams.

He had little regard for many of the New Wave directors of the 1990s — he cordially despised the oeuvre of Takashi Miike and Takeshi Kitano — but went with me to many screenings of new Japanese films, and not only out of a desire to keep up: For several years he wrote reviews for "The International Herald Tribune" and would show me clippings when we met. We were seldom completely out of synch on any given film, including the rare ones he felt came up to his standards.

We also suffered together through the bad ones, with Donald popping breath mints at a faster rate than usual to fend off sleep, not always successfully. Once at a screening of a ponderous indie film, our heads were both drooping as the lights went up and I recognized the young director, sitting in the same aisle. At the door he anxiously solicited Donald's opinion. "The black-and-white photography was superb," he told Sion Sono in familiar Japanese. "Who was your cameraman?"

"He knows I hated it," Donald said with a chuckle as we walked out. "That's the worst thing you can tell a director, isn't it? 'I liked the cinematography.'"

On the other hand, when we saw Hirokazu Koreeda's 1998 life-after-death fantasy "Wandafuru Raifu" at the Imagica screening room in Gotanda, the mints stayed in his pocket. At the end we looked at each other and smiled — words were unnecessary. Again we met the director at the door, but this time Donald introduced himself and exchanged name cards. Koreeda knew who Donald was — this was not a given with directors of his generation — and was suitably impressed when he praised the film warmly. "One thing, though," Donald added. "You shouldn't use 'Wonderful Life' as the English title. People will confuse it with the Frank Capra film." Heeding Donald's warning, Koreeda came up with the English title "After Life" and thus began a friendship that became Donald's closest with any young Japanese director.

I also often attended private film screenings at his small apartment on the eighth floor of a building overlooking Shinobazu Pond in Ueno. ("It's as close as Tokyo comes to Central Park," he told me.) Sometimes it was just the two of us, sometimes a small group of friends. (Four, including Donald, was usually the limit given the size of his dining room/living room/bedroom.)

He typically began the festivities with a simple, but delicious, meal he had prepared himself, Japanese-style curry and a green salad being two favorites. The film, selected in advance by Donald, was usually by the European and Asian auteurs he considered the crème de la crème, such as Robert Bresson, Andrei Tarkovsky and Apichatpong Weerasethakul, though he would occasionally show something more cultish and obscure. Carl Theodor Dreyer's "Vampyr," which he thought the best of the horror genre, was about as close as he came to revisiting the films of his youth; nostalgic for old Hollywood he was not.

His screen was only an old television that fit into his closet, unconnected to a TV antenna, but while the film was playing, he gave it his absolute attention (with never a breath mint in sight). Given my own dissolute home movie-watching habits, sitting upright for two hours on one of his straight-backed chairs was not easy, but I came to appreciate his style of devotion to and respect for the cinema he loved. The film over and the lights on, we could truly discuss because we had truly seen. He was my only film school — and the best I could ever have.

(February 24, 2013, "The Japan Times")

Re-examining Yasujiro Ozu on film

Yasujiro Ozu once had a reputation for making films only other Japanese could understand.

His studio bosses believed overseas audiences wanted the exoticism of samurai and geisha, not Ozu's quietly realistic dramas about contemporary middle-class families.

This explains the reluctance of Ozu's studio, Shochiku, to export his films while he was at the height of his powers, despite the burgeoning outside interest in Japanese cinema sparked by the international success of Akira Kurosawa's 1950 period drama, "Rashomon." Indeed, Ozu's postwar classics only began to penetrate Western cinephile consciousness in the 1960s, with a retrospective of five films curated by critic Donald Richie for the 1963 Berlin Film Festival opening many eyes.

Now, 50 years after Ozu's passing (He died on Dec. 12, 1963, 60 years to the day from his birth in what is presently Tokyo's Koto Ward), not only pioneering critics such as Richie, Noel Burch and David Bordwell, but also generations of scholars, filmmakers and fans have examined, celebrated and canonized his films. In a 2012 poll of leading directors and critics by "Sight and Sound" magazine to select the best films of all time, Ozu's 1953 "Tokyo Story" was voted No. 1 by directors and No. 3 by critics, after "Vertigo" and "Citizen Kane." If this poll result is anything to go by, Ozu is obscure no longer.

What accounts for this amazing rise in recognition, if one too late for Ozu himself to enjoy? After directing his first film, a now-lost period drama, at the age of 24, Ozu made comedies, melodramas and even a gangster film, the 1933 "Dragnet Girl." But as he entered his 30s, he began to develop and refine the style and themes for which he became internationally renowned.

Everyone from Richie to first-year film students has analyzed his work, although the focus is usually on his postwar films, which are considered the most "Ozu-esque." These typically revolve around families in the throes of dissolution or disaffection, with a father scheming to marry off his adult daughter ("Late Spring") or adult children who view visiting parents as a burden ("Tokyo Story"). However, the shouting, caterwauling and other melodramatics of the standard hōmu dorama (TV family drama) are conspicuous by their absence. Instead, strong emotions only briefly roil the calm surface of everyday life with a piercing word, glance or gesture.

In filming his families, Ozu preferred interiors, particularly in Japanese-style houses. He would shoot from a low position, with the camera typically set at the height of a person sitting on a tatami mat in order to give an impression of intimacy.

He also used the camera in ways that defied imported-from-Hollywood convention, such as shooting characters engaged in conversation in alternating frontal head-and-shoulder shots, instead of the more standard over-the-shoulder shots. But as strange as these shots might at first seem to the uninitiated, they gave audiences the feeling of looking directly into the hearts of the characters, past masks of politeness.

Ozu also disliked fades and dissolves. Instead, he preferred straight cuts to transition between scenes, using postcardlike shots of office buildings, alleyways and other mundane subjects that gave audiences a precise, layered introduction to the setting for the upcoming action.

In contrast to standard industry practice, Ozu refrained from underlining emotions with dramatic close-ups and surging background music. Instead, he typically shot such scenes from a distance and confined music to transitions, while using it to offset or contrast the mood of the characters. Thus, lively tunes followed sad scenes.

Ozu would similarly leave out what other directors considered to be obligatory dramatic highlights such as weddings and funerals. Rather than drain his story of drama, however, these omissions helped stir the imagination and kept the audience's focus on what Ozu truly considered important.

In "Late Spring," for example, he focused on, not the wedding ceremony of Noriko (Setsuko Hara), which is never shown, but instead the loneliness her aging father (Chishu Ryu) would feel in her absence.

How did Ozu himself think about filmmaking, including his own innovations (or, as unsympathetic contemporaries regarded them, eccentricities)? One often-quoted statement suggests that he viewed himself as a humble craftsman.

"I only know how to make tofu," Ozu said. "I can make fried tofu, boiled tofu, stuffed tofu. Cutlets and other fancy stuff, that's for other directors."

He may have truly felt this, but he was also no cinematic naïf. Starting as a young assistant director at Shochiku, Ozu diligently studied films and enthusiastically discussed them with his peers. He also wrote his thoughts on cinema in journals (now published in an 800-page volume) as well as in essays for "Kinema Junpo" magazine and other publications. Translating a collection of these pieces, I found a far more opinionated side of Ozu than the "tofu" comment suggests.

One fundamental view — stated and restated in countless essays — is that, unlike written language, films have nothing resembling a "grammar."

Thomas Kurihara, a Hollywood-trained director who was active in the early 1920s, dogmatically believed directors should follow fixed "grammar rules" in every aspect of filmmaking.

Ozu couldn't have disagreed more strongly.

"There's no one form you have to follow," he wrote. "When an outstanding film appears, it creates its own special grammar. If you shoot a film just as you like, you can see that."

This made Ozu an independently minded exception in the hierarchical, formula-driven domestic film industry, despite his image in later years as a conservative director resistant to innovation or change. This defiant streak manifested itself early. In an autobiographical sketch published in 1950, Ozu reminisced about a tyrannical director who forced him and other assistants to toil away for long hours with few breaks.

"The work was so hard that I didn't even have time to smoke and was always famished," Ozu wrote. "My only pleasure was eating."

Sitting in the studio cafeteria after a particularly grueling day, Ozu was anticipating a delicious plate of curry rice when the director strolled in, sat down and was served first. Outraged, Ozu shouted, "Wait your turn!" and nearly got into a fight with a heckler who mocked his presumption. Instead of being punished for his rude behavior, Ozu was rewarded by studio boss Shiro Kido with his first directing assignment. "Perhaps he thought I was an amusing character," Ozu joked.

Kido continued to support this self-described "contrary" director, even when his films did not do so well at the box office. One reason is that Ozu's family dramas exemplified the sort of humanistic cinema that Kido championed, though they may have lacked the uplifting content he preferred. Ozu responded with organizational loyalty — "I'm with Shochiku and Shochiku employees are all my friends, so I have to think of what's good for Shochiku," he later wrote — while going his own artistic way.

That often meant thinking afresh about methods that had become standard industry practice.

One example Ozu himself analyzes in great detail is the filming of two characters in conversation. In order for the audience to understand at a glance that both characters are talking to each other, convention dictates that the camera should first shoot one character so as to be looking left (or right) on the screen and then shoot the other character so as to be looking right (or left). In filming these two shots, the camera should not cross an invisible line that links the eyes of the characters.

Ozu, however, blatantly violated this "eyeline rule." That is, he shot both characters so that they seemed to face the same way on the screen, while moving the camera across the eyeline.

When Ozu screened his first talkie, "The Only Son," his fellow directors at Shochiku criticized his approach.

One, Hiroshi Inagaki, found his unorthodox shooting style "strange only in the beginning," Ozu wrote, "but later he paid it no mind. After that I did not encounter any objections to it."

Ozu did admit, however, that "I am probably the only one in the world who films this way."

Early on in his career, Ozu also discarded the then-common practice of using a fade in to signify the start of a scene and a fade out to mark the end of it. The fade in and fade out, he noted, were "nothing more than mechanical functions of the movie camera," despite claims that they were proper film grammar.

"Inserting them into films," Ozu wrote, "is like sticking extra sheets of paper into the pages of a book before starting to read the first chapter."

While disregarding what he considered to be worthless "grammar rules," Ozu was slow to adopt new technologies. He did not make his first talkie until 1936 ("The Only Son"), his first color film until 1958 ("Equinox Flower") and resisted studio pressure to shoot in the wide-screen format until the end. "Given the short time I have left on this Earth," he wrote in 1963, "I don't want to shoot a film as though I were peering out from a mailbox slot."

This wasn't to say, however, that he didn't welcome fresh ideas, wherever they might have come from. "When I happen to see a film by a newcomer from Mexico or Italy or by an amateur who has suddenly become a studio director, I feel a surprising freshness in their methods," he wrote in 1958. He was also "happy about news from France about a new crop of filmmakers in their 20s shooting controversial films."

The directors of French New Wave of the late '50s and '60s were soon to have their counterparts in a Shochiku-sponsored new generation of young lions such as Masahiro Shinoda, Kiju Yoshida and Nagisa Oshima, all of whom rebelled against Kido and Ozu's brand of humanistic films focusing on the middle class. Instead they and other filmmakers of the postwar era — including Ozu's former assistant director, Shohei Imamura — explored society's margins, from the pathologically violent to the politically radical.

Ozu, however, continued to manufacture his own brand of "tofu" to the end.

"I believe that a good film leaves a good aftertaste," he wrote for the Chunichi Shimbun in 1962.

"A lot of people now equate drama with sensational incident, such as someone getting killed. But that's not drama; it's a freak occurrence," he wrote. "Instead I think drama is something without sensational incident, something you can't easily put into words, with the characters saying everyday things like 'Is that right?' 'Yes, it is,' 'So that's what happened.'"

His genius was to transform everyday things into eternal truths, in ways immediately recognizable as utterly his own.

(December 7, 2013, "The Japan Times")

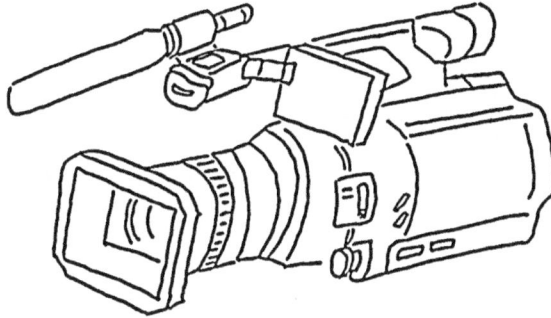

35

Donald Richie's films

Film critics often have a not-so-secret desire to get behind the camera themselves. Francois Truffaut, Jean-Luc Godard and Peter Bogdanovich are among those who made the leap successfully, though Bogdanovich returned to writing after his directing career faltered in the mid-'70s. Even thumbs-up critic Roger Ebert once ventured a screenplay, for "Beyond the Valley of the Dolls." Wrote friend Mike Royko after a screening: "Every young man is entitled to one big mistake." Donald Richie has worn the label of "foremost foreign authority on Japanese cinema" for decades. Arriving in Japan in 1947 as a 23-year-old soldier with the Occupation forces, Richie has lived here, with breaks for work and study, ever since. A film buff since childhood, he witnessed Japanese cinema's Golden Age — and its subsequent decline — first-hand, while getting to know many of its leading figures. He wrote pioneering studies on Akira Kurosawa and Yasujiro Ozu, as well as a history of Japanese cinema with Joseph Anderson that, since its publication in 1959, has come to be regarded as a standard text. Today he teaches a course on Ozu at the Tokyo campus of Temple University and reviews Japanese films for the International Herald Tribune. He has also been, at various stages of his career, a poet, short-story writer, novelist, composer and — no surprise — filmmaker.

According to his filmography, he has made 39 short films, from a 1941 boyhood effort called "Small Town Sunday," shot with an 8-mm camera given to him by his parents, to a 1975 documentary on Kurosawa, with all but three dating from the '50s and '60s. Before first seeing them, at Haiyu-za in Roppongi, I imagined something Ozu-esque. I imagined wrong — the Ozu influence is there, but Richie's work is too individual and diverse to mark him as a disciple of anyone, let alone Ofuna's master of domestic drama. First, there are few, if any, concessions to commercial filmmaking conventions or mass-audience tastes. Though all his films are without dialogue or even intertitles, thus making them easily screenable from Ueno to Ulan Bator, they are also free of censorship, internal or otherwise. They are, in a word, dangerous to impressionable minds, offering not only frontal male nudity ("Atami Blues"), a masturbating youth ("Boy With Cat"), grappling gay lovers ("Dead Youth") and gourmet cannibalism ("Five Filosophical Fables") — now relatively acceptable stuff in mainstream films — but still-shocking glimpses of animal sacrifice ("Wargames") and ritual castration ("Cybele").

Describing his first experience of seeing Richie's films at a Tokyo theater in 1960, artist Tadanori Yokoo later wrote, "I thought then that the man who made them must have been a devil." Yokoo became a fervent fan, a personal friend and a contributor to the program for the retrospective of Richie's films that Image Forum is screening at its Shibuya theater. Richie's films, however, are more than the sum of their shock value — a faded currency indeed. Instead, they are free-ranging investigations into the aesthetics of cinema, black comic looks at human nature, unblinking gazes into the abyss. In form they range from the Imagist poetry of "Dead Youth," with its provocative vision of beauty in death, to the idyllic, erotic haiku of "Boy With Cat." Some, such as "Life" and "Five Filosophical Fables," are laugh-out-loud funny in the best slapstick tradition, while others — such as the 1962 "Wargames," in which a beachside scrap between young boys ends in the death of a goat — are thought-provoking and soul-chilling. Their images seem to come from not only the director's dreams, but the deep memory of humanity, in all its archaic wonder and terror.

These films are very much of their time, especially the '60s, when artists such as Yokoo, Nagisa Oshima, Yukio Mishima, Shuji Terayama and Yoko Ono were challenging orthodoxies, pushing boundaries and moving beyond Japan to the world. Richie's work was, for many of these artists, a window to the outside, a path forward. Through his films, with their borderless aesthetic and sensibility, their insistence on personal honesty and artistic freedom to the limits of society's tolerance and beyond, one can glimpse the later erotic transgressions of "The Empire of the Senses" ("Ai no Corrida," 1976) or the dark satire of "The Funeral" ("Ososhiki," 1984). Though it's an exaggeration to say that where Richie led, others followed, he laid a groundwork and created an atmosphere or, as Yokoo might put it, injected his audiences with the poison of an art that undermined and inspired, upset and liberated. The ferment of that time has long since subsided. The avant-garde affronts of yesterday can be seen in the mall multiplex today, while the cutting-edge young filmmakers are more influenced by anime and arcade games than the films of Robert Bresson and Maya Deren. Nonetheless, Richie's films stubbornly retain their power, passing their special poison to a new generation. Instead of a youthful "big mistake," they remain central to an understanding of not only Richie's protean artistry, but a generation of Japanese cinema.

(March 13, 2001, "The Japan Times")

New Era Launches on Japanese Screens

As a new imperial era begins in Japan, the local film industry is enjoying a renaissance, following a long period of decline, but the digital age is presenting fresh challenges. With the abdication of Emperor Akihito on April 30, 2019, Japan entered a new era — and not only figuratively. The country assigns a name to each imperial era that corresponds to the reign of the country's emperor. When Akihito took over in 1989, the Heisei Era began, and the ascension to the throne of his son, Naruhito, on May 1, heralded the start of the Reiwa Era.

The months leading up to this transition have been a time of national stocktaking, with the movie industry being no exception. In April, "Kinema Junpo," Japan's oldest film magazine, published a special issue looking back at Japanese cinema in the Heisei Era, and the Showa Era that preceded it (1926-1989). In 1989, the Japanese film industry was in the grip of a long decline that started with the widespread diffusion of television in the early 1960s. Admissions for the year totaled 143.5 million, compared with the post-war peak of 1.099 billion in 1957. Meanwhile, local films claimed a 46.6% market share, down from 78.3% in 1960, according to industry organization Eiren (the Motion Picture Producers Assn. of Japan).

Early in the Heisei Era, industry oblivion seemed more likely than resurrection. Younger fans, save for the kids who flocked to popular anime, overwhelmingly preferred Hollywood product. Made for a fraction of the budgets, Japanese commercial films struggled to compete.

What a difference three decades make. In 2018, admissions grew to 169 million while Japanese films claimed a 55% market share, the 11th straight time they had beaten their foreign rivals. Also that same year the number of Japanese film releases rose to 613 and the number of screens to 3,561. Comparable figures for 1989 were 255 and 1,912, respectively. So far this year, Japanese movies have dominated the top of the local box office with home-grown films like "Doraemon: Nobita's Chronicle of the Moon Exploration," "Masquerade Hotel" and "Detective Conan: The Fist of Blue Sapphire" outgunning the Hollywood opposition.

According to veteran industry analyst Hiroo Otaka, a key factor in the industry's recovery was the multiplex boom that began in 1993 with the opening of Japan's first true cinema complex. "The big transition to multiplexes was an epoch-making development," he says. "With the exception of arthouses, 26 years later we're in an era when 'movie theater' means 'multiplex.'"

The current system of multiplexes screening large numbers of films in a variety of formats "has won the strong support of fans, especially young ones," Otaka notes. It has also spelled the demise of the "uniquely Japanese" block-booking system in which studios forced the theaters in their chains to screen their films on a fixed schedule.

The flexibility of multiplexes, which are constantly adjusting their screening schedules in response to audience demand, "means that hit films can achieve higher earnings that they could have before the multiplex boom," Otaka says. And the Japanese industry has learned how to make those hits.

With industry giant Toho in the lead, the major studios have long given over nearly all of their line-ups to films based on proven properties from other media, especially hit comics, novels and TV dramas.

These adaptions are produced by so-called "production committees" (seisaku iinkai) — consortiums of media companies that share the risks and rewards of a given project. Although the production committee system had its beginnings in the 1970s, it hit its stride after Fuji TV and Toho partnered to make and release films based on Fuji's cult hit "Bayside Shakedown" series, which starred Yuji Oda as a cheeky cop in the trendy Tokyo Bay area. The second film in the series, 2003's "Bayside Shakedown 2," earned $155 million, still an all-time high for a live-action Japanese film.

Another trendsetter was Studio Ghibli, the animation studio founded in 1985 by master animators Hayao Miyazaki and Isao Takahata and producer Toshio Suzuki. Ghibli flouted anime industry convention, which was to turn hit kiddy cartoons into endlessly replicable franchises, by making one-off, auteur-driven films that appealed to all ages and became box office powerhouses, starting with Miyazaki's 1989 smash "Kiki's Delivery Service."

For more than two decades, Ghibli films regularly dominated the foreign and domestic competition. The peak was Miyazaki's 2001 fantasy "Spirited Away," whose $275 million take set an all-time box office record for Japan that still stands. The genius of Miyazaki was crucial to this success, but Suzuki's canny marketing and the partnership of the NTV network, which backed all Ghibli films from "Kiki" on, also played a role.

Yet another barometer of the industry's Heisei revival is the iconic Godzilla series. After a decade-long hiatus, Toho rebooted it in 1985 with "The Return of Godzilla," the first in what came to be called the "Heisei Series" of movies featuring the fire-breathing monster.

"Taking a more adult approach [than earlier series entries], the Heisei Godzilla films presented Japan as a world-class nation ready to take its place among the big boys," says Norman England, who covered the series extensively as a reporter for the U.S.-based magazine "Fangoria." This approach proved successful, with the films regularly placing in the annual local box office top ten.

Toho followed up with six films that, released from 1999 to 2004, were known as the "Millennium Series," but the last, Ryuhei Kitamura's "Godzilla: Final Wars," was a flop — and Toho put the series on ice for twelve years.

Directed by animation master Hideaki Anno and sci-fi effects wizard Shinji Higuchi, the 2016 "Shin Godzilla" was a radical revamp of a series long defined by its "man in suit" aesthetics. The all-CG monster, as well as Anno's breathless story of bureaucrats, scientists and military types teaming up to defeat it, was a hit with local audiences: The film made $74 million, more than any of the other 28 series installments to date.

"'Shin Godzilla' was in step with the resurgence of populism here," England says. "In come the young neo-patriots with pure hearts and love of country ready to do whatever it takes to save Japan."

The box office appeal contributed to the industry's Heisei revival, but will that resurgence continue into the Reiwa Era?

Takeo Hisamatsu, a former executive at Shochiku and Warner Bros. Japan, who is now director of the Tokyo Intl. Film Festival, has a laundry list of issues he believes the industry needs to address. "We live in a digital age and film production here has to respond to that," he says. "Also, we need to promote original scripts since the supply of good media properties has become exhausted. And we have to develop more projects with an eye on the foreign market and make more co-productions with foreign partners. Finally, we need to raise the skill levels of young creators and support them when they try something new."

But not, presumably, yet another Godzilla reboot.

(May 15, 2019, "Variety")

Jun Ichikawa — an appreciation

Where is the "real Japan"? Haven't Westernization and modernization killed it off for good? Lafcadio Hearn, the writer best known for explaining the "real Japan" of folklore and legend to the world, asked these questions a century ago and his answers, with some reason, were not encouraging. A Japanese born in 1850 who survived into her eighties would have seen an entire society move from the feudal to the modern era. The sword-carrying samurai of her girlhood gave way, by her old age, to peasant conscripts marching off to conquer Asia with machine guns and tanks.

But core values and beliefs change more slowly than weaponry and, the longer I live in Japan — more than thirty years now and counting — the more I realize that, appearances to the contrary, the "real Japan" is still alive and is a different place indeed from anywhere else.   Among   Japanese directors born after the war, Jun Ichikawa knew that Japan the best, though his one attempt at a period drama, "Ryoma's Wife, Her Husband and Her Lover" ("Ryoma no Tsuma to sono Otto to Aijin," 2000), was also his one big failure.

A common one-word description of his films, especially the ones from his first decade as a director, is jimi — which the dictionary translates as "plain, simple, quiet, modest." His heroes, from Yasuko Tomita's sullen, stubbornly determined school girl in "Busu" (1987), Ichikawa's first feature film, to Masahiro Motoki's struggling manga artist in "Tokiwa: The Manga Apartment" ("Tokiwa-so no Seishun," 1996) and the curiously old-fashioned brother and sister in "Tokyo Siblings" ("Tokyo Kyodai," 1995), fit the jimi label well enough, whatever their outer quirks or inner fires.

Jimi is also one word that pops into my head when I return from abroad, especially from the anything-but-quiet United States, and see the drably, if neatly, dressed commuters silently absorbed in their i-Pods or comics or thoughts on the train from Narita. These are people who never appear in the street fashion magazines, but, with a change of costume and hairstyle, would not have looked out of place in the Japan of Hearn — or Yasujiro Ozu.

Also jimi are the corners of Tokyo where so many of Ichikawa's films unfold, such as his native Kagurazaka, which still evokes the atmosphere of the hardscrabble post-war period, when Ichikawa was a boy, as well as the glory days of the geisha who once flourished there.

But while liking such jimi people and places, Ichikawa was anything but a nostalgist. Like his cinematic heroes, including François Truffaut, Eric Rohmer, Ken Loach and Mike Leigh, as well as the inevitable Ozu, he was interested in revealing human truths behind seemingly ordinary and everyday surfaces, minus the sentimentality and melodrama endemic to Japanese "humanistic" films.

He could be quite unsparing to his heroes, from the humiliating disaster that befalls Tomita's defiant outsider in front of her entire high school at the end of "Busu" to the madness that destroys Hiroyuki Sanada's desperate writer in "Tadon and Chikuwa" ("Tadon to Chikuwa," 1998), but he never treated them as disposable directorial puppets. They had a solidity and dignity as individuals, whatever their eventual fates.

No wonder actors wanted to work with him, even though he could be tough on them. (He told me that Tomita, then a teen idol TV star and singer, "became neurotic" on the set of "Busu." "I was too hard on her," he said wistfully.) He elicited performances that, quite different from the star's usual perky or macho image, were often career peaks. Looking at Rena Tanaka, another pretty teen idol, he saw a loneliness he brought out to stark and memorable effect in Tokyo Marigold, in which Tanaka plays a friendless girl who volunteers to be a "substitute lover" for a guy she likes, while his real girlfriend is abroad.

Also, as much as Ichikawa enjoyed looking back at an earlier Japan, even making "Tokyo Siblings" as an Ozu tribute, he was also in tune with his times. "No Life King" (1989) is a prescient early look at children so absorbed in the virtual reality of a computer game that it begins to invade their non-digital world, with disturbing consequences. Ichikawa's treatment is anything but sensationalistic; instead the film reflects the real-life ways in which "urban legend" memes pass from mind to young mind like viruses.

But the jimi label, though only partly justified, stuck, to Ichikawa's discomfort — and disadvantage. In the 1990s, more raucous voices among his generation of Japanese directors, from Shinya Tsukamoto to Takashi Miike, grabbed the attention of foreign fans and became cult favorites.

At the same time, he did not, like Takeshi Kitano, Naomi Kawase or Hirokazu Koreeda, make films that advertised their seriousness to prestigious festivals with austere stylistics, tamped-down emotions or, in the case of Kitano, extreme violence. A much-in-demand director of TV commercials before and after he started making features, Ichikwa had a gift for revealing poignant moments of transient beauty in everyday settings — the classic Japanese aesthetic of mono no aware (often translated as the "pathos of things"). He could even make a morning sky over a typical Tokyo cityscape look glorious — less with camera or editing tricks than his superbly perceptive eye.

This gift, though, did not make him, to use that 1990s buzzword, edgy. He got his share of invitations and prizes from foreign festivals — Montreal gave him its Best Director award in 1997 for his relationship drama "Tokyo Lullaby" ("Tokyo Yakyoku"), but the highest honors, as well as the critical trends, flowed elsewhere.

This struck me as a gross oversight and I beat the drum loud and hard for Ichikawa's films in "The Japan Times," to little avail. In 2004 I presented four of Ichikawa's films — "Busu," "Tadon and Chikuwa," "Dying at a Hospital" ("Byoin de Shinu to iu koto," 1993) and "Tokyo Marigold" (2001) at the Udine Far East Film Festival, with Ichikawa present — the first such festival tribute in the West.

"Dying at a Hospital," Ichikawa's masterpiece, has been little screened abroad — partly, I suppose, because of its off-putting, if entirely accurate, title. Seeing it on the big screen in Udine's Teatro, I was struck by not only his stories of five terminal cancer patients, told with sensitivity and restraint (all based on a book by a practicing physician), but the interspersed montages of ordinary people doing ordinary things — hunting for clams at the seaside, watching a baseball game, dancing at a Bon festival. Ichikawa filmed them in his spare moments over a period of months, then edited down hundreds of hours of footage.

These montages express the preciousness of life, the presence of the eternal in the everyday with grace and clarity. Much of their power derives from their juxtaposition with the scenes of cancer patients who will never experience those ordinary things again. "Death is the great equalizer — it's something that comes to everyone," Ichikawa told me. "I thought a movie about death shouldn't have one hero. Everyone should be the hero." In other words, the joyously living as well as the painfully dying.

Having had my own brush with mortality just prior to Udine — I was rushed to a Frankfurt hospital coughing blood after coming down with severe bronchitis — I saw that film, sitting next to Ichikawa, with fresh eyes. There is not a single tear-jerking scene in it, but I found myself sobbing uncontrollably, and trying mightily to restrain myself, so I wouldn't look like a total fool to Ichikawa. After the screening, and accepting congratulations from fans whose faces were as tear-streaked as mine, Ichikawa and I walked out of the theater. "I just make films that make people cry," he said with a sigh not entirely ironic.

By this time he had finished the film that he is now best known for — "Tony Takitani" (2004).

Starting with Tadon and Chikuwa, Ichikawa had made film after film in which he tried to break with his jimi image, including the cartoony, if beautifully shot, "Ryoma's Wife, Her Husband and Her Lover," with playwright/director Koki Mitani writing the script ("It was a failure...Mitani probably should have directed it himself," he told me.) Tony Takitani, however, was by far the most successful.

Based on a story by Haruki Murakami about an introverted illustrator (Issei Ogata) with a fashion-crazed wife (Rie Miyazawa), "Tony Takitani" may have had certain affinities with Ichikawa's earlier films, from the withdrawn personality of the hero to the restraint of the shotmaking, but it was in fact another experiment, with a laterally moving camera shifting from scene to scene, like sliding picture cards in a kamishibai (traditional picture play), as a dulcet-voiced narrator told the story. It won the Special Jury Prize, Youth Jury Prize and FIPRESCI Prize at the Locarno fest, as well as many honors elsewhere, but I found it overly stagey and literary (though Murakami himself apparently loved it.)

When Ichikawa died, age 59, of a cerebral hemorrhage on September 19, he was finishing post production on his last film, "Buy a Suit." The winner of the Best Picture Award in the Japanese Eyes section of the Tokyo International Film Festival, this 47-minute film is a return to Ichikawa's indie roots, shot entirely with an HD cam.

The story is simple — a young woman (Yukiko Sunahara) arrives in Tokyo from the countryside to look for her long-lost older brother (Sabakichi) — a brilliant but eccentric man who recently sent her a postcard ending with a vague reference to his current residence

After meeting with her brother's former classmate and close friend, who lost track of him years ago, she tracks him down — and finds him living under a blue tarp near a bridge. He tells her he is planning to get back on his feet with a dubious-sounding business venture, but she is sceptical. An enterprising sort, she arranges a meeting with his one-time lover — a blowzy bar proprietress — hoping for a reconciliation and a return to a more-or-less normal life for her brother.

Ichikawa films this journey into the past — and a possible future — with no sets, no professional actors, nothing but his gift for transforming the mundane and temporal into the transcendent.

There is a certain rhythm to the shots in "Buy a Suit." Scenes of traffic or pedestrians transition to long or medium shots of the principals, finally moving in for close-ups. There is, however, nothing predictable or obvious. Instead, Ichikawa leads us steadily, delicately into his characters' hearts — and the mysteries of life. He makes Tokyo look idyllic, despite its urban clutter and noise, but he also exposes its cruelties and insanities. The ending is a devastating, haunting reminder of our human fragility.

"Buy a Suit" is a brilliant, fitting coda to a life and career cut too short. And, yes, it is the most jimi Ichikawa film of all — small, quiet, real.

(December 15, 2008, "Midnight Eye — Visions of Japanese Cinema")

PART 2:
INTERVIEWS WITH DIRECTORS AND ACTORS

'Afternoon Breezes': Hitoshi Yazaki's pioneer of Japanese LGBTQ cinema is revisited

What was Japan's first LGBTQ-themed film? One often-mentioned candidate is Keisuke Kinoshita's 1959 melodrama "Farewell to Spring," though more for the emotional ties between its young male protagonists than anything explicitly erotic. More upfront in its treatment — and more critically acclaimed — is Toshio Matsumoto's "Funeral Parade of Roses" (1969), a free-form reworking of the Oedipus myth set in the countercultural milieu of go-go-era Tokyo and starring pioneering gay multitalent Shinnosuke Ikehata, aka Peter.

More than a decade later, Hitoshi Yazaki's "Afternoon Breezes" ("Kazetachi no Gogo") also broke new ground with its story of a young lesbian's unrequited love for her straight roommate. This infatuation drives her to desperate acts, such as sleeping with the roomie's libertine boyfriend to force a breakup and, when that fails, stalking the roommate herself. The heroine — the wide-eyed Natsuko (Setsuko Aya) — is clearly deluded about her chances with the roommate — the cool, stylish Mitsu (Naomi Ito), but can't help dreaming of romance in the sultry Tokyo summer.

Shot by Yazaki when he was still a student in the film program at Nihon University, the film was short on the eros found in the era's softcore pornography, but set a house record after it opened at Tokyo's Image Forum theater in December 1980. It subsequently played around the country and at festivals abroad. Despite this success, Yazaki did not direct a feature film again until "March Comes in Like a Lion," his 1992 drama about the incestuous relationship between a free-spirited young woman and her amnesiac older brother. Invited to dozens of festivals in Japan and around the world, the film became another indie hit theatrically and propelled Yazaki to the forefront of the decade's Japanese New Wave.

Starting with "March Comes in Like a Lion," I have reviewed much of Yazaki's work, including his female friendship movie "Strawberry Shortcakes" (2005) and his marital breakup drama "Sweet Little Lies" (2009), but had never interviewed Yazaki himself until his publicist contacted me about the recent re-release of "Afternoon Breezes" in a digitally restored version.

Meeting Yazaki at K's cinema in Shinjuku — one of two Tokyo theaters that began screening the film starting in March — I reminded him we had been introduced long ago at a film event, an encounter he had not surprisingly forgotten.

He then lit a cigarette — the first of many — and began reminiscing about his now 39-year-old debut film. "It was a shocking theme for its time," he says. "But I didn't especially mean the film to be shocking. People around me built it up that way, but I just wanted to investigate the love of one person for another. The sexes of those involved had nothing to do with it."

Since he was a student at the time, I wondered if he faced any opposition from his teachers or school authorities regarding his theme. "I was studying in the scriptwriting course," he says with a smile. "The school was more surprised by the fact that I would direct (the film). The subject matter didn't bother them."

Yazaki also wrote the script, inspired by a contemporary news story about a hair stylist who had come from Okinawa to Tokyo and died of starvation in her apartment. Her end is reflected in the lesbian heroine's fate.

"It's not quite the same as suicide," Yazaki says. "I think of it as one way you can choose to die. But back then most people were just trying to live normally. That someone would choose to die of starvation in a city like Tokyo really shocked me."

Rather than express that shock through the wordy explanations of the typical "problem film" of the time, Yazaki stripped his dialogue to the bare minimum. "I wanted to make a film that lets you rediscover what it is to see," he says. "Film is a medium you can feel something from just by seeing. When ('Afternoon Breezes') was first shown abroad, it had no English subtitles. For me it's more important to get the audience to feel than to understand."

At the time, Yazaki himself was binging on classic films of the past as part of his studies. "Making a new film was like tossing back a ball after having it thrown to me by these other wonderful films," he says. "I felt I had to do it. I had a strong desire to make something — I couldn't resist it."

Among his favorites were works by Yuzo Kawashima and Seijun Suzuki, who carved out distinctive identities while making commercial films for major studios in the 1950s and '60s. But Yazaki tells me he also "strongly rejected" the era's big commercial films.

"They're still the norm even now. In a sense, they've given me the energy to keep directing," he adds.

Made when Japan was on the cusp of its bubble economy, "Afternoon Breezes" is a nostalgic (if at times disturbing) glimpse into a vanished era, but given growing attention to LGBTQ issues now in the Japanese media and online, I suggest it is also timely. However, Yazaki says that "since the heroine's heart is motivated by love, in making the film I didn't feel I had to respond to something like LGBTQ — a term that didn't exist then. This film happens to be about two women, but for me two men would have also been perfectly fine. It's a story about two people."

When the film was first screened abroad, he adds, the response was "really good," but he was most pleased by a New York film critic who wrote that "the director (Yazaki) has created a film in which the fact of being male or female is irrelevant."

He also remembers an encounter with an audience member at the Edinburgh Film Festival who told him she was a lesbian and that "Afternoon Breezes" was not a lesbian film: "My reply was, 'You are exactly right.'"

(April 3, 2019, "The Japan Times")

Kaneto Shindo interview

Films that pay homage to celebrated directors and actors are a venerable cinematic tradition, but when Kaneto Shindo made a film to celebrate the 50th anniversary of his Kindai Eiga Kyokai production company, he paid homage not to another famous filmmaking name, but to Taiji Tonoyama, a character actor known to one and all as "Tai-chan."

Though he appeared in more than 250 films, including many of Shindo's best, Tai-chan considered himself a sanmon yakusha; i.e., a journeyman, with no delusions about his own ability. He was a colorful type, who drank to excess (liver cancer finally killed him) and loved to excess (he shuttled back and forth between his common-law wife and his much-younger mistress for decades), but contributed a distinctive presence to Japanese cinema. (Shindo, who entered the movie business in 1934, rose to the top of the screenwriting ranks in the 1940s and is still going strong at the age of 88, remains a distinctive presence in his own right.)

Kaneto has filmed "By Player" ("Sanmon Yakusha") as a semi-documentary celebrating not only Tonoyama's personality and career, but the history of his Kindai Eiga Kyokai production company, which he started in 1951 with director Kimasaburo Yoshimura and leading actress and wife Nobuko Otowa. Clips of the real Tonoyama performing in "Island" ("Hadaka no Shima") "Onibaba" and other Shindo films are interspersed with scenes of Naoto Takenaka playing Tonoyama, while Otowa, who worked with Tonoyama on many films, provides sharp-tongued, but affectionate, onscreen commentary, as though she were talking to Tai-chan himself.

Shindo, however, did not originally intend the film as an anniversary commemoration. "I had been thinking about making the film for a long time before that," he said, in an interview conducted last May on the set at Nikkatsu Studio. "I did the research, but I found it hard to write the script. For one thing it was about the life of a character actor who played supporting roles. There are many of them, not only here but in Hollywood as well, who do this kind of work their whole lives. Though they may not be the stars, I feel that theirs is the most important role in the drama — they provide invaluable support to the leading actors.

"Toyonaka was a representative of that type of actor. He lived in the shadows, on the same level as the common people, but he was still an important figure. He was an important member of Kindai Eiga Kyokai and an important actor in my films, so I wanted to make a movie about him. Also, in filming his life, I thought I could tell the story of our company and of independent filmmaking in Japan."

"Island" also features the last performance of Otowa, one of the leading actresses of her generation, who died of cancer in 1994. Shindo filmed her reminiscences of Tonoyama long before he was able to begin principal photography with the rest of the cast. "I have clips of representative films in which Otowa and Tonoyama appear, scenes of Otowa talking about Tonoyama, and scenes of Naoto Takenaka playing Tonoyama, with another actress playing Otowa," he explained. "I thought this three-layer structure would be interesting. It's the kind of thing you can only do in films, so I wanted to try it . . . The footage I took of Otowa, especially, is very precious to me now. I shot it six years ago and I've been wanting to use it ever since. But seeing it now, to put it bluntly, is like seeing a ghost."

A veteran scriptwriter, who has worked with many of Japan's top directors, including Kenji Mizoguchi, Kon Ichikawa and Kinji Fukasaku, Shindo admitted to fudging the facts in writing the story of Tonoyama's life with his lover of nearly four decades, Kimie, played by Keiko Oginome. "I made it all up — the interesting parts, the funny parts, the laughter and the tears, wondering all the while if things like this had really happened," he admitted. "The film is a product of my imagination, though some of it was based on what Tonoyama told me and on what I observed being with him for 40 years. I knew a lot about his personal life, but this is not in any way a documentary film."

In a career than spans five decades, Shindo has witnessed significant changes in the conditions of his own job. "It can't be helped," he says. "As you get older your ideas about films change, but film is still film — it's not a novel, it's not a play. You can do things with film that you can't do with any other medium, such as shooting the reminiscences of someone like Otowa and, after she has died, using them in a new film — in effect bringing her back to life. The expressive range of film is limitless."

"In American films they are using technological techniques to show us travel into space or super-realistic violence and all kinds of other things, but I don't think the potential of film is limited to that. I feel that it also has the potential to take us into the inner recesses of the human heart. So there's no reason to be content with what we have now — there's so much more that film can do.

"As a director, it's important to be curious, especially when you're young, but if all you have is curiosity, your films are going to be shallow, you end up saying nothing. You have to direct that curiosity toward expressing the truth as you see it. If you can combine humanism and curiosity then you can make good films."

Kaneto is also not about to put any limits on his own career, even as he approaches his 10th decade. "Why do old folks like me still make films?" he asks. "We don't have any curiosity or youth, so we're good for nothing, aren't we? But in the process of getting old, you suffer setbacks and disappointments — and that's important. Everyone suffers setbacks at one time or other — everyone. The more serious you are about what you're doing, the more setbacks you suffer. You hit a wall. Some people don't get up after they hit that wall — they sink and disappear. But by the time you're in your 80s you've gotten over several walls and that experience is your treasure."

As well as courage and a strong will, Shindo emphasizes the importance of an inquiring mind. "A lot of directors make good films when they're young and then can never equal their early success, like Orson Welles with 'Citizen Kane,'" he said. "Their talent goes sour. They may become technically skilled, but their technique has something rotten about it. "On the other hand, some directors get older, but their films get younger. Those are the real youths — it has everything to do with heart, nothing with age . . . If you've still got the curiosity and the feeling and the vision, you can still make films. But if you're a tired old man, forget about it."

(December 12, 2000, "The Japan Times")

Hideaki Anno interview

Hideaki Anno has had many job descriptions and worked on many projects in his more than three decades as an animator, but he is best known as the creator of the enduringly popular "Evangelion" sci-fi franchise.

Beginning life as "Neon Genesis Evangelion" ("Shin Seiki Evangelion"), a 26-part series broadcast from 1995 to 1996 on TV Tokyo, the franchise has since produced five feature films, as well as manga, games, character goods and even a theme park attraction. From being a cult phenomenon with a small, if dedicated, fan base, "Evangelion" in all its permutations has become a mainstream success in Japan, with fans around the world.

The basic concept is simple: Huge bio-machines called Evangelions, or Evas, piloted by specially recruited teenagers, battle monstrous giants known as Angels that are wreaking havoc on the human survivors of a global calamity.

However, Anno and his team at the Gainax animation studio created a world highly developed not only visually — the mechanics of the Evas in particular were so realistic that they seemed less drawn than designed — but also narratively, emotionally and spiritually. The Eva pilots — especially the troubled, sensitive Shinji, whose coldly calculating dad had developed the Evas — were strongly individualistic types whose turbulent lives were as much a part of the series' appeal as its titanic Eva-versus-Angel battles. The show also incorporated a melange of religious symbolism, and a wealth of psychological and philosophical themes reflecting Anno's own investigations and beliefs, as well as his long struggle with depression.

Anno himself became a sort of hero and role model for legions of "Evangelion" otaku (obsessed fans), although he has not always pleased them — the last two introspective, hard-to-parse episodes of the "Evangelion" TV series drew loud complaints and even death threats. The first two "Evangelion" films, which recapped the story of the TV series and added a new, less murky ending, were made in part to address those complaints.

Now, however, Anno has been anointed as an animation industry giant, with Studio Ghibli producer Toshio Suzuki proclaiming that Anno — a long-time Studio Ghibli collaborator — would "lead the anime world for the next 10 years" following the September 2013 retirement of studio maestro Hayao Miyazaki. For its 27th edition, the Tokyo International Film Festival will present nearly 50 of Anno's works, from animated shorts he made as a student to his animated and live-action features. Long known to be a reluctant interviewee, Anno has cooperated with this project by making himself available to the media, including "The Japan Times."

Arriving at Studio Khara, the animation studio Anno founded in 2006 after leaving Gainax, I was escorted into a meeting room whose walls were lined with models of battleships and other war machinery — a long-time Anno obsession. When the man himself strode into the room — looking taller and more robust than his rather weedy-looking photographs — and I asked him about the models, he told me, as though he'd heard the question too many times to count, that a friend had built them. Given an animator's typically insane work schedule, this sort of delegation made sense, though it popped my thought bubble of Anno, the eternal otaku, busying himself with plastic models in his spare time.

Anno did say, however, that he had involved himself in the Tokyo International Film Festival retrospective, selecting "as many of my films as I was allowed unless there were rights issues that prevented us from screening them." Among them are student shorts that, despite being drawn with little more than paper and pencil, evidence an astonishing talent for the animation craft. Painstakingly detailed mecha (mechanical objects) romp across the screen with a combination of invention, realism and humor that recall Pixar.

Anno, however, denied seeing himself as an animation prodigy.

"When you grow up in rural Japan (Anno was born in Ube, Yamaguchi Prefecture in 1960), it's hard to imagine yourself making animation," he says. "I've never been a confident individual. I kind of stumbled into where I am today."

The most decisive of those stumbles was his hiring as an animator for "Nausicaa of the Valley of the Wind" ("Kaze no Tani Nausicaa"), the 1984 eco-disaster fantasy that first made the name of its director, Hayao Miyazaki, known to the outside world.

"I went (for the interview) because a friend invited me," Anno says. "I never imagined I'd have the opportunity to work there."

Impressed with Anno's drawings, Miyazaki not only gave him a job, but assigned him to animate a key sequence in a film — the beginning of an association with Miyazaki and Studio Ghibli that still continues.

From the very start, Anno's forte as an animator was not only cool mecha, but also visions of destruction with a chilling power as well as a fiery beauty. His early inspirations, he says, "were action movies I watched as a kid," including one whose title he has forgotten but lodged in his brain for "the explosion of a gasoline station — I remember how beautiful the flames were."

In addition to the aesthetics of explosions, Anno was naturally drawn to apocalyptic visions as a child growing up during the Cold War, with its ever-present threat of nuclear war.

"It was imprinted on my psyche that Tokyo could be annihilated any minute," he says. "That kind of imprinting expresses itself in my work. I never experienced the horrors of war that my parent's generation did, but the imagery is very familiar to me, as is the Cold War-era fear of nuclear war. I've read many books and seen many TV dramas and movies that dealt with such themes. They've influenced me greatly. I no longer think we're living on the brink of extinction, but the feeling that it could happen is still with me."

Japan's many natural disasters have also had their impact on his work, as shown by the tsunami that ravages the world of "Evangelion."

"That leads to the beginning of something new," Anno says. "The tsunami wipes out the world and the story then focuses on how the survivors rebuild it. That reflects how I imagine Japan. I don't know about other countries, but if I were to symbolically tell the story of Japan that's what it will look like."

Anno's own success, owes a lot, he admits, to otaku support beginning with the "Evangelion" TV series and the two 1997 feature films based on it — "Neon Genesis Evangelion: Death and Rebirth" ("Shin Seiki Evangelion Gekijo-ban: Shi to Shinsei") and "The End of Evangelion" ("Shin Seiki Evangelion Gekijo-ban: Air/Magokoro wo, Kimi ni"). He denies that once-despised otaku culture and the anime it produced is now widely accepted by the mainstream.

"It looks that way now because animation makes money," he says. "If it didn't, though, the wider public wouldn't care about it. You don't gain public acceptance unless you attract fans and money. … With animation, you see people lined up outside the theater and it's easy to spot as a phenomenon so the media picks up on it, telling the public that animation is hot at the moment. That's how it became more mainstream, I think. We just got lucky."

When I mention Suzuki's comment about Anno becoming the anime industry's next leader, he gives me a wry grin.

"Well, that's Suzuki's opinion so it doesn't make me proud," he says with a laugh. "I try my best but I don't see myself that way. I think that's for the public to decide."

He also doesn't care about always being the director — the summit of the film set or animation studio hierarchy. "All I want to do is to make good films," he says. "I can either be a director, animator, scriptwriter or producer. Any of those roles is fine with me — I don't even mind if I'm not involved as a director."

"Evangelion," he admits, is something of an exception ("I think it's better if I direct the "Evangelion" films," he says), but he balks at comparisons to George Lucas and "Stars Wars," even though he engineered a Lucas-like reboot of the "Evangelion" series.

Starting in 2007 with "Rebuild of Evangelion" ("Evangelion Shin Gekijo-ban"), Anno and his Studio Khara animators have retold the story of the TV series in a planned tetralogy, using the sort of 3-D digital technology unavailable in the mid-1990s. Three parts have been released to date — all massive box office hits, with one more to go, although a release date has not yet been announced.

"I don't want to make ("Evangelion") my life work," says Anno, who turned 54 in May. "I want to do a variety of projects."

He is also not committed the 2-D style of hand-drawn animation (or, as is often done today, digital animation with a 2-D look) that is still the domestic industry standard, years after Hollywood shifted to 3-D computer graphics. "I think there will be more 3-D CG animation (in Japan) in the future and less of the hand-drawn kind," he says. "I can see myself working in 3-D CG if it fits the project. Hand-drawn animation and 3-D CG are only mediums of expression. They're only a tool. Japan's the only place where we're still making hand-drawn animation. To work with the rest of the world, we have to move on to 3-D. Some aspects of hand-drawn animation will remain, but it will no longer be the mainstream."

Anno also sees no future for the sort of tokusatsu (practical effects) shows such as the "Ultraman" series that he loved as a kid and paid tribute to in his 2004 live-action hit "Cutie Honey."

"No one's passing on the techniques," he says. "It pains me to see it go but it's inevitable. All I do is make it last as long as I can. As long as I'm alive, I'd like to see it survive. But in 30 or 40 years it will die out."

Released a decade ago, "Cutie Honey" was Anno's last live-action film. He also made 1998's "Love & Pop," which investigated the enjo kosai (compensated dating) scene, and 2000's "Ritual" ("Shiki-Jitsu"), a drama about two mentally troubled lovers. Despite the long gap between live-action projects, he has not committed himself solely to animation. "I'd love to go back to live-action, but I'm doing animation for now," he says with a resigned shrug.

Asked about the differences between the two, Anno defines animation as more "image centered."

"In live-action, the image exists in reality and you commit that piece of reality to film," he explains. "With animation, you imagine something that doesn't exist in real life and actualize it through drawings or CG."

Anno, however, is not a fan of live-action films derived from his anime. He dismisses "Pacific Rim," with its "Evangelion"-inspired tussles between giant aliens and human-piloted robots, as "not so interesting." Hollywood plans for a live-action "Evangelion" remake leave him cold.

"'Evangelion' was conceived as an animation," he says. "It would be hard to express in live-action."

One reason for the difficulty of the anime-to-live-action leap, Anno believes, is anime's different concept of characters.

"Characters in anime are idealized people" he explains. "Animation is good for that kind of idealized expression because each character is symbolic. But when human actors play those characters, it feels phony. You see the actor's face and think, 'There's no way you're that good of a person.'"

Not, he quickly adds, that the characters in "Evangelion" are all pure-hearted exemplars.

"When we started the 'Evangelion' TV series, we tried things you generally wouldn't expect to see in an anime," he says. "In the symbolic world of cell animation, we tried to make the drama feel as raw as possible."

Anno had a chance to act in an anime himself when Hayao Miyazaki asked him to voice the character of Jiro Horikoshi — the designer of the famed World War II Zero fighter — in his 2013 film "The Wind Rises" ("Kaze Tachinu").

"Since Miyazaki asked me, I couldn't say no," Anno says. He got the role, he explains, because "Miyazaki saw similarities between the person I am and the character of Horikoshi — the way he thought as an engineer."

In the film Horikoshi is more occupied with building beautiful airplanes than agonizing over their use as weapons of war — until the costs of war are brought home to him. Anno, on the other hand, is fully aware of his beloved military mecha's duality.

"I know they're weapons of war," he says. "However, there's a beauty in unadorned functionality totally separate from that. Fighter planes and battleships have a simple, unadorned beauty I'm drawn to. But I don't want to see them in action, killing people."

I decide, strategically, to end the interview with a question about the fourth and final film in the new "Evangelion" series, a question the Tokyo festival PR representative has warned me Anno will not answer. Why not give it a shot?

"Any news on when 'Evangelion 4' will start production?" I ask.

"No comment," Anno replies in English and the entire room, Anno included, erupts in laughter.

(October 18, 2014, "The Japan Times")

Shinji Aoyama interview: not a whodunit but a whydunit

Coming last in a daylong round of media interviews, I was expecting my 40 minutes with Shinji Aoyama to be strained, as in "I'm so tired I can hardly stand." Instead, he came into the meeting room at Toho with a smile and a brisk manner, as in "I'm just getting warmed up." While he was obviously there to talk up his new film, he was also the director-as-film-buff, who lit up when names of his favorites were mentioned, including Alfred Hitchcock, David Lynch and Tai Kato. Speaking about his own work, though, he was less the enthusiast than the sharp-as-tacks analyst, able to sum up, in a few lucid phrases, exactly what he was about and why.

How does "Lakeside Murder Case" fit with the rest of your work? It seems to be something of a departure.

My films are often about how families and other communities are built and fall apart. How one incident can break a community apart. This film is about such a community. It's also about how strangers relate to each other.

I haven't read the novel that "Lakeside Murder Mystery" was adapted from, but the story is along the lines of an Agatha Christie mystery, in which all the action unfolds in one enclosed space, among a small group of people. Was that part of the appeal for you?

For me the mystery element came first, but there were other elements as well. Another interviewer told me he didn't know which genre the film belongs to. That was my intention — it's like a horror movie in some ways. There are various elements in it.

There's a black humor that's almost British, like something Hitchcock might have come up with.

British people might think it funny. There's a Hitchcock film called "The Trouble With Harry" about an inconvenient corpse — if it's found there'll be trouble, so it has to be hidden.

Your approach seems to be more distanced, though, more eye-of-God.

I don't see it that way, as God watching over the characters. Instead I seem them as being in the midst of nature. And nature also between them, dividing them. They're close to nature, they're close to beauty, but a murder is committed among them — that's what's interesting about the film for me.

Your casting of Koji Yakusho is interesting as well. He's got a warm, Tom Hanks quality that's at odds with everything around him.

That's what I paid the most attention to when I was writing the script. An ordinary guy like Koji Yakusho stands out, but he's also being absorbed into the group. There's an American sci-fi film called "The Invasion of the Body Snatchers" — it's as though he's having his body snatched. At the same time, I didn't want to make a 100 percent horror movie — I stopped just a bit short.

What drew you to the mystery genre specifically?

In a mystery, the criminal and the dialogue are important. On the other hand, a film is not interesting when you explain everything with words, so I tried to get away from that. If you can create drama from points of view — from who is looking at whom — and from the conversations [between the characters], the film becomes more interesting. That was the challenge I had, to create that drama. It's a story about ordinary people. At first they don't understand anything — then they find out little by little. There's no professional detective. Everyone is an amateur. It's an all-amateur mystery.

They all seem like good people — but they behave as if they're living in the Warring States (sengoku jidai) period, when any sort of savagery went.
That's Japanese society. The wildness in the [film's] children is like a state of savagery — not at all like a supposedly advanced civilization. The savagery of human beings hasn't changed at all — that's the truth. People wear masks, but at heart they're still wild.

The one who best expresses that may be Akira Emoto, as the doctor.
The doctor is a real gentleman — but being a gentleman for him is like wearing a suit. In reality, he'll do anything. He's a symbol of this society.

As you said, that's a major point of the film — that seemingly ordinary people can do that sort of thing. But the position of Etsushi Toyokawa's teacher is more ambiguous.
He's between the children and the adults. He's calmly watching what the adults are doing, but he's also seeing what the children are doing. He knows that the children do what they do as a result of the adults' actions. He's standing between the two groups.

I know that you do both television and films. If you had made this story as a TV drama, would you have shot it any differently?
Because it was a film, I could shoot it the way I wanted. Because it was a film, I could do this sort of story and think about this sort of problem seriously.

There seems to be a trend now for indies directors from the '90s, including you, Hirokazu Koreeda and Takeshi Kitano and even Takashi Miike to make bigger, more commercial films. I suppose that's a natural process.
Well, these are interesting directors, so there are producers now who will up their budgets and help them make films that people will come to see.

Your producer on this film and other past works was Takenori Sento. He's known for thinking about the foreign market. What about this film?
I thought of it as being for the domestic market. There's a lot of dialogue, so you end up with a lot of subtitles. For people who only understand English, there are a lot of words to process. The characters speak fast.

Also, you can't easily cut the dialogue because it's a mystery.
That's right — you have to explain things.

Are you still thinking of making a film that might be shown at Cannes, Venice or Berlin?
Yes, but I don't really care which. If the producer can say, "This is going to Cannes or Berlin or Venice," it's easier to raise money for the budget. Once the money is raised, then I have to make a film we can submit somewhere.

Now, though, I want to make a film we can take to Cannes. Cannes is interesting — something wild always happens when I go there. I enjoy that.

You've tried a variety of genres — is there anything left?
I'd like to try a melodrama. Then a period drama. Not a samurai film, but something that takes place in the recent past, during World War II or the Meiji Era.

I've talked to several directors recently who said the same thing — they want to make a period drama.
We can think about how we're living now by looking at the past.

That was the approach of Tai Kato — to comment on present-day society by looking at what was happening in the Meiji Era.
I love Kato's films — they've been a big influence on me.

(January 19, 2005, "The Japan Times")

Yosuke Fujita interview: ex-janitor cleans up with comic gem

Winner of the Grand Prize in the short film section at the 1987 Torino Film Festival in Italy, Yosuke Fujita may have been making films for more than two decades, but it's only now that audiences have the chance to see the director's first full-length feature. "Fine, Totally Fine" ("Zenzen Daijobu") is a comic gem of high, flaky brilliance — albeit one that is rather low-key.

In the intervening years, the Hyogo Prefecture native has filmed stage performances for the Otona Keikaku comic-theater troupe and worked on outside film projects with troupe leaders Kankuro Kudo and Masuo Suzuki. He's also done many a day job, including a long stint as a hospital janitor, and utilized his experiences when writing the award-winning script for "Fine, Totally Fine," which centers on the comic rivalry of two close-but-constantly-bickering brothers (played by Yoshiyoshi Arakawa and Yoshinori Okada) for the same misfit, but artistic, girl (Yoshino Kimura).

In person, Fujita said he was nervous because this was his first interview with a foreign journalist. But he quickly grew in confidence as he discussed his latest movie and his philosophy of comedy.

Your realist approach to comedy is quite different from that of your former collaborator Kankuro Kudo, whose directorial style is more cartoony. Were you conscious of any influence?

Not really. The style of the film came from what I was feeling at the time. I didn't think about trends in Japanese films today. I've worked for a long time in Kudo's troupe, as well as with the star of the film, Arakawa. I know Kudo's flashy style quite well, but it's not to my tastes. I like watching his films, but now that I'm 45, his sort of extreme (comedy) gets tiring quickly.

You got your start making 8-mm films. How did that shape your approach to filmmaking?

There's a feeling of freedom you can only get from an 8-mm film. Somebody going directly into commercial films without that experience wouldn't be able to create that kind of feeling. So I think it was a plus for me. It taught me freedom of expression.

There are a lot of sight gags that I imagine weren't in the script. Did you dream them up on set?

Once the script was finished, I started thinking about how to expand on it. I thought of ideas right until we finished shooting. I wasn't going strictly by the script — quite the opposite. Eighty percent of the script came from what naturally popped into my head, the other 20 percent came from thinking more logically. When a script is written with logic alone, it turns out boring. At first I write naturally, then the rest is logical thinking. Otherwise the script doesn't work — balance is important.

The core of the film is Yoshiyoshi Arakawa's character. He reminded me of a silent movie comedian — he can get laughs without saying a word.

I'm happy to hear that. I believe that silent movies are the basis for all filmmaking — making an impact through visuals alone is very cinematic. The first film I made had no dialogue — just music. I think it's good when you can enjoy (a film) with the sound turned off.

Arakawa surprised me in this role — he isn't just playing his usual cartoon, but creating a character.

When he plays minor roles he's mostly there for his comic-book face, but that's not enough for a lead role. You have to express more complex emotions. I think he did that quite well.

There is a lot of detail in the comedic scenes. Did that require detailed instructions from you?

Yes, I made a lot of detailed requests (to the actors). I wanted to create an ambivalent feeling. I really wanted more rehearsal time but because of the tight schedule, we could only rehearse the day before we started filming. I gave acting suggestions at every opportunity, doing retake after retake. We shot on high-definition video, which is a lot cheaper than film.

It looks as though you spent a lot of time casting. All the actors are perfect fits for their roles.
I was really insistent about the casting. Even if they were to appear in only one scene, the actors had to audition as though they were going to play the lead role. I want to film people in a certain way for my films, so choosing the right actor for the role is very important. The naturalness of the performance is what I emphasize. If you're goofing around from beginning to end it's not funny. You need the natural, normal feel of everyday life as the basis — then when the weird stuff appears, it's funny.

As when Akari (Kimura) is pressing the elevator button — and her finger bends.
Yes. That kind of thing, where her finger bends 90 degrees, can't happen in reality. That kind of extreme joke is funny only if the surrounding environment is portrayed naturally. If it's one extreme joke after another, you get tired of it, distanced from it.

It's very realistic how the secondhand book shop and the hospital are portrayed.
I've actually worked as a cleaner in a hospital, so I know the feel of it. I did that sort of job for eight years. An operating room gets bloody and slippery (just like in the film). I also like going to secondhand book shops — the kind of place where you're the only customer and the radio is playing and the owner is staring into space. I wanted to show that kind of situation in a film. If you're never in the sunshine and get no exercise, you'll probably become depressed like the bookshop owner in the movie (laughs).

Speaking of detail, even the props and sets play important roles in getting laughs.
I put a lot of effort into the props and sets. The audience can't enter the world of the film if the props and sets are slapdash. When I make a movie, I pay close attention to the tiniest detail.

The horror figures that look like Arakawa make the biggest impression.
Yes, they look more like him than he does (laughs). They were crafted by a person famous in the world of figures, who is very good at real-life representations.

(January 24, 2008, "The Japan Times")

Koji Fukada interview: young castaways on adulthood's shores

Born in Tokyo in 1980, Koji Fukada released his first film in 2004, but his breakthrough was 2010's "Hospitalité" ("Kantai"), a witty black comedy about a mysterious stranger who talks his way into a job at a small Tokyo printing shop and is soon insinuating himself into the lives of the shop's proprietor and his family. Premiering in the Tokyo International Film Festival's Japanese Eyes section, "Hospitalité" won the best film prize and was widely screened abroad, while its French title and story called up comparisons with the 1932 Jean Renoir comedy classic "Boudu Saved from Drowning."

For his new film "Au Revoir l'Eté" ("Hotori no Sakuko"), Fukada drew on French cinema for inspiration yet again, specifically the oeuvre of Eric Rohmer. And once again his film made its debut at the Tokyo festival, this time in the main competition of the 26th edition. In an interview with "The Japan Times" in the rooftop room of a recording studio (a first for this reporter), Fukada admits that Rohmer "is a director I respect; I was also conscious of (his films) when I was making 'Hospitalité' and 'Tokyo Ningen Kigeki' ("Human Comedy in Tokyo") (2009). But the subject matter of my new film — a young woman spends her summer vacation in a small seaside town — may make it especially easy to understand the Rohmer influence."

Similar to Rohmer, Fukada creates the surface appearance of casualness and discursiveness, but he also carefully weighs the stylistics of each shot. "I've decided that you can really only shoot the surface of people, so I'm a director who's really picky about style, about getting the surface right," he says.

By "style," however, Fukada does not mean slick camera moves or editing tricks. Instead, his approach is to simplify in the name of clarity. This means few to no close-ups. ("A bust shot is about as close as I get," he comments). It also means that his camerawork is relatively stable and straightforward. ("I don't like funny-looking shots," he comments. "I want to create a simple relationship between the subject and the camera.")

This comes from what he calls his "puritanism." "I think that shooting people with a shaky cam or shooting them from below or above distorts the relationship between them and the camera," he explains "I try not to do that."

Fukada also prefers not to let an existing work, be it a novel or manga, get in the way of his own relationship with the film.

Instead, as he did for his previous films, Fukada wrote an original screenplay for "Au Revoir l'Eté." "I'm always asked how I come up with the script," he comments. "And every time I say, 'I don't know.' That's the only thing I can say — every time I write a script, I really feel desperate, wondering how I can make it interesting. It's something like a potter kneading clay, thinking, 'This won't do' and 'That won't do.' If you were to ask a potter why he adds clay to this part or that while he is kneading it, he probably couldn't answer. I'm the same way."

Fukada's usual method is to focus on a group of characters, rather than try to make the audience invest all its emotional capital in one. "I want to make the drama so that the audience can imagine this person is happy or that person is sad by observing the relationships and communications of the whole group," he explains.

In "Au Revoir l'Eté" he may have only one heroine, the 18-year-old Sakuko (Fumi Nikaido), but she is, Fukada says, "a blank slate." "We see the world (of the film) through Sakuko's eyes," he says. "Through this blank sheet of paper called Sakuko the audience can imagine various things, as events unfold around her."

In devising a drama about this girl who sees all but says relatively little about her own dreams and desires, Fukada played what he describes as "a kind of word-association game, with one thing leading to another."

"My first idea was to have a girl come to a certain place on vacation," he explains. "Once the story had that type of drama, I could create something with a Rohmer flavor."

At the same time, Fukada saw no point in making an imitation Rohmer movie. "I thought I had better distance myself from Rohmer," he adds with a wry smile.

He diluted the film's Rohmer quotient by adding his own favorite motifs and themes, from a beloved children's song that one character plays to fluster and frustrate another ("I'd wanted to use that song as a gag for a long time," he says) to the ambiguous relationship of the characters with the truth.

"I enjoy writing lies into movies," he explains. "But more than just depicting lies, I wanted to show how none of us are always expressing our true feelings. Instead, everyone speaks from within a certain web of relationships. Everyone has a certain position in society to uphold, depending on circumstances, be it as a father or a company employee. I give interviews from my position as a director and sometimes I am not speaking my true feelings."

I decide not to ask where the current Q&A falls into the fudging the truth category.

In writing "Au Revoir l'Eté," Fukada was careful to not only separate the truth from lies, including social fibs, but also to differentiate and add complexity to his characters. "If you have two characters who are the same, the drama comes to a halt," he says. "Making them different can, depending on how you do it, give birth to real drama."

(January 9, 2014, "The Japan Times")

Keiichi Hara interview

Ukiyo-e master Katsushika Hokusai is one of Japan's best-known artists. His print "The Great Wave off Kanagawa," with its giant blue wave curling over a tiny Mount Fuji, is seen on T-shirts and coffee mugs around the world. Given his multifarious talent, vast energy and long life — Hokusai died in Tokyo (then called Edo) at age 88 in 1849 — I had long thought of him as a Japanese Picasso.

But as Keiichi Hara's new animated feature "Miss Hokusai" makes clear in scene after gorgeously illustrated scene, he resembled the Spanish master in another way: his vexed relationships with his offspring, particularly his 23-year-old daughter, O-Ei (voiced by the single-named Anne), the "Miss Hokusai" of the English title.

Based on Hinako Sugiura's carefully researched 1983-87 manga, the film focuses on the period when O-Ei was serving as her father's assistant — and coming into her own as both an artist and a woman. Their life together, as the film shows with the manga's dry humor, is hardly conventional. Hokusai (Yutaka Matsushige) is regally unconcerned with housekeeping and O-Ei is coolly disinclined to serve as a surrogate wife for the man she calls "Tetsuzo." So they live in paper-strewn squalor with a menagerie that includes a cute dog and a talkative young disciple, Zenjiro (Gaku Hamada), who would rather carouse than buckle down to work. And so occasionally would Hokusai, much to O-Ei's disgust.

"People in the Edo Period (1603-1868) lived lives very different than the ones we do today," says Hara prior to a preview screening in Tokyo at a theater in Shiodome. "More than us, they looked for pleasure in nearby places. That may have been because they had less in the way of amusement. But when I read Sugiura's comic, I had the feeling that ordinary people were really living intensely and joyfully."

To convey that feeling in the film, Hara and scriptwriter Miho Maruo stayed as close as possible to Sugiura's text, while incorporating the sort of emotional realism that was Hara's trademark in his eco-themed 2007 fantasy "Summer Days with Coo" ("Kappa no Coo to Natsuyasumi") and troubled-teen drama "Colorful," both widely screened and highly praised abroad.

"Sugiura wrote about people who were living their own way," Hara says. "But Hokusai was also stimulated by other people's work. He hated to lose to anyone, so if he saw someone making a good painting, he wanted to make a better one. He had what you might call fighting spirit."

All of this and much more has long been known to Hokusai researchers, including Sugiura, who died of cancer at age 46 in 2005. Hara mentions an "extremely valuable book" about Hokusai published in the Meiji Era (1868-1912) that includes interviews with people who knew the artist — and O-Ei.

"According to researchers, O-Ei painted a lot of the pictures attributed to Hokusai," he says. "He lived to be nearly 90, which was extremely long for a Japanese of that period. There are pictures he is said to have painted just before he died, but they don't look anything like those a 90-year-old would have done. It may just be my imagination, but I believe that more than half the paintings Hokusai made in his latter years were collaborations with O-Ei. In the film it may look as though they don't get along very well, but I think he recognized that her talent as an artist exceeded his."

Hara and his staff, including chief animator Yoshimi Itazu and background artist Hiroshi Ohno, have created a wonderfully detailed evocation of the Edo glimpsed in many of those paintings, combining a hand-drawn 2-D look with 3-D techniques.

"I wanted to see the Edo of the Edo Period," Hara says. "The sky was bigger than it is now, since there were no tall buildings. Also, the Sumida River is not so clean now, but at the time it was a very beautiful river. So people were closer to nature and had richer communications with those around them. The downside was that they had no privacy."

With Hokusai's stranger work as a touchstone, the film also ventures into the ghostly and fantastic realms of the imagination, which, as Hara notes, were not so imaginary to the people of the time.

"People seriously believed in ghosts and goblins and that a giant catfish was the cause of earthquakes," Hara says. "Belief in the existence of the uncanny and nonhuman was taken for granted."

As valuable as Sugiura's manga was as a source of information and inspiration, both visual and narrative, its episodic form, with each installment a stand-alone, made it hard to adapt to film. Hara says he solved the story problem by focusing on O-Ei's relationship with O-Nao (Shion Shimizu), her blind younger sister, who is living apart with their mother, Koto (Jun Miho). (Although still on speaking terms with Koto, Hokusai has a superstitious dread of the disabled that keeps him from visiting her and the girl.)

"Once I got the idea of comprehensively depicting the relationship between the sisters in the first half (of the film), I had pretty much decided on the path I should follow," Hara says.

Often prickly with her father and Zenjiro, O-Ei reveals a softer, more caring side with O-Nao as she introduces the girl to the wonders of the visible world. As she watches O-Nao romp in the snow with a local boy, she is uncomfortably reminded her of her father's stern devotion to work when she was of the same age, as well as his unbending determination to make her follow in his footsteps.

These scenes of sisterly bonding give the film much of its emotional power, as well as advancing the story of O-Ei's development as a person and an artist independent of her father's long shadow. However, the usual sort of Japanese commercial film sentimentality is nowhere to be found.

Also, O-ei's comically awkward interactions with the tall, handsome Kuninao (Kengo Kora), an artist from the rival Utagawa school who is a friend of Zenjiro and a fan of Hokusai, humanize her rather austere character. But they do not lead in the expected romantic direction.

Finally, instead of neatly tying together his various narrative threads at the end, Hara leaves the audience wondering — and wanting to know more.

"That's a good ending for a film, I believe — to make the audience think," he says. "They can imagine what happens to the characters afterwards. I like that sort of movie myself."

(May 20, 2015, "The Japan Times")

Masato Harada interview: a more complex portrayal of Emperor Hirohito

Emperor Hirohito, who is posthumously known as Emperor Showa, had a procession of public images during his long reign from 1926 to 1989 — though none were quite accurate.

There was the pre-1945 Emperor — stern and remote on his white horse — who was viewed as a living god by the Japanese masses and leader of the Japanese war machine by his enemies abroad. After World War II, Emperor Showa transformed into the constitutional symbol of a new, more democratic Japan, who attended faithfully to his endless ceremonial duties while diligently studying marine biology. In his later years, especially to younger Japanese with no experience of the war, he became an eccentric grandfather figure enjoying himself at Disneyland and waving to the crowds at New Year's celebrations.

Masato Harada's "The Emperor in August" ("Nihon no Ichiban Nagai Hi"), released almost a week before the 70th anniversary of the end of the war, presents an entirely different image of Emperor Showa based on the writings of historian Kazutoshi Hando and Harada's own research. In the desperate days of August 1945, this Emperor (Masahiro Motoki) plays a key role in bringing the war to an end, even as young military hotheads mount a coup to thwart his Aug. 15 surrender announcement and fight the American invaders on home soil.

Kihachi Okamoto made a film with the same Japanese title in 1967 (released internationally as "Japan's Longest Day") that was also based on a book written by Hando (but published under the name of well-known social critic and journalist Soichi Oya as "editor").

At a multiplex in Tokyo where Harada's new version was scheduled to open on Aug. 8, I asked him why he felt compelled to remake it.

"(Okamoto's film) was not faithful to the book," he says in fluent English, honed during his six years as an aspiring filmmaker in Los Angeles. "He could not show the Emperor face on, only in long shots or from behind. So he could not show serious discussions in the Imperial Council about important issues that involved both Emperor Hirohito and the 'Big Six,'" Harada says, referring to Japan's six supreme civilian and military leaders in 1945, including Prime Minister Kantaro Suzuki and War Minister Korechika Anami. "I wanted to go more deeply into the characters this time, staying faithful to the book."

Another reason for a remake, Harada adds, was that new research had been published since the '67 film, including a book by Hando titled "Imperial Decision: The Emperor and Kantaro Suzuki" ("Seidan: Tenno to Suzuki Kantaro") that focuses on Emperor Showa's decision to accept the surrender conditions laid down by the Potsdam Declaration of July 26, 1945.

In Harada's film this decision is not immediately approved. The Big Six are deeply divided over the surrender question, with Suzuki (Tsutomu Yamazaki) firmly in the peace camp and Imperial loyalist Anami (Koji Yakusho) among the bitter-enders. But seeing Emperor Showa's strong desire for peace, Anami changes his mind. With the backing of Suzuki and Anami, the Emperor feels emboldened to announce his decision for peace to the Imperial Council.

But if Emperor Showa had truly wanted peace, his critics ask, why didn't he issue a similar Imperial decision before Japan attacked Pearl Harbor?

Harada counters that the Emperor lacked supporters in 1941, but found them by 1945 in Suzuki and Anami.

"These three worked together and stopped the war," Harada says. "Otherwise, the Emperor was not so powerful during the war — that's how I understand it."

What finally motivated Harada to remake "Japan's Longest Day," however, was "The Sun," Aleksandr Sokurov's 2006 drama about Emperor Hirohito in the concluding days of the war. Harada saw the film at a theater in Ginza, a venue chosen "because the distributor was afraid of right-wing attacks," he says. "It was the first time for Japanese to see the Emperor as a leading character," he adds.

While praising veteran character actor Issey Ogata's performance as Emperor Showa as "a courageous effort," Harada says he also found it frustrating.

"He was just mimicking the Emperor's mannerisms," he explains. "It wasn't even true. In 1945 (the Emperor) didn't have those kind of mannerisms. The object was to make him look ridiculous."

Harada wanted to film an Emperor who was truer to life.

At the same time, couldn't Motoki's youthful Emperor, as well as Tori Matsuzaka's fiery Maj. Kenji Hatanaka, who leads the failed coup, become inspirations to the same flag-waving neo-nationalists who long for the militarized, Emperor-worshipping Japan of old?

"This is an anti-war film," Harada says bluntly. "Its message is that only because we lost the army could we save the country. ... Some right-wing politicians or young people might look at Maj. Hatanaka and others and say they're kakkoii (cool), but this movie is a double-edged sword," he says, meaning that none of its main characters are purely good or evil. "I was fair to the Maj. Hatanaka character even though I don't agree with him. I can't deny that some might take advantage of that approach ... but people will take the film whichever way they want."

Harada's hopes "The Emperor in August" becomes a success not only because it would be good for his bank account and distributors' bottom lines.

"It would change industry thinking," he explains. "They'll think, 'We should make more films for mature audiences and not be afraid of taking chances.'"

He confesses, though, that he did not want to risk upsetting right-wingers by depicting Emperor Showa's vexed relationship with his mother, Dowager Empress Teimei.

"She wanted to fight to the end, so Hirohito had a hard time with her," Harada says. "And she didn't get along with Empress Nagako, Hirohito's wife. That would make an interesting film for the future."

(August 5, 2015, "The Japan Times")

Ryosuke Hashiguchi interview: one man, two worlds

Ryosuke Hashiguchi is one of the few gay filmmakers in Japan to have had a measure of popular success making films with gay themes. His third film, "Hush" (2002), about a gay couple whose life changes when one of them is drafted into becoming a father by a desperate woman, was an indie hit, as well as a festival-circuit favorite.

He is, however, not the most prolific of directors — he has made only four features since debuting in 1992 with "A Slight Touch of Fever" ("Hatachi no Binetsu"), a minimalist drama about gay hustlers that screened at the Berlin Film Festival.

His fourth, "All Around Us" ("Gururi no Koto"), not only arrives after a six-year gap, but its main characters are a straight couple with no gay family members, friends or associates in sight.

Unfolding from 1993 to 2001 — with the significant dates shown in subtitles — "All Around Us" presents an ambitious weave of private and public events that illustrate not only the ups and downs of a marriage and a psyche, but the (mostly negative) changes in Japanese society. Meanwhile, Shogo Ueno, who was also Hashiguchi's cinematographer on his last three films, captures a visual beauty, from the natural to artistic, that illuminates moods while dazzling the eye.

The film is the best thing that Hashiguchi has done, but its underlying concerns — including the fragility of relationships and the basic need of human beings for connection — run through all four of his films, as does his puckish sense of humor, his willingness to trash convention and his basic sympathy with his characters, likable or no. He is more interested in understanding them than in moralizing about them, though he is also a close observer of their worst behavior.

"(In my new film), I wanted to depict people who are already connected with each other — a married couple who have been together for 10 years," Hashiguchi explains in a recent interview at the Shibuya office of his distributor, Bitters End. He speaks softly and fluently in Japanese, but with a nervous intensity, as he tries to make his points as clearly as possible for his foreign interviewer.

"All my films are about connections like that. Also, in its structure, 'All Around Us' is no different from 'A Slight Touch of Fever,' which depicted the gay world of (Shinjuku's) 2-chome district and how one boy alternates his existence there with life at college. 'All Around Usi' also depicts how one man alternates between his married life and his work as a courtroom artist. The points of view are similar — one man looking at two worlds as an observer. I like that sort of protagonist."

His couple, Shoko (Tae Kimura) and Kanao (Lily Franky), begin the film in 1993 on the comically quirky side of the scale. Shoko, the slightly ditzy editor at a small publishing house, worries that Kanao, who runs a small shoe-repair shop, is cheating on her — which he is, routinely seducing female customers with his disarming smile and geeky charm. Still, they have their three-times-a-week love-making sessions, carefully marked by Shoko on the calendar. Then Kanao lands a higher-paying job as a courtroom artist for a TV station and Shoko becomes pregnant. Happiness beckons, though Shoko's family, including her self-centered, slatternly mother (Mitsuko Baisho), her loud, crass businessman brother (Susumi Terajima) and the brother's coarse-grained wife (Tamae Ando), remain skeptical of Kanao, whom they regard as little more than a bum.

Cut to 1994. Kanao is still sketching in the courtroom — and becoming accepted by his seniors, including a grizzled reporter (Akira Emoro), who gives Kanao the benefit of his hard-won wisdom. Shoko, however, has been devastated by the death of their infant daughter. By turns irritable, hysterical, tearful and withdrawn, she is falling into a deep depression — and Kanao doesn't know how to stop her.

Her condition seems to reflect a wider sickness in the society that Kanao witnesses in court, from psychotic child-killers to amoral corporate crooks. But it is also quite personal and catastrophically real. Her relatives are mostly clueless or unsympathetic; Kanao becomes her only lifeline to sanity.

Hashiguchi also suffered from depression that deepened after the terrorist attacks in the United States on Sept. 11, 2001.

"I thought of suicide every day — I felt that the atmosphere of the world changed after 9/11," he says. "At the time, I realized that depression and terrorism were very similar. When you are depressed, all the hangups and anxieties that you thought you'd overcome come rushing back at you. You feel as if you're being swallowed by all the pain and hatred. Terrorism is the same. Whenever something big like (9/11) happens, all the dormant problems in the world, like racial conflicts, come pouring out."

For Hashiguchi, those problems first hit home when he saw a news segment about three Japanese who had been taken hostage in the Iraq War and, following their release, were returning home.

"They were met by a smiling woman with a placard that read, 'You asked for it,'" Hashiguchi recalls. "I was shocked. How could she laugh at people who had been hurt like that? I felt that the Japanese had changed."

The turning point, he believes, was the economic bubble era of the 1980s. "It irreversibly changed the value system of the Japanese people," he explains. "All adults talked of was 'money, money.' The bubble burst in 1990, around the time that Tsutomu Miyazaki was arrested for kidnapping, killing and eating little girls, changing Japanese criminal history. It was also around this time that Masako (Owada) married into the Imperial family. As I watched such a glowing personality suffer and sicken more and more each year, I felt that Japanese people were collectively growing mentally sicker as well. I wanted to go back to that (turning) point and also communicate my own experience of depression."

This may sound grim, but illustrator Lily Franky, whose memoir about his relationship with his terminally ill mother was made into the 2007 hit film "Tokyo Tower — Okan to Bolu to Tokidoki Oton (Tokyo Tower — Mom and Me and Sometimes Dad)," brightens the film as Kanao. Instead of trying to compete with the professional actors around him, some of whom have been polishing their shtick for decades, Franky plays himself — a real-life artist with a keen eye and radar sensitivity to his surroundings, and with a natural nice-guy presence. He may have been an off-beat casting choice for Hashiguchi, but he was the right one.

"At first (Kanao) was a happy-go-lucky character, so I thought a comedian could play him, but couldn't think of anybody specific," Hashiguchi comments. "I wanted somebody fresh for the part. Then I happened to read Lily's partly autobiographical book, 'Tokyo Tower,' and felt, 'Here is Kanao.' How Lily feels about people and the world is similar to how Kanao feels. Casting him was a gamble, though. If it turned out to be a failure, there was nothing I could do about it. I had to trust my destiny to our partnership."

Meanwhile, Tae Kimura, a veteran actress appearing in her first starring role, goes deep into her troubled character, holding back nothing, while keeping the performance from becoming over-ripe or monotonous. She shows us that there are several shades of black.

"It's a difficult part," says Hashiguchi. "She had the experience and acting skills, but you can't portray (Shoko) through acting technique alone. You have to open your heart and throw yourself into the character. So I worried about that. But I felt that I had a heart-to-heart connection with (Kimura and Franky) from the start. I could support them when the going got tough. It's hard to open up and throw yourself totally into a role but the two of them did it. They really became Kanao and Shoko."

In the film's third act, colors begin to appear more prominently, particularly in the work of Kanao and Shoko, who takes up art as therapy. Kanao's drawings and Shoko's paintings play an important role in the film, illuminating not only the world around the artists, in all its horror and beauty, but their inner states. They are also an expression of hope — and human connection.

Again, there is a parallel with Hashiguchi's own experience. "When I came out of depression I noticed colors a lot," he says. "When you're depressed, the world looks gray; but when you get better, colors like red jump out at you. I felt that the world had regained its color. So when Shoko gets better she notices the red hue of tomatoes and other colors. Emotion comes back to her little by little. There's more of a spring in her step. That's how it worked for me too — it was a gradual process. I tried to show that in the film."

(June 12, 2008, "The Japan Times")

Ryuichi Hiroki interview 1: having a laugh

A veteran director of "pink" movies, Ryuichi Hiroki won critical acclaim for the 1994 youth drama "800 Two Lap Runners," his breakthrough into straight films. He first collaborated with Shinobu Terajima — star of his new movie "It's Only Talk" ("Yawarakai Seikatsu") — in "Vibrator," a romantic road movie that swept Japanese film awards for 2003 and was widely screened overseas.

Like many other "pink" directors, former or not, Hiroki is a frank, unpretentious type, and during our interview the laughter flowed freely.

How much of Shinobu Terajima's performance came from you?
Not much. She read the script in her own way. All I did was say things like 'Maybe you should be a little more cheerful here.' She encounters five men [in the course of the film] so I told her I wanted her to vary her expressions with each one. Her performance was more part of a group collaboration. In 'Vibrator,' it was all one-to-one.

The men she meets all have their appealing qualities, but they're also all unreliable.
That's right, they're all a bunch of wimps (laughs). I include myself in that group (laughs).

Would you call the film a mirror of Japanese society in that way?
No, no — or maybe. It's a tough call (laughs). But women are more in tune with the times than men. They are living with a firm sense of reality. Japanese women may look sort of quiet and dreamy, but they're really firmly grounded. All women are. I get the feeling that men are just trying to keep up with them.

The first time I saw the film I wondered how you were going to tie it all together.
Exactly, exactly! That was the hardest part about writing the script. [Haruhiko] Arai really struggled with that. There are all these different stories — so what do you do with them? So we focused on the fact that Yuko shares all these memories with her cousin Shoichi, from the time they were both small.

Terajima expresses her character with more than just her face. The way she walks is also very distinctive.
She acts with her whole body, not just her face. She acts with expression in everything — in the way she walks and so on. All I did was tell her she was getting too carried away. I told her [the audience] would understand without the exaggeration.

Even the floppy boots that she wears . . .
Right, those boots. I liked the idea of her clomping around in those boots. She's not one those girls who glides around. She's not one who slips on boots using a shoehorn. She just crams her feet into them and then goes clomping around town taking pictures and them goes clomping home.

If you had pushed it too far, she would have just been this eccentric lady.
Right, right. There was a fine line, but Kamata's the kind of town where you can get away with dressing like that. (laughs) Well, not 'get away with' — it goes with the town.

There's something a little dangerous about the relationship between Yuko and Shoichi.
Yes, no doubt about it.

Even though they're cousins . . .
They're all right, though, even if they've had sex. They're all right (laughs).

There's a difference of opinion about that (laughs). But when they part for the last time, they kiss. That really made a big impression on me as the kiss is so long and intense. Was that your idea or did it sort of happen spontaneously?

We decided from the start to do it in one long cut. Just go for it! Hey, it's not a French kiss. Shoichi wants to kiss her and she responds passionately. That was a really tough scene. I needed about 10 takes. We were filming until morning (laughs). It was a really important scene, so I had to get it right. I agonized over how [the audience] should see it. Is it the end? The beginning?

So you wanted that ambiguity?

Right. But it's really the beginning. He absorbs all of Yuko's weakness and then goes home to the countryside.

A new beginning . . .

A new beginning. I thought that would be all right, that both of them would accept it.

In your films that sort of ambiguity is . . .Common.

Right. I'm living an ambiguous life. So maybe I should have called the film "Ambiguous Life" (laughs).

I couldn't help feeling a bit sorry for Yuko.

You should feel sorry for her. I feel sorry for her. If she'd only met a better guy. A guy with all the good qualities of the men she meets in the film. There actually aren't many guys like that. So filmmakers think they have to put someone like that into their films. But reality is something else.

(June 16, 2006, "The Japan Times")

Ryuichi Hiroki interview 2

Interviews with people you know well can turn awkward if you try to be the probing questioner instead of the coffee-shop companion. No such worries with 61-year-old Ryuichi Hiroki, the former pink film (i.e., soft pornography) director who made his commercial and critical breakthrough with the erotically charged youth drama "800 Two Lap Runners" in 1994.

Though we have met elsewhere many times and once spent a week traveling around central Brazil together, Hiroki quickly slipped into interviewee mode when we met to talk about "Kabukicho Love Hotel" ("Sayonara Kabukicho"), his ensemble drama set in a love hotel in Shinjuku's biggest entertainment district. But when I asked him why the film has been such a hit on the festival circuit — playing to enthusiastic crowds at Busan, Toronto and Tokyo Filmex — he smilingly turned the tables on me. "What do you think?" he asked.

Good question, since I had recommended the film to the upcoming Udine Far East Film Festival.

"The theme is interesting," I opined. "There are places like love hotels in other parts of the world, but they are still distinctively Japanese."

"I've heard that foreigners come from abroad to stay at love hotels," Hiroki said with a laugh. My probing interview was already turning into a coffee shop chat. Here's how it played out:

"The script was an original by Haruhiko Arai, who you worked with on 'Vibrator' (2003) and 'Yawarakai Seikatsu' ('It's Only Talk') (2005). He seems to have a different approach from some of your other scriptwriters."

"True, he has something special."

"What would that be?"

"I haven't thought about it. (Laughs.) His people are weak. He thinks he's weak himself, so that's what he focuses on. But in reality, he's not weak at all."

"The hero, Shota Sometani's hotel manager, certainly fits the 'weak' description."

"Yes, he does. He's close to Arai in that way."

"But Sometani is trying to hide it."

"I guess Arai does too. (Laughs.)"

"By contrast, the 'delivery health' girl (i.e., call girl) played by Korean actress Lee Eun-woo brightens up the film. But Lee also had toughest role, I thought."

"True, but she did a good job. She was very expressive."

"When she came to Japan, she didn't speak any Japanese. Did you have any problems making her understand what you wanted?"

"No, not at all. We had an interpreter. Also, she really knew a lot about films, so I didn't have to say a lot to make her understand. So it was easy for me. But she really agonized over the nude scenes. She didn't say OK to those right away. If a Korean actress goes to Japan and plays a role with nudity, what are they going to say when she goes back to Korea? So she worried about that, but it had nothing to do with the movie itself. It would be the same if a Japanese actress were to go to Korea and do nude scenes. But when we were in Busan (for the International Film Festival), everyone told her she'd done a great job, so it worked out well, I think."

"In Japan, the biggest name in the cast is, of course, Atsuko Maeda (formerly of the pop group AKB48). Did you cast her?"

"I told her I wanted to work with her, yes. I was really taken with Maeda. Since she's been in films by Nobuhiro Yamashita ["Tamako in Moratorium" ("Moratorium no Tamako")] and Kiyoshi Kurosawa ("Seventh Code"), she's become really interesting as an actress."

"You got a great crying scene out of Maeda. And that's your trademark — all of your actresses let loose with the tears."

"That's no good. I've got to make a (Hiroki speaks in English) no-crying movie."

"Did you talk with her about that scene?"

"Yes, I did, and I tried various other things, too — to get her to cry, that is. But she would cry when she ate a kimchi hamburger. That's what did it."

"Looking at her AKB48 videos you can see she had been preparing to be an actress."

"She's not exactly a beauty. On the other hand, she's great as an actress. If she'd been really beautiful, she might have stayed an idol. But she doesn't have an idol's face — it's more suited to movies."

"I was also impressed by the humor in the film. It's not that you'd never had laughs in your films before, but this one is full of them."

"That was the intention. We should have titled it 'My Sister is an AV Actress.'" (Laughs.)

"Was this film relatively easy for you, given your experience as a pink film director?"

"I use that experience when I shoot on a tight schedule — two weeks in this case. Pink films took three or four days to make. We always used to shoot them in one room of a love hotel since they had sex scenes. The movies themselves were different, but we shot them in one room."

"The scenes showing how the hotel is run feel realistic. Did you research how they manage these places?"

"I already knew a bit about love hotels, from my private life and so on. I'd also shot films there, so I didn't do any research. But I went to the places where the staff stays — the staff room, the place where they eat their meals and so on — for the first time. They were dirty and full of stuff."

"I also liked Tomorowo Taguchi as the 'delivery health' club manager. He played him as a nice, kind-hearted guy — not what you'd expect. That job has a kind of dark image."

"The manager was a cheerful guy. I thought (Taguchi) was trying to recruit part-time workers for the 'delivery health' business." (Laughs.)

"The director of the Udine festival told me she left the theater feeling more energetic. I felt that way myself."

"That's good. So there are at least two of you."

"Your next film will be more of an art film, but will you also continue to make the types of commercial films that draw fans?"

"Right, back and forth. Everyone says they like the art films more. (Hiroki speaks in English) Why? In my own mind it's all entertainment."

(January 28, 2015, "The Japan Times")

Director Ryuichi Hiroki interview 3: discussion of "Side Job." and the changing feelings Fukushima evokes

Interviews with Japanese directors tend to be straightforward PR exercises. The subjects may be friendly, but they are also disinclined to deviate from their script, especially if they are on their umpteenth media interview of the day.

Ryuichi Hiroki is different, though, and that's not just because I've known him for years. After getting his start in pinku eiga (erotic movies) in the 1980s, Hiroki directed a steady stream of hit commercial films and acclaimed indie dramas in a pattern that could be described as "one for them, one for me." He has none of the pontificating self-importance of typical industry kyoshō (masters), though. Instead his answers tend to be pithy, delivered with a twist of dry humor.

When we meet at the Gaienmae office of distributor Gaga to talk about his post-Fukushima drama "Side Job.," he starts the interview with a question of his own: "Have you seen the film?" This isn't always a given with the local media, but I surprise him with my answer: Not only did I see the film, I also read Hiroki's own novel on which the Masato Kato-penned screenplay is based. With that out of the way, we can begin.

"Side Job." isn't the first time Hiroki, a Fukushima native, has addressed the Great East Japan Earthquake in his work. He touched on it in 2011, the year the disaster occurred, in his film "River."

"My feelings then were pretty raw," he recalls. "Since it has been five years I'm … what, calmer? Cooler?"

Even so, "Side Job." is very much a passion project for Hiroki, who tossed aside the usual commercial rules in pursuit of honesty and authenticity. Published in 2015, the original novel was a first for the filmmaker, evidence of the thought and effort that went into the film — though Kato's script is quite different from it.

"It's my own original story, so I thought it would be better to have a third party involved," Hiroki explains. "That's why I didn't write the script. I'm usually adapting the original material of others, and sometimes the authors aren't happy with what I do. I thought if I didn't like something then I could just say so … but I didn't," he pauses … and laughs. "It would have been like fighting with myself!"

The story is still far more Hiroki's than Kato's, however, and that includes the long Japanese title "Kanojo no Jinsei wa Machigaijanai" (literally, "Her Life Is Not a Mistake"). The title is used for a play in the film that is based on the 1970 cult classic "The Honeymoon Killers."

"I love that film," Hiroki says. "It's my favorite."

The "her" in the title, however, seems also to refer to Miyuki Kanazawa (Kumi Takiuchi), a disaster survivor who lives with her father in temporary housing and works at City Hall. On weekends, she travels to Tokyo to work a side job as a deriheru (delivery health) call girl.

Unlike the many famous actresses who have graced Hiroki's films and were cast through their agencies, the relatively unknown Takiuchi won the role at an audition.

"One reason I went that route is the nudity," Hiroki says. "There are deriheru scenes and not many actresses will do that kind of thing. Also, I felt it would be better to have someone who came without any preconceptions attached to her."

Takiuchi completely inhabits the role, right down to her perpetual look of exhaustion with life in general. "That's because I gave her a hard time during the shoot," Hiroki jokes. "She got thinner and thinner, but she did an excellent job in the film. That expression of hers is good, right?"

Hiroki switches roles to play the part of the interviewer again by asking me what I thought of the film. My answer contains a bit of a spoiler, so jump ahead two paragraphs if you don't want to read it.

I found Ken Mitsuishi's portayal of Miyuki's father, a farmer whose fields all lie in the disaster's no-go zone, unexpectedly sympathetic.

"He seems pretty hopeless, playing pachinko all day and drinking all night," I reply. "Then one day he tells his friend in the parlor 'I'm outta here' and leaves abruptly. I felt that he was going to change — and the movie brightens."

"I see," Hiroki says with a sense of satisfaction. "But there's no explanation. Kengo (Kora) was also good, right?," he asks.

"Yes he was," I answer.

"He has the line 'You're not the only one I'm protecting,'" Hiroki adds. "That's something hard to say, but he says it to (Takiuchi). I thought that was good."

I realize I am having a two-way discussion about the film, which doesn't happen in too many director interviews.

When he was writing the novel, Hiroki says he made regular trips to the Fukushima disaster area and realized that "It had changed totally."

"My own feelings also changed," he recalls, adding that when he first saw the devastation he could only stand there staring at it, stunned. "Now it's just sad," he says in English.

"It looks as though people will never be able to go back to some of those places. What's done is done."

It was these varied and complex emotions that motivated Hiroki to make a "Fukushima film unlike all the others."

"There are too many films that are simply sad, or just tell people to ganbarō," he says, referring to the word Japanese use to encourage each other to overcome hardship. "I felt that enough was enough. Films like that tend to be over the top, and I wanted to make one that was a little quieter and slower."

But Miyuki's choice of side job, I tell Hiroki, might puzzle foreign viewers, especially. She has none of the usual reasons for prostituting herself.

"They've spent a huge amount of money cleaning polluted land," he says. "She turns her own body into money and for her that money has great value, even though she may be making only ¥20,000 or ¥10,000 each time. By turning her body into money she gains a sense of reality that she had been lacking. She affirms her own existence in the moment."

Another reality, of which she is quite aware, is that she has to move on, but to what?

"I didn't want to show her having found some deeper meaning," Hiroki says. "That would just be fictitious. It's enough for her to simply feel that she is still here."

(July 19, 2017, "The Japan Times")

Mamoru Hosoda interview: Tokyo International Film Festival welcomes audiences to the animated world of Mamoru Hosoda

The Tokyo International Film Festival, whose 29th edition unspools from Oct. 25 to Nov. 3, offers something for everyone — from golden oldies in the Japanese Classics section to films for kids in the new Youth section. However, as Japan's biggest film festival, as well as one of the most important in Asia, TIFF aims to be more than a cinematic smorgasbord.

Under director general Yasushi Shiina, who took charge in 2013, the festival has also become a major event for fans of anime. In addition to offering more animated films in the Special Screenings and other regular sections, TIFF has been presenting retrospectives dedicated to animation masters such as "Evangelion" series creator Hideaki Anno (2014) and "Gundam" series godfather Yoshiyuki Tomino (2015).

This year the honoree is Mamoru Hosoda, who has been an animator for two decades, but truly came into his own with "The Girl Who Leapt Through Time" ("Toki o Kakeru Shojo," 2006). This fantasy about a high school girl who becomes unstuck in time won a shelf of prizes, including an Animation of the Year award from the Japan Academy. Since then, Hosoda has moved from triumph to triumph — commercially and critically — culminating with his fourth feature, "The Boy and the Beast" ("Bakemono no Ko," 2015), the second-highest earning Japanese film last year at ¥5.85 billion.

But when "The Japan Times" interviewed Hosoda about the retrospective and his career, the 49-year-old director wanted first to talk about, not one of his many successes, but a rare failure. In 2000, Studio Ghibli — the creative home of anime maestro Hayao Miyazaki — commissioned Hosoda to develop and direct the film that was to become "Howl's Moving Castle" ("Howl no Ugoku Shiro," 2004). But due to various creative and personal issues, including the life-threatening illness of Hosoda's mother, work on the film was stopped in April 2002 and Hosoda left Ghibli under a cloud. Miyazaki later directed the film himself.

After that, Hosoda worked on an episode of the TV anime "Magical Do Re Mi" (2002), which he specifically asked TIFF to include in the retrospective.

"It has a very deep meaning for me," he explains. "I didn't get to finish my own take on ('Howl's Moving Castle'), so I gave form to my unexpressed feelings about 'Howl' through ('Magical Do Re Mi')."

Did those feelings include a hint of the desire for revenge against Ghibli?

"No," says Hosoda with a laugh that's not entirely nervous. "But not being able to finish your own film is a very frustrating experience for a director. So I had a strong urge to re-create it in another form. 'Magical Do Re Mi' led to 'The Girl Who Leapt through Time,' so it's important to me. It's only one episode of a TV anime, but I made it with the same passion I would put into a film."

One thread connecting Hosoda's features in the retrospective — including "Summer Wars" (2009), "Wolf Children" ("Okami Kodomo no Ame to Yuki," 2012) and "The Boy and the Beast" — is the theme of family, though Hosoda's family groupings are hardly conventional. In "Wolf Children," a single mom raises two children who are half-wolf, half-human. In "The Boy and the Beast," an orphaned boy finds a sort of surrogate dad in the titular beast, who is a bearish, hot-tempered warrior in a parallel "beast" world.

"The image of the 'family' is always changing, it's not set in concrete," Hosoda explains. "Today you have working mothers and stay-at-home dads. Couples don't necessarily have to marry or, even if they do, have children. But all of us need to think about the important things that never change. Why do we need a family in the first place? Why does family make us feel like home, make us feel comforted?"

Though there is a focus on family, Hosoda's films are anything but typical Japanese family dramas; instead of the usual sentimentality their mood is often comic, their imagery vividly fantastic.

"Most of all, I want to make my films to be enjoyable," he says. "So I turn a child into a wolf, a stepfather into a bear. Isn't that more fun than human characters?"

He didn't always want to be an animator, however. As a college student contemplating careers Hosoda wavered between making animation, his childhood passion, and directing live-action films and

TV commercials. When he graduated in 1991, Japan's economy was still booming (soon to go bust), but the animation industry was "at its poorest."

"Normal students would choose to go into the advertising industry, because you could make a lot of money," he says. "So if you went into the anime business you were basically an idiot."

Hosoda, however, reasoned that "a business able to struggle through bad times will be strong when times change. When it's at rock bottom, it has the most potential to grow." So he opted for animation and has never looked back. "I am all about anime," he says.

The director hasn't switched over completely to 3-D computer graphics, the de facto animation format being used in Hollywood these days, though he admits that "every year the amount of handmade animation I use decreases."

However, Hosoda insists he is still attracted to the beauty of hand-drawn animation.

"It's part of Japanese anime's uniqueness," he says. "If all the animation in the world used the same method, like 3-D CG, it would be boring. Every country should have its own unique way of creating anime."

Hosoda is working on a new project at his Studio Chizu animation house, but for now he declines to give any details.

"I found a way to make a film interesting by using new methods," he says. "I can't say much more at this time, but I hope you will all look forward to it!"

Though each of Hosoda's films since "The Girl Who Leapt Through Time" has earned more than the last, he says he feels no pressure to equal his former employer as a box-office king ("Howl's" made a resounding ¥19.6 billion).

"A director should be interested in creating a good relationship with the audience, not in the profits," he says. "I'm just striving to do better from one movie to the next."

(October 20, 2016, "The Japan Times")

Jun Ichikawa interview

What is your new film, "Tony Takitani," about?

Some people mistake the main character for Tony Tani — a comedian who was popular several decades ago. The film has nothing to do with him — it based on a story by Haruki Murakami called "Tony Takitani." Before the war there were Japanese jazzmen working in Shanghai. One of those jazzmen — the father of the hero — returns to Japan after the war. He and his wife have a son and he names him "Tony." He was a jazzman and liked American things, so he gives his son an American-sounding name — but there are no Japanese with that name, are there?

That makes life hard for the boy. The opening narration explains all that. It's a seishun eiga (youth movie) about a boy with this unusual name. He becomes isolated — a kind of hikkikomori (recluse). He has a lonely youth, all because of that name. There's a sort of love story — but a lot of people die too. (laughs) He becomes more and more alone. The film is based on a work of literature, so it's more complex, more philosophical than the usual seishun eiga. The set is like something in a stage play. In fact, we built a stage outside and just changed the decorations for the different scenes, as in a play. It's like "Dogville," the new film by the director of "Dancer In the Dark," Lars Von Trier.

The cuts are quite long. Instead of cutting from one room to another, the camera passes by the walls connecting the rooms. In other words, the camera keeps moving back and forth between the rooms, over and over.

What are your feelings about "Busu" now, nearly two decades after you made it?

Well, it was my first film. At the time I was making TV commercials and having one hit after another. A TV producer approached me about making a film that would be like one of my commercials. When I shot it, though, it turned out to be pretty depressing. (laughs). The producer wanted something light and entertaining, but I took the whole thing seriously.

I was raised in Kagurazaka (Tokyo), where "Busu" was shot — it was a geisha section back then. So going back there to make the film was nostalgic for me. I was about 37. I'd been making these 15- and 30-second commercials, so I wondered if I could really shoot a two-hour movie. I was worried that I was getting in over my head (laughs). But "Busu" ended up being voted one of the ten best Japanese films of the year by the "Kinema Junpo" magazine (critics poll), so that gave me confidence.

Did you have any points of reference for the film? Any specific directors or films that you were thinking of?

Well, I was a movie buff. One of my favorites was Truffaut's "Les Quatre Cents Coups" ("The Four Hundred Blows"). I liked Kenji Mizoguchi's "Gion Shimai" ("Sisters of the Gion") and his other films about geisha. I was also a big fan of Naruse. I saw a lot of old Japanese movies growing up — they had a big impact on me.

I didn't know if I would be able to make a second film so I wanted to put everything I could into the first one. Fortunately, ("Busu") was a success, so I've been able to make films at a fairly constant rate ever since.

You really thought it might be a one-time experience?

Yes, I was afraid I'd never get another chance. I realized how difficult filmmaking is — how hard it is to raise money and so on — so I wanted to pack in as much as I could. The essence of all those old Japanese movies that I loved so much.

A lot of people have told me they like that film, that it affected them strongly. Debut films often have that sort of power. They tend to be good.

It's a film about teenagers, but the ending isn't typical for a film of that type, especially one from Hollywood.

I was young in the 1960s, when there were student protests against the Vietnam War and so on. Young people were trying to start a revolution, blow things up. So a violent ending appealed to me visually. (laughs) I thinking of my own generation when I was making the film — a happy ending didn't seem right to me. I wasn't a very happy teenager myself. (laughs) The heroine expressed some of what I was feeling at the time.

But I felt sorry for her — you were rather cruel towards her in the end. (laughs)

I would have been embarrassed to end with a big triumph — to make her happy. (laugh) That part reflects my own youth — I would have been embarrassed to have all those people applauding me. (laughs)

"Dying In a Hospital" has a more universal feeling to it, as though you're not looking back on your own life so much as making a statement about life in general.

It was based on a bestseller by a doctor. Also at that time there had been several films set in hospitals — it was something of a hot topic. So I was sent the book — it was about people dying of cancer in a hospital. It was depressing and painful reading. (laughs) But my wife told me she thought it would make an interesting film.

Death is a great equalizer — it's something that comes to everyone. I'm going to die, you're going to die, everyone is going to die. When it comes to death, everyone is the same. So I thought the movie about death shouldn't have one hero — everyone should be the hero.

That's why I put the camera back and never moved in for close-ups. I also filmed a lot of scenic shots outdoors. That was the movie, basically — the hospital shots and the scenic shots. Actually, all the shots, even the ones in the hospital, have a scenic quality — they're trying to show the whole picture, not individuals.

The outdoor shots provide a dramatic contrast with the main action.

They're of healthy people, leading active lives, but all of them will die someday. I wanted to show how precious a healthy life is — it won't last forever.

There's seems to be a Buddhist message in there somewhere, though that may not be what you intended. (laughs)

Well, it was a difficult book to film — but I'm not religious really. (laughs) The message, I suppose, is that when it comes to death we're all the same, rich or poor. That may give the impression the film is looking at everyone with the eyes of God. (laughs) I'll be interested to see how a foreign audience reacts to it.

You made several films after "Dying At a Hospital" that had a lot of people comparing you to Ozu, such as "Tokyo Siblings" (Tokyo Kyodai, 1995) and "Tokyo Lullaby" ("Tokyo Yakyoku," 1997). Then you made "Tadon and Chikuwa" ("Tadon to Chikuwa," 1998), which was a complete change of pace.

I got the idea for that one around the time of the sarin subway poisonings (by the Aum Shinrikyo cult) and the Kobe earthquake. There seemed to be something abnormal about Japanese society then — I wanted to put that feeling into a film. I'd been making all these pretty, gentle-spirited films and I wanted a change. (laughs) I had the feeling I was imitating myself.

After that one, I went on to make "Osaka Story" ("Osaka Monogatari," 1999) and "Tokyo Marigold" (2001) — films that were different from the ones I had been making before and a bit different from each other. Then I made "Ryoma's Wife, Her Husband and Her Lover" ("Ryoma no Tsuma, to Sono Otto to Aijin," 2002), but that one was a failure. (laughs) The scriptwriter, Koki Mitani, and I got along well enough, but the film was something of a mess. (laughs) He probably should have directed it himself. Our sensibilities didn't mesh very well.

But Kyoka Suzuki won several prizes for her performance (as Ryoma's wife). You have a talent for bringing out the best in actresses, even idols like Yasuko Tomita (Busu) and Rena Tanaka (Tokyo Marigold). They showed a side that hadn't been apparent in their other work.
[Actors] read the script and come up with a certain interpretation, but it's not really theirs — they've gotten it from somewhere else. I tell them to forget whatever they've picked up. (laughs)

Their first take is usually off somehow. They think they're giving a great performance — but I don't like what they think is great. Maybe on another film they've been praised for it, but I don't like it. They're trying hard, but it's only when they stop trying that I get the expression I want. Sometimes I have to keep telling them to stop, until I get an expression that's natural. That's what my shoots are like — telling people to "stop it, stop it." (laughs)

With young actresses especially, when they think they great, they're usually wrong. (laughs) On "Busu" Yasuko Tomita became neurotic — I was too hard on her. (laughs) "Busu" means ugly but her character wasn't ugly physically — her heart was ugly. That's what I wanted her to show.

The character Rena Tanaka plays in "Tokyo Marigold" is also lonely, but she's more aggressive in her pursuit of love.
I had the feeling that Tanaka herself had had a lot of experience with love. I wanted her to unlock those memories. More than try to act a certain role, I wanted her to open up that part of herself.

So "Tokyo Marigold" wasn't like "Busu," where you were drawing on your own experiences.
When I made (Busu) I was still in my thirties — I could still remember my youth. But by the time I made "Tokyo Marigold" I was in my late forties — I was a bit more of an adult. (laughs).

Most people like festivals, but now I'm more interested in what happens after the festival is over, to the ones who are left behind, like the characters in "Ryoma."

Unfortunately, we can only screen four of your films: "Busu," "Dying In a Hospital," "Tadon and Chikuwa" and "Tokyo Marigold."
Well, that's a good variety.

Are there any others that you would like us to screen?
I like "Tokyo Siblings" ("Tokyo Kyodai"), but it's a quiet film. "Tadon and Chikuwa" is probably better — people are going to be surprised when they see that one. (laughs)

When I saw "Tokyo Siblings," I first thought the brother and sisters were living in a time warp — they're like characters from an Ozu film, but I realized that they weren't as out of place as they seemed. The Japanese haven't changed that much basically – there are continuities from generation to generation.
Maybe, but there's something strange about the Japanese family now. That's really gone off the rails. (laughs) So in my films I want to make sure people don't forget the old ways — otherwise they'll disappear forever.

Japanese society seems to have become conservative lately, at least politically.
There are no social protest movements like in the old days. It's a bit sad. I don't really understand what young people are thinking now. My youth was totally different than what I'm seeing today. Young people are withdrawing into themselves.

The hikkikomori (recluse) phenomenon.
The heroine in "Busu" is something of a hikkikomori, though. The process of how she breaks out of her shell is the theme of the film.

Changing the subject a bit — you came into the film industry through the TV commercial field, but it seems today that more younger directors enter the industry from TV dramas. The director of the "Bayside Shakedown" films is one example, the director of "Kisarazu Cat's Eye" is another. In fact, the films themselves were developed from TV dramas.
When I came in there were several writers making movies. Ryu Murakami was one of the better-known — but they didn't last long. Beat Takeshi, on the other had, made the jump successfully — he was a TV comedian. Peoples from all sorts of fields are becoming directors now.

But there does seem to be a difference between the directors who got their start making TV dramas and ones, like yourself, who were working in other fields. The TV drama directors tend to make films that look like TV dramas.
With TV commercials, I'm trying to make what are really little movies, to pack as much as I can into 15 or 30 seconds. I enjoy doing that because I'm a movie buff. But people who have been raised watching TV end up making movies that are like TV commercials and dramas. It's the reverse from me. After making 15-second TV commercials, I'm so happy to shoot something longer. With movies there are no time limits. Making films is how I relieve my stress. (laughs)

But films have to succeed at the box office, don't they?
That's scary. Also, with TV commercials, my name never appears — there's no "directed by Jun Ichikawa." With films, though, my name does appear — that's scary too. (laughs) Well, I've never had any big hits. (laughs) The videos of my films tend to be long sellers, though. What I need is someone like (Masayuki) Mori, who runs Office Kitano, someone who can push my films commercially. Maybe you can help me, Mark. (laughs)

I'd be honored. (laughs) Thank you very much for you time.

(2004 "Udine Far East Film Festival Catalogue")

Umetsugu Inoue interview

How did you get into films? Did you watch musicals when you were young?

I went to the Kyoto Municipal Number One Commercial High School, which is the third oldest commercial high school in the country. When I was a third year student, the third, fourth and fifth year class presidents and vice presidents were called together and taken to a temple where they were holding a funeral for a graduate (of the high school) who had died fighting in the Sino-Japanese War. I was forced to sit on a wooden floor for a long time listening to sutras until my legs went numb. I had no idea who we were there for — then afterwards I heard that it was a famous film director. Several days after that screenings of this director's films were held at the Kyoto Asahi Hall. That's when I finally learned his name — he was the great Sadao Yamanaka.

My high school also produced Masahiro Makino, Tameyoshi Kubo, Seiichiro Uchikawa and me — five film directors altogether. Kyoto was a center of filmmaking so perhaps it was only natural. Even so it's interesting that five film directors could come out a commercial high school. Anyway, when I learned that the funeral had been for a famous director, I wanted to see his films.

At that time there was a Teachers Association in Kyoto. Its members were junior high school teachers who would take turns patrolling the streets. They would go to the entertainment districts and take the names of students who were going into the movie theaters and coffee shops and report them to their schools. At that time, it was forbidden for junior high school students to go to a movie theater alone. I was the class president, so the Teachers Association caught me, there would be hell to pay. But I managed to sneak into the Asahi Hall by the back entrance. The film they were screening was Yamanaka's "Humanity and Paper Balloons" ("Jinjo Kamifusen"). I was really impressed by that film— it made me realize how wonderful movies were. I became an enthusiastic film fan and snuck into theaters in various ways, avoiding the eyes of the Teachers Association. But I never thought in a million years I would enter the film world myself.

In 1946, when you were still a student at Keio University, you got a job with Shin Toho. How did that come about?

My senior at Kyoto Number One Commercial, Seiichiro Uchikawa, got a job as a assistant director at Toho. That was when Toho was having its labor troubles and some of the actors and staff broke off to form the Shin Toho union. Living in Tokyo, I needed a part-time job, so with Uchikawa's help I was hired as a third assistant director for a film Tamizo Ishida was directing for the Shin Toho union. It was "Alien Green" ("Midori wa I na Mono") — a period drama comedy. They didn't have enough staff, so in addition to my work as an AD, I helped in other ways. I would stand there with the script and the call sheet and the clacker. When the director yelled "start" I'd hold out the clacker, then start the stop watch around my neck and make notes about the dialogue. But I had no idea what I was doing — I was always screwing up and getting scolded. I thought they wouldn't ask me back, but instead Shin Toho hired me after I graduated — that was in 1947.

But to get promoted to director, you had to write scripts, didn't you?

That's right, you had to write scripts if you wanted to be promoted, so I studied scriptwriting. I'd studied economics at the university, so I didn't know a lot about literature. Most of the other ADs coming into the company at that time had. Fortunately, I'd seen a lot of movies and so had a lot of ideas, but I didn't know how to structure them. So I studied scriptwriting. How to plot, how to move the story from point A to B to C.

Toward the end of 1950 a gap opened up in the lineup for New Year's. They only had two months to make a film and no script — no plan, even. One of the producers proposed a film based on a story by Masao Shiro — "The Casebook of the Young Samurai Lord" ("Wakasama Samurai Torimonocho") — but it was too short for a film. I had an idea to use just the atmosphere of the story and write something original, with all the action taking place in one house. So the producer asked me if I could write it up as a script and got me a room in a ryokan (Japanese-style inn).

I dashed off an outline by about seven in the evening. I thought it would take me three for four days to write the actual script, but after dinner I got so caught up in what I was writing that I forgot to go to sleep. I finished the script by about nine o'clock the next morning and took a nap. Then around eleven I went to the studio to wait for the producer. When he finally came in I slapped the script down (on his desk). He couldn't believe that I'd finished it in one day — he thought I was lying. But there was this old woman — Granny Hirata — at the ryokan who told him "What are you talking about — he was hard at work. He was going scratch, scratch, scratch all night long — I couldn't sleep." I'd written it all right. But from a business point of view writing a script in one night isn't a good idea. (laughs)

A critic called Eto wrote a column for the Mainichi newspaper about promising young movie people. He said that this Shin Toho assistant director Inoue has something interesting coming out for New Year's. That he's a promising newcomer. After that the requests flooded in, even though I was just an AD.

It's wasn't because I was that great — it was because I was quick and cheap. I would dash off something in five days and get Y50,000 or Y100,000 for it. That's how I could be promoted to director so quickly. Even so it took me four years to make it to director. When I became a director the studio was divided — all the assistant directors under me were with me, all the directors above me were against me. Also, all the old-timers on the staff were against me.

How did you start writing musicals?

I liked music — I could play the harmonica and the guitar and the ukulele pretty well. A little bit of piano too, but mostly classics. I didn't know anything about jazz. But when I became a director at Shin Toho, jazz was booming. After the end of the war Chiemi Eri appeared. Then she went to America and along came Izumi Yukimura.

Around that time Shin Toho broke off from Toho and got a new president who had come from Korakuen (a Tokyo amusement complex). This president called me in. "You're young, Inoue, and you like music," he told me. "I want you to do something with Izumi now that we have her under contact."

I didn't know anything about jazz, but I met Izumi and tried to learn as much as I could. I met this couple Danny and Mary who had this jazz band. Mary was still going to a women's college. Her father, mother and two sisters were also into jazz — they were all band managers. Also there were all these jazz coffee shops, mainly in the Ginza. I was lucky — with Mary's help I learned all I could about jazz. I went to the Ginza every day with her. This was the time when live jazz was at its peak. The jazz coffee houses were really something. Later I was able to meet Mary's mother and father at Tennessee (a jazz coffee shop) — they really taught me a lot. Her mother even asked me to stay at their place. I ended sleeping in Mary's room

How did you come to make "Tokyo Cinderella"?

"Tokyo Cinderella" had a lot of singing — so much that the drama had to be cut quite a bit, but that may have been what made it a success. It was the first real jazz movie made in Japan. The composer of "Sukiyaki" ("Ue o Mite Aruko") saw "Tokyo Cinderella" and told me that it was unheard of to give (the lead role) to a skinny kid like Izumi. He thought I should have used Ineko Arima or Mariko Okada. But Shin Toho was a small studio — Toho had taken all of the best stars, like Setsuko Hara and Kazuo Hasegawa, and then cut it loose. I had to do what I could with a sixteen-year-old star. There was no way I could have gotten Mariko Okada (a popular ingenue) (laughs)

"The Winner" ("Shorisha") was your first film with Yujiro Ishihara, wasn't it?

It was released in May — Golden Week (a cluster of holidays in last April and early May). There was a ballet scene in an American film — "The Red Shoes" — that went on for fifteen minutes. I did something similar, but mine was about thirteen, fourteen minutes. Reiko Kondo did a great job with that scene — she really got into it. The scene was supposed to be about thirteen minutes, but I ended up shooting three times longer.

That film did well at the box office, so the (producers) wanted to do another film with Inoue and Ishihara for the summer Obon holiday (The Festival of the Dead in August) — That was "The Eagle and the Hawk" ("Washi to Taka"). It was based on a script I'd written a long time before about a detective on board a ship. There had never been a Japanese film shot entirely on a boat like that one.

We took the boat out on Tokyo Bay and got hit by a typhoon. The waves were coming right over the deck as we were filming. I wanted to time the shooting so we'd film the big waves just as they hit — splash! But when we were ready to start filming none of the actors — Yujiro and all the rest — came out. They'd all gotten seasick waiting. (laughs)

We finally had to dock and take rooms in an inn for the night. The waves were dangerous but the boat wasn't built for them — it had a flat bottom like this (demonstrates). That's how they built them during the war. After we finished shooting on that boat they were going to scrap it. (laughs) We shot on the boat a total of four days — after that nothing but sets. It was a hard film to make, but I really love it.

After that I filmed "The Guy Who Started a Storm" ("Arashi o Yobu Otoko") for New Year's. Before that, though, I got married (to Yumeji Tsukioka (one of the stars of The Eagle and the Hawk). That film was really a tough shoot for Yujiro — he had to work like crazy learning drumming so he could look convincing with the real drummers in the film –but it turned out to be a huge hit. Managing director Emori sent me a telegram: (reads) "'Storm' is getting a great reaction. All the theater owners are surprised — and trembling with fear. (They think we're going to raise the rental fee on them.)" (laughs)

When "The Guy Who Started a Storm" opened on the 29th (of December) I was finishing my next film (Horn of the Night/Yoru no Tsuno). I heard that it was a hit, but I didn't really have time to think about it. Then on the 30th it started to sink in — this was a huge, huge hit. The noon siren sounded and ten minutes later we wrapped "Horn of the Night." That's when I realized that Yujiro's era had begun.

Did you think he was going to be big from the very beginning?
I didn't know that he was going to be that big. He wasn't a pretty boy like Shin Uehara. He was really smart — he'd graduated from Keio University. Also he was very modern. And he was a good-looking kid, but just a cut or two above the average. He was a new type — a member of the intelligensia and a man of the people, all mixed together.

How did you happen to make "Hong Kong Nocturne"? It's reminiscent of the "Three Girls" ("Sannin Musume") series with Hibari Misora, Chiemi Eri and Izumi Yukimura.
More than the "Three Girls" films it's a remake of "The Night I Want to Dance, 1963" ("Odoritai Yoru"), a film I did for Shochiku. The three girls in that picture were Yoshie Nieta, Chieko Baisho and Taeko Waniguchi. The story is exactly the same.

The first film I made for Run Run Shaw, the Hong Kong producer, was in a comic style. He wanted me to sign a contact to do more. "You're really good," he said. "Come work for us again."
The first film I did for him (Operation Lipstick) was a spy movie — comic action — something about the Hong Kong government. It was a story of political intrigue, about separatists who wanted independence from England and China...(Run-Run) wanted me to do something else right away, but in three months I had on my visa thought could only shoot one film. I thought I might make the next one in Japan — that's what I thought anyway. (laughs)
Anyway, "Hong Kong Nocturne" had a lot of good actors in it. Run-Run was overjoyed with it. It became a big hit — a million-dollar movie. It really did well in Hong Kong. We screened it for the British governor at a Christmas party. Then Run-Run Shaw showed it to the king of Thailand. In Japan they were making period dramas with a musical flavor. You couldn't make modern Western-style

musicals then in Japan — nobody was doing that kind of thing, including me. So (Run-Run) was surprised to see me do it in (Hong Kong Nocturne).

So when I went back (to Japan), he told me "What do you think you're doing – make another one right away!" I asked him if he wanted me to write something., "I'll have someone else write it — so get over here."

At any rate, I could only make two films in three months — that was the limit. If I'd had it my way I would have spent a year or two (making that sort of film).

The next year when I went (to Hong Kong) and took a tour of the sets, I saw that the actors I had worked with the year before were still there. So I said I'd make two films in three months. This was great news for the (studio) management. At that time one of those films cost 50 million yen to make. If you spend a year or two making a film, that 50 million is not working for you all that time. But I could make two films in three months and then they'd get their money back right away. (laughs) They'd get ten times their money back! So (Run-Run) wanted Inoue. "I'll have someone else write the script – just get over here! (laughs) So I went there every year for six years and made seventeen films.

When I did (Tokyo Nocturne). I wanted to use newcomers (in the main roles). (Run-Run) thought that the foreign director would want to use veterans. "Why newcomers?" he asked. I said that if young people see the film then young people are better (in the main roles). When he said that (casting newcomers) was hit and miss, I said that if you want to make a good movie, it's better to use young people. Then it became a big hit. After that, when I couldn't come, he brought in all these other Japanese directors.

What role in Raymond Shaw play in making your films?
Run-Run Shaw was the one who asked me to come to Hong Kong. He even met me at the airport when I first came over for a look see with my manager. After that Raymond handled all the negotiations. But Run-Run Shaw talked to me about films. He asked me to see this film he wanted me to make — the American film "How to Marry a Millionaire," about these three stewardesses. He said he wanted me to remake it. I said there's a problem with the rights. He said "We don't worry about that in Hong Kong." I said "You say you don't worry, but I'm in Japan, so there's no way I can just remake it as is." Then he said "We want you to make it any way," so I said I would change the stewardesses into dancers and have them go to Taiwan, Japan and Thailand. He said OK — and the film ("The Millionaire Chase") became a big hit.

How was it making films there? Were the shooting schedules about the same as in Japan?
The pace was faster than Japan. I had to shoot quickly because I only had three months, so they would give me priority and work like crazy — they had to getting rolling and shoot something! In Japan I'd have to wait for this or that, but when I went to Hong Kong, I was the first priority. I made the schedule to suit myself. We (Japanese) handled all the post-production — all the editing and music. I had a wonderful editor with me. I did that for six years. One year I filmed in Japan. In five of those six years I made ten films (in Hong Kong) and seven in Japan — seventeen altogether.

Why did you stop going there?
Raymond quit and Mona Hong took over. Mona Hong had been a singer – she had a husky voice and was quite good. Anyway she was tight with money, but she didn't know she was tight. It was terrible. The last time I went there the hotel they had me stay at was a shithole... I stopped going after that. (laughs)

We're also planning to screen "The Performers" ("Hana to Namida to Hono") with Hibari Misora and Shinichi Mori. How did you become involved with that film?
When I said I was going to quit Nikkatsu, the news was in the morning papers. That same day I got a call from Hibari's mother. "Please come to the Toei studio in Kyoto and shoot my daughter's next picture," she said. I was really glad to hear that, but I had several films lined up after I left (Nikkatsu).

I was all booked up. Then ten years passed. In that time Hibari got married and divorced. She performed at Koma Theater (in Shinjuku, Tokyo) twice a year. A lot happened. Anyway, she was celebrating her 25th year in show business. I got a call from her mother just as I was preparing to go to Hong Kong. "Sensei! When can you come? It's been ten years already! My daughter is going to be an old woman!" I said "Uh, I'm going to Hong Kong." "Go to Hong Kong later," she said. "Your promise to us comes first." (laughs) Well. it couldn't be helped — I made a call (to Hong Kong) and asked if I could go in March instead of January. Then I made Hibari's picture.

By then she was this big diva. Did that present any problems?

Yes, she was a big star, but the Toei movie fell through — the one we were going to make in Kyoto. The (film) we did after that was great, though. And the one after that. Just around the time I met Hibari, her younger brother was involved in this pistol incident and was found to be mixed up with the yakuza. She wanted to help him, so she put him in her show. The mass media really made a stink about that. so she had to drop him. So I really wanted to go all out for her.

Then I got a letter from her mother saying she was so happy (Hibari) could meet me after so many years. It was wonderful to see me working so diligently on the set. The mass media has been saying all these bad things about us, but we appreciate your support. We're so happy to be working with you after so many years."

I wrote a reply saying "I apologize for making you wait ten years, but I'm glad that we could work together. Hibari is a wonderful performer."

"She gets up early and, more importantly, her performance is terrific. The mass media has been bashing her, but I am proud to be associated with her and I support her one hundred percent. I'm really rooting for her. You may think that millions of people are against her, but millions are also for her. Please believe that everyone on my staff supports Hibari."

The day after I sent that reply I went to the set and, when I turned on the lights, I saw Hibari and her mother in the shadows. They had been waiting for me in a dark set. They hugged me, saying they were so happy to get that letter. They both kissed me! (laughs) Then the president (of the studio) told me "Inoue Sensei! I heard you sent Hibari a love letter. Hibari and her mother read that letter every night over drinks and just cry and cry." (laughs).

How was her performance (in that film)?

She'd gotten a lot better as an actor. She was originally a natural talent — she had been doing this since she was a child. But as she got older her acting became more powerful. She'd fight with Shogo Shimada (a veteran character actor who played her father in the film). "Sensei! That performance of his is crap!" (laughs)

(2006 "Udine Far East Film Festival Catalogue")

Yuya Ishii interview

Japanese directors with any kind of ambition usually end up making a family drama, which is to Japanese cinema what the Western used to be to Hollywood: the core national genre. Of course, plenty of bad-to-mediocre directors here have made family dramas, just as plenty of bad-to-mediocre

Hollywood directors once made Westerns. But just as the Western was defined by its giants, John Ford and Howard Hawks among them, so is the Japanese family drama exemplified by its masters, including Yasujiro Ozu and Mikio Naruse.

The latest to make the attempt is Yuya Ishii, who was turning out quirky black comedies at a rapid clip in his early twenties and screening them at festivals around the world, including special sections at the 2008 Rotterdam and Hong Kong festivals. Among the honors this wunderkind accumulated was the Edward Yang New Talent Award at the 2008 Asian Film Awards, when he was 24.

Ishii's 2010 dramady "Sawako Decides" ("Kawa no Soko kara Konnichi wa") was still quirky — its twenty-something heroine (Hikari Mitsushima) ran a clam-packing factory she took over from her dad — but it was also tethered to real-life concerns in post-Lehman-shock Japan. Also screened widely abroad, "Sawako Decides" showed that Ishii was growing as a filmmaker, a wunderkind no more.

His latest, "A Man With Style" ("Azemichi no Dandei"), is more Ishii than Ozu in its sudden, if firmly motivated, emotional eruptions and strange but sweet flights of fantasy. At the same time, its story of a father's anxiety over his own authority and his offspring's futures is a genre standard.

In an interview at the office of distributor Bitters End, looking rosy-cheeked and bright-eyed, but already the confidently experienced (if not "veteran") director, Ishii denied any intent to match himself against Ozu and Naruse: "It was the exact opposite," he explained. "The budget was limited, so what we could do was limited. For that reason I wanted to make a film on a very, very basic human theme, something quite simple. But if I could do anything, I might start thinking about making a space ship or filming a war."

The "dandy" of the title is one Junichi Miyata (Ken Mitsuishi), a 50-year-old deliveryman who is still to trying to live up to a vow he made as boy to be a "cool man." Meaning one who lives by the traditional macho code to project strength, protect the weak and never, ever cry. Very important that last one, since the 13-year Junichi was prone to blubbing, even in front of his best pal Sanada, who is still his best and, in fact, only friend, decades later.

In addition to worrying about his manhood, Miyata is facing the usual middle-aged dad dilemmas: His son Toshiya (Ryu Morioka), who is studying for his college entrance exams, and daughter Momoko (Jun Yoshinaga), a high school senior unsure about her future plans, shrug at his warnings and advice (usually delivered at a screech). Sanada (Tomorowo Taguchi) loyally lends an ear at their regular drinking sessions, but Miyata's beloved wife (Naomi Nishida) died at age 39, leaving only memories, including a silly kid's song he can't get out of his head.

He is essentially on his own — but can't bring himself to reach out for help. His macho code forbids it, though his whole personality rebels against the code.

Ishii wrote the script to this story before Ken Mitsuishi, a veteran character actor who had not had a leading role in 32 years, was cast by his producer. "I rewrote the script, trying to make it more interesting for Mitsuishi," he explained. "That goes for the other cast members as well — I tailored the script to them."

Having seen many family dramas by Ishii's seniors, including Kiyoshi Kurosawa's "Tokyo Sonata" (2008), Hirokazu Kore'eda's "Still Walking" ("Aruitemo Aruitemo," 2008) and Sion Sono's "Be Sure to Share" ("Chanto Tsutaeru," 2009) I have often wondered, I told Ishii, why so many of the dads are so hard-headed and, finally, lonely. "That's the traditional Japanese father," Ishii said. "He's short-tempered and not liked by his kids."

But more Japanese fathers today, he added, "are simply ignored by their wife and children." "So rather than a film about a traditional Japanese father, I wanted to make one about what to me is an ideal, a father I'd like to see in this day and age," he explained.

Ishii likes his heroes to be on the emotional boil, but Mitsuishi keeps Miyata's eruptions (barely) under control, while giving hints of the gentler, more caring person under the hot-tempered surface. His heart, we see over the shouting, is in the right place. Even his quixotic quest to be the real man of his boyhood dreams starts to look less foolish, more admirable.

"He's not living a contradiction," Ishii says with some heat. "He living for an ideal. A man should always have something to strive for. It's all right if he doesn't achieve it." And Ishii's own ideal? "I have one. I want to become like (the hero) in the film. I can see myself as that kind of middle-aged guy."

There is, he is quick to add, little overlap between Miyata and his own father. "There is a link in the story itself — my father also lost his wife early," Ishii explains. "But I would never think of putting my own father in a film. He's still alive and well — it would be difficult."

Ishii has his doubts about how well "A Man With Style" will be received abroad, despite the hitherto warm reception foreign fans have given his films. "The person who translated the script told me that foreigners won't understand the father," he said. "In the West fathers have more of a clear position and are respected by their children. So (Westerners) won't get why the father is disrespected so much. But even if they don't understand, I'm OK with it. The foreign opinion (of the film) isn't everything."

At least critics, foreign or no, can't slate him for sentimentality line in "A Man With Style," since it has none. Instead Ishii keeps an objective/ironic distance from dramatic turns that another director would shamelessly manipulate. "I didn't want to jerk tears, but I did want emotion," he says. "...I wanted to make scenes saying that human beings are basically good. But I tried not to put too weight on that. I tried not to overdo it."

One way to accomplish that, he explains, was keep the characters from hugging. "(Westerners) have asked me why a parent and child don't hug when they part from each other in a Japanese film. The Japanese way is not to hug in that situation. Japanese keep a distance between their bodies. I'm always conscious of that Japanese sort of feeling, that good side of Japanese culture."

At the same time, Ishii realizes that Japan, as well as Japanese attitudes towards film, have changed since March 11. He mentions the decisions by Yoji Yamada and Takeshi Kitano to suspend ongoing film projects in the wake of the disaster. "The fans' mindset has changed, both consciously and unconsciously," he says "...But my goal for "A Man With Style" was to make something universal, something with a theme that was the same 50 years ago and will be the same 50 years from now. Even after March 11, I think it has the power to be released just as it is."

Looking to the future, Ishii does not, like many similarly successful indie directors, want to make big-budget commercial films ("I'm not so concerned with the budget — I'd just like to be able to do what I want"), though he is interested in going abroad to work ("It's something I think I should do and want to do").

Meanwhile, he sees big changes ahead for not only his own career, but the Japanese film industry as a whole. "I don't think the media of film itself is going to be the way it is now in ten or twenty years' time. Films are going to be different. They going to naturally change, for the better or worse. So I have to meet that challenge, in various ways. I'm still only 27, so I have the strength to do it."

(June 24, 2011, "The Japan Times")

Kazuyuki Izutsu interview: unafraid of rightist rage

Directors tend to be articulate types, especially when discussing (or rather spinning) their own films, but Kazuyuki Izutsu has few equals in the art of spoken communication, in or out of the director's chair. From snappy one-liners about dull movies to verbal bombshells aimed at local rightists, Izutsu says exactly what's on his active, unorthodox mind to everyone from television viewers of late-night talk shows to this reporter in a recent interview at the headquarters of Cine Quanon, which is distributing his new film "Pacchigi! Love & Peace."

Now 56 years old, Izutsu has had a long, up-and-down career as a director, beginning with his apprenticeship in pink ("adult") films in the 1970s. In the past decade he has become a familiar presence on TV, while making hit after acclaimed hit, including "Pacchigi!," the Kyoto Romeo and Juliet drama that swept local awards in 2005.

In speaking with ""The Japan Times"," Izutsu was more subdued and serious than in his TV appearances, but then the discussion revolved around war movies, social prejudice against Koreans in Japan and the rightist reaction to his latest film, "Pacchigi! Love & Peace."

You seem to have a made "Pacchigi! Love & Peace" as a response to "For Those We Love" ("Ore wa Kimi no Tame ni Koso Shi ni Iku"), the tokkotai (kamikaze) pilot film executive produced by Tokyo Gov. Shintaro Ishihara.
There have been a lot of movies like that one. When major film companies in Japan are stuck for a film, they make one about the tokkotai (pilots). They have a pretty good idea that that sort of theme will draw audiences, so they make it.

But your kind of film is tougher to make.
I never could have made it with a major film company. I was only able to do it because Lee Bong-ou (president of Cine Quanon and an ethnic Korean living in Japan) was backing me. Cine Quanon is about the only company I can imagine doing it.

The film is set in 1974 when Japan's ethnic Koreans in show business were afraid to reveal their true identities because of the prejudice against them inside and outside the industry. Is it different today?
Not really. Japanese society hasn't changed that much, and that includes Japanese show business. Ethnic Koreans are still reluctant to say who they are; they worry that they might not get any more work. There's still a lot of discrimination against them. In a lot of foreign countries, the entertainment business tends to be more progressive than the surrounding society — that's only natural isn't it? — but in Japan it's still feudalistic and conservative.

In "Pacchigi! Love & Peace" you satirize not just Japanese show business, but rightist war movies and the ideology behind them. I can't help comparing it to "The Gentle Art of Japanese Extortion" ("Minbo no Onna") (1992), which got director Juzo Itami nearly stabbed to death by yakuza who didn't like the way he portrayed the gangs. Do you worry that that sort of thing might happen to you?
Actually, a lot of yakuza came to see "Pacchigi!" — they're some of my biggest supporters. (laughs)

But there's a difference between the yakuza and the rightists, isn't there? Won't the rightists be angry with you for disrespecting the tokkotai?
I don't disrespect the tokkotai themselves. They had a certain mission to carry out, a mission that they didn't choose. I don't blame them for carrying out their mission — and the film doesn't blame them. But I do have problems with films that distort the historical reality of what the tokkotai were. I think (audiences) will understand that, so I'm not worried about my personal safety.

(May 18, 2007, "The Japan Times")

Akio Jissoji interview

Japan coordinator Kimiko Ishii and I met Akio Jissoji and his manager at the Imagica studio in Gotanda, Tokyo. He'd had a spell of illness and looked peaked, but was ready to talk — especially about one of his favorite authors, Edogawa Rampo. Jissoji has already made three films based this writer of mysteries dipped in the erotic, the decadent and the macabre — and would like to make one more.

What attracted you to the work of Edogawa Rampo?
I like him as a writer. I especially like his world — he wrote about a Tokyo and a Japan that I was aware of as a boy, but no longer exist. There were more people then who had the leisure to pursue an art or interest — I mean, there were still plenty of poor people — but there were also others whose father was a diplomat or whatever and so had the means to play, while thinking their own thoughts, making their own art.
I like things that don't have a purpose. I don't like films whose purpose is to move people or give them strength. All of my own films are just the opposite — they don't have any purpose. (laughs)

You can find examples of those types in "Watcher In the Attic."
Yes, they're all from the upper classes.

But Kyusaku Shimada's Akechi stands out from the rest. Shimada has appeared in several of your films. Did you think of him first when you were casting the role?
Well, he starred in "Tokyo: The Last Megalopolis" ("Teito Monogatari") as the villain. I liked him (in that role). He seemed like the type who could walk in the shadows of society, so I cast him as Akechi. I thought he did a good job.

Hiroshi Mikami is another stand-out as the hero — but in quite a different way.
I thought he was the type who could be a homosexual. There's something ambiguous about him. When he peeps at women, it's a kind of amusement, a kind of game. It's not just a sexual obsession.

Also when he decides to kill the dentist, it's a kind of experiment. He doesn't really hate him. He doesn't hate him at all. It's like play for him.
On the other hand the hero of Dostoevsky's "Crime and Punishment" kills out of a resentment against God. That sort of resentment doesn't motivate the hero of "Watcher."

No, God has nothing to do with it. Edogawa Rampo took his name from Edgar Allen Poe, but his writings were quite different from Poe's. He doesn't acknowledge the existence of God. Instead he's more interested in the criminal nature of man — not crime as defined by religion but by the society around the individual. There was a film by Noboru Tanaka based on the same story — but totally different from yours. Were you thinking of that film at all when you made yours?
No, not at all. I'm not one to refer to other films. That goes for all films, not just ones based on Edogawa Rampo's work. I don't see very many. I have ones I like — but none very recent. Instead of going to movie theaters, I prefer to go to art museums.

Was there any connection between "Watcher" and "Murder on D Street"?
Yes, there was — in fact, I still want to make a film based on Edogawa Rampo. "Murder" is based on two stories by Rampo His stories are so short that if you don't link two together you can't make a feature-length film. When Noboru Tanaka made "Watcher" he added a story of Rampo's called "The Human Chair." There have been a lot like that.

Your two Rampo films are several years apart, but stylistically they're very similar. Of course, the same director made both. (laughs)

That was because I didn't have any money. I had to compensate (for the lack of money) — I've often had to do that on my films. "Ubume" ("Ubume no Natsu") was the same — I didn't much money. Or for the "The Hell of Mirrors" ("Kagami Jigoku") in "Rampo Noir," for that matter. But I believe it's better not to have money — you can make better films that way.

When you were asked to film a segment for "Rampo Noir" did you have any thing to say about the other directors involved?

No, nothing— I just filmed (my segment). I was the one who first wrote the scenario for that film, though. Originally I was going make one film, but when we took it around to film companies, we couldn't get any of them to make it. Then a producer came along with the idea of making four short films, not one. But I didn't know the other directors — I had never met them. I had never even seen their films.

Was Tadanobu Asano easy to work with?

Yes, he was — he's an accomplished actor. But he's not the kind who develops his role through discussions with the director — he does that on his own. Shimada was more the other way.

Are there any Rampo stories that you'd like to film?

Yes, there is. I'd like to film one of his longer works — "The Bronze Golem" ("Seido no Majin"). I've written the script and found a producer but for some reason I can't get it made. (laughs) It's an interesting story so I can't understand why. But I just can't get the money together. I'd like to shoot it in the Czech Republic. They have a certain kind of doll there that appears in the story.

Maybe we can get the word out when you go to Udine. (laughs)

Yes, that would be good. (laughs).

(Producer Masanobu Suzuki enters conversation): He's been to Italy several times to make commercials.

Are you a fan of Italian films?

I've seen a few — Fellini and Antonioni and Pasolini, but I was raised on French films. When I was young I saw all the French films I could from the 1930s through the 1950s. They were quite different from Rampo, though. (laughs)

You've made all sort of films in your career — ATG (Art Theater Guild), "Ultraman."

I've heard that there are quite a few "Ultraman" fans in Italy. One came all the way from Milano to see me. (laughs)

I'm sure there are a lot more in Italy. (laughs) But is there a similar thread running through all those films for you?

Yes, there is. They're all made about the same way really. That goes for the films and the TV programs. Have you heard of a writer named Kyoka Izumi? He lived about the same time as Rampo and his stories are somewhat similar, but more supernatural. I'd like to make something based on his work as well. Rampo didn't write so much about ghosts and that sort of supernatural phenomena. He was more interested in the strangeness of human beings. The fear that could strike in the real world. How reality could suddenly look unreal —how a human being could suddenly look like a monster. So there is that sort of link between him and Kyoka. Also, they were both interested in old things.

Kyoka's stories have been made into plays — you couldn't do that with Rampo's. Kyoka is broader that way.

Rampo's work reflects a certain time, when Japan was militarizing. Japan had won the war (with Russia) and was feeling its own strength. Rampo also reflects a new type of civilization. Japanese culture had been imported from China — Chinese classics, Chinese writing and so on. In Rampo's day that traditional culture collapsed. That's reflected in his work — traditional culture giving way to a mixture of Japanese and Western culture.

You can see that mixing in his pen name, in the content of his work. The various people who appear (in his stories) are products of the collapse of the old culture and the birth of the new. He was a child of that era himself — that why he could write about it the way he did.

Young people today think of that era as being totally dark — but that's wrong. The Middle Ages also have a dark image, but people then still felt happiness as well as sadness. Japan may have been a militarized country (in Rampo's day) — but that time wasn't dark all the way through — it gave birth to new things as well. The misconception comes from the educational system the GHQ brought to Japan (in the post war period). It painted prewar Japan in dark shades only. That was wrong.

But Rampo remains popular even today.

Yes he is popular — but then his stories contain a lot of eroticism.

For some reason, though, his work hasn't been translated — there's only one collection of stories in English that I'm aware of.

I've thought about that — about why Rampo isn't translated more. Let me ask you — do you have a writer like him (in the West)?

Well — none I can think of.

There are none. Some resemble him in part — but that's all. Yes, I'd like to see (more of his work) translated. It might be interesting. One problem is that his mysteries are a bit cold. They are very logical — you solve them as you would a puzzle. But it's hard for me to express myself logically that way — I haven't been educated to do it. I tend to be more ambiguous. Even so I'd like to try to make a long Rampo film — "The Bronze Golem." I've already written the script.

We'll do our best to promote it at Udine. (laughs)

(2006 "Udine Far East Film Festival Catalogue")

Haruki Kadokawa interview

Haruki Kadokawa is a Japanese soulmate to the Hollywood moguls of old — a master promoter and unrepentant egotist who was the most powerful producer in the industry for nearly two decades.

Taking over as president of Kadokawa Shoten Publishing from his founder father in 1975, Kadokawa quickly began churning out best-selling pop fiction. Beginning in 1976 with the hit mystery "The Inagami Family", Kadokawa also produced and directed nearly sixty films, including the 1990 samurai swashbuckler "Heaven and Earth", which became the third-highest grossing Japanese film ever made.

Most were mass audience entertainments, based on Kadokawa Shoten novels, that Kadokawa relentlessly hyped on the basis of spectacle or star, orchestrating media saturation campaigns of a type familiar to Hollywood, but new to Japan. (Kadokawa launched several unknowns to stardom himself, most notably eighties super-idol Hiroko Yakushimaru.)

Kadokawa promoted himself, however, less as a master showman, more as a poet, adventurer and general renaissance man. He published his haiku and other verses in legitimate poetry magazines — not owned by his company. (His most recent collection of haiku, published this year, is simply titled "Japan.") In 1985 he led a successful expedition to find the remains of the Yamato, a battleship sunk on a suicide mission to Okinawa in the closing days of the war, with the loss of nearly 2,500 lives.

Kadokawa dreamed of playing a leading role on the world stage, with movies as the main vehicle of his ambitions. One was "Virus", a 1980 disaster epic starring Glenn Ford, Chuck Connors and Sonny Chiba that was a hit in Japan, but a disappointment in the US. Another was "Ruby Cairo," a 1993 romantic thriller starring Andie MacDowell, Viggo Mortensen and Liam Neeson that failed to find a US distributor, though it was later distributed there on video.

In August 1993, it all came crashing down when Kadokawa was arrested on a drug smuggling charge. The resulting encounter with the Japanese legal system not only put him into prison for two-and-a-half years, but destroyed his career. In the face-conscious, scandal-shy Japanese film world, he became a non-person.

Now, after years of struggle, including a draining battle with cancer, Kadokawa is back with Yamato, a war epic that recounts the last days of the battleship Yamato, especially its fiery end. His credit as executive producer is the biggest he has had in more than a decade. "This the first film I felt I had to make...this is not just business for me," Kadokawa commented in a recent interview at his office in Kadokawa Haruki Jimusho, the media company that has been his base since 1993. "...Of course, a movie should make money — filmmaking is a business and your movie had better be a hit if you intend to make another one. I'm not against that. But this is first time I've felt this strongly about a film. I'm in the business now just so I can make this film."

The genesis of the film was Kadokawa's aforementioned discovery, in a mini-sub, of the real Yamato on the seabed between Nagasaki and Okinawa. "At that time I was not thinking of making a film," he said. "Just finding the Yamato was a miracle. Better people than me had tried and failed to find it. I think I was guided by the spirits of the Yamato's dead."

Launched soon after Pearl Harbor and sunk in April, 1945 by US planes, the Yamato, noted Kadokawa, has come to symbolize the war, particularly its end, for many Japanese. "'Yamato' is an ancient name for Japan," he notes. "In other words a ship named after the country sank and that tragedy has had a big impact on the souls of the Japanese people."

The people he is hoping to most appeal to, however, are not the oldsters who are the main target of so many Japanese war films, but the young. "Young people in their teens and twenties keep the film business going and I want them to see this film." he says. "I think they'll support it. But the distributor, Toei, didn't believe me when I told them that."

Kadokawa proved Toei wrong with a recent survey showing that the age group with the highest want-to-see was between fifteen and twenty-five. "I find it really interesting that the group I most want to see the film is the group that most wants to see it," commented Kadokawa.

Why the interest? "Because I made the film," Kadokawa notes modestly. "Now there's a Yamato boom." Fueling the boom is a Yamato Museum opened in April in the port of Kure, as well as the open set Kadokawa had built in nearby Onomichi, where a full-scale mockup of the Yamato now on display to visitors. "Last Sunday alone we had 9,000 visitors, giving the local economy a big shot in the arm," Kadokawa said.

The Yamato mockup — 190 meters long and built at a cost of nearly Y500 million ($4.5 million) — would seem to be an anachronism in a CG age. Kadokawa argues otherwise: "The actors' performances and the images are completely different," he says. "If we'd just used CG (for the ship), we'd have shot the film in a studio — and it would have had no depth. When the actors boarded the ship, they felt as though they were really fighting a war. Their expressions changed — their whole consciousness changed."

After the filming, he explained, his formerly pacifistic young cast told a packed press conference, "that they would go to war to protect their families." "In war both the winners and losers are trying to protect their families, their communities, their countries," he added. "At the same time, they're killing each other — that's what war is. It's a tragedy for both sides. I want to say that clearly in the film — that both the winners and losers are victims."

While claiming to being "guided by the spirits of the Yamato dead" in making the film, Kadokawa was also influenced by his own experiences over the past twelve years. "My outlook on life has changed," he says. "I was judged and condemned by the Japanese legal system. Until then I had dedicated myself to Japan — then I was judged and condemned. My anger at that injustice is extremely strong. For the rest of my life I will be an enemy of the Japanese government. That's different from my love for Japan, because Japan and the Japanese government are different...That message appears in the film — I'm saying 'don't trust the government.' You may go off to die in a war, but don't trust the government."

He confesses, proudly, that he is, not a blameless victim, but a "a life-long delinquent." "In any era it's the delinquents who give birth to culture." he explains. "When you forget that, you lose sight of the meaning of culture. The people who create culture are always problem children."

Despite Yamato and other projects, includes plans for remakes and games based on the Akira Kurosawa classics Yojimbo and Tsubaki Sanjuro, Kadokawa has no desire to reclimb the industry heights he first ascended three decades ago. "I don't have that sense of mission any more. When I was in prison I realized that phrases like 'sense of mission' and 'sense of justice' are lies. That sort of thing doesn't really exist.

"I finally understood that human beings are born to enjoy life. More than knowing it instinctively, you might say I learned it the hard way. I have a sense of life as a game — and there's no more interesting game than the business of movies."

(December 25, 2005, "The Japan Times")

An audience with Kyoko Kagawa

Kyoko Kagawa is among the fast dwindling number of living witnesses to Japanese cinema's Golden Age of the 1950s and '60s.

In a career that started in 1949 with the Shintoho studio, Kagawa worked with the giants of the era, including Akira Kurosawa, Yasujiro Ozu, Kenji Mizoguchi and Mikio Naruse. And she appeared in films that have since become regarded worldwide as classics, such as 1953's "Tokyo Story" ("Tokyo Monogatari"), 1954's "Sansho the Bailiff" ("Sansho Dayu") and 1963's "High and Low" ("Tengoku to Jigoku").

To her natural vitality, intelligence and charm she added a sterling work ethic that served her well in the ensuing decades.

Recently the 79-year-old actress appeared in Tokyo at The Foreign Correspondents' Club of Japan to announce that she would receive an award from The International Federation of Film Archives for her film-preservation efforts, and also to promote a nine-film retrospective of her work at the Tokyo International Film Festival and an even bigger retrospective at the National Film Center of 45 films, together with an exhibition of photos, posters and other film-related materials from her private collection.

Looking elegant in a white suit, Kagawa was impeccably gracious in speech and manner. Instead of a remnant of a vanished era, she came across as a still-vital exemplar of that age's best aspects.

Later given a chance to interview Kagawa one-on-one, this reporter realized that she had no doubt answered, ad infinitum, almost any question I could ask — from the obvious to the rude. But during our appointed 30 minutes together, on a day full of media interviews, Kagawa was, to my relief, unfailingly patient.

I had first seen her in the flesh on the set of the 1993 film "Madadayo," Kurosawa's final work, in which she played the long-suffering wife of Hyakken Uchida, the film's eccentric writer/educator hero. I remembered thinking then how Kurosawa seemed to have mellowed from his famously tyrannical days as Toho's top director in the 1950s, when Kagawa worked with him on the Maxim Gorky play adaptation "The Lower Depths" ("Donzoko") in 1957. Did Kagawa, I wondered (hoping she hadn't heard the question today at least), share that view?

"He filmed takes (on 'Madadayo') more quickly," she answered without missing a beat. "When we were making 'The Lower Depths,' I wondered many times if we would shoot even one take that day — and finally realized it wasn't going to happen. On 'Madadayo,' we'd always rehearse the previous day and then the next morning we'd always shoot a take, with one cut per scene. His tempo had really become faster."

She also recalled Kurosawa as being "tough" on veteran character actor Tatsuo Matsumura, who played Uchida, but also saying OK to his first take, which was rare for a director to do — and going to his dressing room afterward to compliment him. "He didn't do that for me, though," she added. "Mieko Harada told me that when she had a good take on 'Ran' (1985), Kurosawa would come over to her applauding. But he never did that sort of thing for me, from a long time back," she said with a big, lilting laugh — and no discernible resentment.

"But it's true that he enjoyed shooting 'Madadayo,'" she quickly added. "He would joke, saying, 'I want to get to the set early, but if I go too early everyone is going to hate me.'"

Having broken the ice (and discovered that Kagawa had a sense of humor), I took the actress back to her beginnings at Shintoho, which at the time was the smallest of Japan's six major studios. When she started appearing in films there in the early 1950s, however, it was home to Kurosawa, Mizoguchi, Ozu, Naruse and other greats of the day.

"It was lucky for me that I was able to make my debut there," she said. "If you were in a big studio then it was hard to make your screen debut even if you had passed what they called the 'new face' (new talent) audition. But because (Shintoho) was a small studio, I could make my debut quickly. Also, my seniors — Hideko Takamine, Ken Uehara and Hisako Yamane — were all really nice people. They were kind to me and it was fun working with them."

Not always so nice were the aforementioned major directors, whom Kagawa described as "big, imposing presences" whose "word was law." Naruse, with whom she first worked on the 1952 family drama "Mother" ("Okaasan"), "was quiet, but his eyes were strict." Also, she explained, Naruse favored short cuts, which made it harder for Kagawa to act.

"I liked longer cuts because they gave my performance more continuity," she explained. "But since Naruse added one small cut to another, it was hard to make the right expression for each one."

Mizoguchi, who cast her as the female lead in his 1954 period tragedy "The Crucified Lovers" ("Chikamatsu Monogatari"), "would never tell me what to do," she said. "'Think for yourself' was his directing style." Then only 22, Kagawa found the experience "tough — it was really hard."

At the same time, being the favorite ingenue for the leading directors of the day made her a major star, as well as giving her confidence that she belonged in the business — and Kagawa is still grateful. "When I tried hard and these eminent directors said 'OK' I thought I might be alright," she said with another laugh. "I could feel a sense of security about myself. They loomed that large. Of course, they were older than me and I didn't feel I could talk to them."

In 1965, Kagawa went with her husband and young child to New York for a three-year stay. When she returned to Japan, the country's film industry was in steep decline and roles were much harder to come by.

"It was the age of television, so I did television work for a while," she reminisced. "That continued for some time, doing period dramas and that sort of thing." She did occasional film work, appearing in Satsuo Yamamoto's 1974 drama "The Family" ("Karei-naru Ichizoku"), a 1979 episode of the "Tora-san" series and Kei Kumai's 1990 period drama "Mt. Aso's Passions" ("Shikibu Monogatari").

Then came a three-year blank, finally ended by Kurosawa's call to appear in "Madadayo." "I was so happy that I could be with Kurosawa again," Kagawa enthused. "It had been 27 or 28 years since my last film with him, 'Red Beard' ('Akahige,' 1965)."

Critics (including this one) called "Madadayo" one of Kurosawa's weaker efforts, but Kagawa won several awards for it, including a Japan Academy Award for best supporting actress. After that she was in demand by not only veterans, but also directors who weren't even born when she rose to stardom, including Hirokazu Koreeda, Chihiro Ikeda and Takashi Yamazaki.

The pressure, I said, must be on the director now, working with the great Kyoko Kagawa. She laughed her loudest of the entire interview. "That's not true," she replied. "For me a director is always a director, even the young ones. So from the beginning I tell them 'Ask me anything, ask me to go anywhere.'"

(November 11, 2011, "The Japan Times")

Keeping it real: Naomi Kawase on filmmaking

Naomi Kawase has always been an outlier in the Japanese film world, if a very successful one. Born and raised in Nara Prefecture, the site of Japan's ancient capital, she started making documentaries while a student at the Osaka School of Photography in the late 1980s, taking as subjects her natural surroundings and immediate family, particularly the great-aunt who had raised her following the break-up of her parents' marriage.

In 1997 Kawase's first fiction feature, "Suzaku" ("Moe no Suzaku"), won the Camera d'Or prize for best new director at the Cannes Film Festival. This film about the disintegration of a family in rural Nara was part of a new wave that brought Japanese cinema to the renewed attention of the world after the Golden Age of the 1950s and '60s. But unlike such new-wave directors as Takeshi Kitano, Kiyoshi Kurosawa and Hirokazu Koreeda, Kawase kept her focus almost exclusively on the personal, local and natural/spiritual, while rejecting the lure of genre and the influence of pop culture.

This independent stance did not hurt her with Cannes: Her 2007 "The Mourning Forest" ("Mogari no Mori") won the Cannes Grand Prix and she has long been a frequent presence at the festival, including a stint on the 2013 main competition jury.

Now in mid-career, when Japanese directors of her stature are typically rushing from one project to the next, Kawase has decided to give back, most recently by conducting a master class on June 10 at the Short Shorts Film Festival & Asia in Tokyo (SSFF&A). Appearing on stage at the LaForet Harajuku department store, Kawase screened clips from her early documentary work and a new short, "Lies" ("Uso"), while promoting the Nara International Film Festival (NIFF), whose fourth edition will unspool September 17-22. "For me, a film is a way to once again spend time with something I will never encounter again — it's a kind of time machine," she told the packed crowd.

To give young filmmakers a chance to construct their own cinematic time machines, Kawase will conduct a workshop on September 16 and 17 at this year's NIFF. The title: "The Road to Cannes."

Also, as an outgrowth of her stint as jury chairman for the Cinéfondation and Short Films section at Cannes last year, Kawase has formed a partnership with the Cannes festival organization. Winners from NIFF's NARA-wave section for student films will be submitted directly to the Cannes Cinéfondation director. Award-winning films from Cinéfondation, which presents student films from around the world, will screen at NIFF.

Sitting down with Kawase at the SSFF&A closing ceremony at Tokyo's Meiji Jingu Kaikan, I asked her why she was taking on the teacher role.

"Life is short and my generation won't be around that long," she says, resplendent in the red floor-length gown she was wearing to the ceremony. "I want to convey my thoughts and feelings to the next generation. They'll take them and pass them on again. That can continue for a thousand or 2,000 years."

As a native of Nara, where traditional ceremonies from a millennium ago are still being performed, long-term thinking comes naturally.

"Nara's history goes back 1,300 years," she explains. "If you want something to continue for another 1,300 years, you have to thoroughly teach it to the next generation."

But when Kawase first traveled her own road to Cannes, at age 27, she had no distinguished mentors guiding her way.

"Everyone thought it was unbelievable," she says. "It wasn't just me; the entire Japanese film industry couldn't process it. Cannes was only for someone like (Akira) Kurosawa — and 50 years had passed since he'd been there. I was the first woman, the first Japanese from the younger generation."

Since she and other new-wave directors first journeyed down the path to Cannes and other major festivals nearly two decades ago, much has changed, and not, she believes, all for the good: "The directors of the (new wave) generation are now around 50, but our successors haven't appeared, at least ones who are Japanese."

The problem, she feels, goes beyond individual talent — or the lack thereof — to general attitudes. "There is this thinking that you're OK as long as you succeed in the Japanese industry, even if you never go abroad," she says. "That may keep the Japanese economy rolling, but internationally our profile isn't so high."

Kawase is doing her bit to raise that profile, such as by producing six short films in collaboration with the hugely successful band Exile and SSFF&A founder Tetsuya Bessho. "We may generate some new possibilities," she says.

But it's not always easy. The Nara festival had its city funding cut at the start of the new fiscal year and Kawase and other organizers have had to scramble to make up for the loss.

"More people have been supporting us, saying 'how could that happen to something so worthwhile," she explains. "So we have to step up our PR efforts and let more people know about us."

Which she proceeds to do on the spot, in a mix of Japanese and English.

"When you think about it, Cannes is a resort, with an old town and the sea," she says. "Nara is also a tourist spot. We've got many temples and shrines — a lot of interesting places. And you can walk everywhere — you don't need a car. It's a good experience for people to do that; you gain a lot of really important things. I'd like foreigners especially to know what a wonderful town it is. They know Kyoto, but they don't know Nara. Nobody knows about Nara."

But not for much longer, if the indefatigable Kawase has anything to do with it.

(June 22, 2016, "The Japan Times")

In the director's chair at 90: Takeo Kimura

Born in Tokyo in 1918, Takeo Kimura debuted as an art director in 1945. In the six decades since, he has worked on more than 230 films. His most famous association is with Seijun Suzuki during his 1960s peak at the Nikkatsu studio, when he made 1966's "Tokyo Drifter" ("Tokyo Nagaremono") and the next year's "Branded to Kill" ("Koroshi no Rakuin") — films that outraged studio executives with their wildly surreal visual flights but have since become cult classics.

In 2004, Kimura launched a new career as a director, shooting four short films that led to the production of "Something Like a Dream" (Yume no Mani Mani), his first feature film, in 2008.

In person, Kimura flows with a fast, never-ending stream of quips and anecdotes. But he is also passionate about the themes of his new film, particularly the still vivid pain of a war now six decades in the past.

Why does the hero, professor Kiya, feel guilty about surviving the war when so many of his contemporaries died?

For Kiya, surviving the war is a kind of shame. A lot of survivors felt that way — that it was shameful to have come back alive. Back then soldiers accepted the fact that they weren't coming back. That's the spirit of the samurai. They also believed that going off to war was the same as going off to die. Young people today don't understand that. They listen to their parents' stories and go to war museums, but they don't absorb anything.

You've made more than 200 films as an art director, but this is your first feature as a director. Was this a chance for you to express yourself in a way that you hadn't been able to before?

I learned various methods of expression (making all those films), but I wasn't always able to use them freely. So in this one, I was able to express exactly what I wanted. I especially didn't want to imitate Suzuki, but we both shoot scenes that don't make sense. (laughs)

Expression and explanation (in films) are different. When you're explaining, you're saying this happened, then this happened. It's a very simple-minded way of telling a story. With the right (visual) expression, you can do it all in one or two images. You can add depths that aren't apparent in one viewing.

You've worked over and over with several directors, such as Suzuki, Kazuo Kuroki and Kaizo Hayashi. Is that because you share the same vision?

With me, its the script, there's something in it the director wants to express. It's not just explanation, there's something symbolic in it that stimulates the imagination. That's what attracts me.

Your relationship with Suzuki is the most famous.

It just turned out that way (laughs).

Suzuki told me that you were a real idea man on the set.

He was the idea man, always coming up with this wild stuff. (Laughs) I just helped him realize his ideas.

He was hard working, wasn't he? Staying up late getting ready for the next day's shoot.

He would drink sake every night and go to bed around eight. Then he would wake up around midnight and work until three. He would be working on continuity (i.e., planning the next day's shooting) when no one was around.

Were you worried that Suzuki might be going too far?

I thought that, yes. "Tokyo Drifter" was going to end with Tetsuya Watari (the gangster hero) hanging on a big dead tree. That was a bit too avant-garde, though. Instead, we reshot (the scene) in a corner of the Nikkatsu studio. We ended it with him just looking, not hanging. But what happened to the original scene? That's a lost masterpiece. (Laughs) Suzuki told me that when the studio executives saw that film, they were angry, but because it was already completed, they had to release it. We were a bit worried whether that film could be released. But worse was yet to come. "Branded to Kill" was released, but the fans didn't come to see it. Young people today, at least the ones living in big cities, have a greater understanding of films. Back then there were a lot of fans whose understanding was rather shallow. It's better now.

You took some chances with "Something Like a Dream" as well.
It's an ordinary drama, but I added some funny business here and there. Stuff that was not really serious, like a ballerina suddenly appearing out of nowhere. I was able to do that fairly easily because I had shot four shorts. I was able to pull together things that I hadn't pulled together before. That gave me confidence. I did some strange things (in those films). Some people got it, though. They came up to shake my hand, the ones who got it. That surprised me a bit. If I had started right away with (the feature), I couldn't have come as far as I have. For me those four shorts were like preparatory drawings (for a painting). I'm preparing to make another film. We'll shoot it in Kyoto in August. I'm also the producer. I'm making it with students at an arts college where I teach.

(October 24, 2008, "The Japan Times")

Takuya Kimura interview

Interviewing Takuya Kimura at the Tokyo International Film Festival was like being a commoner guest on a reception line for show-business royalty — I had media ahead of me, media behind me, handlers all around me and only a short time to say my piece. But Kimura, while glowing with that peculiar aura of superstars whose every wish is someone's command, gave me his full attention and thought through his answers — even to questions he had no doubt been hearing for years. Or was that another flawless performance by the biggest name in Japanese business?

Why was Kimura meeting me and the rest of the journalistic hoi polloi? He and fellow members of SMAP — the pop group that has been everywhere on Japanese television, collectively and individually, for more than a decade — were promoting their latest films at TIFF on a special SMAP day. Kimura's were Wong Kar-wai's romantic drama "2046," which premiered in competition at this year's Cannes Film Festival, and Hayao Miyazaki's "Howl's Moving Castle" ("Howl no Ugoku Shiro"), which screened on TIFF's opening night. Kimura and his fellow SMAPsters long stayed away from the big screen, but are now moving full speed ahead with their film careers. Kimura was kind enough to tell me why.

I thought the role you played in "2046" — a mature man disappointed in love — was not one you could have played a decade ago. It seemed to bring out something in you that your fans in Japan may not have known was there.

That's Wong Kar-wai's style. I went to his shoot after preparing various things that went beyond my character's age and nationality, but he told me I didn't need any of them. He didn't have a script either. We all only really existed inside his head.

Did you find a gap between what you thought you were doing and what you actually saw on the screen?

Yes, here and there. On the set [Wong] would tell me to express "coldness" — then he would shout "rolling, action." I'd try to do what I'd been told, but the scene would have nothing to do with "coldness" at all. So that sort of thing happened. If you wanted to put a bad spin on it, you could call it a sort of scam. If you wanted to. But I don't think of it as a scam really. Directors have different ways of cooking the meal we call a film — and his way is as legitimate as any other.

So you felt you were a well-used ingredient?

Was I being used? Well, maybe. But I was the one doing the expressing. So was I being used really? This may be a heavy way of putting it, but I think allowing yourself to be used implies a certain responsibility. It also gives you a certain confidence.

You were working with a great director, so you had the confidence that, in his hands, you could do anything?

Not exactly. What does it mean to call a director "great" anyway? Even Spielberg, [Francis] Coppola and [Stanley] Kubrick — all those wonderful directors — even a lot of directors at this film festival have this one thing in common: When they start to be called "world famous" everyone thinks they're great, but once a director is on the set all that "world famous" stuff is no longer important.

In a way, that was also true for you when you went to Cannes with "2046." The audience wasn't reacting to Takuya Kimura the television personality but to one actor on the screen.

I was really happy about that. I still remember at the film festival — well, the whole town was the film festival actually — I was at a cafe away from the main theater, when this old couple — they looked like someone's grandfather and grandmother — told me they'd seen my film and they loved me in it. They said it just like that — bang! It was a wonderful feeling. I was also moved when the world media applauded the film and gave it a standing ovation. What can I say? I was really happy.

Here you stand out because you're the only Japanese in the cast, but to the audience at Cannes, everyone in the film was Asian. You might say you were competing with them on an even playing field.

A lot of people have told me that. We're all in the same film so we're on the same playing field. For outsiders, it may seem as though it's actor-vs.-actor or director-vs.-director. They like to pin the "versus" label on us, but I don't see myself as being "versus" anyone in the cast because we're a team. Also, there's this big hard mountain called Wong Kar-wai to climb and to make it to the top everyone in the cast has to pull together.

I'd like to talk about another kind of mountain: "Howl's Moving Castle." That was one you hadn't climbed before. You had to do all your acting with your voice.

Well, I'm 31 now — I'm part of the generation that grew up with animation. That's what excited us the most. So I was thrilled that I could be part of this thing that had excited me and my friends so much as kids — but it wasn't a mountain.

I suppose you'd seen all of Miyazaki's films, so you had some idea of what was expected.

When I got the part, I had all these thoughts — I was nervous and tense, but when I actually got down to work, the film carried me along — the animation, the setting, the colors.

In the case of Pixar or Disney the voice actors record their parts first, then the animators create the characters based on the voices. In Japan it's the opposite. Is the Japanese way easier? Would it have been harder for you to create the character without the visual cues?

I think "harder" or "easier" depends on the case. The way you climb the mountain may differ, but no matter whether you do it the Japanese way or the American way, the peak is the same.

The character of Howl has a certain ambiguity: He's spoiled and temperamental, but he has his good side too. Could you identify with that ambiguity, that sense of mystery?

I truly felt that about him — and when I did the part, that feeling was definitely there. But even if he weren't actually an animation character, even if he were to become a real breathing human being living a real life, I would have the same sense about him. There are things about human beings that you can't understand. But because Howl's an animation character, you can more readily accept it. In a real human being, though, that sort of thing can be a turn off.

Animation has its own style of acting. In Japanese animation in particular, there's a tendency toward exaggeration.

More than being concerned about the voice I was projecting or the sound I was making, I was guided by the character's expression — if he looked surprised or doubtful. But when I look at "Howl" and Miyazaki's other films, I wonder why they have to be animated. The town, the sky look so life-like — and when you act against that backdrop you may seem to be overdoing it. Even though Miyazaki is world famous now, his point of view is still very down to earth — ordinary people can understand it.

You've been in these two projects that have gotten international attention. Do you want to build on that — try your hand at Hollywood?

I don't feel that I have to go to Hollywood. The package is what's important, not who is delivering it. It could be Hollywood, it could be Japan — it doesn't matter which.

You've been in this business nearly 15 years now. Do you have any sense of where you'd like to be in another 10 or 15? Is there a plan?

I don't especially think in terms of plans. But I have these visions — that I'd like to do this or that with a certain person. I'd like to do something similar to "Howl," but in a real situation, not an animation. There are a lot of remakes now — it's a trend — but I'm not so interested in remakes. The

"Taku" in my name means "pioneer." I'd like to be a pioneer of some kind.

I've been wondering for a long time why I haven't seen more Takuya Kimura films. (laughs)
That's just the way things happened. If I want to change that and expand my range of activities, it's up to me.

Talking about expansion, more Japanese films are getting out into the world. The Hollywood remake of "The Grudge" was No. 1 at the U.S. box office — and that's drawn more attention to the original.
There are a lot of problems with Japanese films, technical and financial, but the ideas are there — and the ideas are free. It's not a case of "versus." There's definitely potential in the ideas.

In Japan you have a certain image to uphold — that if Takuya Kimura appears in a TV drama it's going to get high ratings. But abroad that doesn't matter.
I want to trash that image. I want to change my image every chance I get. There's nothing sadder than an actor who only has one image.

(November 24, 2004, "The Japan Times")

Masahiro Kobayashi interview

It's sad but true that Japanese directors with big reputations abroad are often odd men (or women) out at home. Juzo Itami won the hearts of Western audiences with his 1985 foodie comedy "Tampopo," but in the Japanese film industry, he was considered an outsider from the world of television, where he had won fame as an actor and talent. Shinya Tsukamoto became a cult hero worldwide for his ultra-violent cyper-punk fantasies, beginning with his 1989 break-out "Tetsuo: the Iron Man" ("Tetsuo"), but in Japan he often struggled to get his films screened, while many of his industry peers regarded them as little more than freak shows. (Itami and Tsukamoto told me the above themselves; I am assuming they were being truthful.)

Masahiro Kobayashi's case, though, is among the more extreme. As a young singer-songwriter he journeyed to France to meet his idol, Francois Truffaut, but though his quest ended in failure (he couldn't bring himself to push the doorbell to Truffaut's apartment), he later parlayed his passion for European cinema into a successful career as a scriptwriter.

 Then, not satisfied with grinding out scripts for television and the made-in-Japan variety of soft porn called "pinku eiga" (pink films), Kobayashi directed his first feature, "Closing Time," at age forty-two. Deeply influenced by his beloved European auteurs, Kobayashi's early films were barely released in Japan, but three in a row, beginning with the 1999 "Bootleg Film," were screened at the Cannes Film Festival.

This raised the ire of certain critics and colleagues, who suspected the Francophile Kobayashi of benefitting from favoritism. Worse was yet to come. When his 2005 film "Bashing" was selected for the Cannes competition — the only Japanese film to be so honored — his detractors launched an intense Internet hate campaign that Kobayashi later ruefully compared to the bullying inflicted on his heroine — a young woman volunteer who was captured by insurgents in Iraq and, after her release, got the cold shoulder on her return to her Hokkaido hometown.

Her crimes? Causing trouble for her rescuers and embarrassment for her countrymen, though her worst offense was her arrogance for wanting to help strangers in a distant, dangerous land.

Kobayashi's new film, "Travels with Haru" ("Haru to no Tabi") features a similarly young, socially awkward heroine from a Hokkaido backwater, but there the comparisons end. Instead of a stark, unrelenting examination of Japanese insularity and intolerance, the new film is a family-drama-cum-road-movie of a type familiar from local antecedants — Yasujiro Ozu's "Tokyo Story" (Tokyo Monogatari, 1953) is one point of reference, Shohei Imamura's "Ballad of Narayama" ("Narayama Bushiko," 1983) is another — and is clearly pitched at a local audience. Unfortunately, Cannes did not extend an invitation, though Kobayashi is still hoping for other festival screenings.

In person, surrounded by handlers in an Imperial Hotel suite on the day of the film's gala Tokyo premiere, the 56-year-old Kobayashi looked surprisingly young despite his long grayish air — and fragile state of health. (A two-pack-a-day smoking habit evidently had something to do with it, though in his blog, where he describes his aches and pains in bare-bones prose, he doesn't give details.) His voice is soft, if scratchy, and his manner is gentle, if slightly weary. (In his blog he complains about the grind of media interviews, singling out reporters with no real interest in the film as being particularly tiresome.)

The genesis of "Travels with Haru," Kobayashi explains, began in 2001, after he had just completed "Man Walking on Snow" ("Aruku Hito") and was contemplating another project. In September, in quick succession, his wife gave birth and terrorists attacked the World Trade Center. The joy of new life and the shock of mass death inspired him to begin writing a film about family. "It was hard to get what I wanted," he said. "I wrote and rewrote the script, again and again."

He was to finally put it through nearly 100 revisions, but in the interim, he made three films that, including "Bashing," incorporated a critique of society new to his work. "In Japan they were still making a lot of idiotic films (after 9/11), but in the rest of the world, filmmakers were headed in a different, more serious direction, making films about war in Iraq." he explained. "Films can reflect what is going on in society, though not only that, of course. I didn't especially want to make that kind of film, but it seemed to be only kind getting made."

Despite his initial reluctance, Kobayashi shot the three films with he called "a documentary style that I learned from (British director) Mike Leigh." Meanwhile he kept revising the script for "Travels with Haru," but with a new socially conscious slant. "If I hadn't made those three films, I probably couldn't have made this one," he said.

Three years ago, Tatsuya Nakadai, the iconic actor who worked with many of the greats of Japanese cinema in a five-decade career, inlcudng Kurosawa, Naruse and Ozu, saw the script and asked to play the role of Tadao, the old, cantankerous, stroke-disabled fisherman who travels with his granddaughter and caregiver Haru (Eri Tokunaga) to fnd a family member who will take him in so Haru can go alone to work in Tokyo.

Even with Nakadai aboard, Kobayashi struggled to find backers: "It's a simple story about a family, right?," he said as though stating the obvious. "So no one would give us money."

His track record as a Cannes regular, he laments, did not mean much to potential money men. "Japan is not a developed country— it's more like a developing country." he says. "In a developed country, if your film is invited to Cannes, you're treated like some kind of hero. But here that's not the case at all. Instead, it works against you."

While cobbling together the financing, he made his last casting choice — Eri Tokunaga, a screen newcomer, for the role of Haru. "I only met her once before casting her," he said. "We talked for about thirty minutes — and then I decided she would be Haru. I thought I would interview more actresses — we were holding an audition — but after meeting her I couldn't imagine anyone else in the role."

The film's difficult nine-year gestation has paid off in at least one way: Kobayashi is getting his biggest-ever release — nearly 80 screens across the country. Nakadai's presence on the marquee is one reason. Another is that, while being completely a Kobayashi film in style and approach, "Travels with Haru" is in a traditionally humanistic vein more suited to the tastes of the local audience than his artier, more Westernized work. "Maybe I'm getting old, but I wanted to make one Japanese-style film," he says. "I don't like to think that I've become conservative, though."

Despite the film's domestic slant, Kobayashi also wants the world to see it, particularly festival audiences. "If (a film of mine) is not invited to a festival, I feel that it's pointless to have made it," he explains. One reason is that, for indie films like Kobayashi's with no big media backers, festivals serve as free venues for promotion. "Also, the reactions (from the audience) can encourage you and give you confidence in what you're doing," he says. "So there are no down sides."

Kobayashi claims to like even the criticism from the more straight-talking audiences abroad. "At one festival an old couple came up to me in a cafe and said "Your film is no good," he said, with a laugh. "You never hear that kind of thing in Japan."

For his future films, Kobayashi has no intention of returning to socio-political concerns of his 2000s work. Instead he wants to make what he describes as "my sort of entertainment" even though that means, he says with a self-deprecating grin, "the films end up not being entertaining." "But to a certain extent, I want to make films that audiences can enjoy," he adds.

He also hopes to some day escape the low-budget fate of the typical Japanese indie filmmaker. Art films, he notes, have not always been cheap here. "Akira Kurosawa would spend one billion yen — a huge amount of money for the time — making an art film," he notes. "Shohei Imamura would spend 200 or 300 million making his art films, not 20 million. So it's not impossible to do that sort of thing. My wife gets mad at me when I talk that way. 'You're not Akira Kurosawa!' she says. But who said that Akira Kurosawa was so special? I think it's natural to aim for something like that and see how close you can get. When someone says 'You'll never be Akira Kurosawa,' I'd like to ask 'Why not?' From now on I want to make my sort of entertainment. Even though the films don't end up being entertaining." (laughs)

(May 21, 2010, "The Japan Times")

Hirokazu Koreeda interview 1: no easy answers

Directors who have been on the PR circuit long enough often have their answers ready before the interviewer's questions are halfway out of his mouth. Not Hirokazu Koreeda. Despite the dozens of interviews he's given since "Nobody Knows" ("Daremo Shiranai") screened in competition at this year's Cannes Film Festival, he still thinks his answers through, which can be disconcerting for an interviewer confronted with silence instead of the hoped-for torrent of words. But Koreeda, who began his career filming award-winning documentaries for the TV Man Union production company, speaks with directness, precision and flashes of humor that make the waits worthwhile.

How would you say the Japanese audience reaction to "Nobody Knows" differs from the reaction at Cannes? Here people are obviously more aware of the situation the children face.
There's no fundamental difference. The Japanese audience has really responded to the film well, but they tend to connect it with the real incident [on which it's based], while foreign audiences are more inclined to see it strictly as a work of art.

When you wrote the script 15 years ago, the situation it depicted was rare, but in the world now it certainly isn't. When I saw "Nobody Knows" I was reminded of "City of God," the Brazilian film about street children. Somehow you got the same look in the faces of the children — that look of poverty, of abandonment.
I wasn't consciously trying for that. When I explained the story to the children I didn't stress how miserable their situation was or that their mother would never return. For the younger two children especially, I just talked about the scene at hand. I wanted them to concentrate from moment to moment. I didn't want them to emphasize the tragedy of their situation.

The shoot was extremely long — nearly a year — which gave you plenty of time to create the sort of environment you wanted.
Yes, I tried to build a relationship of trust between myself and the children and among the children themselves.

So that you wouldn't have to give them detailed explanations?
So that they could understand what I wanted, so that they could rely on me. It was really important to build a relationship that would enable them to be natural, to look natural.

When you were working with the actors on their characters, did you just use your imagination or did you have images in mind of children you had seen in films or documentaries?
I didn't use much in the way of reference. In any case, I think the situation of the children [in "Nobody Knows"] is somewhat different from what you find in "City of God." Their environment was Tokyo, where there's a lot of everything. If you make good use of the convenience stores here, you can eat.

When we were shooting on the streets I wondered what would happen. But even though the kids were wearing dirty, ragged clothes, nobody paid much attention to them. Nobody asked them what was wrong. This with the camera far back, out of sight. [The kids] would be walking on a shopping street, in these ragged clothes, but nobody said a word to them, ever. "So that's the kind of city it is," I thought as I was shooting. There was no need for them to make any sort of special face. I thought it would be more frightening if they were like ordinary kids, smiling like you see kids smiling anywhere.

I was particularly impressed by Yuya Yagira as Akira, the oldest boy. He matures as the film progresses, both physically and mentally, but he looks totally natural. There's no sense that he's constructing a character.
Well, he got taller, his hair grew, and his voice changed — I had nothing to do with that. Where I mainly directed him was his movements, his point of view and his line readings. His performance had to show the growth [of his character]. So I gave him more detailed instruction than the other children.

Usually in a Japanese film of this type, the children are pure-hearted innocents, so that the audience will sympathize with them. But with Yagira's character there's a darker side as well — you can't always tell what he's thinking. That comes from his lack of trust in adults, I think.
That's right. He's a kid who has to act the role of an adult, who has had the role of an adult thrust upon him.

That's how he is at the start, but there are also times when he throws off that role and reverts to being a kid again. I was reminded of the Hiroshi Shimizu film "Children of the Beehive" (1948), in which the children are living on the street, but still haven't totally forgotten to be children.
I heard that comparison at Cannes. I really like that film, but it was made right after the war when poverty was still a big theme. In my film, though, ordinary people are well-off — that's an extremely important difference, I think.

In "Children of the Beehive," the children's situation is not really anyone's fault, but in "Nobody Knows" the mother is to blame. Even so, she's not an evil figure — she genuinely likes her kids. But there's something mysterious about her — I didn't quite understand her motives, even at the end.
In shooting the film, my viewpoint was close to that of the oldest boy. He can't understand her 100 percent and we can only understand what he can understand. There is a limit to the information we have about the mother. For example, when she leaves the children we don't know how she spends her time with her boyfriend. The children don't know — so it's not described in the film. So in that sense she's a mystery.

Also, when the eldest boy phones her she answers with a different name — Yamamoto. That's how he finds out something about her — and that's how the audience finds out as well. They better understand how he feels. So the mother may be a bit of a mystery, but I didn't want to show her as evil. I didn't want to attack her — in fact I didn't want to make anyone the villain. I just wanted to depict her so the audience would believe she was the type of woman who would make such a choice.

You also don't try to pump the audience for tears — though that would be obligatory with most Japanese films of this type.
That might have been smarter (laughs). That's how a feel-good movie would end. The story would get emotional — there's nothing necessarily wrong with that. But in this film I didn't want to give the audience that sort of release. That's why I didn't make it so people could have a good cry and say how sorry they felt (for the kids). I wanted them to take away something. I think I succeeded, because when I read the comments people have left on my Web site they say they didn't cry during the film, but after they got home they looked at their own children and cried. I don't exactly want them to have flashbacks, though (laughs). So they come away with something more than just a feeling of pity. I think that's really important. A lot of people, especially Japanese, come to the theater to have a good cry. If they come [to this film] with that idea, though, they're making a mistake. Of course, some will cry, but that wasn't my intention. I wanted to be more stoic. In fact, I got rid of anything sentimental.

When I got home after seeing it, I felt that what happened to those kids was not only someone else's problem. I couldn't just blame the mother.
It would be easy to say the mother is a terrible person. Then the audience can relax — you've made this bad guy who has nothing to do with them. They can watch without any sort of uneasiness. But the bad guy is really the indifference of everyone in those kids' lives. That includes the manager of the convenience store and the landlord of the apartment building. But if I were managing that convenience store, maybe I wouldn't do any more than he did.

The film also made me wonder what is going to happen to Akira — he's missed out on so much that ordinary kids take for granted.

I don't think the situation (Akira) finds himself in at the end of the film is going to continue forever. His world will fall apart — and that will be a problem for him. But he does have the neighbor girl with him, though she's not a relative. So although you can't say the ending is happy, at least there is one outsider with him. There's more of a feeling of possibility — at least that's what I thought when I finished shooting. The presence of [an outsider] is really a plus for them. Their world will end by them venturing into the bigger world outside. They'll encounter a new way of life, a new point of view. If their world had collapsed from the inside it would have been really tragic. But instead this outsider enters their world and it starts to open up.

You've been working on this film for 15 years and now that you've made it do you feel that it's put a period on something, that you want to look for a new theme? It seems that all your films have been about human loss.

Now that the film is finished and in the theaters I feel totally wiped out (laughs). For the past 10 years I thought that "Nobody Knows" was going to be my next film, but now that I've finally made it I have to find a new motivation inside myself.

When people tell me that sort of thing [about the theme] of my films, I start to wonder, "Why am I always writing about people who have lost someone important to them?" I don't know myself why all my films tend to be that way, but for my next film I want to do something a bit different. Until now I've been making films that have a basis in reality — that's always been my starting point — but now I want to try something that's more fictional, so I've been thinking about a period drama.

What sort of period drama?

I have a treatment that I was writing while I was shooting "Nobody Knows." Now I'm turning it into a script. I want to start shooting next spring.

Will it have a bigger budget than the films you've made so far?

A bit bigger — it's not going to be a chanbara (swordfighting) film. It's going to be about poor people, not samurai.

Something along the lines of "The Twilight Samurai?"

Something totally unlike "The Twilight Samurai" (laughs).

But that film was nominated for a Foreign Film Academy Award and was well-received abroad. Overseas, there's still a lot of interest in the period drama, it seems.

Was it released in America?

Yes, in New York and a few other big cities. But "Zatoichi" got a bigger release.

Is "Zatoichi" doing well?

So I've heard — but you're not interested in making that sort of genre film?

No — something more like Kurosawa's "The Lower Depths." But maybe I shouldn't say that or no one will come to see it (laughs).

(August 25, 2004, "The Japan Times")

Hirokazu Koreeda interview 2

Hirokazu Koreeda began directing in 1991, while working for TV Man Union, a major TV production company. His first theatrical feature, "Maborosi" ("Maboroshi no hikari," 1995) was selected for the Venice Film Festival competition — a rare honor for a tyro director. His international breakthrough, however, came in 1998 with "After life" ("Wonderful life"), a fantasy set in a way station for the recently dead that was distributed widely around the world, while winning numerous accolades at home and abroad. His 2004 follow-up, "Nobody Knows" ("Dare mo shiranai"), a drama about children abandoned by their mother, was screened in competition at the Cannes Film Festival, where 15-year-old star Yuya Yagira won the Best Actor prize.

This interviewer has known Kore'eda for ten years — and meeting him again to talk about his new film "Still Walking" ("Aruitemo Aruitemo") — was impressed by little he seems to have changed — and not just physically. Open to all questions, thoughtful in his responses, he is still one of the very few Japanese directors genuinely curious to hear an interviewer's opinion — and able to turn what is usually a punctuated monologue into a real discussion.

This is your first real home drama — a basic genre in Japanese films. Did you want to see how you stack up against other directors who have worked in it?

I was raised watching home dramas on TV — I've seen a lot of them, but I didn't make this film because I wanted to make a home drama as such. It came from a personal reason — when my mother died I wanted to express what she had meant to me in a film. I didn't have any bigger reason than that.

It unfolds in such a short period — only 24 hours. Did you have that time frame in mind from the beginning?

Yes, when I started writing the script I knew I wanted to that (time frame). I wanted to show what you can learn about people in the course of an ordinary day, with no big incidents occurring. What you can come to understand about their past and future, their world view.

Not many Japanese films today are being made from original scripts like yours.

It comes down to money, really. Producers are reluctant to put their money into a film that uses an original script, because they don't know how it will work at the box office. If it's based on a novel or something else they feel more secure.

Personally, it's easier for me to write an original script. For the script of ("Still Walking") I used memories of my mother, the personalities of my sister and other people around me. It's easier for me to write that way. If I had to work from another writer's (novel or short story), I'd have to understand that person's worldview — and that would be tough.

The story (of the film), though, is not autobiographical. The setting is not my home town. Also the family relationships are different. But the mother in the film resembles mine. Also, I have an older sister, like the hero in the film. The relationship between the mother and daughter, as they chat in the kitchen and so on, comes from my own experience.

The casting of Hiroshi Abe is unusual. He's a big star who has appeared in a lot of comic roles. Also, he's tall, good-looking — not the usual image of a loser. (laughs).

Yes, this role was something new for him — he'd never played anything similar before. But I thought he could do it. Also, he wanted to do it himself. He looks a bit out of place in a traditional Japanese setting — his face and his size and so on. Just putting him in that kind of setting — in a Japanese-style kitchen, living room and bath — you get a feeling of alienation. That's what I was looking for.

On the other hand Kirin Kiki has the look of a kindly mother figure, but she can say terrible things without batting an eye.

Yes, she was good at that — at sayng awful things in this ordinary, everyday setting, in a matter of fact way. She had the sort of scariness that I was looking for.

The father played by Yoshio Harada is the villain in some ways, but it's hard not to feel some sympathy for him — he doesn't really have a place of his own any more.

A lot of Japanese men are like that when they retire. You feel sorry for them. The father (in the film) has an office to go to, but most men in his situation don't and because Japanese houses are so small, they feel uneasy. Also, they aren't really respected any more. I wonder why it's like that only in Japan. (laughs)

In Japan you have this tradition of the son succeeding the father to keep the family business going. So if a father fails to do that, like the one in the film, he loses face.

Yes, that tradition exists, but I wasn't really conscious of it (when I was writing the story). I was more concerned with how this relationship between the father and son would work out in this narrow space. I'm not all that interested in Japanese tradition and how it is passed from generation to generation, but when I started (writing the script) that aspect started to come out, I guess.

In Japan being a doctor is a special sort of occupation. Everyone calls you "sensei" (master) and shows you respect. It's probably the occupation where the fathers most want the sons to succeed them. Other occupations like that are politicians and entertainers. (laughs)

The character of Atsushi is also interesting. He's just a kid, but he watches everything around him with this appraising look.

He's an outsider, like his mother. They bring an outsider's perspective to the family. His mother has just married into the family and so has to get along with everyone. She has to blend in. Her son, though, is different. He doesn't have any responsibilities, so he can remain an outsider. It's a story of a child who is not child-like and an adult — Hiroshi Abe's character, who is not adult-like, even though he 43 or 44 in the film. That's typical of Japanese men in their forties, including me. (laughs)

I had the feeling that you get to see his whole life in the course of the film.

I'm glad to hear that. That was one of my aims, Without that wider perspective you just have a series of incidents that don't add up to anything. The story takes place in only 24 hours, but I wanted to give a sense of what the family was like in the past and what will happen to it in the future.

There's this mix of feelings toward the dead son.

Everyone thinks of him in their own way. The hero has this complex about the way he is perceived by his father and mother, by the way they compare him to his dead brother. In other words, this ghost from the past fuels his complex. It's not just a story about parents being sad because their son has died. It's about the way a death is like a pebble tossed into a pond, making waves that keep spreading, affecting everyone in the family. It about how that death has changed the family, fifteen years on.

The daughter is another interesting character — she makes nice with the mother and everyone, but she's glad to finally leave.

Yes, she's different — she's just living for the present. She's just trying to live as best as she can.

I wanted to show the various reactions (to the son's death) and how the family has been split apart by it. They've split apart from each other, but they're still connected.

The daughter plays a big role in all this. The family's been split apart but her presence keeps things from falling to pieces entirely. Her way of dealing with (this situation) is very Japanese — she keeps disputes from flaring into the open. She serves as a damper, in other words. She doesn't say anything particularly meaningful — she just chit chats about nothing. (laughs) In fact she and her whole family

— the husband and two kids are sort of irrelevant to the main story, but when they leave, the feelings that have been suppressed break out into the open. The conversation between the elderly couple is one example, the conversation between the mother and (Abe's) new wife is another. When the daughter leaves, the mother and wife start to butt heads, because there's no one to keep (the conversation) nice and meaningless. I just wonder how well I got that across. (laughs)

In any family, you need this balance between the meaningful and meaningless. After the daughter's family leaves, the tension level rises and people start butting heads. That's the turning point of the film — at least I tried to make it that way.

The new wife, played by Yui Natsukawa, is in a difficult position — as an outsider trying to keep the peace.
She's the one who gets the most tired.

So when she finally leaves, she says "Once a year is enough."
But she'll keep coming back — complaining but still coming back. In my experience, most families are like that — they keep going, no matter what.

Even though the mother doesn't get along with the father, they won't divorce. The son may butt heads with the father, but he'll be back next year — and the year after that. Right until the end.

(June 27, 2008, "The Japan Times")

Hirokazu Koreeda interview 3

I interviewed Hirokazu Koreeda in a meeting room in the gleaming new office of TV Man Union, the TV production company where he has worked since the start of his career. Unlike some directors who rattle off anecdotes and opinions sounding like pre-recorded tapes, Koreeda tends to mull over questions, even one he has doubtless heard dozens of times before. He speaks in rapid-fire bursts, as though releasing the pressure of pent-up thought.

Is there any difference between the director who made "Maborosi" and the director you are now?

That's a hard one... Films are difficult, I know that now. (laughs) "Maborosi" was a film about films, a film that was questioning what a film should be. I'm still asking what a film should be, but I'm trying to make films looking at the people in front of me, at the emotions in front of me, without preconceptions. I'm looking more at the overall film, again without preconceptions.

When you made "Maborosi" you had a documentary background, but it wasn't a film that looked like a documentary at all. Who were you're influences for that film?

Hou Hsiao Hsien, (Theodoros) Angelopoulos and people like that. Naruse came a lot later, when I was making "Still Walking." When I was making my first three films, I wasn't thinking of (Japanese) studio films so much. I didn't see any point in reviewing Ozu and Naruse and so on. The way they made those studio films and the way I was making my films were so different, I didn't think they'd have a lot to tell me.

But when I was making "Still Walking" I had another look at Naruse, at how he filmed people, where he put the camera and so on. But in the beginning I put a distance between myself and Japanese studio films.

Abroad your films are often compared to those of Japanese cinema's Golden Age — even though you may not always see the connection. (laughs)

I'm happy to be compared to people like Ozu and Naruse. I'm happy they think that way (about my films). I can't imitate someone like Naruse, so I don't consider myself his descendant, but I've had another look at Naruse, as I said.

One difference between Ozu and Naruse is that Naruse had a darker view of humanity...

Human beings are no good...

And he communicated that more directly in his films. I could especially see that same sort of viewpoint in "Still Walking."

Right. More than Ozu, Naruse is closer to my own feelings about people.

One difference between you and Naruse is that you often incorporate personal — that is, autobiographical — elements into your films. Is that personal element essential to you as a filmmaker? Would you find it hard to make a film without that sort of element?

It's not that I'm trying to include personal elements (in my films). It's just ends up that way. I made "Hana" from the point of view of a son looking at his father. "Still Walking" also depicts a son looking at his mother and father. But now that I've become a father, I'll probably make a film from a father's point of view.

For me it's best if my films reflect changes in my personal life and my view of life in general. I'm not making movies looking at other movies. Instead, I'm looking at my own times and my own situation and making films based on all that.

Some of your films deal with social issues, such as "Nobody Knows," which showed the indifference of society toward the abandoned children in the film. Are you trying to change people's attitudes with that sort of critique?

No, that's not my aim. But after "Nobody Knows" was released, I got a number of letters from fans saying that after they saw the film, they became concerned about children they saw playing late in the evening in a neighborhood park and said something to them. When I got letters like that I was happy. Those fans brought something (from the film) into their own lives, they didn't just leave it in the theater. It wasn't my intention to change their viewpoint, but it's a good thing.

Films that try to communicate a message are pretty common in Japan, but even when your films have the sort of impact you describe, you can't very well call them "message films."

I don't like films that have a social message, either fictional films or documentaries. It's all right if a film reflects something the maker has thought about and agonized about. But a message film doesn't come from that sort of place. The (filmmaker) thinks he has the answer. But the world doesn't work that way.

There's also a tendency in these so-called message films to play on the audience's emotions — to jerk tears and so on. But you avoid that as much as possible. (laughs)

I'm not very interested in that. (laughs)

But I remember that after seeing "Nobody Knows," I walked out of the theater thinking about it and, about thirty minutes later, I started crying.

That's OK. (laughs) It's easy to make people cry while they're watching the film. When two lovers die (on screen) everybody cries, right? (laughs)

Instead of pumping the audience for tears, you create emotional resonance with small, realistic details, as when the mother and daughter make corn tempura "Still Walking." Why corn tempura? (laughs) But that had a personal meaning for you. There's nothing plot-driven about that film at all. Instead it feels totally natural — and the details contribute to that feeling.

That film is nothing but details. That accumulation of small details is life. That's where the drama is — in the small details. When I was constructing each scene, I tried to add details — the pajamas, the toothbrushes, the other sort of things you would actually find in a house, that would contribute to the feeling (the audience has about the characters).

That must have required a lot of preparation before you started filming. At the same time, you also change the script in reaction to what you find on the set. How do you balance the two — being prepared and being responsive to the situation?

I think (being responsive to the situation) comes from my experience making documentaries. I don't make films in a documentary style, but when I come to the set and I'm observing the atmosphere and watching the actors, I'll say "Let's do the scene this way," even though it's not in the script.

That was also your method in "Nobody Knows," when you were working with children.

I was shooting their reactions. It's the same way with documentaries — you're trying to get their reactions. I'm not calling them over and giving them directions. Instead I'm adapting to their expressions and movements. Having done documentaries, I know I'm going to get something (I can use) if I shoot that way. If I hadn't had that experience, I'd be more inclined to decide everything ahead of time.

So your approach was somewhat different than with a film like "Maborosi."

I hadn't had so much experience (as a feature director) then, so I decided everything ahead of time. I still write storyboards, as I did for that film, but on the set I often change them.

In "After Life" you mixed a documentary style and a more formal approach.
Right. That was an experiment for me, doing it that way.

That film was quite easy for overseas audiences to understand. I think. It had certain universality. You didn't have to know anything about Japanese religion or culture to understand it.
Yes, I suppose that's true.

But have there been times when you feel foreign critics or audiences aren't really getting something that a Japanese audience would? Have you ever noticed a gap in perception?
I can't really say that I have. Well, when I went to European film festivals with "Maborosi," people often spoke about Zen. They asked me about the relationship between the film and Zen. That was something I'd never thought about. (laughs)

Also with "Distance," people (abroad) talked about the connection between that film and Hiroshima and Nagasaki. I felt something strange about that. But I've never thought that foreigners don't understand the films — I have different ways of looking at them myself.

When I made "Still Walking" and showed it to my (international) sales agent they said it was too domestic. I was told that only Japanese would understand it. But in reality, foreign audiences understood it. When I made it I thought there was no other mother like (the one in the film) — she was modeled on my own mother — so when people told me she reminded them of their mother I was surprised. I was told that in Spain, Norway, Canada. I started to think that sort of mother was everywhere. I realized that it's not so easy to decide "this is for the domestic audience" or "this is for the international audience."

On the other hand, "Air Doll" doesn't have anything "domestic" about it at all.
Right. I didn't make it as a "Japanese film."

With "Nobody Knows" I felt that you had reached a turning point. Up to that film, you were concerned with the theme of loss — how someone's death or absence impacts the ones left behind. It's not that you've abandoned that theme, but since then you've been trying new things — a period film, a fantasy film and so on. Did you want to be adventurous and try something that wouldn't be labeled a "Koreeda film"?
I don't know if "adventurous" is the right word. I didn't want to change my style as such. I just wanted to find the right method for shooting the material. Once I had decided the theme or motif, I had to think of the best way to film it. For example, what's the best way of filming a period drama? After I had decided that, everything else followed. So I didn't try to change my style, but the films turned out differently.

With "Hana," I wasn't setting out to make a period drama from the beginning, but rather a film about revenge — about the feeling of (wanting) revenge. I started to think about it after the 9/11 attacks in New York. I started to wonder what this feeling called "revenge" was about. I thought of filming a story about taking revenge on an enemy — and that meant a period drama.

It's a common theme in Japanese films, with a lot of stereotypes.
There are a lot of films about revenge in Japan — and not only Japan.

And not only period dramas, but yakuza movies.
I don't care for those very much. (laughs) The hero always uses violence in the name of righteousness. I don't like "righteous violence." I'm not against violence as such, but it's better if it's not for the sake of so-called "righteousness." I don't find that so interesting to watch.

Some of the directors getting a lot attention in the West, such as Miike and Kitano, use extreme violence that's not righteous at all. Theirs is a kind of extremity not found in your films, but has become very popular in the West.
Yes, I suppose we're different that way.

Do you pay much attention to what other Japanese directors are doing? Are there any out there you considers allies or rivals?
Other Japanese directors? I watch Kitano's films. I also like Yamashita Nobuhiro's films. I don't think of any of them as rivals.

What about Nishikawa Miwa? She learned quite a bit from you. You wouldn't consider her an apprentice (deshi)?
No, not an apprentice, though she worked as an assistant director on several of my films. Her films are wonderful. I don't consider her a rival, though. To be honest, I don't watch a lot of new Japanese films. Instead I'm watching films by Korean directors like Bong Joon-ho and Lee Chang-dong. They're really great.

Certain Asian cinemas, like Korea's, become hot with foreign festival programmers and distributors — and then another one comes along, in a kind of wave.
I hate that sort of thing. I hear that a lot from European film festivals especially. This year Korean films are hot, then Mexican. I find that unpleasant. (laughs) Festival programmers have a lot of say-so in the European market — it's all about their preferences, their tastes. Whether they think Korea or Japan or Mexico are hot. They want to show non-Western films that fit their idea of "hot." But movies from Korea or Japan or Mexico or India or China are not competing with each other in that way. I don't try to make films to suit anyone's idea of 'hot."

You have the backing of TV Man Union, which certainly has its advantages. But especially when you make TV documentaries, do you have to listen to people in the company?
I don't have to make anything to please the company. I plan all my projects myself, including the TV documentaries. I'm completely free in that way.

   As for the advantages (of working for a TV production company), with TV I can make something with just three or four people. But with movies I'm working with thirty or forty or sometimes as many as 100.

   Working with three or four people is so simple — that's the appeal for me. It's a good exercise. (laughs) For example, a novelist may a produce major novel every five years or so, but in the interim he's writing short stories and so on. That's the way I like to work as well.

You're not one of those directors who can turn out a film every year.
With me it's like throwing seeds and seeing which ones come up. It takes time to do it that way, so one film a year is impossible for me. I have to give the field a rest.

That seemed especially true with "Nobody Knows" — that one was in development for a long time.
With that one, I couldn't gather the seeds. It definitely took a long time to make, but it didn't have to be ten years. (laughs) I should have made it faster. It doesn't always take that long, though. "Still Walking" didn't take even a year, from the time I wrote the script until I completed the film. That one was quick.

How long does it usually take you to write the script — a year?
Usually it's longer than that.

Is that the most important part of the process for you? That is, once you have a good script, are you pretty confident you can make a good film?

The script is important, but not only the script. When I have material that I might make into a film, I have to keep thinking about it and thinking about it until I can really grasp it. Not all of these ideas become scripts — sometimes they don't. Some novels don't work as scripts. So it's not just about the script. There are also scripts I give up on midway through — I have five or six of those. Sometimes it just doesn't come together.

What are you thinking of doing next? Something adventurous again?

Adventurous? Hmmm. I have a lot (of projects) I'd like to do. I'd like to take a story within "Still Walking" and turn it into a film, somewhat the way Naruse used to do.

If you're talking about adventurous, though, I have one big project I'd like to do. I don't know if I make it a reality, though. There was a studio called Manei in Manchuria during the World War II. I'd like to film a story about Manei. Japanese and Chinese and Taiwanese and Koreans were all working together there. It was a kind of ideal — people of various nationalities making films together. It didn't work out very well, but the idea of different nationalities making films together strikes me as interesting.

Have you ever thought about going abroad to make a film yourself?

I'm not against it. If I had a chance I'd like to do it. It depends on the theme.

You made "Air Doll" with a Korean actress.

Right, Bae Doona. And a Taiwanese cameraman (Pin Bing Lee). That worked well for me. So I think I can make a film without all Japanese. That's why I want to make a film about Manei.

Bae Doona was exactly the right actress for that film. It's hard it think of a Japanese actress who could have taken her place.

Right, it's hard to think of one.

When I saw that film I was thinking it could have almost been made as a silent film, by Chaplin or someone like that.

Yes, Chaplin. When I started to shoot "Air Doll," I was aiming to make something like a silent film.

On the surface it's an erotic film, but you undercut the genre stereotypes. That's how you usually work: You go your own way. That is, you're out there on your own. I sometimes feel that, as a Japanese director, you're lonely that way. (laughs)

Right, lonely. I don't think I'm unhappy, but I am lonely. (laughs) I'm not closely connected to the Japanese film industry, for better or worse. I'm not so closely tied to it. That makes it easy for me.

Does the fact that your films are highly regarded abroad help you keep going?

Psychologically it's a plus. It's not such plus economically, though. That fact that (one of my films) does well abroad doesn't have a big impact on the box office in Japan. Unless you win something like an Academy Award, the domestic market is not going to react.

Overseas recognition has helped Kitano Takeshi. He called "the world's Kitano" (sekai no Kitano) by the Japanese media as a sort of title. (laughs).

But Takeshi's films generally don't do well at the box office.

Now he's going back to his starting point — yakuza films — with his new film "Outrage." Do you have a starting point like that?

Starting point? I've never thought of that. "Still Walking" is my style of film — it comes naturally to me. So if Takeshi's starting point is yakuza moves, mine is family dramas.

I'd like to see more films like that from you.

But I wonder how well the audience would respond to that sort of film. More people came to see it in France than Japan — about twice as many. About 150,000 saw in Japan, but nearly 300,000 in France. I wanted more people in Japan to see it. If more had come in Japan, I could make another one like it.

The market here has become tougher.

Right. In the last ten or fifteen years, it's become tougher. Films that cost about $1.5 million to make and play mainly in arthouses have been flopping one after another. If you don't work with a TV network and promote (a film) heavily on television, the fans won't respond.

The fans, especially the young ones, aren't going to the theater the way they used to. That is, their viewing habits are different.

When I was in college, going to an arthouse theater to see films by Wenders and Jarmusch and Ken Loach and Angelopoulos was considered cool. It was fashionable. Directors of those sorts of films could make a living. But now people don't respond to that sort of thing. They just go to see movies like "April Bride," "Rookies" and "20th Century Boys" made from manga or TV shows.

They may still see art films on television and DVD, but they aren't events the way they used to be.

Right, they're not events. The meaning of "event" has changed. Now films are like attractions at Disneyland.

Everything's being made in 3D now in Hollywood — but what's the point of making a film like "Still Walking" in 3D?

There is no point. I have no interest in making a 3D film. But that's the way things are going.

(December 22, 2011, "Film Criticism")

Hirokazu Koreeda interview 4: 'I wanted to do something different'

Hirokazu Koreeda is best known for intimate family dramas that overseas critics often compare to the work of Yasujiro Ozu (1903-63), the genre's unquestioned master. Koreeda rejects these comparisons, however, and says he feels more of a cinematic kinship to Mikio Naruse (1905-69), one of Ozu's contemporaries.

Koreeda's films — "Still Walking" (2008), "Like Father, Like Son" (2013) and "After the Storm" (2016) — constitute a spiritual autobiography that reflects the 55-year-old filmmaker's own family history and experience with fatherhood. But his latest, "The Third Murder," is a courtroom drama centering on a slippery lawyer (Masaharu Fukuyama) and an enigmatic ex-convict (Koji Yakusho) accused of murdering his former boss. It's Koreeda's first outing in the genre and would seem to be an outlier in his filmography (though he has waded into other genres before: postdeath fantasy "After Life" in 1998 and period comedy "Hana" in 2006). Yet familiar Koreeda themes are found in "The Third Murder," beginning with the two leads who struggle as fathers.

Koreeda, who wrote the film's original script, says one of his prime motivations in this case was to probe the depths of the Japanese justice system, particularly the process of how it hands down judgements.

"The film turned out to be in the suspense genre, but I didn't set out from the start to create a suspense film," he says. The film's gripping suspense element is no fluke; instead it's the result of the filmmaker's thorough preparation and masterly scripting.

For visual inspiration, Koreeda says he revisited the noir classics of the 1940s and '50s.

"I used a wide-screen format, so for reference I wanted to find films that used it well," he explains.

In his script, however, Koreeda downplays the whodunit mystery element found in many of those films he referenced: The ex-con, Takashi Misumi (Yakusho), confesses to murder in the film's opening scene. "I thought it would be better not to make the (murder case) too complicated," Koreeda says. "Instead I came up with a really, really simple story line."

By contrast, the film's depiction of the convoluted legal process is highly realistic, by meticulous design. Koreeda used actual lawyers to enact prison interviews with clients and even conducted a mock trial with his legal experts playing the roles of defense, prosecution and judge. Referring to his video recordings of these exercises, he then wrote his script.

"The whole process took half a year," he says. "That became our base."

His purpose, he insists, was "not to film an indictment" of the Japanese criminal justice system, with its sky-high conviction rates and historically strong reliance on confessions, forced and otherwise. Instead he was more interested in exploring the gap between the public image and the professional perception of the system.

"I came to understand that lawyers see it in a different way," he explains. "I wanted to depict the thinking of the people involved in a process that judges human beings."

His legal sources, however, tried to dissuade him from portraying the realities of what Koreeda describes as "a very Japanese system."

"They told me that a Japanese court trial would not make for an interesting movie," he says with a grin.

One reason is the highly scripted nature of the typical trial here, with defense and prosecution consulting each other in advance and in detail about evidence and witnesses.

"Lawyers told me that sort of actual trial would be boring, but I thought the reality might be interesting," Koreeda says. "Hardly anyone says anything real in the courtroom. Almost everything is decided ahead of time and the truth is found behind the scenes."

The film goes beyond surface realism, however, to a deeper drama focused on the lawyer, Tomoaki Shigemori (Fukuyama), and his client, Misumi. They turn out to be more alike than Shigemori finds comfortable, from their estranged daughters to their predilection for bending the truth.

"I wanted to depict a relationship between two people with an element of dynamic change, in which the one judging and the one being judged find their roles reversed," Koreeda says.

The question of guilt or innocence is by comparison secondary to the story, as is the moral grounds for the death penalty that Misumi faces.

"There are dramas and documentaries that take the stance the death penalty is wrong because the defendant is innocent and the sentence is mistaken — and that's fine," the filmmaker says, "but I haven't made this film simply to oppose the death penalty."

Instead "The Third Murder" takes a more nuanced view, with the truth of Misumi's guilt or innocence a sort of will-o'-the-wisp both defense and prosecution consider somewhat beside the point. Instead, minus witnesses or decisive circumstantial evidence, Shigemori and his colleagues construct plausible narratives that will at least win their client a lesser sentence, if not his freedom.

"They gather only limited information and the judge hands down his verdict based on it," Koreeda says. "He writes his judgement though no one was present at the scene of the crime. Is it scarier if he actually believes he has arrived at the truth? My honest answer is 'yes.' An innocent verdict arrived at in that way is scary to me.

"I didn't want to make a film where a hero appears, solves the mystery, discovers the truth and that leads to a catharsis. I wanted to do something different. I thought it would probably be closest to an actual trial if the hero leaves the courtroom and the audience leaves the theater without the truth being clearly revealed, but feeling that something has been suddenly illuminated."

(September 7, 2017, "The Japan Times"

Kiyoshi Kurosawa interview 1: shooting a work in progress

Directors, a wise critic once said, are devious. After interviewing my share over the years, I understand what he means: Most directors come to media interviews or press conferences with a script more or less prepared in their heads, ready to spin their latest masterpiece.

Kiyoshi Kurosawa is different — he articulates his views clearly enough, in a baritone voice and slow cadences that are an interviewer's delight, but he doesn't spin so much as engage. His film remains something of a puzzle to him — and he would be only too glad if the interviewer could help him solve it. This attitude is so rare — and disarming — that the interviewer is tempted to drop the usual fencing and volunteer as an unpaid script adviser. Also, in person, Kurosawa is not the severe auteur you see in photos of him. Uneasy about this business of interviewing, to be sure — but ready to laugh at himself. Our half-hour talk, in a noisy basement coffee shop, clipped along without a lull — though I felt that silence would have suited him equally well.

Watching "Bright Future" ("Akarui Mirai") for the second time, I was struck by the costumes of the two lead characters, Yuji and Mamoru. Their clothes put them at one remove from the everyday world.
The costume designer, Michiko Kitamura, really understood what I was trying to say in the script. I gave her carte blanche to design whatever costumes she wanted, as long as they had a look of poverty — that was important. She came up with a unique look — out of the ordinary in a stylish way, but at the same time, ragged.

Their clothes seem to draw the two characters closer together. They give you a clearer insight into their relationship. Of course, the film is more than just them. You have the relationship between Yuji and Mamoru, the relationship between Mamoru and his father, Shinichiro, and between Shinichiro and Yuji. And then there's the relationship between Mamoru and his jellyfish.
(laughs) True, the film tells a generational story — but it's not only that. For me two key elements are the costumes and the jellyfish. In a sense, the film is constructed around these elements. I wanted to make something that was not a genre film — something that would be about people who are living in Tokyo today, but are somehow removed from it. The jellyfish is a symbol of that stance: It may look weak, but it's not — it can defend itself with poison. It's off by itself — independent and alone.

The two main characters, Mamoru and Yuji, become enraged for what seems to be little reason, even to the point of murder. It's hard to understand why they do what they do.
They don't understand it themselves. They just flow along with their feelings — their violence is a natural expression of who they are. Violence is a handy tool for injecting drama into a film. When you want to raise the level of tension, use violence. In this film violence also serves the purpose of bringing the characters closer together, much more effectively than talk would.

For me, though, the film was less about violence than a kind of love story.
It's about two young men who try to reach a kind of understanding, but try as they might, they can't understand everything about each other. Still they do understand a lot and come to like each other. So in that sense, it's a love story.

I had the feeling that you didn't understand everything about them either.
I couldn't grasp everything, just bits and pieces. In a way Mamoru and Yuji remain a mystery to me.

As you said, the jellyfish is an important symbol in the film.
Yes, there's something that's fascinating about them. I found myself staring at the one we used for the film. What was it thinking? (laughs) Well, perhaps it's not thinking anything, but I felt like touching it, despite the consequences (laughs). The jellyfish is an important metaphor. It lives in the dark waters

of the sea, but it gives off light — not a bright light, but still a light. Also, it's not headed in any particular direction. Instead, it's floating by itself, protecting its own bit of space.

The character Mamoru is similar. He has a certain charisma, but if you get too close, he can be dangerous.
Yes, he's a lot like the jellyfish. You never know quite what he's thinking. Also, you can't let him go free in society. Jellyfish are beautiful, but in the film, after they're released into the water, they sting people. He's the same way.

He lives by his own rules, outside of society.
In the films I've made until now, the characters find themselves in a world in which the rules are changing — and they have to adapt. The most extreme example is "Charisma" (1999). In that film nature itself is changing. It's a constant theme in my films, including this one.

The title "Bright Future" first struck me as ironic, but as I watched it I realized that, in the case of Yuji at least, you meant it sincerely, that he at least has the chance of a brighter future.
When people use the expression "a bright future" they're nearly always talking about a future they expect to arrive as a sort of gift from outside. I have a different idea — that a bright future is something you make for yourself. I wanted to make a film that expressed that idea, that the future can be bright, at least for certain individuals. I didn't mean the title to be ironic.

At the same time, I can't say for certain what kind of future awaits society as a whole. I can only talk about the futures we create as individuals. Actually, I think the future for Japan and the world may well be dark. But the future of society and the future of the individual can be very different. You can still have a bright future as an individual, despite what is happening in the world. I don't know what kind of future Yuji will have, though.

Did you explain these ideas to the actors when you were directing them — saying that the jellyfish is a metaphor for this or that?
No, not at all, for two reasons. First, these are only my ideas; they may have other ones. I didn't want to force them to think my way. The fact that everyone has his or her way of thinking — and consequently direction in life — is an important theme of the film. Second, I didn't really understand the film myself. I was thinking about it as I made it. Now that I've made it I may understand it better, but I still don't understand everything. Talking to people like you, I start to see it in new ways — I come to understand it more and more.

Was there any particular reason to shoot it in video, other than budgetary considerations?
I shot it on video, but it's being transferred to film. I didn't have a particular desire to shoot it on video — it's just one of several ways of making a film. No matter whether you're using video or film, the things you're shooting are still analog (laughs).

The main advantage of video is that you don't have to light it the way you do film. With film lighting, you get a strong contrast between light and dark. The actors are in the light, the crew is in the dark. With video, however, both the actors and the crew are in the same light — we're all together. It makes it more real somehow. I like that feeling.

(January 15, 2003, "The Japan Times")

Kiyoshi Kurosawa interview 2

Kiyoshi Kurosawa is best known for films about ghosts and other types of strange phenomena that are capable of stirring foreboding feelings through mininal means such as curtains rustling ominously in the breeze or red duct tape stuck incongruously on doors.

His new film, "Before We Vanish," which premiered in the Un Certain Regard section at this year's Cannes film festival, is a first for the 62-year-old director in its sci-fi theme: Unseen aliens infect humans and use their hosts to recruit "guides" and gather gainen (concepts) about human thought and behavior to use in their upcoming invasion of Earth.

Also rare in the Kurosawa filmography is the light, comic tone of the opening scenes, with a newly infected alien host, played to spaced-out perfection by Ryuhei Matsuda, wandering a neighborhood like a dementia patient while his irascible wife (Masami Nagasawa) stews and rages.

But as the aliens rob their victims of core beliefs, the social fabric unravels, thread by individual thread. By the time they launch their invasion the world is falling into chaos and humanity's survival is in doubt. Serious stuff indeed.

In its apocalyptic scenario, "Before We Vanish" resembles "Pulse," Kurosawa's 2001 cult classic about ghosts invading the world of the living via the internet. Speaking to "The Japan Times", Kurosawa smiles at the comparison but insists that his new film is "quite different."

"'Pulse' was a horror film from the beginning, but (in my new film) I pretty much eliminated the horror element and kept the scary scenes to a minimum," he says. "The characters that appear in the first half treat what is going on as a kind of joke; they don't think it's actually happening. Also, for those watching it's not very clear if anything is real. This joking tone gradually changes until what is happening represents a kind of reality."

The 2005 Tomohiro Maekawa play on which the film is based has a similar light-to-dark progression, but the stage on which the play unfolds, Kurosawa notes, "is a symbolic space — everything that happens there is symbolic. You can't really tell if it's real or a lie. It's an interesting play in that way."

The director points out that what works on stage will not work on camera.

"If a character says the line 'I'm an alien' on stage it can sound kind of funny, while expressing a kind of truth," he says. "But when that line is spoken in the middle of a town in a film, you don't think it's serious at all. I was pretty worried how people watching the film would take it."

Kurosawa's solution was to introduce a sinister official from the health ministry, played by Takashi Sasano, who ups the tension by launching a government attack on the aliens.

"From the moment Sasano appears, the film departs from the play and develops in a cinematic way," Kurosawa says. The intention, he adds, is to make the audience feel "something out of the ordinary is really happening."

When I mention that both "Pulse" and "Before We Vanish" signal approaching doom with shots of an eerie-looking airplane passing overhead, Kurosawa says, "That's exactly right. And you're the first one to point that out."

"Of course it's not in the play," he adds, "but I definitely wanted to do it for the film adaptation. I like a shot of an airplane flying across the sky in a dangerous situation, hitting the ground and exploding. (In this film) it expresses the threat to the human race."

However, the architects of that threat — the aliens themselves — make no appearance in the film.

"If you make the audience believe the actors that they're watching are aliens, but then toward the ending show the actual aliens who are using the humans, it's easy to understand," he says. "But then the actors look like phonies. That throws a wet blanket on things. The audience starts to wonder what the point is of even having actors, and feel strongly that the whole film is a lie."

The film's story of an alien attack threatening Japan as a panicked government hunts alien "subversives" also has uncanny present-day parallels, though Kurosawa denies writing it as a reaction to recent events.

"I didn't intend to express that sort of thing, though it's true the sci-fi invasion genre always symbolizes what is happening in that era, so you're not wrong if you can see that sort of thing."

"The world is complex, but a lot of people want to make it simpler," he continues. "It's easy to understand that some country may attack you with missiles, but something scary might happen in a totally different form. An attack may come from within Japan. That's scarier. It's gotten so now that anything could happen and you wouldn't think it strange."

Would it scare him, I ask, if an alien could rob him of his "concept" of film?

"It might be a big blow, like having love taken away," he says. "I'd be scared to have movies taken away from me, but I also might feel really relaxed and happy. I'd think 'What have I been suffering for all this time?' All my stress might go away." He shrugs and smiles. "But I don't know."

(September 13, 2017, "The Japan Times")

Yoshihiko Matsui: the return of the underground king

Born in 1956, Yoshihiko Matsui worked with indie icon Sogo Ishii on his early films, including the seminal 1980 biker pic "Crazy Thunder Road."

In 1979, Matsui made his debut film, "Rusty Can (Sabita Akikan)" about a gay-love triangle, with Ishii serving as cinematographer. His second film, the 1981 "Pig-Chicken Suicide (Tonkei Shinju)," was another love story, this time about a Korean boy and girl, with admixtures of animal butchery, sexual deviance and madness. Experimental theater and film maestro Shuji Terayama, a longtime Matsui associate, screened it at his theater, where it acquired a cult following.

Then in 1988, Matsui released "Noisy Requiem (Tsuito no Zawameki)," a film five years in the making, about a serial killer (Kazuhiro Sano) who wanders about Osaka's Shinsekai homeless district killing birds and women and removing the organs of the latter to deposit in his "lover" — a shop window mannequin. The film set a house record at the Nakano Musashino Hall theater in Tokyo, but roused a storm of controversy. Matsui did not make another film for two decades, for reasons he prefers not to discuss.

His latest film, "Where are we Going?" ("Doko ni Iku no?"), a love story about Akira (Shuji Kashiwabara), a gay man, and Anzu (as herself), a "new half" (transsexual), will open at Shibuya's Eurospace theater.

Matsui recently spoke with "The Japan Times" by phone from his home in Kyoto.

What attracted you to the theme of "Where are we Going?"

In a way, it's a continuation of my three previous films, which were all stories about forbidden love — love between outcast humans, between humans and animals, and even between a man and a mannequin. The new film is another love story, whose two lovers face discrimination. Japan hasn't changed so much — there is still a lot of discrimination against gays, against "new halfs." I wanted to examine that.

Did you spend a lot of time on the script?

I started writing the script in September of 2006 and finished in November — about two months.

The film seems to unfold in a timeless place — it's a bit hard to tell if it's 1988 or 2008.

It was shot in Tokyo. I live in Kyoto, but my staff all live in Tokyo, so I went there to accommodate them (laughs). We had a very low budget, only ¥10 million, so there was no way I could afford to bring them to Kyoto. I used to know Tokyo pretty well, but I hadn't been back in 10 years and the city had changed quite a bit in the meantime. But the film itself is set in the present day.

The character of Akira seems to be the core of the film.

Yes, he was the beginning of everything. I wanted to make a film about a youth who is discriminated against for being gay, and who falls in love, but his type of love is considered abnormal by society. But it's an ordinary film, really. (laughs)

You show not just the prejudice the lovers face, but the anger they feel.

Yes, anger is a big theme. The hero is angry because he is being sexually harassed by his boss. but can't escape. His anger — and what he does with it — are entirely natural.

The boss sees Akira as, not a person, but only an object of lust.

There are a lot of people like that, aren't there? The boss can think of nothing but sex. Other people can think of nothing but money. It's the same thing. The hero has been raised in that sort of environment, so of course he can't trust people.

Kazuhiro Sano, who plays the detective Fukuda, has been with you from the beginning.
Yes, he starred in my last film. We've known each other a long time. Having him on the set made things go a lot easier. He helped me explain the role of Akira to (Shuji) Kashiwabara. When Sano talked to him, he got it right away.

(February 29, 2008, "The Japan Times")

Takashi Miike interview

Japan's most notorious cinematic provocateur, who splatters blood on the screen with manic abandon, in person Takashi Miike was the soul of consideration for this foreign interviewer. When asked questions he had heard dozens of time before, he spoke slowly and measured his words carefully, in a deep baritone voice that was a joy to transcribe. Now in his mid-forties, with more than fifty films to his credit, Miike moves a bit more slowly than when I first met him nearly four years ago. Also he has exchanged his afro for a short cut that gives him the look of a Zen monk, but he is not about to retire to a monastery. As always, he has one film in the video shops, one in the can and one in production. We spoke mainly about the first, "Gozu" ("Gokudo Kyofu Daigekijo Gozu"), which has been described as the first "yakuza horror" movie.

You recently went to Cannes with "Gozu." Was the atmosphere different from the other festivals you've attended?

"Gozu" was in the Directors Fortnight section — it's not the same as being in the competition. Within the larger festival I was able to find a time and place that suited my film — a weekend evening screening. I was also able to get a good reaction from the audience. They laughed and enjoyed the film in a way that was very heartening. So even though my film was selected by Cannes, I was able to find my own space and stance.

Also, I went with staff from the film, including ones who usually work behind the scenes, like the editor. In Japan, unlike in the West, editing is a behind-the-scenes job. My editor has been a partner of mine for a long time, but I had never had a chance to invite him to a place like Cannes. I told him "let's go together" and when he agreed I got him an invitation.

That was the highlight of Cannes for me — seeing my editor, at his first film festival, seeing how the European audience enjoyed the film. In other words, he wasn't just shut up in the editing room, but experienced the film with the audience, breathing the same atmosphere in the theater. That will have a positive impact on his work in the future, I think.

Before seeing "Gozu" I'd heard that, with its mixing of the horror and yakuza genres, it was a new departure for you, but now that I've seen it, I feel that it's very much in line with your other work.

That's right, "Gozu" is not a completely new type of film for me. But was the first one in which I was involved from the planning stage. "Gozu" was originally supposed to be just another yakuza movie — the producer came to me and asked me about making that way. Ordinarily, once I say yes I try to make the film the way the producer wants, but in this case I didn't think the star he had in mind should be doing a yakuza movie.

The star was the producer's son — Hideki Sone. I told him that, as a father, not a producer, he should have Sone do a yakuza movie. Even if this film worked out, there was no future for him there. Instead, I suggested another sort of film, so we started over from the beginning. We called in a scriptwriter and talked about the story and the type of character that Sone should play.

In a short time we were able to come up with a script. We didn't have much money, so we decided to set the film in Nagoya where we could get save on costs. Then we shot the film — it was the father's first film as a producer.

Anyway, the film was selected for Directors Fortnight at Cannes — and I decided to get invitations for everyone who had made it. (laughs)

That film was a big exercise in self-gratification. It's not every day you can have that sort of experience. First the producer was making it for his son. Second, we were able to raise financing from new sources in Nagoya that gave us a freedom we might not have had otherwise. Third, we were able to go to Cannes and enjoy that experience together. In that way, it was different from my other films.

The press materials talk about "Gozu"'s resemblance to David Lynch, but for me the biggest resemblance was to the manga of Yoshiharu Tsuge.

When I read Tsuge's manga as a kid, including "Master of the Gensenkan Inn" ("Gensenkan Shujin") and "Red Flower" ("Akai Hana"), I wondered why I liked them so much. Why were they so interesting no matter how many times I read them? I still don't understand why. But now that I'm an adult I feel attracted to his style, which comes from his own life. So I can analyze it that way now, but when I was a kid I had this very honest reaction of surprise.

Tsuge's manga aren't for children really, but children can understand them in a purer way, not through words, but feelings. I found "Red Flower" extremely erotic. There was nothing pornographic about it, but it was still somehow erotic. The people themselves are erotic.

Tsuge's manga have been filmed any numbers of times. One film we screened at Udine was Teruo Ishii's "Master of the Gensenkan Inn." Of course, Ishii made many films in the "ero guro" (erotic-grotesque) genre — and "Gozu" also seems to be within that "ero guro" tradition.

Where I differ from Ishii and a lot of other directors is that I've worked in all sorts of genres in all sorts of media. I've done TV dramas, films that got a nationwide release, direct to video films and even a film for in Kyushu for a local government body.

Directors usually try to express themselves through the story and images. They try to develop a style that marks a film as their own. I've freed myself of that. (laughs) Instead of aiming for only self expression, I regard filmmaking as a profession that I work at with various partners, trying various modes of expression. I make films that are not violent, that are not "ero guro." I don't want to be put into a box.

But no matter sort of film you're making, there's not much difference in what you're depicting, basically. David Lynch and Nagisa Oshima and Steven Spielberg and Charlie Chaplin are all the same in one fundamental way: They all have to respond to human beings in all their strangeness, with their own astonishment or fear. Whether you're making a film for children or an action film for adults, you're dealing with the same basic themes. The similarities extend to not just the story elements, but the reasons why the scriptwriter wrote the script in the first place. That sort of thing matters more than the particular genre or mode of expression.

Whatever mode of expression you use, you have to answer some very basic questions: "Who am I?" "What are human beings?" "What's going to happen to the world?" I can't claim to know the answers, but I try to express that perplexity in my films. So in that sense, I'm free of genre — it's not my concern.

For me films are about enjoyment. When you think of yourself as an artist, films become a pain. (laughs) I don't like to suffer — I'd rather be free, so I make films for fun. That's how can I make so many of them.

I've still got to think it's strange that, though "Gozu" has been invited to Cannes, it's not being shown in a theater in Japan.

That don't mean very much. (laughs) It was originally made for video. Then, while we were making it, it was selected for Cannes, so we decided to send a print (to the festival). If Cannes hadn't invited it, we might have screened it in one small theater in Tokyo. But once it had been selected for Cannes, we thought it wouldn't look good to release it like that. (laughs)

I'm not a businessman, but if I were I'd know that, even if you release a film like that theatrically, it's not going to be a hit. I didn't want the producer, who is really an amateur, to experience that sort of failure. He would just come away with regrets. He might be thinking that the film could become a hit, but realistically, I know that's not going to happen. It's not that kind of film — I know that from experience. It was better to take it to Cannes and let that be the end of it. It's better for the audience to enjoy it on video, whenever they want. Some people will see it next week and some a year from now — either way is OK.

"Gozu" not like the typical Hollywood horror movie, where there's a shock every second. The pace is slower and there's a greater stress on atmosphere.

It's a road movie, about a guy who doesn't know what to do. He searches for a body and ends up in a place that baffles him. I wanted the audience to experience the hero's journey in, not movie time, but in real-time, just as he would, though they may find it a little boring.

There are already a lot of horror films in which things jump out at the audience to scare them. But to make that kind of film properly you need money. We didn't have it, so we had to try something else.

Actually "yakuza horror" is a play on words — "Gozu" not really a horror film. For one thing, it's not scary. (laughs) It's horror movie that's not scary, in which yakuza show up. (laughs) It doesn't any of the elements that a proper horror movie should have. But it doesn't need them — it's not bound by genre.

We could get away with that because we made it on such a small budget. I'd rather have that kind of freedom than be hemmed in because the budget is too big. That why I think I'd have a hard time if I ever went to Hollywood to make a movie.

At the same time, when I'm forced into a corner — when I'm afraid I can't finish shooting the script because the schedule is too tight — I turn on the power.

If I had to do it just to be a success in life, I couldn't — I don't have that sort of energy. But when I'm on the set, I do to some extent.

I've heard that, once you're on the set you'll often take the movie in a direction that's not in the script.

Writing the script is the scriptwriter's job. He decides what to include and not include and how to develop the story. I respect his work. But there are different ways of interpreting that work. A script is a tool for making a film. How you choose to use that tool is up to you. If one hundred people read the same passage in a script, they will have one hundred different ideas about how to film it. How do you interpret this line? How do you express it? If the script says the character come running in, you have to ask yourself how he runs, why he runs. Maybe he comes flying in? You have to interpret the meaning of "runs."

It's often said that I depart from the script, but I don't agree with that. More than anyone else I read the script with love and respect. All I do is interpret what I read and decide how to put (that interpretation) on film. If I didn't have the script, I wouldn't have any ideas about what to film. I don't think I'm doing violence to the scriptwriter's work. But how that work is interpreted is naturally going to differ from person to person. That doesn't mean I'm changing the theme he's writing about.

For me, a script with defects is a good script. When I come across the boring parts I have to think about how to make them interesting. In that way I can work out my own approach to the script. I'll think that, if I insert a certain cut, I can make a boring scene look interesting.

For a director a perfect script is boring. All you can do is follow it.

Does the film you're working on now have a perfect script?

No, fortunately, Sho Aikawa plays a hero who saves the world. Toei is going to release it nationwide next February.

What's it about?

It's something like the Kamen Rider (Masked Rider) action series for kids. It's called "Zebraman." (laughs). It's more for adults of my generation than for kids, though. It's based on the hero stories I enjoyed as a kid, but I hope that kids of today can also enjoy it. It doesn't have any hard-core violence in it — it's more of a comedy about a hero who makes mistakes, but keeps trying — and ends up saving the world. (laughs)

The story is imaginary — it's about the type of hero I used to dream about being when I was a boy. I want to bring that boy's dream world to the screen. There are scenes of fighting, but it's not really a violent film — it's about a weak guy finding courage and fighting for justice.

But your violent films are what you're known for abroad.

Well, it's not as though I particularly enjoy sending them abroad. I make various types of films, but the people in Europe (who program film festivals) only select my violent ones. They aren't interested in the non-violent stuff.

Well, not all of them. I help program the Udine Far East Film Festival in Italy. One of our films this year was your comedy "Shangri-la" — it came in second in the Audience Award vote.

Yes, I heard that. It's a small film I shot with a light feeling. It's about these homeless people who come to the rescue of a printer who's about to go out of business. It's a simple story, really. I recently met one of the actors, Shiro Sano, on the set. He said he was happy — or rather surprised — at the reaction. It was the first time in a long time he'd had a chance to see one of his own films with an audience and share their happiness and emotion.

Is the budget for "Zebraman" higher than usual for you?

Yes, a bit higher, but with Japanese films bigger budgets don't make much of a difference, do they? You still end up with a film that looks cheap by Hollywood standards.

Most of the time my budgets are really tight. For a direct to video film the budget is about Y40 million — you can't put that kind of film in a theater.

For a theatrical film, producers won't OK a script with a budget of Y40 million. They would rather spend Y80 million and get something flashier. But we can make a Y40 million movie look like it costs Y80 million. The difference is only Y40 million — the staff can make up that gap with their know-how and technique.

But if you try to make a Y200 million movie look like it costs Y400 million, you can't do it with know-how and technique alone. That's why the usual Japanese film is so boring — the people making it are sweating and straining to fill that gap, but they can't. Filmmaking becomes painful for them. You can see that pain up on the screen. You can see how hard they struggled to make an interesting film, but the audience doesn't want to see their pain. It's painful for them as well. (laughs)

With Hollywood movies, the hard work is also up there on the screen, but there's something luxurious as well. Audiences can enjoy each cut.

People who make European films try to put their beliefs and values up on the screen and audiences can get pleasure from that as well. With Japanese films, though, all they can see is the suffering. (laughs) I want to tell the (filmmakers) to chill out. (laughs)

You appeared in an installment of "Detective Festival" ("Deka Matsuri") — a series of short film omnibuses. Most of the directors of those films seemed to be having fun. (laughs)

Takeshi Sato directed that segment — he was the scriptwriter for "Gozu." He also appeared in the film, as the master of the coffee shop who dresses in drag. When he directed that short film, he didn't tell me anything about what he was doing — he just asked where and when he could meet me. Then he showed up with a camera. (laughs) I had no idea what he was shooting.

He's not a director so for him shooting a film for "Detective Festival" was just a game. He did it for fun. Some of the directors of those films were serious — they did it to advance their careers — while other were just having fun. I liked the way both types were mixed together.

Also if one film was boring you didn't have to wait long for the next one. (laughs) But at least the directors were experimenting — trying to be adventurous.

Yes, the audience was willing to accept that. That was a special audience, the one that went to see "Detective Festival." The feeling of this special audience crammed into a tiny theater to watch "Detective Festival" is like the feeling we had watching "Gozu" at Cannes. "Deka Matsuri" itself may not have been that interesting, but the experience of being in the theater watching it with that audience was. That's one way of making and enjoying movies.

There was also something special about the cast and staff of "Gozu" — a lot of them had worked with you on other films.

You couldn't call us "buddies," though — it wasn't that kind of relationship. They were all professionals doing a job. The schedule and budget were tighter than on some of my other films, but atmosphere on the set was a little livelier. We couldn't sleep and that sort of thing because of the hard schedule, but the staff could still enjoy themselves. For the actors as well, that shoot was something of a break from the routine.

After all the producer was a father making a film with his son — it wasn't the usual professional shoot. So I got these people together and said lets have fun with it. That sort of attitude has a way of appearing in the film — the audience knows what's going on.

There's something strange about the world of that film — it's like "Alice Through the Looking Glass." The characters look human enough, but somehow they're not.

None of the characters in that film are considerate or kind. Characters usually exist only for the purpose of the film. They're cooperating with it, you might say, by playing various roles — the guy who helps the hero, the guy who opposes him. But in "Gozu" they could all care less (about the hero). They have no relationship to him. (laughs)

But those people exist in a city. For me they're more real than characters who only exist for the purpose of the movie. They have their own concerns — and the hero is not one of them.

In most films the characters are laughing and crying and dying for the sake of the story. In "Gozu" though there are scenes that have nothing to do with the story. (laughs)

The story itself is not so different from those of other films but the atmosphere is more realistic.

When you become lost in a strange city and ask strangers the way, you might get the same reaction the hero in "Gozu" does from the other characters. People live out their lives in that sort of world, trying to find their own path among people they don't know and never will know. So in that way, "Gozu" is a realistic film. The hero is living an ordinary life when he loses his way. He tries to protect himself, but there are more possibilities out there than he is willing to admit. He's involved in this meaningless struggle, defending what is essentially without value — his own limited view of the world. That's the way a lot of people live their lives. If he left his shell, he might find another, better self.

He not a foreigner, of course, but he is a stranger in a strange land.

That's true, but anyone could have the same sort of experience if they were to get off the train at a strange station. They would enter a world different from the one they encounter everyday — maybe not the same one that exists in the film, but if they were to ask strangers "where is my aniki (older brother)?" they might get the same reaction the hero gets.

If you go on a journey to discover yourself — as opposed to the more usual journey to learn about other people and places — you might find that "Gozu" is a very realistic film. If you go on a journey expecting strangers to confirm your view of yourself, you might find yourself in a different world and you may encounter a different self than the one you thought you knew.

Do you ever feel that way yourself — a stranger in a strange land?

I was born and raised in Japan, but I feel a sense of isolation — that I'm different from others. I'm living a different sort of life than ordinary upstanding Japanese — I'm a dropout, actually. I have the same face, the same blood and the same education as them, but the way I feel about things is different. So even though I'm Japanese I feel isolated. I feel as though I'm in a little stream, away from the main river. That goes for films as well. I'm not in the mainstream film world — I'm a free agent, off on my own. So even though I'm a Japanese, I feel something like an outsider in Japan

(July 23, 2003, "The Japan Times")

Satoshi Miki interview

"Adrift In Tokyo" ("Ten Ten") seems to sum up the themes of your first four films.
Yes, "Adrift In Tokyo" is probably the culmination of all my previous work — my peak. The problem is — where do I go from here. (laughs).

When Takeshi Kitano made "Hana-Bi" I had the same thought — though his films were more serious. Do you have any plans to make a serious movie?
None. (laughs) I get asked that a lot, like Kitano. People say to me "Why don't you make a serious film? You can make one" but I don't think so. (laughs). The ideas that come to me tend to be on the silly side. Some people say I could make a romantic drama but I prefer to stay with the silly stuff I know. If I were to construct a story with more dramatic elements, it wouldn't feel right.

"Adrfit In Tokyo" has a serious side, though. After all Fukuhara kills his wife.
The movie opens with a taboo — that is, wife murder. I tried to separate the journey of the two men from the incident. There are times when people have to deal with major issues in their lives, but they still react to what is immediately in front of them. For instance, even when you are breaking up with your girlfriend, if the waiter spills a glass of water, what goes through your head is 'Oh he spilt a glass of water'. So it makes me wonder if people are actually shouldering these serious issues all the time. Movie narratives are constructted so serious issues and inner conflicts are continuously present in the characters. But I feel that, in reality, the time people spend pondering these isses or conflicts may be quite short. Even if the character is carrying an emotional burden from killing his wife, on a journey to give himself up to the police, if something idiotic appears in front of him, he'll react to that. At that moment, his feelings are focused on that one idiotic thing.

You're carefull to present the main character as something more than a criminal.
Right. When I first brought the script to the production company, they were concerned about the dead body, about whether we should show it or not. My thought was that we need to show that, behind the silly events on the screen, there's another reality, which is the dead body. The first production company I showed the script to took issue with that aspect of the film. They said) It would make the movie too unbalanced, that it would damage the multi-layered structure of the story. There's the guy going to the police to confess, there's the trio from the supermarket, and they're all set in motion by this dead body. The film is structured like a comedy skit — one act can cause unintended consequences for total strangers.

You write all of your scripts yourself?
Yes, even when I'm working from a novel or other original source material. I make drastic changes, so I always tell the author of the original, "I'm sorry, but I'm going to change your story." I only work with authors who can handle that, not the ones who demand that I not change a single line. Mr. Fujita, the author of "Adrift In Tokyo," had a big heart in that respect. (laughs). He believes that novels and movies are two distinctly different mediums. He said, "I feel as if I'm giving you my daughter. Treat her gently." (laughs)

Does filming on a novel adaptation lessen the commercial risk?
There's always a risk. "In The Pool" was also an adaptation of a novel, but from an unknown writer. The author of "Adrfit In Tokyo" is relatively unknown as well. I don't know how much commercial effect being an adaptation has on "Adrfit In Tokyo."

That gives you more freedom of expression then

Yes. And if the original was famous the audience would have an image of the story already and would demand that the film mirror the original, as would the production company. I'm not the right director for that sort of film.

A lot of Japanese films now are based on best-selling novels, comics and games, as well as highly rated TV dramas. Do you think that's a bad trend?

There's are lot of cases where the original best seller is the reason the movie exists. They try to incorporate a lot of elements from the original so that it won't be a commercial failure. It doesn't mean it will be a good film, though.

How much of your work is still for TV?

I did the drama "Statute of Limitations Police" ("Jiko Keisatsu") most recently. I've had a long career as a TV writer but since I started directing movies I haven't been doing as much TV work.

You are a prolific director.

"Dame-jin" was my first film, in 2002. Then "Turtles Swim Faster Than Expected" ("Kame Wa Igai To Hayaku Oyogu") in April 2004. Then "In the Pool" in June 2005. But the order of screening was "In the Pool", then "Turtles" then "Dame-jin" so it's the opposite. I'm the director who's steadily becoming worse. (laughs)

Did you have to change your approach to comedy, from five-minute TV skits to two-hour movies?

If I have a situation like 'going for a walk,' what I do is list the things that will be funny in this situation. For a film, I go through the same process, but for two hours on on-screen time. At this stage there's an unconscious element to my thinking — it's not structured. Then I look for a unifying key word from what I've listed. The writng is tough until I find the unifying key word. For instance when I'm creating two hours worth of skit theatre, as soon as I find what my core ideas is, a kind of linear development naturally emerges from that. It's not exactly a 'theme,' but just something that'll serve as a key word for that production. It's a conscious process to find that.

When you made "Adrfit In Tokyo" did you watch a lot of road movies for ideas?

I don't really watch a lot of movies to sample ideas. I don't know how many movies I watch compared to hardcore film fans, although I do like watching movies. When I decided to do a road movie I thought about American New Cinema — films like "Scarecrow," "Easy Rider," and "Two Lane Black Top." I don't think that last one was a hit, though it's really good. In "Adrfit In Tokyo" I wanted to abruptly end the movie with a character saying 'Nandayo' (What's that about?). Japanese films tend to have long epilogues. The story is over but you still get all these things tagged onto the end, even a song. In American New Cinema films like "Easy Rider" you just get a gun shot — 'bam' and that's the end of the movie. I wanted "Adrfit In Tokyo" to have that kind of conclusion. Takemura says 'Nandayo' at Fukuhara crossing the street and suddenly the screen blacks out and that's the end.

I felt "Adrfit In Tokyo" had a feel similar to that of New American Cinema.

I've always looked up to that kind of ending, that kind of edge. The audience can imagine what happened after that, what happened to Fukuhara and the dead body, I had qualms about depicting it. I know a certain percentage of the audience felt frustration that there was no depiction (of what happened to the body), but that's OK. Like you said, there's a New American Cinema influence on it. I wanted to create the mood more than imagery, because I had looked up to those movies since I was middle school, especially "Easy Rider." I stupidly fell over a lot on my bike because I messed around with the spokes imitating that movie, (laughs). It was cool. So the scene at the beginning at Chofu Air Field, when Fukuhara talks about killing his wife, was influenced by the opening of "Easy

Rider," which takes place at a air field. That's how a road movie should begin, with a suit case at an air field. So I've been influenced in that sense. I wouldn't call it an homage. It's how I decided to make a road movie set in Tokyo.

It would have been hard to make a road movie with motorcycles in Tokyo (laugh)

I actually crossed America, traveling about 2000 kilometers in 1995, on a motorcycle. I left LA, crossed Monument Valley, the Grand Canyon, Lake Powell then back to LA and San Francisco. It was about a ten day trip with a bike tour. I rented a Harley 883. I ride Harleys in Japan as well. I got a feel for places like Route 66. "Adrift In Tokyo" turned out like that, even though it's set in Japan. When I was in that desolate landscape, riding my bike, I started humming music from "Easy Rider," because I'm an idiot. (laughs) "Born to be Wild" gets you in the mood. Your face is dry because it's a desert. You know those scarves that cover people's faces in Westerns? They're actually practical because the place just wrecks your lips. I had one wrapped around my face when I was on my bike.

Do you base your movies on the characters?

I do after the casting is decided. I write the script first, then the actors are cast and I think 'This kind of gag would work better with this person,' so I adjust my script a little. I think about how this actor can be funny or interesting as this character and rewrite a bit. Then I get unique characters and have to figure out how they will fit into the overall flow, where they stand. Maybe it's because I did sketch comedy but I think about where the characters stand in relation to each other and the story. When I read the original for "In the Pool," the only actor I thought of for the lead was John Belushi, or somebody with that kind of destructive tension. Of course there's no John Belushi in Japan so I opted for Matsuo Suzuki, I thought his unique personality would work better for "In the Pool." When Matsuo-san gave me the OK I changed the character so that it would fit him.

Miyako Ichikawa plays a very realistic neuortic. Too bad she can't find a cure. (laughs)

(laughs) She has to live with it. The theme of the original novel, and also my theme in shooting "In the Pool" was that if you permit people their (neuroses) you will ease their suffering. That is, permit what is considered wrong ort a failure of character by the society. People say 'You have to go to school,' but there's no reason why you have to. Everybody vaguely believes that everybody has to go to school, but it never killed anyone not to go to school. Another example is 'You have to fall in love while you're young.' Why?

The movie is good medicine in that way. It's a comedy with a message.

I feel I shouldn't be constrained by those things. In "Deathfix" (Rinko) Kikuchi, who is a wrist cutter, lets Masuo Suzuki grinds wasabi (horseradish) on (her scars) — and it hurts. That to me is a positive action. When he uses the wrist as a wasabi grinder, it makes wrist cutting and suicide look stupid and meaningless. I thought it was a positive scene, but people told me it was quite painful to watch.

That was pushing it to the limit.

The Japanese audience may have a lower threshold for that sort of thing because when I showed "Deathfix" in France I had the feeling the French were accepting of a wider range of humor. Japanese men, on the other hand, have knee jerk rejections especially to humor related to taboos. More women said they liked "Deathfix." it was the men who went (disapprovingly) 'Oh, look what they're doing.'. The men were more conservative.

"Deathfix" deals with mortality — a pretty heavy theme.

It says it doesn't really make a difference whether you're alive or dead. (laughs). It had a grandiose theme but it was loaded with little jokes.

You used a serious actor like Rinko Kikuchi, who not known for playing comedy

Kikuchi came back from the Academy Awards straight to our set (laugh). She was probably thinking 'What is this crap?' (laughs) That was a funny situation for me. From the red carpet to.. this (laughs)

Did you cast her before "Babel" was released?
Yes. At the time she was an unknown actress. I thought she had an interesting feel. Then "Babel" was released, and there was a lot of attention. I thought she was an actress with a strong core, so there was probably no big difference in her basic attitude toward being on the red carpet and shooting "Deathfix." She just goes her own way. That's what it takes to be successful internationally, not to be swayed by who you're with.

What was your reason for making "Deathfix"?
I wanted to make a road movie. It's a coincidence that I felt like making two road movies in a row. One on foot, one by car. After seeing "Fear and Loathing in Las Vegas" by Terry Gilliam and also "Two Lane Black Top," I wanted to do a car road movie. Terry Gilliam came from Monty Python so I took that feeling too. "Fear and Loathing" is about the original gonzo journalist, so that image of (Hunter Thompson and the Samoan lawyer) was in my head. In America it's mostly drugs and marijuana but in Japan it's paint thinner (laughs). The original title for "Deathfix" was 'Don't Inhale Thinner Before Work' (laughs). But that went beyond moral boundaries, so I made the hero a drunk. Originally he was a thinner addict. When I was in high school there were a lot of guys inhaling thinner.

Where was your high school?
It was in Yokohama.

Was there a big foreign influence?
Yes, when I was a kid it was the Vietnam war. The ammunition depot of the US Army was nearby so you couldn't build houses there. There were a lot of open fields. We lived in a small tenement house. When you go somewhere like Chinatown from there you pass the (American) base housing on the bus and you see sprinklers, big lawns, and dogs over the fence. What a way to live!

I lived in Tachikawa near the Yokota base, so I had the same impression. (laughs)
I found out later that, because of the Vietnam War, the situation over the fence was not what I imagined at the time. It was more like Robert Altman's "MASH." But the American base was a source of admiration and influence back then.

So you watched more American films first?
Yes, films like "Easy Rider," Kubrick's films, Macaroni Westerns, "Straight to Heaven" by Alex Cox.

Did the "manzai boom" (the popularity of comedy duos on Japanese TV in the early 1980s) have an influence on you?
Not really. In the 1970s they were showing "Monty Python" in Japan. Also, there was a show called "Geba Geba" that imitated Python. I preferred that sort of thing.

It's said that the irony in British comedy is hard for Japanese people to understand.
There's a strong sense of class differences in Python, and that sort of comedy is hard to understand. But the British are a homogenous race like the Japanese so they're like us in that they don't have to explain the set-up (to a comedy skit). In a multi-ethnic culture like America you have to explain the basic situation so that everybody understands, then you start the gags. In Japan there are a lot of comics on TV and a lot of TV shows with gags. A designer who lived in New York told me that when he came back to Japan and started watching TV he was thinking 'Why are these surrealistic (gags) on at prime time?' Because people here have widely shared belief and knowledge, you can make gags

with little set-up. There's a similar situation in Korea, where their gags are quite developed. In these sort of countries it's easier to develop gags.

In America, blacks and Puerto Ricans find humor in different things. And of course there's the Jewish humor of Woody Allen and Mel Brooks. So to make everybody laugh you have to find something bland or stereotypical or all-purpose. Especially in Hollywood movies, where they want a wide audience to laugh, they need a well-made situation everyone can understand, as in "My Best Friends Wedding," or "Something About Mary." "Something About Mary" is a bit raunchy but it still it aims to make everyone chuckle at well-made situations that are packaged as one story. Hollywood has mastered that technique, but unfortunately I can't imitate that.

Hollywood comedies don't fare well in Japan.

I don't know how many people they attract but TV dramas take the easy route and copy Hollywood romantic comedies. Even if it's a similar formula, when a Japanese actor does it there's a familiarity with the actor, which makes it easier for the audience to laugh. I think it's harder to get into some foreign person you're not familiar with doing the same gag. I personally don't care much for Hollywood comedies and don't watch many of them. I think the Coen brothers and Cheech and Chong are funny, though.

Its more conservative in America now — even Hollywood wants to play it safe, which doesn't make for interesting comedies.

Roger Coleman made a lot of low budget movies for drive-ins and that gave a chance to directors like Steven Spielberg and (Francis Ford) Coppolla. A situation like that gives people the opportunity to make edgy stuff. When there's big money involved its harder to think "This is a funny gag, lets do it.' There will be the story analyst saying "Yeah, this is understandable, so it's ok to invest this much money.' Gags come from a very personal place. Gags everybody accepts tend not to be funny. The best ones have fifty people laughing and the other fifty not. If you start trying to find gags that are acceptable to seventy or eighty people (out of a hundred) the comedy probably won't be funny.

(2007 "Udine Far East Film Festival Catalogue")

Koki Mitani interview

Interviewing Koki Mitani — a playwright and director who is Japan's closest equivalent to Neil Simon in both comic sensibility and success — should have been a barrel of laughs. But Mitani, whose credits include "Welcome Back, Mr. McDonald," "Our House" and his most recent hit, "University of Laughs," was like many comedy writers in being deadly serious about his craft — and explaining it with all due earnestness. Our conversation, in the Hibiya headquarters of distributor Toho, was punctuated by laughter — though this interviewer was cracking most of the jokes.

At the screening I saw at the Tokyo Film Festival, the audience was laughing at every joke — the film was a huge success. Aren't you sorry now that you didn't direct it? (laughs)
(laughs) No, not really. It was originally a stage play. Plays and films are two very different mediums — and I thought that this play would be especially difficult to film. So when I was approached about making a movie, I said I would give my OK only if Mr. (Mamoru) Hoshi directed it. I'd worked with him before and I knew he understood the difference between plays and films. I thought he would be the best one for the material.

How did you come to know him?
He directed a script of mine for a TV program called "Furuhata Ninzaburo." That was a two-man drama about a detective and a criminal — in that way it resembles "University of Laughs." So when the producers came to me with the idea of filming the play, his was the first name that came to mind.

I understand why you chose Koji Yakusho to play the part of the censor, but the casting of Goro Inagaki wasn't as obvious.
I wanted someone who wasn't an "average Joe" type — and that's Inagaki exactly. He's playing a character, Tsubaki, who's something of an intellectual, who makes a living with his mind. He's not living in the everyday world.

He's also very much the professional, who will sacrifice his ego to get his play on the stage.
Being a scriptwriter myself, I know what that sort of character is like. For one thing, scriptwriters may be dedicated to their work, but they're different from novelists in that, whether they're writing for the screen or stage, they're not just writing for themselves, but for a larger community, including the actors who will play their roles. They have to pay attention to human relationships. They have to be able to coolly evaluate what works and what doesn't. Inagaki has the coolness a scriptwriter needs — that's another reason why he was right for the role.

Not only Inagaki's character, but the heroes of the two films you directed — "Welcome Back, Mr. McDonald" and "Our House" — are scriptwriters. Can't you pick any other profession? (laughs)
Well, it's something I understand. (laughs) Also, I like to make films about people who make something together, about the process of creation. There's a lot of drama inherent in that situation — and (scriptwriting) is a profession that lends itself to drama.

When you wrote the script did you imagine yourself in Tsubaki's shoes and what you would do if you were?
Tsubaki is a type of ideal scriptwriter — there's no one like him now. But I've had to write TV dramas where I've had various limits placed on what I could do. Restrictions in terms of schedule or subject or actors. For example actor A and actor B don't get along. So I'll be asked not to put A and B together in the same scene. Or another actor has a poor memory, so I'll be asked to give him shorter lines.

Demands like that are always being made on the set. Some scriptwriters will object, but I'll try to accommodate them as much as possible, while writing the best script I can. So in that way I'm like Tsubaki I suppose.

The film is based on the reality of wartime censorship — but it's also a fantasy.
Tsubaki is lucky to have a censor like Sakisaka, who is both considerate and flexible. In reality censors were scary people, so the story may be somewhat removed from reality in that way. Sakisaka is a complex character. He likes comedy, but can't admit it to himself. In the course of his seven days with Tsubaki he doesn't change so much as recognize what he really likes and who he really is. He finds out that he shares a common interest with Tsubaki.

Tsubaki's case is a bit different. Every day he walks through Asakusa on his way to see Sakisaka and every day the people in front of the theaters are doing the same sorts of things — it reminded me of "Groundhog Day," where Bill Murray is stuck in the same day forever.
True, he goes through the same routine every day — but little by little the war is getting closer. Of course, the political situation didn't change as quickly as it does in the film — so it's something of a fantasy in that way too.

But the political situation in both Japan and America is making the film look more and more timely. The government is now enforcing the raising of the Hinomaru flag and the singing of "Kimigayo" at school ceremonies. We aren't quite back to 1940 yet — but the trend is in that direction.
"University of Laughs" was originally a radio drama, then it became a play. Both times I was told that it was timely. Back then I wondered how it could be timely, but now I'm starting to understand. I just hope we get to the point when no one can call the film timely.

The film also reflects the period — it may start off as a comedy, but towards the end the tone darkens. We realize that Sakisaka and Tsubaki occupy different positions in society and that Sakisaka has to play a certain role. He can't just be Tsubaki's collaborator and friend.
Those two put their heads together and make something they both enjoy — it's a happy time for them. Then the mood changes and becomes more serious. Their relationship changes as a result.
The film may be called a comedy, but I never thought of it as one. I wanted the ending to be serious.

I wonder how it will be received abroad — whether foreign audiences will understand why you had to end it the way you did.
The play was performed in Russia — in a Siberian city called Omsk and then in Moscow. The Russian audiences enjoyed it. The story about a censor and a playwright was more familiar to them than it would be to Japanese.

The world premiere was at this year's Pusan Film Festival — I heard the reaction there was good as well.
I didn't go, but I heard the Korean audience liked the film. What surprised me — there's a lot of word play in the film, but they seemed to get it. I never thought of showing the film abroad when I wrote it. I was just concerned with making the Japanese audience laugh — I wasn't thinking of the foreign audience at all. So I put of lot of puns in the script and I wondered how anyone could translate them. I was surprised to see how the translators were able to find equivalents in Korean and English.

The subtitles are well done. Just one thing bothered me — The name of "Okuni" — one of the characters in the play — is translated as "Ms. Neyshon" — but that's not a real name. "Nation" is a real last name, though. There was Carry Nation — a famous temperance crusader.

Really? Well, we'll have to change it (laughs).

This film resembles the two you directed yourself in so many ways that people will inevitably think of it as a "Mitani film." But it's not.

No, it's Mr. Hoshi's film — and I'm happy now that he directed it. If he hadn't I wouldn't be as nearly as satisfied with the result.

The subject matter and treatment are more distinctively Japanese than in your other films, which have more of a Western flavor. Did you want to write something closer to your historical and cultural roots?

It just so happened that the film was set in that place and period. The situation of two people coming together to make something is not exclusive to Japan. After I wrote the radio drama I saw a film by Woody Allen called "Bullets Over Broadway." It was about a playwright who gets his play financed by a gangster — and then has to change it according to the gangster's whims. I thought it was interesting that Allen could have the same basic idea as me — it had nothing to do with nationality. Comedy is comedy.

(November 17, 2004, full-length version of interview that appeared in "The Japan Times")

Hayao Miyazaki interview: Governors Award recipient says 'I intend to work until the day I die'

At age 73, Hayao Miyazaki is still capable of surprises. He has an atelier, just behind the main Studio Ghibli building, on a narrow and quiet street in a suburb of Tokyo. Surrounded by trees, it looks like the sort of rustic resort cottage a well-off Japanese with European tastes might build in the mountains. When his assistant escorted me through the gate, Miyazaki was in the midst of chopping wood — his preferred method of stress relief. With a big grin and a firm handshake, he walked me into his studio and work space in the center of huge, high-ceiling room. On a big wooden table (imagine a picnic table with chairs instead of benches) was a holder containing dozens of colored pencils and other drawing paraphernalia. Without missing a beat, Miyazaki sat down and started penciling a sketch for a manga that has occupied him since his retirement last year. The esteemed animator talked about his Governors Award (which he will receive Saturday night), the Oscars, about his future animation plans and the changing world of films.

What was your reaction on hearing about Oscar's Governors Award?
I thought, "Somebody must have been pulling strings." Maybe John Lasseter. He's my number one supporter there, so I thought he must have been behind it, though that's pure speculation on my part. I'm not the kind of person who wants more awards. (laughs) Lasseter invited me over to his place, since this may be my last (trip to the States). I don't want to go, to be honest — I don't like riding airplanes. (laughs)

The Tokyo Intl. Film Festival is screening a Hideaki Anno retro this year. Not long ago your producer, Toshio Suzuki, said Anno would be the leader of the Japanese animation industry for the next ten years. Do you agree?
Anno is a friend of mine so I wish him the best of luck. It will be hard work though. The kind of animation he loves, made with paper and pencils, is dying. I still plan on doing small projects with paper and pencils, but no more feature films.

You were talking about making short films for the Ghibli Museum.
We've already released a few and I will continue to make them. I have plans for other projects as well.

Do you have working titles? Any details you can share with me?
Not yet.

I've heard that you're working on a new manga.
Yes, but it keeps getting pushed behind other projects (laughs). I can't work on it as much as I'd like to.

Is it set in the samurai days?
Yes, it is but I have my doubts as to whether I can finish it or not. I wanted to put a lot of effort into it, ignoring costs, like a hobby. I thought I'd have free time, but I keep getting project offers. Not necessarily lucrative ones, but they have a significance for me.

Are you here every day?
Yes I am. I've recently changed my work schedule to five days a week. I didn't know what to do with myself taking three days off a week. (laughs) I try to take Saturdays and Sundays off, though.

So you don't go on long trips?
Well I'm going to go to Kamikochi (a mountain resort area north of Tokyo) for a week. It's the off season then, so there are less people.

When I visited Studio Ghibli in the past, it was always busy. What is the atmosphere like there now?
We've just finished a project (Hiromasa Yonebayashi's "When Marnie Was There"), so it's kind of empty now.

There are rumors that Ghibli is going to focus on managing intellectual rights and abandon feature filmmaking.
I'm working with the museum staff, but as for the whole of Ghibli, I don't know anymore. I don't want to get involved in that sort of thing. I'll be here as long as they let me do what I want to do.
Let me show you what I'm doing now (holds up a drawing of a globe on the back of a turtle). See, this is an island called Kumejima in Okinawa. In this picture, Kumejima is on the top and the rest of Japan is upside down. I don't know what the islanders will think, but it's a symbol I made (laughs). It's a very beautiful island. They made a recreation facility so that they can bring over children and their parents from Fukushima (the site of the March 11, 2011 nuclear disaster). There they can play outside, get stronger, and toughen their immune system. There are parts of Fukushima where children can no longer play outside, you know. I've been asked to help with this project so I agreed to make this symbol for them. (laughs) This has occupied me quite a bit.

Is your son Goro going to take over Studio Ghibli? It seems that he has been preparing for that role. (Note: Goro Miyazaki has directed two films for Studio Ghibli, both box office hits.)
No, I don't think like that. Individual ability should be the deciding factor. It's not something to inherit like property. I think my son would be against the idea as well.

Goro has teamed up with the digital animation studio Polygon to make "Ronia the Robber's Daughter" for television. He made use of 3-D computer graphics, though the program has the look of traditional Japanese animation. What do you think of that trend?
I think talent decides everything. More than the method, what's important is the talent using it. There's nothing inherently wrong or right about a method, whether it be pencil drawings or 3-D CG. Pencil drawings don't have to go away, but those who continue to use the medium lack talent. So sadly, it will fade away.
    I intend to work until the day I die. I retired from feature-length films but not from animation. Self-indulgent animation (laughs). It's nice that I have the mini-theater in the museum. Most of the museum visitors attend the mini-theater screenings and we've never had a complaint about the quality of the films. I'd like to continue to make films that leave the audience satisfied, but I also think it's pointless unless I offer them the kind of animation they can't get anywhere else. They're fun to do. They're short so it's less stressful.

(Assistant question:) Have you ever started making a short film and it became longer than you intended?
A little bit, but I know the limits I'm working with and some stories have to be told succinctly. It's a good opportunity for me to experiment and learn. I won't be in charge of the massive staff at Studio Ghibli, but I will continue to make short films for the museum.

It seems that with the bigger projects, made with a bigger staff, you have to think more about appealing to the audience. If the audience doesn't come, you can't make those kinds of films.
It's challenging, but you always have to appeal to your audience. You always have to consider how well your project will do in terms of admissions. I abandoned many stories because of that. But I don't get too down about it. It's something I accepted from the time I decided to work in films. I could always do something else if I got sick of it, like draw manga, or make my own films like (the late Canadian animator) Frederic Back. But my own tastes are more pop than art (laughs) and that's how I'll continue to work. I found it pointless sitting in my house not working, though I'd like to go on extended vacations from time to time.

It takes a lot of perseverance to do what you did.

Yes, I have more perseverance than I used to think I did. I think my work toughened me. I learned to find time to switch off, by chopping logs.

You've said that too many young animators are otaku (obsessed fans) who have little real-life experience. All they know is the world of anime.

That trend still exists and it takes away from the power of Japanese animation and manga. It was inevitable, though. I managed to work for 51 years with just paper, pencils and film. My wife told me the other day that I should be thankful for that.'You're a lucky man,' she said. My son's generation and the one coming up after can't work with just paper and pencils any more so I can't tell you how that's going to turn out. I managed to avoid using a computer. I don't even have a cellphone. I feel lucky I managed to live like that. (laughs)

Some generations have it better than others, that's true.

Yes, my elders had to quit their jobs to go off to war. Many couldn't fulfill their ambitions because of circumstances beyond their control. I've managed to keep working using the same methods and tools for 51 years, right up until the time film became obsolete. I'm very lucky in that regard. I attribute my success to luck. Who knows how my making films for the museum will turn out, but you don't have to know the future. I'm just mucking about, trying to figure my next project. (laughs)

(November 7, 2014, "Variety")

Kaori Momoi interview: on fire in her new indie film 'Hee'

In her four-decade acting career Kaori Momoi has always been a free-spirited stand-out, indifferent to convention. But beneath her easygoing attitude and signature drawling delivery (which used to make me wonder what she had been ingesting before the cameras started rolling) was a thorough professionalism and boundless curiosity. Unlike most other leading actresses of her generation — she was born in Tokyo in 1951 — Momoi braved the Hollywood jungle, winning roles in such major productions as "Memoirs of a Geisha" (2005) and "The Yellow Handkerchief" (2008), a remake of the 1977 Yoji Yamada road-movie classic that launched her to stardom. She also segued successfully into directing, with her 2006 debut feature "Faces of a Fig Tree" ("Ichijiku no Kao") screening at Pusan, Berlin and other festivals around the world.

Now Momoi is back with her second film as a director: "Hee" ("Hi"), which means "fire" in Japanese. Shot mostly in Momoi's home in Los Angeles, with Momoi starring as a mentally disturbed sex worker who is suspected of murder, the film had a difficult gestation, as shown in a "making of" film that screened at the Kyoto International Film and Art Festival last October.

Based on Fuminori Nakamura's short story, the film had a low budget by Hollywood (or even Japanese) standards and Momoi struggled with everything from the release (in Kyoto she had yet to find a Japanese distributor) to her co-lead, Yugo Saso. In the "making" film Momoi relentlessly criticizes Saso's performance as the psychiatrist who treats her, telling him he is not connecting with her. "You have to be in the moment," she reminds him — an acting lesson Momoi herself has mastered, as indicated by a long list of awards that includes two Japanese Academy Best Actress prizes.

Last February, after "Hee" had screened at the Berlin Film Festival (its subsequent stops on the festival circuit include Hong Kong, Okinawa and, in September, Vladivostok), she spoke with "The Japan Times" about the film and her own illustrious career.

You had a tough time making "Hee."

True, but making an indie film is not just tough for the director. For example, actors work for no fee and the crew is hired for low pay. When I appeared in (Doris Dorrie's) "Fukushima Mon Amour" (2016), everyone worked as a volunteer. Even the people in temporary housing (in Fukushima) appeared for nothing. They didn't even get one omanju (steamed bun). Actually I can't say the director has it tough — the director is the one who wants to make the film to begin with.

But this time you were more than just the director.

I did all the styling, the art direction, the editing. We didn't have the money and I didn't want to ask someone else to do it. You're just imposing on people, since you can't pay them much or you're asking them to volunteer. That's the hardest thing about indie films. So I wanted to make a good film that wins awards. That way I can make everyone who took part feel a little better about doing it.

When I saw the "making of" film I realized how serious you were. It was like a life-or-death struggle.

Of course it is. That's why actors have to beat their directors. As an actress I have to beat my director's imagination. So I experiment with my lines. In any case, I don't try to memorize them, I don't sound them out. I make it a condition that I'm going to say those lines just once, like you do in real life. I'm living the life of the woman (I'm portraying). When I'm acting, the cameraman and the director of photography have only one chance to watch that.

So there were not retakes on "Hee"?

No, none. I think it's cheating to do that if you're both the actor and director. It's not fair. If I can do it only one time I'm going to concentrate. I can lead her life and try to do what she does. One day a fly came into the scene and I caught it like so (demonstrates). Anyway I use everything during the takes.

You gave Saso quite an acting lesson.

He's playing the psychiatrist and this woman has been telling her whole life to him. But when I saw the footage we shot that day, I realized he had not been listening — and that changed the story. Why is it important for him to listen? It's a last chance for her. She has to go away because she killed somebody. She really wants to connect, to trust someone and this is her last chance.

It's like being a soldier. You know you're going to die, but you keep advancing forward. If I'm going to die tomorrow and there's only one person in front of me, I want that person to try hard to understand me so that at the end we can trust each other. I feel that in today's world it's important to have that kind of hope. Nowadays people don't try to understand and believe in each other.

If he's not connecting with your character, the film would have been like a bout of one-man sumo.

Right, one-man sumo. But she can't choose whether the other person is someone she can talk to and trust. All she can do is tell her entire life story to the person in front of her. The theme is connections between people. To live, we have to connect with others, like it or not. But are we truly making that effort? Everybody shuts their doors. Everyone has become like a lonely rabbit in its own cage.

Then there is the connection between the film and the audience.

A film is something people see and understand based on their life experiences. If a movie makes five people feel the same way it's strange. Everyone is different and everyone has different experiences, so the way they feel about things is different too. If 100 people buy your film on television and all 100 feel the same way about it, it's not a good film.

What's the big difference between Hollywood and Japanese films for you?

It's the difference between major and indie films. In Japan, I couldn't appear in indie films — if I did they'd became major. But abroad I can appear in indie films because I'm a foreigner.

Asian women are kind of rare, right? (laughs) So there are still some people who will hire me. There aren't any other Japanese actresses my age abroad, so I get cast. I feel no need to appear in major productions. Those are the kind of films 100 people all like the same way. I like films where five people see it and afterward go to a bar and talk about it.

What is it like working somewhere you are less well-known?

I'm nobody and that's really interesting. How do they see me? For me as an actor, that's fun. Nobody knows how Kaori Momoi will perform, do they? I can try something different and become something new. I'm always a newcomer. Nobody knows my age. I may even be able to play a man. If I don't strip they're not going to know (laughs).

You don't do much television.

I don't do it. I came along at the end of the film era. The era of seeing movies in a theater is just about over. Everyone is seeing them on the internet or on DVD. But for me a movie is something to see in a dark theater. I want to be in a movie that everyone watches with concentration, a movie that you won't understand if you get up to go to the bathroom. That's the kind of movie I want to make. But mine is the last generation to feel that way.

(August 3, 2016, "The Japan Times")

Yoshihiro Nakamura interview

I interviewed Yoshihiro Nakamura on almost the last day he was publicizing "Fish Story" before starting the media rounds for another new film, "The Triumphant Return of General Rouge." We met at the headquarters of Amuse, a major Japanese talent agency, where Nakamura was holding forth all day for the press. He was relaxed and soft spoken, but with a distinctive low rumbling voice. and a ready laugh.

Watching your films, especially "Fish Story," I have the feeling you must be a fan of Charlie Kaufman. (laughs) That is, there's something about the story that reminds me of his films. Are you influenced by him or any other foreign filmmakers?
Yes, I am. I like "Smoke" by Wayne Wang — or any films with that sort of flavor.

The reason I mention Kaufman is because in his film "Eternal Sunshine of the Spotless Mind," memories disappear, but in "Fish Story" the world is about to disappear (laughs).
I don't have any deep purpose — I'm not saying "this is what we should do to save the world." What I'm trying to say is "even if you live an ordinary life, you can have an impact on others." In other words, "you are not alone."

A lot of your heroes, including the ones in "Fish Story" seem to be losers — who somehow end up being winners or at least survivors.
Well, they may have lost on a particular occasion, but if they keep trying, they fulfill their dreams. Or at least they have an impact on others. It depends on how you lose — sometimes you don't make that connection. But what I'm saying in this film is that, even if you keep trying, you can somehow have an impact. You may not win, though.

One example of that is the 1970s punk band in the film.
Right — their music didn't sell, then or later. But even though it didn't sell, they still had a strong desire to say something. (In the film) that strong desire to communicate is what saves the world.

The first scene made a strong impression on me — the whole city has fled to the city in panic and here are these two guys in a record shop talking about music. It's as though you're telling the audience, no matter how bad things get, there's no reason to panic. (laughs)
Right, they shouldn't panic. The message (of the film) is you've got to have something to believe in. The owner (of the record store) believes that something will save the world, that something will happen to put things right. He's believed that ever since he was a kid, watching "go ranger" ("five ranger" superhero) shows on TV. He's grown up thinking that way.

The owner is played by Nao Omori, who also plays the band manager. I understood the difference — but did you worry that audiences might be confused? Why the double role?
Originally one of the band members was going to become the record store owner. But I didn't think it would work to have a former band member playing (the band's) music in the store — it was a little bit strange. Then I thought to have the manager played by Omori manage the shop when he got old. But I was afraid that making him up like an old man would take the audience out of the film. So instead, I had the record owner be the son of the manager.

Is there any particular reason for choosing the years for the various stories, such as 2012 for the end of the world.
Those were the years in the original book. I really don't know why.

139

Not even why for 2012?

That's different — there are various predictions saying the world will end in 2012, including Nostradamus. A lot of people believe in Nostradamus' predictions that way.

I was also impressed by the last five minutes of the film — I really didn't see the ending coming.

Yes, I wanted the audience to wonder how it's going to end.

It reminded me a bit of "The Sixth Sense," though you expand the story more — you're not just flashing back the way that film does.

Yes, I really admire M. Night Shyamalan. There's something beautiful about that film.

Another theme I often see in your films is the strangeness of the world — or rather strange things happen in what look to be ordinary circumstances.

Yes, that's true — but what I'm saying in this film is that if you strongly want to have an impact, you will have an impact — something will get across.

That's also a theme in "The Triumphant Return of General Rouge." The characters are not just trying to solve a puzzle.

That's right. You have people who are trying hard in difficult circumstance — and suddenly they make a break through. I like that sort of moment.

In "Fish Story" and other of your films, it's not always so clear where the story is going, though eventually it does go somewhere. Is it hard to pitch your films to producers for that reason?

Not really, not at the script stage anyway. With "Fish Story," though, they wanted more explanation about the last five minutes. (laughs). There was also a question about the title, "Fish Story." In English it means a "made up story," So it's a kind of joke, but I thought that, through that joke, I could make the audience understand the deeper message of the film.

Perhaps the producers feel that, since you've got a good track record as a scriptwriter as well, they can trust you (laughs)

I don't know about that. (laughs). But I'm always rewriting, even when I'm filming. I'm always trying to see if I can communicate (my message better). That is, make it easier to understand.

Still there's a difference between writing a script and directing it. Do ever find it hard to get across what you've written on the set?

Yes, sometimes. The advantage of having written the script is that I know what I want to emphasize in the film as a whole. I can relax a bit — I don't have to keeping trying so hard.

You have an idea of where the whole film is going, but do you try to communicate that to the actors as well?

No, not really — just the scene they happen to be doing. Thinking about the whole film is my job.

But with Fish Story you have all these different stories — did you worry about consistency, so that the stories wouldn't be all over the map in term of mood and so on?

No, not really. I had no plan (in that way) for this film. (laughs) I wondered how I was going to pull it together in the editing room. But when I was directing, I was just thinking about making these four short films — a college student film, a music film, an action film and an SF film. When it came time to edit it was fun tying everything to together.

You had to have a clear idea of what you wanted to do in the last five minutes, though — you didn't jus throw that together.

Yes, I did plan for the last five minutes, but not so much for the rest of the film. You could do the same sort of thing with other films. Say you have some cuts from "The Sixth Sense" and some cuts from an (Akira) Kurosawa film — it doesn't matter which one. It would be interesting to try to tie them all together. You'd end up with a film totally different (from your sources). It would be fun to try. (laughs).

"Two Guys in Track Suits" is, by comparison, a simple film, but it's got a detail in the running gags and so on. You seem to like that kind of thing. (laughs)

That's right, I do. (laughs)

It was quite a change of pace for you.

It took me five years to get that film made. I talked to different producers, but for two and a half years no one would listen to me. Then one producer happened to say that my idea was interesting — that got things started.

I'm not the type of director who has a strategy, plotting out what sort of films I want to make, but my filmography would be a lacking something if "Two Guys In Track Suits" weren't in it. (laughs) It was a movie I had to make.

You also make films like "The Glorious Team Batista" and "The Triumphant Return of General Rouge" that are totally different, in the which the characters have to solve a puzzle. Is that genre one of your favorites?

Yes, I love mystery and suspense films — I always have. I see every one that comes out. In the past ten years, though, the one director who has really impressed me is Shyamalan. I also like the Coen brothers. I love the reality they create in their films. I love the way they think. The Coens are not only ones who do this, but (in their films) you have a hero who with, just a slight change of perspective, could also be the villain. That not just movies — you can also see that in real life. For example, Mark, in your own life, you're the hero, but to people walking on the street, you're a bit player. Everyone is like that — heroes in their own lives, but in the eyes of others, a bit player — or a villain.

Do you want to make films so that the audience has to see them more than once to get everything? That's the feeling I had with Fish Story — I want to see it again to pick things I missed.

No, one time is enough. If you see the last five minutes of that movie you should understand everything. I want people to walk out the theater with a light feeling, thinking that it's good to be alive.

(March 27, 2009, "The Japan Times")

Tetsuya Nakashima interview

Tall, bearded, bald and craggily handsome, Tetsuya Nakashima stands out in a crowd.

Backstage at Toho Cinemas Roppongi Hills, following the Japan premiere of "Memories of Matsuko" ("Kiraware Matsuko no Issho"), he also dominated an interview with "The Japan Times". Not just reciting talking points, but rattling off answers with passion, clarity and nervous intensity.

His view of his troubled heroine was certainly clear enough: "I wanted to show that Matsuko's life had value, no matter what it looked like on the surface," he began. "That she was able to influence those who came after her, more than if she had lived a normal, happy existence."

Nakashima was first drawn to the project by reading Muneki Yamada's novel. "If I start seeing images when I read a novel I know it's filmable," says Nakashima. "I certainly had that experience with 'Matsuko' — the images came like crazy."

Nakashima, who also wrote the script, realized that filming "Matsuko" as a conventional melodrama would probably turn off much of his potential audience.

"The story is dark — there's no getting around it," he comments. "By making it more colorful — by adding the musical numbers, the animation and all the rest, I thought I could make its central theme easier to understand."

Nakashima's last film, "Kamikaze Girls" ("Shimotsuma Monogatari"), became a box-office smash in Japan and was widely screened abroad. It earned Nakashima a Best Director prize at the 27th Yokohama Movie Awards, while stars Kyoko Fukada and Ann Tsuchiya scooped armfuls of acting prizes, including a Japan Academy Best Newcomer Award for Tsuchiya.

Will "Matsuko" duplicate this success? Nakashima has no box-office crystal ball, but he believes "Matsuko" is more a musical in the Hollywood line than the usual Japanese versions of the genre. "People here think that if a film has songs it has to be nothing but fluff," he comments. "But look at 'The Sound of Music' — that's a film with plenty of sadness in it. Or 'Cabaret' — the heroine hardly has an easy time, does she? The really great musicals usually have something serious going on behind the songs — that's what gives them their power. And that's the sort of film I've tried to make."

(June 2, 2006, "The Japan Times")

Mika Ninagawa interview: Ninegawa paints a vivid picture

Born in 1972, Mika Ninagawa is a photographer with a long list of awards, gallery shows, photo books and credits, from fashion magazine spreads to CD covers. Known for her vivid sense of color and composition, Ninagawa has been branching out into video production and now film, with her first feature "Sakuran." At a recent interview with "The Japan Times", Ninagawa was a ball of verbal energy, rattling off lengthy answers with sub clauses to the sub clauses. Our 30 minutes together were less an interaction than an inundation from her active, fertile mind.

What made you decide to take on this project?

First, I had to be sure that I could bring the (manga) story to life. Second, I had to be sure that it was something only I could do. If it wasn't, there were any number of directors who would be able to film it.

I really liked the original manga. There's a sense of reality in it. (The artist) is not exactly proclaiming her femininity, but she's very accurate in her depictions of women in a way that hadn't been done before. There were certain aspects of the psychology of the (Yoshiwara) prostitutes that I couldn't understand, but as I studied the records of the period, I learned that . . . a lot of their feelings were the same as what women have today. That's when I thought that perhaps I could do this.

Anna Tsuchiya's character resembles the biker she played in "Shimotsuna Monogatari (Kamikaze Girls)," but there are differences as well.

I've known Anna for years and have photographed her in various situations. The performance she gives (in the film) is Anna in the raw. Parts (of the performance) match her image, but other parts reveal a more vulnerable Anna. Her vulnerable, sensitive side is also a big part of her character to those who know her well. She's just not this tough girl — instead there's a good balance of the weak and the strong.

What was hardest about the shoot for you?

Well, it was a hard shoot in general, but the hardest part was communication. . . . If I noticed that something was wrong, when was the best time to say it? Right away, in front of everyone? Or later, in private? . . . I had a lot of arguments with people in the beginning — they were muttering "I'd like to kill that director" to each other as often as they said "good morning." (laughs)

Did you start with the visuals — or did the story come first?

I absolutely wanted to make (the visuals) beautiful, but if a film is just beautiful it's no different from a promotional video. The (visuals) were my lowest priority, actually — I had confidence that I could make them look good, so I sort of shunted them aside. Instead I concentrated in making the script interesting.

Yoshiwara, of course, had its dark side, as a place where women were bought and sold.

Yes, but the oiran there weren't simple prostitutes — they were like superstars, with a lot of impact on fashion. The kimono and accessories they wore became fashionable in the society at large. In that sense, they were the idols of women.

Not just anyone could become one — you had to have the right abilities and a lot of training. The biggest indication (of their social status) was that when clients came it was the oiran who sat in the place of honor. Also, the client couldn't sleep with (the oiran) until he had come to see her at least three times. If she didn't like him, though, she didn't have to take him to her bed. And once a client had chosen an oiran, he couldn't play with oiran from other brothels. I thought that system was interesting. Of course, it was a form of prostitution, but conditions (for prostitutes) then were very different from what they are now. I didn't particularly want people to feel sorry for them. Instead, I wanted to show what their daily lives were like and the sort of conditions they were living in.

Do you want to make another film?

Yes, but this time, I want to do a contemporary story. My staff was always telling me about what a hard project I'd picked for my first film, but since it was my first I had nothing else to compare it with — it was just natural for me. But I'm sure that a contemporary film would be easier.

(February 23, 2007, "The Japan Times")

Teruyo Nogami interview: in the presence of 'Emperor' Kurosawa

Akira Kurosawa's assistant for almost four decades, Teruyo Nogami discusses the master filmmaker's genius, and his weaknesses. No one, perhaps not even Akira Kurosawa's immediate family, knew him better. Teruyo Nogami worked with the legendary director for nearly four decades, beginning with "Rashomon" (1950), the film that launched him — and the Japanese film industry — internationally when it won the Golden Lion at the Venice Film Festival in 1951.

After starting as a script supervisor, Nogami became Kurosawa's production assistant and production manager, but whatever her title on the credits, she was usually by Kurosawa's side from the beginning of the shoot to the end. She was on the set of "Ikiru" (1952), "The Seven Samurai" ("Shichinin no Samurai") (1954) and "Yojimbo" (1961) — classics that made Kurosawa one of the world's most acclaimed filmmakers — and influenced everyone from Sergio Leone, who remade "Yojimbo" as "A Fistful of Dollars," to Francis Ford Coppola, George Lucas, Steven Spielberg and Martin Scorsese, who not only acknowledged their artistic debt to Kurosawa, but supported his work as producers, promoters and, in Scorsese's case, as an actor. (He played Vincent Van Gogh in Kurosawa's 1990 film "Dreams" [Yume].) Nogami was also with him at a low point of his career in the early and mid-1970s, when his professional problems and personal demons, including suicidal depression, threatened to overwhelm him.

Though a loyal member of the "Kurosawa family," she was no sycophant, but rather a keen observer of her boss's character, including his fearsome temper, and was one of the few people able to stand up to him when he flared out of control. She also had intimate knowledge of his working methods, as well as his relationships with his creative collaborators, from Toshiro Mifune, the star of many of his greatest films, to Shintaro Katsu, the volatile action star who stormed off the set of "Kagemusha" (1980) after falling out with Kurosawa on the first day of shooting.

In 2001 Nogami published "Waiting on the Weather — Making Movies with Akira Kurosawa," a collection of articles about her career, centering on her years with Kurosawa. Last year Stone Bridge Press published an English translation [see review below].

Now semiretired, Nogami is a familiar figure at film screenings and events, her mane of white hair and broad, cheery smile immediately recognizable in any crowd. She is usually dressed in casual, practical clothes, as though permanently "on location." She is frank and down-to-earth — the exact opposite of a film-world diva. She is also a thorough pro, who studied filmmaking in the ultimate master class, and has strong views about both the process and the people who make it happen. She reels off anecdote after anecdote with little prompting, while maintaining a critical distance from her most famous subject. Freely acknowledging Kurosawa's genius, she knew him too well to be in awe of his legend.

After "Waiting on the Weather" Nogami published a volume of girlhood reminiscences, "Requiem for a Father" ("Chichi e no Requiem"), that Yoji Yamada, one of Japan's best-known film directors, is using as basis for his next film, "Kabei."

How did you start writing "Waiting On the Weather?"

It began as a series of articles I wrote for a newsletter called "Cinema Club." The readers were people who liked old movies, so [the editors] asked me to write about my memories of the old days — not just [Akira] Kurosawa. I really wish now that I had kept some sort of journal back then; it would have helped me so much in writing the articles. But while you're on a shoot you never think of that sort of thing — you're just trying to get through the day's work. But when I went to Russia with Kurosawa to shoot "Dersu Uzala" [1975] I did keep a journal. That's why that section of the book is so long. When I started the series, I wrote about my association with [director] Mansaku Itami and his son Juzo. Kurosawa was still alive then, so I hesitated to write about him. I started writing about him after he died [in 1998]. If I had written about him while he was still alive, he would have criticized me (laughs). Not that I was telling lies, but he'd say things like "You're exaggerating here" or "I didn't say it that way." I didn't lie, but I did forget a lot — it was so long ago.

You spent a lot of time with Kurosawa on the set, but what about off the set?

When shooting was done for the day he was already thinking about what to do tomorrow. He'd draw pictures and show them to the staff to give them an idea of what he wanted. Also, while eating dinner with the staff, he'd talk about the next day's work. On location we'd all eat together nearly every night. He'd often be telling stories until one or two in the morning. I'd laugh when his stories were interesting, even if I'd heard them many times before, but when he was mad about something it was terrible. Usually he'd lay into the assistant directors or other staff about something that had happened that day. When he really got going, you didn't feel like eating — but there was no escape (laughs).

What impression did you have of Kurosawa when you first worked with him on "Rashomon?"

Kurosawa had had a big hit with his first film ["Sugata Sanshiro" (1943)], so he was quickly elevated to the top rank. When he arrived [at the Daiei Studio to make "Rashomon"], he was still young — only 40. He was like a star. He came with all these famous actors from Tokyo, which made him shine even more. He cut a stylish figure — I was a bit scared of him. But I consider myself lucky. If it hadn't been for Itami-san [Nogami volunteered to care for Itami's teenage son, Juzo, who would later become one of Japan's premier filmmakers, after his widowed mother moved to Tokyo], I wouldn't have been in Kyoto [working at the Daiei Studio]. Kurosawa just happened to come along, and I just happened to be there. It was all a matter of chance. Kurosawa believed in luck; he felt that something would always turn up. In that sense, he had a lot of confidence.

His luck ran out with "Tora, Tora, Tora" [1970].

That was the worst time for him. [Kurosawa was hired to direct the Japanese portion of the Japan-U.S. coproduction about the Battle of Midway, but quit — or was fired, according to some accounts — after several weeks of shooting.] There was a Japanese producer on that film who could speak English, but Kurosawa couldn't really communicate what he wanted to do . . . [the producer] didn't explain [the contract] fully, so [Kurosawa] didn't really know what he was getting into. . . . But people were afraid of him, so they just told him what they thought he wanted to hear. With "Tora, Tora, Tora," he wanted to make an antiwar movie. The Americans, on the other hand, were more interested in battle tactics and that sort of thing. . . . He thought that if you use someone like [Toshiro] Mifune, his star image would get in the way — it wouldn't feel like a real war [on the screen]. He wanted to shoot in a realistic documentary style, using real people. The Americans had the exact opposite idea. Also, there just wasn't enough time to shoot the film [Kurosawa's way]. It would have been tough coordinating the schedules of the amateur actors. Also, it would have been hard to make them learn all the lines. Kurosawa's ideal was one thing, but reality was something else. The whole experience was frustrating for him. He was drinking every night and behaving badly. "Tora, Tora, Tora" was the toughest experience of his career. [After he came back to Japan], he wanted to forget the whole thing. He gave himself some good advice: to empty out his head and become what he called a "fool." His film "Dodesukaden" [1970] is an expression of that attitude. The hero is a simple-minded boy who is a fool for trains — just as Kurosawa was a fool for films. If he hadn't made "Dodesukaden," he might have fallen apart completely. After that he made "Dersu Uzala," which looked like it might be another disaster but turned out to be a wonderful movie. On that shoot, he couldn't understand the language [of the Russian cast and crew] and had to work in terrible conditions, but he was able to finish the film. I admire him for that.

You've mentioned some of his weak points. What about his strong points?

Kurosawa was a great editor — truly amazing. He could just blaze through a reel of film — bang, bang, bang. He remembered every shot.

And you?

I was hopeless (laughs).When Kurosawa came to edit, I had to work like crazy to get ready, putting numbers on everything and so on. . . . He shot tons of footage, as much as he thought he needed, so when it came time to edit there was a mountain of film to deal with. When he was filming, he was always editing in his head. When he was working with two cameras, he was thinking about how to bring up camera A to match a shot with camera B. He had it all figured out; he wanted every bit of film to have his signature on it. Of course, things didn't always go the way he wanted — that's when he got angry.

Did he rage at the actors as well?

He never got angry at Mifune. He never said anything to [Takashi] Shimura, either. In general, he treated his actors well; they were the raw materials for his films. In interviews, though, he used to say all these fine words about the actors (laughs). He'd say that it was better to let them do what they wanted — that it was wrong to give them a lot of instruction. What a bunch of baloney! On the set he'd make some of them do scenes over and over. Well, films are a concrete medium — you can't fool the camera — so sometimes that sort of strictness is necessary. He'd be thinking of a particular expression he wanted, even before the start of filming. He would make drawings to show [the actors] what he wanted, but sometimes it was tough to get the expression that matched his image. It would be a hard struggle day after day. In casting a film, he'd sometimes go for a certain type, instead of a name. For example, for the character of Gorobei in "The Seven Samurai" he cast Yoshio Inaba, who had the right, chunky look for the character. He was a newcomer in a veteran cast, so he had a tough time. Kurosawa was always yelling at him for blowing his lines or some other mistake. I really felt sorry for him.

One actor everyone remembers from that film is Takashi Shimura.

He was the right type for that role. Before then Shimura had been mainly a character actor. He didn't get many leading roles. But Kurosawa made him a star with "Ikiru." When "Ikiru" came out, Shimura's wife was worried about him being cast as the lead. "Do you think the audience will come to see my old man?" she asked (laughs). . . . He was great in "The Seven Samurai," but after that he went back to supporting roles. Kurosawa used to say that different foreign countries liked different characters in "The Seven Samurai." In America, they liked Shimura's character Kambei the best. In Europe, they liked Kyuzo, the samurai played by Seiji Miyaguchi. He had never played a role like that before. Kurosawa was good at that — bringing out something in an actor that was different from what he had done before. That was the finest performance that Miyaguchi ever gave. He was a small man, but there was something intense about him.

In Japan, Kurosawa is best remembered for his period dramas.

That's true. He liked period dramas, but he also liked to remake Shakespeare and other Western classics. "The Lower Depths" [1957] ["Donzoko," based on a play by Maxim Gorky] is an example of that — it's a great picture. The first time he tried that, with "The Idiot" [1951] ["Hakuchi," based on a novel by Feodor Dostoevsky], he failed, but that was a good experience for him — he learned a lot. After that he made many films based on Western classics, but he totally Japanized them — he was really good at it.

When he read a novel he was always thinking about how to turn it into a film. He would think in terms of concrete images. He read "War and Peace" again and again, but always with the images in mind. That's why he was well-suited to be director. He liked various types of literature, including American hard-boiled novels, such as the one by Ed McBain that was the inspiration for "High and Low" ["Tengoku to Jigoku," 1963], but for him the base was always Russian literature. . . . He knew exactly how to turn images into film — he had great powers of concentration. It was as though he was concentrating this energy and then letting it explode on the screen.

You mention in the book that he also knew exactly what was and wasn't in the frame, even if he wasn't looking through the lens.

He knew it all right. He would yell at people who didn't: "What do you think you're looking at?" [or] "What do you think you're doing?" He'd blow up in a second. But all good directors are like that; they know exactly what they're shooting. He was a perfectionist in a lot of ways. He'd have the foreign subtitles for his films translated into Japanese so he could see if there were any mistakes. He'd OK the posters, but just the ones for Japan. He even enjoyed making trailers.

That's hard to imagine in Hollywood; a famous director making trailers for his own films.

The PR people would never tell him, but they'd have an assistant director add words like "genius" to the trailer. He'd never do that kind of thing himself — he'd be too embarrassed.

He didn't seem to care that much about the box office; that is, pander to the audience. Would that be correct?

He worried about the box office, but he wouldn't make films for the sake of it. He did things that would have gotten an ordinary director fired. He'd fight with the studios for the money to make the film he wanted; he had a lot of confidence in his own talent. Movies are a tough business. You have to pour you whole soul into them, otherwise they're no good.

He also fought with his composers. The quarrel you describe with composer Toru Takemitsu is memorable.

Kurosawa wasn't the only one. Fellini also fought with his composers. Music was a problem for Kurosawa because he couldn't write it himself. But he wanted to make his movies his own, completely, so that [inability to write music] bothered him. He often said he wished he could be a composer. He admired Chaplin, because he could compose.

His most famous fight, though, was with Shintaro Katsu, on the first day of shooting "Kagemusha" [1980]. You were there for that one as well.

Do foreign fans even know who Katsu was?

A lot know him from the "Zatoichi" series.

Yes, I suppose so. Anyway, I knew that those two would never get along from before the start of shooting. They were completely different types — like the difference between a school teacher and a gangster. A lot of people think that Kurosawa should have used Katsu in that film and it might have been interesting, but they were destined to fight, if not on the first day of shooting, then sometime after. Katsu was really happy about being cast for the lead, but his personality was that of a playboy. Kurosawa, on the other hand, was a serious type — and he didn't get along with people who weren't. He had no interest in playing around with geisha and that sort of thing. Katsu was the opposite: He loved to go out drinking and to play with his gang. He was known for spending 5 million yen in one night. I found him really, really amusing. He was like the wild character he plays in "Zatoichi," but Kurosawa couldn't stand that kind of person. He tended to shut out what he couldn't control. The actor who took Katsu's place, Tatsuya Nakadai, was more Kurosawa's style: He would do just as he was told. Mifune was also that type — very serious. That's fine, but actors who are just serious tend to be small-spirited. They're cautious to a fault. If an actor is always watching his step around the director and staff, thinking that he's not so great, then his performance suffers.

Could you say what you wanted to Kurosawa?

I was freer to say what I felt than most of the other staff because I'd been with him so long. I'd sometimes speak up to him for the rest of the staff, but he'd still get angry at me. After "Red Beard" ["Akahige," 1965] Kurosawa entered the latter part of his career. A lot of people say the movies he made then were not that interesting, but all directors are like that when they get older. No one makes great movies all the time. Also, when you get older, you lose your physical strength and aggressiveness.

When Kurosawa got older he was not as in tune with the world as when he was young. He wouldn't go out drinking and meeting with different people. He never left his own little world. Also, it became hard to speak freely with him — he was too important. He ended up with the same crowd of people, doing the same things. It was just too bad.

(January 18, 2007, "The Japan Times")

Interview with Nobuhiko Obayashi

We meet Nobuhiko Obayashi at the office of his production company PSC in an apartment building in Seijo, a Tokyo suburb that has long been a filmmaking hub, as well as home to Obayashi's alma mater, Seijo University. Now 78, Obayashi walks less steadily than when I interviewed him a decade ago for his murder mystery "The Reason" ("Ryu," 2004), but his face is still wreathed in his trademark smile. Also present is his wife and long-time producer Kyoko and his daughter Chigumi, who is credited as the writer of his horror/fantasy masterpiece "House" ("Hausu," 1977) and now helps him manage his affairs, including his upcoming trip to the Udine FEFF for a special section of his SF/fantasy films. A born raconteur and teacher, Obayashi tells even often-told stories with an infectious enthusiasm and, behind the smiles, a serious purpose.

We're going to screen SF and fantasy films at Udine FEFF this year, including yours of course. Will this be your first time in Italy?

I went to Italy to film TV commercials every summer and winter in the 1970s. But I haven't been to Udine.

I heard that you wanted to be a film director from the time you were growing up in Onomichi (a port city near Hiroshima).

It started with a toy given to me by my father, who was a doctor. Our family profession had been medicine for generations. And Onomichi is a port town, so many unusual goods were shipped there from abroad, and my father would bring some of them home. We would always store them in our kura (Japanese-style storehouse). So there were always strange things inside our kura and I was always playing with them. When I was small it was wartime and my father was away, so it was only me and my mother and my relatives. Once when I was playing inside the kura I found a gadget called a kinematoscope (toy projector), but I thought it was a toy train.

Onomichi is narrow and long, built on the sides of hills that run right down to the sea, so the trains run through the middle of the town. When I heard the train whistle go 'woo woo" I'd run out into the backyard, but since traditional Japanese houses are all lined up next to each other with roofs made of kawara (thick clay tiles), I could only see the smoke of the train and my heart would beat with excitement. "Something great is coming!" I would think. But when it actually passed by, going "baaaaaa" like a volcano erupting, I'd close my eyes and my ears and pray to God to forgive me. "I'll never do anything bad again. I'll never lie and I'll be a good boy from now on, so please rescue me from this horrible hell!" But when the train started to move away from me, "woo, woo," far away, I'd suddenly feel lonely and the tears would run down my cheeks and I'd wish for the train to come back. This itself is a story, right? Something comes near, I'm glad, and when it passes by, I'm scared, but when it goes away, I'm sad. And then I found this toy in the kura that looked like a train.

The cylindrical lens was like a smokestack, the sprockets were like train wheels and the lamphouse was like a boiler. And when I cranked it, it went clickety-clack like a moving train.

So I really believed that it was a toy train. And when I opened the can and the film came out, it smelled like coal. Then there were the film frames, with twenty-four frames going through (the projector) every second. I cut up the film and put it into the boiler, and when the smokestack started up light flowed out of it and the coal (that is, the film) started to burn. I sang and played, going "woo-woo." One day, I realized that this was not a train. There was a picture on the back of the box, and it said "If you put the "coal" into the "train tracks" and turn on the "boiler" and crank it, light would come out of the "smokestack" and a movie would appear in front of it.

When I did this, the screen was exactly like the front window of a train, and there was movement, and I realized, ah, this is a machine to enjoy like a trip on a train.

One playtime, I cut up ten frames of the film and pieced them together again with string. But they were all in random order and when I projected them the story became very complex. I thought that was very interesting. Then I started to order the film frames my own way. I created a montage.

How old were you at the time?

Three or four. I would use a strip of film like a "Star Wars" sword, or put it over my penis or play with it in the bathroom. Then the pictures on the film disappeared and the film turned blank. I thought "Lucky me!" and drew my own pictures on the film. My own pictures would move. This film was the same as the film in the Leica still camera my father owned, so if I took one frame at a time on the Leica, I could become the star of my own movie. It was negative film, black and white, so I thought again, "Lucky me!" I painted my face black and my eyebrows white. So I learned how to use makeup. That's how learned to make movies on my own. At that time I had yet to go to a movie theater. I was only a child.

So you had nobody to teach you?

No. Children are natural-born geniuses. Our family profession was medicine, so my destiny was to become a doctor. But my father came back from the war after eight years and became a small-town doctor. My father told me, "The world is at peace again and children can live their own dreams in a peaceful world, so do as you wish."

My father owned a double 8mm film camera. In those days it was very expensive. Film was the hobby of company presidents and doctors, like my father. Since I wanted to get into the movie business, when I turned 18 I took that camera with me and rode the train to Tokyo.

Back then a lot of lucky guys got into Toho, Daiei, Shochiku and other major studios as directors, while the unlucky ones became cameramen or lighting men or if they had good-looks, actors. But I didn't know any of those routes (into the business), so I just shot 8mm films in Tokyo.

And you lived near the Toho studio?

Yes, because I loved Toho.

But you never considered becoming an assistant director for Toho?

I had no interest in that. I loved films and I saw all the Japanese and foreign films up to 1960. But when I made films they were in 8mm. While I was in college I met my producer (and future wife) and I became an independent director.

The reason is, and this is very important, I am from the last generation who knows the war. I'm 78 now. Everyone died when the war ended. When we lost, it meant we died. We should have died, but we lived, and my producer survived the Tokyo air raids as well. We were children during the war so we innocently thought that, if we lost the war, the country would perish and we would die.

But after the war, all the adults were like "peace, peace, happy, happy" and dancing around. I couldn't believe it. During the war if we did not study the textbooks exactly as we were told we were scolded, but then we were told to black them out. I couldn't believe anything.

We were also the first generation to grow up in the peacetime of the postwar. In those days Japanese films were at their peak, but all the directors I loved such (Yasujiro) Ozu, (Akira) Kurosawa, John Ford, Howard Hawks, and William Wyler, were of the war generation.

What could we contribute? It would have to be something different from what our seniors had done. Shuji Terayama, Danshi Tatekawa and others were all the same generation as me, born from 1935 to 1940. This was the postwar generation and a very special one.

Some directors of that generation, such as Nagisa Oshima and Masahiro Shinoda, were working in big studios like Shochiku. Did you see them as having different values from yours?

But while they were working at Shochiku they were trying to destroy Ozu's way of making movies. And when I first screened my 16mm film "Emotion" (1966), Oshima, Shinoda and all the rest came to see it. After he retired, Shinoda told me he was heavily influenced by my work and was hoping to create something like my movies but it was hard for him. He was very supportive of me.

So I had friends among the Nouvelle Vague directors at Shochiku. They were of the same generation as the Nouvelle Vague directors in France. I felt we were all creating a new "peace generation" together.

Shinoda and I were simpatico with other, but Oshima became angry at me — probably from jealousy. He was trying to be an anarchist at Shochiku, while I was working in a less constricting environment from the start. That is, we were were friends but he was also jealous of me. That's what our relationship was like. Oshima and the others were trying to make what I call "freedom" movies with the Art Theater Guild. Yoichi Takabayashi, Takahiko Iimura, Donald Richie and I were trying to make 8mm films at the same time. For us 8mm films symbolized "freedom."

I had no intention of joining a major film company, of course, but 8mm films were a bit too small so we started to make 16mm films. At that time, Japanese film magazines proclaimed that the age of the "film artist" had arrived and that "film artists" were cooler than the old-time "movie directors." But it's important to remember that 8mm was just an amateur toy.

To Oshima and Shinoda, Ozu was a master. They respected him while trying to go beyond him. But to Takabayashi, Iimura and me, Edison was the master. We could create films because he invented the film medium.

When we were little, baseball was an extremely important sport for us, since there was nothing else we could do. If Kurosawa was to film a baseball game, the pitcher would throw, the catcher would catch, and behind them he would put a big crane, so when the batter hit a homerun, he could frame up on the ball. But if you simply mimicked that, you would be an amateur. Instead we used the 8mm film camera as the ball. We could hold it and throw it up high for about 30 seconds, with a nice sunset in the back. If the crew caught it, that would be "cut!" and "OK." That way, the viewer can see what the homerun ball sees. Our attempt to do this was a first in movie history.

Movies are a product of scientific invention, so new types of film expression are inventions too. Inventing something new is what movies are all about. That's how we did things.

In those days, the only art film theater in Tokyo was Sogetsu Hall. The directors who screened their films there were a generation before us, such as Shintaro Ishihara and Shotaro Kamikawa. They were creating avant-garde movies on 16mm.

We didn't have anywhere to show our films, but there were many small art galleries in town. My friends would put up a white canvas in them and we'd show our 8mm films there. These galleries were located on 7th Avenue in the Ginza, near Shinbashi Station, and fans would line up to watch our movies starting from 4th Avenue. They were all young people who never watched traditional Japanese films. It became pretty chaotic, but that's how the new era of "film artists" began.

Then Kinkokuniya Hall was built in Shinjuku and that became the new place for the younger generation. We showed our films at the first screening they held there. They told us 8mm films were not allowed, so we used 16mm. They also said that three presenters were not enough, so we brought in Yoko Ono and other undiscovered artists. Nobody from the movie business came. The audience was all musicians or painters or sculptors. The only movie person who participated was probably Yoichi Higashi. We got a good reaction when we did this. I also screened a special version of my film "Complexe" (1964) in a program for two-minute films. This was really well received, and my two-minute film became famous, so offers to do TV commercials came in. I made money from commercials and used it to create personal films.

Some similar was also happening in the United States at the time. For example, when I was a student at the University of Michigan in the 1960s, the Ann Arbor Film Festival was showing independent films – it was the first festival in the country to focus on them. Were you influenced at all by the American independent film scene?

In 1965, Kenji Kasanaga brought the American underground film scene to Japan. And through him I became friends with underground film makers such as Jonas Mekas. Also in 1965 I went to America for the first time and became friends with many underground film makers and they introduced me to Jack Nicolson and such. The first time I went to America and I was supposed to stay at a hotel in downtown LA, but the manager said his father had died at Pearl Harbor and angrily asked us to leave, so the first day we had to sleep on the streets.

The next day we went to Hollywood and it was so pretty. Our shoes were all muddy from the streets of Japan, so we took off our shoes and walked in our stocking feet. You could almost lick the sidewalks. Everybody there wore these enamel shoes. I was thinking that those shoes are so shiny and beautiful, when I saw Frank Sinatra and Dean Martin walking and listening to the radio together.

Do you know a restaurant called Dino's? It was run by Dean Martin near Hollywood. Inside, there was a billboard with "Nobuhiko Obayashi" "Yoichi Takabayashi" "Takahiko Iimura" and "Japanese underground movie festival people" written in Indian yellow letters. I'm walking around in my socks in Hollywood and there's my own name on a billboard. This was my first experience in America!

And there were homeless people with long hair all about, sitting on chairs, painting colors on their clothes, holding guitars, wearing sunglasses. I was, like, who are they? They were hippies. They told me they were against the war in Vietnam and were trying to escape to Canada or New Zealand. This was my first time in America.

That's when I became friends with many underground filmmakers, and that's when I made commercials for Toyota in Hollywood and San Francisco, as well as New Zealand and Australia. Also, a movie theater in San Francisco called The Movie screened my films.

Were you able to speak English back then?
Only a bit. But my English was praised for being "American English." In those days English in Japan was the Queen's English (British English), so you couldn't say "restroom," you had to say "nature calls on me." In a department store in San Francisco, I exclaimed to the clerks "Nature calls on me! Nature calls on me!" and they were like "What? What?" "A restroom!" I said. They asked me if I was a poet from Asia. That's when I realized that English education in Japan was no good.

But I really loved American movies, watching them all the time, so I knew the lines by heart, and if I left my keys at the Hotel, I would sing, "I left my key in my own room" and the clerk would be like, "Oh yeah!". So the lines I learned from movies were very understandable for Americans.

Experimental films were a growing force back then, but so were "New Hollywood" movies. Were they an influence too?
Yes, "Easy Rider." It all started with France's Nouvelle Vague. And before New Hollywood cinema, there were Roger Corman's 'children' (i.e., young directors trained by Corman) — the same generation as us. And after them came directors of a younger generation, like Spielberg. I watched over their success feeling like an elder brother. This was my youth.

When you returned to Japan, did you find the Japanese movie industry to be conservative by comparison?
I was doing TV commercials at that time. For example, the Toho Studio had a huge set, but they couldn't use it for movies. So I was using it to make my commercials. It was about the same size as a Hollywood set. So I was very good sponsor for Toho.

When "Jaws" became a big hit, a Toho producer asked me, "Obayashi-san, can you make something like that?" I said yes, maybe, but back then only Toho contract directors could make Toho movies. The same went for Shochiku and Nikkatsu.

So I simply gave them my ideas for free, thinking that traditional Japanese ideas (for films) were boring, but that they wouldn't use mine anyway. When I was going in and out of the Toho set I used to talk to the producers a lot. They would ask me if I had any new ideas for a monster, the way "Godzilla" ("Gojira") was a combination of gorilla (gorira) and whale (kujira). So I said, how about Dai-kaiju Iko (Monster Iko). Iko is a combination of ika(squid) and tako(octopus). It would have nine legs, because a squid has ten, and an octopus has eight. I thought it was a wonderful idea but they told me it wasn't scary enough.

Toho was that kind of place, so I went home thinking I didn't fit in there. My daughter Chigumi, who was 11 at that time, had just come out of the bath, and was hanging her head to dry her hair in front of the mirror. I asked her, "Chigumi, if I were to do a monster for a Toho movie what do you think would be good?" She told me, "Don't start making those Japanese movies."

I said "I understand but I owe it to my friend the producer," so she replied, "If my reflection in the mirror popped out to eat me that would be pretty scary"

Ah, I thought, this is interesting. After "Jaws" was a big hit, there were movies about bear attacks, rat attacks, but they were all copycats. But the "you" in the mirror coming out to attack you has something philosophical to it. Like "Dracula" or "Frankenstein," it's a Gothic-Romantic fantasy. I asked her, "Can you think of anything else?" and she said, "When you go to the countryside and tie up a watermelon with a string and lower it into the well and then pull it back again, it breaks apart and bites you" or "When you are playing the piano, the keys try to bite you." All my daughter's ideas. I am of the postwar generation, so to those ideas I added my own for a film in which a young girl who has broken up with her lover during the war becomes an old lady and starts eating children who haven't experienced war. I suggested that to Toho, and they said it was a great idea.

In those days an idea like that would usually take half a year or a year to be approved, but mine only took five hours. The problem was there was no director to film it, because no Toho director wanted anything to do with such a ridiculous idea. But Toho producers told me that what was decided was decided and, if worst came to worst, we could simply cancel the film. So I made a huge name card saying "Toho Movie: House," illustrated it myself, and passed it around everywhere I went.

Luckily, all the fans who loved my film "Emotion" from ten years earlier had become important people in magazines and TV stations and department stores, and they supported my project. It became a comic and a novel, as well as department store fashions, record sound tracks and radio dramas. I did this for two years, with ads in newspapers every day about "House." It was a dynamic form of promotion.

When I was directing a commercial in Switzerland, I got a phone call from Toho. They wanted me back right away, saying I was the only director who could make the film. When came back Matsuoka-san (Toho president Isao Matsuoka, now chairman) told me "I convinced all the Toho staff, and we want you to make the movie, even if you are an outsider." I thought, if I just have this one chance, I want to make a Japanese film like no other. I was given a chance to work with a major studio, so I felt I had a responsibility to go over-the-top avant-garde.

At that time it was extremely unusual for an outsider to direct for Toho. Did you feel confident that you could do it?

The Toho crew guys were my friends from making commercials. For three or four years, they'd been telling me they wanted me to come to Toho because there no one but me who could create such commercials. And since I was a sort of Toho sponsor at that time, if I came to the headquarters building the president would welcome me at the front door. So I said to myself, I'm obliged to make one Toho film. I was asked to do it, I didn't ask them.

You were like a young Orson Welles when he went to RKO with carte blanche to make Citizen Kane. (laughs)

That's right. They were thinking "If Obayashi comes here he'll probably make a movie with an alien in it." People were expecting from me the type of radio drama Orson Welles created. But when I came to Toho for the first time as a movie director, the people who had welcomed me before hid themselves and didn't greet me.

When I met Hideo Onchi, the most experienced senior Toho director, at the entrance, he told me, "Obayashi-san, wreck our studio just this once." I laugh about it now, but it was that kind of era.

On top of that, Kihachi Okamoto was the boss of the Toho union, at a time when Toho's films were losing their appeal to the audience. When Nikkatsu director Toshiya Fujita was hired by the studio, Okamoto waved the red flag saying, "We can't let any other directors from the Kanto (Tokyo area) inside!" (Toho's studio was near Yokohama.)

And when Shintaro Ishihara shot a movie for Toho he was not allowed inside the studio. He had to rent a studio out of town and was only given a co-director credit.

So I was the first to be permitted into the very heart of the studio, and that was because of the TV commercials and being a Toho sponsor and being really friendly with the crew. They gave me a warm welcome, because they all wanted to break up the old Toho system.

I was the first to push through the Panavision format at Toho. It required a camera crew of only two, but the union demanded that we employ eight, so six people were wasted. Those people dug holes, or took up part-time jobs elsewhere. Even so, as we worked together to make the picture it started to be fun.

It wasn't just Toho that was so conservative. For example, Seijun Suzuki got fired for making "Branded to Kill" ("Koroshi no Rakuin," 1967).
Back in those days they showed two movies on one bill, one major and one minor. There was an A picture and a B picture. Seijun Suzuki always directed B movies.

You need to be responsible when you make an A movie, but you can have fun with a B picture. So Suzuki's type of film would never appear now. B movies nurture young avant-garde movie makers.

One difference between Suzuki and you is that you were a better promoter of your work, beginning with "House." Suzuki couldn't do because he was a studio contract director.
Something like that even happened to Oshima-san at Shochiku. But Oshima was a sort of anarchist as a director, and created his own breakthroughs in that environment.

I wasn't connected to the movie business. I also was doing a kind of journalism with the TV commercials, so I really understood where I wanted to go. On the other hand, I don't think people in the film industry had a clue. There was that difference.

I always thought that I would only do "House," and never get tied up with the majors. I would do only one, and if it became a hit, that would be it.

And "House" actually did become a commercial hit, but most of its devoted fans were under the age of fifteen. Anyone above that age did not understand my work.

Toho producers were happy to have a hit, but they weren't happy that a film like "House" was successful, since they couldn't understand it. They felt they would rather fail with a movie that they understood than succeed with one they didn't.

Some critics say they hate Obayashi, and half of that is due to "House." They claimed that it wasn't a real movie and they can't back out of that claim anymore.

Around that time, you met Haruki Kadokawa, who was an outsider as well.
Haruki Kadokawa was the son of a bookstore owner, so he had to make movies based on the company's books. He felt that was his responsibility. But he was a movie fanatic so if he hadn't been the president, he would have made a great producer.

As president he had a lot of responsibility, because if he made hit movies but the books (they were based on) didn't become successful, it would mean he had betrayed all the bookstores and book lovers. That was his ball-and-chain. He was limited as a producer that way. He really wanted to create freeform, avant-garde films. That was why we got along so well. In the end I was the director who made the most Kadokawa films. On the other hand, I also made many movies for ATG. I was a very strange type of director, if I do say so myself.

Also, for ATG I created entertainment films, but for Kadokawa I created avant-garde films.

At that time weren't Kadokawa and ATG considered polar opposites?
Japanese movie directors would only do one — Kadokawa or ATG — but never both. But I did, like Orson Welles! (laughs)

That was because of my journalistic temperament. In making both (Kadokawa and ATG films) I was thinking vertically, not horizontally. I felt I could connect with the world more that way.

So maybe I use films more than just make them. My way is to use films to stretch myself, to see what I can do. I personally love to make and watch movies just like any otaku ("obsessed fan"). But when I make films the me who is a journalist me uses the me who is highly personal movie director – it's that kind of relationship. I've always been a 'double personality.'

You were also a pioneer of the 1980s idol movie genre.

Usually in idol movies there is the star, and you make the movie around her. But I used an unknown actress, and made her a star through my film. Nearly all the idols in my films were unknown actresses. Just once, with Hiroko Yakushimaru, did I make what could be called an idol movie.

She had started as an actress, but she didn't become so popular. Kadokawa-san asked me to make Yakushimaru Hiroko an idol, so I agreed. The film was "School in the Crosshairs" ("Nerawareta Gakuen," 1981). That was the only time I used an already well-known actress — all the others made their debuts in my films.

There had been idol movies before that, starring big names like Hibari Misora. In that case, the star came first, the director, second. But you reversed that order.

You have what are called zatsuki directors (i.e., directors attached to a theater troupe). That sort of director takes care of the star and that's his job. But in my case, the director is always the director, the star the star. You can't mess with that relationship. The maker of the film is the director — not anyone else. When I worked with Sayuri Yoshinaga (in "Turning Point" or "Onna Zakari," 1991), my condition was that my name be bigger than hers in the credits. That was my position. I would never take the job where the director's name is not bigger than the rest.

That's because, even though I am not working for an industry major, I still understand how the majors work, and it's the job of the indies to do what the majors can't.

Yoji Yamada of Shochiku has finally had his name put over Sayuri Yoshinaga's for the first time. Until then Shochiku's condition had always been that Yoji Yamada's and Sayuri Yoshinaga's names be treated equally in the credits. But I was not a Shochiku employee so I told them, "You're the one who asked me, so let me do it my way." A director's OK is never a real OK if you don't have that kind of attitude. Now it is all based on the sponsor's OK, the producer's OK, the actor's OK...

So the director's name being smaller than the actress's is no good. I taught my juniors, like (Yoshimitsu) Morita, to always demand that the director's name be the biggest on any poster. If they say no to that, then decline the offer.

"Exchange Students" ("Tenkoseii" 1982) was a case of you using unknown actors.

Back then I did not have enough power and fame as a director, so if I brought in a star who was more famous than me, I couldn't win. I had to use unknown actors.

I've watched all the old-time movies. There have been many movies that became an actor's posthumous last work. It's been my basic policy to cast a "first-time actor" and a "last-time actor" so the past and future could connect. Also, I think it's the job of indies to create movies for the future. That is, the film doesn't have to be a success right now. When I made "House," my generation's philosophy was that the value of a work of art is decided 100 years after its creator's death. I don't listen to what critics say now. I wanted to be judged in 100 years. The majors can't do it that way. That's one reason I'm committed to indie filmmaking.

Back then I thought that "House" would be understood in 100 years, but it only took 30.

"House," "Exchange Students," "The Girl Who Leapt through Time" and "School in the Crosshairs" may have SF elements, but they're about people in the present, not futuristic rockets. They remind me a bit of what Steven Spielberg was doing about the same time in films like E.T. and Poltergeist.

My interest lies more in the Gothic-Romantic rather than science fiction. In Japanese we call it kaiki (fantastic) and genso (illusionary). When there were no Japanese-English words like hora (horror), we called that sort of thing kaiki and genso. The work of Edgar Allen Poe, Frankenstein and Dracula are all kaiki and genso. That's what I liked.

Kaiki and genso focus more on the human viewpoint than the universe as a whole. That's why when Spielberg and Lucas debuted, Spielberg 'prayed,' but Lucas 'played' in their movies. Spielberg doesn't go into space, but Lucas does — that's the difference in the two artists' sensibilities.

I'm the E.T.-type rather than the Star Wars type. That's why I don't blast off rockets very much in my films. It's more fun to be earthbound and look up at the stars from the ground. You want to keep it a mystery. If you simply go out in space, you're like, oh so that's what the moon is like, but looking at the moon from the earth is more romantic. Movies are dreams, and it's better to leave them that way. Dreams are better when you look at things from afar. Imagining the moon is better than taking a step on it.

Movies are a medium for remembering (kioku), not recording (kiroku). I like documentaries. They try to reveal the truth of something but don't quite succeed and I think the irony of that is interesting. Documentaries have a quality of unrequited love, but movies are just being in love without the thought of wanting something back in return. It's one-sided love.

Do you like SF movies? What sorts?

I like "2001: A Space Odyssey" because I like movies I could never make myself. With Spielberg, I feel maybe I could do it a little better. I like the man, but not his movies so much.

Lucas is an interesting guy, so let him do what he likes. Kubrick I like because he does what I can't do. You don't need two of the same kind of artist. So I'll leave Kubrick's movies up to Kubrick and I'll just be a fan. Spielberg and I do things that are somewhat similar, but he's still my junior so I want to tell him what to do. (laughs)

You've made films like "Exchange Students" and "The Girl Who Leapt through Time," with strong elements of fantasy, but they're set Onomichi, which is your hometown. Did you want to ground them more in reality by doing that?

I have a different reason, relating to what I said before about being a haisen shonen (child of a defeated country). After Japan lost the war, the country was left in that condition for a while. Then came the rapid economic growth of the 1960s, when Japan started to destroy itself.

The Japan that our brothers and uncles and fathers had defended was being destroyed by Japan itself. That I couldn't forgive. I thought I couldn't let anyone destroy Onomichi, so I began to film there. It was the age of "scrap and build." Nobody paid any attention to me when I told them we should protect Onomichi. So I dreamed up a scheme, using fantasy.

I filmed that wrinkled, dirty old town in a fantasy, and when the movie was a success everyone came to admire Onomichi. The town leaders were saying they had to cut down all the cherry trees, but I put a stop to that by making those trees part of the movie. Protecting my home town by making it part of a fantasy — that was my plan.

And it worked. Onomichi still looks the same – at least in your movies. (laughs)

I don't call my movies 'hometown movies.' I call them furusato ("native place") movies. Furusato is a state of mind. It has a philosophy behind it. It's not about making a 'hometown movie' to lure in a lot of tourists.

The first movie I saw directed by you was "Beijing Watermelon" ("Pekin no Suika"). It is very imaginative in some ways, but at the same time it's quite realistic. I remember thinking, is there any other director who can range from fantasy to realism like this? And not in just this one film, but over a long period of time?

The most important thing a fantasy movie needs is reality. I basically believe that movies should not be so realistic, but rather fantastic. "Beijing Watermelon" has more reality in it than my other movies, while "The Girl Who Leapt through Time" has a lot more fantasy.

Movies are made from both philosophy and technology. Some movies emphasize philosophy more, others, technology more. For example you can film the branch of a tree or a flower in many ways, but what is the philosophy behind the tree or the reality behind the flower and its fruit?

I love movies more than anything, so I will watch suspense, fantasy, romance, SF, or action. When I make movies I mix that all in. (laughs)

About ten years ago, you remade "The Girl Who Leapt through Time," but not with the CG or the technology we have today. Do you ever think about making a fantasy using modern CG? These days you can do anything visually.

Being able to do anything in a movie is not necessarily a good thing. Art is fun because you're trying to do what you can't do. If you just do what you can do, it's not art. When I think about CG, I don't think about its obvious possibilities, but about what it can't do.

As I said before, look at the history of movies – it's a scientific invention and inventions are usually discovered through accidents. In the same way, modes of cinematic expression were born through accidents. For example, you're filming a car, the film breaks, and when you fix it the car has turned into a horse cart.

Things like that happened all around the world. Some people who made that sort of mistake said "Oops I'm sorry," but others said "I see new possibilities in this," and they were the real artists.

It's the same with 3D – there still hasn't been enough time for interesting accidents to happen. People are still using 3D in limited ways. For example, if I were using it, I'd film flashback scenes in black-and-white, even if it's a color movie. I recently saw the new Star Wars and it was 3D all the way. They could have shot scenes set in the past in 2D. Or shot the young people in 3D and Hans Solo in 2D. I thought it was really strange that they didn't do something like that.

People are just happy about things jumping out of the screen, but now that they can do that, let's have a rethink about using 2D. Or think about how scary it would be if something jumped out at you in black-and-white. I find it very frustrating that no one is trying those sorts of things.

It's because people haven't learned enough from black-and-white and silent films. If the makers (of 3D films) watched those old films, they would understand why it would be interesting to add 2D and black-and-white and silence to "Star Wars."

Films are interesting because you can think about them from so many perspectives. It's not about just using the newest technology. It's not about going higher, but deeper. Politics and economics can simply rise, but art has to go deep. I tried to express myself in different ways in "House" and that film can last 100 years. Since the history of movies is only 120 years, it's best to learn from the past.

(2016 "Udine Far East Film Festival Catalogue")

Issey Ogata interview

Issey Ogata has built his career on virtuoso one-man theater shows in which he changes characters, from drunken salaryman to female fishmonger, as easily as other actors change clothes, while amusing audiences and winning critical accolades with sui generis portrayals that dig down to universal human bedrock.

The chameleon-like quality of the 65-year-old's acting has caught the attention of international filmmakers. He played the savvy video game mogul Ota in Edward Yang's "Yi Yi" (2000), the unworldly Emperor Showa in Alexandr Sokorov's "The Sun" (2005) and the relentless inquisitor Inoue in Martin Scorsese's "Silence" (2016). He has also been a favorite with Japanese directors, including the late Jun Ichikawa, who cast Ogata as the shy, lonely technical illustrator who falls for a shopaholic woman in "Tony Takitani" (2004).

Now Ogata and Kaori Momoi, another acting individualist with a long and lauded career, are co-starring as an unusual married couple in Maris Martinsons' "Magic Kimono" ("Futari no Tabiji"), which is being billed as the first Japanese-Baltic co-production. The film was shot on location in Riga and based on Latvian director Martinsons' original script.

Momoi plays Keiko, a Japanese woman who comes to Riga from her native Kobe with a kimono show — and encounters her husband (Ogata), who went missing during the 1995 Great Hanshin Earthquake. Shocked by his disappearance just as they were about to open a long-dreamed-of restaurant, Keiko seems to resent his return into her life, but as the story unfolds — including Keiko's reluctant rise to local celebrity via a cooking show — we see that she also bears a burden of guilt. In his own enigmatic, sympathetic way, her long-lost spouse helps her to both return to her past and reconcile with it.

Speaking to "The Japan Times" at a share house in Tokyo's Harajuku neighborhood — the residence and office of the film's publicist — Ogata says the opportunity to work with Momoi drew him to the role.

"We'd done live performances together," he says, "but after I went freelance (as a one-man act) we didn't have a chance to act together on stage, so I was happy to be with her in a film."

On first reading Martinsons' story, Ogata says it impressed him "as something like 'Alice in Wonderland.'"

"The heroine is a middle-aged woman, but her adventure in Riga is like (Alice's)," he explains.

Ogata himself found Riga both new and strange. That is, not his usual stage.

"The streets of the old city were like traveling back in time," he says. "It was a place I had absolutely no connection to. I was not just in a foreign city; I was in a distant foreign era. But Riga looks very poetic, beautiful and charming. In that sense it was the right place for the miracle of this couple's meeting to occur. "

The out-of-the-ordinary setting, he adds, made him feel he and his co-star "were doing a play with just the two of us."

"I felt that our performance, whether we could do something good together, was the most important thing," he says. "For me our performance came before the film's story or theme or message."

In shaping that performance, Ogata believes his co-star's experience as both an actor and director were key.

"Momoi is an actress, but she has also been a director for a long time now," he says. "She views her own performance with the eyes of a director and can give advice to other people on their performances. Being a real director, she can see things more clearly. She'll say 'This is the way we ought to do this.' She's strict," he adds with a laugh.

Ogata is primarily a stage performer and views film as a medium "that's quite different from a live stage show in its close-ups, long shots and editing."

"But that's only technique," he adds. "When you take away the technique, what's left is how you perform. And with my own performance I don't see a difference between being in a film and being on stage. There are no cuts in a live performance, but the audience is seeing you in close-up with their eyes. They're also editing in their heads. So in that sense the difference between being in films and on stage is not so big."

As the long-lost husband who has returned from the spirit realm (or wherever he's spent the past two decades) Ogata looks both flesh-and-blood present but somehow detached from the world of the living. In other words, he is quite unlike the usual movie ghost, the result of deliberate acting choices.

"When the dead husband in the (1990) film 'Ghost' appears (to his wife) their eyes lock," he says. "To me that's not a ghost. So (in 'Magic Kimono') the eyes of the couple don't meet; you don't know what they're seeing. I thought it would feel stranger if they had that little rule — no locking eyes. But sometimes their eyes do meet, and then it's surprising."

Ogata finds the finished film "mysterious" and says it's different from the image he had when he was making it.

"It's like with words: Even if the other person is not saying each and every thing with a clear meaning, you somehow understand," he says. "So I didn't feel uncomfortable about connections in the film going missing or being in a different place."

"Real life is bound by a lot of rules," he continues. "And on the set you go from one thing to the next and then the next. But the film doesn't pay much attention to that kind of sequence. Instead what's supposed to happen fifth happens second. It's like shuffling a deck of cards. Everyday life becomes kind of mixed up. But in my mind (the film) felt orderly, not chaotic. I watched it accepting the shuffle."

Then he eyes me and smiles. "What did you think of the film?" he asks.

I smile back, a bit flustered; it's not a question I often get from the people I interview. "It felt like 'Alice in Wonderland,'" I say, "but the Riga version, not the Disney one."

(June 28, 2017, "The Japan Times")

Naoko Ogigami Interview

A Chiba Prefecture native, Naoko Ogigami left for the United States in 1994 and studied at the University of Southern California Film School. Since returning to Japan in 2001, she has won a Pia Film Festival scholarship for her independent film "Hoshino-kun, Hoshino-kun" and directed two features: "Barber Yoshino" (2004) and "Love Is Five, Seven, Five!" ("Koi wa Go Shichi Go!," 2005). In person, she showed little sign of having spent most of her twenties in Los Angeles — no English, for one thing ("I never learned to speak it very well," she explained, in Japanese), no laid-back Angeleno attitude, for another. Instead, she had the sharp glance of a professional filmmaker who misses little, even when making polite small talk with a journalist.

How much of your own youth is in "Love Is Five, Seven, Five!"?
I didn't have a very interesting youth, really, so the film was my chance to (have the characters) do some of the things I wanted to do as a teenager, but couldn't. I went to a very strict high school and had a hard time while I was there. The students in the film have it easier than I did — they make the sort of memories that I wanted for myself. So in that sense the film is my own wish fulfillment

The setting seems to reflect that — it's a kind of rural paradise.
That's right, but for the heroine, a girl who has returned to Japan after living abroad, it a boring place. The fact that the school is in the countryside makes it harder for her to adjust.

If she had been in Tokyo she would have found it easier to maintain an "international identity."
Exactly.

She rediscovers her Japanese identity through haiku. What impressed me about the script was that your haiku sound as though they were actually written by high school students. (laughs)
It was tough getting the haiku right. I had a haiku expert giving me advice, but it was still difficult. I had to write haiku would fit each character's personality, that the actors could recite well.

It's also not the easiest film to subtitle.
No, it isn't. There are haiku in English, aren't there? So the translations have to not just express the meaning of the originals, but be real haiku.
    Haiku is no longer something strictly Japanese — you find haiku in America and Europe — so I want people abroad to see the film as well. That's why we're making a subtitled print.

Haiku is quite popular in America, from elementary school on up — but I've never heard of an American haiku tournament like the one in the film. That would be something new for them. (laughs)
It was hard staging the tournament. There's no movement in haiku — the contestants just stand and recite. The biggest challenge of the film for me was to somehow make that interesting. I beat my brains out. (laughs)
    I had a lot of discussions with the cameraman about how to inject action into (the tournament). The characters don't move, so the camera had to. I also tried to add movement through the editing, by cutting from quickly one character to another.

You studied film at USC and lived in the States for six years. Did that experience make you more interested in filming traditional Japanese themes?
Yes, it did. I was there a long time, so I started becoming nostalgic for Japanese country towns and all that. But I also thought that, because I had been in American so long, I could be more objective about adding traditional Japanese culture (to my films). I wasn't carrying the same baggage as someone who has lived here all their life.

There have been a lot of Japanese films, like "Shall We Dance?" and "Swing Girls," in which the heroes take up an unusual sport or hobby, overcome challenges and achieve success of one sort or another. Did you feel any pressure to do what those films had done better or differently?

I know that (my film) will be seen as belonging to a certain genre — that's a given. I can't do anything about being compared (with other films). All I can do is create my own world as best I can. Then I don't have to be afraid of comparisons, whatever they are.

You found a good balance between the drama and the comedy. The actors are playing types, but in the course of the film their characters become real individuals. If they had been over-acting for easy laughs, they couldn't have done that.

Some of the actors were better at that than others. The girl who played Mako came from a stage background, so she tended to overdo it — I had to sit on her a bit. The girl who played P-chan was a junior high school student — she was still a kid, so she tended to lose her concentration. (laughs) She did a good job, though.

Did you have any problems with the casting?

Not really. When we had auditions I was able to find kids who struck me as just right for each role. I didn't agonize a lot about which ones to choose. Also the actors liked their characters — that was a big relief to me.

You seem to like the borderline between fantasy and reality. I'm thinking of the way P-chan plays the ukulele during the haiku contest. The ukulele is a big part of her identity, so it's possible she would do that, but still... (laughs)

Yes, I like that in-between area. I also did that with the members of the opposing haiku team. They're supposed to be the bad guys, but I didn't want them to look that way. They're all wearing same glasses and t-shirts — they look a bit cute. (laughs) Not just scary.

A lot of Japanese movies about young people today stress the negative — the lack of values, the amorality and so on. One example is Toshiaki Toyoda's "Blue Spring" ("Aoi Haru").

I saw that film — I quite liked it.

You don't ignore the negative, but there's a positive energy flowing in your films as well.

I like to take the negative points of people — the frailties and weaknesses — and try to make something interesting out of them. Like the character of Mako — she thinks she's fat and ugly, but she's also got this cute, charming quality. That's why you can laugh at her. Otherwise, it would be too cruel

The character of Haruko is also a mix in that way — she's strong-minded, but has a softer side as well.

I wanted her to be cool, but from a woman's point of view, not a man's. When male director try to make cool female characters they often end up over-idealizing them. I'm a woman, so I had a different perspective that way — I tried to make her more in line with what women consider cool.

She's also been Americanized — that creates problems for her. Did any of that come from you own experience — of living for a long time in the States and then coming back to Japan?

Yes, it did. When I came back I felt a culture gap, definitely.

But you also didn't feel like staying in the States and trying to start career there?

Not really. For one thing, it's more enjoyable writing scripts in Japanese. I can have more fun expressing myself. Also, I wanted to make films in Japan. All Hollywood is interested in is remakes of

Japanese films — and that's not interesting to me. Finally, it's so expensive to make films there. I didn't feel like getting into that.

And even if I were able to become a director in Hollywood, I don't have the confidence that I could make interesting films, films that I could call my own. In Hollywood they have a system — the producer decides the final cut. I didn't think I could work that way. It's not easy in Japan, but at least I can express myself the way I want. The budgets aren't big, but I can enjoy myself while making interesting films. That's enough.

(March 30, 2005, "The Japan Times")

Kohei Oguri interivew: 'Foujita' struggles to win over foreign audiences

Veteran auteur Kohei Oguri's first film in 10 years, "Foujita" is a biopic of artist Tsuguharu "Leonard" Foujita. The toast of prewar Paris for his elegantly drawn women and cats, Foujita radically switched styles on his return to a militarized Japan and his propaganda art for the war effort was heavily criticized following Japan's 1945 defeat.

Joe Odagiri, known as "Japan's Johnny Depp" for his offbeat role choices, brings Foujita to eccentric — if essentially serious — life, while uncannily resembling the artist, whose fashion trademarks were his pudding bowl hairstyle, round glasses and Charlie Chaplin-esque moustache. But Oguri's deliberately paced, highly stylized approach to his subject makes "Foujita" less a movie than a series of dreamy tableaux vivants, gorgeously filmed by cinematographer Hiroshi Machida.

Premiering in competition at last month's Tokyo International Film Festival, the film divided audiences and critics and left without a prize. Some were puzzled by the abrupt transition from the opening scenes in a stereotypical "Gay Paree," where Foujita, nicknamed Foufou ("Nutty"), lives it up in arty bohemian splendor, to the scenes set in a grim wartime Japan, where a soberly clad Foujita and his kimonoed Japanese wife (Miki Nakatani) escape to a countryside remote, beautiful and mysterious.

Oguri says that from the beginning he had no intention of making a standard biopic. "(Foujita) had two lives and lived in two cultures, so that's how I thought (the film) should go," he said in explaining the film's bifurcated structure.

Oguri had always wanted Odagiri to play his offbeat hero.

"He has a Foujita-like quality," Oguri says. "Like Foujita he speaks in a bit of a mumble and is something of an otaku (geek). ... Also, an actor doesn't construct a performance in his head. In the end, he does it with his body, and Odagiri's body resembles Foujita's."

The film's two locations and eras — the free-spirited, decadent Paris of the 1920s and the politically oppressed, deeply traditional Japan of the 1940s — are starkly different, but Oguri insists that Foujita "always remained the same person inside" in both. "He was a realist whose approach to life was to overcome differences of culture, thought and history," he adds.

This adaptability, Oguri admits, hardly came easy for a Japanese man born in the Meiji era (1868-1912), when Japan was just emerging from centuries of isolation. "It's really amazing that he could sell so well, even though 19th-century Japonism and other such factors laid the groundwork for his acceptance," Oguri says. "But he tried too hard — and the strain definitely showed."

At the same time, major transitions in Foujita's life, be it a change of lovers or countries, occasion no laments or regrets. Switches in style and subject matter, from the pale white nudes of his Paris period to the dying soldiers of his wartime masterpiece, "Honorable Death on Attu Island," faze him not at all. He is instead gratified when a woman viewing the later painting collapses in tears. "My art can move people," he tells a friend.

"Foujita didn't care what people called him, be it war collaborator or whatever," Oguri says. "The only thing that really mattered to him was his art."

Nonetheless, after his successful encounter with Europe, Foujita undergoes a sort of reculturation when he returns to Japan. Living in a world of mountains, rice paddies, clouds and fog, whose inhabitants are still in touch with ancient folkways, he engages with not only his Japanese roots but the mystery of the land itself.

"I don't know if the real-life Foujita did that, but in the film I wanted him to experience Japan," Oguri says. "There's no decadence like that of Paris, but there are legends that still survive, there is a river to cross in the midst of nature. ... I wanted Foujita to cross that river to the other side, to something different from Europe and Paris."

In illustrating that crossing, Oguri and Machida created stunning images, but Oguri says he can't take raves about their beauty as compliments. "When you are asked about a film at a screening, if you are stuck for something to say, you usually say, 'It was beautiful,' "he explains. "Saying that the visuals are beautiful is saying that they aren't really connected to the story, that they stand on their own.

"With a painting you can rearrange the tableau inside the frame with new colors and lines and change the way the work is viewed. The same is true with films, with the difference being that, for better or worse, films have dialogue. If you can tie the images skillfully to a story with dialogue you've done a good job. But with 'Foujita' I had a hard time doing that — it was really tough."

Oguri also expresses disappointment over the film's reception by foreign film festivals to date, despite the support of its well-known French producer, Claudie Ossard. Oguri is no stranger to such festivals, including most importantly, Cannes, where "The Sting of Death" ("Shi no Toge"), his drama of marital discord, won the Grand Prix in 1990. "The foreign festivals didn't think much (of 'Foujita')," he confesses.

One possible reason, he speculates, is the non-Japanese setting. Another is the lack of foreign interest in a Japanese artist who spent the first half of his life in Europe and pre-1945 Japan. "I really don't know," he concludes. "I thought that (Foujita's) time in France would make his story a bit more familiar (to non-Japanese), but basically it didn't go over as well as I had expected."

Festivals, he says, have changed — and it's useless to protest their choices. "They can decide however they want," he says. "You've just got to get on their good side the way (Naomi) Kawase and (Kiyoshi) Kurosawa have. But still it's odd — I thought the film would do a little better."

(November 18, 2015, "The Japan Times")

Tatsushi Omori Interview

Born in 1970 into an acting family — his father is Butoh master Akaji Maro and his brother is rising star Nao Omori — Tatsushi Omori served as an assistant director for Junji Sakamoto and Kazuyuki Izutsu before working for producer/director Genjiro Arato on "Akame 48 Waterfalls" ("Akame Shijuha-taki Shinju Misui") in 2003 — and getting his first chance to direct on another Arato production, "Whispering of the Gods" ("Germania no Yoru"). Articulate and definite in his views, Omori is the young director as-auteur, but without the usual arrogance. Instead he was almost too ready to listen, as I cast for ways to put my various ramblings into questions.

"Whispering of the Gods" struck me as a carefully thought out, deeply structured film — not something you woke up one day and decided to do.
It's my debut as a director, so I wanted to put in everything I had thought and felt in my thirty-five years. I held nothing back.

It's set in a Catholic monastery, but it didn't strike me as a critique of Catholicism per so.
My aim is not to criticize the Catholic church — instead I use it more as a metaphor for Japanese society. The world of the monastery is a microcosm of the larger world outside. I don't consider ("Whispering") to be a "Catholic film."

One of the problems of Japanese society now is the sense of isolation so many young people, especially, feel. That's a big theme of the film.
Yes, it is. Human beings are basically alone and I wanted to express that sense of isolation in a cinematic way. In making a film you use actors and a camera, but there's a separation between the two. The camera can't get inside the actors' heads and tell you exactly what they're thinking. Also, the audience is looking at people on the screen they know nothing about — there's a certain distance between them. Finally, there's a certain distance between the actors as well. I wanted to maintain those various types of distance, within the world of the film.

At the same time, you can help having feelings about people you see on the screen. Usually, a film is trying to make everyone in the audience feel the same thing. I didn't want that. I didn't want everyone to understand the film the same way. It's all right if they don't understand some things. I wanted to get rid of the usual sort of explanations.

It can be enough for a character to just appear on the screen — I don't like to actively explain what he's doing there. I prefer a more passive approach — let the character speak for himself.

Also, when an actor tries to "act," there a gap between what he is and what he's acting. On TV actors are usually trying to explain their characters, so that they'll be easy to understand. But if an actor just stands there, he can still reveal what his character is like. In the scene where Rou is holding a pipe across his shoulders, you can get a feeling for what he is thinking, even though he's not telling you. You don't need an explanation. But to feel that you need time — so I give the audience the time they need, with long cuts. If you cut too quickly, the audience doesn't have time to think.

You underline the sense of isolation with the setting, which doesn't seem to be any particular place.
The film was shot in Iwate Prefecture, but I didn't want to identify the location. If the audience knows the location, they already have a certain image of it. I didn't want that — that's why I didn't shoot in a place with a well-known mountain in the background. Seeing something like that gives the audience a sense of security. I didn't want that, so I got rid of all identifiable landmarks. I wanted the audience to feel insecure.

You also cut explanatory visual transitions to the minimum — sometimes it's hard to tell if the story is flashing back or still in the present.

The film is hard to understand in places. (laughs) But I wanted the audience to be interested in the hard-to-understand bits, not shut them out. At the same time, I didn't want everything to be plain and simple — that's shuts down thinking as well. Instead, I want the audience to wonder why — to try to come to grips with what they don't understand.

You don't judge Rou or the other characters in terms of good or bad.

There's no good or bad as such in the film — everything is mixed up. I didn't want the audience to easily understand what's good and what isn't. Also, there's no clear-cut resolution. That's the way life is — no clear-cut resolution at the end. There's a kind of strength in knowing that.

Rou is a symbol of that strength — he keeps going no matter what. He has the strength to live — it was very important for me to show that. He's always listening to a portable radio — but the "whispering of the Gods" he's hearing is really coming from inside him. In other words, he's not just repeating the thoughts of others — he's thinking his own thoughts and acting on them. That's where his strength comes from — he thinks only his own thoughts. He doesn't trust the words of others. The only thing he values is what he thinks himself.

The monastery stands for Japanese society at large — and Japanese society accepts an American defined global standard, but why? That "standard" is often completely meaningless in a Japanese context. People just repeat what they hear on television as if it were their own idea. I'm really interested in that sort of thing — even though I'm completely different. I'm interested in what people are thinking.

A lot of recent Japanese films show how difficult young people find it to communicate — to say what they're really thinking. That seems to be your theme as well.

The hero, Rou, can't communicate well with words — he prefers actions. He's not a hikikomori — a guy who shuts himself up in his room — he's stronger than that. He prefers violence to words. With Sister Theresa, the nun, he uses sexual violence because he can't communicate his feelings well. But he tries to communicate as clearly as he can. He's not shutting himself off.

You were asking a lot of your actors — they had to show more than explain. Did you have any problems getting what you wanted?

I didn't say a lot to them — I don't like to give detailed directions. If I feel they are getting too far away from the image I have (of a certain scene) I might say something, but otherwise I give them the freedom to create their own interpretations. When directors tell actors how to make every little gesture, the results are usually boring. I want to see what they can do.

I used long cuts for this film, so the actors had to be very clear about what they were doing. When a scene seemed to be going well, I would keep shooting, with no cuts. I went on instinct — on whether or not it felt right. It not something you can easily explain.

Did you have everything worked before you started shooting — or did you leave room for improvisation?

Of course, we had a script, but finding the right settings was extremely important. My cameraman and I were both very particular about that. We were using long cuts, so we had to get the backgrounds exactly right. We looked for settings that were cinematic.

We paid a lot of attention to details — the color of the walls and so on. As much as possible we tried to convey emotions in images — so the images had to have real power. And if we didn't get the camera positions, lighting and so on right, the power wouldn't be there.

You shot on 35 mm film. It's hard to imagine getting the same impact with a DVD camera.
The cameraman decided to go with 35 mm film. He was like me, making his feature debut as a cameraman., so he was very careful to get everything right. He really put a lot of thought into the sort of film we were making.

What about your producer, Genjiro Arato? He has a certain style that seems to carry over from film to film.
He worked a lot with Seijun Suzuki, but though I love Suzuki's films, they didn't have much influence on me.

Mr. Arato is the sort of producer who tells the director to make the film the way he wants. He doesn't talk about what the audience might want or about how to make a good film. He believes in leaving everything up to the director. He says that a director can only connect with an audience when he is making something that is truly his own idea.

The budget for this film was Y120 million — there's no other producer who would give that sort of money to a first-time director. I'm very grateful for that.

(December 16, 2005, "The Japan Times")

Mamoru Oshii interview: talks softly, but carries a big script

Before I interviewed Mamoru Oshii, his publicist asked if I would need an interpreter. "He tends to mumble," she explained. No, I didn't need an interpreter, but I did turn the volume of my tape recorder on high, fortunately. Looking a decade younger than his 52 years, with a mane of unruly black hair, Oshii spoke rapidly in a croaky, whispery monotone, as though, after meeting the press nonstop for days, he was on the verge of vocal collapse. But for all his legendary shyness (it was the most eye-contactless interview I've ever had), his tumbles of words had the assurance and fluidity of one who has long been king of the rich imaginary domain that is "Innocence."

Dolls are an important motif in "Innocence," but the attitude toward them is quite different from that of a film like "Toy Story." There is a sense that the dolls — especially the "gainoids" — have a human spirit, but at the same time are not quite human.

In "Toy Story" the dolls are just objects that humans bring to life, for their own amusement. Japanese have a different view: They think that dolls have a spirit. That's why when they no longer have any use for a doll they just don't throw it away in the trash. They would be afraid to do that; the doll might put a curse on them. So they take the doll to a priest, who performs a ceremony to appease its spirit. I believe that myself, that dolls have a spirit. They're not just objects to have fun with.

Also in "Toy Story," the faces of the toys are extremely expressive — you can read their every thought. In "Innocence" the gainoids have these mysterious expressions — it's hard to tell what they are thinking. They're scary somehow (laughs).

Yes, they are a little strange (laughs). In "Toy Story" the dolls move and talk like human beings. It's hard to tell them from the human characters. But when you animate dolls that way, you lose what makes them special, their individual spirit. It's a lot harder to animate dolls so they still look doll-like. That was the toughest part of the film for me.

The hero, Bateau, is a cyborg — halfway between a human and a doll or robot. The way you animate him reflects that quality. His movements are not quite human but not robotic either.

That's true for not only him, but the other characters as well. Their movements are somewhat doll-like. Even their expressions are more doll-like than human.

The film uses the term "ghost" to describe the spirit that inhabits not just the dolls, but Bateau and the other characters. How does that relate to the Japanese concept of tamashi [spirit] and the Western concept of soul?

That's a difficult question. A soul is not something someone can just show you. But if you believe in it enough, want to see it enough, it will appear. In the West, people don't believe animals have souls, do they? That's not true in Japan, though. I myself believe that dogs and cats have souls — but that has nothing to do with a specific religion. Children have similar feelings about dolls — if they love a doll enough, they feel that it's alive. That feeling is universal. It's not something they're taught — they just feel it somehow. It's not connected with any religious belief.

But your hero in "Innocence" is not a child, as is often the case with animation, but a middle-aged man. What was the reason for that?

Yes, it is an unusual choice (laughs). Bateau is a reflection of my own thoughts and feelings. "Innocence" is a kind of autobiographical film in that way.

Your last animated film, 1995's "Ghost in the Shell," seems very prescient now, with its view of where the Internet was taking us. In "Innocence," though, you seem to be looking backward. The film is set in the future, but it has a retro look — the cars, the buildings, the dolls.

Yes, I'm not trying to make science fiction. The film is set in the future, but it's looking at present-day society. And as I said, there's an autobiographical element as well. I'm looking back at some of the things I liked as a child — the 1950s cars and so on. Basically, I wanted to create a different world — not a future world.

"Ghost in the Shell" was about how technology was making humanity more machinelike. But this time your angle of approach is different.
Yes, back then I was concerned with how technology was changing human beings. In this film I'm more interested in human beings themselves.

In the film, the merging of the human and the machine causes problems. The gainoids experience their "human spirit" not as a blessing, but as a burden.
Yes, as soon as they realize they have a spirit, they start to think of suicide. They want to become fully human — but they can't. That dilemma becomes unbearable for them. The humans who made them are to blame. They try to make a doll that is as human as possible — but they don't think of the consequences.

"Ghost in the Shell" was very popular abroad. In fact, it probably did better abroad than it did in Japan.
Yes, I'm sorry about that (laughs).

When you were making "Innocence," did you feel any pressure to cater to the foreign market? To make the film easier to understand for foreign fans?
No, I wasn't thinking about anything like that while we were in production. My first concern was that the Japanese audience should see the film. Actually, I wasn't thinking about what the audience would and wouldn't like. I was making the film for myself. I only know what I want to see. I have no idea what anyone else wants to see — that includes the Japanese audience — so there's no point in trying to guess. Once you start doing that you end up with a boring film.

Dreamworks plans to release "Innocence" in the United States this fall, which means that it will be eligible for an Academy Award. Does that prospect excite you at all?
Yes, but more than winning an award, I want the film to be seen and remembered. I want people to want to see it again and again. If I can do that, I'll be happy.

One reason that fans, both in Japan and abroad, see your films and those of other Japanese animators again and again is because they can become absorbed in those worlds in a way they can't with a lot of Hollywood animation.
I enjoy making the world [of the film] as detailed as possible. I get absorbed in the finer points — like what the back of a bottle label looks like when you see it through the glass [demonstrates with a bottle of mineral water]. That's very Japanese, I suppose. I want people to go back to the film again and again to pick up things they missed the first time. I'm happier if 10,000 people see the film 10 times each than if 1 million people see it once. I'm not making it for the general public, but for a core group of fans — I hope it will make a big impression on them. If I can do that, I'm happy.

Anyway, I'm sure that "Innocence" has a good shot at an Academy Award nomination. Americans have never see anything like it.
I'd like that — going to the Academy Awards, but I don't have a suit to wear (laughs).

(March 17, 2004, "The Japan Times")

Kiyoshi Kurosawa interview

Kiyoshi Kurosawa is God's gift to film journalists. He speaks slowly and distinctly, in a rumbling baritone, weighing each word — and giving even the most fumble-fingered reporter time to get everything down. He is also patient with questions that, after the 20th media interview, he has heard 20 times before. When I met him on the set of "Pulse" ("Kairo") last spring, he was nearing the end of the shoot and was in a receptive mood, if decidedly eager to get to his lunch.

Somehow the story of the film reminds me of "The Ring" — the dead invade the world of the living via a technology that is still alien to a lot of people.
It's a coincidence. A scriptwriter on "The Ring," Hiroshi Takahashi, has been a friend of mine going way back. We think alike, and our ways of approaching this type of horror film are similar. So perhaps it was inevitable that "The Ring" and this film should resemble each other. . . . But when it's finished it's going to be quite different.

The Internet is an important motif in the film: Do you think that humanity is being absorbed into the Internet, as the film seems to imply?
No, not absorbed, but we are being flooded with information from the Internet. It's not simply information, though, but a kind of message from a world that is a bit different from the real world. That's also true of radio and TV — you're in your home, living your ordinary life, but by turning these things on you're connecting to other worlds. When I think about that, I get really scared, especially in the case of the Internet — you don't know where all that information is coming from. That, to me, is a lot scarier than radio or TV.

At least with radio and television, you don't have viruses.
That's true. So that's the idea I had five years ago — a kind of ghost story, to put it in a word. But if it were an ordinary ghost story, just having the ghosts appear would be boring. It would be like "Ghostbusters." (laughs) Or it could be like the traditional Japanese ghost story, like "Yotsuya Kaidan," in which the ghosts appear and frighten human beings. Then at the end they fulfill their mission, whatever it is, and go to heaven. That's the usual pattern for that kind of story. But in this story, the ghosts come from another world and, after they enter this one, they stay — they don't go back. That's often the case in my films. Something happens that has a big impact on reality — and reality itself changes and doesn't return to what it was before.

You seem to be making a statement about the present state of Japanese society, not just making a what-if entertainment.
That's right. This film is not just about the ghosts; there's another story as well, one about the isolation of human beings. Because we're isolated, we want to connect somehow — with someone on the Internet, say. Or it could be on the telephone. It's all the same. But even when we meet someone in the flesh, we still have this feeling of isolation. At the same time, even when we're home alone, we want to assure ourselves that we're connected somehow. When the ghosts appear [in the film], they're also isolated. They also want to connect. That's a big point in the story.

So the problem is not the technology itself, but the basic nature of human beings.
That's right. I'm not simply saying that isolation is wrong. Even though the people in the film are living in isolation, they connect with each other. In the end, although only one person survives, they still want to live. So it's not a depressing film. (laughs)

Do you want to make "Pulse" more entertaining than your last film ("Charisma"), which was rather serious?

Yes, that's the idea. I want as many people as possible to see it, especially the ones who don't usually go to films. It's not the kind of film that gets sent to foreign film festivals. If they invite me, I'll go, but that wasn't my intention in making it."

(February 27, 2001, "The Japan Times")

Donald Richie interview: being inside and outside Japanese cinema

In his five decades as a writer, Donald Richie has investigated everything from the glories of noh to the mysteries of the Japanese tattoo, while attempting everything from the travel narrative ("The Inland Sea") to the historical novel (the meticulously researched, wittily engaging "Kumagai"). He is best known abroad, however, as the pre-eminent Western critic of Japanese cinema, beginning with the seminal study "The Japanese Film," which he wrote with Joseph Anderson and published in 1959.

He not only brought the works of Akira Kurosawa and Yasujiro Ozu to the attention of the West, but also made experimental films himself that, in the 1960s, injected heady new influences into Japanese cinema while pushing the tolerance of Japanese authorities to the limit.

Image Forum in Shibuya will screen a retrospective of Richie's films in five programs, all in new prints and all selected by Richie himself. They range from the black comedy of "Five Filosophical Fables" and the erotic poetry of "Boy With Cat" to the unsettling sacrifices of "Cybele" and the deadly play of "Wargames."

In a recent interview at his Ueno apartment overlooking the glitter of the night streets and the blackness of Shinobazu Pond, Richie talked with Mark Schilling about the making of the films — and his memories of an era.

What were your feelings on seeing your films again? Is it like looking at another incarnation?

These films are really archaeological. To see what Tokyo looked like back then is a real treat. To me it's really Proustian. It's like Marcel lying in bed and remembering his life. I see a funny combination of things — the beauty of it all, the nostalgia and the "Oh, shit, I shouldn't have done that," you know? It's a combination of critical awareness and, at the same time, a deep emotional sort of nostalgia for the way things were. Remembrance of time past.

You took a film course at Columbia University — but you didn't make the films for it, did you?

No, I didn't make anything for the film course. I just continued (with) my earlier interest in experimental film. Of course, being in New York, I could go see experimental films. I didn't know what they were called, but I was interested in the camera as Orson Welles had used it in "Citizen Kane." In that film, the camera became an extension of the director himself. For me film was a way to make something, control something, put yourself into the world and get the world to come to you — some kind of magic.

So it was another form of writing.

Another form of writing, precisely. As a comparison, I said that if the feature film is like the novel, then the experimental film is like lyric poetry. Some deeper emotion is supposed to appear in an experimental film.

There seems to be a big difference in the way you approached some of the earlier films and the way you approached a film like "Wargames," which you made after coming to Japan.

In the earlier films, I could see Donald Richie in there, but in "Wargames," it's like the eye of God. (Laughs) You're absolutely right. Hani Susumu took me to task for this one. He said, "Why do you step back? Why didn't you go farther and farther inside yourself? Why did you become so objective?" In my earlier films I was so subjective. Then I went on to make more subjective films after "Wargames." "Dead Youth" looks objective, but it's actually a pretty subjective experience. So you could say that I got back to my roots in that film. But it's true, I adopted a presentational mode.

One reason was that I was working with 16 mm for the first time. With 8 mm, you can throw it over to that wall (points), but you can't throw it in the theater. So it's like chamber music — it's not for a large audience. But suddenly I had a machine that could be used in an auditorium, and this changed the shape of what I was doing. Another reason, of course, was that I was here, so I had a different audience. Also, I was in a position to be a new kind of person. So I was interested in Japanese material. How do I use Japanese material? It's not me.

The 8 mm films I had done here, "Aoyama Kaidan," "Shi" and "Shu-e," were much more like the 8 mm films I had done in New York. That's why they're so personal and lyrical. But once I got the machine and once I digested being here, and once I realized that I would be filming Japan in Japanese, I took a more objective stance. Also, I probably wanted to make a more social statement. "Wargames" is a social statement."

We're talking about 1962, before the Vietnam War.
But at the very beginning of the glorious '60s in Tokyo. This was a time when everybody was reinventing Japan. I was watching Hani and (Nagisa) Oshima doing it in film, (Tadanori) Yokoo in graphics, Juro Kara in the theater, Shuji Terayama in literature, Eiko Hosoi in photography. It was an extremely exciting thing.

And I wanted to reinvent, not Japan so much, but the world and myself. I wanted to make a larger film for a larger audience about a larger issue. That's why I tried to get away from lyric poetry. And I took a step toward narrative — sometimes too much narrative. "Nozoki Monogatari" has themes in variations and it's got a narrative, but so what? My tempo is off, my pace is off, in fact I just can't handle it.

My single feature film, "A Couple," is also a great failure. I'd seen (Alain) Resnais and (Michelangelo) Antonioni and they had a big influence on me in devising new narrative devices. But I couldn't begin to control them. "A Couple" is a very strange picture because it has my earlier self-revealing qualities and the lyrical stuff, but it's also a love story, it has a trajectory, it has all of these things that commercial cinema has.

Whereas "Atami Blues" is more like a short story, even though you're using the same basic structure as "A Couple."
But doing it in a lyrical kind of way. At the same time, there's a little ghost of an antidote — about how they meet twice, fuck, bye-bye. Originally it was 40 minutes, but I saw that it was sagging in the middle. Before anybody else saw it, I took out 20 minutes. and it's a much, much better film. It's still a film I like very, very much.

There's a close integration between the music and the images.
Yes, music is used for transitions — it's what Ozu used to call *noren* music. You know, when you go through the noren to get to the next room. I was really lucky about that music. (Tohru) Takemitsu had seen all my earlier pictures and had heard about "Atami Blues." I said, "I don't want to use any music. We won't use any music." And he said, "Use music. Look, here's a tape I was fiddling around with." There were these two jazz pieces and I used them, and it worked very well.

The film itself is like a jazz improvisation, the way the guy picks up the girl, all very much on the spur of the moment.
That's also the way people worked back then — very improvisatory. We shot it in two days. I worked so fast. I shot "Cybele" in one day.

I thought that might have been shot quickly — everyone in the cast was naked. (Laughs)
That whole day they were out of control. (Laughs) Everybody knew what the story was, but there was no directing anyone. Kato, the leader of the Zero Jikken troop that I used for the cast said, "OK, kids, let's go." And then they just acted it out, while I and another cameraman were running around filming it . . .

You had trouble with that film when you screened it in Germany, didn't you?

Everybody thought it was too far-out to be shown in Japan, but we screened it one time and nothing happened. It takes a long run for somebody to complain and for the cops to do something. And then it was brought to France, but the French government denied it a license. It was sent to the London Film Institute and they were going to show it, but (England) still had a very strong censorship policy, and it was rejected out of hand. And, back then, everything in the rejected bin got burned, I was told. At least I never got my print back.

It was shown at the (Robert) Flaherty seminar in Germany where it absolutely infuriated the predominantly political-correct audience. Everybody was saying it was about the slaughter at Auschwitz — all those naked bleeding bodies. I thought it was a feminism statement: Up with the girls. But this was not what they saw. They saw a decadent, savage cult, and they completely missed my major point, which is that you're supposed to contrast the picture with the frame. And the frame is the score — from the elegance of the 18th century — the triumph of the Baroque. You're supposed to take this music and contrast it with the barbarity, but everybody missed it.

It's harder to shock people now — even the police.

Yes, I think the shock value of these films is much, much less now. I think one of the important points in my films is that they are transgressive. And I strongly believe in transgression as a means of self-discovery, sociologically and personally. I think the transgressive is a very versatile, powerful tool. But the transgressive level rises and rises. How do you keep being transgressive today? Now I don't know. Hold hands? Kiss somebody? (Laughs)

Well, "Hannibal" upset a lot of people. I was thinking of that when I saw your cannibal family picnic in "Five Filosophical Fables."

"Baby Hannibal." People have asked me, 'Do you mean that as a statement about the Japanese family?' Of course the answer is no. They may be Japanese, but this film has nothing to do with Japan. That's my comment on families. But not Japanese families. Oh, (Yukio) Mishima loved that picture, because Mishima was transgressive. And he wrote marvelous things about the whole picture but particularly the family picnic — that was really, truly meaningful for him.

Were you out there all by yourself? Was anyone else in Japan making these films that could not be shown without attracting the attention of the police?

Masao Adachi was making movies which were very, very questioning. Hara Kazuo's early films, in the '70s and '80s, also could not be shown. He is perhaps the leading exponent of transgressive cinema, as in the "The Emperor's Naked Army Marches On." He's transgressive in a different way from me. I'm never transgressive sociologically or politically. I'm still on the lyric poetic side, and I'm still talking about expressions of feeling.

We had an audience for this kind of film. People sometimes ask why I stopped making films after '68, and the reason is, I lost my audience. There may be an audience now — we'll find out — but back then there was this dry period when there just wasn't an audience. The people who had been looking at my films all started working for Parco. (Laughs) Everyone had the same problem.

Did you feel that you were part of that avant-garde circle — or were you outside?

I was always outside. We are never inside here, are we? Have you ever felt inside? I've never felt inside. Does any idiot feel inside, I wonder. I wasn't being condescended to, which was nice. I was included in the earliest screenings at the old Sogetsu Kaikan. This was before Hiroshi Teshigahara became the *iemoto* (head of the Sogetsu school of flower arranging). He was the renegade son of the old iemoto. They had all the money in the world and he sort of liked modern art, so they had Yoko Ono doing her gibberish and everybody was doing something, and I was always included as part of that gang.

It was to their advantage to have me, because through me they could indicate that they were not insular. Having me as a member and enjoying my stuff kept them from being marginalized. Nobody talked about it, nobody thought about it, nobody formulated it, but there was a political role I was probably playing as (far as) their image went. In any event, I was always treated extremely well, but this is Japan and they were Japanese so they could not help, even with the best intentions in the world, but to exclude me.

You're not someone parachuting in to do a documentary on the exotic Japanese and, at the same time, you're obviously not Japanese. So your own position is ambiguous.
I felt like Shelley when he was making poems in Italy. He just kept on writing poems. He didn't stop to think that he was in Italy. Byron didn't either. I mean, these are big names to throw around, but still the impulse is the same.

But you were still working with Japanese actors in Japan. In the comedy "Five Filosophical Fables," the type of humor does not seem to be something that the Japanese were doing at that time.
That's right — the film's dedicated to (Buster) Keaton. The genesis of that film was that I saw a mime troupe, a Japanese mime troupe. And they were so good and so funny. I'd been thinking about making little allegorical fables, and when I found them I realized that I could do that. So I got to know them. They were a very young, very struggling mime troupe, and I didn't pay them very much. (Laughs) I wrote the scripts, and they acted them out. I didn't really have to tell them what to do. As soon as they read the script, they knew what it was, so they understood the humor.

It was a precursor of what Sogo Ishii and Juzo Itami started doing in the '80s.
Itami knew my films quite well. At that time, he was an actor going with a girl I was seeing a lot — Kazuko Kawakita, whom he eventually married. He emulated one of my films in the first film he made — a 16 mm film called "Rubberband Gun." He and Kazuko made it, and it had my sense of humor in it, a very funny little film.

"Life" is another one like that. It plays almost like classic slapstick, but the sensibility is still contemporary.
Those comic films were very often allegorical, and that one was, too. The kind of flippancy I showed about serious things was new to Japan; the fact that I could be flippant about something like life. This approach also occurred to (Kon) Ichikawa and (Keisuke) Kinoshita, but they couldn't get the focus so narrow. They couldn't control things to the point where they could be outrageous enough to do this.

These things were very much in the air in the '60s, and that's why the films were popular. What will the younger generation make of these films, I wonder? The people who will go to see them are already half-converted anyway. We're not going to get any dudes with skateboards or girls in platform shoes. (Laughs) It's going to be presumably a thinking crowd. I think they'll find them amusing. I think they'll laugh.

Was that the reaction when you first screened them? Or did people just stare at the screen?
No, it was a very smart audience. Everybody knew exactly what the targets were.

So you weren't ahead of the audience.
I was only ahead of the audience in pictures like "Cybele," but there was hardly any audience, nobody ever saw it here. Occasionally I was behind the audience, I think. "Nozoki Monogatari" was too clunky for the audience of the period. I think they were sharper than that.

The one film that the Japanese consistently admired was "Boy With Cat." They admired the structure. They mentioned the haiku and said that, structurally, I was very much influenced by Japan.

So if you look at the films structurally, you can certainly say, if there hadn't been an Ozu, there wouldn't have been "Atami Blues." And you can certainly say that if Japanese poetics hadn't existed, there wouldn't have been "Boy With Cat." And if there hadn't been a whole layer of Japanese modernist prose poetry, there probably wouldn't have been "Dead Youth," at least in the form that it is in.

That film is very much based on the Japanese poetic structure. It's based on a poem by Mutsuro Takahashi, which is read at the beginning. Anyway, I tried to use the same sort of jump-cutting, lack of narrative and repetition that occurs in poetry. The gay audience didn't like it. They thought the boy was too old. (Laughs) They thought it could not be used for masturbatory purposes, which is what all that Japanese gay pornography is about. And my picture could not be used in that fashion.

It's much too serious a picture. It's too solemn a picture, really. It's all about Thanatos. Some people have called it old-fashioned because of this linking of love and death.

You have the juxtaposition of the tombstone and the boy playing with himself. (Laughs)
That's right. How much more symbolic can you get? There's a long tradition of this in Japan as well. Mishima liked this film a lot, he told me privately. He only wanted to talk about the cannibal picnic in public, but he was deeply stirred by this particular picture. But I think the influence of Mishima on the picture is minimal.

I don't think that, other than structurally, I had too many Japanese influences. I dragged what I could out of myself and I also modeled my stuff on Europeans I'd seen. A lot of the sensibility comes from (Jean) Cocteau.

I was thinking more of (Luis) Bunuel actually.
Absolutely Bunuel. I'd seen "Un Chien Andalou" and "L'Age d'Or" very early, and they had a tremendous influence on me. Cocteau and Bunuel were my patron saints. But among the lesser saints were people like Bruce Bailey and Bruce Conrad — and Maya Deren, whose films had a large influence on me. So you could say Japan for structure and of course for actors and story material, but this sort of self-revealing stuff — that certainly didn't come from Japan. Well there are a few — (Osamu) Dazai and (Ryunosuke) Akutagawa, for example, who killed themselves.
But usually, it's a very careful society. Its very presentational. My films may look representational but I'm doing them in a presentational kind of way. I mean, the elaborate baroque choreography in "Dead Youth," for example. You have to figure out the story of "Dead Youth" from what is not shown. The shape of it is what it's about. The hole in the middle of that picture is the subject. Otherwise, you can't really tell what the picture's about.

In "Cybele," as well, you are bringing in influences that certainly aren't Japanese. When I saw the guys dancing and falling down, dancing and falling down, I was thinking of frescoes from ancient Greek art — it had an archaic feeling to it.
There is an archaic feeling. That was certainly one of the intentions. After all, I was doing a story based on an ancient legend, and doing it with people with their clothes off like in a Greek fresco, and it's framed like a Greek fresco.

There's also a sense of danger. The woman jumps in with the men, and I'm thinking "What's going to happen here?" The ancient Greek rituals weren't always fun and games. They could turn bloody, they could turn dangerous.
The Bacchantes dismembered Orpheus. And Cybele herself emasculated her priests. I think that what some people expect at one point or another is cannibalism. That is one of the few perversions not indulged in this particular picture. Do you think it still has power? I guess it does have power. It does transgress.

That film and "Wargames" were, to me, disturbing films.

Oh good, I'm very pleased. I can still disturb. Why be transgressive if you can't disturb, right? That's wonderful. (Laughs)

(January 28, 2004, "The Japan Times")

Junji Sakamoto interview: on a not-so-sentimental journey to 1947

Born in Osaka in 1954, Junji Sakamoto has set many of his 13 feature films, including his award-winning 1989 debut "Dotsuitarunen," in his native Kansai. He arrived for our interview at the Takanawa Prince Hotel looking dapper in a retro-style suit that he later told me had been worn by an actor friend in a yakuza movie. Not quite 1947, but close enough. He spoke in a baritone voice that somehow seemed big for his slight frame — a good tool for the director of a heavily populated film like "Out of This World" ("Kono Yo no Soto e — Club Shinchugun").

How difficult was it to re-create the look and feel of the period?

It's not a period I'm personally familiar with, so the big question for me was whether the film would be true to reality. No matter how many photos I looked at or books I read or documentary films I saw, I had not experienced that period myself.

I wanted to get the atmosphere right as far as possible. I wanted older people who remember those times to feel as though they were in a time machine. I may have made mistakes on certain details, but I wanted to re-create the feel of the period accurately.

How well do you think you've succeeded? What have the older people who have seen it said?

Some have told me it's like time traveling. Others said I did a good job, considering how young I am (laughs). Nobody came out mad at all the mistakes. (laughs)

A lot of people said that jazz made them feel nostalgic — it wasn't modern jazz but standards and swing. It really brought back the feeling of the period for them. People may have been poor then, but listening to the music of the time, including Japanese music, you get a feeling for how rich their emotional lives were.

Another thing that impressed me was how the actors, even the extras, looked to be of the period. In a lot of Japanese period dramas, the actors look plump and healthy, but in this film they looked lean and hungry. (laughs) Mitch, the musician who played the trumpeter, lost 15 kg for the film (laughs). Also, he's a real jazzman, so he had the period feel for the music right.

Joe Odagiri, who played the drummer, is another real-life musician.

But the way jazz and rock drummers hold the sticks is different. Also the timing for the bass drum is different in rock and jazz, so having experience as a [rock musician] made it harder for him — he had to relearn some things.

Masato Hagiwara, who plays the lead, had no musical experience going into the film — he seems to have had it the hardest.

He practiced the sax for hours in a karaoke box (laughs). He couldn't practice at home — it would have been too loud.

We did a lot of work getting the sets to look period, but more important was to make the playing look real, not phony. The usual way is to shoot the hands of a pro doing the fingering and then shoot the actor's face. We shot the actors actually playing. The music on the soundtrack is by professionals, but when we filmed the scenes [in the clubs], the actors were actually playing the instruments, not just fingering them.

You also paid a lot of attention to the process of how they learn to play jazz and finally become good at it.

In the beginning [of the film] they are playing badly. They aren't just inexperienced — their hearts aren't really in it. All they are thinking about is making money and becoming famous. They don't care about the music itself.

Now that Japan's Self-Defense Forces are on their way to Iraq, the movie is not a period piece, but very timely.
I don't feel good about that. I wish it weren't so timely.

You started planning the film nearly two years ago.
In the summer of 2002. At that time no one in Japan had any idea what would happen in Iraq. So I didn't make the film to be timely. Now Japanese have to think about the changes going on in the world. Before, they felt those changes had nothing to do with them. Now we're in a period when Japan has to become involved in the world — or rather is becoming involved whether it wants to or not. That includes the Middle East, of course.

   Japanese can't easily talk about their own country. They can talk about their own lives, but not their own country. They aren't good at political discussion. They can become emotional, but can't easily express what they're thinking. Koreans and Chinese can do it, though.

Japanese are often afraid of being misunderstood when they talk about politics.
So they end up being vague (laughs). You can't tell if they're saying yes or no (laughs). They're vague because they don't want to hurt other people, I think. That's a plus in some ways. They may be running away (laughs), but they aren't being malicious. They're afraid that if they speak out, they'll be misunderstood — and do some harm.

The characters in the film, especially the ones played by Matsuoka and Shea Whigham, butt heads, though.
The Occupation forces brought democracy to Japan and tried to teach it to the Japanese, but the Japanese equated democracy with individualism — with everyone looking out for themselves. Until then Japanese had been taught that individualism was wrong — they had to unite together as one for the common good, with everyone thinking the same way. Then suddenly democracy came in — and people thought it was all right to do whatever they wanted. They shifted from one extreme to another.

   All the main Japanese characters have shadows in their pasts, in their lives. They're all bearing burdens of one sort or another. Music offers them a way to ease those burdens.

Did you create their stories from your research, from listening to old jazzmen and so on?
I didn't have specific models, but in the course of doing research I found stories that I added to the mix. For example, the Odagiri character lost members of his family in the Nagasaki bombing, but he's still playing jazz for the Americans. I actually heard a story like that — and added it to Odagiri's character

Shea Whigham's character lost a brother in the battle of Leyte — so it's not just the Japanese who have these shadows.
When I was writing the script I knew what I wanted to say about the Japanese character, but I wondered how I should write about the Americans. I did research, but I wondered what the Americans who had come with the Occupation forces were thinking and feeling. I had a problem with that.

I wondered about the casting of Peter Mullan — why a Scottish actor instead of an American?
There's a tune "Danny Boy" that has a lot of meaning for [Mullan's] character. It was originally an Irish tune — so for that reason I wanted to use, not an American, but someone from that part of the world, from Scotland. The character is not necessarily Irish American, though.

(January 28, 2004, "The Japan Times")

Sion Sono interview 1: telling a lengthy tale of lust and religion

Films that are extremely long (say, three hours plus) tend to be extreme in other ways as well — including the megalomania of their director. One notorious early example is Erich von Stroheim's 1924 masterpiece "Greed," which originally clocked in at nearly 10 hours. Von Stroheim, notorious for his perfectionism, spent nine months shooting on location, while spending $500,000 — a fabulous sum for the time. His distributor, MGM, later slashed his film to ribbons — prints now in circulation commonly run to two hours and 20 minutes.

Sion Sono's new film, "Love Exposure" ("Ai no Mukidashi"), may have a 237-minute running time, but its length is about all it shares with "Greed" and other classic — and lengthy — folies de grandeur.

When the film received its world premiere at the Tokyo Filmex Film Festival last November, the packed crowd at the Yurakucho Asahi Hall stayed uncomplainingly to the end — and gave "Love Exposure" the festival's Agnes b. audience award. It has also been selected for the 2009 Berlin Film Festival's Forum section, which specializes in films of an experimental nature. Meanwhile, distributor Phantom Film is juggling offers from festivals around the world.

Why is a four-hour film so popular, with audiences and programmers alike?

Instead of directorial grandiosity, Sono delivered an unpretentious mix of broad satire, much of which targets religion in various guises; stylish, if borderline silly, martial-arts action; and full-throated affirmations of love, voiced by the sweet-faced teenage hero, who also happens to be an enthusiastic voyeur.

Fans of Sono's previous films, including "Suicide Club" ("Jisatsu Circle," 2002), "Noriko's Dinner Table" ("Noriko no Shokutaku," 2005) and "Exte: Hair Extensions" ("Exte: Hair Extensions," 2007), will find much of this familiar. Still, "Love Exposure" represents a departure — and gamble — for Sono, who has directed 14 feature films, beginning in 1990 with "Bicycle Sighs" ("Jitensha Toiki") but never anything so ambitious — or commercially risky.

"I wanted to make it shorter, but somehow I just couldn't," says Sono, wearing his trademark hat, at the office of his distributor, Phantom Films. "I wasn't trying to issue a challenge or anything like that."

The first cut, at six hours, was trimmed at the fervent request of the producers, who no doubt saw their investment going up in smoke. Screenings that long would have to be limited to two a day, and might prove unendurable.

Sono obligingly produced a two-hour cut, but wasn't happy with it. "It was too short," he says. "It didn't explain enough. Also, at two hours, the film was like a kamishibai (picture play for children)."

The script, which Sono wrote himself, originated in his friendship with a habitual taker of up-skirt photos. "He was my friend, but he became a pervert," Sono says with an impish grin. "He didn't do it to get sexually excited. He didn't feel he was doing something wrong. For him it was like bird-watching."

Instead of urging his friend to get therapy, Sono became interested in what made him tick. "I didn't hate him for being a pervert," he says. "I was rather sympathetic in fact."

He also saw cinematic possibilities in his friend's story, despite the ick factor. "I like exploring borderlines," he explains. "In this film, it's the borderlines between perversion and normality, the Catholic Church and cults."

The film's protagonist, Yu (Takahiro Nishijima), goes one step further than Sono's friend, however: He becomes a pervert ninja, leaping and somersaulting as he surreptitiously snaps the panties of passing women. He is doing it not for erotic thrills, but to please his Catholic-priest father (Atsuro Watabe), who insists that Yu confess his sins — even when he has none. Once he takes up "candid" photography, however, he has plenty to tell Dad every day.

Then, while dressed in drag as Sasori — an iconic heroine from an early 1970s "women in prison" series (another of Sono's obsessions) — Yu helps a hard-fisted, if definitely cute, teenage girl battle a gang of punks. Her name is Yoko (Hikari Mitsushima), but to Yu she is a double of the Virgin Mary, who has been his image of the perfect woman ever since boyhood, when he associated her with his dear departed mother.

"In his mind, (these women) are all mixed up together," says Sono "To him they're symbols of perfect love."

This blurring of the boundaries between religion and romance, as well as the film's various comic digs at Catholicism, may strike some viewers as belonging to the long, dubious tradition of mocking Christianity in the Japanese popular media. Sono, however, insists that he has long been fascinated by the religion, though he has no urge to join it.

"If there were a Jesus Christ fan club, I'd join it," he says. "I've been interested in Jesus for a long time. . . . I've often wondered what he would do if he were alive today."

In one scene set on a lonely beach, satire gives way to sincerity as Yoko recites a lengthy Bible passage from the Book of Corinthians to Yu. Its best-known line (from the American Standard Version of the Bible): "But now abideth faith, hope, love, these three; but the greatest of these is love."

"It's the most important scene in the film," says Sono. "It states the central theme — that nothing is more important than love."

The scene also reveals Yoko as a fierce-eyed teller of truths; that is, a woman more complex than Yu's besotted imaginings.

But Biblical verses alone do not a drama make: A villain is also necessary. "Love Exposure" has a great one in Koike (Sakura Ando), a wily leader in a loony cult called Zero Church who takes more than a missionary's interest in Yu — especially after he falls for Yoko.

Always wearing white and carrying her pet green parakeet, Koike is seductive, manipulative, ruthless. But like Yu and Yoko, she is not quite the two-dimensional cartoon she first seems. As a child she was violently abused by her father, until she came to hate all men. But she falls for the pure-hearted (if perverted) Yu.

"She's really the weakest character in the film," explains Sono. "She can't express her feelings because of the way she was raised."

But for all its layers of character and theme, "Love Exposure" is less knotty art than easy-to-digest entertainment. There are plenty of laughs, many of which are supplied by Akiko Watanabe as the priest's blithely devout, daffily hypersexed lover. There is also a terrific score that includes everything from Ravel's "Bolero" to an opening theme song by the psychedelic pop band Yura Yura Teikoku.

For those who know Sono's early indie films, with their solemn ironies and minimalist emotions, the journey to "Love Exposure" may seem caterpillar-to-butterfly extreme. For Sono, however, it's less a change than a coming out.

"Those early films were like school graduation projects: They were a kind of learning experience for me," he explains. "But now I'm through with the New Wave. I'm making the kind of films I liked as a kid. I'm enjoying myself."

(February 6, 2009, "The Japan Times")

Sion Sono interview 2: "Tokyo Vampire Hotel"

Vampires have been staples of Western pop culture since Bram Stoker published his best-selling novel "Dracula" in 1897. But with the five hit "Twilight" films (2008-2012) they became hot again as millions of teenaged girls (and not a few of their mothers) thrilled to the romance of the human teen Bella (Kirsten Stewart) and the ageless vampire Edward (Robert Pattinson).

To the surprise of no one, Japan's entertainment industry has come up with its own version of vampires, just it has with many other Western pop culture phenomena.

But the nine-episode vampire series Amazon Japan announced last April, which its Amazon Prime service starts streaming on June 16, is utterly unlike "Twilight." The story: A vampire clan holes up in an impregnable hotel, with trapped humans as a food source, as civilization collapses outside its doors.

A terrified young woman, Manami (Ami Tomite), ends up inside the hotel, though she finds a defender in the mysterious K (single-named Kaho) and her cohorts, vampires from a rival clan. A Japanese version of Edward is nowhere in sight.

The series creator and, for all but two episodes, scriptwriter and director is Sion Sono. Since his breakout hit, the 2001 shocker "Suicide Club," veteran maverick Sono has moved from the indie fringes to the industry heights, while winning fans abroad for such films as "Love Exposure" (2009), "Tokyo Tribe" (2014) and "Tag" (2015).

Elements from these and other Sono films are found in "Tokyo Vampire Hotel," from the Christian imagery in the set designs and the classical music on the soundtrack ("Love Exposure") to the battling clans ("Tokyo Tribe") and full-bore chase scenes ("Tag") with Manami running frantically through Tokyo streets and vampires in close pursuit.

Speaking to "The Japan Times" in a Daikayama recording studio, a haggard-looking Sono – tired perhaps a long day of media interviews – says the series "is not a big change from my movies." "But of course a drama series is a drama series, so it's a little different," he adds. "You can do detail that you can't do so easily in films."

Sono has scripted and directed series before, including the six-part comedy/fantasy series "Everyone Is Psychic" that TV Tokyo broadcast in 2013. "Each episode of that show was a stand-alone, so it was easy to write," he comments. "But ('Tokyo Vampire Hotel') has a storyline that continues all the way through – that was really tough. On the plus side, I had more freedom."

"There are a lot of things you can't do on television," he explains. "But (with this series) it's totally different. On ('Everyone Is Psychic') I got yelled at a lot by the TV network. Not so with Amazon – they weren't very strict with their rules."

Amazon also gave Sono a free hand in casting. He decided to star Kaho, who had worked with him on the "Everyone Is Psychic" series but had never played an action role, as the hard-charging vampire K. "I thought it would be boring to do the same kind of thing with her she had always done," he says. "I wanted to show her in a different light."

The idea for the series was Sono's though he collaborated with Tomohiro Kubo and Daisuke Matsuo, who each scripted and directed one episode. The show, Sono admits, is not an obvious winner. "Vampires are not so famous in Japan, not so popular," he explains. "The 'Twilight' films were flops here and American vampire TV series all failed in Japan. So, basically, vampires don't work in Japan, but I want to do (the series) anyway."

Sono's fascination with vampires goes back to his boyhood, when he became a fan of the Hammer studio's vampire films, starting with the 1958 cult classic "Dracula" starring Peter Cushing and Christopher Lee. "I wasn't interested in Japanese ghosts and I never much liked J Horror," he adds. Why vampires specifically? "They're really sexy," Sono says, smiling for the first time. "They're unlike other monsters that way."

He denies, though, that his heavy vampire viewing influenced "Tokyo Vampire Hotel." "I didn't want images from all the (vampire) films I'd seen overlapping with (the series)," he says. "I didn't want to anyone to feel I was imitating."

While letting his imagination run free, Sono insisted on a certain authenticity. Since vampires originally came from Romania, he reasoned, he had to shoot there and Amazon agreed. The series features Dracula's Castle, the Salina Turda salt mines and other sites in Transylvania, Romania, where Sono and his crew filmed for five days. "If didn't film in Romania, the series wouldn't have any power," Sono says. "I had to do it. Just shooting in Tokyo would have been no good."

The seeds for the unusual shoot were planted when Sono flew to Romania last May for a retrospective of his films at the Transilvania (note: local spelling) International Film Festival. "I went to Dracula Castle and other places and knew I wanted to film there. So the locations came first. All the places I saw ended up in the script."

The Romanian shoot, as well as the elaborate hotel set (constructed in Tokyo), would have been impossible on a typical TV budget, Sono admits. "We could do it because it was Amazon Prime," he adds. "It really could have been a film, but since it's based on an original story, it would have been hard to raise the money. But if you do a drama series with Amazon Prime, you get plenty of money to make a set like that."

His script, he insists, was also faithful to Romanian history, at least in outline. "There was a (Matthias) Corvinus who actually fought with Dracula (AKA Vlad the Impaler). Corvinus imprisoned Dracula and shut him up underground. So I took a hint from that and had the Dracula clan shut up underground in the series. With that as a backdrop, I constructed my story."

"But the real Dracula was only a prisoner for three years," he adds. "In the series the Dracula clan is kept underground forever."

And Sono smiles again.

(June 14, 2017, "The Japan Times")

Suzuki Seijun interview (Conducted with Mamiko Kawamoto)

Seijun Suzuki was just about to leave for Cannes when I interviewed him with Mamiko Kawamoto at the offices of Nippon Herald Films, which is co-distributing "Princess Raccoon." He was using an oxygen tank — he has been ailing of late — but was still his usual self, quick with a quip and honest to a fault.

Mark Schilling (MS): Were you influenced at all by the "Princess Raccoon" films of Keigo Kimura — or did you try to do something different?

Seijun Suzuki (SS): Those "Princess Raccoon" films of Kimura's exist, of course. It may be strange to call mine a remake, but if those films didn't exist, mine would have never gotten off the ground. I said I wanted to shoot ("Princess Raccoon") about twenty years ago, but you should think about a movie from the moment you decide to do it, not before. It's stupid to be mulling it over for twenty years. When you realize that it's not going to happen, you should forget about it. If you get lucky and someone says "let's do it" — that's when you should start thinking.

Mamiko Kawamoto (MK): Why couldn't you make the film when you first wanted to?

SS: There wasn't enough money. After I made "Mirage Theater" ("Kagerozara," 1981), I talked with the producer about what we should do next. We discussed making "Princess Raccoon." We even had a screenplay and were ready to go, but we weren't able to find enough money to make it the way we wanted. Computer graphics were ridiculously expensive back then — so we gave up.

MS: I heard you were only able to get the film underway after Zhang Ziyi came on board.

SS: That's right. That's the way Japanese films are now — if you don't have a star, nothing happens. She liked my films so she agreed to appear. I'm thankful for that.

MS: She speaks Chinese in the film and her lover (Joe Odagiri) speaks Japanese. The film seems to be saying that love is something you express with, not words, but feelings.

SS: That's right — it's a love expressed through emotion only. They know they love each other through their feelings for each other, not words. They know from the facial expressions and so on.. The fact that they don't understand each other's language adds a nice flavor to the film — the flavor of miso. (laughs)

MK: The songs are an important element. How was Zhang Ziyi's singing of the Japanese lyrics?

SS: That was a problem. (laughs) At first I wondered what I could do. She was singing by rote memorization, without understanding the meaning. There was no way she could really get into the feeling of the lyrics. But with practice she ended up being pretty good. I was relieved. (laughs)

MS: You use various genres of music, even rap. It's like a history of Japanese pop music. (laughs)

SS: It's a hodgepodge isn't it? (laughs) I suppose you could call it a history of Japanese pop music. That's the contribution of the composer.

MK: The story is not just a romance with happy ending. The princess has to fight for a forbidden love — that is, love with a human being. How did you come up with that particular story?

SS: It the "Snow Princess" ("Yuki Hime") story. The basic idea is that of love blooming after the lovers die. Both the man and the woman are dead. Then they come back to life and kiss for the first time. That's a bit different from the love stories we've had till now, wouldn't you say?

MS: You told me before that your job as a director is to make everyone feel relaxed and positive. Was that true on the shoot of "Princess Raccoon" as well?

SS: The director's job is to create a good atmosphere. I think it's his role to liven up the atmosphere, so that the shooting goes smoothly.

MS: Given that it's a musical, did you have a lot of rehearsals?

SS: No, none. Miss Zhang was on a tight schedule. She had to practice before she came to the set. After she arrived on the set we got right down to business — one take.

MK: You didn't shoot any retakes?

SS: Hardly any. If you fail, you fail — that's all right. It's enough if you capture the actor's charisma on the screen. It's doesn't matter that much if their singing is good or bad. As long as you capture what they have to offer, they can be as bad as they want. Fortunately, those two turned out to passable singers.

MS: You had at least one great singer — Hibari Misora. How did you happen to use her — or rather her digitalized image?

SS: I wanted to cast the most beautiful woman in Japan for that role, but she couldn't fit us into her schedule. I was getting desperate when my producer had the idea of using Misora. She's the number one Japanese singer, so I didn't have any objections. Actually, I didn't think that her office would say OK, but the producer won out. He was the one with the idea.

MK: Didn't you have to spend a lot of extra money on the CG scenes with Misora?

SS: We could only use six CG cuts in "Pistol Opera" (2001). When I asked why, I was told that it was a matter of money. But the producer I have now told me I could use as many (CG cuts) as I wanted (in "Princess Raccoon"). CG has gotten a lot cheaper. That's why we were able to make the film.

MK: The scene of the two lovers in the irises really impressed me. Was that done with CG? Also, how did you communicate the sort of image you wanted to the actors?

SS: It was all CG — that's the only way we could have done it. That was a tough scene to do. It's raining and in the background is a Japanese-style painting — that's what I told the actors. But they had no idea how the background was going to be used. Even I didn't know, when I was actually shooting, exactly how it would look on the screen. That's what bothers me about CG.

MS: You tried various things in this film for the first time — how happy were you with the results?

SS: I thought it turned out pretty well. It's not really all that different (from my previous films). I don't think I shot it any differently — I just shot it the way I always do.

MS: What sort of musicals or film music do you like yourself?

SS: I like films where one of my favorite actresses is singing, someone like Mieko Takamine.

MK: I like the sort of charming, sexy, voluptuous women who appear in your films, but Zhang Ziyi's Raccoon Princess is more of a cute, cheerful, energetic type.

SS: No matter how much you tell a director to bring out an actress's sex appeal, if she doesn't have it to begin with, it's impossible. Back in the old days, they'd say that Isuzu Yamada just had to stand (in front of a camera) to look sexy. It had nothing to do with the way she walked. Young actresses now don't have that sort of sex appeal, I'm sorry to say.

MS: I'm sure that when fans heard you were making a period drama, a lot of them were expecting sword-fighting scenes — but you didn't give them any. (laughs)

SS: I had to disappoint them. (laughs) Sword-fighting (in Japanese films) is like buyo (Japanese dance) — it's a kind of dance. Dancing and sword-fighting are the same.

MK: You're going to be 82 soon — we'd like to congratulate you on your birthday.

SS: What's to congratulate? Look at me — I'm a mess. (laughs)

(May 25, 2005, "The Japan Times")

Interview with Yojiro Takita and Yasuhiro Mase

The Japanese film industry now turns out about 400 titles annually, but in a given decade only a few Japanese filmmakers win major international awards — including the biggest of all: the Oscars. One was anime auteur Hayao Miyazaki, whose 2001 megahit "Spirited Away" received an Academy Award for Best Animated Feature Film. Now there have been another — Yojiro Takita, whose 2008 drama "Departures" ("Okuribito") won a Best Foreign Language Film Oscar at the 81st Academy Awards.

I met Takita and "Departures" producer Yasuhiro Mase at the Yokohama Film Festival, where "Departures" won prizes for Best Picture, Best Director and Best Supporting Actress. Smoking one cigarette after another with a long plastic holder, Takita spoke in quick, nervous, if affable, bursts.

"I'm happy and honored," Takita told me — probably the 100th time he had said this to the media since the nominations for this weekend's Academy Awards were announced on Jan. 22. The prizes at Yokohama were among nearly 60 local accolades showered on Takita's film about Daigo, an out-of-work cellist who finds a new calling as a nokanshi — a professional who cleans and clothes corpses for funerals. The first was a Grand Prix at the Montreal World Film Festival last September, followed by a sweep of domestic prizes, including Best Picture, Best Director and Best Screenplay in "Kinema Junpo" magazine's annual critics' poll, whose film awards are the oldest and most prestigious in Japan.

Getting by far the most media attention, though, was the Oscar — "Departures" was the first Japanese film to be nominated for Best Foreign Language Film since Yoji Yamada's 2003 samurai drama "The Twilight Samurai" ("Tasogare Seibei"). Since the start of this award in 1947, only four Asian and three Japanese films have ever won it, beginning with Akira Kurosawa's 1951 classic "Rashomon."

Born in 1955 in Toyama Prefecture, Takita rose up through the ranks of Japan's then-massive erotic-film industry, directing a popular series of porn comedies about commuter-train molesters. In 1985, he made his first straight feature, the black comedy "Comic Magazine" ("Comic Zasshi Nanka Iranai"), but his first big hit was "The Yen Family" ("Kimurake no Hitobito"). Scripted by Nobuyuki Isshiki, this 1988 indie comedy about an avaricious family cleverly skewered bubble-era excesses.

Takita made five more comedies with Isshiki, but his career took a more serious — and mainstream — turn with "The Secret" ("Himitsu"), a 1999 weeper about a high-school girl (Ryoko Hirosue) whose soul enters her mother's body when both are involved in a traffic accident. The film was a box-office success in Japan and later remade by Vincent Perez as "Si j'etais toi."

In the current decade, Takita has tried various genres, from period fantasy (the two "The Yin Yang Master" [Onmyoji] films in 2001 and 2003) to samurai swashbuckler "When the Last Sword is Drawn" ("Mibugishi-den," 2003) and youth drama "The Battery" ("Batteri," 2007), but more with the local mass audience than critical prizes in mind.

In September of 2006, Takita agreed to direct "Departures." Star Masahiro Motoki had first had an idea for a film about nokanshi nearly seven years earlier and finally sold his pitch to producers Toshiaki Nakazawa and Yasuhiro Mase, who proposed the project to Takita. "I thought there was something different and interesting (about this film) when I first read the proposal."

"I had never seen this sort of material before," he said. "But in choosing all my films I find something to be interested in — so it wasn't unusual in that regard. It was hard to imagine how it would do commercially, though."

Takita filmed "Departures" in the winter of 2007, with Tsutomu Yamazaki playing Daigo's grizzled, but supportive, funeral-home boss and Ryoko Hirosue as Daigo's much younger wife Mika, who is at first appalled by his new profession, but comes to understand it. Working from a script by Kundo Koyama, Takita leavened the film's serious drama with touches of his trademark humor, including a memorable opening scene when the hero discovers that the young woman he is preparing for her last rites was really a transvestite.

"It's not easy, getting the right balance between drama and comedy (with this sort of story) — one mistake can throw everything off," commented Mase, who first worked with Takita on "Secret." "But Takita was able to do that well in the delicate world of this film — that's what makes him so special."

Released in Japan last September, "Departures" became a favorite with not only critics but also audiences, recording more than 2.6 million admissions and earning more than ¥3 billion at the box office. These are astounding figures for a Japanese film not based on a popular TV show, anime, manga or novel, and whose subject matter is fraught with cultural taboos.

"It's really hard to know how well a film of this sort will do at the box office until it opens," Takita said. "As for why it's done so well . . . it's a little bit strange for me to be analyzing this, ha ha . . . but I think the people who saw it understood it and told their friends about it. In other words, it was a word-of-mouth success, which is something I'm happy about."

Takita felt from the beginning, though, that "Departures" had the potential to be an extraordinary film with "a positive message."

"The hero is someone who had never had to make choices about his life," he explained. "From the time he was small his life had been decided for him by others. It's the story of how he grows as a human being and discovers his own sense of values."

It's also about how Daigo and his young wife, who at first sees his new profession as both icky and low status, come to better know each other and, in Takita's words, "find love and hope." Initially, however, Mika was supposed to be about the same age as Daigo — that is, their late 30s (Motoki is now 44) — but the search for a suitable actress came up blank. Then Takita suggested the younger Hirosue, who had starred as a teenager in "Secret" — and proposed her for the role to Mase.

"In the beginning (Daigo and Mika) are somewhat naive — they don't know a lot about the world," Takita explained. "Then they are faced with a crisis and have to deal with it — and in the process, grow as people. For that reason, I thought that a younger actress would be better — she would be better able to show that change.

"Also, Hirosue has a wide range. I saw that when I directed her in 'Secret,' where she played a mother as well as a high-school and college student, when she was still in her teens."

But the film's center is Motoki, who rose to fame as a singer with boy-band Shibugakitai in the early 1980s but has since developed a career as a serious actor, working with such leading directors as Masayuki Suo, Shinya Tsukamoto and Takashi Miike. As the nokanshi, Motoki expresses not only a musician's grace and precision, but compassion and respect for the deceased by attitude and gesture.

"More important than the way an actor says his lines are his expressions," Takita commented. "It's really difficult to get that sort of thing right — there are so many ways to see a character. What's good about Motoki is his transparency; he lets you see into his (character's) thinking and behavior."

What are the chances of "Departures" landing an Oscar? Takita would rather not speculate, but Mase noted that the film, with its upbeat story of an unemployed middle-aged man finding a new life, has zeitgeist appeal.

"The whole world is in a recession now," he said. "The timing is right."

(February 20, 2009, "The Japan Times")

189

Yuki Tanada interview: new film sees the humor in societal changes

The Japanese women directors who have been gaining attention in the past two decades, beginning with frequent Cannes invitee Naomi Kawase, tend to be serious types, understandably. Their struggle for respect and recognition in a male-dominated industry is difficult enough — and goofy comedies are usually not going to make it easier.

Yuki Tanada is one such director. "I'm always serious about my work," she tells me in a recent interview about her new film "My Dad and Mr. Ito" ("Otosan to Ito-san").

And yet the first feature of this multi-talented writer, director and actress, 2004's "Moon and Cherry" ("Tsuki to Cheri"), was a lubricious comedy about the members of a college porn-writing club. Also, most of her subsequent films have their laugh-out-loud moments, including the two I programmed for the Udine Far East Film Festival — "Romance" ("Round Trip Heart," 2015) and "One Million Yen Girl" ("Hyakuman-en to Nigamushi Onna," 2008). Like it or not, Tanada has a comic gift that sets her apart from many of her filmmaking contemporaries, male or female.

Based on a novel by Hinako Nakazawa, "My Dad and Mr. Ito" is also in this line: A gloomy 34-year-old part-time bookstore clerk Aya (Juri Ueno) is living with an easy-going 54-year-old man, the titular Ito (Lily Franky), when her cranky 74-year-old father (Tatsuya Fuji) suddenly shows up at their apartment and announces he is going to move in. This is a set up for comedy — and Tanada takes immediate advantage of it. As dad bluntly grills his daughter and Ito about their lives, the former steams and the latter blandly grins.

Instead of turning into a gag fest, however, the film unfolds as a penetrating, affectionate examination of not only the fraught relationship of its central trio, but the various problems they face — from aging alone to living on the economic margins — which reflect larger social currents.

Tanada also had a personal reason for wanting to make the film.

"My parents are getting older — they're in their 70s. They can't move around as well as they did when they were younger, and I have to figure out how to face this reality," she explains. "My generation are the children of the baby boomers, so our parents make up a large part of the population. And now we children of that generation are facing our parents' deaths. We can't run away from that."

Nakazawa's novel, she continues, doesn't dwell on the darker side of this issue: "It doesn't portray this serious social problem heavily and gloomily." she says. "It has a light touch, and that's its charm."

Even so, the novel and film's main character, Aya, is hardly free of guilt.

"She says that if her father dies she wouldn't be able to cry," Tanada says. "Their relationship isn't so terrible, but it's not so close either, so Aya feels she is a heartless daughter. 'I probably would cry more if my cat died,' she says."

This attitude is not limited to Aya, the director adds: "The theme of many films today is 'how kids loathe their parents.' "

"They feel their childhood has been damaged because of them," she continues. "Parents may have meant well, but they were always telling their kids what to do and what not to do, so many people grew up disliking them."

The character of Aya herself, meanwhile represents a problem of another sort: The large cohort of Japanese who, into their 30s and beyond, have yet to find steady, full-time employment, let alone start a family or otherwise join the traditional adult world.

"I think her generation — she is 34 — is experiencing what is called an 'extreme employment Ice Age' (shushoku cho-hyogaki)" says Tanada. "They had a very hard time getting employed in the first place."

Knowing what he does about Aya and Ito's straitened circumstances (Ito is employed as a school cafeteria worker, hardly a high-paying occupation), why does Dad one-sidedly decide to stay with them? Sheer cussedness is one possible explanation, but Tanada has another: "He used to live with his grandfather, grandmother and other family members as a child, but now that he's become their (his grandparents') age there aren't so many family members to live with," she says. "That is a big difference."

One of those members is Aya's wishy-washy big brother, whose whiny wife demanded Dad's exit, precipitating his flight to Aya.

Dad, it appears, would rather sleep on the streets than return to his son, but finally realizes that Aya's place offers no permanent refuge either. He comes up with his own surprising solution to the housing problem, one that hinges on the kindly, if mysterious, Mr. Ito.

Not to give away anything, but the charged family conference that results plays out with Tanada's by-now-familiar combination of pointed observation and wry humor, with a twist the film has been building up to from the beginning.

Rather than remake the story in her own directorial image, Tanada says she "tried to stay faithful to the novel." But, she adds, "I (also) wanted to express the story in a way only a movie can. With writing you can reach the reader by going into detail, but with a movie you can't simply voice-over everything with narrative, so emotions have to be expressed through the actors' performances. In that sense it's hard to be faithful."

She gives an example: In a shot taken from behind Dad, who is sitting alone on a park bench, his slumped posture says more about his loneliness that his words ever could.

"Tatsuya Fuji's back makes him so expressive in portraying the father," Tanada explains. "The book describes Aya's feelings as she looks at her father's back, but in the movie I tried to do it more subtly."

And, I should add, powerfully — or is that my own back I'm seeing, in the not so distant future?

(September 17, 2016, "The Japan Times")

Toshiaki Toyoda Interview

You made "Unchain" with the same company, Little More Films, that made Pornostar.
Yes, but this time I used an inexpensive digital camera and, instead of a low budget, I had no budget (laughs). My own labor was free of course — I spent about five years working on it.

What got you started?
A friend invited me to a bout featuring a kick boxer named Garuda Tetsu. When I went I was immediately attracted by Garduda's style of fighting and became friends with him. From him I heard about Unchain Kaji, Nishibayashi and Nagaishi. I also heard about the attack on the Kamarasaki labor exchange and thought it would be interesting (to make a film about them).

Were you interested in martial arts before you started filming?
I've liked martial arts for a long time, particularly pro wrestling. (laughs) I've been a big fan of Antonio Inoki since I was a kid.

Did you have any idea of a story line when you starred filming? What made you think these four guys were worth a full-length documentary?
They were very appealing in a human sense. It was a kind of instinct or premonition, if you will, but I thought I could make something interesting with them.

I didn't sense much emotional distance between you and your subjects — you filmed them from an extremely close angle.
I don't know whether that's the best way to film, but it was the only way for me. First I had to become their friend, then I could start shooting. A lot of documentary filmmakers keep their distance from beginning to end. I felt like I was standing in the ring with them.

This was your first documentary film.
I never thought that I wanted to film a documentary. In fact, I don't really think of this film as a documentary — to me it's an entertainment film. The usual documentary is made strictly from a journalistic viewpoint. "Unchain" is not that kind of film – it's a drama with a story. It's my way for searching for a great documentary.

Were you influenced by any documentary filmmakers?
There wasn't anything quite like "Unchain" out there when I started filming. But in terms of documentary filmmakers, I suppose one (influence) was Shinsuke Ogawa, who spent years making documentaries (about rural Japan), living with the farmers and growing crops. I really like that kind of approach, and wanted to follow his example, but the film I made turned out to be totally different. (laughs)

It not so much a boxing film as a drama about these four guys and their friendship for each other.
It didn't have to be about boxers at all. I used to be a shogi player — the film could have been about shogi as well. But watching people punch each other is more interesting. (laughs)

But you also have these very human moments, as when Kaji gets out of the hospital and meets his friend Nagaishi again.
I wanted to film that kind of thing — the fact that friendship is not just nice words, but a tie that binds you in a deep way. These guys actually said a lot of nasty things about each other, but at the same time they accepted each other. They had the kind of ties that can't be easily broken. Whatever their differences, they're all fighters sharing a certain experience — and they respect that in each other.

But the film also has its lighter moments — as you said, these guys tell stories and crack jokes about each other.
That's essential. Without the comedy, it would be too sad and serious and real. In Osaka everyone loves to laugh and everyone tells funny stories. Osaka people think it's cool to make others laugh.

You couldn't have made this film in Tokyo?
No way. Osaka is the only place that would allow a guy like Unchain Kaji to act so crazy. In Tokyo they would have caught him and put him in a hospital in no time flat. But in Osaka there are a lot of guys like him running around. (laughs)

(June 6, 2001, "The Japan Times")

Shinya Tsukamoto interview 1: Tsukamoto's great escape

Although his onscreen characters usually range from the demonic to the neurotic, in person Shinya Tsukamoto is the picture of gentle-spirited, well-mannered sanity. One can imagine him as the ideal maitre d' for an exclusive club, able to soothe even the most savage millionaire.

"Vital" is a love story — but one that deals extensively with human dissection. That's something I hadn't seen before in a film. (laughs)
That's right — it's a kind of first. (laughs)

I was surprised by the religious aspect. The students even perform a kind of funeral service for the cadavers at the end of the course.
I'm not religious at all, but it may seem the film is talking about the world after death. I don't want it to be seen that way, though. A girl called Ryoko dies in the film. She and her lover Hiroshi play at strangling each other — she doesn't seem to care very much whether she lives or dies. Then she's in a car crash and she understands what death is and how important life is.

We're living in a kind of virtual reality in Tokyo — it's like being in a dream. At the beginning of the film both Hiroshi and Ryoko are in the world of dreams.

When you're in a dream, you don't feel pain when you're pinched. But a traffic accident is painful, isn't it? (laughs) It's the real thing — it's not a dream. You're afraid you might die. You know that this body of yours is a thing of nature.

Have you ever been in a traffic accident?
No — I'm living in a dream too. (laughs)

I have — I wasn't badly injured, but I did feel that time had stopped, as you show in the film. (laughs)
You got that right. (laughs) People who have been in traffic accidents feel that way, don't they — they lose contact with time.

Most of your films deal, in one way or another, with the human body.
That's right. I've changed a bit, though — I used to favor the body more, but now I feel both the heart and body are equally important. In my previous films I was saying that this body of ours is not a dream in the concrete jungle — it really exists. I wanted to show the feeling when you get hit in boxing. That pain is not a dream — you know you're alive!

Now, though, I'm looking beyond the body, to nature itself. I'm no longer restricting myself to the city. It may be my age. I don't want to be alone in the city, suffering — I feel like getting out into nature.

I want to make a film about experiencing nature, but I haven't actually experienced it myself yet, so I can't write a script. Instead I'd first like to make films on the theme of the city, the body and nature, like the latest one. Almost into nature — but not quite.

"Vital" could have easily been a horror film.
That's right. It's got a typical obake eiga [ghost movie] story. It's about a guy who loves a woman in the world of the dead and gets closer to that world in the course of the film.

Given the popularity of Japanese horror abroad now, you could probably make a big hit in Hollywood.
I've had discussions with people in Hollywood, but nothing has worked out. If I could make something my way and Americans like it, then I'd like to do it. Horror movies are hot now, so I'd like to try one.

What about a remake of "Vital?"

That would be tough — but it would be nice if someone did it. I'd like to do it myself, even if I had to go abroad.

Do you ever feel that you're competing with the impact of your early films?

Not really — I'm just trying to do the best I can with every film I make. I'm happy that my early films had an impact — but they were so strange that Japanese movie people wouldn't talk to me. They all hated me in the beginning. (laughs) "Who is this guy?" That was the attitude. It took some time before people came around.

If I had started out making films that everyone liked, then made strange films, they would have supported me. Instead they hated me from the beginning, so even though I tried hard to make good films after that, hardly anyone supported me.

The opposite is true abroad. They love you in Europe. Do you ever wonder about that gap?

I really don't know the reason. I don't know why they like my films so much abroad. I don't know why they dislike them so much in Japan. (laughs) All I can do is make them the best I can.

(December 22, 2004, "The Japan Times")

Shinya Tsukamoto interview 2: war in the jungle and war in Japan

Actor and director Shinya Tsukamoto often takes violence to strange extremes. In his first film, the 1989 horror "Tetsuo" ("Tetsuo: The Iron Man"), a businessman accidentally kills a crazed metal fetishist (played by Tsukamoto himself) with his car and, becoming "infected" by his victim, horrifically transforms into an ambulant pile of death-dealing scrap metal. The follow-ups "Tetsuo II: Body Hammer" (1992) and "Tetsuo: The Bullet Man" (2010) were made in a similarly hyperviolent style.

So his new film "Nobi" ("Fires on the Plain"), based on Shohei Ooka's semi-autobiographical novel about Japanese soldiers in the Philippines during the closing days of World War II, may seem like an uncharacteristic departure from much of his work to date — until you see Tsukamoto speak in person.

Following a screening of "Fires on the Plain" at the Foreign Correspondents' Club of Japan on July 14, 55-year-old Tsukamoto was the soul of politeness as he answered the audience's occasionally awkward questions, and passionate when the subject of Japan's current drift toward nationalism and militarism was raised.

"When I was growing up (in the postwar period), people generally believed that war was something evil," he said at the Q&A session. That attitude, he noted, changed during the two decades that he struggled to complete "Fires on the Plain" — and not for the better. Though he once assumed that the film's anti-war stance would be universally shared by the local audience, he now feels "a sense of crisis that (Japan) is quickly heading in the direction of war."

"I thought I had to make this film now, more than ever," he added.

That urgency informs every frame. Tsukamoto plays a sick, starving soldier who, after his unit is destroyed in an air raid, wanders the countryside with fellow survivors in search of food and discovers, to his horror, that some have turned to cannibalism. The same shocking motif was present in the Kon Ichikawa 1959 film that was also based on Ooka's book, but "it was not central to mine," Tsukamoto said.

When he interviewed former soldiers who had served in the Philippines, they told him they had more pressing matters to consider than the morality of eating human flesh — namely filling their stomachs. Eventually, they were reduced to eating maggots in other soldiers' wounds and sometimes the flesh those maggots were clinging to.

"In those circumstances," Tsukamoto confessed, "I might eat that flesh. But we should never allow that situation to happen again."

When I interviewed him after the Q&A session, he spoke of the "sense of mission" that drove him and his staff to make the film, despite difficult conditions and a micro-budget. Money was so tight that volunteer extras doubled as equipment carriers. And the sides of a military transport truck that figured in one key scene were constructed of cardboard.

Completed in June 2014, "Fires on the Plain" had its world premiere at the Venice International Film Festival in September that year.

"I didn't aim to specifically release the film on the 70th anniversary of the war's end, but it ended up happening that way by necessity," Tsukamoto explains. "By the 70th anniversary most of the veterans (in Japan) will be over 90. We are losing these precious memories of how painful war is. So I needed to make this film before they die out and Japan forgets the lessons of war even more."

To impress viewers, especially young ones, with the depth of that pain, Tsukamoto filmed his hero behaving with anything but standard war-movie heroism. In one scene he panics and shoots a young Filipino couple who intrude on a deserted church where he is sleeping. Shortly after, he throws his rifle into a river.

"I would never feature a heroic (soldier) in a film about war," Tsukamoto says. "Many great Japanese war movies are told from the viewpoint of the victims but in this film I wanted to tell the story from the viewpoint of the soldiers, that is, the perpetrators. What is terrifying is not that they die; it's how they lose their humanity and become killers once they get into a war."

"They're shocked," he says of audience reactions to prerelease screenings of the film around Japan. "People tend to start talking about it a few days after they've seen it, when the shock has worn off."

Not all, however. One elderly woman, whose husband was a WWII veteran, approached him after a screening.

"She thanked me for making the film," he says. "A lot of mothers have come to see it," he adds. "They have strong feelings about the subject matter because they don't want their own children to be drafted. They want a world without war. What made me the happiest, though, were the young people who told me how anti-war they felt after watching the film."

I ask if he thinks Japan will repeat the mistakes it made in World War II.

"It's a shame that Japan is moving toward war again considering that we have a 70-year legacy of peace," Tsukamoto says. "That's totally wrong."

(July 22, 2015, "The Japan Times")

Koji Wakamatsu interview 1

Walking to Koji Wakamatsu's office near Shinjuku Gyoen park in the broiling August sun, I was expecting a place appropriately dark and bohemian. Instead the building of Wakamatsu Production was painted a cheery yellow and, inside, looked neat, new and organized. Wakamatsu himself presented me with a yellow name card — and looked surprisingly chipper for a man who had recently fought lung cancer to a standstill. But the angry sixties rebel in him was still alive and well — his yellow was not, and probably never will be, mellow.

"Cycling Chronicles: Landscapes the Boy Saw" struck me as a kind of experiment for you, a personal film.

I don't think I've changed that much over the decades, but I'm getting older and with this film I wanted to leave behind a kind of testimony. Through this seventeen-year-old boy I said a little of what I wanted to say about where Japan is heading.

The type of incident you describe in the film is not so rare.

There have been a lot of incidents like that in Japan. I researched about thirty or forty. The kids involved tend to be really well-behaved and smart and get good marks. They nearly all respect their parents. The boy in the film fits (that profile) the best of all.

When I was seventeen I was a typical kid — I rebelled against my parents. I think that's what youth is all about. On the other hand when kids respect their parents and do whatever it takes to please them, when they study hard and run along the rails laid down by their parents, their stress starts to build. That stress has reached a bursting point today. When kids are fourteen, fifteen, sixteen, seventeen anything little thing can set them off. And when they explode, kids often go for their parents, who are the people closest to them. Or if not their parents, they go for their friends — and then they commit crimes.

But the ones who have build this nation and this world are all adults. And adults are only thinking about making money. If they're doing all right money-wise, they're satisfied.

I've seen piles of bodies in wartime — in a camp in Palestine where there had been a mass slaughter. Somehow we have to make kids understand the horror of that sort of war, so it won't happen again. In Japan we've been telling kids (about war) for a long time, but now people who can talk about that sort of thing are dying off. That why, in the film, I had an old man and old woman talk about their wartime experiences. I don't think the boy knows anything (about what they are saying). One reason he doesn't know is that we artists are no longer talking about war the way we used to. And not only artists, but journalists and other people with the ability to communicate have to keep telling young people (about war), but the number who do is getting smaller. Films here are really just copying Hollywood — a lot of them are just showing explosions and people getting killed. In that sense, porno is better. (laughs)

At the same time, you don't explain much in the film, at least on the surface.

I don't explain at all. So the audience has to interpret it for themselves. I want people who see the film to go out afterwards with their friends to a coffee shop or bar and then argue with each other about what Wakamatsu was trying to say. There are different ways to view the film.

For example, I don't like Mt. Fuji. Everyone likes Mt. Fuji — it's a symbol of Japan for them. But for me Mt. Fuji is more like the national anthem or my father. But maybe I'm just talking big. (laughs)

Tasuku Emoto is ideal for the role — it's hard to tell what he's thinking.

You have no idea what's on his mind when he's listening to the old man, the old woman and when he meets people in the village. But though you don't know what he's thinking, you do feel something. That something is what I wanted to communicate in the film.

His father is Akira Emoto so he has acting in his DNA.
He was seventeen and a senior in high school when we made the film. He was told that, if he appeared in the film, he might not get enough credits to graduate, so (the Emotos) had a family meeting. (Akira) Emoto told him that if he didn't appear and saw the film later, he would regret pasing up the chance, but it would be too late. You can't make a film twice, he said, but you can always repeat school. So Emoto told him to do what he wanted.

When you're seventeen you don't like school, right? It's more fun to go on location with a film that to go to school — so he went with us. Usually the parent would tell the kid to finish school first and and appear (in the movie) after they graduate. But Emoto told his son to do what he wanted. In that sense, he was really great.

But the ones who create the society (they live in) are all adults, who only think about making it. But kids usually go through this stage — to use an old-fashioned word, they become punks. (laughs) They become anti-social. But it's better for them to do something a little bad than to kill someone.

When you're seventeen or thereabouts, you're going to rebel against your parents — that's a given. (laughs) But these good kids who respect their parents end up exploding.

(August 10, 2005, "The Japan Times")

Koji Wakamatsu interview 2: the final days of revolutionary struggle in Japan

The West sees the turbulent era of the late 1960s and early '70s principally through the lens of its own protesters and radicals, with America's war in Vietnam the focal point of activist anger. If it thinks about East Asia in this period at all, it is usually the China of Mao and the Red Guards, who became inspirations for the Weathermen and other Western radical groups.

But as Koji Wakamatsu's docudrama "United Red Army — The Path to Asama Mountain Lodge" ("Jitsuroku Rengo Sekigun: Asama Sanso e no Michi") reminds us, Japan had its own hardcore student radicals, who moved beyond peaceful protest to outright terrorism, while conducting bloody internal purges. The Japanese Red Army (Nihon Sekigun), founded in 1971, became the most notorious of these radical groups for terrorist acts that continued for nearly two decades. Their exploits included hijacking airplanes, attacking embassies, bombing buildings and killing 26 victims and injuring 80 more at Lod Airport in Tel Aviv in May 1972. In Japan they first became widely known when five members took a hostage at the Asama Mountain Lodge in the Karuizawa resort area north of Tokyo in February 1972 and fought a pitched gunbattle with police.

Wakamatsu, a gangster-turned-filmmaker who pioneered the "pink" (soft-core erotic) genre in the early 1960s and baited the censors with his cinematic outrages, not only befriended members of the group but joined them in Palestine as a "trainee," an experience that resulted in the 1971 film "Red Army/PFLP: Declaration of World War" ("Sekigun/PFLP — Sekai Senso Sengen"). These and other contacts with the Red Army have made Wakamatsu a target of investigation by Japanese authorities, as well as an "undesirable alien" to the U.S. State Department.

But whatever his past or current political views (he now claims he is neither on the left nor right), Wakamatsu takes a rigorously distanced stance in "United Red Army," which had its international premiere at this year's Berlin Film Festival. While firmly believing, as he told "The Japan Times" at an interview in his Shinjuku office, that "only I could have made this film," he indulges in no special pleading for his former comrades. He refuses, in fact, to editorialize at all.

What he does do, with great meticulousness, using documentary materials and dramatic re-creations, is trace the origin and rise of the group, beginning with the emergence of student activism in opposition to the Japan-U.S. Security Treaty, signed in 1960, and the Japanese government's support of the United States in the Vietnam War. "I wanted to show the youths of today why such things happened, like passing on stories of war," Wakamatsu said. "Whether the actions are judged good or bad is up to each individual viewer. I didn't take sides in the movie. I just documented the paths the (radicals) followed. The rest is up to the audience."

Dramatically, the film truly gets underway in its second hour, after two radical groups merge in July 1971 to form the United Red Army (Rengo Sekigun), a group dedicated to violent revolution by any means necessary. In 1972 the group took to Japan's Southern Alps for intensive training and indoctrination. The remote, idyllic setting certainly didn't induce peace and harmony. Instead, the group's rigidly dogmatic leader, Tsuneo Mori (Go Jibiki), and his manically loyal second-in-command Hiroko Nagata (Akie Namiki) mercilessly rooted out "antirevolutionary elements" whose zeal for the cause was not sufficiently pure and absolute, and they forced them to "self confess" their sins of intellect, attitude and character.

This was a common modus operandi for the extreme left of the period, including the Chinese Red Guards, but Mori, Nagata and their allies give a uniquely Japanese spin to their inquisitions, beginning with brow-beating their victims about minor offenses against group wa (harmony or conformity). One, the cute, naive Mieko Toyama (Maki Sakai), is pilloried by the obviously envious Nagata for her good looks and "coquettish behavior" (i.e., being popular with boys). But this routine ijime (bullying) soon escalates to mass beatings, starvation, exposure and, finally, the death of 12 radicals, while others run down the mountain to escape their coming "confessions."

In filming these episodes, Wakamatsu takes a straight-ahead approach whose stark objectivity and blunt factuality (when the victims die, their names and ages appear on the screen) amplifies the horror.

As their numbers thin and the police close in, the radicals split into two groups and escape. One group is soon rounded up, while the other, consisting of five men, find refuge in an isolated mountain lodge called the Asama Sanso (Asama Mountain Lodge) and take its proprietress hostage. Soon, hundreds of police surround them and urge them to surrender, but their response is rifle fire, precipitating a 10-day standoff watched on television by the entire country. Finally, after two policemen are killed and 23 wounded, the police break into the villa and arrest the radicals.

"From the time the actual incident took place, I wanted to make a film about it," Wakamatsu said. "But it was going to be a lot of effort and I was always hearing rumors about other directors wanting to make similar films. If someone else had made a film that convinced me, there would have been no need for me to make one. But the ones I've seen (about the incident) were very different from what I had in mind. So I felt a need to make this film and communicate the truth."

Among movies taking the Sekigun and the events of 1972 as their subjects are Banmei Takahashi's 2001 film "Rain of Light" ("Hikari no Ame"), which focuses rather theatrically, if powerfully, on the torture deaths, and Masato Harada's 2002 movie "Choice of Hercules" ("Totsunyuseyo! Asama Sanso Jiken"), a commercial film that takes the viewpoint of the cops in the Asama siege — and according to Wakamatsu, is "full of lies." His own film, he says, is "about 90 percent true." He explained, "I have re-created past events in the present, so to some extent there are fictional elements."

"The situation inside the Asama wasn't known — nobody wrote about it," Wakamatsu added. "Of those on the outside, only me and (director, script writer and ex-Japanese Red Army member) Masao Adachi knew." Eight years ago Wakamatsu met Kunio Bando, the only one of the five United Red Army members involved in the siege still at large, in a forest in rural Japan. "He said they fought until the very end as a moral duty toward those who died from the purges," Wakamatsu said. "Bando told me that everyone had pledged to fight to the end. They had committed the sin of purge killings and to make amends, (they) felt they had to fight against authority, even if they had to die."

The dramatic end of the siege, with millions watching the police break-in on live television, also marked a turning point for student radicalism in Japan. "(Masaharu) Gotoda (chief of the National Policy Agency) was a smart man," reflected Wakamatsu. "He showed Japanese people the (events at) Asama for 10 days without rest, while characterizing the (United Red Army members) inside as terrorists. After the Asama Sanso incident, student movements in Japan quickly lost steam."

Now 71, Wakamatsu is at an age when most directors are mellowing out, winding down or just plain giving up. He has no plans to retire, however. "I don't have much longer," says the filmmaker, who has a fought a long, and so-far successful battle with lung cancer. "I don't know how much time I have left, so I want to shoot as many films as possible now. I'd like to shoot a normal movie next time (laughs). But I don't think any film I'm part of will end up normal."

Wakamatsu won't be returning to pink films, the genre in which he created the most celebrated of his films. "Pink films should be guerrilla movies," he explained. "They should be a hidden thing. I quit pink movies because they started to become known and everyone started to praise them. They were no longer guerrilla movies. Being a guerrilla means fighting the government with a small number of people. I'm not a Che Guevara or Fidel Castro, or anything like that, but it's no longer fun or interesting when everyone is praising that sort of thing and bringing it out into the open."

He also doesn't see any successors among the younger generation to his brand of antiestablishment cinema. "I survived as a director for 40-some years because I managed to slip in my own politics and anger while borrowing the label 'pink movie,' "he said. "But now everybody seems to have forgotten how to be angry. Their stomachs are too full (laughs). A country that's striving hard to develop tends to produce good movies. A developed country doesn't. Japan and America have nothing left to strive for, so they don't make good movies any more."

(March 20, 2008, "The Japan Times")

201

Koji Wakamatsu interview 3: "Caterpillar"

Koji Wakamatsu is living proof that a life-long rebel can thrive in Japan's go-along-to-get-along film industry. Today he is celebrated as not just another sixties survivor — he helped pioneer the "pink" (soft porn) genre in that era, while mixing in radical politics and experimental aesthetics with the sex — but a still-relevant director who has done some of his best work in his eighth decade.

Wakamatsu's epic 2007 docu-drama "United Red Army" ("Jitsuroku Rengo Sekigun: Asama Sanso e no Michi") examined the violent apotheosis of the title far-left group that in the early 1970s tortured and murdered its "deviant' members and fought a pitched battle with police, firing rifles from a Karuizawa mountain lodge. Wakamatsu, who personally knew several Red Army members, put the brutal truth on the screen with no punch pulling and no special pleading. The film not only won awards and screened widely abroad but drew audiences, despite its three-hour running time.

His latest film, the WWII homefront drama "Catepillar," has also earned acclaim, including a Best Actress prize for star Shinobu Terashima at this year's Berlin Film Festival. Though based on a story by Edogawa Rampo, a mid-20th-Century writer of the kinky and bizarre, the film is closer in spirit to Dalton Trumbo's 1971 anti-war film "Johnny Got His Gun." Like Trumbo's wounded WWI soldier, Wakamatsu's hero returns to his rural village a decorated hero, but a shell of a man, minus legs and arms, deafened and disfigured, tortured by memories of his war crimes. Instead of pity, Wakamatsu examines his hero (Keigo Kasuya) — and his outwardly dutiful but inwardly resentful wife (Terashima) with a cool, unrelenting gaze that strips away poses and exposes inner lives.

Talking about the film in the office of Wakamatsu Production— a yellow two-story building near Shinjuku Gyoen — Wakamatsu looked greyer and smaller than I remembered from our last meeting two years ago, but his fires were still burning bright, especially when he explained why he had decided to film "Catepillar".

"As much as possible I wanted to make a film that ordinary people could understand," he said. "I wanted to say that war, when you come down to it, is murder. There is no good reason for war, no matter what. Do you know how many people died worldwide in (World War II)? Sixty million! With this film I wanted make even one more person understand that."

Instead of simply looking back in anger at the human cost of Japan's militaristic past, Wakamatsu wants to warn about what he sees as dangerous tendencies in its present. "We've got Diet members who say that Japan has to rearm itself, that women are baby-making machines," he says. "We're going right back to where we were (prewar). We may go back to the old militarism again, to the days when women couldn't vote...We've got college kids now who don't know an atomic bomb was dropped on Hiroshima, students who don't even know we fought a war with America. I'm really fed up with that sort of thing. Now that such idiots are being born I want young people to see this film, to make them understand, even a little, what Japan was once like."

As strong as Wakamatsu's political views may be, "Caterpillar" is anything but simplistic anti-war propoganda. One big reason is Terashima's nuanced, uncompromising performance as the wife, who does everything expected of her as the loyal spouse of a war hero, from proudly displaying her husband medals to patiently tending to his sexual needs, but cannot hide her real feelings, from disgust at his present wretched condition to anger at his past abuses.

"While I was writing the script I never thought she would agree to appear in the film," Wakamatsu confessed. "I thought of various people (for the role of the wife), but I kept coming back to Terashima."

He approached her manager, who rejected his offer, but when she read the script, she told Wakamatsu she wanted to work with him. "The manager said no — we were a poor production company, had no make up (for her to wear), had few people, had no budget, saying she would do it alone, manager or no. "I'll do it without make-up," she said. "Oh, that's wonderful!" I thought. An ordinary actress would never say that sort of thing."

On the set, Wakamatsu didn't direct Terashima so much as allow her to unleash her natural talents. "What a great performance! It gives you goose bumps, right? That performance is not what an ordinary Japanese actress would give. Usually an actress is calculating, asking herself "Will he let me act the way

I want to?" "Will I look strange if I make this face?" They calculate how to cry — that's the usual thing, right? With Terashima there's no calculation. She acts with her feelings alone. She acts with her whole body."

Working with Terashima, he usually finished a cut in one take. "You can't give that kind of performance with two or three tests," he commented. "I'd tell her, "Once I have the camera ready, act the way you want." That's all I said to her about her role...You don't tell someone like her to act such and such a way or make such and such a face."

Just as he didn't want a typical performance from his lead actress, Wakamatsu knew from the start that he didn't want to make a typical Japanese war film. "A lot of Japanese war films are about the tokotai (the suicide or "kamikaze" units), saying how they sacrificed for the good of the country. A lot of them have a victim's mentality. "Oh, we lost, poor us!" is the mentality. But I think there's wrong on both sides in any war. In the last war Japan was like America is now. We were supposedly fighting to free Asia from the colonialism of England and France and so on, just like America is fighting to free Iraq and Afghanistan today...but when things get rough, a lot of the dead are just ordinary people."

What's the solution, if any? Wakamatsu doesn't hold out much hope for Japanese politicians ("They're idiots — all they think about it their own election"). He also thinks they're deluding themselves if they believe that allowing American bases on Okiwawa, over the protests of the Okinawans, will keep Japan safe. ("If China comes to the Japan Sea and starts drilling for oil in Japanese territory America won't say a thing. They won't do anything even if Japanese land is invaded, like Takeshima.")

"Maybe they should fight wars like soccer matches," he says, only half jokingly. "If you fight a war with soccer nobody dies. And when it ends everyone becomes friends. It would be great if everyone opposed war, everyone opposed nuclear weapons. If everyone were to get excited about that sort of thing the way they do soccer, war would disappear from the world. If Japan loses or wins to America in soccer it doesn't matter — Japan won't hate America."

But the Dutch, I countered, weren't overjoyed by Spain's win in the World Cup. "The Dutch only feel that way — 'I hate Spain!' — for the moment. They aren't going to go out and kill Spanish people. They're sorry they lost, but the next day they go out for a drink and forget about it. So let fight wars with soccer. Let's stop people from killing each other."

(August 13, 2010, "Japan Times")

Kenji Uchida interview: a prize-winning director quite happy to have a laugh

With his short-brimmed hat and carefully trimmed goatee, Kenji Uchida looks strikingly like the private investigator played by So Yamanaka in "A Stranger of Mine" ("Unmei Janai Hito").

In our interview at the headquarters of Pia — the media company whose Pia Film Festival launched his career — Uchida looked faintly bemused by the attention his success at Cannes had brought him — or was that fatigue at his umpteenth media interview for the day? His laugh, though, verged on a teenage boy's giggle — and came in reassuringly frequent bursts.

I saw the film twice — once wasn't enough (laughs). Was that your intention — to make people want to see the film again and again?

Not really. I wanted it to be easy to understand. But I'm glad you think it's a film people will want to see more than once (laughs).

Was there a specific reason for the circular story line, for not telling the story linearly, from A to Z?

I wanted to show how different people have different ways of looking at the same incident. I thought it would be interesting to show all the different points of view, one after another. That was the reason for the structure — to make the audience understand how interesting those different perspectives are. When you have an appointment with someone, you usually don't know where they they've been or what they've been up to. Perhaps a chance meeting has opened up a new world for them. In the film, an ordinary salaryman named Miyata has encounter like that. It's not all that exaggerated. It's the sort of thing that often happens in real life. I wanted the audience to see that sort of thing unfolding from God's point of view.

Speaking of God, did the audience at Cannes see the film as embodying Eastern philosophy — reincarnation and so on (laughs).

No, not that I could tell. But when Maki and Miyata are apologizing to each other over and over, the audience started laughing kind of strangely (laughs).

Do you want to stay with comedy for a while — or branch out?

I'm not so particular about the genre. But I don't want to make the sort of film that chooses its audience. In other words, films that only a select few can understand. I want to make films that anyone can understand and enjoy. I like well-made films by people like Billy Wilder and Alfred Hitchcock. Their scripts, especially, are really great. With a good script and good cast, you can't go all that wrong. Movies cost a lot of money to make. It's better to make them as perfect as you can at the script and casting stage, when they don't cost a lot of money.

Given that you spent a year writing the script you probably had a clear idea of what you wanted to see on the screen. How close did you come?

That's hard to say. The film is full of faults, but the actors gave me exactly what I wanted. So in that sense, I'm really satisfied with it. We only had two weeks to shoot and only a short time to prepare. So given all that, I'm happy with what we were able to do.

Did making this film help you to graduate from amateur to pro in your own mind?

Not really. I didn't know what I was doing. Fortunately, I had a lot of experienced staff around me who helped me a lot.

The film is not quite what people abroad think of as typically Japanese.

I was surprised that it got invited to Cannes (laughs).

I'm thinking in particular of the gang boss, Asai. He's always smiling, well-mannered — not what you would expect of a yakuza (laughs).

Yes, people at Cannes told me that they had never seen anything like Asai — he's totally different from their image of the yakuza. They found him interesting.

What are you making next? Not a comedy?

It's a suspense film, but it has comic elements. It's comic suspense.

(July 6, 2005, "The Japan Times")

Yoji Yamada interview

A director since 1961, with 77 films to his credit, Yoji Yamada, 71, is a Japanese film industry icon. His "Tora-san" series, about a wandering peddler who is forever falling in love, but never gets the girl, generated 48 hit installments — and made Yamada the most successful Japanese director of his generation. He has also won his share of prizes, both domestic and international.

His latest film, "The Twilight Samurai," has garnered the largest haul at home, including "Kinema Junpo" magazine's Best One prize — considered Japan's most prestigious. On March 7, it also won 12 Japan Academy Awards, including Best Picture and Best Director — the second-highest number ever after Masayuki Suo's 1997 "Shall We Dance?" Ironically, the film is Yamada's first-ever samurai drama — but he is now planning another.

Why did you decide to do a samurai drama, after more than 40 years of making contemporary dramas and comedies?

First of all, I liked the work of [Shuhei] Fujisawa — he wrote period fiction about the samurai and the common people. I thought I would make a film based on three of his novellas. This was about four or five years ago. Secondly, I had seen many period dramas over the years, but I wasn't satisfied with them. They were full of lies and said nothing about how the samurai really lived.

Akira Kurosawa told me that also bothered him [about the genre]. He wanted to make a realistic film about the lives of the samurai. He had a lot of trouble getting the information he needed — the materials just weren't there — so in 1954 he ended up making "Seven Samurai" — a totally different kind of film. (laughs)

Anyway, I wanted to try to make a film that would show how the samurai lived, ate, talked and felt. I thought I could understand that sort of thing — after all, these people were my ancestors.

The climactic fight scene between Hiroyuki Sanada and Min Tanaka is especially impressive. It gives a sense of the way it really might have been.

I wanted to shoot more realistic fight scenes than you see in [samurai movies], even Kurosawa's. I mean, when the bad guys have the hero surrounded, why do they always attack him one at a time, so he can pick them off? Why don't they all go for him at once? (laughs) Also, when the bad guys are cut, they die right away. In reality, it's a lot harder to kill someone in a sword fight, unless you get in a good cut. According to period accounts, samurai sword fights could go for two or three hours. They'd cut each other again and again, until they turned white — and the weaker one finally fell. That's how it was — they would slowly die of blood loss.

Also, back then women didn't usually wear the sorts of flashy clothes that you see in samurai films. They dressed more plainly. They didn't do their makeup as nicely or wear their hair as elaborately. I wanted to show that.

There have been good period dramas — Sadao Yamanaka's "Humanity and Paper Balloons" (1937) and of course Kurosawa's "Seven Samurai." When I saw those films, I was surprised. I realized that there were period dramas that you could watch just as you would contemporary dramas. Those films were my touchstones.

Even though "Twilight Samurai" is a period film, it has a lot to say about contemporary Japan — the hero deals with the same sort of social and economic turmoil that you find today.

I tried to include plot elements that present-day Japanese could relate to. When you're ordered to do something by the boss, you have to do it — or it might be the end of your job. That's something everyone can understand — and that's the kind of situation the hero faces. Some people buckle under the pressure and commit suicide. In Japan, nearly 30,000 people kill themselves every year — a lot of them men in their 40s and 50s. Some of them have been fired, some have been told to fire others. The hero deals with his situation differently, of course — but the pressure is similar.

The heroine, played by Rie Miyazawa, is also a contemporary type — when her husband beats her, she leaves him. That's not the sort of thing you see in traditional period dramas, where the woman is supposed to stick it out, no matter what.

She has a modern way of thinking, that's true. In a way, her story is a critique of the feudal system, though the film doesn't spell it out as such.

In the Edo Period (1603-1867) women weren't allowed to have their say. In the Middle Ages, Japanese women were fairly strong and made important contributions to culture, but in the Edo Period and the Meiji Era (1868-1912) women more or less disappeared from public view. Particularly in the Meiji Era, women were discriminated against. They were supposed to be impure. That way of thinking still exists — women aren't allowed to step into the sumo ring, for example.

But while injecting modern elements into the film, I tried to make it exciting. When a company employee is restructured he can't reach for a sword. (laughs) But a sword fight makes the film easier for the audience to understand. It also has more impact.

Min Tanaka, the butoh dancer who plays the hero's opponent in the climactic fight, is particularly impressive, even though it was his first film role. Did you have to give him any special training or instruction?

He had never used a sword before, so he had to practice that. He really worked hard. (laughs) Also, in butoh, the dancers hardly say anything, so he had to study how to deliver his lines as well. Fortunately, he had a good voice. He had a great death scene — only Tanaka could have done it that way. It took him two minutes to die on camera. I just told him, "Do it your way." (laughs) He had a scary face — that helped. You need a long face to be scary, like Seiji Miyaguchi in "Shichinin no Samurai." Tanaka has that kind of face.

The film was also something of a departure for Hiroyuki Sanada. Before this film, he had usually played comic roles — not many serious ones.

He had been in a lot of period dramas, but he told me he was also dissatisfied with them. He wanted to know why everything had to be so beautiful, when it wasn't like that in reality. He told me it was his dream to make this kind of film. That was encouraging.

His training in the martial arts helped a lot — I felt confident that he knew what he was doing. Real samurai stand differently, somewhat like noh actors. Not straight up, but with their hips forward a bit. They take small steps, without lifting their feet from the ground — they do that to keep the sword steady.

There's something of a period drama boom now, but unlike "Twilight Samurai" many of the new period dramas use computer graphics to create fantasy elements. They aren't about realism at all.

Yes, that kind of fantastic film is popular. Also, there are a lot of horror films now. In troubled times like these, more films like that tend to get made — fantasy and horror. People want to escape, and that's what they go for.

But "Tasogare Seibei" has done well at the box office, even though it's taken quite a different approach.

That's true, but it's drawing a different kind of audience. First of all, older people came to see it. Then they told their sons about it — men in their 30s and 40s. Then their sons saw it and told their sons about it — junior and senior high school students. (laughs) So there are three generations seeing it. That's helped it have a long run — the audience keeps changing.

It has universality — you don't need to be a period drama fan to enjoy it. The message — that you can find happiness even without a lot of material possessions — appeals to people.

Japanese are wondering what is going to happen to the country. They feel anxious — and so do I. What's going to happen to the banks? Is my money going to be there tomorrow? But at the end of "Twilight Samurai," Seibei is with his children — and as long as he has his family and they all love each other, he can go on. The audience leaves with the feeling that everything will somehow turn out all right. They're thinking, if I have something like that in my life, I can make it, even if the company goes under. That thought gives them comfort and courage.

The film is in tune with the mood in Japan now, but do you think the same will be true abroad?
That worries me — how will people from other countries react? But we're living in anxious times, when people everywhere don't know what is going to happen next. What is the Bush administration going to do? Will they start a war? That is certainly worrying. Why have things come to this pass? Why can't this be settled by the United Nations? Why do we have to have this sort of international conflict? What is going to happen if a war starts?

People from Iran and other Islamic counties who took part in February's Berlin Film Festival certainly felt this sort of anxiety. The world has come to a strange and unpleasant pass. So in that sense, I think people abroad will be able to relate to the film, even though Americans and Europeans don't feel the same economic anxiety as Japanese.

(March 16, 2003, "The Japan Times")

Mitsuo Yanagimachi interview

Mitsuo Yanagimachi is enjoying a moment in the sun after nearly a decade in the twilight: His new film "Who's Camus Anyway?" was screened in the Director's Fortnight section at Cannes, picked up for distribution in the United States and showered with rave reviews from everywhere (Manola Dargis at "The New York Times" called it "a shocking testament to the power of representation."). Yanagimachi, however, is not quite ready to play the smoothly affable comeback kid: In a recent interview at the bare-bones Ginza office of his distributor, he was more inclined to engage than spin, with a quick smile, ready wit and open manner verging on the bluff, but also flashes of a tougher, pricklier side. If were his student — he taught film at Waseda for three years — I'd come to class prepared, both to avoid his wrath — and keep up with his restless, probing mind.

None of the main characters are quite what they seem — they're are all playing roles. At the same time there is a balance between them.
That's something I got from Truffaut, the balance between characters' various sides. There's a balance between strength and weakness, sadness and joy. People are like that in real life as — they have more than one side. I wanted to express that.

One example is the character of "Adele," whose name is taken from a Truffaut heroine. I wanted to show her good, giving side as well as her other, less attractive side. She's a character with breadth — she's more than one thing.

The opening scene plays a double role as well. It's not just a piece of virtuoso camerawork but something more.
I wanted to show the relationships between the main characters in an interesting way. That's comes from Mizoguchi, among others.

Did it take you a long time to work out those relationships?
I worked them out in a diagram, then I wrote the script. The whole process, from start to finish, took about ten years. It became very complicated. (laughs)

I used the settings (in the school) to underline those relationships. I used the stairs a lot, as well as the lounge, the studio, the staff room and so on. Each setting has a role to play in tying together all these relationships.

You refer to various films, beginning with Truffaut's "The Story of Adele H" and Visconti's "Death in Venice." Were they your influences when you writing the script as well?
My first influence was Hollywood. I owe a lot to the films of William Wyler. Also Robert Altman's "The Player." He's a hard director to imitate. He's made some great films — he's really talented.

I taught at a university for three years — that's when I got the idea. I thought it would be interesting to make a film together with students.

The actors you cast really look and act like students. One exception is Meisa Kuroki, who stands out from the others. There's something mysterious about her — she acts quite mature, but she's really the youngest of the cast.
Kuroki was 16 when she made the film. I thought I would have to give up on her because she was so young. She's beautiful but she doesn't look 16 — or Japanese for that matter. She's of Okinawan and Panamanian background.

Actually when casting college students it's usually better to get actors who are 25 or 26. They can still remember what it's like to be that age, but they have some perspective on it as well. They can give a good performance that way.

Everyone is going to say, of course, that the character of Professor Nakajo is modeled on you.
I took a bit of a chance with that one. When I was drawing the (character diagram) I added one old guy. At first I wasn't going to make him a character like Nakajo, but then I thought I could use a film director in the story. I didn't want to make him anything like me, though.

I thought I would film on the Waseda campus, where I had taught, but the negotiations didn't go well so I had to give up that idea. Then we decided to shoot at Rikkyo University. The campus is quite Western — something like you would find in Boston, with all the bricks.

It's got a borderless feeling — you're not quite sure if you're in Japan or not. There's that feeling in the story as well.
It's a story about a making a student movie — so it goes back and forth between fiction and reality. There are "Adele" and "Aschenbach" — characters who are a mix of the fictional and the real. The murders (in the student film) mix fiction and reality as well.

The aim, frankly, is to confuse the audience, keep it off balance. Toward the end the tone changes — you're no longer sure if you're just watching a scene (in a student film) — or actual murders. There's a surface reality — and a deeper reality. Again, the mix of reality and fiction.

The students in the film are livelier than the ones I used to see in the classroom. But maybe that was just me. (laughs)
Well, they're working together toward a common goal. It's like a festival for them, so of course they're going to be lively.

Also, it's not true that college students today just sit there like sticks. They jabber away when they get the chance. (laughs)

Their choice of subject matter for the film — "The Stranger" — is rather unusual, however.
There's no way they would have known "The Stranger." On the other hand, if Nakajo had let them choose their own subject, (the film) wouldn't have been interesting for him, so he had them do Camus.

In the same way, the film didn't strike me as a typical "seishun eiga" (youth film), even though it's about young people.
I wanted to make it more universal. I wanted both adults and young people to see and enjoy it.

It's also more realistic about the way young people interact than the typical "seishun eiga," which is often just the director's fantasy. .
My three years of teaching experience was important. Without that the film would have been totally different.

(January 19, 2006, "The Japan Times")

Shinobu Yaguchi interview in Chicago

When I met Shinobu Yaguchi at a Chicago sushi restaurant, I made my usual mistake with well-known directors: Mention that I had once interviewed him. He, understandably, blanked, since the interview was twenty years ago for his 1997 indie comedy "My Secret Cache."

His response may well have been the even if I had had one-to-ones with him about his other films that I had reviewed, starting with his 1993 feature debut "Down the Drain" and continuing with his 2001 breakout smash "Waterboys" and his new film "Survival Family." In general a journalist begins to dissolve in a director's mind the moment the former exits the room. After about five introductions, if you're lucky, you begin to stick.

This time, though, I was going present "Survival Family," a comedy about the desperate journey of a Tokyo family across Japan after the world's electrical grid goes down, at Asian Pop-Up Cinema, a festival founded and run by Sophia Wong Boccio, a long-time friend and colleague.

The "Pop-Up" points to the festival's unusual scheduling: The eighteen contemporary Asian films of its fourth season would unspool over two months, from March 1 to May 3 at various venues. As the season's premiere, "Survival Family" would play at the largest: AMC River East 21 – a multiplex in downtown Chicago.

With his trademark glasses, short hair and serious air, Yaguchi looked more the nerdy scientist than the maker of hit commercial comedies, all of which he had scripted, mostly from his original ideas.

But the full-house crowd laughed in the right places and gave Yaguchi a big round of applause as he came down to the front of the theater for our Q&A. At the same time, the film was more than a gag fest. Inspired by the March 11, 2011 triple disaster – the earthquake, tsunami and reactor meltdowns that devastated the Tohoku region and caused major disruptions in Tokyo – the film presents a realistically chaotic country, from panicked crowds to trash-strewn highways. And all with no CGI assists whatsoever.

This emphasis on the analogue, as well as the film's warning against over-reliance on the digital, Yaguchi told me, came from his own deep techno skepticism (or, given his aversion to smartphones and other digital gadgets, phobia). "Use of CGI in film is growing so much that it's becoming hard to find a film without it," he said. "The audience has gradually started to notice and now they watch a film with a sense of security, thinking 'That's not really happening. The people are in no danger.'"

With "Survival Family," he said, he wanted to make something "simple and honest." That is, an "anti-CGI movie." "The family really goes to the places (in the film)," he explained. "They really ride their bicycles on a highway, catch fish, build a raft and cross a river on it. They ride in a real steam locomotive."

This old-school approach to shooting the family's arduous journey to Kagoshima, where the wife's father (Akira Emoto) is a farmer, was also hard on the cast, Yaguchi admits. "When their faces look as though they've suffering, they really are, but I wanted the film to truly reach the audience, so that's the way I had to do it."

During the two-and-half-months shoot – longer than usual for Japanese films – Yaguchi and his staff traveled to multiple locations across Japan. But some scenes, such as one of a mass exodus on a major highway, weren't as labor-intensive to set up and film as they looked. "That freeway scene took us only one day," Yaguchi said. "We had a truck full of trash following the shoot. It would dump the trash on the location and they we would film it. We caused a lot of trouble for the local people," he added with a laugh.

At the same time, the family's odyssey is more than a disaster simulation. The film shows them not only learning to survive, but also become closer and more considerate, especially the teenaged daughter (Wakana Aoi) and son (Yuki Izumisawa), who were barely interacting with their housewife mom (Eri Fukatsu) and salaryman dad (Fumiyo Kohinata), let alone with each other, before the blackout.

Also, the family's Kagoshima life of farming, fishing and otherwise living much as their ancestors did makes them and those around them personally happier and generally more likeable. Yaguchi admits that "at least part of the film's message" is that the old days were better. "But when the electricity comes back on and the family returns to Tokyo I don't think they are sad about leaving their country life," he adds. "Human beings, me included, are foolish. When the convenience of electricity returns, they may go back to their old way of life. But I realize how you could get the impression the family has grown and become a little better than they were at the beginning (of the story)."

The Q&A ended, Yaguchi spent the next half hour outside the theater taking photos with fans — another sign the screening had been a success. Sophia, who had programmed the film partly on my recommendation, was overjoyed with the audience reaction. "I want to take this film to schools," she said. "It teaches values people here are losing."

I thought of Yaguchi's response to an audience question about his preparation for the film. He and two staff members, he said, had made the family's trip themselves — and had some of the same experiences. "We tried battery liquid to see if you could actually drink it," he said. The result: One of the film's funnier gags. And an object lesson on the value of doing instead of Googling.

(March 22, 2017, "The Japan Times")

Koji Yakusho interview

"Toad's Oil" is your first film as a director. How did you come to make it?
The script was the starting point. It was about these two young lovers. The guy dies and the girl (not knowing it) tries to call him on her cellphone — and gets the guy's father. By adding the episode about the older guy doing the "toad's oil" sales talk, we could depart from reality and tell a story about how the son is watching everyone from heaven and the connection between his world and ours. That's why the toad's oil story made its appearance.

If we had just stuck to the realistic story about the father losing his son, it would have been just sad and the movie would not be so interesting. The toad's oil salesmen and his wife don't live in this world — they are like angels. They also add humor to the story, as well as offering hope. Instead of just being the sad, the story gives people energy.

The toad's oil sellers were orginally one of the peddlers at festivals, like the guys who make yakisoba. They had connections with the yakuza and all that. They would do magic — anything to draw a crowd.

You have a very international background, but when you made your first film, you use some very domestic only-in-Japan elements.
When I think of the theme of death, I can't help thinking of butsudan (Buddhist altars). From the time I was a kid I had an image of it being the gateway to another world, with the ihai (Buddhist memorial tablets) being dead people. When I was little and realized that there was an end to human life — that I would some day die — that my mother had died, that my grandfather had died — I would get scared and crawl inside my futon. (laughs) I would sleep near the butsudan.

Watching the film, I was reminded of "Departures" ("Okuribito"), which also deals with death. It was also a film that was considered for domestic audiences only, but now it is been seen around the world. Do you have the same ambition for your film — do you want it to be seen by foreign audiences as well?
The theme of death is universal. Also, the film has nothing to do with a particular religion. I think Japanese will easily feel something in common (with the story) I don't know how foreign audiences will see it, though. But if they can think back and relate it to their own lives.

Your own films until now haved ranged from comedies to serious dramas — but this film is something in the middle. (laughs) Did you want it that way so you could show your full range as an actor?
The story is about a father losing his beloved son — but I didn't want to make it just sad. I wanted to make it a film that makes people laugh and feel cheerful at the end.

The story is about a son's death and how the father reacts to it. The spirit of the son doesn't appear until late in the film, but he's always present — he goes on the road trip with the father and leads hims in different direction. I wanted people to feel that there's a guiding spirit in the background.

When actors direct films they often leave the camerawork up to the cinematographer and concentrate on the actors. Was that true in your case as well?
Well, I trusted the cameraman to do his job. I also had people from the company there giving me support — but I was in charge of directing the actors.

There's also an interesting mix of veteran actors and newcomers in the casting.
The newcomers were a real plus for the film. They had a freshness in their performance that veterans don't. They have something that veteran have lost. Actors are really afraid to work with children and animals. (laughs) They bring a sort of tension to the set.

But the two newcomers in this film had something natural in their personalities that was just right for their roles. The girl (who played the son's girlfriend) had a smile that really fit her role. She wasn't performing so much as just bringing out her natural personality. Also the boy who played Akiba had something in his personality that fit the character. When you see him on the big screen you realize that that's just who he is. But we rehearsed them before we started filming.

You also have a sharp contrast between the wife and girlfriend, who are rather ideal types of Japanese women, and the hero, who is not an ideal at all. (laughs)

The hero is a man who thinks that money can solve everything, but finally he encounters problems that money can't solve, such as the dissolution of his family, the death of his son. The women, on the other hand, have big hearts — they support the men. The "gama no abura" couple is an example. The guy is still not that good at it, even though he's had hundreds of years to perfect his act. (laughs) His wife, though, is still cheering him on. (laughs) She gives him the courage to go on. That also the image of the modern-day couple — the day trader and his wife.

She doesn't seem to mind that, instead of living in a huge mansion, they have to survive in a camping car. (laughs)

Right, she feel more at ease when they don't have a lot of money. She likes living (in the camper) better than living in the mansion.

What is your next film?

It's a period drama — but I can't announce it yet.

(June 7, 2009, "The Japan Times")

Takashi Yamazaki interview: box office smash 'The Eternal Zero' reopens old wounds in Japan with its take on wartime kamikaze pilots

Based on a best-selling novel by Naoki Hyakuta about the pilots of the famed Mitsubishi A6M Zero fighter plane used in the second world war, Takashi Yamazaki's "The Eternal Zero" has soared at the box office in Japan, earning nearly US$84 million since its December 21, 2013, release — the second highest box office total of any film for the year to date. "The Eternal Zero" has inspired controversy, however, with master animator Hayao Miyazaki publicly blasting Hyakuta's novel as a "pack of lies" and Yamazaki's film for propagating "a phony myth" about Zero fighter pilots. Ironically, the Studio Ghibli doyen's latest and last film as a director, "The Wind Rises", is loosely based on the life of Zero fighter designer Jiro Horikoshi.

One reason for the uproar is that the pilot hero (played by J-pop singer and actor Junichi Okada) volunteers for one of the kamikaze suicide squadrons flying one-way missions in the closing days of the Second World War. Over the decades, the kamikaze pilots have become objects of veneration for Japanese rightwingers, while their leftist opponents view this sympathy as suspect, since it is not matched by similar sentiments for the Japanese military's many war victims.

Another is that Hyakuta, an avowed nationalist, made headlines early this year with his revisionist pronouncements that the Nanjing Massacre "never happened" and that the postwar Tokyo Trials of Japanese war criminals were a "cover up for America's own atrocities," including the atomic bombings of Hiroshima and Nagasaki.

But Yamazaki, whose long string of hit films includes the warmly nostalgic "Always: Sunset on Third Street" trilogy along with 2010 live-action sci-fi fantasy "Space Battleship Yamato", describes "The Eternal Zero" — whose title refers to the Zero plane deployed by the Japanese military during the second world war — as less of a war film than "a love story," with the hero, Kyuzo Miyabe (Okada), vowing to return alive to his young wife (Mao Inoue) and young child.

"It's centred on its human drama, with the war era as a backdrop," the filmmaker tells me when we meet in a coffee shop next to the Toei studio in a Tokyo suburb, where he is working on a new movie. "It's similar to 'Titanic,' which was a love story set against the backdrop of the Titanic sinking."

At the same time, Yamazaki admits that "The Eternal Zero" falls squarely in the "war movie" category. "In Japan, the box office limit for war movies is about US$15 million, but I thought that if we tried hard we could do better than that," he says. "Even so, I never expected it to become such a hit," he adds with a laugh.

Unlike many Japanese Second World War films that assume an acquaintance with that era's die-for-the-emperor mentality, "The Eternal Zero" frames its hero and his times in ways that a younger audience, whose knowledge of the Second World War is spotty, can understand. "A hero who is called a coward [by his fellow pilots] for clearly saying he wants to survive the war is something new to Japanese war movies," Yamazaki explains. "But people now can relate to the feeling of wanting to live for the sake of your family."

He also believes that such a hero can appeal to foreign audiences. "The character of Miyabe is simple to understand on a human level," the director says. "Even if you were to remove him from the context of Japan, you can still sympathise with him. He says he wants to return alive to his family, which seems like common sense to us now. But he says it in an era when he isn't supposed to say it. And more than that, he acts on it."

The story largely follows Hyakuta's novel, though Yamazaki and co-scriptwriter Tamio Hayashi had to excise many characters and incidents. "More than just making cuts, we were making choices," Yamazaki explains. "We really struggled at the script stage, trying to extract the essence of the novel." Hyakuta, however, had no objections to the finished script.

When casting for the film, Yamazaki wanted, "young actors who had something of the atmosphere of that time about them", he says. "We cast them on the basis of whether they were right for the role, not their popularity," he adds.

That was especially true of Okada, though he is a founding member of V6, one of the most popular Japanese boy bands. "He was extremely close to our image of Miyabe," Yamazaki says. "In the film the character knows martial arts, so Okada studied hard. He got so much into it that he became a shihan [qualified teacher]. He's a guy who's really thorough when he focuses on one thing."

But while trying hard for a period look and feel, Yamazaki was not interested in replicating the hanky-wringing sentimentality of so many older Japanese war films. "We tried to suppress that kind of thing, actually," he says. "But people cried anyway — they really cried."

As for its critics who complain that "The Eternal Zero" celebrates war, Yamazaki has little but contempt. "That kind of thinking is strange," he says. "The film depicts the war as a complete tragedy, so how can you say it glorifies war? I'd like [the critics] to explain that. I really don't get it. In the end, people see what they want to see. If you think from the start that 'this movie glorifies war' you're going to see it as a movie that glorifies war, no matter what."

The 49-year-old filmmaker's own understanding of the Second World War's realities was deepened by not only watching newsreel footage of kamikaze attacks, but meeting some of the surviving pilots from the suicide squadrons. "I realized that they didn't want to be pitied," he says. "When they were in that situation in that era, they felt they had to do this one thing. They didn't want anyone to feel sorry for them. They were just doing their duty."

Nonetheless, Yamazaki says, "Of course, I do feel sorry for them." Elaborating on his point of view, he says: "I think they had feelings they kept to themselves. To understand it you really have to experience it yourself and then you probably think about it your whole life. When I met the pilots, I felt that."

(May 11, 2014, "South China Morning Post")

Hitoshi Yazaki interview

Once a leader of Japanese cinema's 1990s New Wave, Hitoshi Yazaki dropped off the radar for more than a decade, returning triumphantly in 2005 with "Strawberry Shortcakes" a widely praised drama about four lonely women in search of, not just a partner, but reasons for living. In his new film, "Sweet Little Lies," the heroine has found the partner — is still looking for fulfillment.

In person, Yazaki was soft-spoken and polite, but also quick to smile and laugh, despite the interviewer's at times convoluted questions. Though he may have been away a long time, he was anything but the shy, socially inept auteur.

Did you have Miki Nakatani in mind when you wrote the role for Ruriko?

When I met her for the first time, I saw that she had the sort of tension and personality that could make the character come to life. If I didn't have her (in the role) there would have been no reason to make the film. I was really lucky to come across an actress like that. I didn't want to force her to play my image of the character — I wanted to film Miki Nakatani as she is now.

So you didn't have to instruct her to do this or that.

Right, I left it up to her.

Juichi Kobayashi, who plays Haruo, is a dancer inexperience in acting. Were you concerned that Nakatani might be too much for him? (laughs)

Actually, yes. (laughs) I think he himself was kind of nervous. But I was glad that a world-class dancer could play the role. When I first met him I was impressed with his softness — that is, his ability to adapt quickly to situations. I thought he would be fine just as he was.

The bed scenes, in particular, must have been difficult for someone inexperienced.

The love scenes expressed something deep inside the characters. What was really important was what came before and after, not just the bed scenes themselves.

The married couple — Ruriko (Miki Nakatani) and Satoshi (Nao Omori) — seem to represent the "sexless marriage" phenomenon that has been written about so much. But I somehow I doubt that your intended to make a social statement.

This couple is something of a puzzle. They aren't defined by any set of rules. I don't think of them as representative of any sort of social phenomenon.

In the usual melodrama about a marriage, you can pretty much tell how the couple is going to turn out, but with your couple I didn't have that feeling at all. (laughs)

Actually, I don't know myself. (laughs) That's the theme of the film — that we don't know about a marriage. But by the end they're definitely heading in a positive direction.

It's can be hard to put something so interior into images.

Right. So I had to try different approaches. For example, there is a scene in novel where Ruriko is talking about her feelings on the phone with a friend. But that sort of long phone conversation is not very cinematic, so I had to think of how she could express herself more directly.

There's a pared-down quality to the images, the feeling that you've focusing only on the essentials. I'm thinking of the scene where Ruriko declares her love to Haruo. She just looks straight into the camera and says "I love you" but it has a big impact.

That's all because of Miki Nakatani's power as an actor, not me. (laughs) There were difficult lines (in the script) that worried me a bit — I wondered how she could say them — but she did a great job with them. I was really impressed.

I thought of Yasujiro Ozu when I was watching that scene. Were you thinking at all about classic Japanese films, since your theme is one they treat quite often?

When I was brought this story I was happy to do it since I had been wanting to make a film about a couple for a long time. I was really influenced by Naruse and other great directors — they made me want to (try this sort of film) myself.

You use certain symbols, such as the red and white flowers, to express themes and feelings. Did you get any of those from the novel or were they all you own creation?

When I read the novel various images occurred to me. Some of this was in the novel, but I also wanted images that would express what was in the words. Those I had to create myself.

The teddy bears that Ruriko makes are not just toys, but works of art. Also, when she is making them we can see her expressing her feelings, as when she jabs one hard with a needle. (laughs)

Before making the film, I had never met a teddy bear artist, but in preparing for the film I was able to meet several. Also, Nakatani made some bears herself. My staff and I — everyone made bears. (laughs) What impressed me what how much imagination goes into making them — it's not not just (following a pattern). For me the scenes (with the teddy bears) were extremely important. Without them I couldn't have told this sort of love story.

For about ten minutes at the end there were several places where I was thought, "Is it going to end here?" — but it didn't. Then, when it finally ended, I thought "OK, this feels right." (laughs)

I had a lot of trouble with the ending. I thought of several ways to end it before I came up with one.

Your previous films have been screened widely abroad. Is that also what you plan to do with this one?

Yes, I want to take it abroad. I hope that foreign audiences will find some of it funny. (laughs) I put in some humorous touches. In Japan audiences generally don't laugh very much. Abroad, though, they laugh a lot — even in places where there's not a lot to laugh at. I'm looking forward to that.

I was also impressed by Chiharu Ikewaki, since she makes you really understand why Satoshi would be interested in her character — she's got a natural warmth that Satoshi seems to be missing in his own marriage.

Ikewaki conveys something more than just the physical relationship — there's a depth to her performance as well. She's really great.

In your previous film, "Strawberry Shortcakes," you end on a positive note — with the characters eating the title sweets. But in this film I wasn't so sure about the ending. (laughs)

Right, you're not so sure what's going to happen to them. (laugh) But for me it was a positive ending.

(March 12, 2010, "The Japan Times")

Director has whale of a time making experimental 'Mind Game'

Now an animation veteran, with 17 years in the business, Masaaki Yuasa still looks young enough, acts deferential enough and dresses down enough to be mistaken for a rank-and-filer. Instead, he is a rising industry star hailed for his work on the "Crayon Shinchan" franchise, the nearest Japanese animation has come to "The Simpsons," and his directorial debut, "Mind Game," which is to most Japanese feature animation what extreme skiing is to a schuss down a bunny slope.

In person, Yuasa was comfortable enough with his new role of director, but that of interviewee seemed to strike him as a bit odd — though maybe that was the fault of his interviewer. He was polite and forthcoming enough — and relieved when the last question came. (True, I was the last in a day-long media procession.)

You use live actors in certain scenes of the film in a way reminiscent of Richard Linklater's "Waking Life" — but unlike anything I've seen in Japanese animation.
I've heard of "Waking Life," but I haven't seen it. The story in the original comic deals with some pretty deep themes, but it's drawn in a rough style, very much like a gag manga. But it's hard to get that rough feeling into an animation. Usually in animation you have several people working on an image and they tend to make it cleaner as they go along. When I thought about how to preserve that rough feeling, I came up with the idea of throwing various styles into the mix, almost at random. It may sound strange, but I wanted it to look as though we hadn't worked very hard on it, though of course we had.

That look goes with the characters, especially the hero, who is something of a rough type himself (laughs).
We wouldn't get that feeling across if we were to draw him too cleanly. We'd lose the atmosphere. Also, if we had made the film as a conventional cel animation, people wouldn't come to see it. For adults an animation that's a little offbeat is more interesting.

Kazuaki Kiriya, the director of "Casshern," told me something similar. He went for a rough look partly so he could express everything he wanted to express on a limited budget. If he had tried for a smooth Hollywood look, he said he wouldn't have been able to do that.
That was true in my case as well, but the look also suited the film. Instead of telling it serious and straight, I went for a look that was a little wild, a little patchy. When I'm trying to convey a theme that's a bit embarrassing, a bit hard to say straight, I tend to end up with that sort of look. Of course the budget was low, so that was also a factor.

A lot of recent animation, like "Steamboy," is done to perfection and costs a ton of money to make. When you make something like that, you're under a huge amount of pressure. I couldn't handle that [sort of job] and I know it. But when you've been given a small budget, you just figure out how to make the most interesting film you can with the money you have. You can take a more casual approach.

Also, I think that Japanese animation fans today don't necessarily demand something that's so polished. You can throw different styles at them and they can still usually enjoy it. In the past, if you had used different styles, you would have pulled [the audience] away from the story. Audiences today don't mind it as much when the style changes. They may feel a bit of discord, but it doesn't take them away from the story.

The film is based on a manga, but it's not a best seller. In other words a lot of the audience will not be very familiar with the material. Did that allow you to express yourself a little more freely?
That's right. I didn't have to draw [the film] to look exactly like the original [manga]. So in that sense I was free to express myself. At the same time, I respected the original story — I didn't depart from

it. But even though I was using the same [story as the manga], I tried to make it my own. For me, that sort of approach is the best.

"Waking Life" has its comic moments, but mostly it's a serious examination of the meaning of life, the universe and so on. By contrast, "Mind Game" has a lighter, more playful feeling. God appears, but it's not the sort of god most Westerners would recognize.

I would be embarrassed to talk about that sort of thing seriously. I'd rather joke around (laughs). For me the best way is to allow the audience to enjoy themselves while giving them something to think about. In other words, film as entertainment.

The god changes to reflect changes [in the hero's] own feelings. That's one of the themes — that the world reflects your own feelings toward it. Even when you're in a negative situation, if you think about it positively, your feelings will change as well.

When Nishi and the others end up in the whale, the obvious Western comparison is Pinocchio, but you took that situation in a very different direction. Were you trying to avoid comparisons or just following the manga?

That's in the manga. It's like a memory you might have from when you were 4, when you imagine the inside of a whale as being like a shell. When you're inside [a whale] nothing from the outside can attack you. It's fun, to be shut in like that, but you also can't stay there forever. The outside may not be as fun, but you have to go there.

You make it look inviting. Nishi and the others don't have to work, their food comes to them. It's something like being at a seaside resort (laughs).

Yes, it is enjoyable for them. When they're inside they start to remember things they had forgotten on the outside. They figure out what's important to them. They're eating, sleeping — and remembering everything, including the dreams they had when they were children. For the first time, they think things through. What are our dreams made of? That sort of thing.

So they seem to be drifting along, but inside they're thinking. Then they start to remember the outside and decide to escape. I had discussions with my staff about this part — some of them didn't want [the characters] to leave (laughs). They wanted them to stay inside. I thought that was really strange: If it were me I'd want to escape (laughs). But I had to give them a reason for leaving. What I said was that, basically, the world is an interesting place with various types of people. That was the reason for leaving.

They don't mind being inside, but they finally decide they want to leave. And when they do, they're like Pinocchio — changed.

Exactly. Pinocchio was reborn, wasn't he? In that sense so is Nishi.

But the way they work together to escape struck me as Japanese somehow. You don't see that in the Disney version.

That's true. When they enter [the whale] and after, they receive help in various ways, from the fish and so on. And they're also able to escape with various kinds of help. I wanted to make it tough for them, though. I didn't want them to have an easy time getting out. The pain is the price they have to pay. When they leave this little enclosed world, where they've enjoyed themselves, they let in all this culture and history. They endure a lot of suffering. They have to overcome all that to escape.

And yet when Nishi does get out, he leaps over ships, bridges and buildings. I wanted to tell him it was all right to stop (laughs).

When he gets out he has this very positive feeling that he can do anything. The world puts various kinds of obstacles in your way — it's not all fun and games. But you can find the strength to overcome that. You may face various global problems as well, such as war, but you can find the strength to live with them as well.

This particular job is your first feature film as a director. Are you satisfied with it, or are there more obstacles you have to overcome?
I still have some areas where I want to learn more. In this film I worked in areas that were my strengths. I'd like to learn more in areas that aren't my strengths.

"Mind Game" is more on the experimental, cult side than the commercial film side.
I wanted to make something that would be experimental, but also popular entertainment. I'm satisfied with it, but next time I want make something that has a wider appeal, in a different way. That's why I want to learn more.

I heard that the company is thinking of inserting the faces of foreign actors for the overseas version. How do you feel about that?
It's sad if the actors who appeared [in the original] are not [in the overseas version]. But that may be necessary to get foreign audiences to see it. There is also text that may have to be redone. But I want a lot of people to see and know about the film, so I don't mind if it's changed somewhat. The ideal would be to have a lot of people see it the way it is, but that may be difficult.

The storyline, though, reminded me of "Pulp Fiction," the way it doubled back on itself at the end.
Yes, but it doesn't double back in a complicated way. It's simple — ta da! — and you're back at the beginning.

I got the feeling that things had come full circle, but that Nishi had changed. There's a sense of liberation in the final images. A feeling that life is wonderful.
I'm glad you feel that way. In any case, he goes inside [the whale], suffers, then comes out and — then pow! — the world opens up for him. He finds out that the everyday lives of ordinary people are wonderful, even if they're not doing anything so great. Some images in the film may seem to say something negative — that his life from now on will be a waste, but I also wanted to say that if he lives life to the fullest it's not that terrible at all. It may look bad from the outside, but for him it's not bad at all.
   In the beginning, Nishi is really miserable — he can't say what he feels and he can't tell the girl he likes that he doesn't want her hanging out with another guy.

But by the end he has grown beyond that.
Exactly. From now on he'll be different.

But it's hard to imagine a sequel.
That's right. I just hope that he will try hard to live his life [to the fullest].

So now you're interested in making a more commercial film.
Yes, something that a lot of people will enjoy.

But I hope that, once in a while, you'll make this type of film as well.
I'll try (laughs).

(July 28, 2004, "The Japan Times")

Kazuo Hara returns to form as a documentary filmmaker with 'Sennan Asbestos Disaster'

Kazuo Hara became famous — some would say notorious — for the documentaries he made about individuals who defied Japanese social norms and laws. One such individual was Kenzo Okuzaki, the subject of Hara's 1987 film "The Emperor's Naked Army Marches On." A veteran of the Imperial Japanese Army's disastrous New Guinea campaign in World War II, Okuzaki relentlessly tracked down fellow survivors with information about the executions of two privates, ostensibly for desertion, shortly after Japan's surrender. In the film's climax, Okuzaki violently attacks a former sergeant who, as Hara's camera records every punch, kick and groan, confesses that he and others killed and ate fellow soldiers.

The 72-year-old Hara says that he stopped making documentaries for nearly 14 years after the release of "A Dedicated Life," his 1994 film about iconoclastic novelist Mitsuharu Inoue, because he had basically run out of material.

"I couldn't find fierce individualists (like Okuzaki) anymore," he explains. "People like him now never appear in Japanese films; Japanese have all become nice and compromising."

What drew Hara back into filmmaking was a group from the city of Sennan in Osaka who were fighting a long, wearying court battle against the government over compensation for deadly respiratory diseases caused by asbestos. Long the center of Japan's asbestos products industry, Sennan was a magnet for workers from poor rural areas and marginalized groups, such as Koreans living in Japan, in the postwar period.

Though aware of the dangers asbestos poses to human health, the Japanese government did little to effectively regulate the industry, prioritizing economic development instead. A 1995 ban against the most carcinogenic forms of asbestos, and a final total ban in 2012, came too late for the 31 people in the first group of Sennan plaintiffs, many of whom were already severely ill when they sued the government in 2006. Many died in the years that followed.

As he began filming the plaintiffs together with their families, supporters and lawyers, Hara struggled to find a theme. Not only was the issue unfamiliar, but his subjects were not rebellious and out-sized personalities like Okuzaki was.

"I personally like strong people," Hara says. "I myself am weak. I want to turn my weakness into strength and so I've made films about these strong people who attract me.

"However, the people in this film are not strong. I shot them for over eight years and during that time I'd always have this image of strong people in my head. I'd compare these images to the weak people I'd see before me, thinking that they ought to be angrier at their opponents, even violently angry."

After two years of editing, Hara screened the completed film, "Sennan Asbestos Disaster," at festivals in Busan, Yamagata and Tokyo last fall. Despite its 215-minute length, audiences responded with laughter, tears and applause, and the film won prizes at all three festivals.

The first screening for the general public was at the Yamagata International Documentary Film Festival, Hara explains. "Afterward people came up to me and told me how interesting the film was. I could tell by their expressions and words that they meant it, they weren't just trying to spare my feelings. That gave me a bit of confidence."

Even so, Hara says he regrets not finding a protagonist like Okuzaki. The nearest he came was Kazuyoshi Yuoka, an outspoken former asbestos factory manager and plaintiff group leader. In the film, Yuoka becomes ever more exasperated as the government loses trial after trial but continues to file appeals. Over the opposition of his group's lawyers, Yuoka tries at one point to push past a security detail to personally present Prime Minister Shinzo Abe with a petition asking him to halt a government appeal to the Supreme Court. When that fails, he is among the plaintiffs loudly demanding a meeting with the health minister. After 21 days of daily meetings, the plaintiffs work their way up a ladder of sweaty, stone-walling junior bureaucrats, but not to the minister himself.

The story has a happy ending, of sorts. In October 2014 the Supreme Court sided with the plaintiffs, though some were shut out of the compensation judgement since their claims dated after the 1971 cut-off decided by the court. Then, in January 2015, then-health minister Yasuhisa Shiozaki visited Sennan to meet and apologize to the plaintiffs and their families. He even lit incense and prayed beside the body of one woman who had died three days before his arrival — an emotionally charged scene recorded from beginning to end by Hara's camera.

In a final interview with Hara, however, a still-dissatisfied Yuoka says the plaintiffs should have expressed their true anger to Shiozaki, instead of being pleased, as some evidently were, that such a high official should bow his head to them.

"Yuoka became the hero (of the film), and people compare him to Okuzaki, but they're fundamentally different," Hara says. "Okuzaki would say that he was going to do something, and no matter how much people opposed him, in the end he would do it."

By contrast, Yuoka argued with the legal team about strategy "but in the end he compromised," Hara notes. "And Yuoka agonized about compromising; that made him relatable on a human level. Okuzaki, though, never compromised, which I think is wonderful. Japanese with that sort of iron will are extremely rare."

Hara says he can see similarities in how the victims of the Great East Japan Earthquake are praised by the foreign media for their silent stoicism.

"I wanted to tell them 'Are you joking? Stop it!'" Hara says. "I hate it when Japanese are praised for being so patient in a situation like that. In the film I clearly criticize Japanese who are like that. I mean, I love them but we ought to detest those who call someone like Shiozaki a 'nice guy.' That's the message of the film.

"If we don't, we'll never have real peace in this country. The willingness of the Japanese to forgive the powerful is a danger to our democracy. You don't forgive them. But Japanese people are indifferent to that."

(February 28, 2018, "The Japan Times")

Yoichi Higashi and Takako Tokiwa interview: the delicate notes of "Someone's Xylophone"

Japanese directors now routinely do dozens of media interviews to publicize their new films, especially if they are on the indie end of the spectrum. The stars of said films also sit down with the press, if not as commonly, but though I have been writing about local film folk since 1991, an interview with a director (Yoichi Higashi) and an actress (Takako Tokiwa) together was a first. Here to talk about their new film "Someone's Xylophone" ("Dareka no Mokkin"), neither are newcomers in need of a helping hand.

Born in 1934, Higashi has been directing feature films since 1969, ranging from hard-hitting social dramas ("The River with No Bridge"/"Hashi no Nai Kawa,"1992) to dream-like explorations of childhood memories ("Village of Dreams"/"E no Naka no Boku no Mura," 1996). Meanwhile, Tokiwa has successfully transitioned from her 1990s fame as television's "queen of trendy drama" to a career as an in-demand film actress, starring in both indie experiments ("Cut," 2011) and big-budget spectacles ("20th Century Boys"/"Nijuseiki Shonen" trilogy).

But as the two talked about their first film together, in which Tokiwa plays an ordinary housewife who falls for and obsessively stalks a handsome hair stylist (Sosuke Ikematsu), their unusual united front began to make more sense. A big name in both Japan and Asia, Tokiwa was glad to lend her star wattage to a director she obviously respects. Meanwhile, Higashi was clearly happy to have Tokiwa by his side since she was not only eloquent about the film's talking points but quick with apt anecdotes. In other words, theirs was a mutual admiration society, not a marriage of PR convenience.

It's rare for me to interview a director and actor together.

Higashi: It's all right if you just interview her. No one wants to see me. I'm just here to support her. She's the one who should be the center of the conversation.

Takako, why this project and Yoichi Higashi?

Tokiwa: I love his films and was really happy to get an offer from him.

Higashi: It hard for her to answer this kind of question if I'm here. (Laughs)

The heroine, Sayoko, is something of a mystery. Did you have any trouble understanding her motivations when you read the script?

Tokiwa: I didn't, no. You don't need a special reason for liking someone. Also, the definition of who is and who is not a stalker is vague. Some may view her actions as stalking, but you can also see them as an expression of pure love. The choice of where to draw that line is up the individual.

Higashi: I'd like to add something to what she just said. The film is about a person leading an ordinary life who enters a strange world, There's no clear borderline with one side normal and the other abnormal — both can exist in the same person. When she read the scenario she really understood that.

You've often dealt with the theme of "borderlines" in your films.

Higashi: That's true — it's something I've given some thought to. I'm not trying to sound difficult, but there is a history of philosophers and psychiatrists studying that kind of thing. What I've learned from them is that we can't divide insane people and normal people into two groups. In Japan, we do tend to divide them, but I'm strongly against that. I don't like seeing people judged that way. It frightens me. In the film I didn't want to clearly state what she really is.

Tokiwa: I also feel that way. I often go to see court cases and I've noticed that sort of thing. For example, you may think a person who has committed a crime would say crazy things, but that's not the case at all. He talks plainly about what he did. I nearly always find myself wondering if that person really did something so bad.

Higashi: (Handing over a sheet of paper) I've written something about that here. Please read it for reference later. It basically says that at a certain point in the film, Sayoko's spirit becomes like a chrysalis.

Tokiwa: It's for the program sold in the theaters.

Higashi: I don't know exactly why, but her heart becomes like a chrysalis, a pupa. From the outside the pupa of a butterfly seems to be still, but inside big changes are taking place. Then one day the butterfly emerges. Sayoko is grappling with that kind of major change. She's being reborn in a different form.

This is the first time, Takako, that you worked with Sosuke Ikematsu. I've seen him in a lot of films, but his character in this one is quite different.

Tokiwa: One thing Ikematsu has been doing right all along is to take long pauses between lines. It's because he's being honest about his feelings, I think. He waits until he wants to say his next line. So the pauses become really long.

Higashi: When you think he's finally going to speak, he doesn't say anything. Takako was surprised at that and so was I. I told him just once to make the pauses a little shorter.

The most important element in a film is rhythm. Not a simple rhythm, but the interior rhythm between two actors. But if you ask me what sorts of things create a good rhythm, I don't know. I just feel it instinctively.

Sometimes you do it bang, bang, bang and sometimes it's good to leave a little pause between lines. A director has to pay attention to that. My job is to watch the action and give some advice.

You inject surreal elements, such as the scene of Sayoko sleeping when two pairs of hands reach into the frame to touch her. You seem to be saying there's no difference between the real world and the dream world.

Higashi: Human beings basically cannot live deeply and happily without some kind of illusion. That is, we can't always distinguish between dreams and reality. I don't want to list the reasons; it's also something I feel instincively.

Tokiwa: I went to see noh for the first time yesterday. It really reminded me of the world beyond. That may because it's based on Japanese classic stories. Noh and the way Mr. Higashi makes films are really close.

Higashi: But noh is superior.

Tokiwa: No, your films are! (Laughs)

Higashi: She's extremely perceptive and extremely intelligent. I didn't have to consult with her about a single scene or single cut when I was shooting the movie.

Tokiwa: I can really trust him. He would always tell me when I was getting off the track. The moment I brought in the pedestrian world of TV drama he would tell me, "That's not it."

There are a lot of films about women of a certain age making a last try for love. Is that also true of Sayoko?

Tokiwa: I don't know. Her story may be one that is (in English) "to be continued."

Higashi: Right, you don't know if it's her last love. Women don't think about their "last love," not at all. For them, it's a (in English) "never-ending story."

(September 7, 2016, "The Japan Times")

PART 3:
SELECT FILM REVIEWS

When the Rain Lifts, Ame Agaru, runtime: 91 min.

"When the Rain Lifts," a period drama scripted by Akira Kurosawa, has some tough acts to follow, namely the 30 feature films that Kurosawa directed from "Sugata Sanshiro" in 1943 to "Madadayo" in 1993. The obvious question is whether this homage, made by former "Kurosawa family" members, with long-time Kurosawa assistant director Takashi Koizumi helming, meets the standards of a "Rashomon," "Ikiru" or "Seven Samurai."

The short answer is "no." As narratively unadorned as a folk tale, with an affirmative message as straightforward as its samurai hero is upright, the film will no doubt strike many who know and love Kurosawa's work as Kurosawa and water — and I can't disagree. Nonetheless, after seeing so many new films whose mental atmosphere is cold, cynical or downright psychotic, I found "When the Rain Lifts" a refreshingly warm, if retro, change. Perhaps, in writing this last script in his early 80s about a wandering ronin's search for redemption, Kurosawa was recalling, not only the triumphs of his earlier career, but the silent period dramas of his youth, whose sterling heroes and simple good-vs.-bad storylines gave pleasure to millions.

Also, in transferring this script to the screen, the staff and cast, including Kurosawa regular Akira Terao as the samurai, have channeled Kurosawa's spirit without being slavishly imitative of his methods. Instead of a dull memorial service, the film has the feeling of an affectionate farewell from the master himself.

Misawa Ihei (Terao) begins the film as a ronin without employment or destination. Unlike the wild, impetuous samurai of Kurosawa star Toshiro Mifune, Ihei is a gentle-spirited, mild-mannered type who would rather smile than glower, and make peace than war. Unable to cross a river swollen by heavy rains, he and his wife Tayo (Yoshiko Miyazaki), a paragon of patience and loyalty, stop at an inn whose guests are poor but good-hearted folk. A prostitute (Mieko Harada) disturbs group harmony by raging over the disappearance of her meager portion of rice, but Ihei quickly restores it, treating everyone to a feast on his winnings from a street-corner sword fight.

When Tayo berates him for breaking his promise to stop fighting for money, he sheepishly tells her that he could not bear to see the people in the inn quarreling — so he drew his sword to buy them a meal. This sensitive soul, however, is no mean warrior, as he proves the next day when, out on a walk, he stops a sword fight between two hot-headed young samurai, then quickly proceeds to disarm them when they attack him for interfering. His heroics are witnessed by several admiring samurai on horseback, including the local lord, Nagai Shigeaki (Shiro Mifune), who invites Ihei to his castle.

Receiving an invitation from one of Shigeaki's young retainers, Gonnojo (Hidetaka Yoshioka), Ihei visits the castle the next day. He charms the bluff, good-natured lord with tales of his wandering life and his training under the renowned swordsman Tsuji Gettan (Tatsuya Nakadai). Shigeaki is so charmed that he asks Ihei to become a teacher of swordsmanship to his retainers. Overjoyed, Ihei tells Tayo the news, but remembering the previous times when her husband had similar chances and lost them, she is reluctant to celebrate. Then, several days later, Shigeaki invites Ihei to demonstrate his skills at the castle. Ihei goes, but though he beats all comers, he is no politician, and ends up enraging both the lord and a local fencing school, whose master wants his job.

The rain may let up, but Ihei's troubles remain.

In playing Ihei, Terao avoids the inevitable comparisons to Mifune by approaching the role from the opposite direction. Whereas Mifune's samurai were often traditional tachiyaku ("manly warrior" types) for whom affairs of the heart were out of the question, Ihei is a New Age ideal: dedicated to his profession, while being sincerely devoted to his long-suffering wife. Terao, a pop-musician-turned-actor who appeared in Kurosawa's "Ran," "Dreams" and "Madadayo," is not as comfortable with a sword as Kurosawa's previous generation of samurai (he had reportedly never handled one before taking the part) but he brings a deadpan panache to his fight scenes.

Also, he is not embarrassed about or contemptuous of the idea of heroism. Instead, in his own low-key way, he embraces it. While not dominating the screen like Mifune, he brings a quiet authority and likeability to his role. Given an impossible assignment — reviving a vanished heroic type — he does a better job than expected.

As Shigeaki, Shiro Mifune displays some of his father's talent for broad comedy, but his bombastic lord is more of an attitude than a true character. Even so, in his first encounter with Ihei, he looks every inch the medieval aristocrat, both confident and commanding as he loudly praises Ihei's swordsmanship while firmly reining in a high-spirited horse.

First-time director Koizumi has what must be the hardest assignment of the "When the Rain Lifts" staff: making a film worthy of the man Steven Spielberg called, rightly, "the pictorial Shakespeare of our time." Working with veterans of Kurosawa's staff, including cinematographer Shoji Ueda and photography consultant Takao Saito, he has created images, such as Ihei and Shigeaki's ferocious duel at the castle, that recall the mentor's work. All that is lacking is the tingle down the spine that separates genius from craftsmanship.

It's easy to dismiss "When the Rain Lifts" as sub-Kurosawa, a last faint hurrah from the period of the master's final decline, but I prefer to see it as one last message from his heart, a distillation of all he learned in nine decades of living and five decades of filmmaking. A commonplace message, perhaps, but a necessary one: Despite all evidence to the contrary, the essence of life is love, its highest expression, joy.

Charisma, runtime: 104 min.

Is it a coincidence that one of the first Japanese films made for release in the new millennium should be something of a cinematic Nostradamus? "Charisma," Kiyoshi Kurosawa's eco-allegory about a mysterious tree that obsesses all who come in contact with it, resembles the prophecies of the 16th-century French astrologer in being oblique and enigmatic, but with a strange power and persuasiveness. The film, however, does not make grandiloquent, if gnomic, predictions about the future. Instead it poses questions that go to the heart of modern attitudes toward not only nature, but society and even life itself.

What one of the film's contending factions regards as life-giving, another sees as life-threatening. What one wants to save, another tries to exploit — or kill. For this outsider, it was next to impossible to sort out which group, if any, had right on its side. In the end, I could only rely on my not-always-reliable instincts. Logic, save of the dream variety, couldn't make sense of it. The truth is out there, says "The X-Files." "Charisma" makes the less popular, if more defensible, assertion that the truth is not absolute, but individual, not out there, but in here.

What is this tree that is alternatively celebrated and despised? What you make of it, for better or worse. A directorial design is evident, but no directorial moral, neatly wrapped and ready for easy delivery.

"Charisma" could have easily degenerated into a pseudo-Beckettian exercise in intellectual paradox — sterilely theatrical and unbearably pretentious. But Kurosawa, who spent much of the past decade making low-budget horror and gang films for the video shelves before becoming a festival favorite with the 1997 psycho-thriller "Cure," would rather connect with his audience than lecture to it. Instead of allegorical figures behaving, well, allegorically, his characters act with a disconcerting, almost childish directness, as though their social masks had been surgically removed. While looking and speaking like normal flesh-and-blood Japanese, they seem to move in an unusually vivid dream, one that invites interpretation while defying it.

The film's principal dreamer is Yabuike (Koji Yakusho), a detective who has been suspended from the force after botching the rescue of a kidnapper's victim. Fleeing to the countryside to escape the media and sort out his life, he finds himself alone in a mountain forest. Then, while he is sleeping, his car explodes in flames and he barely escapes. Wandering about, Yabuike encounters a tree strung with what look to be I.V. bottles and tubes. Then, he meets a forester, Nakasone (Ren Osugi), who tells him that the forest around them is dying. Could the cause be that strange tree in the clearing?

But the tree has its defenders, the foremost being an intense young man named Kiriyama (Hiroyuki Ikeuchi) who lives in an abandoned sanitarium together with the widow of its owner and tenderly cares for the tree, while violently attacking anyone who would do it harm. He calls the tree "Charisma" and says that it has lived for thousands of years. He is also convinced that Charisma is about to transform — and end as the last survivor in nature's battle for life.

Soon after, Yabuike steps into a trap while walking in the woods and is rescued by Mitsuko Jinbo (Jun Fubuki), a university botanist who lives nearby with her eccentric younger sister Chizuru (Yoriko Doguchi). Mitsuko tells Yabuike that Charisma excretes toxins that poison everything around it. The only solution is to destroy it — or risk losing the forest.

Finding himself in the middle of these warring factions, Yabuike can't easily decide which side he is on. Mitsuko seems to have hard science on her side, while Kiriyama exudes fervent conviction. Meanwhile, Nakasone and his associates simply want Charisma out of the way. One day Nakasone and a group of men appear in the clearing and, after chasing off Yabuike and Kiriyama, uproot Charisma, and drive off with it in a truck. Later Yabuike happens upon the tree, set ablaze by the Jinbo sisters.

End of story? Not quite. In another part of the forest a giant, leafless tree appears. Is it Charisma in a new guise? But when Kiriyama sees this new tree, he is not overjoyed. "This is no good," he says. "I can't understand it."

Yabuike, on the other hand, is beginning to emerge from his personal fog. Unlike the others, he claims no special knowledge or insight. He is, he confesses, "an ordinary man." He does believe, however, that Charisma and the forest can live together. Or can they?

It is tempting to call Charisma the life force, and tag Kiriyama as the good ecological warrior and Jinbo and Nakasone the evil forces of scientific arrogance and capitalist exploitation. (Nakasone seems to hate the tree because it interferes with the lumber harvest.) The film, however, resists such easy labeling. Charisma remains, from beginning to end, an ambiguous symbol.

At one point Kiriyama even tells Yabuike, "You are Charisma." What does he mean? That Yabuike is the life force — or that he alone knows how to save the tree? With the broadest range of any Japanese actor working today, Koji Yakusho is well equipped to portray Yabuike's slow coming to awareness, while never losing sight of his common man appeal. Nonetheless, his Yabuike is not a hero in the usual sense. He also has blood on his hands — and knows no easy way to cleanse it.

The rest of the cast burst with an energy and spontaneity — perhaps because Kurosawa gave them a chance to act out as well as act. Most movies are good for a few moments of post-screening coffee shop chat, if that. "Charisma" almost demands a longer thrashing out.

Is it a work of twisted genius? An out-of-control example of directorial self-indulgence? What, if anything, is this man trying to say? Go see for yourself — but make sure to check the time of that last train.

The Dentist, Shikai, runtime: 84 min.

Young directors were once encouraged to think of their careers as a steep, costly climb up the film stock ladder, from the 8 mm of their student movies to the 16 mm of their first arthouse films and finally to 35 mm, the stock that marked their arrival as full-fledged professionals. That ladder still exists and still has many climbers, but with the monster box-office success of "The Blair Witch Project," shot with the kind of video equipment that Dad uses to record Daughter's high school graduation, thousands of would-be Scorceses have received confirmation that there are other, less expensive and arduous ways to make their filmmaking dreams come true.

Thus the flood of digital movies made with little more than chutzpah and a credit card; thus the emergence of digital film festivals (Tokyo hosted its first last fall); and thus the concept of Movie Storm, a five-film project produced by Gaga Communications, Excellent Film and Bonobo. All five are scheduled to be shot with video cameras, reducing the cost of production to one-tenth that of the average Japanese commercial film. All five are on the theme of "Eros" and several feature directors who have won awards and box-office success.

The aim is less to confront conventions of mainstream cinema in the manner of the Dogma group, whose "vows of chastity" include the use of handheld cameras, natural light and "found" locations, than to fill distributor Gaga's line-up with salable product. Even so, if the second of this quintet, Shun Nakahara's "The Dentist" ("Shikai") is any indication, the use of less cumbersome digital equipment and the lack of budgetary pressures has given Movie Storm directors the kind of freedom that produces interesting films, not just more video shelf space-fillers.

A graduate of the University of Tokyo, Nakahara began his career in the early '70s, grinding out soft porn for Nikkatsu, then graduated to straight films with the 1986 "Don't Touch My Woman" (Boku no Onna ni Te o Dasu na), a vehicle for idol star Kyoko Koizumi. In 1990 he swept local awards with "The Cherry Orchard," a subtly sensuous, movingly lyrical, beautifully photographed film about the members of a girls school drama club.

While injecting similar qualities into his subsequent films, Nakahara could not direct his way past the clotted comedy of "Lie, Lie, Lie" or the turgid melodramatics of "Coquille." In "The Dentist," however, he returns to his porno roots and produces a film that recalls the erotic power and humanism of his earlier work, while venturing farther out on the sexual and emotional edge. Think of the Nagisa Oshima erotic classic "In the Empire of the Senses" ("Ai no Corrida") — only with the roles reversed.

The dentist of the title is Tomoya Matsunaga (Ken'ichi Endo), who runs a thriving practice out of his house. Taller, darker and more handsome than the average tooth puller, with a piercing gaze and caressing rumble of a voice, Matsunaga would seem to be a dream catch — and so he is in the eyes of his smoky-eyed young bride, Noriko (Amiko Kanaya), save for one problem — Matsunaga has become impotent since the recent death of his loving tyrant of a mother.

Noriko tells a freelance writer friend named Ritsuko (Ayana Inoue) about this problem in graphic detail, complete with embarrassed giggles, for an article Ritsuko is doing on the "sexless couple" phenomenon. When Matsunaga hears the tape he explodes with rage, slapping a cowering Noriko to the floor. But instead of reacting in the usual way of battered wives in Japanese movies — with tears of submissive contrition — Noriko stares at her husband with an unsettling combination of silent reproach and steamy satisfaction.

The slapping continues, this time on Noriko's willing rump, as she screams with pain and joy. Matsunaga and Noriko end up making explosive, ecstatic love. Scratch one prescription for little blue pills — this odd couple's real honeymoon is about to begin.

There is a large market for S&M fantasies in this country — see all those video racks that look like photo manuals on ways to hog-tie the female form. Harder than devising knots not in the Boy Scout manual, however, is filming an S&M relationship frankly, without exploitative leers or PC frowns. Nakahara, a veteran observer of the erotic in all its variations, pulls off this trick with stylistic grace and narrative impact. (Too well, perhaps — his bosses at Gaga would no doubt have preferred more leers.)

Going to a hot spring where Matsunaga's parents once honeymooned, Matsunaga and Noriko enjoy an S&M idyll. No longer content to cut panties with scissors or fondle nipples with knives, Matsunaga tries a different game — pushing his wife's head under water and keeping it there, then panicking when she nearly drowns. Noriko emerges from this near-death experience ready for more. What began as a game to keep Eros alive in a troubled marriage, now becomes a prolonged flirtation with Thanatos — that Matsunaga becomes all too ready to consummate.

A story that began with a thrill, finishes with a series of chills. Say good-bye to "In the Empire of the Senses" and say hello to "Psycho."

Working from a script by Shotaro Oikawa, Nakahara films this descent with a directorial gaze both unflinching and understanding. Also, together with cinematographer Satoru Maeda, he creates images that not only take the digital medium where most news cameramen could never follow, but plunge the audience into his characters' trance dance of love and death. Imagine a coffin with a live naked occupant, curled in a fetal position and hurling toward oblivion.

Veteran character actor Ken'ichi Endo, whose credits include films by Yoichi Sai and Takeshi Kitano's "Violent Cop," portrays Matsunaga's transformation from man to monster without losing sight of the man in the monster, or forgetting to foreshadow the monster in the man.

But it is Amiko Kanaya as Noriko who gives the film its true charge, not only in her mask of a face, with its standing invitation to forbidden pleasures, but in her stance when she finally displays her body to the shocked eyes of her friend. Unrepentant and unashamed, she reveals her bruises and scars not as the proofs of her victimhood, but the testimony of her love.

Audition, runtime: 115 min.

Be careful what you wish for, because you just might get it. Cynical advice, perhaps, but for the middle-aged male, too often true. With more responsibilities and fewer options than his younger brothers, he can easily find himself in free fall, when he was only longing for freedom.

His new business can be thrilling, until he winds up in bankruptcy court at age 50. An affair with a woman half his age can be wonderful, until it ends in a messy, expensive divorce, with hungry looks from his lover replaced by reproachful glances from his children. He tells himself he can always pick himself up and start over, but with each fall, the pavement gets harder, the climb back, longer.

Nonetheless, he keeps wishing. Time, he realizes with an urgency his younger brothers can seldom fathom, is running out. Happiness, whatever his vision of happiness may be, has to be now. His pursuit of it can look selfish, stupid or plain wrong-headed to those around him, but he can stop chasing his particular rainbow as easily as he can stop breathing.

The hero of Takashi Miike's new film, "Audition," is one such middle-aged man — a representative type, especially in his talent for self-delusion. Miike has explored similar territory before, in such films as "Rainy Dog" and "The Bird People in China," but in "Audition" he goes far deeper. The film is reminiscent of "The Sixth Sense" in its hallucinogenic persuasiveness, but whereas M. Night Shaymalan's hit extols the power of love, "Audition" exposes the inexorability of evil, in all its cold, mocking fury.

Most Hollywood films about the dark side are little more than effects-driven melodramas without a particle of conviction behind them — see Al Pacino's ham turn in "The Devil's Advocate" for an example. "Audition" doesn't just put on a Halloween costume and make scary faces — it gives us a jolt of pure, unrefined terror, while reminding us, with skin-crawling starkness, that actions have consequences. If "Fatal Attraction" made millions of married men swear off cheating (at least for the duration of the ride home from the theater), "Audition" may convince more than a few over-40 males to give up younger women altogether (or at least confine their leching to the Internet).

Its hero is an industrious sort, who runs his own small video distribution company. Also, far from being a haunter of Thai hostess bars, Aoyama (Ryo Ishibashi) is a widower still in mourning for his wife seven years after her death. His teenage son tells him he ought to remarry — he is starting to look old before his time — and Aoyama is inclined to agree, but how can he find the right woman? His ideal is modest, refined and accomplished in a traditional art, Western or Japanese, but where is he to find such a paragon among the vulgar, grasping, empty-headed masses of the younger generation?

His friend Yoshikawa (Jun Kunimura), a worldly-wise movie producer, has an ingenious, if underhanded, solution: Hold an audition for the starring role in an upcoming film and take his pick from among the thousands of women certain to send in applications. The audition won't be a total sham, Yoshikawa assures the conscience-stricken Aoyama — he really does intend to make a film, but the best bride material won't be among the finalists.

Why not, Aoyama wonders. "An actress able to play the lead in a film wouldn't marry you," his sage friend replies. "And women like that aren't suited for marriage anyway." What Aoyama does find, after sifting through piles of resumes, is Asami Yamazaki (Eihi Shiina): an attractive young woman with a haunting gaze, 12 years of ballet training and a refreshing seriousness about life. After suffering an injury that ended her ballet career at the age of 18, she writes in her resume essay, she underwent a shattering personal crisis and "learned to accept death." Clearly a woman after his own heart!

Aoyama is even more enamored when he meets the mysteriously lovely Asami at the audition. He all but declares his intentions in a passionate outpouring that leaves his friend Yoshikawa gaping.

Undeterred by Yoshikawa's urgings to go slow, Aoyama decides, after a couple of dates and one passionate weekend at a hot spring, that Asami is the one for him. What he doesn't see, when Asami answers the phone in her psychotic wreck of a room, is the sack in the background filled with a writhing human form. Love is blind, goes the cliche — Aoyama is about to discover how dangerous blindness can be.

Working from a novel by Ryu Murakami, Miike and scriptwriter Daisuke Tengan play straight with the audience in laying a trap for their unsuspecting hero, leaving subtle hints while refraining from "Fatal Attraction"-like manipulations. But however aware we may be that Asami is bad news, we can't imagine how bad until she removes her mask — and stands revealed in all her sweetly smiling, sugary-voiced, cruelly implacable rage.

As Asami, newcomer Eihi Shiina is perfectly cast. (I would have loved to attend her audition.) A pale-faced beauty with large, liquid eyes that can look soulful one moment, stone cold the next, she plays Asami to double-jointed perfection. Meanwhile, rock-vocalist-turned-actor Ryo Ishibashi turns in another finely edged performance in a long series, though one far removed from the tough guy types he usually plays. He injects an appealing vulnerability into a character who might, in other hands, have become irritatingly obtuse.

Among the film's few irritants is a smarmy, snarly bad guy turn by Renji Ishibashi as Asami's wheelchair-bound ballet instructor. He is a reminder of where too many other Miike films have headed — straight for the video racks. But "Audition," which won an international critics' prize at this year's Rotterdam Film Festival, proves that Miike is ready for a bigger role — as one of the leading Japanese directors of his generation.

Bullet Ballet, runtime: 87 min.

Shinya Tsukamoto is one of a madly obsessed, brilliantly talented, perversely likable kind. In the past decade, when the emotional temperature of most Japanese independent films ranged from medium low to icy cold, he boiled over with "Tetsuo: The Iron Man," "Tetsuo II: The Body Hammer" and "Tokyo Fist" — films that were the essence of late 20th century urban alienation and rage.

But in their very extremity — especially in their bizarre metamorphoses and operatic violence — there was something comic as well as horrific. Think Godzilla on speed. Also, in his stance as the ultimate cinematic otaku, obsessing over every detail of his fantastically complex creations, Tsukamoto stood in refreshing contrast to many of his young indie colleagues from the worlds of music video and advertising, who seemed to be playing at moviemaking.

In his latest film, "Bullet Ballet," Tsukamoto continues to work out his various artistic and personal obsessions, including, as he states in a program note, "the relationship between the metropolis and human physical existence." But in place of writhing robots, slamming fists and other images straight from the seething core of the Japanese pop culture imagination, Tsukamoto creates an underworld more recognizably like the one we see in Shibuya at three in the morning. In short, he has returned to earth, if not quite to everyday life as most of us mortals know it.

The change is not all for the better. Along with the extremity, the outre originality of his earlier work has largely disappeared. Instead, "Bullet Ballet" is a grim, if essentially romantic, journey through a noirish urban jungle where fashionable young outlaws play violently nihilistic games. This theme is a popular one with younger Japanese directors, but too often the aim is to attitudinize rather than to truly explore or expose.

Tsukamoto is still blazingly sincere in his rage against the Japanese social machine, but in "Bullet Ballet" he also has a tendency to fall into mangaesque poses more self-regarding than self-revealing.

Once the most personal of filmmakers, exposing his very nerve endings on the screen, Tsukamoto has become more distanced from his material in this film; he focuses more on coordinating his lighting and camera moves than in journeying to the heart of his hero's obsessions.

Despite its great visual invention, sophistication and intensity, the film plays curiously flat, like a drummer slamming out the same beat at the same tempo for a 10-minute solo.

The story is that of Goda (Tsukamoto), a salaryman type who is distraught after losing his love of 10 years, Kiriko, to suicide. He is also obsessed with guns — the method Kiriko used to end it all. In the course of his drunken wanderings through the back streets of Tokyo, he encounters Chisato (Kirina Mano), a sultry cutie in skintight leathers who belongs to a gang that once pounded him to a bloody pulp. When Goda raves at her for the beating, the other gang members appear — and continue where they had left off. Humiliated and enraged by this fresh insult, Goda decides to blow his tormentors away. First, however, he has to find a gun — no easy task, as he discovers.

He tries to make his own, but learns he is as ineffective a gunsmith as he was a street fighter. Failing to off his tormentors, he is drawn irresistibly into their orbit.

The long-haired leader, Idei (Tatsuya Nakamura), is a nightclub manager with a dark charisma and a deviant mind. His right-hand man, the darkly handsome Goto (Takahiro Murase) is the stone-coldest of the crew. But the gang's male members are bad boys playing naughty games compared with Chisato, who has a genuine death wish.

Goda finds himself attracted to her: She shares his fascination with Thanatos — and is less hesitant to indulge it. The film's climax comes, however, not in a suicide pact, but in a war with another gang that offers Goda — a working gun finally in hand — a chance for his long-contemplated revenge, and Chisato, for her long-desired end.

In telling this story, Tsukamoto uses harshly lit black-and-white photography and jittery, jumpy camera work to create the right end-of-the-tether, edge-of-the-night mood. The industrial noise score, by Chu Ishikawa, adds to this mood, as does a spare, intense performance by Tsukamoto as Goda. But all the atmospherics cannot disguise yet another recycling of familiar themes and motifs. What was stunningly sui generis in "Tetsuo" has started to feel banal in "Bullet Ballet." We've taken this particular death trip once too often.

Monday, runtime: 100 min.

New directors need something unique, in terms of talent, technique or theme, if they are to distinguish themselves from the digicam-wielding hordes. Mere competence doesn't do the trick any more.

Sabu, an actor who turned director in 1996 with "D.A.N.G.A.N. Runner," became an immediate stand-out for two reasons. First was his name, which appealed to foreign festival programmers everywhere, for not only its nostalgic reference to the Indian star of those old Hollywood jungle epics, but its blessed pronounceability (compared with such tongue-twisters as Hirokazu Koreeda and Takashi Miike).

Second and more importantly were his chase scenes, which became the dramatic engines of film after film. Sabu designed them much the way Buster Keaton did, with wacky ingenuity and blithe indifference to the laws of probability. Also, like the director of "Sherlock Jr." and "The General," Sabu was not just manufacturing laughs, but making statements about the arbitrariness of fate and the absurdity of life.

But whereas Keaton preferred to slowly accelerate to a bang-up finish, Sabu slammed the pedal to the metal and kept it there. Also, as befitting a young Japanese director in the recessionary '90s, his vision was bleaker and more violent than his American senpai's.

But as terrific as his first acts were, Sabu had trouble keeping his frantic pace, as exhilaration gave way to exhausted genre cliches.

In his fourth film, "Monday," Sabu finally gives the chase a rest, while continuing to explore familiar themes. Distinctly Sabu in its one-damn-thing-after-another structure, this comedy of errors about a salaryman's disastrous weekend is, in its dark comic style and inventive nonlinear storytelling, more Danny Boyle than Buster Keaton. It brilliantly realizes the promise of his previous work.

In its third act, "Monday" threatens to falter — a chronic Sabu problem — but recovers with a twist equal in its cleverness and rightness to anything in "Trainspotting." With "Monday," Sabu may well climb out of his "festival favorite" niche and into the audience-favorite mainstream.

Sabu regular Shin'ichi Tsutsumi ("Postman Blues," "Unlucky Monkey") stars as Takagi, a salaryman who wakes up hungover one Monday in a hotel bedroom with no memory of how he got there — or where his weekend went. Then he discovers a packet of salts, the kind given to mourners at funerals, and the fog lifts for a moment. He remembers attending the wake of a young colleague and being inadvertently responsible for the horribly funny way it ended.

No need to detail this comic disaster — only to say that, by clipping the wrong wire, Takagi gives his colleague a send-off unique in the history of film, if not fireworks. The rest of "Monday" segues between the past and the present, as Takagi pieces together more fragments of his lost weekend.

As his past actions, both the idiotic and the deadly, begin to impinge on his increasingly desperate present, the film moves toward its explosive, surreal, finale.

After the wake, a shaky Takagi meets his girlfriend (Naomi Nishida) at a coffee shop. He tries to tell her his story, but she barely lets him get a word in edgewise. When he finally blurts it out — and dissolves into giggles at its absurdity — she storms out in disgust. Takagi, we see, not only has a big communications problem with women, but a strange personality.

After this fiasco, he winds up in a bar where he encounters, in quick succession, a gay fortuneteller (Hideki Noda) with an interest in more than his palm and a woman (Yasuko Matsuyuki) whose sultry looks and slinky sheath dress make him steam at the ears. Unfortunately, he also attracts the attention of her man (Toru Yamamoto), a snarling gang boss who invites Takagi to drink at his club. Under the glare of the boss's permanently pissed-off subordinates, the poor simp can't refuse.

By now, however, Takagi is thoroughly soused and beginning to lose his Mr. Nice Guy inhibitions. At the club, he dances an impassioned disco solo, a la John Travolta, under the stony gazes of the gangsters and club hostesses, then grabs his host's lady friend and performs a sensual pas des deux. His host is starting to lose his carefully studied cool. After the dance, he invites Takagi upstairs for a private chat. It ends with one dead yakuza and Takagi walking out of the club, shotgun in hand, for a date with destiny.

Sabu's previous films all had similar small-actions-have-big-consequences plots — but in "Monday" the elements click into place with a new precision and effectiveness. I found myself laughing on the beat, an experience I hadn't had with a Japanese film since Koki Mitani's superb, sitcom-ish, "Welcome Back, Mr. McDonald," but Sabu's brand of comedy is far drier.

Also, "Monday" delves deeper into not only the psychology (or pathology) of the salaryman, but the eternal tug of war between fate and free will, peaceful hopes and violent realities. Though Takagi initially seems to be the helpless plaything of malevolent gods, his tribulations force him to assert, define and justify himself. While abandoning the comforts of traditional fatalism, Sabu also rejects the "zero to hero" formula of Hollywood. There is something heartwarming in Takagi's transition from corporate mouse to outlaw lion, roaring his defiance at the guardians of the law, but there is also something ridiculous. He remains, from beginning to end, irredeemably and hilariously weird. A nerd triumphant, but a nerd for all that.

Dora-Heita, runtime: 111 min.

"Dora-Heita," the 74th film by the 84-year-old Kon Ichikawa, is one of those ideas that sounds terrific on paper, but becomes more problematic, if not impossible, in practice. In the case of this serio-comic samurai drama about a canny-but-fearless machi bugyo (an Edo Period sheriff) who cleans up a corrupt castle town, the various problems involved its production became so formidable that it spent three decades in development hell (or rather limbo) before finally going before the cameras in February of last year.

The idea: Four master directors pool their talents for a film, with the aim of revitalizing the struggling Japanese film industry. The idea man: Akira Kurosawa, who was recovering from the disaster of "Tora Tora Tora" — the World War II epic from which he had been recently fired by Twentieth Century Fox. (Accounts vary — Kurosawa insisted to the last that he resigned.) He wanted to film "Diary of a Town Magistrate" ("Machi Bugyo Nikki"), a novel by long-time favorite Shugoro Yamamoto, but rather than do it himself, he asked three distinguished colleagues — Ichikawa, Masaki Kobayashi and Keisuke Kinoshita — to make it with him.

They called themselves, romantically, the Four Musketeers (Yonki no Kai) and began with big dreams of recruiting talented unknown musketeers and producing a series of films. But though the musketeers eventually came up with a script, which bore a family resemblance to Kurosawa's 1961 hit "Yojinbo," they went on to other projects and "Dora-Heita" went into a drawer — until Ichikawa rescued it in 1998.

The resulting film is not, as one might expect, a Kurosawa tribute: "Dora-Heita" was already scheduled to start shooting when Kurosawa died in September 1998, and it is very much an Ichikawa film in look and pace. It is also, quite deliberately, a period piece — even the credits look as though they have been recycled from a 1960s jidaigeki (period drama).

This was a reasonable choice on the part of Ichikawa and his veteran staff — too much updating would have undermined the film's raison d'etre. On the other hand, by shooting "Dora-Heita" in 1998 much as he might have shot it in 1969, Ichikawa shows why dozens of scripts by other famous dead directors remain in drawers.

Films may not have sell-by dates, but they are of their time. If Ozu were alive today, he wouldn't be making Ozu movies — the Japan and the Japanese film industry of "Tokyo Story" no longer exist. Samurai movies are somewhat different, but not entirely so — though set in a pre-modern Japan, they are still influenced by the Zeitgeist outside the studio walls and the state of the art within. Ichikawa, one of the great stylists of Japanese films, has put his antique script on the screen with his characteristic visual sumptuousness and flair, but he can't hide all the yellow on the pages, or the lumpiness of the material itself.

Four cooks may not have spoiled this particular broth — the movie has its entertaining moments — but they also failed to give it a strong, distinctive taste. "Dora-Heita" is not so much "Yojinbo" and water as "Yojinbo" and several types of thickeners, as though its four writers decided to combine their four scripts instead of blend their best elements.

The story is stamped from the mold of a million westerns. A new machi bugyo, Mochizuki Koheita (Koji Yakusho), arrives in a provincial town from Edo. Because he embodies the legal authority of the shogunate, the local clan officials and other power brokers defer to him, at least on the surface, but as the town metsuke (superintendent officers), Yasukawa Hanzo (Tsurutaro Kataoka) and Senba Gijuro (Ryudo Uzaki) make clear, trouble is brewing in River City in the form of smuggling, prostitution, gambling and murder-for-hire.

Three oyabun, (gang bosses), led by the white-haired, black-hearted Nadahachi (Bunta Sugawara), run these rackets, with the knowledge and acquiescence of the town authorities. Mochizuki, or Dora-Heita ("Scapegrace Heita"), as those who know him (and dislike him) call him, would seem to be worst possible choice for battling this corruption.

Instead of dealing sternly with the offenders, he holes up in a cheap inn and, using the money the town fathers have provided him, proceeds to blow it on riotous living — indulging all the vices he is supposed to suppress.

But Mochizuki is crazy like a fox. While gambling and wenching, he is becoming friends with the town's yakuza and geisha and learning where all the bodies are buried. When three young righteous samurai get wind of these disgraceful goings-on they decide to rid the town of this wastrel — and learn that Mochizuki is as good with his sword as he is free with the treasury's koban (gold pieces). This man, they see, is more than meets the eye.

He is not, however, without weaknesses, one being his love for a feisty, sharp-tongued Edo geisha named Kosei (Yuko Asano) and his undying reluctance to commit. He took the bugyo job partly to escape her clutches, but she finds him and takes up exactly where she left off — whereupon Mochizuki suddenly changes from warrior to wimp.

He is less at a loss, however, in pursuing his anti-corruption campaign, finally rousing the wrath of the gangs and moving the film toward its epic, one-against-all climax.

Appearing in his first samurai drama, Koji Yakusho acquits himself well enough as the jaded, sarcastic, but coolly competent Mochizuki. He gives the film whatever contemporary edge it possesses, but I couldn't help noticing that the part was written for Toshiro Mifune — and wondering how much more physical dynamism and emotional voltage Kurosawa's favorite samurai might have brought to the film.

Yakusho slices dozens of baddies with commendable panache, but his triumph is also one of skillful editing to disguise his middle-aged moves. I also couldn't help wondering why a supposed action movie was so everlastingly talky and why the joke of the shrewish mistress seemed so stale. But then I wasn't the producer who greenlighted the script — three decades too late.

Love/Juice, runtime: 78 min.

On Oct. 13, 1999 a new late-night program started on Fuji TV starring Tsunku, a pop musician and producer whose acts include the red-hot idol group Morning Musume. Tsunku, however, did not intend to devote his "Tsunku Town" show to discovering yet more cutesy singing sensations. Instead, he announced that he had been given 100 million in cold, hard yen by an unnamed angel to produce creative projects. After a lengthy hashing out with his guests, he decided to make — ta da! — movies. Over the next several weeks the show resembled an ongoing production meeting as Tsunku and company thrashed out the details, finally settling on a budget of 10 million yen, with story ideas to be solicited on the "Tsunku Town" Web site (www.tsunku-town.net). By March the first "Tsunku Town" film, a drama about the group dating phenomenon called go con (literal translation: "mixed company") was in the theaters.

Two more have since joined it: Kaze Shindo's "Love/Juice" and Shugo Fujii's "Living Hell" ("Ikijigoku"). On the basis of these two films — I have not yet seen "Go Con" — I would say that "Tsunku Town" is batting .300: Shindo's is an impressive, if slow-footed, debut, while Fujii's is a risible over-the-top shocker that may find second life as a campy Midnight Madness favorite.

"Love/Juice" is billed as the story of an unusual friendship between two women: one lesbian and the other supposedly straight (or as the flier blurb puts in gairaigo, "normal"). But short-haired, fiery-eyed Chinatsu (Chika Fujimura) and pouty-lipped Kyoko (Mika Okuno) not only live together in a ramshackle little red house, but club together, sleep together and share every intimacy together. Kyoko, in other words, is "normal" if one accepts Gore Vidal's theory that only homosexual acts, not homosexuality, exists.

Chinatsu and Kyoko begin the film in a giddy, carefree romantic dream, in which even a trip to the supermarket becomes a delightful romp. This kind of thing is fine in small doses — I was reminded of Charlie Chaplin and Paulette Godard playing house in "Modern Times" — but first-time director Shindo gives us too much of Eden, until we begin to understand Kyoko's growing restiveness.

While Chinatsu is snapping picture after lovingly framed picture of the object of her adoration, Kyoko is battling boredom and having thoughts of . . . men, including the beefy bartender at their favorite club and the silent-but-dishy manager of a local pet fish shop.

Ostensibly the dominant partner in this relationship, Chinatsu tries to force Kyoko to stop wandering — even turning away the bartender when he shows up at their house with a smile and a six-pack — but Kyoko rebels and, in doing so, exposes another side to her winsome childishness — a hard core of selfishness.

Kyoko's only love, we see, is the girl in the mirror; her only aim, to satisfy that girl's every whim, both the innocent and the cruel. She begins to probe her partner's weaknesses: "You've never had an orgasm, have you?" she asks Chinatsu one day in bed, with the merciless persistence of a 6-year-old.

Finding the power balance suddenly reversed, Chinatsu tries everything to restore Eden, including the desperate expedient of seducing the husky, hard-eyed manager of the hostess club where she and Kyoko work. But her brush with straight sexuality devolves into a hellish fiasco.

Finally, she abases herself before Kyoko, declaring her undying love — with devastating results.

The granddaughter of master director and scriptwriter Kaneto Shindo, Shindo demonstrates that talent does indeed run in families, with an explosive third act that redeems the longueurs of the first two. Also, she builds to this climax with the kind of professional skill and cunning she may have learned at granddad's knee, but there is nothing derivative in her execution. Trained as a documentarian, she is sensitive to the ambiguous realities of her characters' unusual relationship — and is willing to allow those realities to unfold, without pushing them into PC molds or box-office formulas.

Zawa Zawa Shimokitazawa, runtime: 105 min.

Some directors become hometown heroes, whose favorite cities appear again and again in their films and become indelibly associated with their names — think Federico Fellini and Rome, Woody Allen and New York.

Jun Ichikawa, however, went one step farther in not only setting a film entirely in a beloved neighborhood — Tokyo's Shimokitazawa — but premiering it in a theater there. Why Shimokitazawa, a bohemian enclave and theater district? In a program interview, Ichikawa cites the place's "strange appeal." "People from different generations live quietly and peacefully together," he explains. That is, it's a fortunate exception to the fractious and isolated rule of urban life.

"Zawa Zawa Shimokitazawa" may be somewhat out of the ordinary in its localization, but it marks a return, after the stylistic experimentations of "Tadon and Chikuwa" and the Kansai earthiness of "Osaka Story," to essential Ichikawa. Shot after perfectly composed shot poetically evokes rather than conventionally explains, and the naturalistic dialogue sounds more improvised than written, but expresses character and advances the story.

Ichikawa has often been compared to Yasujiro Ozu (and has invited such comparisons with homages to Ozu's work) but his films also resemble those of Eric Rohmer in their affectionate attention to the realities of relationships in today's advanced societies. The principals may seem freer than their tradition-bound parents, but their romantic transactions are also more fragile and fragmentary.

In love with the slower-paced, more human-centered Tokyo of his youth, the 51-year-old Ichikawa is also no nostalgist spinning cliches from a rosily misremembered past. He seeks the essence of that Tokyo in contemporary faces, gestures and inflections, in cityscapes that everyone knows but few see. He reveals the pathos and beauty that exists, not on an exalted plane, but in everyday lives.

At their best, his films are gifts of a fresh, but intimately familiar spiritual vision.

As with many Ichikawa films, "Zawa Zawa Shimokitazawa" begins as a group portrait but coalesces around turning points in the lives of its principals. One is Yuki (Tomoko Kitagawa), a 20-year-old waitress in a cafe near the station. Another is the cafe manager, Kyushiro (Yoshio Harada), who leads a troupe of actors that has been performing regularly at a local theater for more than a decade. The cafe mama, Yoko (Lily), is also a longtime Shimokitazawa resident, whose relationship with Kyushiro has remained firmly one of friendship. Something of a throwback — she exudes a purity more reminiscent of an Ozu heroine than a Shibuya girl — Yuki faces a very New Millennial dilemma. She is, she feels, running down an endless track, while her relationship with her boyfriend, Tatsuya (Masayoshi Ozawa), is on the cusp of a change — but of what kind she cannot clearly say.

Meanwhile, Tatsuya drifts in and out of a job with a publishing company, takes photos, plays the bongos and hangs out with his slacker friends. He also becomes involved in a desultory affair with a woman who works in a Shimokitazawa secondhand shop — and offers him what Yuki cannot.

In thrashing out her various issues, Yuki draws comfort from her aunt (Ingrid Fujiko Hemming), a gravel-voiced dowager who plays a soulful classical piano and has survived life's battles with her salty sense of humor intact. Yuki is also inspired by Kyushiro's performance in a swordplay drama that he's staged dozens of times, but still injects with sparks of passion. He may think he's just going through the motions, but he still yearns for something more. (He talks, without conviction, of quitting show business and retiring to Okinawa.)

Yuki, too yearns for something more. By the end of the film, she decides to find it and move on.

In filming these and other transitions in his characters' lives, Ichikawa uses supporting metaphors, including the usual one of changing seasons (the film begins in the heat of the summer and ends in the chill of winter) and the unusual one of a small Tengu-like object that Yuki gives to Tatsuya. In the course of the film, it changes hands several more times, not only linking the characters in a karmic chain, but underlining the transience of their relationships.

There is sadness in the Tengu's journey from love token to good luck charm, but there is also hope. Ichikawa believes in the essential goodness of its owners, who may not be perfect, but appreciate its value. In Ichikawa's Shimokitazawa old things and old ways still matter and still live. In a modern Japan dedicated to eradicating and Disneyfying its past, it's comforting to know that such pockets of resistance still exist.

As Yuki, Kitagawa gives a performance at once interior and transparent. Not because she expresses every thought literally, but because she truly inhabits her character, in all her reserve and directness. It's interesting that Kitagawa spent most of her school years in Saipan, but still impresses as "purely" Japanese — perhaps another case of an expat preserving aspects of the home country culture long after the natives have abandoned them.

Meanwhile, Ozawa (the son of conductor Seiji Ozawa) heats up the screen as the restless Tatsuya. With brooding good looks and a confident presence reminiscent of the young Yujiro Ishihara, Ozawa hits the power chords the film needs to make it more than yet another minor-key essay on postadolescent angst.

In his 13th film, Ichikawa again shows why he is among the best and most consistent filmmakers of his generation. The man has never made a bad movie and, as his latest proves, he is only getting better with age. A lot like Shimokitazawa itself.

The New God, Atarashii Kamisama, runtime: 99 min.

Fiction and nonfiction films are commonly put in separate boxes, with the former considered entertainment and the latter, not. Documentary filmmakers here, as elsewhere, have long accepted this commercial sentence of doom and sought rationales for their work outside the mainstream standards of box-office success, often in leftist political movements and social causes. With the decline of the Japanese radical left into factional infighting and political irrelevancy, young documentarians who might have once manned the cinematic barricades have shifted the focus of their work from the public to the personal.

Several of the most talented, including Naomi Kawase, Nobuhiro Suwa and Hirokazu Koreeda, have made fiction films using not only documentary techniques, but also the themes and motifs of their documentary work. Meanwhile, in recent years fiction filmmakers such as Jun Ichikawa, Ryosuke Hashiguchi and Satoshi Isaka have injected a documentary flavor into their work, examples being Ichikawa's extended montage sequences of ordinary people doing ordinary things in "Dying at a Hospital (1993), Hashiguchi's long climactic one-cut scene in "A Touch of Fever)" (1994), with its hand-held camera and improvisatory feel, and Isaka's decision to make "Focus" (1996), his expose of media corruption, as a faux documentary.

This blurring of the boundaries continues in Yutaka Tsuchiya's "The New God," a documentary that begins as a meditation on the search of the younger generation for meaning in the political and spiritual void of modern Japan, but becomes an unlikely relationship film, reminiscent of the work of Ken Loach and Woody Allen.

I never thought I'd hear "Annie-Hall"-like lines in a movie whose star is a fervent rightist — until I saw "The New God." Tsuchiya, who was born in 1966 and began making films in 1990, is serious about his theme of Gen-X angst, but his directorial stance differs significantly from that of documentary filmmakers of the previous generation, who often took farmers and other common folks for their subjects.

A self-described lefty, who filmed two documentaries on the issue of the Emperor's war responsibility, Tsuchiya has focused "The New God" on two members of that seeming oxymoron, a rightist punk band.

The band's leader, Hidehito Ito, and its vocalist, Karin Amamiya, may look like typical rockers (with her heavy makeup, long blond hair and throaty, sexy voice, Amamiya is a Japanese cousin to Courtney Love), but both belong to a rightist fringe group and harangue the crowds at their live-house appearances with appeals to prewar patriotism. (Their reception from these crowds is not always the warmest, however.)

One might expect Tsuchiya, whose politics are diametrically opposed to those of his subjects, to demonize or satirize them. But while confronting Ito and Amamiya about their beliefs, he refuses to type them as villains or mock them as fools. Instead, his attitude is one of curiosity and even active sympathy.

What has made them embrace the politics and values of their grandparents, when the only "isms" embraced by most of their generation are materialism and careerism? Are they really filled with the old fervor to revive the glory and defend the honor of Dai-Nippon? Or are other motives at work?

The more interesting of this pair, he soon decides, is Amamiya, who had a troubled youth (she was a target of classroom bullies and attempted suicide several times) but later found a measure of fulfillment and release in art. She made dolls that exuded, not the usual asexual cuteness, but an ethereal beauty and a strange loneliness.

Then she discovered something larger than what she described as her "empty self": romantic nationalism. In the sacrifices of the war generation, all those boys who went off to die for the Emperor and Empire, she saw something bigger than the Western-style individualism of the postwar period, which had devolved into mere narcissism. She began to worship a "new god."

Tsuchiya, who also questions the prevailing ethos and seeks a way out of a personal impasse, finds a kindred spirit in this straight-talking young woman. He gives her a digital camera to record her every thought and mood, and sends her off to North Korea, to visit Red Army members who fled there after hijacking a JAL flight in 1975.

The object is to engage, provoke and, not incidentally, get some interesting footage. Amamiya comes through, but probably not the way Tsuchiya expected. Instead of lecturing the aging radicals on their dereliction of their patriotic duty, she drinks their beer, laughs at their jokes and finds them to be (surprise, surprise) human. She perceives that her new friends and their North Korean hosts are, like her, searching for a "new god." She sympathizes with their quest, and begins questioning her own assumptions about the meaning of "left" and "right."

Thus begins a personal journey for Amamiya that continues to the end of the film (and, one suspects, beyond). It is also a revelation for Tsuchiya, who becomes attracted to Amamiya not only as a subject for his film, but also as a woman. His own "new god" is more personal than he had thought.

More than the earnest talk about the end of ideology and the search for meaning, I found the film's real message in Amamiya's absorption in the camera, as though it were a best friend who would vibrate sympathetically with her every change of mood, and give its undivided attention to her every word. The real "new god" of her generation has but a single eye.

Face, Kao, runtime: 124 min.

When a film was based on a true story, I used to wonder why the actors always looked better than the real people they were playing. Take away their scowls and even most tough-guy actors are handsomer than the real-life thugs they portray. That was before I learned the first rule of the box office: Moviegoers of whatever stripe, be they Brad Pitt worshippers or Robert Bresson scholars, like to see beautiful people on the screen. There have been exceptions throughout film history (the matronly Marie Dressler, the basset-houndish Walter Matthau), but they only prove the rule. When Hollywood makes a movie about a plain Jane who can't get a date, it hires Michelle Pfeiffer.

Junji Sakamoto's "Face" ("Kao") is thus a rara avis indeed. Its heroine Masako, played by stage actress Naomi Fujiyama, is a plus-sized frump and an eccentric recluse, who spends her lonely days in the ratty upstairs room of her mother's ancient dry cleaning establishment, sewing clothes, mainlining cookies and indulging in bizarre fantasies (one being a desert idyll with zoo animals).

Watching the opening scenes, I thought "Face" was going to be another version of the ugly duckling story, but Masako never turns into a swan. Rather than slim down, shape up and live happily ever after with Mr. Right, she remains frumpy and strange, but begins fulfilling long-deferred dreams, however small. In her own odd way, she remains true to herself. Despite all the masks she wears in the course of the film, she is, inevitably, Masako.

Given this realism, both exterior and interior, it's a wonder that "Face" ever got made. It's based on the true, widely reported, story of a bar hostess who murdered one of her coworkers and spent years in hiding, only to be caught as the statute of limitations was about to expire.

In writing this story for the screen, however, Junji Sakamoto and Isamu Uno tossed nearly everything save their heroine's flight and profession. Dramatic chase, capture and trial scenes are absent. There is not even a murder scene; we see a body, but can only guess how it got that way. But minus all the usual melodrama, "Face" manages to be a deeply engrossing and quirkily entertaining film about the survival and education of a contrary spirit.

"The Fugitive" it isn't, but a hit it is: The screening I attended at Theatre Shinjuku was packed, with the management thoughtfully handing out cushions to late arrivals.

Masako is drudging away at the side of her sharp-tongued mother (Misako Watanabe) while her pretty younger sister Yukari (Riho Makise) rakes in the money at a hostess bar and flits off to Disneyland with her latest boyfriend. Naturally, these two can't stand each other and, when their mother suddenly dies at the steam iron, fireworks erupt.

Yukari ends up dead at the foot of the stairs, and Masako flees with the condolence money. She is torn between guilt — even visiting a police box with the intent of turning herself in — and a fierce, animal desire to escape and live. But after years in her room, with her television as her only companion, she is as unsocialized as a bear freed from its cage. Her movement through the world is full of awkward fits and starts, but somehow, with a kind of instinctive radar, she seeks out sympathetic souls, safe refuges.

One is a love hotel, where she first stays as a guest (no registers for snoopy cops to peruse), then works as a maid. The manager (Ittoku Kishibe), a silent type, knows she is hiding something but doesn't care; he has a more important problem, financial ruin, to contend with.

Before the final debacle, he teaches her to ride a bicycle — a task her long-absent father couldn't be bothered with. Fleeing again when the police make a call, she winds up in a seedy Kyushu resort town where she encounters a friendly bar mama (Michiyo Okusu) and her sullen ex-yakuza brother (Etsushi Toyokawa). Working as a hostess, she begins, for the first time, to find a measure of acceptance and happiness.

In a regular (Jun Kunimura) with a sad-sack face and bad marriage, she even discovers the glimmerings of romance. Improbably and wonderfully, Masako begins to bloom. Then the ex-yakuza's past catches up with him and her little world comes crashing down.

Masako's past will catch up with her as well, on a small island off the coast of Kyushu. Ironically, it will be because she is no longer the shuffling loner with no friends and no future. She has come out of her shell and no cop or ghost of remorse is going to force her back into it.

Playing Masako, most actresses would go for crowd-pleasing caricature. Naomi Fujiyama creates a character whose prickly, wary individuality is anything but conventionally charming. She is unique, this Masako, almost simple-minded in expressing her fears and needs, but capable of telling home truths in a level voice with a disconcerting seriousness.

Her many faces make "Face" a most extraordinary movie. If there is any justice in the Japanese movie business (and there is, occasionally), Fujiyama will sweep this year's acting awards, but she may have trouble finding a suitable followup — unless she morphs into Masako's younger sister.

Gojoe, runtime: 138 min.

Period dramas (jidaigeki) once accounted for nearly half of all films made in Japan. Then, in the 1960s, top-knotted heroes began moving their act from the big to the small screen and the genre went into a long decline.

In the past year there has been a revival of sorts, led by directors on the far side of 50. But whatever merits Masahiro Shinoda's "Owl's Castle," Kon Ichikawa's "Dora-Heita," Nagisa Oshima's "Gohatto" and Takashi Koizumi's "When the Rain Lifts" may have as films, they are less reinventions of the genre than late-career reworkings of familiar themes.

Among younger filmmakers, the period drama has inspired scant enthusiasm. Their sporadic attempts to pump new life into the genre, such as Kaizo Hayashi's 1990 "Zipang" and Hiroyuki Nakano's 1998 "SF Samurai Fiction," have been little more than mangaesque parodies.

For producer Takenori Sento this lacuna represented an opportunity. If the "Ring" horror series, which he helped produce, could hit at the box office by applying a teen-friendly gloss to genre conventions, why couldn't he do the same for jidaigeki?

"I'm not going to make a period drama," he told me in a 1998 interview. "I'm going to make an action movie — a Japanese action movie." In other words, goodbye to tired cliches, hello to Gen-X attitude, stud star power and eye-popping visuals.

Sento found a willing collaborator in indie director Sogo Ishii, who had long been mulling a period-drama project based on the life of Minamoto no Yoshitsune (1159-89). A general of the Minamoto clan, whose brilliant victories over the rival Taira have long been celebrated in story and song, Yoshitsune fell from grace when his jealous older brother Yoritomo (1147-99), the clan head, suddenly turned against him.

Pursued to the wilds of northern Japan by Yoritomo's troops, Yoshitsune found a protector in Fujiwara no Hidehira, a local warlord, but when Fujiwara died, his son yielded to pressure from Yoritomo and offered to surrender Yoshitsune. Rather than endure disgrace at his brother's hands, Yoshitsune ended his life by suicide in 1189.

Ishii intended to focus on the fabled tussle between Yoshitsune and Benkei, a fighting monk, on Kyoto's Gojo Bridge. Yoshitsune won and Benkei became his loyal retainer, accompanying his master throughout his career, on his flight north and into his subsequent exile.

The story of this struggle, like the one between Robin Hood and Little John in Sherwood Forest, has acquired an accretion of legend and symbolism. In both the young, handsome hero overcomes his larger, stronger, simpler opponent with skill and wit, while winning his heart with his star charisma. The facts have long ceased to matter — and rightly so.

In "Gojoe," the visually extravagant film Sento and Ishii finally made from this story, not only facts but reality has taken a holiday. In place of the effete youth of legend, the film's Yoshitsune, played by Tadanobu Asano, is a two-sworded killing machine with supernatural powers, whose hatred for the triumphant Taira has become a madness.

Accompanied by two young retainers, Yoshitsune has established a base in a wood near the capital, where he wreaks havoc on hapless Taira troops, slashing through their colorful armor as though it were so much marzipan. In pursuit of this fiend in human form goes Benkei (Daisuke Ryu), once a warrior consumed with a devilish rage of his own, who became a monk after accidentally killing his son in a fit of anger.

Though possessed of spiritual powers himself (he casts out a demon who possesses a pregnant woman) Benkei doubts his fitness for this ultimate challenge. Instead of the stout-hearted hero of tradition, this Benkei is a conflicted soul, who may carry a big two-edged sword, but is reluctant to use it. At the urging of his saintly teacher (Saburo Teshigawara), and with a disillusioned swordmaker (Masatoshi Nagase) as a guide, he ventures into the woods, where he encounters forces beyond the ability of a mere mortal to comprehend, let alone conquer.

Most terrifying of all is his opponent's ability to confront him with his own past.

Ishii and cinematographer Makoto Watanabe express the mythic grandiosity of the story, particularly its climactic duel to the death, by shattering reality into hallucinatory fragments, while the camera performs stunts worthy of an Olympic gymnast. Ishii is not merely making a two-hour music video (though the program comes with a CD of Hiroyuki Onogawa's pulsing techno score), but creating a sensory and narrative experience of hypnotic intensity and density.

Those who expect a Heian Era jidaigeki to have a wispy ethereal beauty may go into shock at the pounding the film delivers. Those who have experienced the wilder matsuri (festivals), with their audio-visual overloads, will be better prepared for what transpires.

In the midst of all the hyperactivity is a rock-solid performance by Ryu as Benkei, which combines the lean intensity of a monk who has just descended from the mountain with the spiritual fragility of a man who has wrestled with the dark angel and won an uncertain victory.

In the end, however, the film recalls the more excessive episodes of the "Dragonball Z" cartoon show. "Gojo" may do what Sento intended — bring in the same kids who made the "Ring" films an event — but it's not going to make anyone forget "Seven Samurai." Kurosawa's masterpiece delivers the essence of battle with authority; Ishii's struggles are all behind the eyelids, eidetic images from a strange and troubled dream.

Freeze Me, runtime: 101 min.

Takashi Ishii loves to see women suffer — and triumph. Thus the rapes in film after film (Shinobu Otake was the victim in "Original Sin," Kimiko Yo in "A Night in Nude," Maiko Kawakami in "Angel Guts: Red Lightening," Yumi Takigawa and Yui Natsukawa in "Gonin 2"). Thus the scenes of revenge, in which women kick their male tormentors silly or blast them into oblivion. (Reona Hazuki did both with ruthless efficiency in the first installment of the aptly titled "Black Angel" series.)

This mix of exploitation and entitlement (if you consider films about avenging angels with assault weapons as "entitlement") is hardly unusual in the Japanese film business, but Ishii takes it to new levels of obsession — and art. Though he may be making product for the video shelves, Ishii is clearly in love with his work and talented at making us feel the heat of his fixations. This is not always a pleasant experience, but when Ishii is at the top of his form, it is a powerful one. Think Brian De Palma, but of "Body Double," not "Mission to Mars."

In "Freeze Me," Ishii reveals yet another side of his artistic personality — a fascination with horror and a blackly humorous, flesh-crawling way of expressing it. The obvious comparisons are with David Lynch's walks on the weird side, but the core of this film about a woman's ultimate nightmare — gangbangers with the persistence and implacability of Terminators — remains unmistakably Ishii. One wants to say, "There he goes again," but instead of simply repeating a formula, he uncuts expectations to sensual, sickening and memorable effect.

His heroine, Chihiro (Harumi Inoue) whom we first meet getting uproariously drunk with her office mates and stumbling back to her apartment, impresses as a deserving victim in Japanese movie terms, being both trashy and ditzy. But Inoue, a former idol whose skinhead look for a Kishin Shinoyama nude photo book brought her outlaw notoriety, also projects a street-girl cunning and toughness.

Chihiro may have made the worst possible choices in men at one point in her life, but this O.L. with the copper-colored hair is not about to let her past mistakes ruin her present, which is happier than she once dared hope. She has a job she likes and a man she wants to marry (a goateed colleague who is nice, if a bit slow). Then, suddenly, it all falls apart.

One day she spies a man riffling through the mailboxes in her apartment building. He is, she senses, a predator, whose mocking smile inspires fear. Then she flashes on a moment in her past that she has been trying to put behind her for five years — a rape by three men on a snowy day in her native Tohoku. Her visitor was one of them.

To her horror, he spots her, chases her and forces his way into her apartment. With a terrible insouciance, he plays the long-lost lover and, when she tries to escape, responds with violence, intimidation and stills taken from a video of her rape that he begins stuffing in her neighbors' mail slots. The intruder, Hirokawa (Kazuki Kitamura), tells her that her other two rapists are on their way for a reunion. The occasion: their leader, a gangster named Baba (Naoto Takenaka), has just been released from prison and is eager to take up where he left off. "We'll have a four-way sex party to celebrate his release," says Hirokawa, but as Chihiro soon discovers, he is not about to wait for his turn.

Even worse is yet to come, however. Her boyfriend (Shunsuke Matsuoka) pays an unexpected visit and, when Hirokawa tells him about the rape, leaves in anger and confusion. Not content to destroy her personal life, Hirokawa next shows up at her office and creates a scene designed to get her fired. By this time, the audience is aching for the catharsis of Hirokawa's richly deserved end — and Ishii delivers, with a killing that makes the shower scene in "Psycho" look like a child's bathtub romp. But Chihiro now has a body to dispose of. Time is pressing: The other rapists might arrive any moment. Then she notices the big empty space inside her fridge . . .

Chihiro's unusual hiding place is funny, but Ishii's primary aim is not laughs. Now still and silent, Hirokawa has become, as Chihiro notes with delight and awe, ethereally beautiful. In life a monster, in death he has become a frozen specimen of ideal manhood — as well as a perfect listener. Now that her life has been returned to zero, she decides to keep him. Every girl needs someone she can talk to, at least until the next visitor comes calling.

Kazuki Kitamura, who displayed a similar feral energy as a gangster in Rokuro Mochizuki's "Minazuki," plays Hirokawa to chill perfection. Shingo Tsurumi and Naoto Takenaka are also creepy as the other two rapists, but their moral monsters are also all-too familiar (Takenaka has been playing variations of his for years).

It doesn't help that Chihiro uses the same basic murder method for all three. Boiled down, "Freeze Me" is the Three Pigs story with the numbers reversed. There is, however, nothing childish about Ishii's vision of evil, which is universal and specific. His demons would be familiar to Thomas Aquinas, but their attitudes and actions reflect the realities of today's Japan, in which stalkers prey.

No social reformer, Ishii sees more clearly than many of his directorial colleagues how that evil still too-often roams unhindered. Chihiro's solution is extreme, but her worst fears are not illusions.

2001

Party 7, runtime: 104 min.

Writing about Japanese films in English, I am usually flying below the radar of the local industry — I can skewer a director's latest triumph on this page and meet him later at a party secure in the knowledge that he has not the foggiest idea of what I've said about his movie. Once in a while, though, I do catch it. One memorable evening the producer of Katsuhito Ishii's feature debut, "Sharkskin Man and Peach Hip Girl," called me to cuss me out in English for my review, in which I described the film as "less an eiga (movie) than an eiga gokko (movie game)" and compared Ishii unfavorably to Quentin Tarantino, whom he obviously worshipped (and who, incidentally, raved about "Sharkskin" to its director after seeing it at the Hawaii Film Festival).

It was an interesting experience, hearing the f-word 20 times in five minutes from an urbane Japanese man fluent in English, though in the heat of the moment his favorite insult began to sound like a katakana rendering of "far king."

Now Ishii's second film, "Party 7," is on the screens, and I'm afraid that the wrath of my producer friend, who is listed in the credits, is going to descend on me again.

Nearly everything I said about the first film applies to the new one, an over-hyper, over-produced comedy about a pair of peeping Toms who spy on a pompadoured punk and his tarty ex-girlfriend, with unexpected consequences for both sides. Ishii, an in-demand TV commercial and music video director, brings the technique and sensibility of his day job to his films.

The technique involves digital games with film speed reminiscent of the Keystone Cops (i.e., fast=funny), with a sensibility heavily influenced by manga and anime and the work of not only Tarantino but also Luc Besson (the cartoony costume designs look lifted from "The Fifth Element").

What might have looked fresh and funny in a three-minute clip becomes grating after 104 minutes. To give him credit, Ishii wants to entertain, not merely show off, and has original ideas about how to do it. Also, he gives his two-dimensional creations a hint of a third, while refusing to condescend to them. (Have fun with them, yes, condescend to them, no).

It's a film that a Japanese pop culture otaku like Tarantino would like — it comes from enough inside that culture to be credible, while paced and structured to be accessible to anyone, including American moviegoers who only know anime from the latest Pokémon.

The protagonist, Miki (Masatoshi Nagase), decides to ditch his career as a petty hoodlum and rip off his boss for 200 million yen. On the recommendation of an eccentric travel agent, he ends up at the Hotel New Mexico, which is appropriately rundown and out of the way. It is managed by a middle-aged Peeping Tom (Yoshio Harada) who has not only built a special "peeping room" that gives him intimate access to all his guests, but assumed a special peeping identity as Captain Banana, complete with a yellow superhero costume and a mask that makes him look like a lascivious salamander.

He is joined in this lair by Okita (Tadanobu Asano), the puffy-faced son of a former peeping companion, who is a peeper himself. Though at first taken aback by Captain Banana's act, Okita soon realizes that he has met a man after his own heart — and together they sit down to watch, through a one-way mirror, the goings-on in Miki's room.

It is lively enough, this show, though hardly sexy. Miki is visited by the leggy Kana (Akemi Kobayashi), an ex-girlfriend, who wants to collect money he owes her, even though she is about to marry a wealthy man, one Todohira (Yoshinori Okada). Miki, understandably, objects, even more vociferously when Todohira himself appears and reveals himself as runty, combative and suspiciously unaffluent.

Miki's quarrel with his new rival soon pales into insignificance when the gruff Sonoda (Keisuke Horibe), an aniki ("elder brother") from the gang, swaggers into the room to kill Miki and recover the money. Meanwhile, a gang wakagashira (lieutenant) with an Afro hairdo and a hair-trigger temper is on his way to check up on Sonoda and become the seventh member of this party from hell.

The film's gangsters are cartoons, though Masatoshi Nagase's has a low-life Lothario appeal reminiscent of his teenage Elvis fan in Jim Jarmusch's "Mystery Train." Funnier are the pair of peepers, who pass the time between incidents in Miki's room by comparing their "10 best peeps" and giving each other high fives.

This kind of naughty otaku fun finds its parallel in Ishii's own approach to filmmaking. Does he has a life, one wonders, outside the screening room and studio? Perhaps he should think of getting some fresh air. It's a big world out there — and one wilder than anything in "Party 7."

Avalon, runtime: 107 min.

Dark future movies are, by now, as established an SF subgenre as creature features or space operas. Their world view is usually a cross between an Orwellian nightmare and a Jean Paul Gaultier fashion show: grim, oppressive and dangerous but sexy, radical and cool. In other words, you wouldn't mind visiting, but you'd hate to live there.

It all goes back to "Blade Runner," which has had a bigger impact on dark-future films — and their art directors — than any other. But times have changed since Ridley Scott was updating the definition of human for the '80s, while introducing the word "replicant" to the language.

Today, instead of artificial entities who look, talk and act like us, dark-future films are speculating more about the unreality of reality and the merging of humanity with the bit stream that threatens to engulf us. Among the best is "Ghost in the Shell," a 1995 animation by Mamoru Oshii set in a future Hong Kong menaced by a cyber criminal who has no mortal form, only malicious control over an enormous sea of data.

Now Oshii has returned with a live-action film that takes up where "Ghost in the Shell" left off, in a future Poland instead of Hong Kong. Place, however, is less important than post-apocalyptic mood, in which the risky thrills of a virtual-reality game coexist with economic depression and social collapse.

There is little recognizably Polish about this world — it could be any Eastern European country with picturesquely decaying cityscapes, wheezing streetcars and statuesque brunettes with an air of experience and an aura of danger.

There is also something Oshii about it — "Avalon" is his anime otaku vision transposed to a world of flesh and blood, brick and mortar. Watching it, I found myself mentally "animating" the characters and sets and realizing that, though Oshii may have left animation behind, its esthetics still inform his every frame.

Not to say the film is "cartoony" — it is, if anything, too lost in the noirish gloom — but it is shot in a way familiar from the world of SF anime, with its affection for techno detail and retro style. Oshii even processed most of the film in the sepia shades favored by art photographers and printmakers of a century ago. They are lovely to look at — and further blur the line between dream and reality.

The heroine is Ash (Malgorzata Foremniak), one of the aforementioned brunettes, who lives alone in a run-down apartment block with her basset hound. She makes a precarious living playing Avalon, a virtual-reality RPG (role-playing game) with a military theme, in which the losing players end up as "lost" — i.e., burned-out shells whose connection with reality has been permanently severed. The grimly ironic name of the game refers to the mythical island where warriors go after their deaths in glorious battle.

An expert player, who vaporizes enemy soldiers and equipment with ease, including a deadly looking monster of a chopper, Ash wants to move to the next, highest level of the game: Special A, which has no reset and, for all but the winners, no return. She is also determined to play solo, despite the urgings of the aged Game Master (Wladyslaw Kowalski) to join a "party" or team.

She once belonged to Wizard, one of the best parties in the game, which dissolved after its leader Murphy (Jerzy Gudejko) took a disastrous hit and became a member of the blank-eyed lost. Enough, she decided, was enough — if she tackles Special A again, it will be alone.

Then two men enter her solitary existence and jolt her out of her rut. One is the mysterious Bishop (Dariusz Biskupski), a skin-headed hulk who mockingly challenges her supremacy on the field of battle. The other is Stunner (Bartek Swiderski), a former Wizard member and a shifty-eyed, food-bolting slob who wants to renew his relationship with Ash — and has information she needs if she is to return intact from Special A.

So far, fairly standard woman-on-a-mission stuff. The story unfolds, otaku-like, too slowly for strangers to the RPG culture, not as enthralled as initiates with Ash's quest to battle through to the "mission complete" screen and rack up more points on her Avalon gold card.

But once she enters Special A, the game, and the film, moves to another, more complex, level, in which the quest becomes more inner than outer and the objective begins to shift in ways that Ash cannot not foresee or humanly understand. What is "virtual reality" when you're no longer sure what is virtual and what is real?

This is the same question posed by the Wachowski brothers' "The Matrix" and David Cronenberg's "eXistenZ," and, for fans of those films, Oshii's answers may have a familiar ring. (Though Oshii first got the idea for "Avalon" nearly a decade ago, long before his American and Canadian competition.) I liked Oshii's, though: He is not trying to graft heady New Age philosophy onto Hollywood SF and Hong Kong martial arts cliches ("The Matrix") or film the equivalent of a bad acid trip with gross-out effects ("eXistenZ"). Instead, he is taking his personal RPG obsession to the outer limits, giving "Avalon" a feeling of conviction the other films lack. Hit the play button — if you dare.

Eureka, runtime: 217 min.

Filming inner lives is hard. Too many voiced-over scenes of a protagonist's stream of consciousness induces audience catatonia. See Joseph Strick's misbegotten "Ulysses" (1967) for an example.

Trauma is among the hardest of inner states to get right in any fictional form, since its effects are incomprehensible to those who have not experienced it. When a man goes to a war and is still having nightmares about it years later, those who stayed home often wonder why he can't suck it up and move on. They've never faced a shock or a loss that shredded the core of their beings. They just don't get it and, if they're lucky, never will. Even so, with the proliferation of everything from weapons of mass destruction to powerful mind-altering drugs, trauma has become central to our time. Even in Japan, a society dedicated to avoiding conflict, is no longer immune. Trauma is found in the subways, the schools and the most intimate relationships.

Trauma and its consequences is the theme of Shinji Aoyama's "Eureka," which was awarded the FIPRESCI prize at the 2000 Cannes Film Festival, while dividing critics. Stephen Holden of "The New York Times" slammed this three-hour-and-37-minute film as "dawdling" while David Stratton of "Variety" praised it as "majestic."

Asian festival films often regard the fixed camera and long cut as indicative of art, so before watching "Eureka," I was more inclined to agree with Holden than Stratton. But Aoyama who has made four films since his 1995 feature debut "It's Not In the Textbook," has made intelligent choices in "Eureka," the story of three bus-hijack victims struggling to recover from their ordeal. Working with cinematographer Masaki Tamura, Aoyama uses sepia shades that reflect, with austere beauty, the victims' inner landscape. He avoids cliches such as voice-overs, swelling music, anguished confrontations and tear-filled eyes. Instead, he strips the victims' search for renewal to its essence, with his model being John Ford's "The Searchers."

"Although 'Eureka' might not seem so, it is indeed a western!" he says in a program interview. There is relatively little dialogue or incident, instead he has imposed a sophisticated unity of style and mood.

A bus in rural Kyushu is hijacked by a disturbed salaryman, who shoots everyone but driver Makoto Sawai (Koji Yakusho) and two children before he is killed by police. The driver is reduced to a trembling wreck, while the children, Kozue (Aoi Miyazaki) and her older brother Naoki (Masaru Miyazaki), lapse into a zombielike silence.

Two years pass. Having lost his job and wife, Sawai is slowly returning to a semblance of normality. Meanwhile, the children's mother has divorced and left them and their father has died in a car crash, an apparent suicide. They live alone in the big family house, in near total isolation.

Then, after failing to fit in with his family and his co-workers in a new construction job, Sawai re-enters their life — first as a visitor, then as a member of their world. An obnoxious cousin (Yoichiro Saito), a college student seemingly on permanent vacation, intrudes, but never penetrates their silence. Sawai is arrested as a suspect in a murder investigation (he was seen with one of the victims on the night of her death) but is released for lack of evidence. A free man again, he wants to find a place where he can heal. He fixes up a bus and takes the children and their reluctant cousin on a voyage of redemption. His starting point: the parking lot where the hijacking ended in blood and terror.

The problem with this voyage is not so much its length as the motivations of the voyagers and the means Aoyama uses to express them. Sawai I understood well enough: the versatile Koji Yakusho more than adequately portrays Sawai's anguish, guilt and need for human connection (though his tubercular cough labors the point that he's a sensitive sufferer). The children, meanwhile, are mute bundles of anger and resentment that serve as living symbols of the film's central themes.

What horror has stricken them dumb? What makes Naoki explode with violent rage? Aoyama answers with stylized gestures, spare images of Kyushu as Monument Valley. His vision, finally, is too abstract and orderly to reveal the true face of trauma's father: chaos.

Brother, runtime: 114 min.

Are Asian films ready for the mall cineplexes of America? The $60 million grossed so far in the U.S. by Ang Lee's "Crouching Tiger, Hidden Dragon" would seem to an emphatic "yes."

But on mailing lists devoted to Asian cinema, the response has been less than ecstatic. "CTHD," claim posters, is not a real Hong Kong movie, but a Hollywoodized hybrid. American mall moviegoers, they imply, are going into raptures about the cinematic equivalent of a California restaurant that serves white wine with stir fry.

The lukewarm response in Asia to the film adds credence to these claims. In Japan, "CTHD" barely made a box-office ripple, while disappointing in Hong Kong and Korea as well.

Takeshi Kitano's gang movie "Brother" follows another, older model for Asian films trying to appeal to Western audiences. Unlike Lee, Kitano never went to Hollywood to master the local filmmaking codes. Though set mostly in Los Angeles and starring American actor Omar Epps, "Brother" is all Kitano in nearly every frame, meaning about as non-Hollywood as you can get.

Instead of Hollywood hyperkineticism, Kitano opts for the frontal compositions and elliptic editing, minimalistic dialogue and uninflected acting, brutal violence and pawky comedy that have constituted his style for more than a decade. The typical Hollywood action film is all extroverted expression, the typical Kitano film, all introverted compression — and never the twain shall meet.

He has also included nearly the entire catalog of clichés that have characterized Japan to the West since the heyday of "yellow peril" pulp: Amputated pinkies, a disemboweling, a severed head, a suicide, and in one memorable scene, broken chopsticks jammed up the nose of a rival hit man. Just about all that's missing is a banzai charge and kamikaze attack (though the film considerately furnishes near-equivalents).

Compared with the makers of "Battle Royale," who correctly figured that blowing up 15-year-olds in a government-sponsored murder game would be better box office than wasting yet another roomful of gangsters with semiautomatic weapons, Kitano's attempts at crowd-pleasing are touchingly old-fashioned. The brouhaha over "Battle Royale" (Diet members and the minister of education waxing wroth over its bad effect on youth) insured that every teenager in the country would want to see it. The reaction to the on-screen mayhem in "Brother," however, has been mild indeed, and its earnings has been correspondingly less.

It's hard to imagine American mall rats tuning into Kitano's brand of arty machismo. They may buy the severed digits, but not the chopped-up narrative or chopped-down performances. Culturally, the film is a plate of squid sushi in a soul food restaurant.

The hero is Yamamoto (Kitano), a yakuza sub-boss who is left with two choices after a defeat in a gang war: get whacked or get lost. He decides, wisely, to fly to Los Angeles to find his long-lost half-brother, Ken (Claude Maki). On his first day in L.A., however, he becomes involved in a street fifght with an African-American man nearly twice his size, who tries to shake him down for $200. Grabbing a broken bottle, Yamamoto cuts his opponent a new eye socket and goes on his way, without having changed his expression or mussed his black designer suit (courtesy of Yohji Yamamoto).

Speaking not a word of English — or hardly a word, period — Yamamoto quickly tracks down Ken, who is dealing drugs with a black gang. One eye-patch-wearing gangster, Denny (Omar Epps), greets

Yamamoto with a suspicious stare. This bad moment passes, however, when Ken assures Denny that his big brother didn't do the deed. "All Japanese look alike," he jokes. This is the beginning of a beautiful friendship.

Yamamoto, who everyone is soon calling "Aniki" (older brother) in imitation of Ken, establishes his tough-guy credentials by whacking members of a rival gang. With Aniki as the muscle and brains, Ken and his confederates become powers in the drug trade, as well allies with the handsome, ruthless Shirase (Masaya Kato), the gang lord of Little Tokyo. Instead of battling roaches in a crummy apartment, they cruise the streets in a stretch limo and shoot hoops in a spacious penthouse office.

Aniki, however, wants to take on the Italians, who still hold the keys to the drug kingdom. He wants, in short, to live his version of the American dream. Once war is declared, it's hell in the Pacific all over again.

"Brother" has its moments of lyricism and pathos, as well as laughs and chills, but it never develops momentum either as a thriller or an essay on East-West friendship. Aniki rarely ventures from his shell (save to explode), while Denny never becomes more than a trash-talking sidekick. The ending, which aspires to soul-wrenching catharsis, is simply an embarrassment.

Kitano may have gone to America, but he clearly needed to get out more.

Kaza-hana, runtime: 116 min.

Pop idols are not only a Japanese phenomenon — Britney Spears sells from Zurich to Zimbabwe — but Japan produces more idols, of both sexes, than anywhere else in the world and has refined the idol aesthetic to an extreme. Japanese idols must be not only cute enough to make your teeth hurt, but everlastingly chipper and bright, with never a negative thought crossing their unfurrowed brows. Idols are permitted a bit of naughty sexuality — the pouting of Ryoko Hirosue or the booty-shaking of Morning Musume — but they are essentially wish projections of ideal youth.

Kyoko Koizumi, or Kyon Kyon as she is still universally known two decades after her debut, is among the most successful idols ever. When she was at her peak in the 1980s, it was impossible to open a newspaper or flip on a TV without seeing her perky 1,000-kilowatt smile.

Yet Koizumi's act was slyly subversive; as though she not only knew the idol gig was a sellout, but was letting us in on the joke. The trademark smile, which she varied about as much as a Mickey Mouse logo, expressed a complacency that bordered on contempt. "I'm giving you what you want," it seemed to say, "but that's all you're getting." The subtext was, "This is a silly way to make a living, isn't it? And I'm going to milk it for all its worth."

At the dangerous age of 34, Koizumi is now playing a washed-up, wised-up sex worker in Shinji Somai's "Kaza-hana," a role that is being described as a courageous leap in the dark. Kyon Kyon is changing her image! My feeling is — what a brilliant piece of casting.

The film itself is another of Somai's excursions into high-minded melodrama, but Koizumi has transformed it into "All About Eve." Her performance is all Koizumi and she steals every scene, just as she stole all those hundreds of now-forgotten TV music and variety shows. Only now the mask is off and the darkness has crept in (but not too far — this, after all, is a Kyon Kyon movie).

Koizumi is Yuriko, a Tokyo pink-salon hostess who services anonymous men in dimly lit booths with a blowsy detachment, but also with a creeping exhaustion. One spring morning, she finds herself under the cherry trees with a hung-over salaryman who has totally forgotten who she is and what they did together the night before. This makes her angry, but not very — the salaryman, Renji Sawaki (Tadanobu Asano), is scrumptious-looking and somehow different from her hundreds of other johns.

Sawaki also feels an attraction, but can't articulate it — or much of anything else for that matter. An elite bureaucrat in the Education Ministry, he is on a perpetual bender and has long since quit caring about his career or his life, including his relationship with his ever-patient lover (Kumiko Aso). One night, drunker than usual, he shoplifts beer at a convenience store and ends up arrested and in the pages of the weeklies. His bosses are not pleased.

Sawaki is seemingly content to drift into oblivion, but Yuriko has other plans. After five years in the big city, she wants to visit her hometown in Hokkaido, where her mother and her Buddhist priest stepfather are caring for her young daughter. Something about her night with Sawaki — a glimpse into the abyss perhaps — has stirred her into action; she buys a plane ticket and is about to board at Haneda, when she spies a familiar face: Sawaki, drunk again.

The scene shifts to the back roads of Hokkaido, where Sawaki is sullenly driving a depressed Yuriko to her destination in a pink rental car. What these two lost souls are really searching for is not an exit ramp but a way out. Given the way they snap at each other, love would seem to be the obvious answer, but first Yuriko has to keep an appointment with easeful Death.

Somai has often dealt with the theme of spiritual transformation and rebirth, most notably in his 1993 masterpiece "Moving" ("Ohikkoshi"), but in "Kaza-hana" he is also exploring the way memory shapes our vision of the present, as well as our perception of time. Bravely, he violates the ironclad movie convention of presenting flashbacks in chronological order. Instead, he opts for the way the mind really orders memories: by emotional significance. This method results in a certain confusion — Yuriko is seen dandling an infant before she becomes pregnant — but it gives us a clearer view of the characters' interior landscapes.

Also, by frequently delving back into the past, Somai creates the illusion that Yuriko and Sawaki's journey is much longer and more epic than the three-day drive it is in reality. What he cannot hide, however, is that their problems and solutions are only a step away from soap opera and that, for much of the film, Sawaki is an unpleasant fellow to be around — a bad drunk and a boor. Asano plays Sawaki with his usual combination of outer blandness and inner fire, but the fire comes too late.

He and the rest of the film's generally excellent cast, however, are little more than foils for Koizumi, whose performance is all of a piece. Like Bette Davis as Margot Channing in "All About Eve," she seems to be playing, not a role, but her life, with a heady frisson of self-advertisement and self-parody. At the end, she performs a strange, hypnotic dance of death in the snow. The idol brought to earth, the idol eternal.

Firefly, Hotaru, rating: ★★★, runtime: 164 min.

In 1997, a young documentary filmmaker named Naomi Kawase won the Camera d'Or prize at the Cannes Film Festival for "Suzaku" ("Moe no Suzaku"). A first feature about the disintegration of a family and community, set deep in the mountains of Kawase's native Nara Prefecture and shot almost entirely with amateur actors, "Suzaku" became an art-house hit and made Kawase a celebrity. Even the sports papers covered her marriage to her producer, Takenori Sento.

Her second feature, "Firefly" ("Hotaru"), is a story of turbulent love told in her usual visually poetic, narratively impressionistic style, but with a new emotional power and narrative dynamism.

Even so, Kawase is still very much the conscientious documentarian, who would rather have the characters tell their own story, in their own way, than force them to express a preconceived directorial vision. The aim is an examination of inner realities, free of commercial restraints — and "Firefly" achieves it more often than not.

A tenacious type, Kawase can't rest until she has worked through her lovers' roiling surfaces to their sulfurous core. It is not where every director can or even wants to go — human volcanoes can be as dangerous to explore as the natural kind — but Kawase returns alive, with nuggets of emotional truth

At nearly three hours, the film is a long sit. Certain scenes drag on interminably, as though Kawase, absorbed in her character's personal journeys, forgot to bring the audience along.

"Firefly" begins dramatically enough. After a raging argument with her lover, an exotic dancer (Yuko Nakamura) storms out of her ramshackle house and, thoroughly depressed, absentmindedly walks into the path of an oncoming car. Among the first on the scene is a brawny potter (Toshiya Nagasawa), who thinks that the woman lying on the street and staring up at him has tried to kill herself.

Shaken, but attracted, he invites her to a local festival. Working in the nearby mountains at what was once his father's kiln, he has fashioned hundreds of ceramic holders for the festival's spectacular outdoor display of votive candles — one of the film's life-force symbols. The dancer's club, however, is raided by the police and she spends the night in jail.

The potter, thinking that she may have tried to do herself in again, searches frantically for her and, in the process, learns what she does for a living. It doesn't matter — by this time he is mad about her. The dancer reciprocates, hesitantly then passionately, the old boyfriend by now forgotten.

Both potter and dancer are wrestling with demons in their past, but those of the dancer, who was abandoned by her mother as a child and ran away from home a decade ago, are larger and more immediately threatening. With the support of her new lover, she decides to return to her birthplace to confront them.

Playing the potter, Nagasawa exudes a rough masculinity and wounded sensitivity. His love scenes with newcomer Nakamura smolder, but Nakamura more than matches him in intensity, especially when she destroys everything in her house but the kitchen sink, and then only because she can't lift it. Is it any coincidence that, when she made the film, director Kawase was in the process of divorcing producer Sento?

Merdeka, rating: ★, runtime: 114 min.

War movies have a hard time telling the truth about one of humankind's most universal acts. Even when filmmakers loudly proclaim their intention to get it right, they nearly always make their films as Americans or Russians or Japanese, with the accompanying social, political and, needless to say, commercial filters.

Be that as it may, there is still a wide gap between the red-white-and-blue, black-and-white approach of Edward Dmytryk's 1945 "Back to Bataan," with John Wayne as an American officer leading brave Filipino freedom fighters against the evil Japanese invaders, and that of Terrence Malick's "Thin Red Line," in which war is stripped of ideology and reduced to its essentials, including its awful beauty.

On that spectrum Yukio Fuji's "Merdeka (Freedom)," which depicts Japanese soldiers fighting for Indonesian independence, is far to the right, deep in John Wayne territory. But the straight-up jingoism of "Back to Bataan," made when Americans were still dying in Philippine jungles, is less understandable in a film made at the turn of the new millennium, when Japanese have had half a century to distance themselves from wartime propaganda.

Not a few Japanese, however, both reject the victors' interpretation of Japan's war, and want to present that war in the best possible light. The result, in "Merdeka," is a revisionism that, in the guise of telling the truth about a little-known historical episode, luridly distorts it.

The film is based on the experiences of the 2,000 Japanese soldiers who remained in Indonesia after the end of World War II — and never returned home. Nearly 1,000 died in combat, by the side of Indonesian freedom fighters battling their Dutch colonial masters. This is a story that deserves to be told, and the filmmakers had the cooperation of the Indonesian authorities in telling it. They shot on location in Indonesia, using Indonesian actors and crew.

But the film's war is mostly the one imagined by sound truck rightists — all guts and glory for the warriors of Dai Nippon. The hero, Lt. Shimazaki (Junta Yamada), is a red-blooded samurai in modern dress who battles fearlessly to free Indonesia from the corrupt Dutch. Bursting into the headquarters of the Dutch commander at Bandung after the Japanese invasion in December 1941, he does not negotiate surrender so much as imperiously order it, with his eyes glaring, his voice thundering and his hand firmly on his sword.

How can a rabble of Westerners and their native puppets to resist such an overpowering display of yamatodamashii (Japanese spirit)? The commander can hardly wait to sign the surrender papers.

Soon Shimazaki and his men, including the gentle-spirited, poetically inclined Lt. Miyata (Naoki Hosaka) and the doggedly loyal interpreter Yamana (Naomasa Mutaka) are training bright-eyed local youths as an elite fighting force.

"You must struggle for your own independence!" Shimazaki tells them. The training is harsh — and some of the young soldiers rebel — but Shimazaki whips them into shape, while winning their understanding and allegiance. He is later undercut by the Japanese High Command, anxious to exploit Indonesians for the greater glory of the Empire, not raise up a potential third column. Even so, Shimazaki perseveres, never losing sight of his ideal.

When the war ends in Japan's defeat, he faces a difficult choice: protect the Emperor's arsenal, as is his soldierly duty, or follow his heart and open it to his Indonesian charges, now guerrilla fighters. He decides to not only turn over the weaponry to his former students, but take up their cause. Many of his men join them — with a paragon like Shimazaki as their leader, how could they not?

Together they wage a desperate struggle against the colonial oppressor. One by one, they die as Shimazaki, with the fiercely patriotic sister (Laura Amaria) of one of his fallen Indonesian students by his side, sternly presses on to victory.

Playing Shimazaki, Yamada is a war-recruiting poster brought to life — all clenched jaw and burning patriotism. He emerges from the war with his fighting spirit stronger than when he went into it.

Save for one token bad Japanese soldier, a ruffian who treats the local women like whores and the men like servants, Shimazaki's comrades are similarly upright types. Meanwhile, their foes, particularly a gay Dutch interrogator who tortures Miyata with slithery glee, are cartoon cutouts.

And the dark side of the Japanese occupation? The inhumane treatment of Allied prisoners and the slaughter of Chinese residents? If you expect to see that in "Merdeka," you've come to the wrong movie.

Tokyo Marigold, rating: ★★★★★, runtime: 97 min.

Film is art, commerce — and fashion. Actors, directors and even national cinemas are in vogue one year, out the next. What does all this have to do with Jun Ichikawa? Despite a long string of awards for his television commercials — his day job — and his 11 feature films, Ichikawa has been out of step with trends that have boosted several of his colleagues to international acclaim. Unlike Takeshi Kitano, he has never gone in for the sort of black-comic violence that Quentin Tarantino made trendy. Unlike Hideo Nakata and other purveyors of "Japanese horror," he has never latched onto a hot genre.

What he has done instead is produce a body of work that redefines the best traditions of humanist cinema for contemporary Japanese society. Ichikawa may pay homage to such masters as Yasujiro Ozu and Eric Rohmer, but he has developed his own distinctive style and vision.

In his new film "Tokyo Marigold" Ichikawa finds a fugitive loveliness in birds flitting across the sky of a Kichijoji dawn or in headlamps flickering through the streets of a Shinjuku night. Though he may give his cityscapes a beatific glow that most of us miss when we're running for the train at 7 in the morning, Ichikawa is not merely prettifying but seeing more deeply than the average straphanger — or director.

Also, with dialogue that sounds less written than recorded, he patches together a mosaic of urban moods and lives — of Tokyoites who may be freer of the restraints of the past than their parents were, but who lack their connection with the world around them and are falling into desperate isolation. Oases of an older, more human-scaled city still exist, but for the film's heroine — Eriko (Rena Tanaka), who has broken up with her boyfriend and is drifting through her days — they offer only temporary refuge.

From the first scenes of her wandering through the streets of Daikanyama and Aoyama, she is at one remove from shopping and dating masses around her. While proclaiming a love of solitude, she is really adrift. She visits her mother (Kirin Kiki), an earthy type who makes Henry-Moore-like sculptures and prepares scrumptious-looking noodles, but nothing in her larder can fill the gaping hole in Eriko's life.

She finds a new job as an office worker for a foreign car dealership, but the real change comes when she attends a go-con — a group matchmaking party — and meets Tamura (Yukiyoshi Ozawa), an elite salaryman who is charmingly awkward and tongue-tied. Also, instead of asking for her cellphone number, he gives her his — a bit of sexual role-reversal that she finds irresistible.

But when she calls Tamura and they go on what seems to be the perfect date, he makes an unsettling confession: He has a girlfriend studying in America. The end of a budding affair? Not quite. Eriko can't get him out of her mind. When she happens to see him again, laughing unrestrainedly at the performance of a comedy troupe in a Shimokitaza theater, she falls even harder — and they soon resume their interrupted romance. Throwing caution to the wind, she asks him to stay with her for a year, until his girlfriend returns. He agrees, and Eriko begins to move from the shadows into the light.

But as the weeks turn into months, Mr. Right proves to be a wrongo. He may claim he likes Eriko's pure-hearted personality, but he is taking advantage of her for his own murky ends.

In the hands of another director, "Tokyo Marigold" might have become a weepy cautionary tale. But Ichikawa subsumes the he-done-her-wrong story line into an evocative portrait of a relationship from its passionate beginning to its troubled middle and unexpected end that depicts Eriko's longings and doubts with sympathy and clarity.

Tanaka, an actress of uncommon ability, expresses Eriko's turbulent moods with unforced conviction. We feel her pain because it is really ours as well. And Ichikawa is the nearest thing we've got to a master. Maybe someday the rest of the world will realize it as well.

Unchain, rating: ★★★★, runtime: 98 min.

Boxing movies have one advantage over action films with high body counts and world-shattering explosions: It's not written that the hero has to blast all the bad guys into oblivion and finish the third act in triumph. In fact, some of the best-remembered movie boxers, from Marlon Brando's Terry Malloy to Sylvester Stallone's Rocky Balboa, did not win their big fights.

When Toshiaki Toyoda started filming "Unchain," his new documentary about four young boxers in Osaka, in 1995, he had no idea whether one or more of his subjects would become a Rocky Balboa — or trundle down the slope to oblivion. As it turned out, none of them made it big. (One, whose ring name Unchain Kaji supplied the title of the film, never won a bout, period.)

Toyoda did not, however, simply record whatever fate (or his heroes' opponents) dished up. He fiddled with chronology and even staged several scenes, though not in a blatantly obvious way. So it might be more accurate to call "Unchain" a docu-drama — not that it matters.

Toyoda's feature debut "Pornostar" (1998) explored some of the same themes as "Unchain," including the charged one of violence as purification. Both the hit-man hero of "Pornostar" and the boxer Unchain Kaji are unsocialized types for whom violence is expression, identity and destiny. But while their actions may seem bad or mad, they are seekers who, in wrestling with their various demons, attain a kind of grace.

Toyoda plays the standard documentarian role of dogged, meticulous observer, but with a skilled storyteller's feel for dramatic structure. He is not yet a Martin Scorcese with the camera — his usual approach to his key boxing scenes is to poke his digicam through the ropes and let it run — but he also brings his characters and their world to vivid life. A serious aspirant for a career as a professional shogi (Japanese chess) player who gave up training at the age of 17 and later turned to film, Toyoda can sympathize better than most with their struggle — and its costs.

The film belongs, most of all, to Unchain Kaji, who was born in Osaka in 1969 and was raised by his uncle at his mother's request. At the age of 20, sporting a goatee and an attitude, he made his pro-boxing debut and lost his first seven bouts — another sad case of a big heart and slow hands. Forced to quit on doctor's orders, Kaji became a jack-of-all-trades who was willing to do anything but — he announced with pride — contract killings. While scuffling at various jobs, he kept up his connection with the ring, serving as a cornerman to a former biker-turned-boxer named Garuda Tetsu. Watching Kaji's antics at one of Tetsu's bouts, such as climbing into the ring to strike champion poses while the referee introduces the fighters, it's not hard to sense a blowup in the making.

It comes when a day laborer working for Kaji's tiny "trading company" calls to demand his back pay. Enraged by what he considers his employee's insolence, Kaji pours yellow paint over his head, girds himself for battle and, together with a "shoot boxer" named Seiichiro Nishibayashi, invades a labor exchange to teach its aging and alcoholic habitués "a lesson." Instead the two get the worst of it from three yakuza, and Kaji ends up in a mental hospital.

This, however, is not the end of his story. There is much more to tell about Kaji and his three fellow boxers, particularly the dramatic (and staged) reunion, two years later, between a chastened and wiser Kaji and Osamu Nagaishi, a marginally successful boxer who married Kaji's former girlfriend while Kaji was in the hospital. There is, however, nothing fake about Kaji's change — or his friends' affectionate recollections of his wild and crazy past and their own long, ultimately losing battles for a title shot — and a measure of self-respect.

Toyoda combines every means at his disposal — montages of old snaps, flashbacks of faded videos, interviews with the principals and gong-to-gong footage of their bouts — to bring us close to their raucous joy and frightening chaos, brief triumphs and lasting disappointments. By the end we understand more about the primal power and terrible harshness of their trade than all but the best boxing films can tell us. We also feel an admiration for his heroes, though no one will ever confuse them with Sly Stallone. In a society that rewards the conventional and mediocre, they have dared to embrace the dangerous dream of warrior's glory. If nothing else, they have lived.

Distance, rating: ★★★★, runtime: 133 min.

Directors, it's often said, keep making the same movie over and over, though the sameness is more evident with some than others. Akira Kurosawa filmed everything from Shakespearean drama ("Throne of Blood") to popcorn entertainment ("The Hidden Fortress"), but he kept returning to the problem of being a hero in an unheroic world.

Hirokazu Koreeda, who made acclaimed documentaries before his feature debut with "Maborosi" in 1995, has placed memory, in both its lighter and darker manifestations, at the center of his work. In "Maborosi" a young woman loses her husband to an inexplicable suicide — and needs years to work through her grief and guilt. In "After Life" (1999), the newly dead select their most precious memory to take with them into eternity.

In his new film "Distance" the theme of remembrance takes a topical cast, as four people whose loved ones were members of a murderous cult — and died at the hands of their fellow cultists — gather on the anniversary of their deaths. The obvious parallel is the Aum Shinrikyo cult, which released poison gas on the Tokyo subway system in a mad plot to unleash Armageddon. Koreeda's approach, however, is anything but sensationalist. In a way by now familiar, he uses documentary techniques to create the illusion of immediacy, while exploring how memory illuminates the past and shapes the present.

Like the masters he admires — Andrei Tarkovsky, Robert Bresson and Hou Hsiao-hsien — Koreeda rejects the conventional devices of cinematic storytelling: There is no voice-over to explain the plot, no music to cue the emotions. One danger of such an approach is over-intellectualization: a film that is all theorizing head, no feeling heart. Another is self-indulgence: In making his personal statement, the director shuts out the audience.

Koreeda has been accused of both sins, unfairly. He is a filmmaker of extraordinary talent, intelligence and integrity, who strips his story to its essence and gets at its emotional truth. And as a good documentarian, he wants to show, not tell; to be the fly on the wall, not the performer in the spotlight.

"Distance" starts slowly, with a narrative approach that resembles a game of go in its diffuseness. Also, it assumes an understanding of topical references that, in the case of non-Japanese, may not be there. Finally, in places it becomes too much like a shot-in-real-time documentary, with the camera recording chitchat and soulful staring into space. Koreeda evidently let his actors improvise much of their dialogue, thus the flavor of life as it is lived, including its banality.

Nonetheless, as revelation follows revelation of both past and present we come to understand the characters directly, especially, with chilling clarity, their isolation. Despite the commonality of their experience and the links they form, they are alone with their memories, mirrors that reflect only a personal reality.

The four survivors — a sensitive teacher (Yui Natsukawa), gruff salaryman (Susumu Terajima), punkish freeter (freelancer) (Yusuke Iseya) and soulful student (Arata) — drive together to a remote lake where their loved ones once lived in a cult cabin. There they encounter a shy, soft-spoken former cultist (Tadanobu Asano), who narrowly escaped the holocaust that consumed his comrades.

When, in an improbable twist, they find themselves stranded in the wilderness, they are forced to spend the night in the cabin, now abandoned for three years, but still haunted by the ghosts of their respective pasts. With the former cultist serving as an unwilling catalyst, they begin to confront those ghosts.

Some of the revelations are what we expect from movies of this type, such as that the student is not quite what he seems. But the insights are mostly of the inner variety, as the protagonists flash back to scenes from the past, from brutal confrontations to wrenching separations. They are, we see, trying to answer the one unanswerable question: Why? In doing so, they find the imperfect accommodation that is called, tritely, "closure." Also, in a way very Japanese, they achieve a kind of mutual understanding that is not the same as closeness. At the end, they go, as they must, their separate ways.

All this plays out much the way it would in real life — little feels staged or strained. By the final cut I felt as though I was on the train home with this odd quintet, alone with memories of my own.

Spirited Away, Sen to Chihiro no Kamikakushi, rating: ★★★★★, runtime: 125 min.

Hayao Miyazaki and his Studio Ghibli animators had their biggest-ever triumph with "The Princess Mononoke," an eco-fable set in premodern Japan that broke box-office records in 1997. Unlike animation studio heads in Hollywood, who are not expected to personally animate their creations (Walt Disney was a famously mediocre artist), Miyazaki is a hands-on type; he took a pencil to nearly 80,000 of the 144,000 cels used in "The Princess Mononoke." Aged 56 when he completed his herculean three-year task, he was badly in need of a rest and announced his retirement from directing.

Fortunately for us, he is also an incurable workaholic, and now, four years later, there is another Miyazaki film, "Spirited Away." While "The Princess Mononoke" was targeted at teenagers and adults, with graphic violence that would have never passed the first reader at Disney (though the Mouse House signed a deal with Studio Ghibli to distribute the film), "Spirited Away" is aimed, says Miyazaki, at 10-year-old girls. Accordingly, it is simpler in everything from language to story line.

It is also a masterwork, my new favorite among Miyazaki's many masterworks; whose story of a girl's separation from her parents is the most primal of all. It is told with all the resources at Miyazaki's command, from the richness of his imagination and the force of his moral intelligence to the superb craft of his Studio Ghibli animators. "Spirited Away" may be the culmination of Miyazaki's four-decade-long career, but far from being monumental it is a joy and wonder, like revisiting the emotional landscape of childhood in a fantasy world both universal and uniquely Miyazaki.

The inevitable comparison is with Lewis Carroll's "Alice" books. "Spirited Away" has the same queerness of atmosphere that seems to come from a dream or another life. It has, too, the same sense of purposeful playfulness, with characters and situations that may seem absurd or grotesque, but illuminate our deepest fears and desires.

At the same time, Miyazaki is expanding on themes that occupied him in "The Princess Mononoke" and his other films, notably the vexed relationship between humanity and nature. In doing so, he reworks motifs that have often appeared in his work, such as the pastel Europeanesque architecture that exists only in his films, and flying scenes expressing a freedom and exhilaration like little else in animated or even live-action movies.

But, as hinted at in the title, the narrative core of the film lies in how the young heroine's search for her parents transforms into a struggle for a new, independent identity. In short, the age-old story of the Quest, in which the goal is less important than the character-building, consciousness-expanding encounters on the way.

The heroine begins the story as Chihiro, a 10-year-old on a holiday drive with her parents. Her father, an adventurous type, tears along a mountain road until he comes to the entrance to a long tunnel that has been blocked so cars can't enter. When he suggests they walk through it, Chihiro resists because the tunnel frightens her. Mom and Dad, however, stride off into the dark and Chihiro, even more afraid of being left alone, tags along.

At the other end of the tunnel they find what appears to be an abandoned theme park, whose Western-style buildings have a seedy, uncanny look. Dad, however, notices nothing but the smell of food wafting from one of the restaurants. Finding no proprietor, only heaps of scrumptious grub on the counter, he digs in, followed by Mom. Chihiro, feeling the bad vibes even more strongly now, refuses to eat and runs off to explore instead. When she returns, Mom and Dad have been transformed into huge, snuffling pigs.

She flees in horror — only to find that there is no waking up from this, the worst dream in her life. Somehow, she has fallen into another world, one populated by all manner of strange gods and goblins, and where she seems to be the only human being. Then she encounters Haku — a 12-year-old boy who helps her find her feet in a place where nothing (including Haku) is what it seems.

One rule, she learns, is that everyone must work — no slackers allowed. Another is that she cannot keep her name — she must find a new one: Sen. Haku warns her that she must not forget her old name, or she will never be able to return to her former life. He also introduces her to Kamaji, a grandfatherly, if madly busy, creature with four hands and two legs who runs the boiler room in the town's hot-spring resort, and Rin, a short-tempered teenage maid who takes Sen under her prickly wing. The owner of the place, however, is the forbidding Yubaba — a crone with an enormous head and a personality that is a cross between Scrooge and the Queen of Hearts.

The guests, Sen discovers, are gods returning for a spell of R&R after exhausting tours among humanity. As a kind of initiation, she is assigned to wash Okutaresama — a river god who is a huge, moving pile of filth. She bravely tackles her loathsome task, despite nearly drowning in a flood of sludge, and begins to earn Yubaba's reluctant approval and Rin's friendship.

While adapting to her strange new environment, though, she has not forgotten her parents. Where are they? How can she return them to human form? How can they find the tunnel when it and indeed all of their former world seems to have vanished like a dream?

Filmed and projected using the latest digital technology, "Spirited Away" is as gorgeous as anything Miyazaki has ever done, packed with dazzling images, such as a mysterious train that runs through water in a way reminiscent of the Catbus in "My Neighbor Totoro." But some of the best scenes are the smaller ones, as when Sen, alone in a garden, collapses in tears of relief because in Haku she has found kindness. A scene that would probably not have occurred to Disney, or Lewis Carroll for that matter. Dickens? Yes, definitely Dickens. Perhaps the true model for this extraordinary film is not "Alice's Adventures in Wonderland" but "David Copperfield."

Firefly Dreams, Ichiban Utsukushii Natsu, rating: ★★★★, runtime: 95 min.
For decades, foreign directors have been going to Hollywood and making movies with American settings, stories and stars that American audiences have accepted as their own. Charlie Chaplin's "Modern Times" and John Woo's "Mission: Impossible 2" may reflect the backgrounds of their makers — be it the low comedy of the British music hall or the high-wire choreography of the Hong Kong action film — but few Americans have found these films "foreign" in their concept or execution.

No Japanese filmmaker has successfully made this leap, though several have tried. Some who set films in the United States or other overseas locales, but target them at domestic audiences, are often deaf to the inflections of foreign cultures, blind to the individuality of foreign peoples. Their versions of the American Southwest or Southeast Asia bear about as much relation to the real thing as beef curry rice does to the cuisine of Kerala.

Meanwhile, the film industry here has long been all but closed to non-Japanese entrants. The exceptions — mainly the Koreans who have emerged as directors and screenwriters in recent decades — usually come from families that have been in the country for two or more generations and are themselves "foreign" in only the color of their passport.

The made-in-Japan films of Hollywood directors, on the other hand, seldom do more than skim the exotic surface, while, to Japanese audiences, their images of Japan are little better than caricatures, be they mindlessly entertaining ("You Only Live Twice") or gratuitously offensive ("Black Rain").

In his first feature "Firefly Dreams," which is set in a remote region of Aichi Prefecture and uses only Japanese actors, British filmmaker John Williams has made this leap with agility and assurance.

How did he succeed where so many have failed? For one thing, instead of parachuting in with a few guidebook phrases, Williams took the trouble to learn the language and live among the Japanese — since 1989 to be precise.

For another, though he wrote his script in English, he made the Japanese translation sound as native as possible by having his Japanese staff check it and his actors woodshed it. For still another, in telling his story of intergenerational conflict and reconciliation he used a naturalistic approach reminiscent of classic Japanese cinema (and, together with cinematographer Yoshinobu Hayano, created images of rural Aichi mountains and streams that recall the beauties of that cinema as well).

Watching "Firefly Dreams" without the credits, I might have mistaken it for a film by a Japanese director, albeit one a decade older than the 38-year-old Williams. There are, however, telltale signs that it is not a family drama of the old school.

Though conventional enough in its storytelling and shot-making, "Firefly Dreams" departs from the typical family drama of a generation ago in both its rejection of sentimentality and its refusal to exalt the everyday into a melodramatic ideal.

Also, unlike the many older Japanese filmmakers who explained plot and motivations so that even the salaryman nodding in the back row could get the point, Williams prefers the simple-but-apt visual metaphor that says what needs to be said, with an impact all the greater for its indirection.

His heroine is Naomi (Maho Ukai), a teenage girl of today's Nagoya, right down to her carroty hair, year-round tan and umbilically attached cellphone. After sullenly enduring dull classes with clueless teachers and fractious mealtimes with her quarreling parents, she comes alive at her favorite club, where she can engage in her two favorite activities — dancing and schmoozing with her friends.

Then, one day, Mom (Chie Miyajima) packs up and leaves to be with her lover. Not ready to deal with Naomi now that his marriage has collapsed, Dad (Atsushi Ono) packs her off to spend the summer working at a countryside inn run by his elder sister and her family. Predictably, Naomi hates being stuck in the middle of nowhere. She would rather be working on her attitude at the club than schlepping trays of food to drunken middle-aged men.

Seeing that the job isn't working out, her aunt asks Naomi to look after Mrs. Koide (Yoshie Minami), an elderly relative who lives alone on a small farm and is slowly losing her memory to Alzheimer's. Naomi readily agrees — she has fond memories of playing at Mrs. Koide's as a girl — but she finds that the old woman has forgotten her existence. Still, she likes Mrs. Koide's down-to-earth manner and the stories she tells about her past.

This frail old woman in a kimono was once a much sought after beauty that married her girlhood love and, after his death in World War II, became gossiped about for her forays against social convention. She even took up the dubious profession of acting and made a film, "Valley of the Fireflies," whose poster Naomi discovers in the old woman's attic. The girl keeps coming back to learn more.

Meanwhile, she is having romantic adventures of her own with a liquor-store delivery boy (Tsutomu Niwa) who gives her rides on his motorbike and enchants her with his quick-witted repartee. "The ones with the clever tongues are the ones you have to watch," warns Koide.

This episode draws the girl and old woman closer together as Naomi realizes that, despite their difference in ages, they are two peas from the same wayward pod. Though the wounds of the heart never completely heal, Mrs. Koide's steadying presence gives Naomi the strength to go on — and the girl loves her for it.

The film, however, is about more than this meeting across the gulf of age and values. Naomi's real tests, including the ultimate ones of death and final separation, are still to come.

Williams' casting of newcomer Ukai as Naomi is as perfect as it is unusual. Most Japanese directors with an eye on the box office would have chosen the latest elfin embodiment of the teenage male ideal over the tall, chunky Ukai. But she is credible as Naomi in her moodily rebellious mode, while expressing her inner life — and its growth — with nuance and assurance.

Another casting coup is Minami as Mrs. Koide. A veteran actress who worked with Ozu and Kurosawa, she gives the film a gloss of professionalism, while quietly abstaining from diva displays. Her performance is a reminder of the glories that were once Japanese cinema.

"Firefly Dreams" is proof that today's filmmakers can still cherish and revive those glories, even if they happen to have been born in St. Albans instead of Sendai.

Waterboys, rating: ★★★★, runtime: 91 min.

Serious is easy, funny is hard — this is a bit of wisdom that everyone who makes screen comedies believes, but that those who bestow the more prestigious awards seldom acknowledge. Those zany foreigners who present the Golden Globes may have their quirky Best Comedy prize, but the Hollywood powers-that-be rarely deign to honor a comedy with a Best Picture Oscar.

In Japan, young directors hungry for recognition as auteurs — i.e., nearly all of them — are busy churning out one-scene/one-cut exercises in postadolescent angst or cutesy genre parodies. Those ambitious to be the Harold Ramis of Japan can be counted on one hand. Among the best is Shinobu Yaguchi, who labored long and successfully on the indie fringe with such films as "Adrenaline Drive" and "My Secret Cache," before hitting the box office jackpot with his latest comedy, "Waterboys."

The film adheres to the sports-oriented zero-to-hero formula perfected by executive producer Minoru Masui, whose credits include Masayuki Suo's 1996 smash "Shall We Dance?" But though the third act is hardly a mystery (the film's trailer gives away the feel-good ending) "Waterboys" avoids boring predictability.

Suo integrates every element of his films — from gross slapstick to eye-misting pathos — into a seamless whole. By contrast, Yaguchi may have mastered technique — his big finale in "Waterboys" evidences an intense study of Busby Berkeley — but is irredeemably adolescent in his approach to humor. This sensibility — 34-going-on-14 — gives Yaguchi a handle on his gawky teenage protagonists that most directors could only fake. He truly feels their pain — and embarrassment at their various stupidities.

Not that "Waterboys" is a low-comedy masterpiece on the order of "Dumb and Dumber" but it is funny, rousing and, depending on taste, sexy. Given that Japanese school boys in their throat-clutching collars and black uniforms — a legacy from 19th-century Prussia — are not always the most attractive specimens, this last is no mean accomplishment.

It opens with the arrival of a new adviser to a mediocre boys' high school swim team — the chipper, luscious Sakuma-sensei (Kaori Manabe) — who immediately wins 28 admirers. But infatuation turns to shock when she reveals her secret dream: to start a synchronized swimming team. One member, the sweet, dorky Suzuki (Satoshi Tsumabuki), becomes the nucleus of a squad that includes rock-god-in-embryo Sato (Hiroshi Tamaki), with his Afro wig; disco-mad Ota (Akifumi Miura), with his red bikini-briefs; math-geek Kanazawa (Koen Kondo), with his Coke-bottle glasses; and swishy Saotome (Takatoshi Kaneko), with his crush on Sato.

This motley crew is training — or rather flailing — hard when Sakuma Sensei breezily announces that she is quitting to have a baby. Disheartened, Suzuki and the other members decide to disband and give the pool over to the basketball team, who want to use it to raise fish (don't ask why). Then, taunted by their classmates for being losers and realizing that they like doing leg kicks in unison, they have a change of heart.

But now they have no coach and no place to practice: The pool is already alive with finny invaders, dumped there by a skin-headed guy (Naoto Takenaka) who tells them that if they want to swim there, they will have to catch his fish — the first of many challenges.

The path to synchro glory is full of twists, some frankly ridiculous. Suzuki acquires a girlfriend (Aya Hirayama) with an angelic face and a vicious karate kick. The skin head, a dolphin trainer by trade, becomes their coach, but puts them to cleaning aquariums instead of practicing. The boys even acquire a supporter: the mama-san (Akira Emoto) of a local transvestite bar, who knows nothing about synchro but loves a well-filled Speedo.

There is a production number in which the boys strut their stuff — and pretty amazing stuff it is. If you laugh at synchro as neither sport nor art, but camp — the Rockettes with chlorine — nothing in "Waterboys" is likely to change your mind. But you may appreciate the athleticism required to execute all those sweeps and circles while paddling for dear life.

Also, training for the film in midsummer burned every ounce of fat off Yaguchi's young actors, while roasting them to a perfect tan. A good argument for getting in the water yourself — even if you never lift a leg out of it.

Go, rating: ★★★★, runtime: 122 min.

A few years ago, Asians were the hot thing in Japanese films, and then, suddenly, they were not. The peak was Shunji Iwai's "Swallowtail" (1996), a dystopian fantasy about a near-future Tokyo overrun by hungry young Asians who would commit any crime for a yen, but were more vital than the gray Japanese masses around them. With its stylistic borrowings from Ridley Scott's "Blade Runner" and its peculiar mix of xenophilia and xenophobia (its Asians were great people to party with, but not to trust with the CD player), "Swallowtail" became a hit — and more local money and talent went into movies with an Asians-in-Japan theme.

Unfortunately, none equaled or surpassed the success of "Swallowtail" and the Asian boom died down. Isao Yukisada's "Go" is something like "Swallowtail Redux": a hot film by a promising new director featuring an ethnic Korean hero with the spunk and soul most of his Japanese age-mates have either lost or never had to begin with. But in contrast to Iwai's Asians, who were cool figments of the director's imagination, the hero of "Go" — a teenager with a lion-mane hairdo and a temper to match — is the creation of Kazuki Kaneshiro, the author of the best-selling novel on which the film is based and an ethinic Korean himself.

He is Sugihara (Yosuke Kubozuka), who simmers with a rage that comes from being different in a society that celebrates homogeneity and defines membership by blood. Though they may be the third generation of their families in Japan and look, talk and act like the Japanese around them, Sugihara and his Korean pals are excluded, in ways subtle and not so subtle, from the mainstream. They are, the film notes in a fast-paced opening sequence, more likely to end up in a police lineup than behind a company president's desk.

This is not a new theme — films such as Nagisa Oshima's "Death by Hanging" (1968) and Kohei Oguri's "For Kayoko" (1984) tackled it, usually from the Koreans-as-victims angle. Probably the most accurate and certainly the funniest take was that of ethnic Korean director Yoichi Sai in his 1993 film "All Under the Moon" with its black-comic tale of a Korean cabby who is just trying to get by, shrugging off slurs from his Japanese passengers while fending off the demands of his bar-mama mother to find a nice Korean girl and settle down. Instead of a social problem demanding redress, Sai treated his hero's ethnicity as a condition admitting no easy solution.

Though he may not have Sai's background, Yukisada is well-equipped for the task of making Koreans trendy again. In addition to working as an assistant director for Iwai, including on "Swallowtail," he has made everything from music videos to features ("Sunflower," "Luxurious Bone"), while becoming fluent in the new language of the digital visual artist, with its large vocabulary of computer editing techniques and its blithe rejection of traditional boundaries between high and low art. "Go" is by turns, cheeky, cartoony, witty and stylish — but never dully self-important. It also has a vitality that makes up for its irritants, primarily the gratingly coy Ko Shibasaki as Sugihara's love interest.

Most of all, it has a star-making performance by Yosuke Kubozuka who brings a brash attitude and boyish charm, raw toughness and comic flair to the role of Sugihara.

The film traces his journey from his lock-step education at a Korean junior high school, dedicated to the greater glory of Dear Leader Kim Jong Il, to his entry into an ordinary Japanese high school and his fateful encounter with Sakurai (Shibasaki), she of the copper-colored hair and dramatically arched eyebrows. A bit of a rebel herself, Sakurai is attracted by the fire in his eyes — and makes him believe, for the first time, that "Korean" is a category he can escape.

The film, as Sugihara keeps reminding us in a voice-over, is thus a "love story," but it is also a coming-of-age story, with a frenzied energy and satiric bite. Instead of running standard oppressed-versus-oppressor changes, Yukisada and scriptwriter Kankuro Kudo turn them inside out. Trained from boyhood by his former pro-boxer father (Tsutomu Yamazaki), Sugihara knocks off a succession of bullies as though they were so many arcade-game villains. His big eyes-lock moment with Sakurai is preceded by a free-for-all, inspired by Hong Kong martial arts movies, in which he takes on an entire hostile basketball team (his own, as it happens).

He might appear to be a local version of that familiar figure from Hollywood films — the Super Minority Hero. (Yosuke Kubozuka, meet Will Smith.) Only he is not. Dad, a testy eccentric who changed his nationality from North to South Korean so he could take Mom (Shinobu Otake) on a trip to Hawaii, regularly knocks the stuffing out of him, while his delinquent pals at the Korean school get him into idiotic trouble, such as running down the tracks ahead of an approaching subway train with only a suicidally slim head start. Then Sakurai weaves her spell – and he becomes a gawky kid who can hardly talk to a girl, let alone bed one.

Sugihara is something more as well. Refusing the loser's role in which society has cast him, he tries again and again to break out — and nearly has his heart broken in the process.

He makes "Go" worth going to.

All About Lily Chou Chou, rating: ★★★☆, runtime: 146 min.

Teenagers live on another planet, adults have long liked to complain. But in today's Japan that planet is more like the asteroid belt — tumbling rocks of teen culture that are both harder to reach and inhabited by ever smaller communities.

Those communities still gather at places like Harajuku, where goths in black leather warily eye girls dressed like Little Bo Peep, but more are meeting in the chat rooms and on message boards that attract everyone from death-metal fans to hamster lovers.

Among the more knowledgeable adult adventurers in these realms is Shunji Iwai, the director of "Love Letter," "Swallowtail" and "April Story." Trained in the craft of the music video and TV commercial — which is the craft of keeping itchy fingers off remote buttons — Iwai has a sophisticated grasp of digital tools to keep eyes and brains engaged. He and cinematographer Noboru Shinoda are joint authors of a cinematic style that is postmodern on its surface, but romantic at its core; that finds truth more in glancing impressions than sustained observations; that would rather lose itself in deliquescent dreams than thread its way through labyrinths of plot.

Iwai have been accused, rightly, of navel-gazing and ego-tripping. He also has clung to adolescent attitudes and concerns as if, in his mid-30s, he were still trying to be the coolest guy in school. With his pop-star good looks and long, tea-colored hair, Iwai is everywhere in the media — and in every frame of his work.

This style and sensibility are well-suited to his latest film, "All About Lily Chou Chou." The hero, Yuichi (Hayato Ichihachi), is a second-year junior high school student in an idyllic countryside, whose life revolves around Lily Chou Chou, a pop singer with a throaty voice, a druggy sound and mysterious charisma. Together with his classmates, Yuichi indulges in petty crime, such as shoplifting CDs and selling the rejects to used-record shops, while running into trouble, including bullying by older boys that leaves him a shattered wreck.

Yuichi, we see, is a wimp and a tool, who survives the perils of adolescent life by attaching himself to the stronger and sullenly doing their bidding. Then, when he can't stand it anymore, he retreats to his private world of CDs and Internet chat, where he is free to express his true feelings to strangers, particularly a girl who goes by the handle "blue cat."

Flash back to 1999, when Yuichi was a first-year junior high school student — before the fall from grace. He becomes friends with Hoshino (Shugo Oshinari), a boy in his class and his kendo club who is a natural leader and an excellent student — i.e., everything Yuichi is not. Yuichi also has a crush on Kuno (Ayumi Ito), a girl in his chorus club who is an accomplished pianist — and is barely aware of his existence.

Then summer comes and Hoshino, Yuichi and other kendo club members go to Okinawa on money they rip off from a gang of punks (who in turn ripped it off from a man in a parking lot). There they meet pretty girls, friendly locals and have the time of their young lives. The good vibes turn bad, however, when an acquaintance nearly loses his life in a road accident and Hoshino nearly drowns. It is almost as though the island gods have cursed them. When the new semester begins, Hoshino returns with a new, darker personality, beating and bullying with a casual cruelty. He makes Yuichi's life a living hell.

Hoshino and his henchmen expand their criminal career beyond petty larceny, forcing a classmate, Tsuda (Yu Aoi), into prostitution, with Yuichi serving as go-between. Then a clique of punk girls take a dislike to Kuno and, with Yuichi's assistance, subject her to tortures worthy of the Taliban.

Meanwhile, Yuichi pours out his love for Lily Chou Chou on the Internet nightly, while in the daytime he retires to a nearby rice field to listen to her music — and wrestle with what remains of his soul.

This tale of the teen-world-as-jungle has a persuasive authority, as though Iwai is not observing these kids so much as getting inside their heads. But the lushness of the imagery (all those gorgeous shots of blue skies and waving rice) and the beauty of the music (Debussy's "Arabesque" providing accompaniment to the torments of the damned) begins to feel distanced and smug. Also, as its 146-minute running time indicates, "All About Lily Chou Chou" lives up to its title all too literally, with the hero's self-involvement mirroring the director's self-indulgence.

The film's neverending journey across the howling moral wilderness of its characters' lives is nonetheless entrancing. By the end we understand why Yuichi can't live without Lily: In a world gone wrong, she is the only one who will never betray him.

Triple review of "Ka-chan," "Warm Water Under a Red Bridge" and "Pistol Opera"

Ka-chan, rating: ★★★, runtime: 96 min.

Directors seldom retire — voluntarily at any rate. But for every Manoel de Oliveira, the 92-year-old Portuguese master who made his first film in 1931 and released his most recent, "I'm Going Home," this year, many once-celebrated directors have been rendered unemployable by the vagaries of the movie business.

In Japan, directors who have attained revered master status are more likely than their Hollywood counterparts to keep working into their 60s, 70s and beyond. Kaneto Shindo — at 89, Japan's oldest active director — released "By Player" last year, a film commemorating the 50th anniversary of his production company, Kindai Eiga Kyokai. Among the over-65 set Nagisa Oshima, Masahiro Shinoda, Kinji Fukasaku, Shohei Imamura, Kon Ichikawa and Seijun Suzuki have also all finished films within the last year or so, with Fukasaku's ultraviolent "Battle Royale" becoming one of this year's big box-office hits.

Three of the aforementioned Japanese masters now have films on release — a cause of celebration for the Japanese film industry as a whole. Though Ichikawa, Imamura and Suzuki could not be more different in career paths or directorial styles, they have all brought a touch of genius to a business badly in need of it. They are three big reasons why anyone outside Japan cares about the films being made here. The most senior of this trio, the 86-year-old Ichikawa, freely admits that many of his more than 80 films have been works-for-hire. But he is a consummate craftsman and professional giving a high sheen to otherwise routine genre product. As a result, he has kept working steadily through the decades.

His most recent film, "Ka-chan," is the latest in a long line of literary adaptations that includes "Conflagration" (1958), "The Key" (1959) and "The Makioka Sisters" (1983). This time his source is a story by Shugoro Yamamoto, a popular writer whose tales of life among the common folk also inspired three films by Kurosawa. "Ka-chan" was co-scripted by Hiroshi Takayama and Natto Wada, Ichikawa's wife, who wrote some of his best films in the 18 years before her death in 1983.

The setting is Edo (feudal-era Tokyo), which in the grip of an economic depression after a series of failed government reforms. Sound familiar? A strong-willed matriarch (Keiko Kishi) struggles to keep her brood of five — including three grown sons and a pretty, marriageable daughter — on the road to financial survival, if not success. She has also given them a strong moral core, as evidenced by their collective effort to save a friend of the oldest son from ruin.

She faces a sterner test when a thief (Ryuji Harada) invades her humble abode and demands her money — including the coins she and her children have scraped together for the oldest son's friend. Instead of calling on her sleeping boys to beat the invader to a pulp, she sweet-talks him out of his demand — and invites him to join the family. The thief, a young first-timer driven to this desperate strait by poverty, accepts her offer, though he can't help feeling uneasy about the secret he has to keep from his new "cousins," especially the daughter.

Ninety-six min. long, "Ka-chan" plays like a short story with an improving moral. The characters are types, while every scene is in service of the heartwarming climax, with an aim to affirm and reassure rather than challenge. Its principals, most notably Ka-chan, are all upright, gentle-spirited types intended to make the audience feel better about being Japanese.

The dry humor in the tone and sophistication in the execution are distinctively Ichikawa; he may traffic in sentiment, but rarely in sentimentalism. The usual mass-audience period drama presents premodern Japan as a glorified folk museum, with everyone and everything colorfully and impeccably traditional. Ichikawa, however, shows the poverty of the era in all its grim horror, with even Ka-chan and her family one shaky step above destitution.

Warm Water Under a Red Bridge, Akai Hashi no Nurui Mizu, rating: ★★★, runtime: 119 min.

Shohei Imamura is another director with an interest in the lower levels of Japanese society — an interest that has informed much of his career. Instead of being a populist, however, Imamura has gone about his investigations in such films as "Pigs and Battleships" (1961), "Vengeance Is Mine" (1979) and "Why Not?" (1981), taking a more anthropological, or even entomological, view. At the same time, he has long been fascinated with the lower half of the body, particularly that of his lusty, strong-willed, decidedly eccentric female protagonists.

These strands of Imamura's work come together in his latest film, "Warm Water Under a Red Bridge," though with a kinder, gentler, more whimsical touch than formerly. But what might have been daring in 1961, particularly the "oceanic" sensuality of the heroine, now looks almost willfully out of step with the times.

A restructured salaryman (Koji Yakusho) befriends a homeless philosopher, who tells him about a treasure in an old house near Toyama Bay, next to a river crossed by a red bridge. When the philosopher dies, the salaryman, Sasano, sets out in search of the treasure. Instead, he finds, in a supermarket, Saeko (Misa Shimizu), a woman with a sensuous air, who drips water from underneath her skirt as she leaves the store.

Sasano learns that she lives with her senile mother in the house he is looking for. Rather than ferret out the treasure, however, he becomes her lover and learns her secret: She is a human reservoir who accumulates water to bursting point. It is only by having sex and making the dam burst, so to speak, that she can find relief.

Instead of recoiling, Sasano is enraptured. He finds a room at a local inn, gets a job on a fishing boat and comes running each time Saeko signals distress with a flashing mirror.

The woman-as-lifegiving-sea metaphor is crashingly obvious and literal, especially when water spews like a geyser from between Saeko's thighs at the critical moment. Yakusho and Shimizu bring off these scenes with unflinching elan, which doesn't mean they unembarrassing. There is a puckish sweetness to the unusual love story, and flashes of Imamura's trademark vitality, but the film is a private joke.

Pistol Opera, rating: ★★☆, runtime: 112 min.

Seijun Suzuki is something of a prankster. As a contract director for Nikkatsu in the 1960s, Suzuki churned out yakuza programmers with a growing disdain for genre convention. He used everything from kabuki to Pop Art and the French Nouvelle Vague to create a cheeky blend of hypercharged action and wacky surrealism, offered up with the straightest of faces.

The culmination was the 1967 thriller "Branded to Kill" in which Joe Shishido played a hitman with appealing insolence. The hero falls for a death-obsessed Japanese-Indian client — and finds himself locked in a duel with the mysterious No. 1 in the hitman's guild. The film got Suzuki fired from Nikkatsu (the studio president found it incomprehensible) but it became a cult classic in Japan and abroad.

Now, Suzuki has returned with "Pistol Opera," a reworking of "Branded to Kill" with women playing the main roles. Shot in black-and-white, "Branded to Kill" was — for all its Mod flourishes — a gritty, noirish film. By contrast, "Pistol Opera" has been shot in gaudy primary colors and staged with flamboyant theatricality. Call it Taisho Decadent entertainment. There are even long set pieces in which the actors declaim to the audience and the action comes to a dead halt.

Suzuki still has his old stylistic flair and is even more outrageous than he was in 1967: Think Takarazuka channeled through the antic spirits of Salvador Dali and Jean Cocteau. But with only the flimsiest of stories to tether it, "Pistol Opera" spins off into the ether, where its gyrations become tiresome.

No. 3, aka Nora Neko ("Stray Cat") aka Miyuki Minazuki (Makiko Esumi), is given an assignment by hitwoman guild representative Kayoko Kamigyo (Sayoko Yamaguchi): Whack No. 1, the elusive, deadly Hyakume ("Hundred Eyes"). This job soon becomes the most elaborate and deceptive of puzzles. In solving it, Miyuki meets Goro Hamada (Mikijiro Hira) — the No. 3 of "Branded to Kill," now retired from active duty and elevated to the honorary title of No. 0. She also encounters various rivals, including a mysterious man in black (Masatoshi Nagase), while a little girl tags after her, begging to learn her trade. Finally, she receives an invitation she can't refuse, from No. 1 himself.

As played by Esumi, a former fashion model with a commanding presence, Miyuki is a striking vision in kimono and leather boots. She is, however, little more than a swaggering pose, without the sweaty desperation of Shishido's original No. 3.

Suzuki no doubt had a ball putting Miyuki and his other fantastic inventions through their paces. Having ascended to Japan's cinematic pantheon, he, Ichikawa and Imamura are now amusing themselves on screen. Better that than gateball.

Godzilla, Mothra and King Ghidorah, rating: ★★★☆, runtime: 104 min.

Live long enough and you figure out a few things. That was my thought as I sat through the double feature "Skippy Hamutaro — Big Adventure in Hamuhamuland" and "Godzilla, Mothra and King Ghidorah: Giant Monsters All-Out Attack." My plan had been to slip into the Godzilla film and slip out of the Hamutaro cartoon, an entertainment for under-7s based on a popular TV show. The guy I called at the theater assured me that "Godzilla" started at 4:30 p.m.; actually, he said, "The show starts at 4:30" — a crucial difference.

So I ended up seeing the adventures of Hamutaro and his pals in Hamuhamuland, while the kiddies squirmed and their mothers silently endured. I also wondered what marketing genius had paired this cutesy bauble, whose villain is a kitty in a cape, with the latest installment in the Godzilla saga, which prerelease publicity had assured me would be the scariest yet. Wouldn't the Big G's titanic battles with Baragon, Mothra and King Ghidorah — the last, a flying three-headed monster 50 meters long from fangs to tail — give the tykes a nasty turn? Wasn't this like screening a Rugrats movie with "Alien 3" — a mismatch verging on child abuse?

Well, no. The tykes liked the Big G and his friends just fine. In fact, the boy sitting next to me giggled through the monster fight scenes. The folks at Toho who made and marketed this film knew exactly what they were doing. Instead of trying to go mano a mano with creature features from Hollywood — the mistake of the ill-fated American Godzilla movie — Toho has stayed with the formula that made Godzilla an international icon. That includes the monster's portrayal by a man in a rubber suit.

In 1954, when Ishiro Honda directed the series' first installment, the suit was the only feasible option. Now, however, with computers being used to animate everything from "Shrek" to film students' shorts, it would seem logical to digitize Godzilla as well. But the man-in-a-rubber-suit aesthetic — the presentation of the monsters as costumed big kids — distances the onscreen action so much from reality that even kindergartners can enjoy it. So Toho once again corrals its target "family" audience on the cheap, while conceding to Hollywood the CGI extravaganza market in which it could not expect to compete anyway.

Directed by effects-meister Shusuke Kaneko, who has brought dynamism to a genre in desperate need of it in such films as "Crossfire" and "Gamera III," "Godzilla, Mothra, King Ghidorah" is a return to basics — more precisely, to what the 46-year-old Kaneko found thrilling about Godzilla when, as a boy, he first saw him stomping across screens big and small. Instead of misguided attempts by other recent movies in the series to soften or update the Big G's image — giving us a cute Godzilla Junior or a hypertrophied "new" Godzilla seemingly trained on nuclear steroids — the film alludes to ancient myth, modern warfare, natural catastrophes and show-business legend. This Godzilla is not only a mean fighting machine, able to vaporize rivals with one mighty atomic blast, but a symbol of our collective fears, be they earthquakes or Armageddon.

A human-centered story must unfold, however, before Godzilla and his opponents climb into the ring. Kaneko, who wrote the script, follows the series' tradition of cutting between shots of fleeing crowds and scenes of tight-lipped officials bandying pseudo-scientific theories and bellowing orders in military jargon. But unlike previous installments that took the monster-bashing business with a risible seriousness, Kaneko's injects welcome touches of black humor.

As the film begins, Godzilla is stirring from his half-century-long sleep in the waters off Guam, where he retired after his last rampage in 1954. But when the commander of a Japanese submersible spots suspicious monster activity in the area, near a sunken U.S. nuclear submarine, officials back home are reluctant to act — save for Adm. Tachibana (Ryudo Uzaki), who witnessed Godzilla's power as a 5-year-old and knows how destructive it can be.

Meanwhile, Tachibana's daughter Yuri (Chiharu Niiyama) is working as an announcer for a struggling BS station. While making a documentary near Mount Myokozan in Niigata Prefecture, Yuri and her crew experience a disturbing earthquake. That night, a gang of marauding bikers are buried in a tunnel collapse — and a truck driver they have been harassing sees a huge, fiery-eyed beast stir in the rubble. Soon after, at Lake Ikeda in Kagoshima Prefecture, a group of young revelers are attacked by a horrific Thing arising from the waters. What in the name of all unholy is going on here?

A writer friend of Yuri's, the gangly, Jeff-Goldblum-ish Takeda (Masahiro Kobayashi), reads a book on monsters of ancient Japanese legend — and wonders if they aren't so legendary after all. Then Yuri, Takeda and Murao (Takashi Nishina), an eager-beaver assistant director who is Takeda's rival for Yuri's affections, meet the eccentric old author of the book, who says that Godzilla is a living, raging embodiment of the souls who lost their lives in the Pacific War. Wouldn't you know? — he happens to be right.

Inevitably, the monsters emerge, while the authorities dither (the most realistic part of the film). Godzilla stomps a few islands on his way north, while Baradon, a four-legged creature with a pug nose and ears that look like radar dishes, tromps south from Mount Myoko. Finally, they converge in the mountains of Hakone, where an air-headed woman, catching sight of the rampaging Baradon in the distance, poses her uneasy hubby for the ultimate tourist snap. "Isn't it cute?" she coos. Then she hears a roar and sees Godzilla glaring down at her from the peak behind. The kick that follows atomizes mountain, tourists and all. How can you not love this guy?

Ichi the Killer, Koroshiya Ichi, rating: ★★★, runtime: 128 min.

Edge-wise, violence has replaced sex as the last frontier in the local film business — and Takashi Miike knows it. A self-styled outlaw with out-sized ambition, energy and talent, Miike has rapidly upped the violence ante to heights that look, depending on one's point of view, sickening, awe-inspiring or absurd. I admit to being shocked by "Audition," a brutally effective horror show about the perils of May-September love, especially if May happens to be a psychotic sadist. The last 30 min. are like major eye surgery without anesthesia — almost as painful for the spectator as the victim.

Despite the hints of fetishism in Miike's work — he has the same kind of thing for body-piercing that Hitchcock had for icy blondes — he has a comic and even humanistic side. He's like the naughty kid who dreams up neat tortures, but who would never think of wielding the pliers and meat skewers himself (save, perhaps, on the stray toad).

His latest assault on all that's decent is "Ichi the Killer," a gang thriller based on a cult comic by Hideo Yamamoto. The premise has a "Revenge of the Nerds" appeal: A wimp has transformed himself into a deadly fighting machine, but stokes the fires of rage with tears of remembrance for boyhood humiliations. Though reminiscent of "Crying Freeman," a popular manga about a weeping hit man, "Ichi the Killer" adds a new, perverted twist: The hero climaxes each time he kills (and Miike, considerately, shows the results in closeup, starting with the opening credits).

Ichi's serious strangeness is only the beginning; it's as though Miike and his staff sat up nights topping each other with outrages designed to drive the more tender-minded out of the theater. But the splatter is so over the top — certain shots are a broom's-eye view of the slaughterhouse floor — that the movie becomes a grotesque gaman taikai (endurance contest).

That said, if you happen to share Miike's warped sense of humor (and to some extent, I confess I do), you will enjoy the way he propels the cartoony violence far beyond anything a Hollywood director would venture, even if his name happens to be Quentin Tarantino. Or the action will leave you staring at the screen in stony-eyed disgust. There's not much middle ground.

The story starts with a standard-enough gang-movie trope: The boss of the Anjo-gumi and his young lover are murdered, and the survivors, led by Anjo's hot-blooded top lieutenant, Kakihara (Tadanobu Asano), boil through Shinjuku in search of revenge. Because this is a Miike film, the victims are not only slaughtered, but sliced, diced and spattered from floor to ceiling. Included in the gang's three-man cleanup crew is Jijii (Shinya Tsukamoto), a shifty-eyed man of indeterminate age who takes a certain grim pleasure in his work.

There is, we discover, a reason: The hit man was Jijii's protege — the aforementioned Ichi (Nao Omori), a doe-eyed shlump who works as a waiter in a coffee shop. Though Jijii's willing tool, Ichi is a delicate type who was traumatized by bullies when he was a lad (or at least that's how he obsessively remembers it). He also happens to be in love with Sarah (Mai Goto), a pink-salon hostess who is brutalized by her pimp (Hoka Kinoshita). But while the pimp is beating Sarah to a monstrous pulp in their apartment, Ichi is standing outside, writhing in agony — and ecstasy. The boy clearly has problems.

So does Kakihara, whose face is crisscrossed with scars and whose mouth splits into a huge rictus when he loosens the pins that hold the corners, like a demon in a folk tale. He pursues his boss's killer with an eerie calm, punctuated by eruptions of inventive cruelty. When Jijii fingers a hood named Suzuki (Susumu Terashima) from an affiliate gang as the probable perp — the Anjo gang stole Suzuki's profitable porn-video business — Kakihara has him strung up with meat hooks, like a flying bat, and douses him with boiling oil. This is not a scene to see before your tempura dinner. Suzuki somehow survives this deep-fry — and vows to kill every member of the Anjo gang.

At Jijii's urging, Ichi goes on more rampages, shredding his victims with a blade concealed in his boot. Meanwhile, Kakihara conducts his own investigation, using the services of a straight-arrow former cop (Sabu) who is prone to remorse — and homicidal rage. As the body count mounts, we see a showdown coming: Ichi vs. Kakihara. The loser, it seems, will not sleep with the fishes, but be pureed into a bloody action painting.

Tsukamoto and Sabu, both acclaimed directors in their own right, are effective in their respective roles, adding a third, human dimension to their manga models. But Asano as Kakihara is this extreme movie's grinning malevolent center. Usually cast as a quiet type who seethes with inner fire, Asano plays the flame-haired gang boss with a chilling psychopathic glee. If Miike had used him to better purpose, instead of diddling with prop innards, "Ichi the Killer" might have been more than the latest exhibit in his Traveling Geek Show.

The Happiness of the Katakuris, Katakurike no Kofuku, rating: ★★★, runtime: 113 min.

When I heard that Takashi Miike was remaking the Korean hit "The Quiet Family" with songs and dances, I knew it wasn't going to be "The Sound of Music."

In films such as "Audition" and "Ichi the Killer," Miike's images of demented torture and depraved sex wiped smirks off the faces of even hardened deconstructionists, who thought they celebrated "irony," until "irony" came straight at their eyeballs.

Miike delivers his gross and gruesome effects with a cheek that is the essence of rock/punk/rap rebellion. Call his bad attitude adolescent if you will, but Miike, who has said his second career choice after film director was lead singer in a band, has a performer's instincts that make his brand of outrageousness work.

Making a musical, even one like Miike's "The Happiness of the Katakuris" means choreographing all those leaping and strutting bodies, while segueing from speech to song. It helps, in other words, to have a bit of Stanley "Singing in the Rain" Donen in your soul, even if several of your performers are zombies.

Miike may not be the most obvious choice for such an assignment, but the story — a hapless family runs a failing B&B, dealing with guests who mostly end up dead — is right down his outlandish alley. Also, his staging of the songs by Koji Makaino and Koji Endo, which range from comic rap to uplifting uptempo numbers, is always energetic and occasionally inspired. He has made what could have easily become a mess into a film that is unmistakably by Miike, who slams nihilistic shivs into his most life-affirming moments.

The title family are patriarch Nihei (Tetsuro Tanba), dad Masao (Kenji Sawada), mom Terue (Keiko Matsuzaka), daughter Shizue (Naomi Nishida), son Masayuki (Shinji Takeda) and tot Yurie (Tamaki

Miyazaki), Shizue's offspring from a failed marriage. They live in a B&B many lonely kilometers from civilization, in the midst of natural splendor.

Why are they there? Restructured from his job as a shoe salesman, Masao fulfilled an old dream of running a B&B with the whole family pitching in. He bought this place because he had heard that a highway would be built nearby, but he was misinformed.

The first guest arrives, a weary little schlump who goes straight to his room. When Masayuki brings him a beer, the guest glumly asks him what he would do if he knew this night were to be his last. The next morning the Katakuris find him lying dead on the floor — and immediately burst into song. Like I said, a Miike musical.

Terrified that this untimely death will kill his fledgling business, Masao decides to bury the evidence. After overcoming opposition from Terue, the others agree to dispose of Mr. Loner, with all the appropriate rites.

Next to arrive is an enormous sumo wrestler and his diminutive girlfriend, who promptly set the floorboards squealing with their enthusiastic lovemaking. Masao is soon confronted with a logistical problem in the form of the wrestler's dead body after he expires from his exertions.

Then, when ditzy Shizue makes an excursion to Karuizawa with Yurie, she falls head-over-heels for Richard (Kiyoshiro Imawano), a guy in white uniform who says he is a half-British, half-Japanese fighter pilot with the American Navy — and claims Queen Elizabeth as his aunt. She and her new sweetheart sing a love duet, with Richard floating up into the sky and Shizue in seventh heaven. Too bad about all those bodies piling up back home.

This sounds funnier on paper than it is on the screen, at least for the first hour. The chuckles stuck in my throat when the first victim appeared, a knife rammed in his jugular and his neck splattered with gore. Wes Craven couldn't have done it better.

In the second hour, the comic momentum builds as the family accepts its peculiar fate (even digging holes for prospective victims), while plot complications start to bear absurd fruit. Several of the songs, such as Masao and Terue's karaoke hymn to marital love and the final all-family dance number, are hummable and funny. And a claymation cliffhanger battle between Richard and Nihei add a bizarre spice to the already strange goings-on.

I wonder, however, who Miike's producers thought they were making this movie for. Pop star/actor Kenji Sawada is a relic to Miike's mostly young fan base, bur the film is too sardonic and strange for the oldies who remember Sawada as Japan's answer to David Bowie. Miike, though, seems to have had a swell time — and that's all that counts, isn't it?

Harmful Insect, Gaichu, rating: ★★★★, runtime: 92 min.

The heroes of seishun eiga (youth films) used to be idealized types, usually played by the teen idols of the moment. In the 1960s, Sayuri Yoshinaga became the ultimate fresh-faced school girl for a generation — and her career has lasted far longer than the bloom on her cheeks.

Today teens in Japanese films are more likely to seethe than sparkle, while battling to survive in dysfunctional families and schools.

Far from sensationalizing, the best of these films show clearly what real teens are experiencing. Among them are Akihito Shiota's "Moonlight Whispers," "Don't Look Back" and now "Harmful Insect." Unlike directors who project their own agendas or egos onto their underage characters, Shiota films them without filters.

Which does not mean that he simply points the camera and shoots. Instead his films combine the stripped-down style of today's minimalism and the character-centered focus of traditional humanism. He unerringly finds whatever makes a scene comes to life, be it the early-morning beauty of a waterfront canal or the hard glint of understanding in a young girl's eyes, while excluding everything that might distract. His images may be austere, but each shot is telling. Shiota is, at heart, a portraitist. If he were a war photographer, he would shoot a single face that sums up the horror.

In "Harmful Insect," that face belongs to Sachiko (Aoi Miyazaki), a seventh-grader whose mother (the single-named Ryo) has attempted suicide and whose handsome sixth-grade teacher (Seichi Tanabe) was forced to quit after falling in love with her (whether he molested her or not is left unstated). These scandalous goings-on are common knowledge among her classmates, who regard her as a creature from another, sadder planet. Their relentless gossip and ostracism finally drive her out of school, to the privacy of her room and the freedom of the streets.

There she meets Takao (Tetsu Sawaki), a carrot-haired boy who lives in an abandoned factory and survives by petty crime, and Tama (Koji Ishikawa), a mentally disabled man who veers from childish frolics to fearsome rages, but is basically sweet-tempered and harmless. They form an unlikely trio, enjoying an idyll amid the ruins and back streets, interposed with the occasional scam.

One day Tama is hit by a van, whose driver was jabbering on his cell phone instead of looking at the road. He is uninjured, but the driver, fearful of losing his job, pays a wad of hush money to the only witness — Takao, who set up the entire "accident." At first worried for Tama, Sachiko is delighted by the outcome. There are more ways to move in the world, she discovers, than along the ruts worn by straight society.

Even Mom seems to be recovering, as she rediscovers love in a pleasant man who tries his best to make friends with Sachiko. The girl is slow to respond, but after a classmate, Natsuko (Yu Aoi), hunts her down, she makes the momentous decision to return to school. She joins the chorus as an accompanist and even attracts the attention of a boy who seems unfazed by her reputation. Natsuko, however, has her eye on him as well — and when he chooses Sachiko, she is hurt.

This crack in Sachiko's happiness soon widens, as a series of calamities strike. Finally she finds herself on the road, hitchhiking to the nuclear power plant where her old teacher now works. She has been corresponding with him, pouring out her heart in letters and, though his answers have been sporadic, she feels he is the only one left who knows and understands.

This may sound like twisted melodrama: A 13-year-old girl flees to the arms of her adult abuser. But her choices have an emotional logic that make them, if not ideal, at least comprehensible. As Sachiko, a girl who has seen too much and been loved too little, Miyazaki has the look of innocence hardening into experience Though not a passive victim, she has been neglected and used by the adults around her, while Takao and Natsuko prove to be no substitute for the family she never had.

Extraordinarily talented child actors can be creepy to watch — the magic they work is not quite human — but Miyazaki, who also starred in Shinji Aoyama's "Eureka," can nail an emotion without making it look like a sleight-of-hand trick. Her Sachiko is as real as it gets, which makes the crimes committed against her all the more loathsome. The true "harmful insects" in this film are not the kids, who are mainly decent sorts, but the adults, who are poisoning their young.

Hush!, rating: ★★★, runtime: 135 min.

Say what you will about the Japanese attitude toward sexuality, it has traditionally been more tolerant than that of more puritanical societies. Hence the many foreign gay men who over the decades have found in Japan a refuge where they can live in relative safety. But for every cross-dressing celebrity on late-night TV, thousands of gay men here remain in the closet, for social or professional reasons. The Japanese equivalents of media mogul David Geffen and U.S. congressman Barney Frank are hard to find.

Japanese filmmakers have explored these and other contradictions of gay life here in the past decade, but few as penetratingly and honestly as Ryosuke Hashiguchi. Openly gay himself, he has provided an insider's view of the lives so many gay men here lead in such films as "A Touch of Fever" and "Like Grains of Sand." While portraying them with a candidness that can be raw in its impact he succeeds in humanizing them.

His latest film, "Hush!" sounds like the type of gay comedy Hollywood makes with Robin Williams and Nathan Lane (that is, the Williams and Lane who starred as gay characters in "The Birdcage" in 1996, not 2002). A gay couple — pet groomer Naoya (Kazuya Takahashi) and civil engineer Katsuhiro

(Seiichi Tanabe) — are living together more or less happily, but the less is threatening to undermine the more.

Closeted from family and colleagues, Katsuhiro is being pressured to do the "normal" heterosexual thing, especially by Emi (single-named Tsugumi), a cute, flaky co-worker who is obsessed with him. Naoya, who is more open about his sexuality, even with his busybody mother, feels that something is missing in his life with Katsuhiro and muses out loud about the fragility of gay relationships. ("I wouldn't have been able to make it if I hadn't accepted being alone," he says at one point.)

Then a woman stumbles into their lives and everything changes. She is Asako (Reiko Kataoka), a dental technician who, after two abortions and an attempted suicide, has given up on not only men and marriage, but humanity as a whole. Her sex life reduced to fumblings with strangers, she dreams of a baby of her own. When she encounters the tall, handsome Katsuhiro — and quickly realizes he is gay — she sees the answer to her prayer. Barging into his company lab, she asks him point-blank if he will father her child. No need for marriage or sex — all she needs is a vial filled with the required fluid.

Here is where Hollywood would turn the story toward comedy, with a bundle of joy arriving sometime in the second act. Hashiguchi seriously examines the problem of being different (or in Asako's case, clinically disturbed) in a society that demands conformity as the price of membership.

There are light moments along the way, as well as the sort of intimate character portrayal more associated with Eric Rohmer than Mike ("The Birdcage") Nichols. Hashiguchi's one-scene, one-cut style, with its preference for the lengthy playing out of turbulent emotions from the detached middle distance, recalls another of his French idols, Robert Bresson.

But for all Hashiguchi's sympathy with his principals' dilemmas, he misses a crucial point: The true test for this odd trio will come after the reason that unites them arrives in their lives. Picking out baby clothes is not the same thing as dealing with their wearer 24 hours a day. Who will not just play at being parents, but change, feed and soothe a squalling bundle of joy at three in the morning? Take it to day-care and read it stories at night?

Instead, Hashiguchi focuses on a melodramatic distraction: Emi's mad attempt to smear Asako's reputation with Katsuhiro's brother and Naoya's mother. In dragging out the resulting contretemps, he makes "Hush!" feel longer than its 135-minute running time. When Asako finally collapses in a faint from stress, we are ready to join her.

Sometimes, Hollywood gets it right. At least, in "The Birdcage," Albert and Armand raised a kid — and a good one at that. It would have been interesting to see how Hashiguchi's threesome did it.

Dog Star, rating: ★★★⯪, runtime: 125 min.

Movies with animal stars have long been box-office winners in Japan, though the genre fell out of audience favor in the 1990s, after greedy producers, both in Japan and Hollywood, went to the well (or rather the pet shop) too often. Now it is back, with the 3-D animation "Dogs and Cats" drawing audiences and Tatsuya Nakadai starring in Takashi Tsukinoki's "To Dance With the White Dog," a romantic drama about an old man whose dead wife returns in the form of the title pooch. The newest film in this often-dismissed genre, "Dog Star," may be mass audience entertainment, but is intelligently different from its predecessors.

Director Takehisa Zeze, once proclaimed as one of the "four kings" of the "pink eiga" (softcore porn film), is a fearless trasher of cinematic conventions. His caper film "Rush" scrambles narrative logic to the point of total confusion but there is a method — and humor — to the madness that gives the film an undeniable charge.

I suspect Zeze took on the assignment to make "Dog Star" because he saw a similar chance to deconstruct familiar material. The resulting film is about as hard to understand as "Lassie Come Home," while extracting more than the standard quota of tears. But Zeze, who also wrote the script, turns genre formula on its head. A lovable old seeing-eye dog is the film's star, but he spends most of his screen time in the form of Etsushi Toyokawa, he of the mysterious hooded eyes and glorious long legs.

In Hollywood terms, it's as if Richard Gere were set to sniffing trees and romping through the grass. But while being a heartthrob, Toyokawa is no empty-headed hunk. Since making his screen debut in "You Will Love Me" (1989) Toyokawa has played everything from a psychic with destructive powers ("Nighthead") to a gangster with a split personality ("The Man with Two Hearts"), while proving to be one of the more talented actors of his generation. So with Toyokawa cast in the lead Zeze no doubt felt delight and relief. "With this guy," he thought, "this crazy thing can work" — and it does.

The plot takes a few curious turns before Toyokawa appears. Shiro is a white seeing-eye dog who was raised by a volunteer family before being taken away for training. Now 12, he still has fond memories of Haruka, the girl who was his inseparable companion. His master is Gong (Ryo Ishibashi), a blind boxing trainer who coaches his charges by hearing their mistakes.

One night, after a drink too many, Gong is hit and killed by a truck. Shiro survives, but is racked with guilt over his failure to protect his master when a ghostly Gong reappears. God won't let him into heaven, he says, until he does at least one good deed — and he wants that deed to be for Shiro. You have one wish, he tells the dog — what will it be?

Shiro's wish is to take human form and visit the family that raised him. Transformed into a man dressed entirely in white, he sniffs out their house — and learns that all but Haruka were killed in a plane crash. Now grown to womanhood, Haruka (Haruka Igawa) is teaching at a kindergarten in the countryside, far from painful memories. Shiro hitchhikes there (the deal with Gong did not include train fare) and finds her, but how can he get back into her life? When she discovers him sniffing her bike seat and calls him a pervert, all seems lost.

Shiro gets a job as a helper with a traveling petting zoo. The eccentric coot (Shigeru Izumiya) who runs it sees that Shiro is good with animals. On a visit to the kindergarten, Shiro renews his acquaintance with Haruka. This time she notices his kind heart — and affection blooms. On her summer vacation, she comes to help with the petting zoo. Her insecure boyfriend (Kenjiro Tsuda), however, suspects that her new interest has more to do with Shiro than ducks and rabbits.

Meanwhile, Gong is warning Shiro against falling in love with a human. He only has a year left to live — and love can only lead to sadness. Shiro, however, has a doglike determination to be with Haruka that Gong can't shake. But how can he reveal his real identity to the only woman who has ever meant anything to him?

Toyokawa could have gone full Jim Carrey with this role (Ace Ventura as the pet instead of the detective), but he opts for hot-eyed sincerity, instead of manic clowning. He plays a dog, to be sure, but a dignified dog of few words who sees through humans ("You're a half-assed man," he tells the discomfited Gong). And the way Shiro holds himself (alert, attentive, determined) and runs (with a loping, straight-backed grace) is all dog.

If he were playing a brilliant schizophrenic scientist, Toyokawa would get a Japan Academy Award for this performance. He'll probably have to settle for a citation from the Japan Seeing-Eye Dog Foundation.

As Haruka, newcomer Haruka Igawa plays a standard pure-hearted heroine with a couple of welcome twists. First, she has the aura of a real dog lover. Second, she looks as though she might have a real sex life. Give credit to Zeze, who may have spent much of his career making dirty movies but in "Dog Star" shows us the power of love, in different forms — and different species.

The Laughing Frog, Warau Kaeru, rating:★★★★☆, runtime: 96 min.
Some people float through life, taking their ease, while others have to paddle like crazy just to keep their heads above water. Ojosama — the pampered daughters of Japan's upper and upper-middle classes — often find themselves in the previous category. Secure in the knowledge that Papa or Hubby will pick up the tab, blissfully deaf to feminist calls to take up stressful careers, they seem to be above the clouds, swathed in Prada, forever journeying to that great gallery opening at the end of the rainbow.

But what happens when an ojosama is brought to earth, when Hubby turns out to be a philanderer, a debtor and, finally, a fugitive? In Hideyuki Hirayama's finely tuned comedy of manners, "The Laughing Frog," the heroine's response to such a catastrophe is true to ojosama form.

Ryoko (Nene Otsuka) may be living in her parent's countryside villa after her banker husband disappears trailing 85 million yen in debt, but she is looking out for No. 1 and doing a decent job of it, thank you. She still has her youth, her looks and that ineffable ojosama air of entitlement. On the Titanic, she would be standing at the rail with a sweet smile, certain of getting the best seat on the first lifeboat.

When hubby Ippei (Kyozo Nagatsuka) shows up, looking like a tramp, she promptly crumples in a ladylike faint — that feminine defense mechanism beloved of Victorian novels. But when Ryoko comes to, it is as though panic never entered her well-ordered mind. Coolly, she tells Ippei to put his dirty underwear in the washing machine and hide in the storeroom when visitors come.

In the storeroom wall Ippei discovers a peephole and soon learns several distressing facts. One is that Ryoko has a lover, Yoshizumi (Jun Kunimura), the father of a girl she is tutoring. ("How is Daddy in bed?" the sassy kid asks. "He's terrific," Ryoko answers without batting an eyelash.) Another is that the local cops who think Ippei is in the neighborhood. ("He's probably at his girlfriend's place in Yokohama," Ryoko helpfully tells one.)

Yoshizumi arrives on the third day of Ippei's stay. A carver of arty gravestones, he is all that the disgraced Ippei is not: charming, neatly turned out, successful at his chosen profession and a wonderful cook. Even Ryoko's raffish mother (Izumi Yoshimura) likes him. "He's loaded with sex appeal," she says with a knowing grin, as poor Ippei chokes on a pit.

Mom, it turns out, has a new man herself, an antique dealer who is a spry 58, but no match in the sack for her dear, departed husband. "He was like a symphony orchestra," she reminisces, rhapsodically.

Ippei makes Ryoko promise not to bed Yoshizumi until he is out of the house. But when Yoshizumi shows up and administers a soothing foot massage, Ryoko weakens. Ippei, bursting from the beers he downed to prepare for this ordeal, pees a torrent into a bucket as Ryoko's moans merge with the croaking of the frogs in the pond. A symphony indeed — and not the last; frogs croak similar commentary throughout the film. Thus, I suppose, the unusual title.

Hirayama resists the temptation to turn this material into a sitcom. Instead of feeding his characters comic zingers, he quietly, relentlessly peels away their evasions, delusions and lies.

Based on the novel "Toriko" by Yoshinaga Fujitsu and scripted by Izuru Narushima, "The Laughing Frog" is closely observant about the way society sorts out its winners and losers, in relationships as in everything else. Ippei believes he can get back into the game, even though he lost his touch ages ago. Ryoko, all soft, yielding femininity on the surface, calculates her every move with an icy inner logic far beyond Ippei's ability to outthink.

Kyozo Nagatsuka, who also starred in Hirayama's "The Games Teachers Play," restrains his usual strong on-screen personality enough to indicate the devastation wrought on Ippei's masculine pride. Though pathetic, he is not yet a clown (the operative word being "yet"). Nene Otsuka, a model and TV drama actress with a scattering of film credits, is effective both as an object of desire and an agent of change (representing one client).

The excellent supporting cast is headed by Yoshimura, an idol star of the 1950s who is making her first screen appearance in 15 years, and Kunimura, one of the best character actors now working.

If anything, Hirayama dials down the comic spirits of this cast a touch too far. But the ambiguity of tone — is it a comedy or drama? — keeps us guessing about Ippei's fate, until the entire cast of characters descend on the villa for a get-together and final reckoning. Some directors would play this climactic scene for clever twists; Hirayama opts for the more difficult existential chill.

Henry James, that expert on the 19th-century American version of ojosama and master chronicler of social subterfuge and cruelty, would approve, I think, though I wonder what he would have made of the froggy Greek chorus.

Chicken Heart, rating: ★★★⯪, runtime: 95 min.

When Takeshi Kitano started directing films, beginning with "Violent Cop" in 1989, he went for punches over punch lines. In spite of being one of the most popular comedians on Japanese television, Kitano preferred to play a tough guy on the big screen, whose sense of humor was black and who usually went down in a self-destructive blaze.

When he finally turned his attention to comedy, in 1995's "Getting Any?," the result was closer to "Dumb and Dumber" than Dirty Harry. The film's half-witted hero, played by longtime "Kitano Army" member Duncan, embarks on a futile quest to get laid, by any means necessary — and ends up as a happy voyeur.

Veteran Kitano assistant director Hiroshi Shimizu has absorbed both strands of his boss's comic mind: the black and the barmy. His 1998 directorial debut "Ikinai" was a comedy about a bus tour for losers whose last scheduled stop is a plunge over a cliff — the culmination of a suicide-for-insurance-money scam. His new film "Chicken Heart," which screened in Critics' Week at this year's Cannes Film Festival, also features characters at the bottom of the social barrel, but its take on their predicament is lighter — and goofier.

The film echoes Kitano's minimalist style, with its deadpan economy and inventiveness. Despite the influences, however, Shimizu's touch in "Chicken Heart" is less mannered and often funnier than that of his boss. Blasphemy? Maybe, but Kitano, whose big-screen gags tend toward sadistic pranks and lame pratfalls, often stands apart from his performers, playing the ringmaster. Shimizu is more willing to let his cast wing it, with hilarious results. His heartwarming climax falls a bit flat but does not dull affection for his three heroes, particularly Matsuo Suzuki's Maru — a nerd who stumbles away with the film.

The ostensible focus, however, is Iwano (Hiroyuki Ikeuchi), a former professional boxer who has been reduced, at age 27, to being a nagurareya — a human punching bag who lets drunken businessmen take potshots at him for cash. (A real nagurareya was Shimizu's inspiration for the character.) He is assisted by Maru, a 36-year-old former teacher who serves as timekeeper, and Sada (Kiyoshiro Imawano), a 53-year-old drifter who collects money from customers. This trio lives in the same run-down rooming house and, after hours, drinks together at an outdoor stall run by a mysterious old man (photographer Nobuyoshi Araki) who fixes electronic gadgets when he is not evading the police.

All three have day jobs: Iwano washes graffiti off walls, Maru helps his elderly uncle mind his hat store (while sitting in front of it blowing bubbles), and Sada hands out promotional packets of tissue to passersby (or simply chucks them at the uncooperative). All three want something better — they just don't know what.

Iwano's businessman brother offers him a real job, but Iwano doesn't want responsibility he can't escape. Maru tries to better his lot with lucky charms and colors, with little success. Sada, a free spirit, dreams of repairing a broken-down boat and heading out to the open sea, but can't get the engine to start.

Three hopeless cases? Not quite. Each, in his own roundabout way, makes progress toward something or other, in fits and starts that would be the despair of a self-help guru.

Iwano's case is supposedly the most serious, but his babe-magnet looks keep him in the running, even after he has dropped out of the race. When a bored young woman (Misayo Haruki) from Osaka engages him as a board game partner, the question of whether he will make it takes on a different nuance — but one not terribly interesting. If the film were his alone, it would be another sweet-sad exercise in post-adolescent angst.

Fortunately, it also belongs to veteran rocker Imawano, who makes no attempt to act but gets laughs anyway as the unconventional Sada. Whether slapping paint on his boat or tossing off quips at the bar, Sada couldn't care less what impression he is making. But his brusqueness has a charm and his loneliness a pathos that make him more than a one-note character.

Suzuki is the film's real find, however. A veteran stage actor who has suddenly become in-demand in the movies, he plays Maru as a child in a man's body — a gawky klutz who, in classrooms of a more innocent day, would have been a running invitation to a spitball volley. Suzuki's comedy seems to come from a personal place – his inner goofball — and bubbles to the surface with no filters. It's a natural spring of wackiness.

In its third act, as the trio embraces their respective fates, "Chicken Heart" takes a serious turn. Even death makes an appearance, though more gently than it would in a Kitano film. The concluding moral: Everything changes, but the spirit, nutty or otherwise, endures. A Buddhist thought, perhaps, but one that, in Shimizu's hands, translates into a universally appealing comedy.

Shangri-la, Kin'yu Hametsu Nippon: Togenkyo no Hitobito, rating: ★★★★, runtime: 105 min.

Yuji Aoki has made a fortune with comics about such mundane money troubles. His latest is "Japan's Financial Collapse" ("Kin'yu Hametsu Nippon"), which appears in "Gorakuo" magazine and has now been made into a film by Takashi Miike: "Shangri-la." Best-known abroad for outrages like "Audition" and "Ichi the Killer," Miike also has a more conventionally humanistic side, as shown in such films as "Bird People in China" and "Guys From Paradise."

In "Shangri-la" Miike comes as close as he probably ever will to being his generation's Yoji Yamada, whose Tora-san series made its peddler hero an icon of common-man values. It's not as though he's gone squishy; a Miike movie wouldn't be a Mii`ke movie without blackly funny, graphically explicit scenes of kinky sex and brutal violence — and "Shangri-la" has a few.

The film also illuminates the realities of life as lived by the millions who are just one uncollected bill away from ruin, as well as by the human slime who try to exploit them. But mainly it's a clever romp, with financially savvy Robin Hoods outwitting malefactors of great wealth, not to mention garden-variety hustlers and thieves.

It begins with the bankruptcy of an Osaka supermarket chain. The news hits the small printer of the chain's flyers hard — if the 10 million yen check from their biggest client bounces, the company is history. The printing company president, the hyper Umemoto (Yu Tokui), begs for mercy from the supermarket magnate (Maro Akaji), but the old rogue protests that he doesn't have a yen to his name, even as his tarty young wife luxuriates in their gaudily furnished mansion.

In a panic, Umemoto returns home, where his wife has been getting a tongue-lashing from her brother and sister-in-law. Guarantors of the printing company's debt, they are in deep doo-doo as well. Umemoto goes next to his lawyer, who advises bankruptcy court. He would rather die first.

Umemoto is making careful preparations for gassing himself in his car when he is rudely interrupted by an attack on a nearby homeless camp by a gang of punks. After rushing one of the injured homeless folk to the hospital Umemoto is warmly welcomed into their camp, which they call Togen Village, by Kuwata (Shiro Sano), a writer who is down on his luck, and the village "mayor" (Show Aikawa), a mysterious chap wearing sunglasses and an Afro wig. Overcome by the kindness of these strangers, Umemoto pours out his tale of woe. Moved, Kuwata and the mayor vow to help him save his company.

The first step in their business recovery plan is for Umemoto and his family to abscond, leaving their persistent creditors behind. The second is to raise gap-financing by selling off everything not nailed down and pressuring a sleazy loan shark to extend credit. The third step is to run an elaborate scam on the supermarket magnate and to use the money raised to make a quick killing on the stock market.

Watching all this play out is great fun. Masakuni Takahashi's script moves the story along briskly while carefully explaining the various subterfuges and stratagems. Miike's direction is uncharacteristically unobtrusive, with an unsprung rhythm that flows rather than pounds. He is also still the provocateur who likes to give the audience a jolt of strangeness every now and then to keep it alert — and remind it who is directing.

Tokui is engagingly frantic as Umemoto. Small and wiry, he acts from a deep-seated need — call it desperation — that is touching as well as funny. He is not just a comedian doing shtick, but a man in a whirlpool, paddling for dear life as his life vest deflates.

Aikawa, the best tough guy in Japanese movies, and Sano, the best geek, work well together as Umemoto's saviors. Aikawa plays up to his image — swaggering and glowering to cow the bad guys

— while well aware he looks absurd in that Afro wig. Meanwhile, Sano is convincingly scruffy and beaten down as the writer, but his unforced joy in gaming his opponents gives his character a satisfying upward arc.

I especially liked the way the film walks the audience through the details of the scam — the sign of a good caper movie. The art of printing has seldom looked so fascinating — but why add a spoiler? Suffice to say that "Shangri-la" is a welcome ray of light in the recessionary gloom.

Dolls, rating: ★★☆, runtime: 113 min.

When Takeshi Kitano won the Golden Lion at the Venice Film Festival in 1997 for "Hana-Bi," he was already being hailed as the most important Japanese director of the decade, with comparisons ranging from Ozu to Scorsese. Since his triumph at Venice, however, Kitano has been struggling both artistically and commercially. His road movie, "Kikujiro" (1999), got mixed reviews (David Rooney of "Variety" called it "klutzy" and "treacly"; Kevin Thomas of "Los Angeles Times," "totally irresistible"). His gang epic "Brother" (2000), which was shot in L.A. with an international cast, made only a modest box-office splash, though it was intended as Kitano's calling card to the multiplexes of the world.

With "Dolls," a film about three pairs of star-crossed lovers, Kitano is making a break with much of his cinematic past, particularly the savage violence that, tinged with black humor and presented in a minimalist style, first brought him to international attention. At this year's Venice Film Festival, where the film screened in competition, critical opinion was once again divided, with some calling it a masterpiece, others an exercise in cheap Orientalism. The nays had it — "Dolls" left without a prize — and I found myself agreeing with them.

The film's unusual structure — a bunraku puppet play segues into a modern love story whose protagonists are the puppets brought to life — has its interest, especially for those who like their Asian cinema traditional and exotic. But I balked at the literal-minded symbolism (a dead butterfly standing for dashed hopes, etc.), the tired sentimentalism of the principal couple's lonely journey to a foreordained oblivion and the awkward fit between the feudal-era story of tragic love and the realities of present-day Japan, where young people choose marital partners as freely as they do charge accounts.

The third act, in particular, is like "Way Down East" in a Japonesque mode, complete with an interminable trudge through the snow, but no heart-stopping leaps across the ice floes. D.W. Griffith could at least evoke pathos; Kitano in "Dolls" is the director as technician, who is more concerned with costumes and cinematography than the story he happens to be telling. He's jiggling the strings expertly enough — but there's no life in his puppets.

"Dolls" begins with a performance of "Meido no Hikyaku," a bunraku play by Chikamatsu Monzaemon (1653-1724), based on the true story of a young money courier, Chubei, whose love for the beautiful courtesan Umegawa takes a tragic turn when he is accused of the capital crime of seal-breaking and forced to flee, his lover accompanying him. The authorities are in hot pursuit, however, and the couple ends up committing suicide.

Switch to the present. Under pressure from his parents, Matsumoto (Hidetoshi Nishijima), an elite businessman, breaks off his engagement with the sweet-but-delicate Sawako (Miho Kanno) to marry the company president's daughter. On the day of the wedding, he hears that Sawako has attempted suicide and been committed to a mental hospital. Abandoning his bride, Matsumoto rushes to Sawako's side, finds her a gibbering wreck and escapes with her in his car. Thus begins a long odyssey that ends with the couple tied together with a red rope (Matsumoto cannot let the dangerously impulsive Sawako out of his sight) and wandering forlornly through the picturesque countryside as the seasons change and death closes in.

To give the audience relief from his couple's slow walk to a self-appointed doom, Kitano has woven in two other stories of love gone wrong. One concerns an elderly gang boss (Tatsuya Mihashi) who discovers that the lover of his youth (Chieko Matsubara) is still faithfully making a box lunch for him every day, decades after he abandoned her. (Like the ill-fated Sawako, she has gone batty.)

Another focuses on the pathetic fan (Tsutomu Takeshige) of a fatuous pop singer (Kyoko Fukada), who takes desperate measures when he hears she has damaged her face in an auto wreck and is retiring. (Enough to say they involve piercing parts of the body that would be the last choices of all but the deranged.)

In "Dolls," love is either deadly or maddening to one or both of the parties involved. This sort of high romanticism — love as the most dangerous of emotions — has a long tradition in Japan, but Kitano uses it as yet another way of avoiding the subject of real adult relationships in the here and now.

There are bright spots amid the gloom, including the gorgeous nature photography of cinematographer Katsumi Yanagishima, the resplendent costumes by fashion designer Yohji Yamamoto and, most of all, the art of the bunraku puppeteers, whose astonishingly lifelike performers outshine Kitano's stars. "Dolls" is aptly titled, but it cries out to be either a period drama — or a bunraku documentary.

Out, rating: ★★★☆, runtime: 119 min.

Every once in a while a Japanese movie comes along that cries out for a Hollywood remake. Hideyuki Hirayama's "Out," a black comedy about three women who chop up bodies for cash, gave me a bound-for-Hollywood vibe — partly because Hirayama's previous feature, the sci-fi drama "Turn," has already attracted Hollywood interest, but mostly because it has the kind of catchy plot line that grabs producers with short attention spans, while offering terrific roles for veteran actresses. Susan Sarandon, call your agent.

It helps that the film lives up to the promise of that plot, with spot-on casting, vibrant ensemble performances and a virtuoso job by Hirayama, who smoothly mixes comedy and drama to entertaining effect. Though the mainspring of the story is a high-concept gimmick, the film uses it to delve deeper not only into the women's relationships and souls, but also a society in the throes of a decade-long recession. It's not a pretty sight, but Hirayama and company make it an absorbing — and uncomfortably accurate — one. As grisly as the principals' new part-time job may be, who can say that, given their unpleasant alternatives, one would not do the same?

They start as four friends — Masako (Mieko Harada), Yoshie (Mitsuko Baisho), Kuniko (Shigeru Muroi) and Yayoi (Naomi Nishida) — working together at a box-lunch factory. But as monotonous as life on the o-bento assembly line may be, what is waiting for them when they arrive home is worse.

Masako is in a loveless marriage with a restructured salaryman, while trying to raise a sullen teenage son. Yoshie is a widow who spends her days taking care of her senile, bedridden mother-in-law. Scatter-brained Kuniko is a shopaholic who is hopelessly in debt to her friendly neighborhood loan shark, Jumonji (Teruyuki Kagawa). Yayoi is eight months pregnant, but her husband beats her when he loses at gambling, a near daily occurrence. One day, after a particularly ferocious thrashing, she strangles the snoring brute until he stops breathing.

In a panic she calls Masako and begs her to help hide the body. Not wanting to see Yayoi carted away to jail just as she is about to deliver a child, Masako reluctantly drives over and, after much huffing and puffing, shoves the corpse into the trunk of the car. Yayoi, for whom out of sight means out of mind, stops going to work — and tearfully asks Masako to dispose of the evidence, for a fee, of course.

A practical sort, Masako knows that dumping Yayoi's hubby is risky. The only thing to do, she decides, is to dissect him and chuck the pieces, in carefully wrapped packages, in dumpsters around the city. For this gruesome task, however, she needs a helping hand — and calls on her best friend Yoshie to provide it, with money from Yayoi as a lure. Yoshie, who could use the cash for a much-needed vacation, agrees. Then, after Masako and Yoshie have dragged the body to the bathroom and are about to carve it up, Kuniko arrives in a flutter to beg for a loan. They enlist her, over her loud protests, and after donning plastic rain gear, goggles and surgical masks, the three women do the dirty deed.

Kuniko, however, is careless about disposing her assigned bundles. The crows arrive, followed by the police, who arrest the most likely suspect: a gangster who runs a casino where the victim ran up huge losses. The discovery of the remains also draws the attention of Jumonji, since the too-clever Kuniko asked Yayoi to guarantee her loan shark debt in lieu of payment — and the doofus agreed. He puts two and two together, and comes to the women with a business proposition: There's this body, you see . . .

This is where many a Japanese director would go slapstick and cute, but Hirayama keeps "Out" firmly on the rails he first laid down for it. Absurd complications ensue, but the three women do not devolve into cartoons. Instead they become adept at their unchosen task and start to discover what really matters in their lives. Even Kuniko begins to imagine an existence beyond Prada and Gucci. This may sound like a women's bonding film, but it's not, quite. Though targeted at women who fit the profile of the three principals (mature, experienced, frustrated), "Out" is less a sisterly revenge fantasy than a comic examination of human behavior at its most extreme, with the operative word being "human."

Scriptwriter Ui-shin Chung keeps this examination focused on the characters themselves, not plot points or abstract themes. Everything his odd quartet does makes a wacky sort of sense. They don't plunge into their gory dilemma so much as slide into it. Once they take the first, fatal step, they just keep going, straight onto thin ice. Watching them, it's hard not to feel sympathy, especially for Masako, the prime mover, who wants to do the right thing by a friend in desperate need and learns why no good deed goes unpunished.

The three leads — Harada, Baisho and Muroi — are veterans who lend quality to even dire material. Rather than go head to head with them, relative newcomer Nishida spends most of the film apart, in a ditzy universe of her own. Her character's unconquerable selfishness may comfort over-40s who want to believe in devolution of the younger generational and the blessings of maturity. But as "Out" illustrates so vividly, whatever your age, you'd better have that do-re-mi.

The Twilight Samurai, rating: ★★☆, runtime: 129 min.

"The Twilight Samurai," Yoji Yamada's 77th film, is also his first period drama, though the 48 episodes of his Tora-san series were period dramas in all but name. Tora-san, that perpetually lovelorn peddler, may have traveled all over Japan in the last three decades of the 20th century, but he and his extended family from downtown Tokyo were throwbacks to another era — a friendlier, warmer, slower-paced Japan.

In " The Twilight Samurai," which is based on a best-selling novel by Shuhei Fujisawa, Yamada finds in the last days of the Edo Period (1600-1867) a Japan uncannily like the one we're living in today, complete with premodern versions of yen-pinching recessionary lifestyles, corporate restructuring, office politics — and men who can't say what they feel. Yamada's trademark humanism is also much in evidence, tempered by a darker, more tragic view of human nature than that found in the Tora-san films. This view, however, does not appear until the third act, after more than an hour of warmed-over melodrama about star-crossed lovers, aimed at Yamada's core audience.

The hero, Seibei (Hiroyuki Sanada), is the mid-19th-century equivalent of a rank-and-file salaryman: a samurai scraping along on a stipend of 50 bales of rice a year and working as a clerk in the clan office. He is, however, not a conformist. When his colleagues head for a drink after work, he goes straight home. Since he disappears every day as the sun goes down, he is derisively tagged with the nickname Tasogare (Twilight) Seibei.

His reasons for his early departure are his two young daughters and senile mother — all that is left of his family after the death of his wife from illness. Everyone pitches in, but Seibei does most of the work, from tending the garden to making cricket cages for extra money. But for all his ceaseless labors, he remains desperately poor.

Then a friend and fellow samurai, Rin-no-Jo (Mitsu Fukikoshi), tells Seibei that his sister Tomoe (Rie Miyazawa) has left her drunken brute of a husband and returned home. The next day Tomoe appears at

Seibei's house — she and Seibei were childhood friends — and her cheery smile brightens the gloom. Seibei's daughters fall in love with her — as does he, though he would rather die than admit it.

The ex-husband (Ren Osugi) reappears to beat and harass Tomoe. When Seibei defends her, the ex challenges him to a duel. Seibei wins using only a wooden stick against his opponent's sword, and his fame spreads throughout the town. Tomoe becomes a frequent visitor to Seibei's house, but when Rin-no-Jo proposes a match to Seibei, he refuses. "After three or four years of living in poverty, she would regret marrying me," he explains — but his heart says otherwise.

Impressed by what it has heard of Seibei's bravery and skill, the clan orders him to dispatch Yogoemon (Min Tanaka) — a samurai on the losing side of a clan succession struggle who is taking out his dissatisfaction with a sword. Seibei is reluctant, but the clan elders insist — and promise to end his financial worries. Just as he is about to set off to perform this distasteful task, however, Tomoe tells him she has accepted an offer of marriage. Then he discovers that his intended victim is a poor man much like himself. How can he kill him with a clean conscience? Why should he even care, now that the love of his life belongs to another man again?

Why should we care either? Rie Miyazawa's Tomoe is a wish-fulfillment figure, who lives only to worship the hero and care for his brood, from the moment she enters their lives. Also, her sweetness-and-light act belies her recent history as a battered wife — nary a scar remains. Miyazawa's performance, charming as it may be, offers few clues to her inner life.

Sanada brings a quiet conviction to the role of Seibei. A former gymnast who trained for action stardom under Sonny Chiba, he can also, at 42, still wield a mean sword. But while Seibei's dogged determination to do the right thing is admirable, his long slog through his twilight existence becomes tiring — and puzzling. Why, I couldn't help wondering, is the hardworking, clean-living Seibei dirt poor, while his colleagues live lives of pleasure and ease? Don't they have families to support as well? Or is there a background story I'm missing?

In any case, the climatic showdown between Seibei and Yogoemon redeems much of what has gone on before. The tepid romance forgotten, Yamada finally presents his main themes — the imminent disappearance of the samurai way in the coming tide of Westernization, the absurdity of mortal combat (and, by extension, war) once the combatants see each other as human beings, and the incurable contrariness of human nature. Sanada and celebrated butoh dancer Tanaka, as Yogoemon, perform their dance of death with power and grace, while connecting as comrades in injustice and misery. I don't want to add spoilers, just to say that this scene could stand alone as a one-act play — and is one of the best things Yamada has ever done. At the age of 70, he is just beginning to show us what he can do. But please, no more angels in kimono.

In Prison, Keimusho no Naka, rating: ★★★★☆, runtime: 93 min.

We live in overstimulated times. Sometimes we need to step back from the e-mail, cable TV and the rest of the media stream that flows ceaselessly over every waking hour and realize how different existence can be without it. It's not easy for the more connected among us, for whom gadgetry has become an extension of self — my cellphone is me! — but it can be done. There are still mountaintops and islands out there where one can find peace, quiet and not a single Internet provider.

But after semipermanently leaving the modern world behind, one still has to fill the hours, not to mention put food on the table. For every self-sufficient Robinson Crusoe, many more would find the tranquillity maddening, the freedom overwhelming. They crave community, structure, security and all the rest. What is the solution? A monastic order? A mental institution? Or, as Yoichi Sai's new film suggests, prison?

Based on a comic by former prisoner Kazu'ichi Hanawa, "In Prison" ("Keimusho no Naka") presents prison as, if not a paradise, an excellent place for relearning to appreciate the little things amid well-ordered surroundings, while not sweating the small stuff, like a roof and three squares meals. The tone, as might be expected, is gently ironic, but the film's underlying message is sincere. Want inner serenity? Check into the Gray Bar Hotel.

This message is counter to everything Hollywood has taught us about prison, going back to the 1930s Warner exposes of Big House life. And not only Hollywood; in his 1999 novel "A Man in Full" Tom Wolfe presents life in a California prison as a Dante-esque hell. The prisoner protagonist spends his nights listening to the ravings of the demented and depraved, and his days struggling to survive in a society of human wolves, with the ultimate trauma — gang rape — an ever-present threat.

In Japan, as Sai makes clear in scene after wryly funny scene, they do things differently. The Hokkaido prison where the hero, the elderly-but-spry Hanawa (Tsutomu Yamazaki) is sent for a three-year stretch is organized and operated along lines derived from the old Imperial Army. The guards never beat or otherwise abuse the prisoners, but they constantly order them about, with curt, shouted commands. The prisoners march or jog in formation everywhere and are forever falling in line, either standing or in seiza (i.e., kneeling in the formal Japanese style). Every minute is accounted for, every act is circumscribed by a myriad of rules, each one of which must be obeyed to the letter.

If a prisoner carving wooden tissue boxes in a workshop wants to take a toilet break, he must first raise his hand, be acknowledged by the guard, step up and state his request, receive the appropriate tag, hang it over the toilet door (thus notifying the world whether he is doing No. 1 or No. 2), complete his business and return the tag, with the appropriate bow and thanks. No variation is tolerated in this minutely choreographed drama, one of dozens that play out in the course of a day.

The prisoners, in short, are deprived of every speck of autonomy, if not human dignity, and are treated more like unruly boys than men. This is the sort of feudalistic, paternalistic mentality that half a century of democratization was supposed to change — but in Sai's prison it thrives, as though the clock had permanently stopped in 1942.

Hanawa, his four cellmates (Teruyuki Kagawa, Tomoro Taguchi, Yutaka Matsushige, Toshifumi Muramatsu), and the other cons not only get with this program, but internalize it to an absurd degree. They follow their rigid routine without major complaint, while delighting in the smallest privileges. The prospect of osechi ryori (traditional New Year's food) prompts one prisoner (Houka Kinoshita) to deliver a rapturous monologue on the delights awaiting them, accompanied by mouth-watering shots that would not be out of place on a cooking show. Treated to a movie, a can of Coke and boxes of cookies for "good behavior," one of Hanawa's cellmates (Taguchi) revels in each crunch and sip as he watches the show ("Kids Return" by Sai pal Takeshi Kitano).

There is no story as such, just the unfolding of prison routine, in incident after pointed incident, to ever more amusing effect. But though nothing much happens, save for Hanawa's brief stretch in solitary for a minor violation of the rules, many things are revealed. One is that, for all the fussing and shouting, the regime is generally humane: The food is plentiful and healthy, if plain, the prisoners live in clean, if Spartan, quarters and the various jobs, games and diversions keep them productively and, for the most part, happily occupied. Far from being an indictment of the Japanese prison system, the film is a backhanded love letter.

This is because Sai closely followed Hanawa's manga, if minus its obsessively detailed descriptions of prison life, while faithfully reflecting Hanawa's own fascination with the penal system. Like his onscreen hero, Hanawa was arrested for altering model guns to make them more like the real thing but, as the program notes explain, as a first-time offender, he probably could have won a suspended sentence. Instead, he opted to serve his three-year stretch — and gather the material that later became "In Prison."

Sai, maker of the comedies "All Under the Moon)" and "Dog Race," may gloss over some of the system's darker realities, but he captures the way prison life strips away superficialties and, in a fundamental way, makes the world new again.

As played by Yamazaki, in a uncharacteristically quiet performance, Hanawa is less an actor in the small dramas of prison life than a close observer. Forced to live like a 13-year-old on a school excursion, he comes to think and feel like one. Though approaching his dotage, he finds himself thrilled by the spectacle of falling snow. In a culture jaded with electronic sensation, this moment has the force of revelation — and is the ultimate luxury.

Suite de Jeudi, Mokuyo Kumikyoku, rating: ★★★✫, runtime: 113 min.

Films about women — and for women — are enjoying something of a boom now. They are also diversifying beyond the righteous sisterly bonding stories of the past.

One is Tetsuo Shinohara's new film "Suite de Jeudi," in which five women gather to remember a deceased writer who was a mentor and friend. But what begins as a reprise of "The Big Chill" takes another direction entirely when the women realize that the cause of death may not have been suicide, as they had thought, but murder. They decide to stay in the writer's house until they find an answer, or at least a suspect.

At this stage, I expected the bodies to start falling as accusations fly and the mental gears spin. That is, a local version of the Agatha Christie locked-in-a-room mystery. I was wrong, but not disappointed. Working from a novel by Riku Onda and a script by Sumio Omori, Shinohara has made a complex drama about admiration and envy, trust and betrayal, pride and ultimate defeat.

"Suite de Jeudi" is almost all talk, but it is smart, impassioned and, at times, devious talk, by some of the best actresses now in Japanese films: Mieko Harada, Kyoka Suzuki, Yasuko Tomita, Naomi Nishida and Ruriko Asaoka. There are moments of laughter and terror, but few moments that are simply dead air.

The film's story is what the Japanese call doro doro, which literally means "muddy" but describes the sediment of feelings that accumulate in any long-term relationship. In melodramas the principals stir up this sediment by raging and tearing at each other for offenses imagined and real. By contrast, the characters in "Suite de Jeudi" barely raise their voices — but their barbs are all the sharper for it.

As in all films about fictional writers, when the women tell us how wonderfully talented the departed sensei was, we have little choice but to take them at their word. Asaoka is suitably imperious and difficult as the author Tokiko Shigemura, but for the audience her novels remain closed books. Thus the initial suspicion that her five survivor are making a mountain out of a literary molehill. They dispel it when they reveal themselves as literary professionals with mixed feelings about both Tokiko and her work. In yet another realistic touch, they are also competitors of their dear departed sensei.

Eriko (Suzuki) is a nonfiction writer; Tsukasa (Nishida), a literary novelist; Naomi (Tomita), a mystery novelist; Shizuko (Harada), an essayist; and Eiko (Tokiko Kato), Tokiko's long-time editor and literary executor, living in Tokiko's house as a caretaker. They were at dinner together the Thursday night Tokiko killed herself with poison, and in the four years since, have gathered annually on that day to reminisce and try to resolve their feelings about her untimely end.

This year something happens to jar them out of their mood of reverie and regret: A delivery boy arrives with a bouquet from a certain Mr. Fujishiro, with a message implying that Tokiko's death was not as it seemed and that all of them are implicated in the crime.

Is this a sick joke, or does Fujishiro know something they don't? The women start spinning conjectures, while hesitating to fling accusations. Three of them, Eiko and Eriko excepted, are related to Tokiko by blood, while Eriko is Shizuko's cousin, adding family ties to the mix. All save Eiko were disciples of the dead writer to varying degrees, though as writers in different fields, they don't vie with each other directly. They also don't want to destroy their bonds of friendship — without good reason, that is. For much of the first half of the film, they tiptoe carefully around the elephant in the room: that one or more of them might be murderers.

Perhaps I shouldn't say more, save that the story takes a sharp twist midway that, in retrospect, makes perfect sense. There is an element of the bizarre in this development that Dame Christie herself would have admired. It adds the right frisson of fear, while launching the film toward its surprise conclusion.

Omori's script may be too low-key to inspire a Hollywood remake, but is true to the dynamics of this group of women, all of whom have strong personalities and are good with words — weasel and otherwise. Nishida is particularly strong as the baby-faced Tsukasa, who speaks her mind with disconcerting frankness — and keeps the proceedings from becoming too sedate. Suzuki also stands out as the cigarette-smoking skeptic Eriko, who is tougher-minded than the rest about Tokiko's failings. Playing Tokiko's half-sister, who agonizes over her responsibility for Tokiko's demise, Harada burns with nervous energy, but never descends to hysterics. As the sweet, soft-spoken Naomi, Tomita at first fades into the background, but emerges with a show of spunk. The oldest and the only non-actor of the group, singer Kato is appropriately reserved as Eiko, the woman who guards Tokiko's memory, including her secrets.

As a cinematic suite, "Suite de Jeudi" makes intelligent, absorbing music — on any day of the week.

Travail, rating: ★★★★, runtime: 118 min.

Director Juzo Itami once sagely observed to me that Japanese society is one in which "men are weak and women are strong." The work of Itami's younger colleague, Kentaro Otani, is built on this observation, starting from his 1999 debut feature "Avec Mon Mari (2 + 2)," a study of two intersecting couples whose female halves control the relationship dynamics, to amusing and instructive effect.

The films of Eric Rohmer were an obvious influence in their naturalistic dialogue, unforced pace and careful accretion of details, though Otani brought a distinctively Japanese perspective to the eternal theme of sexual power-politics.

In his new film, "Travail" (French for "work," as well as the title of a popular employment-listings magazine for women), two couples again intertwine, with the women doing the tying. This time, Otani had a bigger budget, resulting in a more professional look and bigger names in the cast, including Asaka Seto, a TV drama star, and Shinya Tsukamoto, the director/actor responsible for the "Tetsuo" films. Otani is also aiming at a larger audience; the comedy is broader and the ending brighter than in "Avec Mon Mari."

But, like the best of Rohmer's work, "Travail" gets beneath its characters' skins while recording the minutiae of their lives. Its plot is cleverly constructed, but not overtly mechanical; it doesn't click along so much as flow. The principals are lovably goofy and some of the lines are laugh-out-loud funny, but they can also convey deeper emotions than the usual sitcom. "Friends" has payoffs; "Travail" offers up epiphanies. That doesn't make the film a superior comedy, but it is more than the sum of its gag lines.

Asami (Seto) is a professional player of shogi (Japanese chess), as is her younger sister Rina (Mikako Ichikawa). Married to Kazuya (Tsukamoto), an elite salaryman, Asami is living a comfortable life in a spacious new apartment whose furniture looks as though it has been crafted in a Scandinavian atelier.

Asami is in a slump, however, and one night, after yet another loss, she tells Kazuya that their marriage is the cause. Though Kazuya dotes on Asami (he agreed to postpone their wedding for three years while she pursued her career) he objects and they fall into an argument, which is to be the first of many.

Then Rina come calling with her new boyfriend, Hiroki (Jun Murakami), a struggling musician who is living with her and doing all the household chores. Asami praises Hiroki's progressive attitude and complains that Kazuya does little more than collapse on the sofa, exhausted from work. Meanwhile, Rina is eyeing the gorgeous digs and wishing she were with an earner, not a loser.

The next holiday, Asami goes to the racetrack with a girlfriend, telling Kazuya a fib on her way out the door. There she spots Rina with a former lover, a bearded charmer who looks more prosperous than the woebegone Hiroki. That night, Rina shows up at Asami's apartment alone, saying that she and Hiroki have had a fight. But when she asks her sister to cover for her and tell Hiroki they have been together all day, Asami explodes and calls Rina a liar — but in explaining why in front of an astonished Kazuya, she exposes herself as one as well.

The sparks continue to fly and the losses at shogi continue, until Asami and Kazuya are on the verge of a breakup — and Asami is facing demotion to C class, a humiliation she would die to avoid. Then Kazuya gets transferred to the company's one-man office in Indonesia — a demotion he regards as an effective dismissal — while Asami is matched against her sister in the game that will decide her fate. What, if anything, can save their marriage and her pride?

Both Asami and Rina are not only deadly serious about their careers, but also dominate the men in their lives with almost contemptuous ease. As played by Ichikawa, a model-turned-actress, Rina behaves less like Hiroki's lover, more like a baby sitter with a balky charge. Though more mature, Seto's Asami is both a steely pro and a bossy big sister — a combination overwhelming to the wishy-washy Kazuya.

The obvious conclusion is that these women are mismatched — lions lying down with house cats — but it's not that simple. Unlike Katharine Hepburn in "Woman of the Year," secretly longing for all-man Spencer Tracy to put her in her place, Asami and Rina can hardly imagine having it any other way. Their will to power is hard wired.

Otani may be having fun with this role-reversal story — his casting of the short, balding Tsukamoto against Seto is one indication — but its sexual dynamics are no fantasy. Today's geisha may still pour her lord's sake, but she spends his money at the host club of her choice — and woe be the host who is slow with his lighter.

Alexei's Spring, Alexei to Izumi, rating: ★★★★, runtime: 104 min.

Documentaries get no commercial respect. As Robert Redford recently commented: "Nobody wants to fund them. Nobody wants to show them, but almost all the people who don't want to fund or show will tell [documentary filmmakers], 'You've got to make them. It's so important to get this film made. It's a noble idea.' Well, nobility doesn't have a huge place in an industry that's just about business."

Redfords are in short supply in Japan, although a few Tokyo theaters do screen documentaries. One is Box Higashi Nakano, where Seiichi Motohashi's "Alexei's Spring," will open Feb. 2. The film is a compelling argument for Redford's cause.

In 1998 Motohashi released "Nadja's Village," about a girl and her family who lived in a village near the site of the Chernobyl nuclear power plant in a region of Belarus declared uninhabitable because of radiation pollution. Most villagers had long ago left, but a few, mainly older people, were too attached to the land to leave. Motohashi and his crew got to know the villagers and filmed their lives minus the usual journalistic slants and cultural filters.

His subjects had endured a terrible disaster and were scratching out a subsistence existence. Nonetheless, they had a vitality and humor that shone through his camera, while their land, despite the poisons in its soil, had the look of a rural paradise. Watching "Nadja's Village" was like stepping into the world of the classic Russian novel: the horse, plow and well were still in common use, the telephone, television and private automobile were in little evidence. While pointing to the devastation wrought by Chernobyl — the abandoned homes and ruined lives — thr film was also a poetic evocation of a nearly forgotten past and a quietly moving celebration of the human spirit.

Early in 2000, Motohashi and cameraman Masafumi Ichinose returned to Belarus to film another village in the same region. The result, "Alexei's Spring," is not a sequel — none of the people from the first film appear in the second — but its central story is, if anything, stronger.

Located 180 km from Chernobyl, the village of Budische lies deep in a pine forest — but not deep enough to protect it from the radiation that fell from the skies on April 26, 1986. Alexei, a 34-year-old disabled man who lives in Budische with his elderly parents and narrates the film, remembers that time: The wind blew, the sky turned orange, the rain briefly fell — and everything changed.

What kept 56 villagers from leaving with the rest? "We stayed because of the spring," says Alexei. The spring, which serves the entire community, has remained miraculously free of radiation, refreshed by what the villagers claim is "100-year-old rain water." Without it, the people would have no pure water for drinking or cooking. They regard the spring as a lifeline, replacing the timbers that line it and worshipping the icon that safeguards it.

The film follows the lives of Alexei, his parents and other villagers through the seasons; beginning with the harvest, for which the villagers use an ancient combine and, to dig the potatoes that are a staple food, their bare hands. They receive small government pensions, which the women use to buy household necessities and the men use for vodka, but given sky-high inflation rates, no one bothers to save. Instead, at the Apple Festival in mid-August, they celebrate, holding a feast at which the women dance and the men look on. It is a happy time, but a sad one as well; nearly everyone is old — and their numbers, as Alexei notes, decrease every year.

Nonetheless, they do the work that needs to be done; five men, all over 70, cut and shape the logs that will be used to repair the spring — the big job of the summer. They use only hand axes and skills gained from decades of experience. When they finish their arduous labors, for what will probably be the last time, they share a bottle and a laugh, until an elderly woman complains: The frame is too small to do the laundry comfortably. "Don't listen to her," her husband — one of the workers — tells the others. "She's always sounding off like that." Some things, we see, never change. (Later, we see women washing clothes on the crossbars the men have provided, talking and smiling, glad to have the spring renewed.)

An Orthodox priest comes from the city to bless the spring. Younger than all the worshippers, he flings purifying spring water at them with his whisk. It is as though seven decades of communism never happened. The film records these and other moments in the life of the village unobtrusively, with a sharp eye for the revealing detail or comment. The villagers speak to the camera freely, with little of the stiffness or self-consciousness of the typical talking-head interview. Meanwhile, the score by Ryuichi Sakamoto is a model of elegance and restraint, underscoring without intruding.

Some might argue that Motohashi is prettifying a grim reality. Where are the shots of the smoking reactor, the children dying in the hospital? But the film belongs less to the director — and his agenda — than the people of Budische. They have much to tell us about not only coping with adversity, but what we need to live in the world.

Ju-on: The Grudge, rating: ★★★★, runtime: 92 min.
"Japanese horror"is a hot genre. Hideo Nakata's 1998 shocker "Ring" has spawned a hit Hollywood remake and Nakata is in negotiations to direct a film in the United States. Meanwhile, foreign fans have been eagerly consuming the products of the boom, including Nakata's "Ring" followups — "Chaos" (1999) and "Dark Water" (2002).

Meanwhile, Japanese fans — after being burned by bad and mediocre films that cashed in on the boom — have been turning away from horror.

"Ju-on: The Grudge," the scare-a-minute sensation by newcomer Takashi Shimizu, is drawing them back. Shimizu himself has been hired by Ghost House Pictures, the production company of "Spider-Man" director Sam Raimi, to direct a Hollywood remake.

The groundwork for this success has been well-laid. Shimizu, who studied under the "Ring" series scriptwriter Hiroshi Takahashi and horrormeister Kiyoshi Kurosawa, scripted and directed a straight-to-video "Ju-on" duo in 1999. The films became a cult sensation, and Shimizu later made shorts, TV films and even dramas webcast on the Internet in the horror genre. His feature debut was the 2001 "Tomie Re-birth" — the latest entry in a series about a teenage girl with supernormal powers. Finally, with Takahashi and Kurosawa serving as "supervisors," Shimizu scripted and directed "Ju-on: The Grudge," a feature that continues the story begun by the two "Juon" videos.

Acquaintance with the videos, however, is not needed to understand the film, despite its long back-story about the dead wreaking vengeance. It is more like a whirl through a house — or rather a world — of horror than a film with a beginning, middle and end. Like many films that aspire to edge, "Ju-on" scrambles its chronology, but once you are in its grip, the plot puzzles matter less than the atmosphere of impending doom. It's like being caught in a bad dream with no way out — save a death too horrible to endure.

But as quickly as Shimizu keeps the shocks coming — following the classic formula of one grabber every 10 min. — he cannot completely mask the chintziness of his production. Against the CGI ghosts and goblins of Hollywood, little boys in scary makeup don't quite cut it.

That said, Shimizu makes a virtue of necessity by emphasizing the everydayness of his Ghost World, which looks very much like our own, especially if you only get around to cleaning the house once every five years.

The house where most of the action unfolds is a moldy wood-and-mortar firetrap that sits apart from its neighbors in a jungle of weeds. Its first visitor is Rika (Megumi Okina), a "home helper" come to care for the bedridden woman who is the owner's mother. When she announces her presence from the entryway, no one answers and when she enters the mother's room, she finds her in a state of shock, unable to utter a word.

Hearing rustling on the second floor, Rika climbs the stairs (which emit the obligatory creaks) and finds, in the children's room, a closet door covered with duct tape. She removes it and sees something that frightens the living daylights out of her.

Backtrack a few days, when mother's salaryman son, Katsuya (Kanji Tsuda), returns home from work to discover his wife Kazumi (Risa Matsuda) upstairs — prostrated and speechless. Knowing too well that strange things have been happening ever since they moved in, he becomes determined to learn why. What he finds is a boy who looks like a pint-sized mime with terrifyingly empty eyes.

Later Katsuya's sister, Yoshimi (Misaki Ito), arrives to check on Katsuya and his family — no one answers her calls and she is getting worried. She finds Katsuya — now mad and murderous — and flees for her life, but the ghosts that sucked out his life and soul pursue her. Is there no peace, she starts to wonder, this side of an unquiet grave? What can stop the spread of this unholy circle?

The premise of the angry dead is a standard of Japanese folk stories, popular fiction and films. Also, some of the scares, such as the implacable black shadows and the photo that looks like a reflection in a diabolic fun-house mirror, are familiar from other recent J-horror flicks.

Although the film's long daisy chain of death makes it easy to lose track of relationships — by the time victim No. 10 came along, I was getting dizzy — it builds an irresistible momentum. Instead of exaggerating for effect — the typical strategy of Hollywood horror — the film tries for psychological realism. In other words, it reproduces what we dream about in nightmares — or see out of the corners of our eyes in dark and spooky places.

Every horror movie needs a girl with a good scream — and "Ju-on" has several, particularly Okina. Though she may not have the decibels of Naomi Watts in "The Ring," Okina has the right look — of someone who can't believe this is happening to her — and the determination to stop the horror. Does she succeed? Does the screaming stop? Yours will, when the lights go up, but on the train ride home, try not to sit opposite that kid with the creepy stare.

A Snake of June, Rokugatsu no Hebi, rating: ★★★★, runtime: 77 min.

Since bursting onto the scene in 1989 with "Tetsuo," Shinya Tsukamoto has been a one-man show: writing, filming, editing and acting his private visions of a nightmare world in which humans are fused to machines, set to a pounding soundtrack of industrial noise. After becoming a cult sensation, however, Tsukamoto hit an impasse, recycling the same outrages to ever-diminishing effect. In "A Snake of June," he has returned triumphantly to form while breaking new ground.

For all the extreme violence in his work, Tsukamoto displays a fascination with the erotic, as well as a poetic sensibility that owes as much to the masters of the silent film as the avatars of punk. Though some of the imagery in "Snake of June" is familiar — including a mechanical serpent that serves as a grotesque torture device — the film a departure for Tsukamoto that is comic and disturbing, revealing and enigmatic. While the film's couple in crisis is less an independent entity than an expression of the director's obsessions, they are more identifiably human than his earlier robotic creations.

They are Rinko (Asuka Kurosawa), a counselor for a telephone crisis service at the county health center, and Shigehiko (novelist Yuji Kotari in his acting debut), a prosperous, workaholic businessman. Rinko is dedicated to her career and devoted to her husband, though he is balding, stocky and old enough to be her father. They live together in an ultra-modern flat that is all angles, shadows and concrete surfaces.

One day Rinko receives an envelope filled with candid snaps of her masturbating. Then she gets a phone call from the photographer (Tsukamoto). Instead of money, he demands that she go out wearing a micro-miniskirt and buy a vibrator. She says she will never comply — until he tells her she has already been shopping for a vibrator on the Internet. Unsettled and excited, she goes on this unusual expedition and later learns that the mysterious stranger has been photographing her every move. Not long after, she finds out she is suffering from breast cancer.

When Shigehiko hears about his wife's illness and discovers her secret sex life, his carefully ordered world shatters. Meanwhile, the photographer is revealed as not only a marriage wrecker, but a catalyst for revelation and change.

Tsukamoto has filmed the story of this odd threesome in cool, silvery, otherworldly black-and-white. Also, in its striving for detachment and transcendence the film recalls the work of Robert Bresson and Alexander Sokurov. Rather than fall into homage, however, Tsukamoto creates a vision of sexual repression and longing reminiscent of his previous work, but chillier and more serpentine.

The two leads, Kurosawa and Kotari, may be a physical mismatch but connect as codependents who feed each other's deeper needs. Kurosawa, with her air of imploding from fear and desire, brings immediacy to what could have been a cliched transition from severe to sensual. Frequent collaborator Chu Ishikawa's soundtrack provides the techno throb and propulsion expected in a Tsukamoto film, without overwhelming the on-screen action.

In "Snake of June" Tsukamoto connects with his audience on a new level, giving it an Eros even stronger than his trademark rage. Rampaging robots are no match for Kurosawa in a micro mini.

2003

Shara, Shara Soju, rating: ★★★✩, runtime: 99 min.

Naomi Kawase has acquired an international following for films that are autobiographical and stylistically distinctive, beginning with "Suzaku," a study of family disintegration that won the Camera d'Or prize at the 1997 Cannes Film Festival.

Born and raised in Nara, the cultural heartland of Japan, Kawase has quietly, stubbornly gone her own way. Where many of her documentary-making seniors invested their talents and energies in leftist causes, she has made films about her family and region in which politics is conspicuous by its absence. Where many of her directorial contemporaries have injected pop-culture references into their films, she has gone in an opposite, technically minimalist direction, rejecting the media-saturated side of Japanese life.

Though her stories may unfold in present-day Japan, her people adhere to traditional ways of living and working, while their central concerns would have been familiar to Yasujiro Ozu or Mikio Naruse: relations between parents and children, men and women. But more than the humanist filmmakers of earlier generations, Kawase is conscious of the natural world, using the forests, fields and gardens of Nara as not just backdrops, but living, breathing presences. In her ideal Japan, people live in peaceful harmony with their natural surroundings, but that ideal, she reminds us, is under constant attack.

In "Shara," which screened in competition at the 2003 Cannes Film Festival, Kawase returns to the themes of "Suzaku" — the pain of loss and the possibility of love. Once again she strips her story to its essentials, while using point-of-view shots to put the audience into her characters' world. She may wander at length in the greenery, but compensates with moments that simply, powerfully deliver her message of renewal and hope. "Shara" is not so much a feel-good movie as a feel-real experience. It begins with twin brothers chasing each other through the summer streets of an old Nara neighborhood. Then one, Kei, turns a corner — and is never seen again, despite a frantic search by his parents and neighbors. The other brother, Shun, is devastated by this loss.

Five years later, now 17, he is still grieving. As a project for his high school art club, Shun (Kohei Fukunaga) paints a life-size portrait of Kei; not the real boy, but the youth of his imagination — or rather the one he sees in the mirror.

His confidante is Yu (Yuka Hyodo), a classmate who has been his friend since childhood. Shun has feelings for her that go beyond friendship, but can't breath a word of them. Yu, though, knows what he wants and is willing to reciprocate.

Meanwhile, Shun's soft-spoken, hard-working mother (Naomi Kawase) is pregnant with her third child and his outgoing, indolent father (Katsuhisa Namase) is helping to organize the Basara Festival, an annual summer event.

Shun remains obsessed with the past, but through his father's expansive optimism, his mother's quiet strength and Yu's youthful vitality (and sexuality), he comes to see that change has another side — bringing not just death and defeat, but new life and hope.

Cinematographer Yutaka Yamazaki brings a hazy, summery beauty to this story, while locating it precisely within its Nara milieu. Filmed in only 12 days, "Shara" may occasionally devolve into patchy improvisation, but Yamazaki's camerawork smoothes the rough edges, while expressing Kawase's sensibility.

Kawase impresses in the role of the mother. Directors who appear in their own films tend to show themselves in a flattering light — witness the cool heroes of Takeshi Kitano or the aging Lotharios of Woody Allen — but Kawase gives herself the permanently exhausted look of late pregnancy. Also, watching her character in the throes of labor, I wondered, as I never had about similar scenes directed by men, whether it might not be the real thing. Kawase may have been forced into this role (the professional actress she had cast as the mother dropped out before the start of shooting), but she creates an extraordinary moment — and a rare identification between a director and her vision.

Gozu, Gokudo Kyofu Daigekijo Gozu, rating: ★★★☆, runtime: 129 min.

"Straight to video" has long been the kiss of death for any Japanese film hoping to get attention from critics and the media. In other words, no theatrical release, no reviews or press coverage, save perhaps from the stray fanzine.

But distributors have been giving their better straight-to-video titles, called "V Cinema" films in Japan, token theatrical releases since the start of the "V Cinema" boom in the early '90s.

Many of the films for which Takashi Miike is known abroad, from his international breakout "Shinjuku Triad Society" (1995) to the film currently under review, "Gozu," are V Cinema titles. But for foreign festival programmers and fans a Miike film is a Miike film — the more extreme, the better. The "theatrical release" label so important in the Japanese market is of no matter

Certainly not to the programmer who selected "Gozu" for the Critics Fortnight section at this year's Cannes Film Festival. And not the critics who named this yakuza horror flick as one of the festival's finds.

Miike is notorious for shocking the unshockable — including hardened cineastes who celebrate "transgressive cinema" but hid their eyes when the psychotic heroine sawed off her middle-aged lover's foot in "Audition."

By that measure "Gozu" is mild indeed, despite its "horror" label. It is, in fact, more in Miike's comic vein, though it doesn't mean you can take your grandmother to it, unless her fantasy life resembles the work of Hieronymous Bosch. A local reference point is Yoshiharu Tsuge, an underground manga artist whose loner heroes are forever stumbling into awkward, usually erotic, situations in strange, forgotten corners of Japan.

"Gozu" may ramble for scene after bizarre scene, but it draws us, together with its flummoxed hero, ever deeper into a creepy, sex-charged dreamscape, until it springs its climax like a razor-toothed trap. This is not the video to watch before nodding off — unless you wants to wake up screaming.

The hero is Minami (Hideki Sone), the doggedly faithful subordinate to Ozaki (Sho Aikawa), a wakagashira (second-in-command) in the Azamawari-gumi. But when Ozaki flakes out — calling someone's pet Chihuahua a "yakuza assassin" and swinging it around his head like a bolo, the gang's sybaritic boss (Renji Ishibashi) decides he is a threat and orders Minami to take him to a "yakuza disposal site" in Nagoya. Minami may respect his nutty aniki (gang brother), but his higher loyalty is to the boss. He reluctantly accepts the assignment.

As Minami drives Ozaki to his date with destiny, Ozaki flips out yet again — and ends up dead. When Minami dashes into a roadside restaurant to call the boss for instructions, the corpse somehow disappears. Now panicked, Minami goes in search of the body. The cop at a nearby police box, a Hong Kong Chinese, is little help, as is a blond foreigner who reads her lines, in stumbling Japanese, off cue cards taped to the wall (an impatient Minami reads along with her). Finally Minami runs across a chap, sitting in a field, whose face is painted half-white — and who happens to work at the "yakuza disposal site," a junkyard run by gangsters.

Ozaki is not there, however, and Minami ends up staying at a seedy ryokan managed by an eccentric older couple. The man seems to be brain damaged, while the woman has a raging libido and a problem with . . . lactation. By now, Minami is convinced that all of Nagoya is a madhouse. He doesn't know how mad, however, until he meets a guy with the head of a bull . . .

This may sound like complete nonsense — "Yakuza Through the Looking Glass" — but Miike has more on his mind than a comic reel through a crazy-clock universe. By betraying Ozaki, he shows us, Minami has violated something deeper than his phony gangster code. His descent into nightmare, as a dull normal in a world of scary weirdos, is a fitting karmic punishment. He rages at this world — but in the end it devours him.

Miike fans will enjoy the latest in a long series of I-can't-believe-I'm-seeing-this finales. The rest of you? Just make sure you have at least one hand free; you'll need it to block that screen.

Bayside Shakedown 2, Odoru Daisosasen the Movie 2 — Rainbow Bridge o Fusa Seyo!, rating: ★★☆, runtime: 138 min.

Based on a popular Fuji TV series, "Bayside Shakedown" was the Japanese film industry's surprise hit of 1998. Its 7 million admissions and 10.1 billion yen gross earnings made it the fifth most successful Japanese film of all time. Instead of merely recycling its rebel-cop-on-a-mission formula from Hollywood, producer Chihiro Kameyama and his collaborators localized it with wit and flair.

Hero Shunsaku Aoshima (Yuji Oda), may have been defiantly unorthodox and badly groomed in the best Hollywood cop-movie tradition, but he was not another tough-guy loner working the mean streets. Instead, he was a former salaryman whose beat was the trendy Odaiba waterfront district where Fuji TV's headquarters building happened to be located. Also, in the whole film, Aoshima did not dodge a single explosion or kill a single bad guy while uttering a deadpan one-liner. Instead, "Bayside Shakedown" derived most of its comedy and tension from Aoshima's conflicts with the police bureaucracy, from precinct timeservers more intent on their own petty perks than on catching crooks, to the elite of the Metropolitan Police and National Police Agency, who regarded beat cops like Aoshima with barely disguised contempt.

This focus on Japan-specific issues, particularly the organizational sclerosis that thwarts innovation and initiative, may have limited the film's international prospects — it sold to only a handful of territories — but resonated with local audiences. They bought not only movie tickets, but also books that investigated every aspect of the film's densely populated, highly detailed world. Some otaku (obsessed fans) even gave themselves Aoshima makeovers, while Oda emerged as one of Japan's few bankable stars.

A sequel was all but inevitable — the only surprise is that it has taken nearly five years for "Bayside Shakedown 2" to reach the screens. As Kameyama explains in a program interview, the first film's originality meant that the sequel could not be a mere re-tread. "We had to come up with something that no one could imagine," he said.

But the film that has finally emerged after endless hashing out of "original" ideas has perhaps the most obvious plot engine of all: a terrorist threat to the Rainbow Bridge. Also, submitting to the iron law of the Japanese movie business — that fans come to series films looking for more of the same — the producers have brought back almost the entire cast of the first film, playing characters mostly still locked into the attitudes and styles of half a decade ago (including Aoshima's trademark rumpled overcoat).

Some things have changed since 1998, however. Though Aoshima is once again battling the powers-that-be, his main adversary is no longer Muroi (Toshio Yanagiba) — the grim-faced Metropolitan Police investigator who, in the first film, ended by siding with Aoshima against his superiors, but another elite cop from the same agency, a woman named Okita (Miki Shinya) who is more than a match for any male bureaucrat in sheer arrogance.

Also, Aoshima is still assigned to the same Tokyo Bayside precinct, the station house is now cheek-by-jowl with the Fuji TV headquarters in Odaiba — the opening sequences offer a virtual tour of the building and its environs. It even operates its own gift shop, presumably to catch the visitor spillover from its more famous neighbor.

The story gets underway with a bizarre murder committed under the noses of the precinct's cops, with the corpse tied elaborately in a spread-eagle pose (an obvious homage to Hannibal Lector's most creative murder in "Silence of the Lambs"). Though Aoshima, his feisty female colleague Kashiwagi (Miki Mizuno) and the rest of the Bayside crew are soon on the case, the higher-ups decide that they cannot handle it alone — and assign the command of the investigation to cops from Metropolitan Police, led by the imperious Okita. Meanwhile, Muroi serves as an uneasy bridge between the Metropolitan Police elite and the Bayside beat cops, who are relegated to a supporting role in their own precinct.

Then another murder occurs — and though the police investigation goes into full gear, with meetings that look like cop conventions, the killer's motives, let alone identity, are a mystery. Okita and her colleagues assign a specialist negotiator to deal with phone calls from the alleged perp, while installing hidden cameras in every nook and cranny to catch him in the act. Their prey remains elusive, however, even daring the cops to ID him at a crowded party. Meanwhile, with the Metropolitan Police outsiders keeping them from their normal duties, the Bayside cops are forced to let other criminals roam free, including a pervert whose MO is to bite the necks of his young female victims.

Eventually, the cops realize that they are dealing with something more dangerous than a deranged individual and that the threat is greater than just another serial-murder scare. Okita's high-tech, flood-the-zone tactics are obviously not working. Perhaps Aoshima and his fellow foot soldiers have a better idea.

Katsuyuki Motohiro, who also directed "Bayside Shakedown," films this familiar material with a smooth professionalism. Newbies who know nothing of the TV series or first film may find the profusion of characters and incidents baffling — but they are in a minority. The film's numbers so far — its first-week grosses set a new box-office record for domestic films — indicate that fans can handle its density of information, while enjoying its satiric commentary on the Japanese Way.

The film's take on its villains, however, struck this non-native viewer as oddly 1998. In the universe of "BS2," terrorists are still comic misfits and bumblers. The world may have changed since 9/11, but at the movies, at least Japan is still very much an island unto itself.

Zatoichi, rating: ★★★★, runtime: 115 min.

Old-timers in the Japanese film industry often complain that no one makes entertaining movies here anymore. Animation, in their view, doesn't count. They also don't much like the romantic dramas that are gussied-up TV shows or the CG extravaganzas that are video games without the controls.

What the old-timers often really mean by "entertainment" is guys wearing top-knots and slashing at each other with swords. They still have fond memories of the "Zatoichi" series — 26 films, as well as a spinoff TV series, about a blind masseur who makes his living less by kneading aching muscles than by gambling and swordfighting.

The title character, played in all 26 episodes by Shintaro Katsu, had powers that were close to psychic — he was blind but could read the moves of his opponents by their sounds or smells. In the first installment of the series, Kenji Misumi's "The Tale of Zatoichi" ("Zatoichi Monogatari") (1962), Katsu's superman could split a lit candle in mid air or place a winning bet after listening to the way the dice rolled. Audiences loved this flimflam, as well as Katsu's earthy onscreen persona. A dirty hero, willing to get his hands bloody for money, Katsu's Zatoichi was also the era's definition of I-did-it-my-way cool.

Fourteen years after the last "Zatoichi" film and six years after Katsu's death, Takeshi Kitano has loosely reworked the first film in the series. Titled simply "Zatoichi," it won Kitano the Best Director prize at this year's Venice Film Festival and is currently packing theaters in Japan.

It is very much a Kitano film, which means quirky, violent and self-indulgent. It is also the most entertaining thing he has done, quite deliberately so. I never thought I would write "crowd pleaser" in a Kitano film review — but there it is.

Old-timers may balk at the tap-dance finale, with its postmodernist wink at everything that has gone before, but they will like the way Kitano stages the swordplay, with brutally efficient choreography and spurts of realistic CG blood.

Also, instead of ploddingly developing his characters and their relationships before getting to the good parts — the strategy of many a period drama director — Kitano plunges right in. Bang comes the opening title — and out come the swords.

Despite the flying limbs and falling bodies, the film is hardly a typical samurai swashbuckler. It nimbly jumps back and forth in time, while freely violating genre rules. Also, though it takes the side of the common folk in their never-ending struggle against corruption, it is anything but a moral tract. Instead it is Kitano's homage to both the series and the genre.

"Zatoichi" begins with assorted wanderers drifting into a town. One is Zatoichi (Kitano), also known as Ichi, who makes his entrance by slicing and dicing three yakuza. Another is Hattori (Tadanobu Asano), a haggard-looking ronin (masterless samurai) who hires out as a yojimbo (a feudal-era hit man) to buy medicine for his beautiful, tubercular wife (Yui Natsukawa). Others are Okinu (Yuko Daike) and Osei (Daigoro Tachibana) — a pair of sisters who work as itinerant entertainers and are as deadly as they are lovely.

The town is run by the slimy yakuza boss Ginzo (Ittoku Kishibe) with the aid of a weaselly merchant (Saburo Ishikura). Before tangling with this pair, Ichi comes to the aid of Shinkichi (Guadalcanal Taka), a lunkhead who is losing at a Ginzo-run dice game when Zatoichi puts him on the winning path. Then Hattori, at the suggestion of a cagey old sake shop owner (Akira Emoto) and after a dazzling display of swordsmanship, enters Ginzo's employ.

When Ichi and Hattori meet, in the old man's shop, they clash immediately, if not fatally. Meanwhile, the sisters want to get next to Ginzo, for dark reasons of their own. Fate is also drawing them to Ichi — their natural ally in the looming battle with Ginzo and his minions. But how can two women and a blind man take on a yakuza army? For one thing, it helps to be unbeatable with a sword.

The showdown between Zatoichi and the ronin swordsman was also the dramatic centerpiece of the Misumi film, but Kitano's path to it is far more winding. Few of the principals are what they seem. They have hidden identities, secret lives. They are survivalists, first and foremost. Hattori, being both dutiful and doomed, is a glaring exception. There is a contemporary ring to these poses and masks that Kitano advertises by sporting blonde-dyed hair. Not of the period? No one notices or cares, including, after the first shock, the audience.

The injections of humor that often devolve into variety-show slapstick in other Kitano films are more pointed in "Zatoichi," as well as funnier. A portly simpleton dashing about with a spear, dreaming of samurai glory, is not just a running joke, but Kitano's way of telling us (and himself?) not to take this sword stuff so seriously.

What does it all mean? Maybe not very much. Kitano's intent is less penetrating social commentary than a rousing good time. And there is something about "Zatoichi" that chases the endless-recession blues. How many samurai movies leave you humming as you walk out the door? One, for now — but can a sequel be far behind? Kitano told the press that he already has a title for it: "Zatoichi vs. the Terminator."

Doppelganger, rating: ★★★★, runtime: 107 min.

Some directors keep making the same movie over and over. Others, after becoming known for a certain type of film, struggle to escape their own typecasting. Kiyoshi Kurosawa falls into neither category. Early in his career, while making genre films for the video market, Kurosawa developed a distinctive style notable for its indirection, economy and sure grasp of dream logic. No matter what the story, be it revenge ("Serpent's Path," 1997), the search for a serial killer ("Cure," 1997) or the end of the world ("Pulse," 2001), Kurosawa creates an atmosphere redolent with dread, in which the barrier between the real and the unreal, the living and the dead becomes terrifyingly permeable.

This atmosphere — at once dreamlike and mundane — has the feel of inner reality, as though Kurosawa is giving shape to his personal demons, whose features have remained remarkably consistent from film to film.

At the same time, Kurosawa is constantly shifting his angle of approach, while conjuring fresh "what if" situations. For "Pulse," he came up with a high concept — ghosts coming out of computers — that might have sold at a Hollywood pitch meeting. In this year's "Bright Future," his central metaphor — a poisonous jellyfish — was simple enough, but his story was as shape-shifting as the jellyfish itself.

Kurosawa's new film, "Doppelganger," is closer to "Pulse" than "Bright Future " on the pop/art spectrum. The premise — a stressed engineer (Koji Yakusho) starts to see his own double — has fictional antecedents going back to Edgar Allen Poe. Writers of the stature of Goethe and Guy de Maupassant reported encounters with their own doppelgangers, long fueling paranormal speculation about the reality of such beings.

The engineer, Michio Hayasaki, is attempting to build a wheelchair with robot arms controlled by impulses from the brain. A star at the medical instruments maker for which he works, he has high expectations for his latest contraption. Buckling under the pressure, he lashes out at not only his assistants but also his boss, the phlegmatic-but-understanding Murakami (Akira Emoto).

Soon after, he encounters his doppelganger (Yakusho) briefly at a coffee shop and later, more gut-wrenchingly, in his own apartment. He dismisses it as a figment of his imagination (or a sign of a mental breakdown), but the doppelganger is persistent: It has come, it says, to help.

And help it does — by trashing Hayasaki's lab. No more lab, it reasons, no more stress. When that results in Hayasaki's dismissal, the doppelganger pitches in again by carting off the wheelchair and hiring a dodgy, determined man named Kimijima (Yusuke Santa Maria) as a new assistant.

From here the film becomes a waking dream — or rather nightmare. Events unfold in a matter-of-fact way, but their contents are impossibly bizarre. Hayasaki becomes involved with the pixie-faced Yuka (Hiromi Nagasaki), who is similarly vexed by her dead younger brother's doppelganger. The solution proposed by Hayasaki's doppelganger: kill it. He also murders and robs to raise money for Hayasaki's research. In short, the doppelganger is Hayasaki's id — acting out desires Hayasaki has repressed. It is also growing intolerably in power and influence. Who will win this struggle for his soul: Hayasaki or his diabolical twin?

Viewed as a psychological thriller, "Doppelganger" soon becomes tediously preposterous. Kurosawa makes no attempt to persuade us, with editing or effects, that we are seeing something conceivable in the real world. Instead he uses the techniques of naturalism to create a dreamlike realm of pure psychodrama, in which the barriers between impulse and action have weakened or dissolved.

Hayasaki begins the film with all the usual inhibitions. Despite his outbursts, he realizes that he is dealing with a shadow self that is moving, with cool insolence, into the light. In the climax, his battle with his doppelganger threatens to devolve into a car chase straight from an action film.

Kurosawa, though, is not pumping up excitement so much as bringing the film to its inevitable conclusion, with the evil entity inexorably closing in on the dreamer. A subplot revolving around Murakami's reappearance distracts, but Kurosawa never completely wakes us from his dream.

He gets able support from Koji Yakusho who relies solely on his acting skills to distinguish between Hayasaki and his doppelganger; in appearance, they are exactly alike. He does this with little more than an impish gleam in the eye — that nonetheless chills. At times he deliberately blurs the distinction between the two, to even creepier effect.

What is more horrifying: to glimpse your doppelganger, emerged from some inner hell, or realize that you and it are becoming, forever, one?

G@me, rating: ★★★★, runtime: 145 min.

Based on Keigo Higashino's best-selling novel, Satoshi Isaka's thriller "G@me" has "Hollywood remake" written all over it. It also has sharp insights into the way Japanese companies really work — not as the harmonious, conformist business juggernauts once beloved by foreign management gurus, but human institutions in which strong egos clash and jealousy and envy run rife.

Satoshi Isaka is the ideal director for this material. His 1996 feature debut "Focus" was a brilliant espose of media manipulation in which the exploited geek hero violently turned the tables on his exploiters. Isaka also made the semi-comic thriller "Doubles" (2001) in which two bickering thieves find themselves trapped in an elevator and must con their way out.

"G@me" combines elements of both films, together with a love story that is uncommonly clear-headed about the importance of trust — and its betrayal. The story is too twisty by half — take an aspirin before seeing it if your head throbs after too many narrative loop-the-loops. It is also one of the rare Japanese films that respects the audience's intelligence, while delivering the expected package of suspense and romance.

The film's primary gamester is Shunsuke Sakuma (Naohito Fujiki), a young advertising executive whose career stock is skyrocketing. His theme park plan for a big agency client, a beer company, promises to bring in billions. Then the company's vice president, Katsutoshi Katsuragi (Ryo Ishibashi), brutally kills the plan and humiliates Sakuma in front of his peers.

To add insult to injury, his goateed boss (Ryudo Uzaki) takes him off the account and gives it to a smarmy rival. Once a cocky winner at the corporate game, Sakuma has now been branded a loser.

Seething, he goes for a midnight walk in front of Katsuragi's house — and spies a young woman jumping over the wall around it. The escapee turns out to be Juri Katsuragi (Yukie Nakama), the illegitimate daughter of the VP's mistress, who is fed up with her bossy half-sister and angry at her father for not taking her side.

These two size each other up — and Juri decides that Sakuma might have his uses. "I want you to kidnap me," she tells him. He agrees — and sets the ransom at 300 million yen. Then he sends a note to Katsuragi using an untraceable e-mail address. The game has begun.

The kidnapping goes according to plan but Juri is a spoiled brat who expects Sakuma to cater to her every whim. Made of sterner stuff than the other men in her life, he refuses to play that particular game. Still, Juri has her charming side — and Sakuma has a healthy libido. The sex that follows has its moments of tenderness, but love is a different matter altogether.

Here the Hollywood formula would call for a quarrel, a parting and a final kiss-and-make-up, while saying goodbye to the ill-gotten gains. "G@me" takes this this formula and makes it do somersaults, but through it all the two principals, as well as their opponent Katsuragi, retain an internal consistency. All are gamesters to the core — and all pay a price for it, win, lose or draw. Instead of a trumped-up happy ending, the film plays it straight to the end.

Fujiki conveys the anger and ambition burning deep inside by a bruised look that never quite leaves his face. Nakama initially impresses as a self-involved ditz, but later drops the mask to reveal the trickster beneath. She gives the proceedings a sexy zing and comic lift, while bamboozling men with her huge, innocent-looking eyes. She would be perfect in the Barbara Stanwyck role in "The Lady Eve." Great conwomen are forever.

Karaoke Terror, rating: ★★★⯪, runtime: 76 min.

The story of Tetsuo Shinohara's "Karaoke Terror" — amoral punks battle spoiled middle-aged women — has a built-in absurdity, but is hardly fluff. Like the best satire, it illuminates certain truths with clarity and bite. Thinking I was walking into a gimmicky farce, I walked out knowing I'd seen the best black comedy of the year. OK, scratch "black."

It begins in present-day Chofu, where six guys drifting through their early 20s have become close friends and co-conspirators. At night they gather at an abandoned pier to sing songs from the Showa Era (1926-89) — mainly '60s pop standards. They even go in for period costumery. Think the punks of "Clockwork Orange" turned old-pop-song-loving Japanese.

One day one of their number, the soft-faced Sugioka (Masanobu Ando), ventures out with his favorite knife. In the street, he bumps into a middle-aged woman (Shungiku Uchida) in a hurry. He tries to pick her up and, when she curtly rejects him, slashes her. Watching the blood spray out with a bemused detachment, he turns and walks away, his irritation replaced with a surge of satisfaction.

The victim belongs to a circle of six women — all past 30 and all with the first name Midori. One of the Midoris, the feisty Henmi (Kayoko Kishimoto), discovers the body and alerts the others. Using a clue from the murder scene, they soon track down Sugioka. This, they decide, is more fun than the karaoke sessions that had been their only real bond. (They also prefer Showa Era tunes.) They proceed to terminate the evil-doer using a similar weapon, if a more spectacular method.

This means war. Using a tip from a spacey college girl (Miwako Ichikawa), the boys soon ID the Midoris and, with the boyish Ishihara (Ryuhei Matsuda) in the lead, go off in search of weapons.

Working from a script by Sugio Omori, Shinohara places the two opposing camps squarely in their proper social milieu. Also, they may be familiar types — the young slacker male and the pushy middle-aged female — but they and the other characters act out their true feelings, murderous rage included, with a matter-of-factness funny and true.

When traditional bonds are replaced by random collections of social atoms, as is happening in today's Japan, group violence becomes an elixir for deadened souls, with a bigger charge than any karaoke tune.

Unless maybe "My Way."

Vibrator, rating: ★★★★★, runtime: 95 min.

Japanese mainstream films and TV dramas commonly feature young actresses who fit current notions of beauty (the big-eyed gamine look, the leggy beauty-queen look, the sleek computer-generated look) in starring roles, even if they couldn't act their way out of a ramen commercial. Those with genuine acting skills who want to play something more than the lead's best friend, often end up on the stage.

Naomi Fujiyama, who swept acting awards in 2001 playing an eccentric recluse in Junji Sakamoto's "Face," first made her reputation in the theater. Shinobu Terajima, who plays a bulimic, alcoholic freelance writer in Ryuichi Hiroki's "Vibrator," is also a stage veteran.

Her performance is so far above what commonly passes as acting in Japanese films that it exists on a plane of its own. The Japan Academy should save time and trouble and send her its Best Actress trophy now. (The Tokyo International Film Festival and the Yokohama Film Festival already have).

Not that her portrayal of a woman on the edge of madness and despair is a diva turn. Terajima plays with, not off, costar Nao Omori's preening, self-promoting truck driver. Her performance also fits Hiroki's concept of his film, which is more multi-layered and realistic than the typical local "problem drama," anxious to assure the audience that, after the obligatory wringing of tears, all will come out right in this best of Japanese worlds.

Based on a novel by Mari Akasaka, "Vibrator" offers no such easy affirmation. At the end the heroine's demons still exist, if for the moment calmed. We can only hope they don't stir again. At the same time, the film throbs with infectious energy, erupts with raw emotional force. It is an ode to the open road, leaps of faith and the transforming power of love.

Terajima plays Rei, a freelance writer buying liquor at a convenience store when she spies a truck driver with spiky blondish hair and decides, as an intertitle expressing her thoughts explains, she wants to "eat him." She ends up in the cab of his four-ton truck, heading off to who knows where.

The driver, Okabe (Omori), greets his new traveling companion as though he had been expecting her all along. As his truck rumbles through the night streets, he eases her over her initial embarrassment until she can tell him what is really on her mind. The sex that follows is fumbling, passionate and seals a bond between them. Rei begins to open up to Okabe, telling him of her past and her addictions, and the adventure she has chosen.

She eagerly listens to his boasting stories of running drugs for the yakuza and being a gangster himself. She even imagines herself as one of the whores he used to pimp for. She joyfully absorbs all the lore of his world, particularly his slangy exchanges with fellow truckers on his CB radio. This new language seems to open doors to a new, bolder self.

But she is terrified of losing her old self, for all its insecurities and anxieties. Feeling it slipping away, she finds herself staring into a void. At a gas station, she vomits up her fear, rage and humiliation, but Okabe lifts her up and cleanses her. There is another side, we see, to this smooth operator. He too is on the verge of telling truths.

This may sound like a fantasy of love conquering all but Okabe is not a wish-fulfillment figure, just as Rei is not a woman-as-victim. Their talk and on-screen thoughts, scripted by Haruhiko Arai, express with poetic economy and force what these strangers-turned-lovers are and what they are becoming.

Also, as Okabe and Rei, Omori and Terajima don't meet cute; they meet lonely and hungry. They have few illusions, but have not given up hope. Emerging from their ride together, they are like tired swimmers who have reached a distant shore after abandoning everything, including their lies. They have an exhausted purity that is beautiful.

And Terajima does it looking as though she spent three minutes, not three hours, getting ready to leave the house. I think it's called acting.

9 Souls, rating: ★★★⯪, runtime: 120 min.

Toshiaki Toyoda makes films about males behaving violently — which might be said of dozens of directors, both in Japan and Hollywood. Mr. Toyoda, meet Mr. Bruckheimer. But his protagonists differ from Hollywood action heroes in being marginal types already close to the edge from scene one, who explode into unthinking rage when nudged over. They are rebels with neither a cause nor a clue.

In "Blue Spring" (2002) Toyoda's teenage heroes play deadly games out of terminal boredom. Even so, they rather like their high school — it offers a large, graffiti-smeared stage for their chaotic performance art. But their nihilism is more of a blank shrug than an articulate howl.

"9 Souls," Toyoda's followup to "Blue Spring," is similar in theme, if several shades lighter. Instead of flirting with oblivion, the nine heroes — all cons on the lam — are determined to make the most of their new freedom. At the same time, they can't rewind the past or easily change the bad behavior that got them into trouble in the first place. The salvations and absolutions they seek remain distant shimmering goals — like the image of Tokyo Tower that opens the film, standing tall and bright over a blasted plain.

There's something overdetermined about the journey of the nine toward their appointed fates; they are less men with free wills than shogi pieces in the hands of a player who can see a dozen moves ahead. But Toyoda also combines an original visual imagination and a twisted comic mind to advance his themes.

Japanese road movies have a way of getting lost in their own picaresque conceits; Toyoda keeps his film traveling down a road with scenery that is consistently engaging, if at times outright strange.

It begins with that shot of Tokyo Tower — overlaid by a long knife held in the hand of Michiru Kaneko (Ryuhei Matsuda). The knife is soon plunged into Michiru's domineering father and Michiru, a recluse (hikikomori) for the past 10 years, is sent to prison for 13 more.

There he finds himself in a cell with other cons — all hard cases serving long sentences. Their boss, the gruff Hasegawa (Yoshio Harada), is serving a 16-year stretch for killing his own son. But as awful as some of their crimes are, at mealtimes they are as subdued as accountants in the company cafeteria. Then one, Yamamoto (Jun Kunimura), starts raving about a fortune hidden in a time capsule at his old primary school, near the foot of Mount Fuji.

The guards drag Yamamoto away, but the other cons believe him. Soon after, led by Shiratori (Mame Yamada), a midget escape artist, they go under the walls and scamper off into the woods. Flagging down a dilapidated camper advertising a strip club on its side, they tie up the driver and sail off down the road, free at last.

Their first stop is the house of Nakayama (Jun Inoue) — an old prison mate of Hasegawa's who is now trying to go straight with his stocky Filipino bride. There they find food, clothes and showers, but a cold welcome from the bride, who sees them for what they are: louts on a spree.

And they are uncouth and clownish as they steal coins from a temple donation box, rob a roadside store and sashay into a restaurant, dressed in drag to avoid detection. But as their journey continues, their personalities emerge, from the gentle-spirited, bull-strong Ushiyama (Genta Dairaku) to the wimpy, weasely Inui (Takuji Suzuki), who becomes the gang's butt. A rough group solidarity forms that includes all but Michiru, the youngest, the quietest — and the most dangerous, as Hasegawa soon finds out.

When they discover that Yamamoto's "treasure" is a pipe dream they go their separate ways and meet their individual fates, for better or worse. Shiratori is the first to leave, reuniting with a former student and lover (Misako Ito) — now a stripper at the club advertised on the camper van. Most of the nine are not so lucky — death claims some, disappointment greets others. But the camper finally rolls into Tokyo and Michiru goes, brick in hand, to take care of unfinished business.

Unlike films that treat life on the run as an adventure or lark, "9 Souls" tells dark, unpleasant truths: Japanese society is stingy with second chances and children are slow to forgive the sins of their parents. But as hard as Toyoda can be on his heroes, he allows them their humanity and their moments of bliss.

They too have souls, even if their idea of heaven is a camper crammed with junk food. Not such a terrible idea, really. Freedom is where you find it — and just consider their alternatives.

2004

Josee, The Tiger and The Fish, Josee to Tora to Sakanatachi, rating: ★★★★, runtime: 116 min.
Why does one small indie film pack theaters week after week, while others with similar themes vanish without a trace? There is no sure-fire formula for success, but there is a kind of alchemy. The

philosophers' stone that transforms base metal into box-office gold is often not just talent, but also a knack for knowing what the audience wants — and giving it a bit more.

This week's example is "Josee, The Tiger and The Fish," Isshin Inudo's romantic drama about an ordinary college boy who falls for an extraordinary girl with cerebral palsy. Since opening Dec. 13 at Cinema Quinto in Shibuya it has become a box-office sensation, scoring a whopping 9.4 million yen screen average in its third week on release.

Heroes who triumph over physical disabilities and social prejudice have become a staple of Japanese films, TV dramas and best-selling memoirs — most of which preach uplift and jerk tears as predictably as the waves lap at Kamakura.

"Josee" does it differently. Yes, the heroine is spunky and yes, she finds a measure of love and happiness, but her story will not make the audience snatch for its collective Kleenex — the genre's nearly universal aim. Instead it plays with its own conventions, with an offbeat humor and style that recalls Jean Pierre-Jeunet's indie hit of 2001, "Amelie."

Though Inudo was born in 1960 and started making films three decades ago, "Josee" has a youthful feel — it views the world of its characters as they might and not through a nostalgic haze.

Oldsters, including members of Inudo's own generation, may be baffled by the ending, which seems to contradict everything that has gone before. But younger viewers, wiser to the ways of their contemporaries, may find it more convincing. An oldster myself, I was thrown by it at first, but later realized I should have seen it coming. It was a "Sixth Sense" moment — and made me appreciate the brilliance of Aya Watanabe's script.

The film begins with Tsuneo (Satoshi Tsumabuchi), a fresh-faced college kid, working a part-time job at an Osaka mah-jongg parlor and listening to the patrons' gossip about a crazy old woman who pushes a huge baby buggy around the neighborhood. What's in it, they wonder. Her secret fortune? Drugs? The mummified body of her grandchild?

One morning, while out walking the parlor owner's dog, Tsuneo encounters the old woman (Eiko Shinya) and her runaway buggy, which he tries to stop. Inside is a young woman (Chizuru Ikewaki) who is not happy at being exposed — and flashes a knife at her exposer.

The granny invites him to her rickety little house, where her granddaughter Kimiko — the buggy rider — reluctantly prepares him an omelet. He finds the food delicious and the cook charming, despite her perpetual frown and her distressing habit of throwing herself from her stool onto the floor. Stricken by cerebral palsy as a child, Kimiko has been living under her grandmother's care, while reading voraciously and accumulating a large store of arcane knowledge. A fan of Francoise Sagan, she has taken the name Josee (joh-SAY) after one of the writer's characters.

Tsuneo becomes a regular visitor. His girlfriend (Juri Ueno) does not take kindly to his new interest in the disabled, however. Also Josee's hot-tempered tough of a friend (Hirofumi Arai) has a seemingly inexplicable grudge against the grandmother. But though well populated with these and other characters, eccentric and otherwise, the story is simplicity itself.

As Tsuneo and Josee become friends, then lovers, her narrow world begins to open up. They go to a zoo to see the tigers and on a drive to see the ocean — both firsts for her. When the aquarium they had planned to see is closed, she persuades Tsuneo to spend the night at a love hotel where holographic fish swim on the walls. Her happiness seems complete, but then . . .

Watching the film, I thought I could complete this sentence, but I was wrong. I also thought Tsuneo was something of a saint, but I was wrong about that too. Casually confident of his attraction to women, whom he beds as easily as he shuffles mah-jongg tiles, Tsuneo is intrigued by the challenges Josee presents. She is the spicy kimchi to all the bland takuan pickles he has had till now. Josee, however, offers not just an exotic sexual flavor — she is a woman whose dark inner recesses Tsuneo can barely imagine, let alone comprehend.

Chizuru Ikewaki, who also starred in the Inudo-scripted "Osaka Story" and Inudo-directed "Across a Golden Prairie," plays Josee less as a tough, wary survivor who has built a private world and is not sure she wants to let anyone in. Josee's drawling Osaka dialect is just this side of irritating, but she is a prickly original.

It's easy to see why Tsuneo keeps coming back and why Theater Quinto keeps filling. "Josee, The Tiger and The Fish" is as memorable as its title, if in some ways as puzzling. Where did granny get that enormous buggy? And where is that hotel where the guests sleep with the fishes?

Kirishima 1945, Utsukushi Natsu Kirishima, rating: ★★★☆, runtime: 119 min.

Why has the flow of Japanese movies about Japan at the end of World War II never stopped, more than 50 years after the event? Why have they far outnumbered the films set in the earlier years of the conflict? It is as if, instead of "Saving Private Ryan," "The Thin Red Line" and "Pearl Harbor," Hollywood filmmakers had made endless variations on "The Best Days of Our Lives."

One reason often advanced is that the Japanese prefer to see themselves as the war's victims rather than its perpetrators — hence all the movies set in Japan, 1945 rather than in China, 1937.

But most makers of these films — Shohei Imamura, Masahiro Shinoda and Kazuo Kuroki among them — can hardly be described as war apologists. Like the vast majority of Japanese alive today who remember the war, they experienced it only on the home front — and became strongly antiwar as a result. It's only natural that their most vivid memories should be of bombings, starvation and chaos rather than victorious battles and parades. The end of the war rather than the beginning.

With this period fading into the mists, most recent films set in it, including Imamura's "Dr. Akagi" (1998) and Shinoda's "Setouchi Moonlight Serenade" (1997), take a softer-focused view. One exception, however, is Kuroki's "Kirishima 1945," a film based on the director's own youth in Miyazaki Prefecture, in southern Kyushu.

Instead of affectionately recalling eccentric characters ("Dr. Akagi") or dutifully recycling cliches ("Setouchi Moonlight Serenade"), the film evokes the era with a precision only possible from someone who was there and remembers everything, the dark as well as the light.

Kuroki meticulously re-creates period atmosphere, including the general air of exhaustion and repressed trauma. But he also keeps violence at a distance — instead of explosions and corpses, we see the beauty of old Miyazaki, with its thatch-roofed cottages and mountain vistas.

This may have a basis in reality — Kuroki spent the final days of the war in this setting — but for viewers who lack the background of Kuroki and his generation, it may seem like a turning away from unpleasant facts.

Kuroki's stand-in is Yasuo Hidaka (Tasuku Emoto), a gangly, withdrawn youth who is recovering from a lung ailment at his grandfather's house, while his parents are presumably escaping from the Russians in Manchuria and his classmates are working at a nearby war plant. When one of those classmates was fatally wounded in an air raid, Yasuo ran away instead of finding help — and he has been wracked with guilt ever since. He is fascinated by a print of Caravaggio's "The Entombment of Christ" that he keeps in his bedroom. Perhaps like the resurrected Christ he can find a new life and beginning, but is such a thing possible?

Meanwhile, soldiers repatriated from China drill and dig trenches in a nearby forest to prepare for the expected Allied invasion. One, the jaded Toyoshima (Teruyuki Kagazwa) steals government rations being kept in storehouse belonging to Yasuo's grandfather and takes them to his lover Ine (Eri Ishida), the wife of a soldier who has probably died in the war. Ironically, her daughter Natsu (Erika Oda) is working as a maid at grandfather's house and becoming closer to Yasuo, despite her son Minoru (Takashiro Kuranuki) being Yasuo's bitterest enemy, for reasons unknown.

Grandfather (Yoshio Harada) is more occupied in marrying off another maid, Haru (Hiroko Nakajima), to a discharged soldier (Susumu Terajima) who lost his leg in the Philippines. A former army officer who fought with the White Russians against the Bolsheviks, the old man also wants to put some steel into Yasuo's backbone — but the values he has defended all his life are collapsing around him.

Yasuo would seem to embody that collapse — but despite his interest in the enemy's religion, he is no traitor. After a military policeman publicly humiliates him for being a malingerer, he becomes desperate to find absolution through a glorious death. In the forest he digs his own trench and sharpens his own bamboo spear. Even Japan's surrender does not chill his ardor — bring on the Americans!

There are other characters and subplots, including a secret romance between Yasuo's beautiful Westernized aunt (Riho Makise) and a young navy officer, but Kuroki weaves them into his main narrative while keeping the focus where it belongs — on Yasuo and his struggle to come to terms with the horrors he has seen and the mass of contradictions he has become.

Named the best film of the year in a "Kinema Jumpo" magazine critic's poll — long the Japanese film industry's highest honor — "Kirishima 1945" is a valuable act of witness. Its war, however, is like the American planes that buzz in formation through its far away skies — vaguely ominous, but not immediately dangerous.

With the SDF now embarking on its Iraq adventure, a new generation of Japanese may discover that war leaves scars that never heal. Fade, but never heal.

The Hunter and the Hunted, Yudan Daiteki, rating: ★★★★, runtme: 110 min.

Cops and crooks aren't supposed to be pals, but they often become . . . acquaintances, if not quite allies. In Japan the relationship between the two sides has long been a symbiotic one, with the police turning a blind eye to yakuza activities, as long as they stay within certain bounds, while the yakuza support poorly paid beat cops in ways the tax office will never discover. In other words, live and let live as one hand washes the other.

A true cop-crook friendship, though, is a rarity — in Japanese movies at least, where many cops take a familiar, even roughly affectionate approach with crooks — but few exchange confidences or unburden their souls. That would make them look ridiculous — a fatal flaw in a hard-boiled hero.

But the cop hero of "The Hunter and the Hunted" is soft-boiled. Tousle-haired and eternally boyish, Sekikawa (Koji Yakusho) is too good for this corrupt world — or perhaps I should say the cop trade. There are decent men among his colleagues and superiors, but they want results — and Sekikawa hasn't been getting them. Since the death of his wife, he has been too busy taking care of his 8-year-old daughter, Mika, to devote himself to his job.

When a thief rips off 600,000 yen from a local daruma doll factory, the cops are baffled, until Sekikawa comes across a grizzled middle-aged man fixing Mika's bike — and discovers a clue from the robbery in his tool box. Reluctantly, he takes out his badge . . .

This Good Samaritan is Nekoda (Akira Emoto), a.k.a. Neko (The Cat) — a master thief who knows all of his interrogators' tricks. Instead of trying new ones, Sekikawa thanks him for helping his daughter and apologizes for arresting him. Touched by the cop's sincerity and contrition — a first in his line of work — Neko decides to spill. Sekikawa is suddenly elevated from department pariah to hero.

Soon after, Sekikawa meets a pretty day care-center teacher (Yui Natsukawa), but Mika objects to this possible replacement for her dead mother. The film's narrative heart, however, is the relationship between Sekikawa and Neko. The latter decides to take the former under his wing and make a real crook-catcher out of him. Little do both know that this bond will last for years — and dramatically change their lives.

This may sound like sentimental hokum — hands across the legal waters — but first-time director Izuru Narushima presents this unusual friendship more in the style of bickering screwball comedy than warm-hearted drama. Based on a collection of short stories by veteran ex-cop Jun Iizuka, the film also has the feeling of observed reality, not scriptwriter vaporings.

"The Hunter and the Hunted," however, is mainly a showcase for its two leads — Yakusho and Emoto. Yakusho doesn't stretch very far as Sekikawa, a role that plays straight to his nice-guy image. Nonetheless, his Sekikawa shows flashes of professional steel under his rumpled exterior.

Yakusho is overshadowed by Emoto, a veteran character actor best known abroad as the eccentric doctor in Shohei Imamura's "Dr. Akagi." With a heavy-lidded, tired-looking mug that has seen (and no doubt drunk and smoked) everything, Emoto usually plays world-weary types who run the emotional gamut from gray to black.

In Neko, he creates a character more multicolored, not the standard thief-with-a-heart-of-gold, but something deeper, even mysterious. For Neko, a master trickster, laughs at the very idea of sincerity, even when he is being sincere. This is not to say he is simply toying with Sekikawa — he likes him well enough — but he knows the gap between them can never be closed. (Bridged, yes; closed, no.) When Sekikawa innocently starts to believe otherwise, Neko quickly brings him up short.

In its final act, "The Hunter and the Hunted" tries to pluck a few heartstrings, but Neko remains true to his stoic crook code. He also keeps dropping pearls of thiefly wisdom. "I want to be a first-class thief until I die," he says. "I'm taking care of my health so I can still do this when I'm 100." Given the state of pension systems in Japan and elsewhere, that might be a sensible goal for all of us.

Ramblers, Realism no Yado, rating: ★★★⯪, runtime: 83 min.

Underground manga artist Yoshiharu Tsuge occupies a cultural niche in Japan similar to that of Robert Crumb in the United States but remains all but untranslated into English. This is sad, but in commercial publishing terms, understandable. Tsuge's comics, which often concern the wanderings of struggling artist types in the stranger reaches of the country, have achieved classic status since he began publishing in Garo magazine in 1965. Several have been made into films, the latest being Nobuhiro Yamashita's "Ramblers."

A selection of the 2003 Toronto Film Festival, "Ramblers" is less a Tsuge homage than Yamashita's own contemporary interpretation of his work. Tsuge's world may resemble the Japan of his youth (he was born in Tokyo in 1937), but with its preference for odd backwaters and its flashes of surrealism, it has a timeless, dreamlike quality. Also, it is no easier in 2003 for unknown filmmakers — the job description of Yamashita's two protagonists — than it was for unknown manga artists in the 1960s, especially if they lack anything resembling ambition or the simplest of survival skills.

They are the hulking, boyish Kinoshita (Hiroshi Yamamoto) and skinny, nerdish Tsuboi (Keishi Nagatsuka). Young enough to think of themselves as having a future they are old enough to doubt what, if anything, that future might hold. Then they discover they are the punchlines of a cosmic joke. Based on Tsuge's personal observations of how this joke unfolds in real life, the film is so comically spot on, if understated, that by the halfway point, I had laughed so hard I was choking.

True to Tsuge's spirit, "Ramblers" also suggests the not-so-comic loneliness of human beings and the strangeness of the world. There is something very Japanese about its outlook, which is less nihilistic than we-are-flawed-but-lovable humanistic. Though Tsuboi and Kinoshita find themselves down to their last yen, they do not give in to rage or despair. Wary of each other at first, they become brothers in defeat and misery — and come to laugh at the crazy hopelessness of their situation.

They don't know it, but they are doomed from the start. Tsuboi, a scriptwriter, and Kinoshita, a director, are supposed to meet Funaki (Takeshi Yamamoto) — an actor who wants to work with them on a film – in a provincial town. Funaki, however, doesn't show and the boys finally set off to find accommodations.

They end up at an out-of-the-way inn where they enjoy lavish meals — that quickly eat up their money. Desperate for something to do, they go fishing, but catch nothing. Then the inn's master (Sunny Francis), a burly foreigner, offers them his catch for a fee. More yen notes fly away. They talk desultorily about making a film together, but Funaki still doesn't show.

On the beach they encounter a pretty girl (Machiko Ono) walking alone, who sets them to thinking of various scenarios. Was she jilted by a lover? Is she here to drown herself? Tsuboi snags what looks to be a piece of flotsam — and it turns out to be her bra. The girl, naked, chases after them.

Named Atsuko and evidently having nothing better to do, she joins Kinoshita and Tsuboi in their wanderings. A sort of romantic triangle develops — and brings out a new, idiotic competitiveness in the heroes. Atsuko, tiring of the tug of war, abruptly dumps them. Now down to their last yen, they end up at a ramshackle inn that doubles as the family home of the owners. Here they begin their final descent into misery, amid watery soup, filthy bath water and the dying wheezes of an old man. Will Funaki ever arrive?

Nagatsuka's scrawny Tsuboi and Yamamoto's puffy-faced Kinoshita are a slacker Stan Laurel and Oliver Hardy — if Stan had less of a temper and Ollie weren't such a klutz. Their brand of comedy isn't for everyone, but I could relate, probably more than I should admit. Tsuboi and Kinoshita, c'est moi.

Casshern, rating: ★★★★, runtime: 141 min.

The great age of the megalomaniac director, who dreamt of making big, visionary, no-expenses-spared movies, ended with the silents. D.W. Griffith and "Intolerance" (the set for Babylon!), Eric Von Stroheim and "Greed" (the 9.5-hour first cut!), Fritz Lang and "Metropolis" (the Tower of Babel!), Abel Gance and "Napoleon" (the title says it all). The studios tired of backing geniuses who wasted millions, while the sound era required new talents, who were better with intimate glamour shots and witty repartee than crowd scenes. Only Lang, whose first talkie, "M," became an international hit, had a real career after 1928. (He also later disowned "Metropolis," which he told interviewer Peter Bogdanovich was a "patchwork" that he "detested after it was finished.")

Today, with digital technology, it is possible to create big, visionary movies without breaking budgets — even those of the Japanese film industry. The result has been a spate of Japanese films that take up where Lang and company left off in the delusions-of-grandeur department, Mamoru Oshii's "Innocence," and Katsuhiro Otomo's "Steam Boy" being two recent examples.

But what to make of "Casshern," the first feature film by Kazuaki Kiriya, a fashion photographer, music video director, and husband of pop diva Hikaru Utada?

Beginning directors, even wunderkinds like Shunji Iwai ("Hana & Alice") and Ryuhei Kitamura ("Azumi"), typically make their critical and commercial bones on indie films before moving to the big time.

But Kiriya, who is also "Casshern's" scriptwriter and cinematographer, is starting at the top in terms of budget, resources and staff. It's as if, instead of shooting all those one-reelers for Biograph, D.W. Griffith had made his debut with "Birth of a Nation." Like that 1915 epic, "Casshern" is madly ambitious, visually stunning. Though based on a mid-'70s manga and TV anime set in a postapocalyptic world, the film has the same relation to most SF animation that Duchamp's "Nude Descending a Staircase" had to "September Morn." It redefines its genre.

Why the early 20th century references? Because the look of "Casshern" — its cities, robots and weaponry — draws heavily from the period, from World War I newsreels to Futurist art. Instead of giving this look a nostalgic spin, Kiriya takes his vision of a future society seriously, much as the Futurists did themselves. (Most ended up supporting various forms of utopian totalitarianism, from Mussolini's Fascism to Lenin's Communism.) There is a scary power to this world, with its robot armies of thousands marching in lockstep, but a nightmarish beauty as well.

If only the story matched this vision, but it falls into operatic grandiosity and prolixity that makes "Intolerance," with its four parallel story lines, a model of simplicity by comparison. At the end, I felt as battered as if I had gone through the film's 50-year war, battle by titanic battle.

It begins with Dr. Azuma (Akira Terao), a brilliant genetic scientist, explaining his research to the leaders of the Greater Eastern Federation. Following the aforementioned war, which ravaged the planet with nuclear, chemical and biological weapons, the Federation has won control of the Eurasian continent. The survivors have rebuilt using Machine Age technology, but the long struggle has left them physically and spiritually spent. Azuma proposes developing a revolutionary "neo-cell" treatment to repair the bodies of the afflicted. He also has a more personal reason for his research: his wife Midori (Kanako Higuchi), a botanist, has been blinded by a pollution-caused disease.

His request for funding is rejected by Health Ministry bureaucrats, however. Then, with a slithery businessman (Mitsuhiro Oikawa) acting as go-between, he receives backing from General Kamijo (Hideji Otaki), the Federation's elderly dictator, who is in declining health and in desperate need of

Azuma's genetic miracles. Before he can deliver them, a mishap in the lab gives birth to a new race of mutants. Though most are slaughtered by security forces, a few escape to fight underground against their human persecutors. They are led by Brai (Toshiaki Karasawa), a supermutant with a mad vision for a peaceful world.

Meanwhile, Azuma's son Tetsuya (Yusuke Iseya) has joined the army, over the objections of his father and fiancee, the gentle-spirited Luna (Kumiko Aso). On the battlefield he encounters horrors that shake him to his core. Is his father right in wanting to save humanity? Where do his loyalties lie? What is his true identity?

Kiriya and CG supervisor Haruhiko Shono, visual effects supervisor Toshiyuki Kimura and production designer Yuji Hayashida take the film's B-movie premise — eccentric scientist unleashes mutant hordes! — as the merest starting point. Their real interest lies in, not astonishing the audience with CG marvels, but seeding its consciousness with a vision so richly imagined and grounded in past dreams of the future that it exists in a universe of its own, if with debts to Jules Verne, Albert Robida and H.G. Wells, to name a few.

How can Kiriya top this folie de grandeur? Lang wisely never attempt another "Metropolis," but he never had Kiriya's digital tools, which make the impossible possible at a keystroke (OK, thousands of keystrokes). So the real question, I suppose, is "why not?"

Kamikaze Girls, Shimotsuma Monogatari, rating: ★★★☆, runtime: 103 min.

Youth fashion in Japan used to march in lockstep from trend to trend, led by magazines with names like pandas (An An, Non No). No more. Harajuku on a Sunday afternoon swarms with teenage nails that refuse to be pounded down, in everything from biker leathers to Little Miss Bo Peep frocks. Come Monday morning many of them are back in classrooms in sailor dresses, looking very pounded down indeed — until next Sunday.

It's easy to laugh at these weekend rebels — and Tetsuya Nakashima's "Kamikaze Girls," based on a novel by Novala Takemoto, has fun with its two fashionista heroines, who occupy opposite ends of the sexual role-playing scale. But Nakashima goes beyond clever, cartoony sight gags to uncover his heroines' psychic underpinnings, from their messed-up childhoods to their philosophies of life.

His brand of absurdist, stylized filmmaking is verging on cliche by now (see the recent movies of Tim Burton and the Coen brothers), but Nakashima soars past any models into a candy-colored realm of his own. The giddy, grrrl-powered energy of his latest film is infectious — and has made it a surprise hit here and abroad.

Its two principals, frilly Momoko (Kyoko Fukada) and punkish Ichiko (Anna Tsuchiya), are both non-conformists to the core.

Momoko, as she explains in a voice-over narration, was conceived following a chance encounter between a cowardly, oafish yakuza (Hiroyuki Miyasako) and a drunken, scatter-brained bar hostess (Ryoko Shinohara). Unable to make it as a tough guy, Dad starts hawking cheap Versace knock-offs (with misspelled labels) that turn out to be a hit with brand-conscious consumers.

When the story starts, Momoko is 17 and living with Dad in Shimotsuma, Ibaraki Prefecture — a burg in the middle of the rice paddies. Mom has long since vanished, while Dad is still an irresponsible lout.

To Momoko none of this matters: She is living in her own fantasy world, inspired by the Rococo Era, with its blissful frivolity and gloriously ornate fashions. The good folks of Shimotsuma may do all their clothes shopping at Jusco — that temple of the cheap and prosaic — but Momoko journeys three hours by train to Daikanyama, where she spends every last yen on the lacy concoctions of Baby, The Stars Shine Bright, a boutique that takes its fashion cues from Victorian dolls.

It takes guts to wear this stuff in Ibaraki, but the stoic Momoko ("We are born alone, live alone and die alone," she intones at one point), ignores the stares and taunts.

Peddling fake Versace on the Internet to finance her shopping sprees, she attracts the attention of Ichiko, a biker on a 50cc scooter, but a tough cookie nonetheless. One day, Ichiko barges into

Momoko's house on business — and detects a kindred rebel spirit, however buried in froufrou. The two girls become allies — if not yet friends.

The story, such as it is, revolves around their quest to find a legendary embroiderer in Daikanyama, the only one Ichiko feels is worthy of stitching a design on a tokkofuku for the leader of her all-woman biker gang, The Ponytails. Ichiko also wears this garment — a long, loose-fitting coat much favored by antisocial types with rightist tendencies — but her background, we learn, is strictly middle-of-the-road, while in her childhood she was more wimp than warrior.

In the course of their adventures, Momoko learns these and other facts about Ichiko, while revealing her own talents for embroidery — and pachinko. Clearly neither of these girls are quite what they seem. But can they truly close the culture gap that yawns between them?

Nakashima's script underplays this gap. Instead of warily pacing on either side of it, as they would in a real high school, the two girls quickly, if tentatively, bridge it.

The chemistry between super-idol Fukada as Momoko and model-turned-rocker Tsuchiya as Ichiko is genuine enough, though. Also, instead of condescending to their extreme characters, Fukada and Tsuchiya throw themselves into their roles, while displaying, especially in Fukada's case, hitherto unknown comic talents.

Having seen "Kamikaze Girls" and the similarly frothy but entertaining "Cutie Honey," I'm wondering if we're on the verge of a trend. Instead of vengeful spirits in videotapes ("The Ring"), maybe the next big thing from Japan will be quirky loner girls with devastating punches — and a thing for pink.

A Taste of Tea, Cha no Aji, rating: ★★★☆, runtime: 143 min.

Brimming with invention and seemingly inspired by the stranger manga, Katsuhito Ishii's "Sharkshin Man and Peachhip Girl" (1999) and "Party 7" (2000) were hits at home and found admirers abroad, including Quentin Tarantino. Now, Ishii is back with "A Taste of Tea," the opening film in the Directors' Fortnight section of the 2004 Cannes Film Festival.

My first thought on hearing about this film — a leisurely paced family drama shot in an idyllic corner of Tochigi Prefecture — was that Ishii had gone from the Tarantino-esque to the Ozu-esque. But it's not quite that. Ishii is still Ishii; less a Tarantino or Ozu disciple than a unique talent with his own bent take on reality (or rather surreality).

Nonetheless, "A Taste of Tea" marks a departure. In place of the alternate universes of his previous films, Ishii's latest unfolds in a world much like our own, though located in a rural cultural bubble from which cell phones and convenience stores have been excluded. Also, his family of Mom (Satomi Tezuka), Dad (Tomokazu Miura), Gramps (Tetsuya Gashuin), 6-year-old Sachiko (Maya Banno) and 16-year-old Hajime (Takahiro Sato) has an average-enough makeup, but its members are distinctively quirky.

Mom is an animator at work on a project that requires her to try out superhero poses, which she does with diligence and abandon. Gramps is going senile, but has enough of his wits about him to help Mom with said poses. He also periodically holds a tuning fork to his head, as though to make sure his brains are still on key. Fresh-faced kid Hajime races awkwardly through the countryside on a comically tiny bike, his mouth flapping with gormless exertion. Little Sachiko doesn't say much, but is constantly seeing a giant doppelganger and wondering if she can ever make it disappear. Ostensibly the most rational of the bunch, Dad works as a hypnotic therapist, ushering his clients into soothing dream worlds.

In the course of the film, the Haruno clan encounters various strange characters; have small, but significant, adventures; and achieve what is now called closure, but might be more accurately described as moments of pure joy. Leaving the audience with a clean taste and warm glow, "A Taste of Tea" lives up to its title.

Though all the Harunos, together with various friends, relations and strangers, get screen time, the two main protagonists are Hajime and Sachiko. A serious, dreamy girl, Sachiko decides that the solution to her doppelganger problem is to do a back flip on the monkey bars, thereby changing her relationship to the world. She finds a set in an abandoned playground in the middle of a forest and practices until blisters appear on her hands. Meanwhile, Gramps, like a guardian angel, watches from afar.

Hajime's story is the usual adolescent one of unrequited love. A new girl at school, the big-eyed, sardonically grinning Aoi (Anna Tsuchiya), makes his heart do flip-flops, but he can't imagine speaking to her. Then she joins the school go club, and he is recruited by two male members who find him to be a go whiz. Happiness beckons if he can work up the courage to ask her for a game.

Ishii, who also wrote the script, works in several subplots, including the awkward reunion of Mom's soft-spoken brother (Tadanobu Asano) and an old flame (Tomoko Nakajima) and the quest of Dad's loud-mouthed brother (Ikki Todoriki) to record a song he has composed for his birthday. (Called "Yama Yo," the lyrics are little more than a repetition of the title, sung to a catchy tune and accompanied by hand gestures.)

Ishii films this mix of the odd and the ordinary in a semirealistic, semisurrealistic style. Much of the dialogue and action, particularly of the minor characters, resembles the clowning of manzai comics. It can grate, depending on your tolerance for TV variety shows. Meanwhile, CG imagery, such as the doppelganger, transports the film into a realm of the imagination far removed from the annoying static of the everyday.

Like Ishii's other work, "Taste of Tea" is very much an exercise in style, if one less frantic and eager to impress. Instead, its world is mostly a pleasant, if flaky, place, in which even the odd man (or girl) out can feel at home. It's a fantasy, this world, but it also holds out reasonable hope. Happiness is not always up in the clouds, it says. Sometimes, like a set of monkey bars, it's in your hands, in front of your face. But to put yourself over, you've got to practice that kick.

Mind Game, rating: ★★★★, runtime: 103 min.

Animators have always had a thing for Surrealism, going back to Disney's "Silly Symphonies" in 1934. (Disney, in fact, collaborated with the most notorious Surrealist of all, Salvador Dali, on 1946's fabled "Destino" project.) Japanese animators are no exception, and their bizarro characters and worlds make Dali look relatively sane.

Based on a manga series by Robin Nishi, Masaaki Yuasa's animation "Mind Game" is what used to be called a "head movie," meaning that its rush of images replicates the experience of ingesting certain mind-altering substances. One sequence, in which God Himself appears in a myriad of guises, from the loony to the sinister, recalls that trippiest of '60s animations, "The Yellow Submarine." Like, psychedelic, man.

But this not 1968 — and Yuasa and his animators at Studio 4⁰ doubtless have no intention of encouraging anyone's bad lifestyle choices. They are, however, quite serious about obliterating the psychic boundaries between the inner and the outer, between dream and what is usually called reality.

They also make a full-bore inquiry into the persistence of human folly, desire and hope, and deliver a full-throated paean to living what Henry Miller called "life on all fours" — that is, with the sort of freedom belonging to children, madmen and saints.

Their film is by turns silly, frantic and strange, but it's also funny, sexy and energizing in primal ways that sweeps critical quibbles aside. Instead of the pounding headache I was dreading, I left the theater with an "I can't believe I saw that" grin, as though I had just watched someone run a marathon in five minutes, leaping tall buildings along the way. Wrung out, in other words, but astonished as well. What's the old hippie phrase? My mind was blown.

The story starts ordinarily enough, in Osaka, with college boy Nishi-kun (voice actor: Koji Imada) chancing to meet the voluptuous, sweet-spirited Myon-chan (Sayaka Maeda), his childhood crush. Brushing aside his awkward attempts to make up for lost time Myon takes him to a yakitori joint she runs with her older sister Yan (Seiko Takuma). There he meets her philandering, impecunious lush of a father (Rio Sakata) and her tall, tanned, beaming fiancee Ryo (Tomomitsu Yamaguchi).

Then just as Nishi's spirits are sinking into his shoes — how can he ever compete with this hunk? — two yakuza come to collect a debt from Dad and end up blowing poor Nishi to Kingdom Come, in the most embarrassing way imaginable. There his spirit meets a terrifyingly mutable God, who points him in the direction of extinction. Instead of accepting his fate, Nishi tears off in the opposite direction — and finds himself alive and back in the yakitoriya again.

Following the Almighty's parting instructions to "live for all you're worth," Nishi escapes in a car with Myon and Yan in tow and the gangsters in hot pursuit. In the heat of the chase, he takes a header off a bridge and the car lands inside a passing whale. There he and the others meet a white-bearded old man (Takashi Fuji) who says, in rusty Japanese, that he has a radio. He has also built a Swiss Family Robinson house in the whale's belly, complete with all the amenities, scavenged from his ruined ship. He has spent 30 years in this one-man paradise, and it looks as though Nishi and company have joined him for 30 more.

But Nishi, burning with the energy of the recently saved, refuses to let his blubbery prison depress him. Doesn't he have all the time in the world to woo Myon? Not really, if he ever hopes to see daylight again. But getting out of the whale's belly will take even more determination than he needed to escape Paradise.

Just as the God in "Mind Game" changes form the way Madonna changes costumes, the film switches from animated characters to human actors who resemble their animated simulacrums (and also provide their voices). This approach — the real intruding on the unreal and vice versa — is reminiscent of Richard Linklater's in "Waking Life" (2001), a film in which human actors were animated using rotoscoping technology. The two films also both wrestle with ultimate issues, though the lost-in-a-dream hero in "Waking Life" is more inclined to abstract verbalizing; Nishi to acting out. Both are caught in impossible traps, but only Nishi, the eternal optimist, fights with every fiber of his being to escape.

Comparisons with other films abound, including the most obvious, Disney's "Pinocchio." But Yuasa, a first-time director best known for his work as a key animator on the "Crayon Shinchan" series, has a style all his own. It's crude and lewd at times, especially in the early Osaka scenes when the gags seem to have sprung from the nether regions of Kansai comedy, but it's also capable of erotic lyricism, as when Van, huge balloons strapped to her breasts and crotch, performs an exotic dance that takes that old hippie art — body painting — into a new, aerial dimension.

Towards the end, "Mind Game" surges into a realm of pure speed, adrenaline and will, in a long, mad sprint toward the ultimate paradise. That is, this dull, prosaic, everyday Japan of ours, which has rarely looked sweeter. Dali was never like this.

Nobody Knows, Daremo Shiranai, rating: ★★★★★, runtime: 141 min.

A generation ago, Japanese TV moms were selflessly devoted to their offspring, bringing them bowls of nutritious noodles as they crammed for those all-important school entrance exams. TV dads, though workaholics, usually had time for a game of catch or gruff words of fatherly advice. Like the moms, they were always going to be there for what they called their kodakara — literally, "child treasures."

But in recent Japanese films, the kyoiku mama ("education mother") of old has given way to clueless, distraught parents who are all but irrelevant to their kids' lives. Junior is no longer at his desk sucking down Mom's home cooking, but hanging out in the streets of Shibuya.

By comparison, the mother in Hirokazu Koreeda's "Nobody Knows" seems a sympathetic type. Though emotionally still a child herself, she is pals with her children: 12-year-old Akira (Yuya Yagira) and younger siblings Kyoko (Ayu Kitaura), Shigeru (Hiei Kimura) and Yuki (Momoko Shimizu). They love her dearly, though Akira knows, more than the others do, that she is not to be trusted.

Mom (You), who had each of her kids with a different father, but is married to none of them, is flighty, scatterbrained and pathologically irresponsible. Soon after moving into a new apartment (and sneaking in the three younger kids so the neighbors won't talk), she leaves and doesn't return. Used to their mother's frequent absences, the kids go about their business with Akira serving as a surrogate parent —

shopping, cooking and enforcing Mom's rules: Don't talk loudly, play on the veranda or leave the apartment. That means no school, no neighborhood friends — nothing but whatever life they can create in the confines of their flat on the 200,000 yen Mom left them in an envelope.

As the weeks pass, they manage well enough — like most children they are resourceful — but they are also almost totally alone. Akira visits two of Mom's former boyfriends, but they give him only a few yen notes and words of sympathy. He forms a tentative bond with the staff of a neighborhood convenience store, but can tell them nothing of his true situation. Meanwhile, the younger children withdraw into private worlds of fantasy and play.

After a month, Mom returns with presents, but little in the way of apologies or explanations. Then, just before Christmas, she leaves again — not saying when or if she will come back.

Based on a true 1987 incident, "Nobody Knows" has been 15 years in the making, since Koreeda wrote his first draft of the script in 1989. Usually such a long gestation is not a good sign: By the time a director brings his labor of love to the screen it feels . . . labored. Scenes that burst with vitality in the auteur's brain look inert on the screen.

Koreeda typically works from personal concerns and memories, using methods he developed in his early years as a documentary filmmaker, when he would spend months and even years getting to know his subjects. In making "Nobody Knows," however, he was not just a fly on the wall with a camera: He had a script and a shooting schedule — the usual movie-making apparatus.

But he also wanted his young cast to interact, grow, and express their personalities freely, with as little adult dictation as possible. Momoko Shimizu, who played the youngest child, Yuki, liked Apollo Choco better than Strawberry Pocky (if you are familiar with neither, you have probably not spent much time in Japanese convenience stores with a 5-year-old), so Koreeda changed his script — and her on-camera smile when she sees a box of her favorite treat is brighter as a result. A minor point, but illustrative of the way the film reflects the fabric of the children's lives over the course of a year.

Koreeda may be editorializing about how kids can become invisible in modern, urban society, but he is also showing us how they really talk, play, and otherwise live when no one but his (ever-discreet) camera is looking. The lack of the usual structuring and cueing — no music swells as Mom leaves her little ones for the last time — may make the film seem, in places, unfocused and slow, but in its last third, Koreeda's faith in his methods and patience with his young actors, pays off.

By this time the children's money is gone, together with the water, gas and electricity, and their only real friend is a quiet, ethereally pretty girl (Hanae Kan) who has stopped going to junior high school. Their utter isolation, the fact that no one in their building or neighborhood cares if they live or die, is wrenching precisely because we have been with them so long, getting to know them so well, in the everydayness of their struggle and decline.

All the film's young actors are superb (as is pop singer You as their unreliable mother), but it was Yuya Yagira, as Akira, who won the Best Actor prize at this year's Cannes Film Festival, where "Nobody Knows" screened in competition. A newcomer when he auditioned for the role, Yagira has little of the professional child actor about him. His Akira is a complex personality, who can be cynical, furtive and world-weary beyond his years, but then light up with boyish enthusiasm when he is playing schoolyard baseball or riding a playground roundabout.

What will his future be? "Nobody Knows" offers no easy answers, allows for no easy pity. Instead of giving us a good, self-congratulatory cry, it leaves us with one lingering truth: His mother wasn't the only one who abandoned those kids — we all did.

Vital, rating: ★★★☆, runtime: 86 min.

When Shinya Tsukamoto released his first feature "Tetsuo" in 1989, many critics compared this crazed speed dream about the merger of man and metal to the work of David Lynch. This critic couldn't see it: Lynch is an ironist and nostalgist, Tsukamoto is neither. In fact, he is not like anyone — a mark of distinction in a country where many directors pepper their work with references to revered seniors, foreign and domestic. (Admittedly, he does have his influences, including the Ultraman series.)

Tsukamoto takes the rage and emptiness of modern urban life to their natural conclusions — violence, murder, psychosis. He is the poet of fists, bullets and drills shattering flesh, the dreamer of ultimate nightmares that are also ultimate fulfillments. His heroes not only desire degradation and annihilation — they revel in it. In "Tetsuo" the faces of two enemies conjoined in a bizarre ambulant junk pile are suffused with mad glee. They are free at last from the pain of being human.

He would seem a natural for the now-trendy genre of horror, but unlike Hideo Nakata ("Ring") and Takashi Shimizu ("Ju-on"), who made scary movies in Japan, then trooped off to Hollywood to turn out more of the same, Tsukamoto resists genre conventions. He made genuflections toward the mainstream in "Hiruko the Goblin" (1990) and "Gemini" (1999), but remains an apostate to the religion of the box office.

His latest film, "Vital," is again Tsukamoto being Tsukamoto. The result of his long fascination with the inner workings of the human body, culminating with two months as an observer in a university anatomy class, the film is another entry in a cinematic spiritual diary kept by a director who can see both beauty and beastliness of human life. Now in his forties, Tsukamoto depicts a romantic idyll at a tropical beach and a joyous solo dance, complete with stop-motion balletic leaps, in his latest work. Is the cyber-punk Prince of Darkness going soft?

No, unless your definition of "soft" encompasses shots of cadavers being ripped open like so many sides of beef or sex scenes that consist of two people strangling each other to the point of asphyxiation.

The film's Tsukamoto surrogate is Hiroshi Takagi (Tadanobu Asano), a medical student who survives a car wreck that kills his lover, Ryoko (Nami Tsukamoto) — but leaves him with no memory, even of his worried parents (Kazuyoshi Kushida and Lily) or, for that matter, of himself. His only anchor to a world gone adrift is the old anatomy texts in his closet. There he finds meaning and hints of a past. Enrolling in medical school, he takes the anatomy class required for second-year students, which involves cutting open cadavers.

He and his team are assigned the corpse of a young woman with a blue tattoo on her arm and a bag over her head. She is thus anonymous — but to Hiroshi disturbingly individual. He dissects her with a passion bordering on obsession. He also stirs the curiosity of Ikumi (single-named Kiki), a fellow student who looks, with her squarely cut straight black hair and theatrical air of doom, as though she has wandered in from a beatnik coffee shop, circa 1960.

Like Hiroshi, she is also inadvertently responsible for a death, that of a middle-aged lover (Riju Go) she toyed with like a cat mauling a weak-minded mouse. Hiroshi, though, is made of stranger, more elusive stuff. When he and Ikumi enjoy the delights of mutual strangulation, he enters another dimension where Ryoko still lives, dances, loves. Are these flashbacks of real events? Or are they fantasies that he — or possibly Ryoko — has created to symbolize a future that never was? They keep growing longer and more explicit. Confused and upset, Hiroshi goes to Ryoko's parents (Jun Kunimura and Hana Kino) to find answers and perhaps absolution.

Tsukamoto presents this contemporary gothic material without a hint of irony — though the performances of his two death-fixated lovers border on self parody. Kiki, a model with little acting experience, crosses over, while Asano, who has been playing outwardly blank, inwardly seething characters for years, knows where to draw the line. His problem is more one of lighting — in certain underlit scenes he looks a death-warmed-over 40. In character perhaps, but not the most likely second-year medical student.

In his scenes with Nami Tsukamoto, a professional ballerina who is also an acting neophyte, Asano finally gets to bask in the sun — and lighten up. There is a feeling of paradise lost — or rather of a dream more real than reality — new to Tsukamoto's work. And "Vital"'s central message is one of hope: A scalpel can not only expose the secrets of the flesh but awaken the spirit — in the memory, if not on the autopsy table.

Lakeside Murder Case, rating: ★★★⯪, runtime: 119 min.

More Japanese directors, young and not so young, are following American-style career paths: After an indie success or two, they move on to bigger and more lucrative things. Is no one immune to the lure of the box office?

This thought was prompted by the news that Shinji Aoyama, director of "Helpless" (1995), "Wild Life" (1997) and the Cannes-prize-winning "Eureka" (2000), was making "Lakeside Murder Case," a film based on a best seller by Keigo Higashino about a murder at a lakeside resort.

With his minimalistic one-scene-one-cut style, Aoyama did not seem the most obvious choice to helm what looked to be multiplex fare.

"Lakeside Murder Case," however, is less a commercial whodunit with than a multilayered psycho-drama, whose subjects include the ills of the Japanese educational system and the moral limits of parental love. In other words, right down Aoyama's alley after all. It is also more mainstream than the Aoyama norm. Mystery fans will enjoy the plot twists, as well as the dark undercurrents of illicit passion and murderous rage, presented in a chilly, mannered style reminiscent of late period Hitchcock.

Aoyama doesn't deliver Hitchcockian shocks, but with a cool efficiency he lifts social masks to reveal the creepy-crawlies underneath. I didn't buy his ending, but given what came before, it has a certain inevitability, like cram school flyers in the mailbox.

Shunsuke Namiki (Koji Yakusho), an ad agency art director, has a mid-life-crisis affair with a scrumptious photographer, Eisako (Yuko Mano), and separates from his wife Misako (Hiroko Yakushimaru). As the film begins, he is rushing off to meet Misako and her daughter from a previous marriage, who are attending an intensive study session sponsored by the daughter's cram school.

Unsually, the setting is an elegant rustic villa by a quiet lake. Also, instead of the usual uniformed masses, the class consists of two boys and a girl, all cramming for admission to the same elite junior high school. The head of this establishment, Mr. Tsukumi (Etsushi Toyokawa), has the excruciatingly proper bearing of a manager at an exclusive club — which, in a way, he is.

Most of the parents are dressed as for a funeral. They answer Tsumiki's mock interview questions about their parenting practices and goals as though reciting from a manual. Shunsuke, by contrast, is casual in both his choice of clothes and answers, as though he could hardly be bothered.

This bad attitude sends Misako into a rage. Her mood is not improved when Eisako arrives, ostensibly on business, and slinks about with a naughty grin. She might as well be wearing a big "A" on her forehead.

That night someone is murdered, and, shortly after, one of the parents confesses. But if they go to the police, they will put their kids' studies — and thus their futures — in jeopardy. Instead, they decide to hide the corpse. One parent, a dour-looking doctor (Akira Emoto), is something of a body disposal expert, but he needs help — and soon everyone is implicated save Tsukumi and the kids, cramming away in another cabin. Shift the story a few degrees, and "Lakeside Murder Case" could be a black comedy of the "Shallow Grave" variety. A few degrees in the opposite direction, and it could fit into the horror bin, next to "Village of the Damned." Aoyama's aim, however, is neither laughs nor shocks — though he does raise goose bumps showing us how much unpleasant work a perfect crime can entail, and how easy it is to make one fatal mistake.

Koji Yakusho as Shunsuke is our link to ordinary humanity, but his performance, though winningly rumpled, is not enough to warm the film's frigid emotional air. To scale this country's educational heights, the film seems to say, one must be as ruthless as the feudal lords in the Warring States days, who would commit any outrage to advance their interests or extend their domains.

This nihilism may be overdone — most parents don't have to bury bodies, not yet anyway — but the film does pose a timely question. In a winner-take-all society, how can one compete successfully and stay human? The answer may be staring us in the face, from the bottom of a lake.

Tony Takitani, rating: ★★★★, runtime: 75 min.

Jun Ichikawa is an admirer of Yasujiro Ozu's highly ordered, less-is-more aesthetic. In his recent films, he has tried to shake his "Ozu disciple" image, but in his latest, "Tony Takitani," he returns to a key Ozu-esque theme: The drama in seemingly quiet, unexceptional lives. His source, though, is a short story by Haruki Murakami about a shy technical illustrator (Issey Ogata) stuck with an unusual name by his jazzman father — and about his trying to escape the isolation the name and his own nature imposes on him.

Famously reluctant to permit film treatments of his work, Murakami is reportedly delighted with "Tony Takitani" — as well as he should be. In place of the usual revisions (or butcheries) to make the story more cinematic, Ichikawa has opted to make his film more literary. As the camera moves laterally from scene to scene, somewhat like the cards in a kamishibai (picture play), a narrator tells the story, from beginning to end, less like a raspy-voiced kamishibai man entertaining antsy kids, more like a dulcet-voiced radio storyteller soothing drive-time adults.

The story relates Tony's life, starting with the decision of his father (also played by Ogata) to give him that fatal name, but centering on his relationship with Eiko (Rie Miyazawa), an elusive beauty mad about designer clothes. He falls for her, marries her — and feels alive in a way he never imagined possible. Then, as she maxes out her plastic to feed her obsession, he realizes that with human connection comes human pain. When he tries to change Eiko, he discovers another emotion: loss. Ichikawa's distancing strategies, including tamped-down, hollowed-out performances by Ogata and Miyazawa, may evoke Murakami's prose with pitch-perfect fidelity — but when I realized the narration was never going to stop, I felt a vague panic, as though I were being absorbed, word by velvety word, into Tony's lonely world. Or rather locked into Eiko's airless closet, without hope of rescue until the closing credits.

Break Through!, Pacchigi!, no rating, Running Time: 119 min.

Kazuyuki Izutsu's "Break Through!" packs a big, raw, revitalizing jolt, like walking from a present-day Tokyo street, with its dull, closed-off faces, into a wild student-party-cum-riot, circa 1968. The film is partly Izutsu's look back at his own '60s youth. Mostly, though, it is "Romeo and Juliet" redux, with Kyoto standing in for Verona and the Japanese and Korean communities substituting, respectively, for the Montagues and Capulets. Romeo, a.k.a Kosuke Matsuyama (Shun Shioya), is a second-year high school student. A nice, normal, nonviolent type, he suddenly finds himself in the middle of a rampaging crowd of ethnic Korean boys, outraged by insults perpetrated by several of his idiot classmates on two Korean girls. He makes a narrow escape, but soon after, he and his best bud Yoshio (Keisuke Koide) are sent by their homeroom teacher to invite the Korean students to a friendly soccer game as a way of restoring the peace.

Trembling like black-uniformed leaves, they enter enemy territory, where Kosuke encounters a doll-faced, serious-looking girl (Erika Sawajiri) playing a Korean folk song, "Imjin River," on a flute. He and Yoshio are also nearly lynched by her older brother Lee Ang Son (Sosuke Takaoka) and his gang, but he is already smitten — and eager to learn that haunting tune.

The story centers on Kosuke's struggle to not only master a song, but win the love of a girl who seems to live in an alien, hostile world. Meanwhile, Ang Son and his crew are street fighting with Japanese toughs as though playing a contact sport, with one side scoring hits, then the other. He is macho to a fault, but when he learns that his girlfriend (Kyoko Yanagihara) is pregnant and determined to keep the baby, he faces a choice that makes him quail: grow up or cop out.

"Break Through!" may be based on the Takeshi Matsuyama novel "Boy M's Imjin River," but it is Izutsu's film in every frame. A native of Nara, Izutsu debuted in 1975 with an independently produced porno film, but became best known for films like "Empire of Kids" (1981) and "Boys Be Ambitious" (1996) that depicted, with gritty realism and rough affection, the lives and brawls of Kansai bad boys.

In recent years, Izutsu has become popular as a tart-tongued TV film critic, but as "Break Through!" proves, his celebrity has not softened his style or concerns. If anything, he has upped his already high violence ante. His young toughs fight knock-down, drag-out battles at every opportunity, made or found. It's their release, their raison d'e^tre and, finally, their path to mutual understanding. As I beat you, I know you.

This insight may not occur to the middle-class, college-educated, movie nerd types who now make most of the films about Japan's marginals and minorities, but it comes naturally to Izutsu. He knows his people and their world inside out. He doesn't interpret them so much as give them a voice (while inserting his own wry asides).

Love is Five, Seven, Five, Koi wa Go Shichi Go, rating: ★★★★, runtime: 105 min.

Movies about losers who become winners through a combination of grit, talent, luck and love are common everywhere, though the Japanese have come up with a twist on this formula: The losers win at something considered "dasai" (uncool). Masayuki Suo was the pioneer, with 1989's "Fancy Dance" (hero takes up zazen), 1992's "Sumo Do, Sumo Don't" (sumo) and 1996's "Shall We Dance?" (ballroom dancing).

The latest in this line is "Love is Five, Seven, Five," Naoko Ogigami's film about high-school outsiders who take part in "Haiku Koshien" — a team haiku competition named after the Koshien baseball tournament. Held each August, it's conducted much as it is in the film, with competitors critiquing each other's poems and a panel of judges choosing a winner by raising flags.

As we see in the opening scenes, the film's high-school haiku club is considered the lamest of all, beneath even that perpetual repository for the unathletic and uncool — the English club. The task that Ogigami has set herself is to raise one school's club to the level of cool.

In the process she has produced an old-fashioned seishun eiga (youth movie), but without the old-fashioned sentimentality about the purity, innocence and general splendidness of youth. The downsides, including teenage jerkishness, are also on display.

Also, she does not go in the opposite, now familiar, direction of making her outsider types part-time hookers, apprentice gangsters or other parental nightmares. Instead she reveals them in all their quirky, but essentially normal, humanity. She uses the techniques of caricature to deepen and intensify her portraits, not cheapen or degrade them.

The first is that of Haruko Takayama (Megumi Seki), a sharp-eyed beauty who has grown up abroad and is now stuck, against her will, in a provincial high school, whose ways strike her as absurd. Why does she have to stuff her head with kanji now that she can find them with a few keystrokes?

One day she discovers a chubby classmate, Mako (Kinako Kobayashi), being abused by a nasty boy and sends him flying. This act of heroism is witnessed by P-chan (Akane Hasunuma), a ukelele-strumming pixie, who is immediately smitten — and attaches herself to Haruko like a leech.

But Mako, who has also been kicked off the cheerleading squad, remained unconsoled. She is about to throw herself off the school roof when Tsuchiyama (Takahito Hosoyamada), a handsome photography buff coolly asks her to recite her suicide poem. She complies ("In the next world/I want to be born/as a better me") and he praises it without sarcasm. She becomes smitten with him, but he is secretly in love with Haruko — and has dozens of candid snaps to prove it.

Over the upcoming summer break, the school haiku club is supposed to prepare for the Haiku Koshien, but has only one regular member: the burr-headed Yamagishi (Ryo Hashizume), who also rides the bench of the school baseball team. The milquetoasty teacher who advises the club, Masuo

Sensei (Tetta Sugimoto), is thus surprised to see Haruko, Mako, P-chan and Tsuchiyama all present at the first meeting.

Haruko was drafted by her Japanese teacher — and the rest followed. None, save Yamagishi, have any interest in haiku. And he knows the rules, but not the rhythm. The situation looks hopeless, but Masuo turns out to be a good teacher. Instead of belaboring formulas, he takes his charges out in the natural world, where they can see haiku in action, with their own eyes. Also, the kids turn out to have that essential requirement for poetry — passion, though at first more for each other than for haiku.

Still, it's not obvious how the team can win even the moral victory — de rigueur for films of this sort. Especially when they encounter the winners of last year's Haiku Koshien, guys wearing identical geek glasses, geek haircuts and rattling off their kanji-laden poems with contemptuous geek precision. Our heroes are not just beaten in a "friendly" contest, but pounded and crushed, reduced to silence and tears.

But when they face the geeks again, at Haiku Koshien, we not only know that the result will not be the same, but, poem by poem, exactly how and why. Shinobu Yaguchi's 2004 hit "Swing Girls" did something similar with girls and jazz, but in a big, splashy, faintly incredible finale. Ogigami's film is more precise and convincing. Haiku, Yamagishi tells us over and over, is pop. It is also, as "Love is Five, Seven, Five!," shows us, cool. But who ever doubted it?

The Whispering of the Gods, Germania no Yoru, rating: ★★★★☆, runtime: 107 min.

A full-frontal plunge into acts of depravity and violence, set in the faux idyllic confines of a rural Catholic monastery, "The Whispering of the Gods" falls squarely into the love-it-or-loathe-it category. Screened in competition at this year's Tokyo International Film Festival, Tatsushi Omori's debut feature evoked fervent praise from some — Japanese film scholar Donald Richie called it the "the most powerful Japanese film I have seen during 2005" — but equally fervent damnation from others. I'm with Richie — especially about the "powerful" part.

Filmed in rural Iwate Prefecture and based on a prize-winning story by Mangetsu Hanamura, "Germania" has a borderless, timeless feel, while relying more on iconic images and gestures than words for its impact. It leaves certain disturbing acts open to interpretation — suggesting, but not insisting. In other words, those who prefer clearly defined heroes, villains and resolutions had best give it a pass. That said, Omori's visionary, uncompromising direction (actress Leona Hirota described the shoot to the press at TIFF as "hell" in which she came down with pneumonia, damaged her liver and broke two bones) has resulted in a film of rare beauty and force.

At its center is the unreadable face and explosive presence of Rou (Hirofumi Arai), a killer of two strangers, who escapes to the Catholic monastery and orphanage where he was raised. The head priest, Father Komiya (Renji Ishibashi), offers him refuge. In return Rou masturbates him while he reads the Bible in Latin — and a dog looks on inquisitively.

Father Komiya, we are given to understand, has been abusing Rou since boyhood.

Rou is also asked to bring slops to the monastery's pigs and shovel the droppings of its hundreds of chickens. When the smarmy farm manager, Ukawa (Nao Omori), assigns Rou the former task and walks away whistling, Rou remembers — and later beats Ukawa into a sniveling heap.

More outrages follow, including Rou's naked romp with a young novice (Megumi Sawara) in the storehouse, sexual assault on a nun (Leona Hirota) in the kitchen and a teasing confession of future crimes that drives his elderly mentor, Father Togawa (Kei Sato), to despair.

Meanwhile, Rou stirs the desires of the angel-faced Toru (Keita Kimura), another of Father Komiya's teenage victims, and the pudgy pervert Scoutmaster (Genta Dairaku), who wants to . . .let's leave it at that.

Rou, however, is not just another sociopath indulging appetites and urges at will, but a damaged seeker after a private truth, who no longer trusts words — only deeds. He does not so much destroy as expose hidden desires — and decay.

Telling this story with long cuts and a minimum of clutter, Omori gives each of his images a vivid presence and emotional weight. They are less heavy (or ponderous) than just there — with depths and echoes that are less stated than felt. He adds underlayers of black humor (the antics of the Scoutmaster being the most risible), but your laughs may stick in your throat (as you suppress the gag reflex). Also, though the pace is deliberate, the tension stays high — mainly because Rou is a volatile enigma. Arai plays him with a coiled power that makes his very blankness eloquent and, occasionally, threatening.

The photography by Ryo Otsuka ("Akame 48 Falls") has an Old Master richness, as in the scene of Sister Theresa cutting vegetables in the kitchen and looking like a subject for Vermeer. But when the violent or erotic occasion calls for it, beauty gives way to starkness.

What are the gods whispering? Like every other element of this disturbing, provocative film, their message is ours for the parsing. But first, like Father Komiya's dog, we have to watch — and listen.

Princess Raccoon, Operetta Tanuki Goten, rating: ★★★⯪, running Time: 111 min.

Seijun Suzuki was, like Orson Welles, a wayward genius who used and defied the studio system, before he was crushed by it. Suzuki's arc of rise and fall was longer than Welles', however: He directed 39 films at Nikkatsu before his most outrageous act of defiance — "Branded to Kill" — got him fired from the studio in 1967. His fatal error was baffling his audience and, more importantly, his studio boss, with a story that had all the logic of a Kafkaesque dream.

As his latest film, "Princess Raccoon" shows, the 82-year-old Suzuki is still dreaming private dreams, but they have taken an older, more domestic form. In place of the anarchy and eroticism in "Branded," Suzuki has drawn on native folklore, with its stories of trickster tanuki (raccoon dogs) assuming human form to bewitch and bedevil. His sensibility, though, derives more from his beloved Taisho Era (1912-1926), when the Japanese traditional and the Western new were blending with more freedom — and license — than possible in the straitlaced days of Emperor Meiji.

He is not the first to film the legend of Princess Raccoon, but he has made it his own, which is to say visually brilliant and theatrically stylized, in opposition to the quasi-realistic integration of story, dance and song that defined the classic Broadway and Hollywood musical from "Showboat" on. This is squarely in the Japanese theatrical tradition that celebrates, rather than conceals, its own artificiality. Suzuki's characters don't strike kabuki-like poses, but they are fantasy creatures of the stage (or rather studio set), with no imaginable existence beyond it.

Their world is a blend of Western and Japanese, with foreigners in Elizabethan era garb chatting in the castle of one Azuchi Momoyama (Mikijiro Hira) as the action begins (or rather, the curtains part). This lord is, like the Queen in "Snow White," a self-infatuated sort. When he asks his seer-in-residence, the white-haired Biruzen Baba (Saori Yuki) — who is the most beautiful of all — she peers into a bubbling bowl of soup and delivers the expected answer: Azuchi Momoyama.

But then, to her distress, the lord's visage disappears, to be replaced by that of his son, Amechiyo (Joe Odagiri). Upset at the thought that his handsome offspring will supersede him, Azuchi Momoyama banishes Amechiyo to a distant mountain, with a ninja (Taro Yamamoto) serving as escort/assassin.

Amechiyo frees himself and encounters the lovely Princess Raccoon (Zhang Ziyi), who has come from China to the Raccoon Palace. Despite the language barrier — the Princess speaks and sings mostly in Mandarin, Amechiyo in feudal-era Japanese — they promptly fall in love. (The heart, we are given to understand, can interpret what the rational mind cannot.)

Among the barriers to their bliss, however, is not only Biruzen Baba, determined to uphold the supremacy of her lord and master, but Ohagi no Tsubone (Hiroko Yakushimaru), Tanuki Hime's nurse, who is opposed to this unnatural union. Will true love prevail?

If this were kabuki, the answer would be a simple "no." But since it is an "operetta," tragedy is not required — or even hinted at. Instead, we get elaborately, if statically, staged musical numbers in various styles, from prewar pop to — believe it or not — rap. The digital ghost of enka (Japanese ballad) diva Hibari Misora even makes an appearance.

Chinese star Zhang Ziyi may have displayed dancerly athleticism in the martial arts epics of Zhang Yimou and Ang Lee and smoky eroticism in Wong Kar-wai's "2046," but in "Princess Raccoon" she shows a softer, if elusive, side more in keeping with Suzuki's vision. Both she and co-star Joe Odagiri are required to do little more than embody archetypes.

By comparison with Suzuki's 2001 "Pistol Opera," a mannered exercise in style, "Princess Raccoon" is lighter in spirit and touch. His affection for his material and his showmanship in presenting it still charm, as does his puckish sense of humor.

But halfway though "Princess Raccoon" I was longing for the snap and sass of the Hollywood musicals that succeeded Suzuki's beloved Taisho operettas. Zhang Ziyi may be sweet, but give me Fred and Ginger.

In the Pool, rating: ★★★★, runtime: 101 min.

In the West, the funnier forms of neuroticism have long been the subject of comedy, with pioneer Woody Allen using stand-up as a sort of public therapy session, but what about Japan, with its keep-it-under-wraps, gut-it-out ethos?

Satoshi Miki's "In the Pool," a comedy based on Hideo Okuda's Naoki Prize-winning novel of the same title, offers the answer in the form of one Hideo Irabu (Suzuki Matsuo), a staff psychiatrist at a large hospital (that his unseen father runs and will one day, we are told, bequeath to him).

Wearing a fake leopard-skin shirt under his white coat, ensconced in a moldy basement office with only a gorgeous nurse (Maiko) in a distractingly tight dress for company, Irabu treats patients as though they were punch-lines in a private joke. Played by Suzuki Matsuo, a veteran stage comedian with a lengthening list of screen credits ("Chicken Heart," "Cutie Honey" and his 2004 directorial debut, "Otakus In Love"), Irabu combines the con-man impudence of Groucho Marx with the antic moods of a younger Jim Carrey. Imagine a shrink who has absolutely no idea what is he doing, but does it anyway, with an uninhibited, unhinged gusto that somehow carries his patients along like leaves in a crazily shifting wind.

Though his shtick can be blow-it-out-your-nose funny, Matsuo does not dominate "In the Pool" — to the film's detriment. Instead, he shares the screen with three mostly ordinary neurotics. Two are Irabu's patients, one is his acquaintance — and all three discover that the root causes of what ail them are the mostly humdrum disasters of everyday life. It's as though a Marx Brother movie were to detail the pearl-collecting mania of Margaret Dumont — not as much fun as watching Groucho chat her up, while simultaneously taking her down.

Miki, an in-demand director of TV comedy and variety shows, keeps the comic pot bubbling merrily. Along the way he creates — or rather makes room for — moments of inspired madness, whose ultimate message is reassuringly sane: It's almost never as bad as you think, folks. Not that neurotics will listen.

The film's first case, who gives it its title, is Kazuo Omori (Seiichi Tanabe), a busy young executive in charge of an outlet mall development. Stressed by the demands of his job — and his affair with a pretty subordinate — he finds relief in swimming laps every day, without fail. When his pool routine is interrupted, he goes to pieces, though he finds temporary relief by plunging his hands into sinks full of water. Meanwhile, a fellow swimmer, Irabu, always seems to have time for a carefree splash and paddle. What, Omori begins to wonder, is his secret?

Stranger is the case of Tetsuya Taguchi (Joe Odagiri), a mild-mannered salesman at a manufacturing company who awakes one day to find himself with a permanent erection. Horrified by this Kafka-esque transformation, Taguchi does everything to hide his condition from his colleagues, even if it means shaking hands from a crouch. Desperate, he consults Irabu, whose first request is to drop trou — and whose first response to what he sees is a cackle.

More common, and funnier, is the case of Suzumi Iwamura (Miwako Ichikawa), a magazine writer and obsessive-compulsive who can't leave her apartment without wondering whether the gas and electricity are off and rushing back to check . . . and check . . . and check. Irabu begins by kidding her about the size of her bag, crammed with gear she needs "just in case," then sticking her with a coffee shop bill and borrowing her umbrella, soon after which . . . but it should be obvious shouldn't it? Not getting results with insults, he tries other, bizarre treatment options, while Suzumi blows yet another big assignment, obsessing on an imaginary flying beetle.

Of the three actors playing these characters, only Ichikawa — with her wide Julia Roberts mouth and big Shelley Duvall eyes — is a real comedian, who can get laughs just by counting "off" switches. Odagiri and Tanabe are capable enough as slightly warped Everymen, but Jim Carrey they are not. Instead they serve primarily as straight men to Irabu — and the various low tricks life plays on them.

Hollywood will probably cast Ben Stiller and Owen Wilson in their roles in the remake. But who can replace Suzuki? No one can — or should. Comic genius speaks a universal language, even in fractured English.

A Stranger of Mine, Unmei Janai Hito, rating: ★★★☆, runtime: 98 min.

Kenji Uchida's "A Stranger of Mine" arrives at theaters here after netting three awards at this year's Cannes Film Festival, where it screened in the International Critics' Week section. Not the biggest prizes — the Young Critics Award, SACD Screenwriting Award and something called the Grand Golden Rail Award — but impressive nonetheless, especially given that Uchida was unknown outside local film circles prior to his Cannes triumph.

Interestingly (or, depending on your place in the directorial hierarchy here, infuriatingly), "A Stranger of Mine "is not a typical festival film. Instead it is a circularly plotted, slickly made relationship comedy that abounds with witty lines and twists.

Uchida sees himself asan entertainer — Billy Wilder is one of his idols — whose talents lie more in casting the right actors and giving them funny things to say than in the nitty-gritty of lighting, shooting and cutting (for that he relies heavily on his staff, beginning with cinematographer Keiichiro Inoue).

He hasn't quite mastered the art of comic pacing and momentum, lingering too long in medium tempo, while his script, which doubles back on itself over and over for yet another point of view on a key scene, begins to feel gimmicky.

But as a Hollywood calling card, as well as a comedy in a minor key, "Stranger" succeeds well enough. Next time, though, I hope Uchida takes more risks — and releases more inner demons.

As the film begins, a straight-arrow salaryman named Miyata (Yasuhi Nakamura) and a sad-sack girl named Maki (Reika Kirishima) have both been dumped by their respective lovers. Maki is left with only a 3,500 yen engagement ring, Miyata with a few boxes of stuff his ex deposited six months ago in his new condo, which he bought in anticipation of wedded bliss.

In the normal course of events, these two would never meet, but Miyata's best buddy — a wised-up private eye named Kanda (So Yamanaka) — introduces the still-sniffling Maki to a protesting Miyata at a restaurant. To be more precise, he hands her over to Miyata — and makes his escape.

One awkward thing leads to another and Maki, now homeless, ends up at Miyata's apartment. Gentlemanly to a fault, with no obvious thought of hanky-panky in his head, Miyata is settling her in for the night, when in waltzes the ex — the leggy, slinky Ayumi (Yuka Itaya). She has just come for her things, she says, but Maki, embaraased, makes her exit. Miyata, sensing the love of a lifetime slipping away, pursues her.

So far so a conventional-enough romcom, but the film flashes back to earlier that evening — and we start to see that nearly everything we know about Kanda and Ayumi, as well as a smiling, stylish yakuza boss (Sasuke Yamashita) who is now Ayumi's boyfriend, is wrong.

A con game starts to unfold, involving a suitcase full of money, death threats and other shenanigans, all of which are tied together as neatly as a Christmas ribbon at Takashimaya.

Another Wilder fan, Koki Mitani, makes similarly talky, twisty comedies by keeping the energy level high and the actors mugging away. Uchida's approach is lower in key, while his characters are truer to life.

The most interesting is Maki, who comically blubbers and frets, but talks straight enough to keep Miyata — and the audience — from taking her too lightly.

The most worldly seems to be Kanda. "After 30, forget about meeting women naturally or by fate," he admonishes Miyata. "You aren't going to find them in the hall after class or at the school festival any more." In other words, step up to the plate, slugger. Fashionably dressed and bearded, with a smooth line of patter, Kanda is as good as his word, chatting up Miki with ease, but he is also less on the ball than he looks.

All five principals, in fact, turn out to be more complex than first impressions suggest, a testimony to not only Uchida's writing skills, but also the talents of the well-chosen cast. I especially liked Yuka Itaya as the conwoman, Ayumi. Unapologetic about her outrages and crimes, slick and cool as chilled glass, Ayumi is the Darwinian principle personified. When the world ends, she and a few cockroaches will survive.

How would have Wilder, that ultimate survivor (and cynic), cast Itaya, I wonder? The Barbara Stanwyck role in "Ball of Fire?" The Greta Garbo role in "Ninotchka?" Note to Itaya's agent: Wilder may be gone, but the world awaits.

Linda, Linda, Linda, rating: ★★★☆, runtime: 114 min.

Nobuhiro Yamashita is a deadpan minimalist in the Aki Kaurismaki and Jim Jarmusch line, making films whose comedy derives from exact, wry observation of the offbeat in the midst of the mundane.

His latest, "Linda, Linda, Linda," would seem to be his leap (or shuffle) into the mainstream. Set in a provincial high school, and with a storyline about a girl band's dream of school-festival glory, it stars Yu Kashi ("Lorelei") and other idol talents, as well as a soundtrack by James Iha, formerly of The Smashing Pumpkins.

But Yamashita is still Yamashita — that beat poet of the quotidian — and "Linda, Linda, Linda" makes the many local teen movies about struggling athletes or musicans look fake to varying degrees. Nearly all the conventional tropes — the initial defeats and humiliations, the clashes with unsympathetic teachers and classmates and the final triumph before a huge, cheering crowd — are conspicuous by their absence. Instead, he shows us the way Japanese high-school life actually unfolds, the tedium of band practice included. He also gets the way teens really relate to each other, with the emotional temperature set on cool and the verbal volume on low, and the way they can suddenly downshift maturity gears from 16 to 10 — or upshift to 25.

He first introduces us to three band members: cute, quiet Nozomi (Shiori Sekine) on bass; bossy, steely willed Kei (Yu Kashi) on guitar; and perky, boy-crazy Kyoko (Aki Maeda) on drums. Just before their performance at the school festival — their one real chance to shine — their lead guitarist and vocalist drops out with an injured hand.

Now unable to perform the original songs they have so laboriously rehearsed, the girls instead decide to do "Linda, Linda, Linda," a three-chord rocker by the 1980s band The Blue Hearts. Kei can sub on lead guitar, but they still need a vocalist. They search unsuccessfully until, out of desperation, they ask a gawky Korean exchange-student named Song (Bae Doona), who immediately agrees even though she can barely speak Japanese, let alone rock in it.

How can the girls get their act together, with the festival only three days away? Here you might expect the film to kick into high gear, as though a three-minute performance in a high-school gym were a Broadway opening. And to be sure, Kei, Nozomi and Kyoko work hard — we see them passed out around their instruments more than once — but they refuse to overdo it.

Also, despite a glare that looks as though it could slice titanium, Kei never goes ballistic, even when Kyoko is late for a practice after dallying with a male classmate at a festival crepe stand. Instead, she stays resolutely on task, dragging everyone to a rehearsal studio where her guitarist boyfriend plays. A stocking-capped dropout, he can barely string two coherent sentences together.

Song takes her new role – lead vocalist — with a grim seriousness that her bandmates smile at — but never mock. This forbearance is another departure, this time from the many Japanese films and TV dramas showing teens as cruel to outsiders.

Song, though, is a pure-hearted girl of the old school — a type her bandmates find refreshing and one boy finds captivating. (His fumbling declaration of love is one of the film's comic high points.) Also, her voice has a power and drive that is perfect for The Blue Hearts' song, if only she can unleash it.

As Song, Korean star Bae Doona steals every scene she's in, with no effort or self-consciousness. "Linda, Linda, Linda," however, is less her vehicle than Yamashita's affectionate look at that short, precious moment called youth. He gets it right, while making it look easy, which is quite an accomplishment.

Other, slicker, teen movies may make more box-office noise, but tune into Yamashita's little low-watt film. It will be playing in your head long after the rest have vanished into the ether.

Cycling Chronicles: Landscapes the Boy Saw, 17-Sai no Fukei — Shonen wa Nani o Mita no ka, rating: ★★★★, runtime: 90 min.

We're all familiar with the figure of the old director, a power in his time, who has fallen into a slump, but longs to recapture former glories, while lamenting the sad state of movies and the world in general. Then there is Koji Wakamatsu, an enfant terrible of the 1960s, who made experimental/political/erotic films that scandalized guardians of public morals, and who associated with notorious radicals, including scriptwriter and Japanese Red Army member Masao Adachi.

In the 1970s Wakamatsu became "king of the pinks," churning out soft porn flicks on the cheap and by the dozen, until the video revolution of the 1980s marginalized pink-film production. He also took on more mainstream assignments, but with patchy success, and in recent years, plagued by health problems, has struggled to keep working. Instead of descending into embittered codgerdom, however, Wakamatsu has made a film, "Cycling Chronicles: Landscapes the Boy Saw," that expresses the sort of personal passion and formal boldness I seldom see in the work of directors half his age.

It's also the film of a veteran who, after decades of flouting conventions and pushing boundaries, now has the confidence and daring to be simple and direct. "All you need for a movie is a girl and gun," Wakamatsu idol Jean-Luc Godard famously declared. For "Cycling Chronicles" Wakamatsu has substituted a teenage boy for the girl and a bicycle for the gun, while sharply critiquing Japanese society and showing us the world through his troubled hero's eyes. A film that at first seems little more than spinning wheels and labored breathing develops a hypnotic power, poetic resonance and narrative momentum, despite a lack of standard movie incident.

It is based on the true story of a 17-year-old boy in Okayama Prefecture who, in the winter of 2000, killed his mother with a baseball bat and fled north on his mountain bike, pedaling for 17 days until the police ran him to ground. What intrigued Wakamatsu about this story was not just the boy's crime, but his form of escape. Why north in the dead of winter? Rejecting easy explanations, Wakamatsu retraced the boy's steps, trying to see what he had seen. In the rugged mountains and sea coasts of the Tohoku region, he found intimations of the boy's state of mind. He also found the makings of a film.

On January 6, 2004, Wakamatsu and a tiny crew started a 17-day shoot that approximated the boy's route, though their starting and ending points (Ikebukuro and the northern tip of Honshu) were different. They filmed on the fly, without a script, though Wakamatsu and three collaborators wrote one later.

Playing the boy, newcomer Tasuku Emoto spends much screen time climbing hills and battling winds, while saying little or nothing to the various people he encounters on the way.

This may sound like the very definition of boredom — a two-wheeled trip to nowhere, with a sullen teenager as a reluctant guide. And yet the sight of the boy's whirling legs and mask of a face, as he slogs though a winter landscape of desolate beauty, compels attention and invites speculation. Is he trying to obliterate feelings of guilt and regret — to sweat and freeze them out? Or is his journey a form of atonement through self-inflicted suffering?

Instead of giving us clear answers, the film supplies the boy's unfiltered thoughts, in captions and narration. As he passes though a Shinjuku crowd, at the start of his journey, captions flash on the screen: "Why are you gathered here? You have nothing to do with me. You are just scenery."

But he listens attentively to an old man in a station waiting room and an old Korean woman in a mountain hut, as they tell stories of being teenagers in wartime Japan. Unlike him, they want their memories to endure — and are articulate and passionate in relating them.

Though he never drops his mask, the boy connects with them in a way he never could with his own parents: They have no need or desire to judge him, while also having experienced deadly violence, if in extremely different circumstances.

Finally, he arrives at a rocky coast, with no other human beings in sight. His bike chain is broken and his memories — of his neat room, his smiling mother, his bat descending in a vicious arc — are still with him. Is he trapped in a hell of his own making? Or can he be saved?

The climax, like much of the rest of the film, is open to interpretation. The boy is not a protagonist in a morality play, but an empty vessel that will accept anything poured into it — from rote education to parental expectations — until it cracks and shatters. His journey is also ours, to make of what we will, as we pedal with him into the night.

Hanging Garden, Kuchu Teien, rating: ★★★★, runtime: 114 min.

Some people have all the luck — and some can't get a break. Toshiaki Toyoda falls into the latter category. After completing "Hanging Garden" — the best film of his career — he was arrested at his home for possession of 3.9 grams of stimulants.

In Hollywood, news of this sort — talent in drug trouble with the law — becomes tabloid fodder, but the career damage can be often managed. Thus the serial resurrections of Robert Downey Jr.

In the scandal-shy Japanese entertainment world, however, drug arrests are bad news indeed.

There was speculation that the distributor, Asmik Ace, might pull "Hanging Garden" from the theaters entirely. It would be somewhat like the Fox network dumping "Ally McBeal" because Downey went off the wagon yet again.

Toyoda, who debuted in 1999 with the surreal gangster film "Pornostar" and later directed "Unchain," "Blue Spring" and "9 Souls," still has his legal cross to bear. "Hanging Garden," however, has been rightfully saved from straight-to-DVD oblivion; it opens at Eurospace in Shibuya.

Based on Mitsuyo Kakuta's best-selling novel, the film sounds like yet another in a long line of black-comic takes on the Japanese family.

The Kyobashis are an average family (salaryman Dad, housewife Mom, two teenage kids) living in an average apartment complex in an average Tokyo suburb. Mother Eriko (Kyoko Koizumi), however, rigorously enforces a non-average rule: everyone must tell the truth about everything. So when daughter Mana (Anne Suzuki) asks early one morning how she was conceived, Eriko and hubby Takashi (Itsuji Itao) smilingly tell her they did the deed in a love hotel called Nozaru (Wild Monkey), which is still in business.

When Mana relates this story to her boyfriend (Ryo Katsuji), he is flummoxed — his parents would certainly never say such a thing and he would certainly never ask them. Undeterred, she goes to check out the hotel, with the reluctant boyfriend in tow.

So far, so funny. Toyoda, however, does not allow us to sit back and laugh at his family of eccentrics — instead he pulls the curtain on the fake family-harmony act to reveal the dysfunctional reality: Dad is a feckless philanderer, Mana and younger brother Ko (Masahiro Hirota) are slackers who rarely show their faces at school — and all three routinely lie to Eriko and each other.

Eriko is not what she seems either. While assiduously playing the role of the good wife and mother and carefully tending the flowers of her roof garden, she is a woman on the verge of a nervous breakdown, who blames her ailing mother (Michiyo Okusu) for her miserable, lonely childhood. Her ironclad "rule" and her "perfect" persona are her ways of controlling a disorderly reality, of pretending that the lies don't exist — or hurt.

In protraying this reality, Toyoda's camera spins, rocks and sways to the point of vertigo, while his close-ups of objects (a blaze of candles on a birthday cake, a blood-soaked rose) vibrate with symbolism ranging from the vaguely disturbing to the outright menacing.

We get it — and then it starts to get to us. The Hanging Garden of Babylon decorating the lampshade over the family dinner table — the film's first image — may be a winking allusion to the familial paradise that is about to crumble, but once we are inside the Garden's walls as they shake and fall, we are in no mood for a giggle.

This approach is more Luis Bunuel, the master Surrealist and exposer of bourgeois hypocrisies, than the typical Japanese humanist director, always looking for the good side of even his worst characters. Toyoda doesn't despise his family for their various sins, though he exposes Dad, in thrall to his bossy longtime mistress Asako (Hiromi Nagasaku) and his fiery new lover Mina (Sonim), as a weasel and a wuss. He strips away their masks as coolly as he might peal the cellophane from a convenience store rice ball. We also learn that Ko is an architecture buff, whose investigations lead him to the Nozaru, a temple of 1970s kitsch excess. Meanwhile, Mana is trying to maintain some semblance of order and continuity in her life by keeping a small stuffed bear in the Nozaru room where she was conceived (unbeknownst to the other guests, of course). A comforting presence, it is there for her each time she returns.

The most fully revealed characters, however, are Eriko and her chain-smoking, straight-talking, terminally irresponsible mother. Their ping-pong battle of recriminations and justifications, fought over Mom's blazing birthday cake, is as sparely poetic and piercingly real as anything in a David Mamet play. Bust Toyoda, if you will, but don't bury his movie.

Rampo Noir, Rampo Jigoku, rating: ★★★, runtime: 134 min.

The stories of Edogawa Rampo, born Taro Hirai in 1894, exert a continuing fascination over Japanese filmmakers. Modeled on the work of Edgar Allan Poe (from whom he took his pen name) and Arthur Conan Doyle, Rampo's tales of the mysterious and the macabre are far better known in Japan than abroad.

An Amazon search reveals only one Rampo title in English, a 1956 collection titled "Japanese Tales of Mystery and Imagination."

Two young Japanese directors — Suguru Takeuchi and Atsushi Kaneko — and two older ones — Akio Jissoji and Hisayasu Sato — have joined forces to make "Rampo Noir," a four-segment omnibus based on Rampo's stories. All four-star Tadanobu Asano, the king of the indies.

As the segments show, Rampo differed from his namesake in not only era and nationality, but also sensibility. Poe, an early Victorian romantic, made his women into sexless angels. Rampo was a roue, whose famous story "The Human Chair" is about a chairmaker who, obsessed with a woman, sells her an upholstered chair made so that he can climb inside when she is sitting in it.

The film's first segment, Takeuchi's "Mars Canal," takes this idea one mind-bending step farther. A naked long-haired man (Asano) wanders through a desolate wasteland (Iceland, standing in for the "Mars" of the title). He happens upon a circular pond and peers into the water. Seeing his lover's face, he flashes back on a scene of violent sex with her — a tall, muscular woman whose hair is as long as his own. Then he notices that he now has the body of his lover. With his long fingernails, he begins to tear at his flesh.

Takeuchi films this shortest of all segments with only silent images flashing like a nightmare that, horror of horrors, might not be a nightmare at all, but rather karmic retribution.

The second segment, Jissoji's "The Hell of Mirrors," is more conventionally shot — but equally primal in its shocks. Kogoro Akechi (Asano) — Rampo's version of Sherlock Holmes — takes an interest in the sudden deaths of two women. In both cases a Japanese-style mirror was present in the room where the death occurred, made by one Toru Itsuki (Hiroki Narimiya), a wickedly handsome stationery shop master who knew the victims intimately. In his hands, mirrors become powerful occult objects, able to suck out their victims' souls. Then Toru seduces his sister-in-law (Harumi Ogawa) and presents her with his latest mirror, the deadliest of all.

More than his collaborators, Jissoji brings out the characters of his principals, including the sexual current flowing between Toru and the poker-faced, hyper-aware Akechi. He also generates more narrative excitement, despite the pseudo-scientific rationales for the mirrors' powers.

More straightforwardly "ero-guro" (erotic and grotesque) in the classic Rampo style is Sato's "Caterpillar." Lieutenant Sunaga (Nao Omori) returns from the war a mangled human stump, with no arms or legs, able to communicate only with grunts and moans — and his agonized eyes. His young, nubile wife Tokiko (Yukiko Okamoto) tires of caring for her "caterpillar" of a hubby and begins to use him as a sex toy. Then she discovers a more exciting game: torture. Meanwhile, a resident artist (Ryuhei Matsuda) begins to take a twisted interest in the erotic goings on. To him Sunaga is a human objet d'art, who needs further work to become truly "perfect." Unknown to this pair, Akechi (Asano) is on the case, intrigued by images of Sunaga's severed limbs, preserved in formaldehyde.

One of the so-called "four emperors" of the "pinku eiga" (pink film) scene, Sato films his story's S&M horrors with an undisguised relish and a pronounced black comic streak.

The final segment, Kaneko's "Crawling Bugs," is the most extreme and confusing. Asano plays two roles — the first as a shy, allergy-prone driver for a sultry actress (Tamaki Ogawa), the second as the actress's commanding lover, who can make her do things the driver — a secret witness to their rough sex — can only dream of. When the driver finally screws up his courage and, bouquet in hand, confesses his love, she cruelly rejects him and he snaps. Employer and employee finally unite — in a bizarre fantasy land of his psychotic imagination.

Kaneko lays on the steamy S&M atmospherics, but he is too clever by half with his editing, making it hard for the inattentive to keep the two Asanos straight. All in all, though, Edogawa is well served by his four interpreters, who have made him cool again for a new generation of fans. A truly sick — and talented — mind never goes out of style.

2006

Who's Camus Anyway?, Camus Nante Shiranai, rating: ★★★★★, runtime: 115 min.
Beginning with his 1976 debut film, the biker documentary "God Speed You! Black Emperor," Mitsuo Yanagimachi has repeatedly dealt with alienated youth and isolated individuals in modern Japanese society. His heroes, such as the god-maddened woodsman in "Fire Festival" (1985) and the socially marginalized Chinese slaughterhouse worker in "Of Love, Tokyo" (1992) are enigmas whose actions can be selfish, criminal or simply insane. Their stories, told with stark, arresting images, go to straight the dark heart of the world in all its manifestations, human, inhuman and divine.

After making "The Wandering Peddlers" in 1995, a documentary about Taiwanese peddlers, Yanagimachi did not direct another film for a decade.

He has broken his silence with "Who's Camus Anyway?" a drama about a student film production, supervised by a teacher (Hirotaro Honda) who is a Yanagimachi stand-in. The film was screened in the Directors Fortnight section of the 2005 Cannes Film Festival and won the Best Picture Award in the Japanese Eyes section of last year's Tokyo International Film Festival.

As one of the Japanese Eyes judges, I was struck, not only by Yanagimachi's ability to take up essentially where he had left off, but also by how far his film stood above the other 10 section entries. Though in a lighter key than usual for Yanagimachi (only prop blood is shed, for one thing), "Camus" is an intricately structured, deeply meditated film, made by a master at the top of his form.

It begins with a dazzling traveling shot of students and their teacher, Professor Nakajo (Honda), walking and intersecting across the Rikkyo University campus. It sets the stage for what is to come — a film about a film that comments on the process of filmmaking.

The students, members of the literature department's film workshop, are preparing to shoot "The Bored Murderer," a film based on Albert Camus' "The Stranger." Things start going wrong almost immediately, beginning with the lead actor's sudden departure. The director, handsome, smooth-talking Matsukawa (Shuji Kashiwabara), soon recruits Ikeda (Hideo Nakaizumi), whose blond-haired androgyny (though he insists he is straight) makes him perfect for the role of the alienated antihero, who decides to murder an old woman just to see what it feels like.

Meanwhile, Matsukawa's clingy girlfriend, Yukari (Hinano Yoshikawa), who has transferred schools to be near him, is dubbed "Adele" by one film-literate student, after the love-obsessed title character in Francois Truffaut's "The History of Adele H."

Professor Nakajo's air of gloomy preoccupation inspires another student nickname: Aschenbach — the doomed middle-aged hero of Luchino Visconti's "Death in Venice." Unbeknownst to the students, or anyone else, Nakajo is secretly infatuated with Rei (Meisa Kuroki), a mixed-race beauty he watches (from a discreet distance) dance each day with a campus hip-hop crew.

At the center of the film's romantic roundelay, however, is Hisada (Ai Maeda), the cute, intense assistant director of the "The Bored Murderer," whose boyfriend has gone off mountain climbing for a week. Matsukawa, Ikeda and the film's cameraman, Motosugi (Shinnosuke Abe), all take this opportunity to hit on her, with the first two stealing kisses. They may only be blowing off erotic steam in the pressure-cooker of a film shoot, but Hisada, a serious type, is wracked with guilt because she did little to discourage their advances.

At his point the film may sound like an arty campus love comedy, but as it moves into it's middle section, the story deepens and darkens. "Adele" abases herself before Matsukawa at every opportunity — until she cracks under the weight of his indifference and disdain. Meanwhile, Aschenbach arranges to have lunch with Rei through their mutual acquaintance Oyama (Tomorowo Taguchi), an intense 35-year-old grad student with an important secret of his own. When Aschenbach's plan goes awry — never mind how — he plunges into drunken oblivion.

Meanwhile, on the set, Ikeda is getting deeper into the role of the student murderer. Will he, like Adele and Aschenbach, also cross a dangerous line? When the frenzy of production ends, what will have changed — and who will remain?

The climax, in which that fake blood comes out, seems like a radical departure from all that has come before. But its very intensity — as well as its blurring of fiction and reality — powerfully sums up all that has happened. The blood, not being real, can be expunged — but never the unholy impulses it symbolizes.

In making this leap in the dark, Yanagimachi risks of baffling his audience. But he meticulously prepares it to leap with him, through gestures and acts whose whole meaning only becomes apparent later, and through an intricate web of relationships whose flawless design is less displayed than suggested (though it is certainly there to see).

His use of Ikeda typifies this process. Sexually ambiguous and emotionally opaque, he first impresses foppishly strange. And yet in rehearsal he clicks into his murderous character with a focus that, in retrospect, chills. In their suddenness and arbitrariness his attempts at seduction foreshadow later, deadlier acts, while shining a revealing light on his targets.

But who is this interpreter of Camus, anyway? Like the other principals in Yanagimachi's masterfully choreographed dance of art and life, youth and age, desire and death, he is what real people often are: a multitude in one skin, whose mysteries can take a lifetime to plumb.

Gratitude, Aogeba Totoshi, rating: ★★★★, runtime: 82 min.

Jun Ichikawa's "Gratitude" depicts one man's response to an approaching death in his family — but from an unexpected angle. He is Koichi (Terry Ito), a middle-aged elementary schoolteacher whose father (Takeshi Kato), a teacher once himself, has been diagnosed with terminal cancer and has returned home to die. Koichi, his wife Mari (Hiroko Yakushimaru), and his mother (Miyoko Aso) are all there to care for him, but the strain begins to show, as when Koichi discovers a boy in his fifth-grade class looking at the photograph of a dead body on the Internet. Usually avuncular with his charges, Koichi curtly orders the boy to turn it off his screen.

The boy, it turns out, has lost his own father and is now obsessed with death. When he asks Koichi why looking at a corpse is wrong, Koichi has no ready answer. Meanwhile, his father, a prickly type who was always strict with his students, is passing his final days alone. Koichi has the idea of bringing volunteers from his class to visit him, but the boy is the only one to come a second time.

Thematically, "Gratitude" is a continuation of "Dying at a Hospital)," Ichikawa's 1993 masterpiece about five terminal cancer patients. Dramatically, though, it's quite different, since the focus is less on the last days of the father, who is mostly a mute presence, than on how his survivors cope with the ultimate fact of death.

Ichikawa films this story in his usual elegiac style, including shots of Tokyo cityscapes that capture the evanescence of life with poetic clarity and grace. At the same time, he doesn't prettify the actions of his principals, which in the boy's case verge on the morbid and, in Koichi's, on the exploitative. He embraces their humanity in all its complexity and suffering.

Terry Ito, a sharp-tongued TV talent making his film debut, gives a firmly grounded performance as Koichi. His casting was an inspired choice, in a film full of them.

"Gratitude" takes its title from a traditional song students sing on graduation day to express gratitude to their teachers. It proves again what I've been saying for years — Ichikawa has long since graduated to the ranks of Japanese masters.

The Sea Gull Restaurant, Kamome Shokudo, rating: ★★★★, runtime: 92 min.

Don't we all have the urge to chuck it all in, hop on a plane and fly to the Great Good Place, where we'd live in peace and contentment forever — or until our cards max out? This urge is particularly strong in urban Japan, where images of tropical islands beckon from fliers at street-corner travel agencies or posters in crowded commuter trains, and where the racks at the neighborhood bookstores are crammed with travel guides offering ultimate getaways that ultimately require more time and money than the average punter can afford.

As Naoko Ogigami's "The Sea Gull Restaurant" demonstrates so enticingly, a lucky few live the dream — or rather their best approximation of it. Her film about three women, all single and past 30, who find new lives in Helsinki is not another you-go-girl celebration of female empowerment, however.

Like the films of Finland's Aki Kaurismaki that Ogigami so obviously admires, it is more of an engaging and perceptive essay on the basics of existence — food, friendship, work, love, home. It gives us glimpses of the tourist's Finland, including the gulls circling Helsinki harbor, but its usual perspective is the intimate and everyday. We see far more of the interior of the title restaurant than the outside world, but then so do its three main characters.

For those used to the more common panoramic-famous-views approach of Japanese films set in foreign lands, "Kamome Shokudo" may start to feel claustrophobic. Even I, no travelogue fan, started to long for a long shot or two. But Ogigami, knows exactly what she is doing and why. Patterns and motifs that at first look cutesy or mundane begin — through repetition and expansion — to acquire resonance and weight.

The gulls in the harbor, seen in shot after shot, end up being more than feathered bits of local color. They come to resemble the three heroines — free spirits who, after much wandering, have found a home.

The proprietor of the title establishment is Sachie (Satomi Kobayashi), a spunky, forthright type who wants to bring home-style Japanese cooking to Finland. But she gets only skeptical looks from passersby, particularly a trio of middle-aged women who serve as a comic Greek chorus. She perseveres, however, and finally a teenage boy (Jarkko Niemi) shuffles into her small, spotless eatery and reveals himself as a speaker of (very limited) Japanese and a fan of anime, especially Gatchaman. Does Sachie, he wonders, know the lyrics to the Gatchaman theme song? Sachie, to her embarrassment, does not.

That evening in a bookshop cafe, she encounters Midori (Hairi Katagiri), a tall, gawky woman with a perpetually startled look, who happens to know the words of the stupid song that has been plaguing Sachie all day. Relieved, Sachie asks her new acquaintance why she has come to Finland. Midori tells her one day she closed her eyes, jabbed a finger at a world map — and it landed on the Land of a Thousand Lakes. Feeling she has found a kindred spirit, Sachie asks the hotel-less Midori if she would like to stay at her place. Soon, Midori is waitressing at the restaurant, though her only customer is the boy, who comes in every day for free coffee and a dose of Japanese culture.

One afternoon another customer (Markku Peltola) walks in — a big, shambling man with a knowing look who shows Sachie how to brew the perfect cup of coffee — then walks out the door, seemingly never to return. This brief encounter, however, works a magical change in the restaurant's fortunes. Attracted by the aroma of the coffee and Sachie's mouth-watering cinnamon buns, customers trickle in, including the Greek Chorus.

Then another Japanese woman appears on the scene — the bespectacled, polite, decidedly eccentric Masako (Masako Motai), stranded in Helsinki, her luggage having gone missing. Sachie and Midori soon have another hand in the kitchen, whipping up scrumptious omusubi (rice balls), or as Sachie calls it, "Japanese soul food."

As far as drama goes, there isn't a lot more. A plump, frowzy woman, after glaring through the restaurant's window day after day (and scaring the impressionable Midori half to death), lumbers through the door and, through a chain of events I won't describe here, finally forces the trio to leave their island of Japanese-ness to encounter the Finnish world around them. It is bit too cozy, this island, with a slightly complacent air of spreading Japanese culture to the natives. But it is real enough in its feeling of freedom and loneliness — the crown and thorns of expatriation.

Toward the end, Ogigami takes the story to another, surreal level. Nothing outlandish — just an overt, liberating expression of the magic that had been there all along, in the hearts of its three heroines and their new home. Maybe it's something in the water — or the omusubi.

Route 225, rating: ★★★☆, runtime: 101 min.

Lewis Carroll first sent Alice down the rabbit hole with "Alice's Adventures in Wonderland" in 1865, but today it is the Japanese who are most fond of stories about plucky females in fantasy lands or parallel worlds. Anime master Hayao Miyazaki has made a thriving career from this sort of story, from his classic "My Neighbor Totoro" in 1988 to the megahit "Spirited Away" in 2001.

Many recent live-action Japanese films also take up variations of this theme, from Hideyuki Hirayama's "Turn," about a young woman who is hit by a truck and finds herself alone in another dimension, to Kaze Shindo's "Korogare! Tamako (Tumble! Tamako)," whose flaky, steel-helmeted heroine is almost as fantastic as her brightly colored, severely circumscribed world.

In his new film, "Route 225," Yoshihiro Nakamura takes an approach somewhere between stranger-in-a-strange-land fantasy and coming-of-age parable. His 14-year-old heroine and her pudgy younger brother may make a wrong turn into an alternative reality, but instead of plunging into Miyazakian adventures with strange creatures, they find themselves trying to unravel a maddening puzzle, with no logical clues to its solution, somewhat like Alice trying to decipher the nonsensical commands of the Queen of Hearts.

More than its plot machinery, however, "Route 225" is concerned with the primal fears that grip us all at one time or another, from kindergarteners separated from Mom in a busy department store to adolescents grappling with the scary business of growing up. At the same time, its heroine is a normal-enough kid, if one with more sang-froid than usual. As played by newcomer Mikako Tabe, she is bracingly within the realm of the believable.

If anything, the film stays too close to the reassuringly everyday to deliver more than an existential tingle, instead of a chilling plunge into the void. Also, its occasional attempts to squeeze tears feel forced, because the world the two children have lost verges on the absurd. But its unexpected ending is exactly right — and heartening. You may not always get what you want, it says, but you can usually cope.

Eriko (Tabe) is a second-year student in an average junior high school who leads an average middle-class existence with her housewife Mom (Eri Ishida), salaryman Dad (Kyusaku Shimada) and younger brother Daigo (Chikara Iwata). Ever-busy, ever-chirpy Mom, who turns out cutesy flower arrangements and glops milk into the dinner stew to make it "richer" (that is, inedible) is a bit too much for the down-to-earth Eriko. Dad is nice, but is rarely home long enough to make more than a fleeting impression.

Then, one day, Mom asks Eriko to fetch Daigo from a nearby park. She finds him sitting on a swing, in his undershirt, looking disconsolate. A fun-loving classmate scribbled something insulting with a magic marker on his white uniform shirt — and Daigo knows that Mom is going to kill him when she sees it. Eriko gets him moving homeward, while teasing him for being such a loser. So far, so typical. Then they turn a corner and see the sea, which is odd because they live nowhere near it.

Global warming in action? No, it's weirder. Leaving the beach-that-shouldn't be, they wander down suddenly unfamiliar streets, unable to find their way home. Then they come across one of Daigo's classmates, a girl named Kumanoi — and Eriko asks her the way, while Daigo hangs back, looking confused — and horrified.

It turns out that Kumanoi shouldn't be there either, for a reason best left unexplained. Eriko and Daigo finally make it home, but find their parents missing, though the stew is on the stove.

Somehow, they have stumbled into another dimension that is the same as their own save for a few critical differences, the biggest being the absence of Mom and Dad.

How to get back? Eriko and Daigo struggle to find a key that will unlock the dimensional door, somewhat like Bill Murray's desperate reporter in "Groundhog Day." Unlike Murray, however, they have a link to their old world — a phone card with agonizingly little time left on it.

Nakamura, who has written scripts for films by directors Yoichi Sai ("Quill") and Hideo Nakata ("Dark Water"), has obviously studied Danny Rubin's masterpiece, which has been called both a flawless piece of comic writing and a profoundly religious statement about the meaning of salvation. Nakamura's script for "Route 225" is seemingly simpler, closer to a children's story than the New Testament. I kept waiting for Eriko and Daigo to discover the magic formula, say the magic words.

But Nakamura turns out to be deeper — and wiser — than I'd suspected. He does not, however, exploit an unsettling fact about the folks who inhabit the children's new dimension — all of them are utter strangers. The Kumanoi that Eriko and Daigo meet on an unfamiliar street is not the same Kumanoi who was once in Daigo's class. They are actually all alone, like two space explorers stranded on an alien planet, surrounded by doppelgangers of people they once knew. It's enough to drive you mad — or make you stronger. Which is it going to be?

Memories of Tomorrow, Ashita no Kioku, rating: ★★★⯨, runtime: 122 min.

The usual point of view in Alzheimer's films is that of the caregivers, who may suffer agonies of impotence, frustration and grief, but at least end their ordeals with their minds intact — and their characters strengthened. The elderly they are tending, on the other hand, are typically shown from the outside and, by the last reel, become the lovable, harmless boke rojin (senile oldies) of cultural stereotype. The object is to inspire sighs and tears for human frailty — at one remove.

"Memories of Tomorrow" falls into the medical melodrama genre category, but its Alzheimer's victim is a man not yet 50, in what should be his professional and personal prime. Also, director Yukihiko Tsutsumi takes the victim's perspective with a gut-wrenching specificity. This, I thought as I watched the film, is what it's like to have, not just the occasional senior moment, but one's entire mental world dissolve away like ice crystals in the sun, leaving nothing but a puddle, mist — vacuum.

Ken Watanabe, who is now Hollywood's best-known Japanese actor for his work in "The Last Samurai," "Batman Returns" and "Memoirs of a Geisha," plays the afflicted hero with the sort of heart-and-soul performance that wins Oscars. The technical and emotional grandstanding common to these performances, however, is conspicuous by its absence. Instead, Watanabe, who has fought his own life-or-death battle with leukemia from age 30, plays his character — a successful ad agency executive — from the inside, in all his confusion, terror and despair.

Those who know Watanabe only from his more macho roles will be surprised (or shocked) at how convincingly he declines to a shrunken, prematurely aged shell. Think Nicolas Cage in "Leaving Las Vegas," minus the booze pallor and shakes. Watanabe, who also executive produced the film from a novel by Hiroshi Ogiwara, may have slimmed down for the part, but the core of his performance is spiritual transformation — and a terrifyingly natural emptying out.

The story begins with the exec, Saeki (Watanabe), directing a pitch for a major account. He and his team snag it, but his chronic memory lapses — a forgotten name here, a missed meeting there — begin interfering with his job. Together with wife Emiko (Kanako Higuchi), a dutiful but much put-upon sort, he goes to the hospital for tests and gets the devastating diagnosis. Tempted to end it all, he is dissuaded by his young doctor's vow to do everything possible, and Emiko's reminder that their only daughter (Kazue Fukiishi) is about to get married and have their first grandchild.

With the goals of a wedding and childbirth to spur him on, he begins treatment, but despite all Emiko's efforts, including health foods and detailed memos, his decline continues. He manages to get through the wedding speech — an ordeal for even the healthy — but finally realizes he can no longer keep up pretenses at work — or anywhere else. He resigns first as department chief, then from the company.

Meanwhile, Emiko is beginning a new career as a saleswoman at an upscale pottery shop, continuing an interest both of them shared in their youth. Saeki starts to make pottery himself, but becomes increasingly confused, lonely and angry. How could this be happening to him, so relentlessly and soon? He lashes out — but finds no escape.

This downward spiral is standard for an Alzheimer's drama, but Tsutsumi, takes us into his hero's mental world, whirling the camera, distorting the image and otherwise expressing Saeki's disorientation and isolation. The result is reminiscent of the last scenes of "2001: A Space Odyssey," when Dave Bowman is alone in an alien world, watching his life slip away with an eerie rapidity.

As Emiko, Kanako Higuchi first impresses as a strained, sexless paragon — but as her husband disappears before her eyes, her mask of empathy and composure shatters — and she explodes with anger and resentment over what she is losing — and never had. She still loves him, though, with a fierceness that is all the more powerful for being so contained.

"Memories of Tomorrow" may smooth over certain aspects of the disease, including the final, irreversible descent, but it also captures something of its horror and pathos. And it also proves that Watanabe can act, in a role he was meant to play. Who knows if he will find another, but this very personal film proves that, in at least its movie stars, Japan is exporting its best.

Memories of Matsuko, Kiraware Matsuko no Issho, rating: ★★★☆, runtime: 129 min.

Directors of TV commercials have to quickly grab easily distracted viewers against a blizzard of competition. When they move into feature films, many still assume short attention spans — and blitz audience eyeballs accordingly.

Looking at the trailer of Tetsuya Nakashima's new film "Memories of Matsuko," it's easy to believe this veteran director of commercials, as well as the international hit "Kamikaze Girls," falls into this category. The rush of CG-assisted images, beginning with a musical stage show about a fairy tale princess, are colorful, bubbly and glitzy to point of self parody. The title character, a girl we first see watching the show with her dour dad (Akira Emoto), is so smiley and bright-eyed that she might pop from sheer delight. Surely this has to be a comedy?

But the girl (Miki Nakatani) grows up and, instead of meeting the Prince Charming of her dreams, suffers every possible calamity: A popular teacher at a provincial junior high school in the early 1970s, she nobly takes responsibility for a student's theft — and is fired. Considered a disgrace by her family, she reels from one bad relationship to another. Seeking love, she finds only abandonment and abuse. Then she becomes a massage-parlor whore, kills her pimp and goes to prison.

Her salvation, ironically, is Ryu (Yusuke Iseya), the young thief who cost her the teaching job.

Now a gangster, he encounters Matsuko on her downward slide and falls in love with her. She returns his passion and, after her release from prison, finds happiness with him. It can't last, though — and Matsuko begins her final descent to loneliness, madness and death.

Sounds depressing, doesn't it? But asked to clean Matsuko's disaster zone of a flat (she was a pathological hoarder in her declining years) her slacker nephew (Eita) discovers mementos of her checkered past, and realizes that she lived life to the full, never giving up her dream of love.

The splashy visuals and brassy musical numbers that initially seemed to channel "Chicago," including its slick cynicism, take on new meaning and weight.

They express the inner Matsuko, in all her irrepressible vitality and optimism.

Nakashima's approach — including uptempo song-and-dance numbers to celebrate Matsuko's downer existence — may look outright odd, but he used a similar one in "Kamikaze Girls," an exuberantly surreal, candy-colored romp about two outsider girls — one a sneering punk biker, another a frilly fashionista — who become unlikely allies and friends. "Matsuko," in other words, is Nakashima being Nakashima. Expecting this master of visual fireworks to film a sober, tasteful social document is like expecting Tom Wolfe to write a measured, balanced, dull-as-dust editorial.

At the same time, in "Matsuko" Nakashima is trying to move beyond the cult can base of "Kamikaze" into the mainstream. Thus the impression of strain — since he is more naturally a black humorist than a feel-good entertainer. Also, the gap between the sheer awfulness of what befalls Matsuko and the film's glitzy look and upbeat tone would be hard to bridge for anyone, entertainer or no. Nakashima succeeds better than most — for his stylistic chutzpah, if nothing else.

Based on Muneki Yamada's eponymous best-selling novel, "Matsuko" in almost any other hands would be a dark melodrama about a woman who loved too well, lived too recklessly and drew no winning numbers in life's lottery. Nakashima's approach avoids — or rather explodes — genre cliches, but he also keep the focus firmly on his central message: Love gives life its value, despite appearances to the contrary.

The question is whether Matsuko's love for her hot-tempered, violence-prone gangster boyfriend is worth the physical and mental pain. I say walk quickly in the opposite direction — to freedom, safety and that rainy day stash in a postal-savings account. But that's just me.

Miki Nakatani, who played the nerdy hero's love interest in last year's smash "Train Man," shows more of her comic side in "Matsuko," especially in her scenes as a fallen woman, but she never loses sight of her character's passion — and persistence. There is a direct line from the little girl bubbling with romantic dreams and the woman holding onto her soul, while living a nightmare.

For all its box office ambitions, "Matsuko" is not really for the "Life Is Beautiful" crowd that wants its uplift straight. It's too contrary and strange, if gorgeously made. Something like Matsuko herself.

Hana, Hana Yori Mo Naho, rating: ★★☆, runtime: 127 min.

When I interviewed Hirokazu Koreeda about "Nobody Knows," his award-winning 2004 drama about children abandoned by their mother, I finished with a question about his new film, "Hana." Would it, I wondered, be anything like Yoji Yamada's "The Twilight Samurai," which depicted the samurai rank-

and-file with more realism than the genre standard, while satisfying the mass audience taste for flashing swords? "I want to make it as unlike Yamada's film as possible," he said.

Instead, Koreeda made it more like Akira Kurosawa's "Dodesukaden" (1970) and "The Lower Depths)" (1957). In other words, he removed the swashbuckling, while sympathetically, if comically, portraying the swordless lower classes of the Genroku Era (1688-1704).

"Dodesukaden" and "The Lower Depths" famously flopped. Will "Hana" meet the same fate? Not necessarily — though it is one of Koreeda's rare stumbles.

Not because of the performances, which are almost uniformly excellent. Koreeda has always been good with actors and in "Hana" he has drawn performances that both stand on their own and form part of a well-balanced whole. Nearly everyone plays a shade or two bigger than life — just as they do in countless other Japanese period films, but even the minor characters have histories and personalities, not just labels and ticks.

His staff, including cameraman Yutaka Yamazaki, who also photographed "After Life," "Distance" and "Nobody Knows," and costume designer Kazuko Kurosawa, who worked with her father Akira Kurosawa on his last three films, is also first rate, creating a nagaya (tenement house) neighborhood that looks lived in, not merely populated. More than most of the dozens of period films set in this Edo (old Tokyo) milieu, "Hana" illuminates the true conditions of the time, from the flimsiness of the houses, which with one good shake might be reduced to a giant wood pile, to the spirit of the people, with its mix of never-say-die grit and all-too-human weakness.

But for all its minor pleasures the story lacks anything major — change, catharsis, you name it. This, Koreeda suggests, was the way the unheroic, unexceptional majority really lived. True enough, perhaps, but since Koreeda's samurai hero remains the same affable, peace-loving fellow from beginning to end, who dodges challenges instead of facing them. I found myself taking only a mild interest in his doings. Yamada may have been guilty of using that chestnut — the big, character-testing showdown — as the climax of "The Twilight Samurai," but he also made his audience feel the anger of one man, the fear of another and the desperation of both.

Koreeda's hero is Sozaemon (Junichi Okada), a samurai who has come from Matsumoto to Edo to take his revenge against his father's killer. If he succeeds, he will not only fulfill his duty as a son, samurai and successor to his father's sword school, but receive 100 ryo from his clan.

He takes up residence in a nagaya and teaches the neighborhood children to supplement his meager funds — meager mainly because he spends so much on eating, drinking, bathing and other dissipations with his pleasure-loving buddy Sadajiro (Arata Furuta). He is also friends — and something more — with the lovely widow Osae (Rie Miyazawa) and her young son.

One day Sozaemon's skill with the sword — or rather wooden staff — is tested in a street fight with an unarmed tough. Sozaemon comes out the battered loser, with half the neighborhood, including the boy, looking on. Not long after, he is challenged by real samurai swordsmen, who are plotting their own revenge and suspect him of being a spy. This time, Sozaemon doesn't even put up a bumbling fight, but beats a hasty retreat instead. So he is not only a lousy swordsman, but a coward to boot. Finally, he crosses paths with his father's enemy (Tadanobu Asano), a big, silent man with a terrible facial scar, who has abandoned the sword and is living a quiet life with his wife and son. Will Sozaemon redeem himself?

That, the film soon makes clear, is the wrong question. Sozaemon's true test, we see, is whether he can reject the false, inhuman values of his caste. Koreeda treats this test as something of a joke — one that is cute, obvious and falls flat.

One fix would be to make "Hana" a straight comedy — but then it wouldn't be a Koreeda film. Another would be to cast an actor who can play both sides of the good/bad, strong/weak divide as Sozaemon instead of boy-band singer Junichi Okada, who is too handsome and cool to be a sympathetic coward. Too bad Bill Murray isn't 20 years younger — and Japanese.

It's Only Talk, Yawarakai Seikatsu, rating: ★★★★, runtime: 126 min.

In 2003 Shinobu Terajima made a career breakthrough in Ryuichi Hiroki's "Vibrator," playing Rei, an emotionally fragile writer who finds sexual and spiritual release on a road trip with Nao Omori's loquacious, mendacious, but ultimately understanding truck driver.

The daughter of 1960s' yakuza film star Junko Fuji and a veteran stage actress, Terajima was more than ready for this demanding role. Instead of indulging in the histrionics that often pass for screen acting here, she revealed Rei's every emotional tremor with a luminous delicacy and conviction. Playing a character who was a walking psychological disaster area — alcoholic, bulimic, neurotic — Terajima made her not only human, but sympathetic and attractive. Rei's triumph over her fears came not from a cliched story arc, but the depths of her being — and lifted the audience up with her. In her new film, "It's Only Talk," Terajima reunites with Hiroki and, briefly, with Omori.

Based on a novel by Akiko Itoyama, the film centers on Yuko, another single woman in her mid-30s with an unbalanced psyche and a life on hold. In other words, it starts as "Vibrator Part 2."

But instead of falling back on familiar attitudes and gestures — and then complaining about typecasting — Terajima creates a character who is subtly, but clearly, different from Rei. She is supported by some of the best male actors currently working, including Omori, Etsushi Toyokawa, Satoshi Tsumabuki, Shunsuke Matsuoka and Tomorowo Taguchi, but "It's Only Talk" is her vehicle.

It rambles in a way the tightly constructed "Vibrator" did not. It also lacks "Vibrator" 's feeling of urgency — of swimming through a choppy sea of lies and fears to something like truth, and a temporary peace. It opts instead for a more languid pace, including long minutes watching a depressed Yuko hibernating in her futon, but brings us finally to a bittersweet resolution.

Unlike Rei, Yuko has no career, no job — not even the standard-issue movie mother worrying back home. She lives alone, off the insurance she received after her parents' death. Her residence of choice is Kamata, a town that was once home to the Shochiku studio, but has since subsided to an out-at-the-elbows tackiness that Yuko finds comfortable and endearing.

As the film begins she is engaged in unorthodox sex with a self-confessed pervert (Taguchi) she met on the Internet. The pervert, a ratty-bearded, shifty-eyed middle-aged man, doesn't know quite what to make of his new playmate, who acts as though they have been sorting laundry together. Then a handsome, if cowardly, gangster (Tsumabuki) finds her blog about her life in Kamata and contacts her. They meet and compare medications — both are bipolar — but romance is not in the cards.

She also hooks up with two college pals, both of whom still have crushes on her. Homma (Matsuoka), a struggling politician, is the more persistent, though when he and Yuko find themselves alone he tries to beat a quick escape, claiming impotence. She chides him, saying that sex shouldn't come between friends — and persuades him to spend the night cuddling with her in her futon.

Before she can cure him and start a proper affair, her ne'er-do-well cousin Shoichi (Toyokawa) shows up, saying that he left his mistress, after his wife in Kyushu kicked him out. His karaoke business a failure, his personal life a bust, he has nowhere to go but to Yuko — his childhood friend, his confidant and something more.

She is wary of him at first — this 40-year-old guy tooling around in an ancient Thunderbird he bought when he was flush (or pretending to be so). But he is all she has left of family and, unlike nearly everyone else in her life, he knows her secrets and lies.

When the depressive side of her personality takes hold after an upsetting encounter, he is also the only one there to cook for her, medicate her and otherwise watch over her. Shoichi is no saint — he hits up Yuko for money when she is least able to resist him — but his natural buoyancy slowly, surely lifts her up, beyond the reach of her demons. But he has yet to get the better of his own.

Toyokawa, a versatile actor who has played everything from the mad serial killer in "Scissors Man" to the valiant Ainu brave in "Year Zero in the North," supplies all the requisites for the rascal Shoichi — including a credible combination of good-heartedness and unreliability.

Shoichi's duality is more than matched by that of Yuko, who is free-spiritedly clomping around Kamata in her brightly colored skirts and clunky boots one moment, the next collapsing into a lifeless heap, as though she were an inflatable toy popped by a needle.

She requires something more than Shoichi or the other broken men in her life can supply. By the end of her long journey, she knows what it is, just as she's probably known all along. We all need a soft life — the literal meaning of the Japanese title "Yawarakai Seikatsu" — once in a while, but as Yuko discovers, there's also something to be said for this hard thing called reality. What else is there, really?

Bashing, rating: ★★★★, runtime: 82 min.

Japan can be a pretty harmonious place, unless you're out of tune by appearance, personality or the model of cell phone you bring to school. Then you start to learn the meaning of the large Japanese vocabulary for exclusion, including *ijime* (usually translated as "bullying") and *murahachibu* (social ostracism — literally, "cast out of the village"). Foreigners often encounter mild forms of this — the seat beside you that stays empty on a crowded train — but it is Japanese themselves who usually bear the full brunt, as Japanese filmmakers have noted again and again.

They often portray schools as snake pits of merciless bullying, including viciously creative varieties that could give CIA interrogators pointers. Exaggeration for dramatic effect? Certainly, but in most of these films, the perpetrators are finally brought up short. Lives may be shattered or lost, but justice prevails.

Masahiro Kobayashi offers no such assurance in "Bashing," a sparely told, emotionally walloping film suggested by the real-life experiences of a Japanese woman who was on a self-styled volunteer mission in Iraq when she was captured by insurgents, held hostage and finally released unharmed. Back home, she was widely criticized by the media and public for going to Iraq in the first place, as well as for causing trouble for her rescuers and embarrassment for the nation.

Screened in competition at the Cannes Film Festival last year, "Bashing" represents a breakthrough for Kobayashi, who also won invitations to Cannes for "Bootleg Film" in 1998, "Film Noir" in 2002, and "Man Walking on Snow" in 2001. A veteran scriptwriter with nearly 500 TV credits, Kobayashi has had a harder time establishing himself as a major director here than in France. Critics were not always kind to his at times labored attempts to channel his beloved French auteurs, while audiences mostly stayed away. "Bashing," however, has enjoyed what, for a Kobayashi film, is a flood of media attention, and is still drawing crowds a month after its opening at Image Forum in Shibuya.

It deserves this attention not so much for the originality of its stripped-down aesthetic — Kobayashi is once again channeling, this time the Dardennes brothers ("L'Enfant," "Rosetta") — as its unsparing look at the Japanese way of ostracism, carried to its ultimate extreme. His heroine, Yuko (Fusako Urabe), is first seen after she has returned from her ordeal to her home in a bleak industrial town on the Hokkaido coast. When she arrives for work as a hotel maid, none of her colleagues acknowledge her greeting and she works her shift in total silence. Then her boss (Teruyuki Kagawa) tells her she's been fired. She's "disturbing the atmosphere of the workplace," he says.

Her real crime, we see as the story progresses and more people around her make themselves brutally clear, is that, by being in the wrong place at the wrong time for the wrong reason (i.e. trying to help distant foreigners), she brought shame on herself, her family and her community. Every encounter — with a trio of bullies who surround her in a convenience store parking lot, with a former boyfriend who demands a meeting, with married acquaintances she encounters on the street — drives home her utter isolation, the utter lack of anything resembling sympathy for her ordeal or recognition of her simple humanity.

It is not enough for her tormentors to abuse her physically and mentally; they must assert their moral superiority to this arrogant woman, who either ignored or never learned the first rules of living in what is still a village society: Go along to get along and never stand out from the crowd.

She finds no refuge at home, where harassing e-mails and phone calls follow her and her factory worker father (Ryuzo Tanaka) and part-timer mother resent her. They are, according to the laws of society, guilty as charged for raising such a thoughtless, irresponsible daughter. Their punishment is also severe, and Yuko's father is less able to withstand it. His reaction — let's leave it vague — precipitates Yuko's final decision: Should she stay and fight it out, surrender to despair or return to the only place where she ever felt truly human?

Fusako Urabe plays Yuko with a clenched, headlong intensity. She pumps her gaily colored mountain bike through the gray streets as though battling through a fog of hatred and contempt. At the same time, Urabe exposes the bleeding wounds beneath the defiant, closed-off exterior. Her look of fierce bitterness and resentment, after hearing a cutting remark or the latest bad news, has a raw, unmediated quality. Far more actresses would opt for a sympathy-grabbing sob over her nakedly revealing scowl.

"Bashing" is the sort of grim, unrelenting film that the entire Japanese industry is trying strenuously not to make. What the public wants, nearly everyone says now, is tear-wrenching, heartwarming drama, preferably with a touch of fantasy or a sprinkling of CG fairy dust, which makes "Bashing" so refreshing: It shames the devil and tells the truth.

Sway, Yureru, rating: ★★★, runtime: 120 min.

The Cannes film festival invited only one feature from Japan this year: Miwa Nishikawa's psychological drama "Sway," which screened in the Directors' Fortnight section. This was disappointing, but not unexpected. For all its flirtations with the pop/genre end of the spectrum, Cannes remains a stronghold of auteur cinema. The Japanese film industry, meanwhile, is producing fewer true auteurs and more young directors plucked from the television industry who just want to entertain.

Nishikawa, who debuted in 2002 with the black comedy "Wild Berries" and has since directed an award-winning docu-drama for NHK and segments for the omnibuses "female" (2005) and "Ten Nights of Dreams" (2006), has resisted this trend. Instead of making commercial films developed from popular manga and TV dramas, Nishikawa has written and directed her own scripts. Her producer and mentor is not a network hack but director Hirokazu Koreeda, for whom she first worked as a freelance staffer on his film "After Life."

"Sway" shares one of Koreeda's principle themes — the centrality of memory to human relationships and identity. The film, however, is anything but a Koreeda clone. It begins as a sensitively observed drama of family and fraternal strife, but in the second act the action shifts to a courtroom, with conflicting testimonies that recall Akira Kurosawa's "Rashomon."

Nishikawa uses her trial as a stage on which two brothers — one a defendant being tried for manslaughter, the other the only witness to the alleged crime — act out their personal psychodrama of envy, rage and love. The case is as simple and deep as a fable, with the line between truth and untruth shifting and indeterminant.

Instead of a setting in the distant, mythical past ("Rashomon") or the realm of metaphor and nightmare (such as Kafka's "The Trial"), however, Nishikawa opts for a present-day setting and conventional realism. In doing so, she introduces genre expectations that don't really belong and distract from her dramatic arc.

The brothers are the younger Takeru (Joe Odagiri), a photographer based in Tokyo, and the older Minoru (Teruyuki Kagawa), a pump jockey at his father's gas station in the countryside. Though close as boys, the two siblings are now like night and day: Takeru is handsome, stylish and successful in his work and love life; the quiet, serious, suicidally depressed Minoru is none of the above.

When Takeru returns home, reluctantly and late, for a ceremony commemorating the first anniversary of his mother's death, he has sharp words with his irascible father, Isamu (Masato Ibu), while Minoru tries to smooth things over. Takeru later meets Chieko (Yoko Maki), an old flame who works at the gas station, and spends a passionate night with her at her apartment.

The next day, Minoru, Takeru and Chieko go to a river where they once played as children. Takeru crosses a shaky pedestrian bridge high over the rushing waters below and heads upstream to take pictures. Minoru and Chieko follow. Midway across, Chieko somehow falls to her death.

How could such a tragedy occur? We see Chieko tell Minoru she wants to go to Tokyo and start a new life with Takeru. We see Minoru's shocked reaction — he has feelings for Chieko himself — and their consequent struggle on the bridge, but we do not see if, in his disappointment and anger, Minoru pushes her off.

The police call Chieko's death an accident, but soon after Minoru cracks — and confesses his guilt. Isamu hires a lawyer — his brother Osamu (Keizo Kanie) — and the case goes to trial. On the stand, Minoru recants his confession: When Chieko fell on the bridge, he says, he tried to help her up, but she slipped off. Will Takeru, the only witness, back him up?

If this were "The Sopranos," with Tony Soprano on the stand, family loyalty would trump all, including dead girlfriends. But Takeru hems and haws, as his memory of the incident on the bridge keeps shifting.

Here is where my fine legal mind, honed by countless courtroom dramas, began raising objections. There is zero circumstantial evidence, a lone witness who keeps changing his story and a mentally disturbed defendant with no clearly substantiated motive. Does that not, your honor, indicate a reasonable doubt?

Here is also where my sympathy for Takeru began to evaporate. Given that he doesn't really know what he saw, the honorable course is to admit it, instead of grasping for an elusive (and emotionally colored) "truth." Why doesn't he? Takeru has his reasons, but they are self-serving.

Joe Odagiri and Teruyuki Kagawa both have their strengths, but they are not complementary. Odagiri is a movie star — all smoldering charisma, playing variations of himself in film after film. Kagawa is an actor's actor, who disappears into each part. On the screen together, they are oil and water in not only their characters but their approaches to their roles, sharing hardly a strand of actorly DNA.

Their casting exemplifies the disjointed nature of the entire enterprise: Brilliant in its parts, "Sway" is built with structural flaws. The title, at least, was well chosen.

The Youth of Etsuko Kamiya, Kamiya Etsuko no Seishun, rating: ★★★☆, runtime: 111 min.

Film directors are often "in production" to the last, even when they're breathing on a respirator (John Huston) or recovering from a stroke (Nagisa Oshima). There's something valiant about this, even if the late films are a falling off from the best work. Sometimes, though, they are a precious final statement about saying farewell to the passion of your life.

Kazuo Kuroki, who died of a stroke at age 75 last April, summed up an era for his entire generation in his last four films, starting with "Tomorrow" (1988), about the Nagasaki atomic bombing, and concluding with "The Youth of Etsuko Kamiya," which became a posthumous film — and a fitting coda to Kuroki's four-decade career.

All four films are either set in or refer to the war's chaotic closing days. "The Youth of Etsuko Kamiya," however, differs from the other three in that it's based on a play by Masataka Matsuda. Also, though it starts with a borderline-sentimental framing device — an elderly couple on a hospital rooftop, viewing one of their last sunsets together — its overall tone is surprisingly comic, in the folksy manner of Yoji Yamada's "Tora-san" series.

Comparisons are likewise possible with Yamada's Shochiku senior Yasujiro Ozu — both Ozu and Kuroki extract major truths from seemingly minor acts and words, more by well-timed suggestion than blatant underlining (though the sunset is about as blatant a metaphor as it gets). But "Kamiya Etsuko" is also austere — hardly any music, mostly long takes and only straight cuts — in a way identifiably Kuroki. It is as though, knowing the end was approaching, he concentrated his remaining energies to make a strong-but-simple drama, with maximum efficiency and minimum distractions.

The film begins with the eternally patient title character (Tomoyo Harada) and her cranky, but ever-loving husband (Masatoshi Nagase) having a conversation about the weather, the landscape and the war that is as comically banal and repetitive as "Waiting for Godot."

Then the scene shifts to a house in rural Kumamoto in the last spring of the war. Etsuko is living with her sweet-tempered older brother (Kaoru Kobayashi) and his testy beauty of a wife (Manami Honjou). Once again the conversation verges on a comic routine in its short seesaw rhythms, punctuated by gag lines.

The situation: Her brother wants her to have an informal omiai (meeting with an eye to marriage) with an air force officer, Nagayo (Nagase), who is a comrade of an old school friend, Akashi (Shunsuke Matsuoka). Etsuko is willing — though she also has unstated feelings for Akashi.

Then the brother is called away to Kumamoto on urgent business. His wife decides to go with him, and Etsuko is left alone to deal with her two military visitors. Nagayo, a straight-as-an-arrow innocent, earnestly bumbles his way into her heart. In the ordinary course of events, she would have to choose between these two suitors — one self-effacing and one not, but Akashi volunteers for the tokkotai (suicide squad) — and everything changes.

Kuroki evokes the poignancy and bitterness of this situation, while never losing sight of his principals' ordinary humanity. He also gets nuances that a younger director might miss, such as the undercurrent of wartime anxiety that runs beneath the banter. I had to wonder, though, at his casting choices — Nagase and Harada are both two decades too old to be playing fresh-faced youths. On stage, this wouldn't matter, but the camera's eye is merciless — and Kuroki refuses to filter it.

Ishii Teruo Fan Club, rating: ★★★☆, runtime: 80 min.

Masaaki Yaguchi's documentary "Ishii Teruo Fan Club" is an elegy. His subject is Ishii Teruo, the "king of cult," whose eroguro ("erotic and grotesque") films of the 1960s and 1970s were once considered trash exploitation, but are now rightfully hailed as works of an original, brilliantly warped talent. His masterpiece from this period, "Horror of Malformed Men" (1969), based on stories by Edogawa Rampo and starring butoh founder Tatsumi Hijikata as the deranged leader of deformed outcasts living on a remote island, has never been released on video or DVD, supposedly for its un-PC language and content, but when it screened at the Udine Film Festival in 2003 the audience gave the film and its director a thunderous standing ovation for its inventiveness, audacity and sheer lunacy.

Yaguchi's camera followed Ishii on the production of his last feature, the minor eroguro gem "Blind Beast vs. Killer Dwarf" (2003), capturing Ishii's puckish sense of humor, inexhaustible energy and uncanny ability to create his distinctive world in the chaotic conditions of a low-budget shoot. One moment he is joking with his crew of mostly young film students, and next he is totally focused on the work at hand, be it demonstrating a bit of business to his bemused actors or staring through the viewfinder of his digital camera, alert to the slightest deviation from his vision (which he never recorded on story boards — a practice he detested — but instead drew from his fertile imagination and immediate surroundings).

I had the privilege of knowing Ishii before his death last year at 81 of lung cancer. I also appear in the film, in segments shot at the 2003 Udine Far East Film Festival — a fact I didn't know until I walked into the theater. But don't let that discourage you from seeing this master in action. His love of filmmaking and unflagging professionalism was an inspiration and delight. "It was over too soon," Ishii tells the camera after the film wraps. I say the same about him.

Hula Girls, rating: ★★★★, runtime: 108 min.

"Hula Girls" sounds, from its title, like the many Japanese movies about loser heroes who take up minor sports or performing arts (sumo wrestling, ballroom dancing, rowing, synchronized swimming, swing jazz) and find their respective grooves. These films usually end with a big, rousing finale, in which the heroes exhibit their hard-won skills and show us that the waltz, say, is, guess what! — really cool. Thus the boom in ballroom dancing prompted by the 1996 Masayuki Suo hit "Shall We Dance?"

Though it follows this formula, the latest film by director Lee Sang-il ("69," "Scrap Heaven") also departs from it in ways reminiscent of "The Full Monty" and "Brassed Off" (show biz brightens up an industrial hinterland) and Kirio Urayama's 1962 classic "Foundry Town," in which Sayuri Yoshinaga plays a spunky girl struggling to rise above her rough, factory town environment.

That is to say, Lee and co-scriptwriter Daisuke Habara blend straight-up melodrama and social commentary into their pop entertainment mix. Their film is a frothy, campy pineapple drink, but spiked with a jolt of old-fashioned, eye-tearing Japanese *shochu*. This mix doesn't always go down easily — especially in the long middle section, when the heartstring-tugging crises come along once every 10 minutes — but the ending is an all-stops-out crowd pleaser that bursts with the sexual dynamism and exuberance of hula (not the sweetened-for-the-tourist-trade version). Purists may complain that the moves are more "Tanko Bushi" ("Coal Mining Song") than the real Hawaiian deal, but these girls can shake it.

The story begins in a setting as far removed from Waikiki as could be imagined: a dreary coal-mining town called Joban that, in 1965, was in an irreversible decline that the town fathers were trying desperately to reverse. One of them, the fluttery, bumbling but determined Yoshimoto (Kishibe Ittoku), has the brainstorm of starting a Hawaiian Center as a tourist magnet, whose main drawing card will be hula performed by local lasses. (This is not another high concept fantasy, but based on the true story of Joban's still ongoing contribution to Hawaiian culture.) He hires a professional dancer from Tokyo, one Madoka Hirayama (Yasuko Matsuyuki), as a hula teacher. She arrives looking Mod (white sheath dress, big shades, dangling cigarette), bored and out of place.

To many of the local folk, particularly the no-nonsense, quick-tempered Chiyo (Sumiko Fuji), the whole idea of bringing Hawaii to the mines is an affront to community dignity, tradition and mores. When the local girls Yoshimoto lures to a recruiting session see a scratchy film of hula and realize that it involves shaking their hips and exposing their midriffs, they blanch and take flight. The only survivors are the bubbly, stage-struck Sanae (Eri Tokunaga), her reluctant pal Kimiko (Yu Aoi), the geeky Shoko (Shoko Ikezu), who is a clerk in the mining company office, and the big, lumbering Sayuri (Shizuyo Yamazaki), whose eccentric, show-biz-loving father dragooned her into coming.

The girls are predictably hopeless and Madoka, who has taken the job under duress (from what, is to be revealed), barely goes through the motions of teaching them, while drinking and smoking herself into oblivion. But when the feisty Kimiko rebels, Madoka feels a stirring of conscience — and ambition. She will turn this motley crew into hula dancers if it kills them, but first she has them relearn movement, from the feet up. (The hip shimmy comes later.)

Meanwhile, she has some lessons of her own to learn about local pride, taught by a drunken Yoshimoto (in an outburst that surprises him as much as her) and Kimiko's loutish, but good-hearted, older brother Yojiro (Etsushi Toyokawa), who becomes Madoka and Kimiko's defender against the wrath of his mother, the aforementioned Chiyo, while having his own designs on the sexy, stylish Madoka. Finally, the girls who had first fled return — and Madoka has the rough makings of a dance troupe.

This is same basic pattern as Shinobu Yaguchi's 2004 hit "Swing Girls," but where Yaguchi kept the tone consistently bubbly and light, Lee ladles on the dramatic complications, from the usual one of parental opposition to various setbacks and disasters that reflect the hardscrabble realities of life in mid-1960s Japan — and at times feel dragged in from another movie.

In its last act, however, the film comes triumphantly to life as the girls strut their stuff, particularly Yu Aoi in a bring-down-the-house solo, with Lee's camera capturing every erotically explosive moment. Sayuri Yoshinaga was never like this. Forget Honolulu — Joban, here I come.

Strawberry Shortcakes, rating: ★★★★, runtime: 127 min.

Hitoshi Yazaki was once an avatar of the 1990s Japanese New Wave. "March Comes In Like a Lion" (1992), his lyrical, elliptical drama about incest, was championed by the likes of Asian film doyen Tony Rayns and screened at dozens of festivals around the world.

It made the West aware that something was happening in Japanese cinema beyond bloated bubble-era period dramas, while setting the pattern for dozens of Japanese indie films that followed with its plotless story about a flaky, if determined, young woman adrift in an urban wilderness, looking for pure love — and finding it in her mentally disabled brother.

After this triumph, however, Yazaki dropped out of sight, reappearing briefly in 2000 with the little-seen "The Girl Who Picks Flowers and the Girl Who Kills Insects." Now, 14 years after his breakthrough, he is back with "Strawberry Shortcakes," a romantic drama based on a popular manga, with a name cast headed by Chizuru Ikewaki, Yuko Nakamura, Ryo Kase and Masanobu Ando: In other words, a film that is more commercially-minded '00s than purist-indie '90s in subject, source and stars.

"Strawberry Shortcakes," however, is less a sell-out than a shading toward more digestible, if not always sweet, entertainment. And Yazaki is still Yazaki, defiantly indie in sensibility and style. Compared with the local romantic melodramas that underline every emotion with big pink markers, "Strawberry Shortcakes" is a small marvel of compression, subtlety and realism. Instead of boldly proclaiming their feelings to the skies or their significant others, the four principals mostly mumble them to themselves — or to God. That's a bit sad, but reflective of the isolated state of many singles in today's socially fragmented Tokyo. Yazaki may have been away a long time, but he's still in touch.

The film tells parallel stories about two sets of young women. The first we meet is Satoko (Ikewaki), who, after being cruelly dumped by her rocker boyfriend, is working as a receptionist at a *deriheru* (an abbreviation of "delivery health" — meaning she answers the phone from customers wanting call girls). Back in her apartment, she swigs beer on the veranda swing and prays to a small, black stone that fell from the sky and is now her resident "god."

At work, Satoko becomes friends with Akiyo (Nakamura), who is older, quieter and more aggressive than the other girls. She is squirreling away her yen to buy a condo on the fifth floor — so that, when she starts to go senile, she can jump out the window and kill herself quickly and efficiently. She is also sleeping in a coffin — to keep her mind focused on her final exit. Her one escape from her death-worshipping present are her drinking sessions with Kikuchi (Ando), a former classmate who is also drifting and knows that beneath Akiyo's buddy-buddy exterior beats the heart of a woman madly in love. Unfortunately, he cannot reciprocate.

Also lonesome is Toko (Toko Iwase), an illustrator whose ex, she learns, is about to marry someone else. Meanwhile, she is sinking into a miasma of bitterness and bulimia, while working herself to a nub on a publisher's commission to "draw the face of God" for a book cover.

Her roommate is Chihiro (Noriko Nakagoshi), a sweet, chipper office lady into shopping, makeup, fortunetelling and her self-absorbed salaryman boyfriend Nagai (Kase), who treats her abysmally. In short, she and the boho Toko have zero in common. But Chihiro is not as brainless as she seems. Instead, she is another lonely soul, who desperately wants a normal married life and worships the boyfriend as her "god," the poor thing.

This may sound like a long, dreary wallow in feminine self-delusion and depression, but Yazaki's four heroines are all struggling toward self-awareness and their various versions of "the light." Also, they are all people in their own right, not directorial sock puppets, who, like many of us, are playing roles with the people they work with, live with and love. But when they are alone — or have tired of the game, they let the mask slip.

The film is really less about the search for love than finding the courage to live in one's own skin without the usual neurotic or religious crutches, but with a like-minded soul or two.

Working from Kyoko Inukai's script, Yazaki depicts this journey more through the small incidents and rituals of everyday life than the standard drag-out-the-hankies scenes — though he doesn't shy from the occasional big flareup or flakeout.

Even the humble stuff of the heroines' rooms expresses their personalities, and dreams. Nearly everything of Toko's has edges; nearly everything of Chihiro's has curves, right down to her heart-shaped alarm clock. Toko displays her art proudly on the walls, but hides her feelings. Chihiro puts her feelings on open display in her "private" diary (which Toko reads daily for amusement), while keeping her decorative urges under wraps (though the makeup bottles crowding her vanity case send a message of their own).

This is hardly a new strategy for adding color and depth, but Yazaki uses it with unusual thoroughness, to extraordinary effect. When the title treats finally show up, in the last scene, they pack more than the usual meaning because the film has been preparing for their appearance in dozens of ways, from scene one. Dig in, enjoy — and let's hope we don't have to wait another 14 years for a second helping.

Paprika, rating: ★★★★, runtime: 90 min.

Can dreams drive you crazy? Is the boundary between dream life and so-called real life permeable? Satoshi Kon has been making brilliant animations based on these and similar questions since "Perfect Blue," his 1998 feature debut about an idol singer whose life, inner as well as outer, is invaded by an obsessed fan.

His latest and, he says, last investigation of this dream-vs.-reality theme is "Paprika," which premiered at this year's Venice Film Festival and has been selected as a possible nominee for an animation Oscar. I have no idea if his film will make it into the final five, but it is definitely different from not only the CG animation for kiddies that is now standard in Hollywood, but also the manga-based, sci-fi fantasy that the Japanese animation industry exports in large quantities.

True, it has SF elements, the main one being a gizmo called the DC Mini that looks like a futuristic hearing aid and can transmit the wearer's dreams — think of an MP3 site that allows you to share dreams instead of tunes.

But instead of focusing on his hardware or spinning the usual good-vs.-evil SF story, Kon takes his audience on a wild, fantastic ride into a land of extreme dreaming, where primal desires and fears (absolute freedom, appropriation of one's identity by a malevolent Other) come to gaudy, phantasmagorical life.

His imagery is at once everyday (marching household appliances) and nightmarish (Japanese dolls with uncanny grins that walk, talk, and in one memorable case, makes like Godzilla). His story, based on the fiction of Yasutaka Tsutsui, may not make much rational, left-brained sense, but works at a deeper, right-brained level, like a fairy tale for adults (or at least older teens), told with affection for its mostly oddball characters and a puckish sense of humor about their mad adventures.

Sounds like good, trippy fun, doesn't it? But this movie is cunningly designed to mess up minds — even the characters lose track of the many transitions from dream to reality and back again.

Kon's heroine exemplifies this duality. Atsuko Chiba (voiced by Megumi Hayashibara), a psychotherapist at a mental hospital research center, is the epitome of cool, poised professionalism, who has the absolute trust of her short, balding, excitable boss, Dr. Shima (Katsunosuke Hori). More importantly for the story, she not only investigates patients' dreams, but is able to enter them with the aid of a "psychotherapy machine."

The alter ego she assumes on these inner trips is the polar opposite of her real world self, being a sexy, sprightly pixie named Paprika who trips through dreamscapes with blithe abandon and shape-shifting ease. She is less a therapist than a sort of angel of deliverance who appears when her patients are confused — or endangered.

The only ones who know Paprika's true identity are Dr. Shima and Tokita (Toru Furuya), the nerdy inventor of the DC Mini. Then three of the devices are stolen from the lab — and Atsuko and Tokita fear that the thief may use them not to cure minds, but instead destroy them.

Their fears prove well founded when Dr. Shima starts spouting bizarre nonsense. Atsuko, in the persona of Paprika, enters his dreams and finds a parade of dolls and the aforementioned ambulant appliances. One of the marchers is a sinister talking Japanese doll who resembles one of the doctor's assistants, Himuro (Daisuke Sakaguchi).

Is Himuro the culprit? Is the doll truly Himuro? What exactly is going on here? As the dream invasions continue and spread, the saturnine hospital director, Inui (Toru Emori), takes notice, as does a macho police detective, Konakawa (Akio Otsuka). Inui responds by forbidding the development of more psychotherapeutic hardware, but the malevolent force behind the invasions is already beyond the control of mere technology. Meanwhile, Konakawa, a comically square-jawed, down-to-earth sort, finds himself caught in a recurring bad dream — no longer the pursuer but the pursued.

In films like "Millennium Actress," (2001) and "Tokyo Godfathers" (2003), Kon worked in a far more realistic vein than the fantastic Japanimation norm — making some fans question his use of animation to begin with. Why not just film real actors in real settings and be done with it?

In "Paprika," however, Kon states the case for animation with an imaginative force and clarity that blows such objections away. His imagery, poised uneasily between the cutesy and the creepy, is more richly suggestive of the dream state, with its visually abstracted, emotionally unstable flights of the psyche, than the usual sort of live-action film, even with CG additions.

The character designs, supervised by Masashi Ando, may have a reassuringly conventional Japanimation look — Dr. Shima is the brother to eccentric hakase (professors) in dozens of anime — but there is nothing conventional about Kon's vision, which undercuts realistic expectations at every turn with a visually strange, but persuasive internal logic. (Somehow those appliances and dolls belong together.)

Did I understand that logic at first go? Not really, and "Paprika" would reward a second viewing — and more. But not just before bed, please.

Love and Honor, Bushi no Ichibun, rating: ★★★☆, runtime: 121 min.

Some directors, like the recently deceased Akio Jissoji, have careers that look from the outside to be wildly eclectic. Jissoji's filmography encompassed everything from the early "Ultraman" shows to the arty films he made for the Art Theater Guild in the early 1970s.

Yoji Yamada, on the other hand, would seem to be the ultimate journeyman, churning out 48 episodes of the Tora-san series from 1969 to 1996 — a feat that lifted him into the Guinness World Records. In discussing the series, Yamada often compared himself to a noodle cook, who aims for consistency as well as quality.

But Yamada's trilogy of samurai films — "The Twilight Samurai" (2002), "The Hidden Blade" (2004), and the new "Love and Honor" (2006) — differ from much of his earlier work not only in subject matter but also treatment and sensibility. The folksy humor and sentimentality that were once Yamada trademarks are seldom in sight. Instead, the dominant mood is autumnal, verging on somber; the stylistics spare, if visually rich.

If Yamada was once a sort of Japanese Norman Rockwell, giving the big audience warm tinglies with his idealized portraits of national archetypes, he has since become more like Andrew Wyeth: still popular with the masses, but striking deeper, darker emotional chords.

Based, like the first two films in the trilogy, on the fiction of Shuhei Fujisawa, "Love and Honor" also resembles them in its story arc. Once again, a low-ranked samurai faces character-testing difficulties that he overcomes with the support of a pure-hearted woman, culminating in a sword duel with a rival. In other words, a third serving of soba.

But just as one bowl of noodles is not like the next, "Love and Honor" stands apart from the other trilogy films. First, its star, Takuya Kimura, is not, like Hiroyuki Sanada of "Twilight Samurai" and Masatoshi Nagase of "The Hidden Blade," a middle-aged screen veteran, but a youngish TV megastar with limited film experience. Rei Dan, who plays Kimura's wife, is a screen newcomer, in contrast to Rie Miyazawa and Takako Matsu, established stars who played the female leads in the first two films.

Also, the situation of Kimura's samurai, Shinnojo Mimura, is more dramatically desperate. A food taster for his clan's lord, he is poisoned by bad shellfish and goes blind. Though poor by samurai standards, Shinnojo and his wife Kayo (Dan) have a happy marriage, and his career prospects as an expert swordsman are bright until suddenly it all goes crash.

Kayo and the couple's elderly servant Tokuhei (Takashi Sasano) remain devoted, but Shinnojo feels worse than useless. He contemplates suicide, and turns bitter and violent. Kayo, an orphan who married up, can bring no allies to this struggle. Meanwhile, Shinnojo's relatives, beginning with his aunt Ine (Kaori Momoi), are selfish, coldly practical sorts who, at a family conference, tell Kayo to find a powerful patron. She remembers Toya Shimada (Mitsugoro Bando), a clan banto (captain) who had once expressed sympathy for her plight.

Shimada proves to be as good as his word, using his influence to allow Shinnojo to keep his status, income and house. All seems to be saved — the once light-hearted Shinnojo cracks his first jokes in ages — but he can't escape the feeling that Kayo is slipping away from him, into the arms of another man. When a rumor confirms his fears, he goes off the deep end — this time, it seems, for good.

This material is ripe with melodramatic potential, but Yamada films it with a minimum of histrionics. He keeps his scenes, even ones in which crockery is thrown, simple and pointed, with plenty of strong emotion but little overacting.

This sort of paring down is common in films by older directors, but "Love and Honor" does not share other familiar features of "geriatric" cinema: staginess or outdated-ness. One reason is that Yamada's principal couple is young and he allows them to act that way.

Kimura disappears into his role more completely than I would have thought possible, while Dan, a former star in the Takarazuka revue, is a revelation — thoroughly professional, refreshingly natural. Not an aughties idol or diva, but an actress who could have walked in from a Mizoguchi film.

Also, instead of falling back on the tricks of his earlier career — Tora-san redux — Yamada is working in what for him is still a new genre, using new approaches. Even Tokuhei — whom Yamada could have easily turned into yet other lovable version of Tora-san — is a hard-bitten original.

Viewers of the other trilogy films will recognize familiar tropes, including the climactic duel that, true to Yamada's keep-it-real code, has none of the fantastic flash of other films about blind swordsmen, including the "Zatoichi" series. The sword moves are the real deal, the battle intensely personal, the results grippingly final. That is to say, if you liked the first two films, you'll like this one even more. Cooks tend to improve with practice — and Yamada's third batch of noodles is his best.

2007

I Just Didn't Do It, Soredemo Boku wa Yattenai, rating: ★★★★, runtime: 143 min.
Like many foreigners here, I have had my brushes with the Japanese justice system, from ID checks by cops wanting to practice their English to one memorable appearance on a witness stand. I have also seen it in action as a moviegoer, from prison comedies (Yoichi Sai's "Doing Time" being the funniest) to courtroom dramas (Yoshimitsu Morita's "Keiho" being the most mind-twisting).

One lesson that I have learned from these experiences and observations is that the Japanese are a law-abiding people for a very good reason — once the system here has you in its grips you are well and truly in the meat grinder. Safeguards exist for the accused, who are entitled to a defense lawyer, but the legal scales are tipped in favor of the police and prosecution, who want to save face by convicting as many "criminals" as possible — and nearly always succeed.

Meanwhile, before and during their trials, prisoners and their supporters are reminded, through a thousand rules, exactly who has the power and who has been stripped of every particle of individuality and will.

Masayuki Suo's new drama "I Just Didn't Do It" drives these and other points home with an unrivaled forcefulness. Suo's first film in a decade — his last was the 1996 hit comedy "Shall We Dance?" — it is carefully researched. At the same time, Suo hasn't forgotten to tell a story that anyone can understand, about an ordinary man in an extraordinary situation that starts as a brief, apparently innocent, encounter with an anonymous person, but becomes an all-consuming descent into a legal hell.

To those who think of Suo only as an entertainer this may seen like a radical departure. But he has long been an explorer of Japanese society's more obscure, uncool corners, while his unheroic heroes struggle against not just their own weaknesses but also social prejudice in films like "Fancy Dance" (1989), "Sumo Do, Sumo Don't" (1992) and "Shall We Dance?" (1996). "I Just Didn't Do It" is along these lines as well, but with a new turn toward serious social commentary and advocacy. If a film can change Japan's legal system, this is the one — but don't hold your breath.

Teppei Kaneko (Ryo Kase), an unemployed man, is arrested for molesting a 15-year-old girl on a crowded commuter train. But after he is taken to the station office for questioning, together with the girl and a portly male passenger who helped apprehend him, an embarrassed young woman appears at the office door, mutters "he didn't do it" — and vanishes into the crowd.

The detectives investigating his case, however, have nothing but contempt for Teppei's protestations of innocence. Locked away in a detention cell with hardened criminals, he begins to realize the seriousness of his predicament, but he rejects the advice of the cops and his court-appointed attorney to confess. Why should he, when he did nothing but try to loosen his coattail, caught in the train door? Yes, he may have brushed against the girl, but his right hand was nowhere near her body. Yet she continues to insist that he groped her with it. Who is right?

Teppei finally finds two lawyers willing to defend him — the shrewd veteran Masayoshi Arakawa (Koji Yakusho) and his smart-but-green junior partner, Riko Sudo (Asaka Seto). At first reluctant to defend an accused molester, Sudo is persuaded by Arakawa's observation that Teppei may well be the victim of a legal miscarriage. But even with these two behind him, Teppei's chances of winning acquittal in a court trial are slim — about 0.1 percent.

The rest of the film follows the usual pattern of a courtroom drama, but with an unusual devotion to detail, so much so that "I Just Didn't Do It" serves as an excellent introduction to Japanese court procedure. The approach is not without its dryness, as one hearing follows the next, through a dense haze of legalese. But Suo uses it to demonstrate, with quietly devastating thoroughness, the system's rigidities and contradictions.

Supposedly dedicated to uncovering the truth, Teppei's trial, we see, begins with a presumption of guilt. In other words, the defense must not only introduce an element of doubt, but must completely overturn the prosecution's case. Also, instead of wooing a jury with the emotional appeals of Hollywood, the defense must persuade a judge. The first one they draw seems sympathetic, but he is replaced midway by a hard-case type — and the odds of acquittal suddenly look longer.

The cast includes familiar faces from other Suo films, including Koji Yakusho, Hiromasa Taguchi and Naoto Takenaka of "Shall We Dance?" fame. Ryo Kase, who also stars in Clint Eastwood's "Letters from Iwo Jima," is outstanding as the mild-mannered but stubbornly determined Teppei, who simply can't understand why he should confess to a crime he didn't commit. An unlikely legal hero, he is also totally credible when he delivers the title line. Until the Japanese justice system can come up with an answer that makes human, as well as legal, sense, all of us, natives and outlanders alike, are its potential victims.

Nightmare Detective, Akumu Tantei, rating: ★★★★, runtime: 106 min.

Shinya Tsukamoto has long labored on the fringes of the Japanese film industry, not always by choice. The original cyberpunk bad boy of Japanese movies, Tsukamoto burst onto the scene in 1989 with "Tetsuo," a film so extreme in its violence, sex and general insanity, including an interlude with a whirling penis drill, that it made most local attempts at transgression look tame. Written, directed, filmed and edited by Tsukamoto, with a score by Chu Ishikawa that was like a buzz saw ripping through a live skull, the film's vision of man (and woman) merging with machine had a crude vitality and startling originality that suggested genius and madness — or both.

Few would have been surprised if Tsukamoto had flamed out after his initial brush with notoriety. Instead he persevered like one of his unkillable on-screen heroes, making films that were either uncompromisingly Tsukamoto ("Tetsuo 2," "Tokyo Fist") or nominally commercial ("Hiruko the Goblin," "Gemini").

His latest, "Nightmare Detective," is hardly a formulaic play for mass appeal, despite its remake-able — and remarkable — story line. Instead it's reminiscent of David Lynch's stranger imaginative flights, presented with Tsukamoto's trademark straight-to-the-throat directness. Be prepared for a viral infection of your dream life.

Keiko Kirishima (the single-named Hitomi) is a cop investigating two bizarre unnatural deaths. In the first, a punk girl is found dead in her bed, her throat slit and the door locked, with no signs of an intruder. In the second, a pudgy salaryman cuts his own throat while lying on the futon, apparently asleep, next to his horrified wife.

Kirishima's jaded middle-age partner, Sekiya (Ren Osugi), writes off both cases as suicides, however odd the circumstances. Kirishima is not so sure. She notices that just before their deaths the two victims answered a call from somebody identified only as "0" on their cellphone screens.

This caller may have said something that drove them to kill themselves — but what? She decides to find out, enlisting the support of the skeptical Sekiya and Wakamiya (Masanobu Ando), a younger, more sympathetic detective.

Kirishima comes to realize that the perpetrator (played by Tsukamoto himself, in full psychotic flower) has insinuated his way into his victims' dreams. To catch him she enlists the help of Kyoichi Kagenuma (Ryuhei Matsuda), a troubled young man with unusual psychic powers — the "nightmare detective" of the title.

This may sound like something out of Edogawa Rampo — an early 20th-century writer best known for Sherlock-Holmes-like puzzle mysteries. Tsukamoto's take on this story, however, is both unpuzzling and unironic. For Kagenuma, dreams are not wispy recyclings of daily life, forgotten immediately on awakening. Instead, they are alternative realities packed with meaning — and real danger.

Tsukamoto has long had a thing for leading ladies with strong personalities and smoldering presences and in singer Hitomi, an acting neophyte, he has found an ideal embodiment of his erotic vision. Compared with the men around her, who mostly range from the ineffectual to the disturbed, her Kirishima is a beacon of determination and sanity, whose reactions to the strangeness she encounters may be limited in range, but are charged with emotion. When her eyes light up with fear, you want to believe.

In most horror pics, the female leads play women in peril. Tsukamoto not only reverses the usual gender roles — his male "nightmare detective" is the one in gravest danger — but refuses to pander to audience expectations.

There are no jack-in-the-box ghosts — just the creeping dread that evil dwells deep within — an implacable, alien presence ready to pounce as soon as the lights go out. Sweet dreams.

Sakuran, rating: ★★★★, runtime: 111 min.

How did "Memoirs of a Geisha" get it so drearily wrong — and Mika Ninagawa's new film, "Sakuran," get it so gloriously right? Experts on geisha culture slammed Rob Marshall's film for its inaccuracies in everything from obi (kimono sash) patterns to Zhang Ziyi's glitzy solo dance, which had about the same relation to real buyo (Japanese dance) as "The Chorus Line" does to kabuki. The decision to cast non-Japanese in the three main female roles also came in for criticism, for reasons ranging from the xenophobic to the commerical.

I found Ziyi's dance ludicrous and the casting obtuse — it was like starring four Commonwealth actresses (say a Brit, a South African, a Kenyan and a Jamaican) in the quintessentially American "Dreamgirls," but my main objection to the film was its phony exoticism, echoing the Hollywood films of the 1950s set in the "mysterious East," but with less of an excuse.

Ninagawa, a photographer-turned-director whose father is stage director Yukio Ninagawa, takes as her subject not the done-to-death geisha, but the Edo-era prostitutes of Yoshiwara, the nightlife district that served as an emporium of the flesh for hundreds of years. (It still exists, though "soaplands" [sex parlors] have replaced the once-storied brothels)

True to her background — and her own uninhibited tastes, Ninagawa dresses her actresses and decorates her sets in a theatrical riot of color, with a cheeky indifference to period fidelity. Did the bordellos of the period feature the gorgeously extravagant flower arrangements found in "Sakuran?" Did even the elite oiran wear such fabulously glam kimonos every working night? I suspect the answer is "no" — but I didn't mind the visual overload, quite the opposite.

Unlike Marshall, who imposed a romanticized Western template over his geisha, Ninagawa sees her oiran as young women with desires, dreams and tastes recognizable to their 21st Century peers. Also, she is not a slipshod curator of dusty cultural artifacts, but a sui generis artist who flamboyantly but perceptively re-imagines the era. Her Yoshiwara may be more highly colored than the real thing, but it aptly expresses the glamour and beauty at the heart of the place's appeal, while exposing its everyday realities, from the trivial to the tragic.

Her heroine is Kiyoha (Anna Tsuchiya), who was brought to the Tamagikuya brothel in Yoshiwara while still a child — and hated it. A feisty sort, she tried to escape its walls at every opportunity, but was always brought back by Seiji (Masanobu Ando), the brothel's relentless-but-sympathetic bancho (chief clerk). Kiyoha chafes under the supervision of Shohi (Miho Kanno), a senior oiran who looks down on her an as an untutored peasant, but she finally decides to become an oiran herself.

As one of Yoshiwara's elite, she will command enormous sums for her favors and perhaps, like Shohi, eventually leave on the arm of a rich danna (patron). That, she knows, is her only realistic avenue of escape. At the age of 17, Kiyoha takes her first customer, a kindly old sybarite (Sadanji Ichikawa) who is a patron of the brothel's top oiran, the arrogant Takao (Yoshino Kimura). Then she falls in love with the young, sensitive Sojiro (Hiroki Narimiya) — and lets her various masks slip. In doing so, she risks ruin. In a business that sells the illusion of love, the real thing is the most dangerous emotion of all.

She also incurs the jealousy of Takao when one of the oiran's patrons, the painter Mitsunobu (Masatoshi Nagase), begins to show an interest in her. Despite the romance and rivalry, Kiyoha is promoted to oiran, receives a new name — Higurashi — and becomes a Yoshiwara star. Finally, a rich, indulgent samurai, Kuranosuke (Kippei Shiina), appears as the answer to all her prayers — the danna who will set her free. By now, however, she is like the fish that swim about in the brothel's aquariums — a creature of her enclosed, protected environment. Has freedom come too late?

Anna Tsuchiya plays Kiyoha/Higurashi with a swaggering, profane verve that recalls her biker girl in "Kamikaze Girls" — the role that made her a star — but with flashes of a previously unseen vulnerability. She also makes no attempt to ape period drama cliches, and thus comes across as authentic. Perfectly expressing the old-is-new vision of "Sakuran" is the soundtrack score by pop diva Sheena Ringo that swings ferociously in a mix of jazz and pop idioms. Did I mention that the artist of the original manga (Moyoco Anno), the scriptwriter (Yuki Tanada), the art director (Namiko Iwashiro) and the producer (Chikako Nakabayashi) are also women?

Mr. Marshall, face it — you passed over these and other Japanese women of talent because you were blind. But now the world will see "Sakuran."

5 Centimeters per Second, Byosoku 5 Centimeters, rating: ★★★★, runtime: 63 min.

As the boundaries between animated and live-action films blur and finally become meaningless perhaps a new category is needed — call it live-mation. In any case, animators in Japan are breaking free of whatever limits on theme and treatment were once imposed on them by the public or technology. An avatar in this regard was Hayao Miyazaki, who proved with his 2001 masterpiece "Spirited Away" and other animations that he could create worlds as rich as any in live-action films.

In his new animation, "5 Centimeters per Second," Makoto Shinkai makes his own vision of an animated paradise from the materials of the every day: trains, birds, snowflakes, sky — and three teenagers with no magical powers whatsoever, only the common experiences of longing, love and loss. If this were a run-of-the-mill seishun eiga ("youth movie") there wouldn't be much reason to celebrate — just to wonder why Shinkai didn't shoot a live-action film and save himself the labor of animating the ordinary. But Shinkai, who has been hailed as the "next Miyazaki" since the 2002 release of "Voices of a Distant Star" — an awarding-winning sci-fi short he created entirely himself on a Macintosh computer — is an extraordinary talent.

In "5 Centimeters per Second," his imagination may not leap to Miyazaki's strange and wonderful heights, but he pierces the veil of the everyday to reveal a poignant, evanescent beauty most of us notice only in rare moments. Or maybe not so rare if you are, like Shinkai's three heroes, a sensitive adolescent in love.

Many of these images may derive from photographs — Shinkai and his staff diligently scouted real-life locations, principally in Kagoshima, Tokyo and Tochigi — but they become impressions of life lived at its most intense — and heartbreaking. They capture the meaning of the title: Five centimeters per second is the speed at which cherry blossoms — those ancient Japanese symbols of youth's brief flowering — are said to flutter and fall.

The story, divided into three episodes, is a seishun-eiga standard. A boy named Takaki (voiced by Kenji Mizuhashi) meets Akari (Yoshimi Kondo) in a fourth-grade class in a Tokyo suburb in the early 1990s. Both new to the school, they have the same tastes in books, the same aversion to sports. They become inseparable friends, to the derision of their classmates.

Soon after graduating from elementary school, Akari moves to a town in Tochigi Prefecture. Takaki exchanges letters with her for months but, just before cherry-blossom season, he learns that his family is going to leave for far-away Kagoshima Prefecture. He arranges to meet Akari in Tochigi, after an absence of nearly a year, knowing that this may be the last time he sees her. Then, on the way, the snow starts to fall and the train is delayed. Will she still be there when he arrives?

Shift to Tanegashima, the island used by the National Space Development Agency of Japan for rocket launches, in 1995. Kanae (Satomi Hanamura), a shy third-year high-school student, finds herself peeking around corners at Takaki, now an accomplished surfer, who came to the island from Tokyo when he was a junior in junior high. She becomes friends with him — and wants to become something more, but senses that he has someone else on his mind.

Shift to a time near the present. Takaki is now an adult who has recently quit his job, left his girlfriend — and is remembering a past that now seems incredibly distant, as the cherry blossoms fall. Meanwhile, Akari (Ayaka Onoue) is still in Tochigi, alone with her own memories.

There is little conventional drama in this story — no dramatic runs after a departing train, no lonely walks in the rain as car headlights blink like fireflies. There is much, though, that will be familiar if you were ever the new kid in school or had a hopeless teenage crush that turned you into a gibbering idiot in the presence of The One.

The usual Hollywood response to these adolescent rites of passage is comedy of the grosser sort. In treating them seriously and tenderly Shinkai runs the risk of sentimentalism, a risk he doesn't entirely escape. Though the lengthy voice-overs by the main characters have a poignant lyricism ("How fast do I have to live until I can see you again?"), they are a bit much.

Not that real-life teens are incapable of the film's finer feelings, but they are also capable of changing moods as quickly as they change hairstyles.

In creating the temperamental Chihiro in "Spirited Away," Miyazaki showed he knew that quite well. Shinkai may know it, but he doesn't yet show it.

Is he really the "new Miyazaki?" He won't become one by imitating the master — geniuses are by definition sui generis — but at age 34 he is the anime world's bright new hope. That and a brilliant gem like "5 Centimeters per Second" are enough, for now.

The Coin Locker of the Duck and Drake, Ahiru to Kamo no Coin Locker, rating: ★★★, runtime: 110 min.

Many directors keep returning to the same themes and motifs again and again. Alfred Hitchcock liked to torture ice queens (Grace Kelly, Kim Novak, Tippi Hedren), while Luis Bunuel, the master surrealist, subverted everyday reality with bizarre imagery, like a sleeper returning to a familiar nightmare. Scriptwriter-turned-director Yoshihiro Nakamura likes plots where the facade of ordinary reality begins to crack — or dissolve altogether.

The obnoxious late-night DJ of Nakamura's horror film "Booth" (2005) is taking calls from listeners when the voice of his dead lover comes over the wires, calling him a liar. The 14-year-old heroine of the same director's "Route 225" (2006) and her pudgy kid brother are walking home from the park when they find themselves not only lost in their own neighborhood, but trapped in another dimension.

The story of his latest film, the oddly but aptly titled "The Coin Locker of the Duck and Drake" fits this things-are-not-what-they-seem pattern, but with a twist: The hero — and the audience — do not find out how strange the film's world truly is until well into the third act, but the clues are there to see from the beginning. So I have to be careful in describing the story for fear of giving the game away.

It's clever, this story, in a way familiar from Christopher Nolan's "Memento" and David Lynch's "Mulholland Drive" — films that subvert conventional narrative expectations at every turn, with an internal logic (or in Lynch's case, illogic) that spells confusion to the literal-minded.

But Nakamura's use of a Bunuelian device — two actors in the same role — is less successful, since he is less clear about his rationale than the more artful Bunuel, who used double casting to brilliantly illustrate his heroine's duality (among much else) in "That Obscure Object of Desire." In other words, Nakamura takes the audience out of the picture. Devotees of trick plots may not mind, while those who prefer to dance with the one that brought them may feel jilted — or simply baffled.

Nakamura, who based his the script on a novel by Kotari Isaka, is trying to, not just mess with his audience's mind, but interject the sort of Buddhistic message that would never have occurred to the atheistic Bunuel: People have the power to change — in the next life if not this one.

The story unfolds over the course of six action-packed days, with flashbacks. On the first Shiina (Gaku Hamada), a freshmen at a university in Sendai, moves into a new apartment. A Bob Dylan fan, he is singing "Blowin' in the Wind" to himself when he is greeted by his new neighbor, Kawasaki (Eita). Imposingly tall, with an air of confidence, Kawasaki is the polar opposite of the short, nervous, but determined Shiina, though he announces himself as another Dylan fan. Dylan's singing, Kawasaki proclaims, is like "the voice of God."

Soon Kawasaki is taking Shiina into his confidence, telling his new friend that he wants to steal a Kojien dictionary for another neighbor — an exchange student from Bhutan — and needs Shiina's help. He also gives Shiina a warning that sounds as loopy as his plan: Beware the owner of a nearby pet shop, the sexy but dangerous Reiko (Nene Otsuka).

If Shiina were smart, he would run in the opposite direction, but instead he finds himself drawn irresistibly into Kawasaki's orbit. The next day, Kawasaki confesses to Shiina that he is the former lover of Kotomi (Megumi Seki), a girl who once worked at Reiko's shop, but threw him over for the Bhutanese. So what is his motive for helping the guy? While puzzling this over, Shiina agrees to aid Kawasaki with his seemingly absurd robbery, standing guard outside a bookshop's back door with a replica pistol.

Here is where I should stop, though I should add that Reiko later gives Shiina a similar warning about Kawasaki. How do ahiru (duck) and kamo (drake) come into it? The former is the domestic variety of quacker, the latter, the wild. Similar but different, something like a character in the film who starts as one thing, but becomes another. The coin locker of the title is in the film too, at the end, with a connection to the Dylan song at the beginning.

As this detail indicates, Nakamura has thought of every way, plot- and theme-wise, to make "The Coin Locker of the Duck and Drake" an intriguing puzzler, but he shot and cut it in a flatly realistic style more suitable for comedy — I was half expecting laughs, not existential mysteries.

Eita plays Kawasaki with a combination of outward openness and palpable weirdness that puts Gaku Hamada's Shiina rightly on edge, as well as giving the audience a foretaste of what is to come. Ryuhei Matsuda does his usual cool, not-of this-world thing, which happens to be exactly right for his character, who is . . .

The answer, my friend, is blowing in the wind.

How to Become Myself, Ashita no Watashi no Tsukurikata, rating: ★★★★, runtime: 97 min.

Jun Ichikawa, who began his directing career with the seishun eiga ("Youth film") "BU★SU" (1987) and "Tsugumi" (1990), has long been interested the struggles of adolescent outsiders to find their own path in a conformist society. Ichikawa is hardly alone — many Japanese directors have tackled this theme, seeing their teen characters as kindred spirits (if not actually based on the filmmakers' youthful selves) or as vehicles for explorations of society's ills.

Ichikawa, though, presents the two heroines of "How to Become Myself" as young women in their own right, not directorial stand-ins or representatives for this or that social malaise.

Based on a novel by 30-year-old Kaori Mado, his film also does not romanticize or stereotype. If anything, his style may be too uninflected for an audience used to the melodramatic or comic exaggerations of the pop-cinema mainstream. But Ichikawa also has a keen eye for the moments of truth or flashes of beauty that suggest a larger, transcendent reality. Like many directors, he uses shots of trees, clouds, crowds and other "found" phenomena for transitions, but he somehow finds images that suggest the eternal in the present, the universal in the mundane.

His heroines, though, are not Zen monks seeking the Absolute, but ordinary girls faced with that typical adolescent choice — fit in or be cast out. Juri (Riko Narumi) goes the former route, more out of fear than inclination. She acts the part expected of her (perky, cool, etc.), but lives in fear of the mask slipping and her true, unperky, uncool self showing. She admires a classmate, Kanako (Atsuko Maeda), who is better at the popularity game and seems to play it effortlessly.

Meanwhile, at home, things are not going well between Mom (Mariko Ishihara) and Dad (Yoshizumi Ishihara): Juri feels she has to be the perfect daughter to hold the family together. Where, she wonders, is the real Juri? Does she even exist?

Then, in the blink of an eye, Kanako falls from grace and becomes the class pariah. Juri sympathizes, but can say nothing until the primary school graduation ceremony, when she and Kanako have a rare moment alone — and can speak their hearts. A bond is sealed between the two outcasts, one actual, the other potential.

Fade to junior high school, where Kanako is still the class butt and Juri still strives to be liked — and left alone by the bullies. Fade again to high school, where Kanako finally makes her escape — moving with her parents to a distant town. Now a budding writer, Juri anonymously e-mails Kanako installments in a story about a girl named Hina who becomes popular with the aid of sage advice mostly culled from the Internet. Inspired, Kanako adopts the Hina persona — and achieves a Hina-like success — but knows her act is a fake. What happens when her benefactor, known only as "Kotori (Little Bird)," stops feeding her lines?

The performances of Riko Narumi, as Juri, and Atsuko Maeda, as Kanako, are a study in contrasts, though both underplay by seishun eiga standards. Maeda, a pop idol making her film debut, is inscrutably dark, while Narumi, an acting prodigy who has starred in three films so far this year, is sympathetically transparent in portraying Juri's doubts, fears and self-preserving deceits.

Their on-screen relationship is characterized by indirection, subterfuge and flashes of candor. Thin dramatic gruel? In Ichikawa's hands, it's more like a bowl of perfectly prepared ochazuke (basically, green tea over rice). Simple ingredients, delicate taste, but so satisfying — because so real. Imagine — a movie about text-messaging teens that even Ichikawa's idol, Yasujiro Ozu, could admire.

Double review of "Glory to the Filmmaker!" and "Big Man Japan"
Glory to the Filmmaker!, Kantoku Banzai!, rating: ★★★⯪, runtime: 104 min.
Big Man Japan, Dai Nipponjin, rating: ★★★★, runtime: 113 min.
It was a marketing gimmick of the first order to open Takeshi Kitano's "Glory to the Filmmaker!" and Hitoshi Matsumoto's "Big Man Japan" on the same weekend. This head-to-head duel between films by the two reigning kings of Japanese comedy can only boost the box office of both.

A preliminary verdict of sorts was rendered by the Cannes Film Festival, where "Glory to the Filmmaker!" was rejected for the competition and "Big Man Japan" was selected for the Directors Fortnight section.

"Glory to the Filmmaker!" is a film Kitano has described as part of an ongoing "creative destruction" of his career, beginning in 2005 with "Takeshis'." In that film he played two versions of himself — one "Beat," a famous TV comedian, the other, "Takeshi," a scuffling actor who idolizes Beat. The film's many shifts between dream and reality are head-spinningly hard to follow — and "Takeshis' "was a box-office disappointment.

In "Glory to the Filmmaker!" Kitano has made his first all-out comedy since 1995's "Getting Any?," a feature-length naughty joke that falls flat. His new film is more accessible and funnier, especially to anyone who has been following his long TV and film career. Kitano stars as "Kitano" — a director who is rummaging around the genre bin for his next film and coming up empty-handed. This, Kitano insists, is not only fiction — he hit an impasse and "Glory to the Filmmaker!" was his way of working through it, somewhat like Fellini with his crisis-of-confidence masterpiece "8½."

So we get Kitano trying and failing to make an Ozu-esque home drama, a tear-jerking love story, a gritty 1950s family drama, a ninja actioner and a J-horror movie. All have their comic moments, but only the family drama achieves something more than (deliberately lame) parody. Its alcoholic house painter father (Kitano), abused housewife mother, studious older brother and mischievous younger brother are all based on Kitano's own dysfunctional family — and its incidents, including the way poor shitamachi (old downtown Tokyo) residents fasten onto a new car like vultures on prey, give the lie to current nostalgia about the glorious warm-hearted 1950s.

The film truly gets underway in its second act, in the tale of a mother (Kayoko Kishimoto) and daughter (Ann Suzuki), both grifters, who attach themselves to a rich political fixer/philanthropist Mr. Big (Toru Emori) with the aim of marrying off the daughter to Mr. Big's idiot son. Kitano plays Mr. Big's hapless private secretary, who gets into ridiculous scrapes in the service of his boss.

The gags come from the unfettered late-night-TV side of Kitano's brain, not the serious-film-director side. One funny touch is the frequent appearance of a "Kitano doll" that takes the brunt of the punishment (getting dumped off a bridge, beaten to a pulp by goons, etc.) for Kitano in his various incarnations. A sign that the 60-year-old Kitano is getting too old for action scenes? Not really, since he also appears as a high-flying, sword-wielding ninja, taking on 60 opponents at once.

But the doll does get laughs and reminds us that Kitano's mind, creative blocks or no, is still one of the most original in Japanese show business. Its big joke: Kitano, who has ostensibly sworn off the violent gangster pics that made his reputation, has made — guess what? — another violent pic. Ho ho — but Kitano gives his 13th film the biggest possible send-off, taking the joke to another, higher, more explosive level.

If "Glory to the Filmmaker!" is a treat for core fans, "Big Man Japan" is an ambitious gagfest for everyone from kiddies who like "Ultraman" to pointy-headed critics who can spend hours parsing the film's multilayered take on the Japanese spirit. Matsumoto, the boke (dim-wit) of the manzai duo Downtown, reportedly spent five years developing the film, his first as a director. But instead of subjecting the audience to his rejects, Matsumoto builds on a simple-but-brilliant comic premise with subtlety and daring. The laughs come slowly at first, but pick up steam as the story progresses.

The premise: the hero, one Daisato (Matsumoto), is being interviewed for a documentary, but looks and talks like a middle-aged loser. He lives alone in a cluttered firetrap of a house and is hated by his neighbors, who have decorated his front gate with exhortations to die or disappear. His business is being a superhero, but though he is fifth in the family line, the character he becomes — Dai Nipponjin (The Great Japanese) — has long since gone out of fashion. With his stand of straight black hair (imagine the electroshocked hero of "Eraserhead"), short arms, long trunk and purplish pro-boxing briefs, Dai Nipponjin looks like a compendium of everything uncool in this age of long-limbed, artfully coifed, stylishly dressed Japanese superstars.

Also, Dai Nipponjin becomes as gigantic as the monsters he battles, through a process absurdly dated. How can the masses identify with this throwback to old, unstylish Nippon? The short answer is, they can't, and despite his feats of derring-do (with monster introductions by a nasal-voiced narrators in the style of pre-war radio broadcasts), his TV ratings are slipping.

Matsumoto plays this character with a straight face, while fleshing him out with dry comic strokes. This approach is reminiscent of Ricky Gervais in "The Office," but Matsumoto has a wackier imagination — and gives it full rein, ending with a finale that threatens to degenerate into a violent free-for-all.

But it also satirically reflects similar free-for-alls staged countless times on TV comedy shows, as well as the distance Japan has traveled from its cultural and spiritual roots. Matsumoto, the hippest and smartest of comic puppetmasters, is never preachy or obvious. Also, unlike Kitano, he keeps his ego firmly on a leash. Give him round one of this battle of comic giants, by a decision.

The Mourning Forest, Mogari no Mori, rating: ★★★★, runtime: 97 min.

In her methods and concerns Naomi Kawase resembles other documentarians turned fiction film directors, such as Hirokazu Koreeda and Nobuhiro Suwa, but she has also gone her own way, quietly, stubbornly and successfully. In May she reached a new career peak by winning the Cannes Grand Prix for her drama "The Mourning Forest." It's an extraordinary work, fulfilling the promise of "Suzaku," the Kawase film that won the Cannes Camera d'Or a prize for first-time feature directors a decade ago.

Both films are set in rural Nara, which has been Kawase's spiritual home since childhood. Both also deal with the themes of loss, memory and the relationship between humanity and the natural order. "The Mourning Forest," however, is more technically accomplished, with rich high-definition colors and compositions that make Nara's woods and fields look like visions of eternity. It is also stronger both dramatically and thematically.

Instead of borrowing from a sure-thing manga or best seller, like so many of her contemporaries, Kawase wrote an original script light on dialogue and heavy on visuals that her backers had to take largely on trust. Also, instead of a bankable star, she cast freelance writer and used bookstore proprietor Shigeki Uda as her lead. This amateur had to play, not a version of himself, but a 70-year-old man in the last stages of senility — a challenge for even a veteran actor. Uda rises to it magnificently, in an egoless performance that is wordlessly eloquent.

Uda lives in the best of possible old folks homes: a clean, airy, comfortable place in a beautiful natural setting, run by a youngish woman (Machiko Watanabe) with a genuine affection for her charges. But he can barely speak and among his few remaining words is the name of his wife Mako, dead now 33 years. Something clearly bothers him, something that he can't express, something that causes problems for the home's staff, particular newcomer Machiko (Machiko Ono, who also appeared in "Suzaku").

Shigeki is attracted to her, first because her name is only one syllable different from his wife's, but more importantly because she is a sympathetic soul, who sees not only the disease that has stolen his memory and personality, but also the human being who still lives. Together they romp amid the tea bushes like two children, enjoying each other's company, beyond the conventional bounds of caregiver and patient. At the same time, Machiko is dealing with the recent death of her child and trying to rebuild her life. Her relationship with Shigeki contributes to this process, but he is also a handful, pushing her roughly in a fit of pique and falling out of a tree as she helplessly looks on. Then, one sunny day, she takes him for a drive and everything goes wrong. The car falls into a ditch on a country road and Shigeki wanders off when she goes for help. She manages to catch up with him, but can't control him as he steals a watermelon from a field, smashes it and gobbles the fruit.

Following his impromptu meal, he strides off into the nearby hills with Machiko close behind. His destination? "Where Mako is," he says, whatever that means.

The film follows the pair into the night and the next day through various crises and coming-togethers, including one memorable scene in which Machiko strips to warm a water-chilled Shigeki with her bare flesh. There is nothing sensual in this act; instead it simply but powerfully symbolizes the bond that has grown between the two while underlining their common humanity.

In filming this story, Kawase rejects the melodramatics of the usual local Alzheimer's film. She uses few cuts and explanations, while allowing her characters a full range of emotions, from rage to tenderness.

"The Mourning Forest" demand attention and patience, but it also sinks in, like a memory that takes on a greater meaning through time. It defies the tendency to define human worth in terms of beauty, power, possessions and other exteriors attributes. Its message: The loving soul endures, even when the mind departs. Skeptics may laugh; I'm sure Kawase won't care.

Funuke, Show Some Love You Losers!, Funuke Domo, Kanashimi no Ai o Misero, rating: ★★★⯪, runtime: 112 min.

Black comedies about dysfunctional families are common in Japan, from Sogo Ishii's anarchic "The Crazy Family" (1984) to Takashi Miike's batty "The Happiness of the Katakuris" (2001), the first Japanese zombie musical. "Funuke, Show Some Love You Losers!," which has one of the best English titles I've run across in a while, is the latest in this loopy line. Screened in the Critics' Week section at this year's Cannes Film Festival, this first feature by Daihachi Yoshida has a clever script, talented cast, vivid characters and, as might be expected from a veteran CM director, ample eye candy, including an inspired sequence in which real life segues into manga.

What it does not have is a consistent tone, as it veers from sitcom yoks to drama shocks. This is calculation, not incompetence — Yoshida wants to make, not just a laugh fest, but an unblinking examination of how families can become swamps of crushed hopes, suppressed rage and sexual deviance. Was he inspired by similar examinations by Todd Solondz ("Happiness"), Wes Anderson ("The Royal Tenenbaums") and Noah Baumbach ("The Squid and the Whale")? No telling, though Yoshida's script is based on a novel by Yukiko Motoya.

What is clear, though, is the scarcity of real laughs, with most coming from the brilliant Hiromi Nagasaku as a strenuously "normal" housewife. This may help "Funuke" qualify as festival-worthy art, but it lessens its value as stress-relieving entertainment. Minus Nagasaku, it would be just mildly funny and vaguely creepy, like taking a bus trip with a gorgeous neurotic and learning that she has has carved her beloved brother's forehead into a checker board. You might feel like making an unscheduled stop, no?

Or you might make an exception for Eriko Sato, who played a superpowered robot in the SF-romp "Cutey Honey" and a child-abusing teacher in the horror "A Slit-mouthed Woman."

In "Funuke" she plays a failed actress who has both a dark and a comic side. Sato's performance is all of a piece, even when her character stinks up an audition and has a fit when she is booted. She is brilliantly awful, superbly enraged.

She plays Sumika Wago, who returns to her home in rural Hokuriku for the funeral of her parents, killed in a freak road accident. There she meets her mousy little sister Kyomi (Aimi Satsukawa), who works at a part-time job in town, her sullen big brother Shinji (Masatoshi Nagase), who is a wood-cutter, and his new bride, Machiko (Nagasaku). A frantically cheery loner who has exiled herself from Tokyo to the boonies in pursuit of a normal family life, Machiko finds herself a bystander in a sibling war, with strange undercurrents that surprise and appall her in various measures — though she never loses her chirpy manner and eagerness to smooth things over in the name of "family harmony."

The battle lines, however, were drawn long before Matsuko arrived on the scene. Four years ago, Sumika was quarreling with her hard-headed father over her dream of going to Tokyo and becoming an actress. Sharp words led to violence — and left Shinji with the aforementioned scarred forehead and Kyomi, then 14, with the desire to draw the family drama in manga form. She submitted her finished work, depicting Sumika as a latter-day Lucrezia Borgia, to a horror comic and won a newcomer's prize. The ensuing uproar, with the whole village devouring Kyomi's roman a clef, led to Sumika's departure (though the money she raised by turning tricks with a former classmate eased the way).

Back now, dead broke, to claim her share of the inheritance she is angered to learn from Shinji that the money is not forthcoming. Soon after, she is dumped by her manager and takes out her disappointment on Kyomi, as fearful as ever of big sis's bullying, but still drawing on the sly. Then Sumika reads in a magazine that a famous director is looking for a "new type of heroine" for his next film, which will be on the theme of "communication." She decides to communicate with him by letter — and is overjoyed when she gets a reply hinting that she might be the one he is looking for. Will all finally be forgiven and Machiko's impossible dream of a happy, loving family come true?

The problems of the Wago clan run too deep and weird to admit of an easy solution, however. To begin with, the three women are all infected with the artistic virus: Sumika is obsessed with acting, Kyomi with drawing and Machiko with making bizarre dolls out of yarn, buttons and other household scraps. All three are dreamers unsatisfied with the status quo — and all three are punished for it. Stolid Shinji, whose idea of recreation is a nightly bottle of beer, seems immune from the feminine madness swirling around him — but he, in fact, is the most vulnerable of all.

A Shohei Imamura or Akio Jissoji might have made a dark human drama from this story, with real knives and murder. Yoshida prefers toys and paper as his characters' weapons of choice — and his film is neither comic fish nor dramatic fowl. But I'd watch it all again for Nagasaku's hilariously twitchy reactions to humiliations and outrages, which elevate the arts of self abasement — and the double take to new levels. She deserves a TV show of her own: "Desperate Housewives — Japan Style."

Adrift in Tokyo, Ten Ten, rating: ★★★★, runtime: 101 min.

With the films of Satoshi Miki, beginning with "In the Pool," a 2005 comedy about the three wacky patients of an even madder psychiatrist, there has always been a "but": terrific gag ideas, but shaky plot structures; likable quirky characters, but they don't develop so much as shamble. In short, his films, including the inventively titled "Turtles Swim Faster Than Expected" (2005) and "Insects Unlisted in the Encyclopedia" (2007) have been patchy affairs, with flashes of crazy brilliance.

In his new film "Adrift in Tokyo," Miki finally puts together a great comedy from start to finish. His two principals — an eternal college student and a middle-aged debt collector — still shamble through the story, but have a definite goal, and their relationship grows as they pursue it.

The gags are still funny, but also reveal character and advance the story. The premise — two strangers spend a few strange days walking around Tokyo — is typically Miki in its improbability, but by the end their journey makes a kind of poetic sense.

There is no obvious lesson-learning, but real bonding takes place, and real changes occur. The same is true of heroes in other offbeat road pics, but Miki sets the credibility bar high, which make his clearing of it all the most impressive.

He also drawn inspired comic performances from his leads, Tomokazu Miura and Joe Odagiri. Miura, who shot to fame in the 1970s as pop diva Momoe Yamaguchi's love interest in film after hit film (and husband since 1980), has since matured into a versatile character actor who deftly works both sides of the comic/dramatic divide.

His turn as the irascible debt collector, Fukuhara, is his best yet, the sort of performance that reveals as much about the tired tricks of other actors in similar roles as it does about the character itself. Instead of coasting with prickly-old-guy shtick, Miura creates an inner world for Fukuhara with its own cast-iron logic that may seem bizarre to outsiders, but makes absolute sense to Fukuhara himself.

Odagiri's student, Takemura, is at first baffled and intimidated by Fukuhara, but at the same time charmed and fascinated by his oddball honesty. Something of an oddball himself in the Japanese industry — think a Johnny Depp with stranger hair and role choices — Odagiri is perfectly in tune with what Miura is trying to do, while going beyond slacker cliches into a cooler dimension of his own: Odagiri World.

Takemura begins the film as an 8th-year college student who has somehow managed to accumulate ¥840,000 in debt. Abandoned by his parents in childhood, he has no one to turn to for the cash. One night a stranger with a grubby trenchcoat and grizzly beard, Fukuhara, bursts into his apartment, puts him in a chokehold and demands the dough, or else. Takemura agrees to scrape it up, but his feeble attempts, including a losing pachinko session, fail miserably. Then, the day before the debt comes due, Fukuhara comes to Takemura with an unusual offer: walk with him from Kichijoji to Kasumigaseki for ¥1 million, paid on successful completion. Takemura has no choice but to go along.

On the first day of the walk, Fukuhara tells Takemura his reason for it: He killed his wife and intends to give himself up at the Sakuradamon police station. Takemura, a law student, urges Fukuhara to go to the nearest cop shop — if the police discover the body before he turns himself in, the hand of the law will be heavier, Takemura explains — but Fukuhara refuses to change his plan: It's Sakuradamon or nothing. They have many adventures and make many stops along the way, including a stay at the home of a club mama (Kyoko Koizumi) who serves as Fukuhara's "emergency wife." Don't ask me to explain that one.

Meanwhile, his real wife's scatter-brained colleagues at the supermarket where she works note her absence, but can't get it together to find out what happened to her. Fukuhara and Takemura will have plenty of time to make what is not just a hike around picturesque Tokyo landmarks, but a journey of remembrance. Fukuhara, we see, loved his wife: Her (unseen by the audience) death was evidently an accident, though he admits responsibility.

Doesn't sound like the material of the next Ben Stiller comedy, does it? But in Miki's hands, Fukuhara's long march to the clink starts to feel, if not normal, at least possible. Also, the types he and Takemura encounter, including an elderly gent in a white superhero costume and a busker with a guitar and portable amp who plays power riffs as he strolls, make this odd couple look almost average.

"Adrift in Tokyo" made me feel better about living in Tokyo — other cities may have better housing or wider sidewalks or cleaner air, but we have more interesting weirdness.

Summer Days with Coo, Kappa no Coo to Natsuyasumi, rating: ★★★★, runtime: 140 min.

"Summer Days with Coo" is Keiichi Hara's anime about a family's encounter with a kappa — a mythological creature that might be described as a Japanese leprechaun, if leprechauns could swim, sumo wrestle and absorb water through a little bowl on their head.

Disclosure: I have a personal connection with this movie, since much of it is set in the town where I live, Higashi Kurume, including my morning jogging course.

Located in western Tokyo, Higashi Kurume usually draws a blank when I mention it to foreigners, even ones who have lived in Tokyo for years. Many assume I have buried myself in a faceless bedtown (while they live the urban high life in a six-mat flat in Harajuku). The place, however, has its charms, among which are two small rivers — the Kuromegawa and Ochiaigawa — that bisect it and whose banks are lined with bike paths, masses of flowers and much greenery, which the city cuts several times yearly to keep the bug population down. The rivers are also home to many ducks, carp and other creatures, though kappa are probably not among them.

Should I have recused myself from writing about "Coo?" Maybe, but the film, which Hara spent five years making, is that rarity in the anime world: a mass-audience entertainment made as a labor of love, with the focus on quality, not formula. One comparison is with Studio Ghibli, whose animators have reportedly raved about "Coo," but Hara's imagination is more solidly rooted in the here-and-now than that of Ghibli auteur Hayao Miyazaki, whose settings may derive from Japanese and European models but exist only in Miyazaki Land.

Hara, though, has a Miyazaki-like talent for bringing common fantasies to vibrant, spine-tingling life. And Miyazaki-like, his characters have specks of grit in their natures, from pettiness to selfishness, that aren't all scrubbed away by the end.

Hara also shares Miyazaki's skill at depicting the natural world — and his understanding of its beauty, mystery and fragility. Biking around the neighborhood after seeing "Coo," I realized that my eyes had been dulled by familiarity. Yes, Hara and his animators have improved on reality — making even moldy gray stucco look atmospheric, but they see what remains of the old, original Higashi Kurume that many of its natives are all-too ready to pour concrete over.

Hara's hero is Koichi Uehara (voiced by Takahiro Yokogawa), a boy who finds a mysterious stone on the bank of the Kuromegawa, which looks like a fossil inside. But when he takes it back home and washes it, while chasing away his annoying little sister (Tamaki Matsumoto) and trying to placate his dubious mother (Naomi Nishida), a boy kappa (Kazato Tomisawa) pops out, woken from a 300-year sleep. The kappa saw his father cut down by a frightened samurai and, as he was trying to escape from the murderer's blade, fell into a crack opened by an earthquake.

With the help of his kappa-conversant dad (Naoki Tanaka), Koichi slowly brings the kappa back to the land of the living and dubs him "Coo" for the first sound he uttered. Coo can speak antiquated Japanese, toss Koichi and even Dad in sumo bouts, and eat pretty much anything put in front of him, including sis's pet snails. Koichi sleeps with him, takes him on tours of the neighborhood in his knapsack and otherwise does what he can to keep Coo thriving and happy, but the kappa is lonely. There seems to be no one like him in Higashi Kurume — and Koichi and his family, fearing for his safety, discourage him from independent exploration.

One day Koichi and Coo set out by train for Tono, a town in Iwate Prefecture in the far north of Japan known for its kappa lore. If any kappa remain in Japan surely they must be somewhere in Tono's lush green paddies and sparkling rivers.

There is much more to the story, including the uneasy relationship between Koichi and a shy-but-pretty classmate, and the depredations of the mass media, so much so that "Coo" would have benefited from judicious cuts. But it's hard to blame Hara for wanting to realize his kappa's world as completely as possible — especially since I happen to be living in it.

But I honestly feel you'll enjoy "Coo," even if you don't own a house in Higashi Kurume — emphasis on "honestly."

Sex is no Laughing Matter, Hito no Sex o Warau na, rating: ★★★★, runtime: 137 min.

The romantic combination of an older woman and a younger man is common now in Hollywood films, which have come a long way since the day when a young (actually 30-year-old) Dustin Hoffman threw over a middle-age (actually 36-year-old) Anne Bancroft in "The Graduate."

This combination, however, is not often found in Japanese films. One reason, I suppose, is that women over a certain age — traditionally 25 — have long been considered past their romantic sell-by date, especially to younger guys, who might regard them as an onesan (older sister) or obasan (older woman) but rarely a potential kanojo (girlfriend). This is changing, though, as Nami Iguchi's "Sex is no Laughing Matter" makes refreshingly clear. Based on an eponymous novel by Naokora Yamazaki, the film is an unusual combination of drama and comedy within a relationship, shot in the by-now standard indie style: longish cuts, no close-ups, and naturalistic dialogue and acting. Expecting, from the stylistics, a subdued and downbeat look at age-inappropriate love, I was pleasantly surprised by the film's sly humor, freeform eroticism and refusal to treat its theme as inherently sad.

Iguchi and her collaborators, including co-scriptwriter Yuka Honcho and star Hiromi Nagasaku, turn the usual May-September romance tropes on their head. They have created, not a fantasy figure, but a down-to-earth heroine who, on the verge of 40, is still willing and able to take what she wants sexually, despite society's norms.

She is Yuri, a teacher of lithography at an art college. We first see her stumbling along a mountain road at dusk, with a broken heel, after missing a last train. She is rescued by a girl and two guys in a pickup truck, one of whom, the tall, boyishly handsome Mirume (Kenichi Matsuyama), helps her into the back, rides with her to the nearest bus stop — and hands her his own flip flops.

Later, Mirume, who is a student at the college, borrows a light from a woman smoking next him on a campus bench — and realizes she's Yuri. Giving no sign she knows him, she walks away — and Mirume follows her to her classroom. When he peers in the window of the classroom door, she pops up from the other side and sticks out her tongue, scaring him half to death. This is clearly no ordinary obasan.

As she instructs a curious Mirume in the art of lithography, we realize she is also thorough professional, as well as obviously older than her new student, despite her youthfully trim figure and vivacious — if mischievous — personality.

She asks him to be her model and, when he arrives at her house for a drawing session, seduces him with sly calculation. Unlike the girl he spends time with at college, the tomboyish En-chan (Yu Aoi), Yuri is unembarrassed by sex, treating it as a game. Mirume is soon an eager player. When he starts taking the game seriously, however, Yuri stops coming to school. A worried Mirume arrives at her door, where he is greeted by a kindly gray-haired fellow (Morio Agata), Yuri's artist husband. Yuri is unapologetic about her duplicity, while Mirume is flabbergasted but not discouraged. The husband remains blissfully oblivious — or is perhaps simply resigned.

Meanwhile, En-chan, now aware of what is going on, decides to confront Yuri. Yet another player in this romantic roundelay is the nerdy Domoto (Shugo Oshinari), who is head over heels for En-chan and best friends with Mirume.

Iguchi could have taken this setup in the direction of farce — or tragedy. Instead, she finds a middle way that is truer to life — or rather Yuri's unconventional character. Also, where most directors would turn up the volume, with towering rows and thrown crockery, she turns it down. The volatile En-chan expresses her frustration at her rejection by bouncing on a bed around Mirume's passed-out-drunk form. The scene is cute but unfolds without a word.

Life, of course, is not always a low-volume affair, and the film might have benefited from a comic row or two, but the title has it right. Sex, even for a free spirit like Yuri, has consequences, not all of which can be laughed away.

Nagasaku, who gave the funniest performance of 2007 as the batty housewife in "Funuke Show me Some Love, You Losers" is also excellent as Yuri, striking the right balance between the manipulative and playful sides of her character. She is a bit of a devil, this woman, but a likeable one. Her boy toy strikes it lucky indeed — and unlike the witless Benjamin, knows it.

Fine, Totally Fine, Zenzen Daijobu, rating: ★★★★☆, runtime: 110 min.

Japanese comedies today come in two broad categories: frantic, surreal ones of the Kankuro Kudo ("Maiko Haaaan!!!") sort and ironic, realistic ones from the Nobuhiro Yamashita ("Linda, Linda, Linda") corner.

Yosuke Fujita's "Fine, Totally Fine" falls firmly into the latter category from the first scenes, which slowly but inventively introduce the oddball characters and set up the love-triangle story. And the film, which Fujita also scripted, stays focused and funny, but relaxed, to the end.

Two brothers — dough-faced, developmentally arrested Teruo (Yoshiyoshi Arakawa) and the mostly grownup Hisanobu (Yoshinori Okada) — live together with their father (Keizo Kanie), who runs a failing used bookshop and is slowly going crazy from boredom.

Teruo, a horror buff, dreams of building the ultimate amusement-park haunted house, but his reality is a part-time job trimming trees. Hisanobu, a human-resources manager at a local hospital, tries to be Mr. Nice Guy to everyone, but secretly hates his dull, purposeless life — and vents his frustration on Teruo.

Into this dysfunctional little family stumbles Akari (Yoshino Kimura) — shy, clumsy and unworldly, but also pretty, literate and artistic. Hisanobu hires Akari as a cleaning lady at the hospital, even though she arrived at the interview with torn clothes and a bloody nose. He sees something real and pure in her — something he wants to investigate further.

Then she comes into Teruo's orbit as well — and he sees in her not just a kindred soul but a future wife. The romantic battle of brothers is growing to absurd heights when a sensitive but facially flawed art restorer (Naoki Tanaka) walks through the bookshop doors and threatens to sweep Akari off her feet.

From this bare description, "Fine, Totally Fine" may sound more like a fraught relationship drama than a knee slapper; but in Fujita's hands plot points take second place to character-based gags, which are plentiful — ranging from the gross (Teruo's colleague absent-mindedly exposing himself to Akari) to the strange (Teruo's collection of monster figures that all feature his perfectly modeled head) and everything in between.

The film's comic core, though, is Arakawa, who looks like an overgrown kid and can get laughs just by wrinkling that baby-smooth brow. Rather than rely on his cartoonish looks, Arakawa plays Teruo as a real, if ridiculous, human being — existential angst included. It's not always fun, we see, being trapped in a 12-year-old's body and mind when you're pushing 30. A kid may be happy with play and dreams, but an adult has to eventually make it real, and somehow Teruo knows it.

Holding the dramatic center is Kimura's Akari, who begins by apologizing for her existence but gradually emerges into the light of her own quirky day. Without fuss or strain, Kimura shows us why three guys compete for the hand of this seemingly mousy dweeb — and why she ends up with the one she does.

The English title, "Fine, Totally Fine," not only describes the mood of this quietly brilliant film but also sounds like a three-word review. This film is more than daijobu — it's totemo, totemo subarashii. Really, really wonderful.

Where Are We Going?, Doko ni Iku no, rating: ★★★★, runtime: 100 min.

Japanese indie directors who made their reputations in the 1970s and '80s often have big gaps in their feature-film resumes. Sogo Ishii didn't make a feature for 10 years following 1984's "Crazy Family,"a groundbreaking black comedy. Mitsuo Yanagimachi, who burst onto the scene in 1976 with the legendary biker pic "Godspeed You! Black Emperor," took a 13-year break after "All About Love, Tokyo" in 1992, a gritty drama about Chinese students in Japan.

The record for the longest such hiatus must belong to Yoshihiko Matsui, who worked as an assistant director for Ishii before directing three indie films that were released between 1981 and 1988. The last, "Noisy Requiem," was a black-and-white film set in Osaka's down-and-out Shinseikai district where a mad serial killer disembowels his victims and stuffs their insides into a female mannequin. The film became a love-it-or-hate-it underground sensation. Then Matsui himself went underground for 22 years.

His re-emergence with "Where Are We Going?" is a cause for celebration. The film tells an unusual love story, with an unusual power that comes from Matsui's absolute sincerity. Despite what sounds like a gimmicky premise — a gay shophand falls in love with a transsexual bar hostess — the film contains not a single wink. Instead it views the world through the eyes of its outsider pair and allows us to directly experience their isolation and rage, as well as their all-too-brief moments of release and joy. Matsui is not merely sympathetic to these characters — he artistically inhabits their skins.

Much of the authenticity comes from the casting of Anzu, a real transexual Matsui found working as a hostess at a Shinjuku club. She is not required to act so much as play herself (even her character name is Anzu). She is somehow apart from the run of humanity, as though living in a universe separate from the "normals" around her. Her character is wise in the ways of the world, but also quiet, sensitive and, once she has her mind set on something, almost scarily focused.

Matsui's hero, however, is the passive-aggressive Akira (Shuji Kashiwabara), who lost his parents as a child, was sent to a orphanage and now works in a machine shop whose owner (Genjitsu Shu) is enamored of him in a creepy, obsessed way. He has been sexually harassing Akira for years, but lacking the will or any alternatives, Akira can't break free from the owner's clutches. His only escape is his motorbike so, with the goal of buying a bigger one, he fellates Fukuda (Kazuhiro Sano), a grizzled, cynical police detective, for cash. Fukuda is also infatuated, but Akira treats him like a human ATM. He feels, in fact, little for anyone.

Then one day, riding his bike too fast, he clips a woman walking on the side of the road — and takes her to his apartment to recover. Bruised and battered, she is strangely silent and calm — and Akira finds himself attracted. Several days later, she returns for her bag, which she had forgotten — and the jealous Fukuda, who has been watching Akira's apartment, rushes to head off what he thinks is his new rival. But he doesn't stand a chance — Akira is already in love and so, soon, is Anzu.

What follows includes a lyrical romantic interlude and a murder, both of which feel natural and the latter, in Akira's case, fated. As we watch Akira and Anzu methodically dispose of the body, we realize that they are not just bonding but expressing their outcast anger at a world that uses them, mocks them and has never really cared for them. But they care for each other — and that's all that matters, for the moment.

"Where Are We Going?" has something of a time-capsule feel, as though Matsui picked up where he left off in 1986. Made for a tiny budget, it also has a few technical rough spots, such as a shot of a burning body that is too obviously a dummy. But it has two decades of stored up passion behind it, the sort of passion conspicuous by its absence in the Japanese film world today. Matsui-san, welcome back and, this time, stick around.

Gachi Boy Wrestling with a Memory, Gachi Boy, rating: ★★★★, runtime: 131 min.

Pro wrestling gets no respect, save from the fans who love watching it, and the schoolboys who practice its moves. I was once one of those boys, trying out head butts (learned from Bobo Brazil) and karate chops (acquired from Rikidozan) on my little brother.

Pro wrestling is also a popular theme for Japanese and other Asian filmmakers for box-office reasons. In Japan especially, the sport has long been a big draw with top performers from Rikidozan to Antonio Inoki and Giant Baba winning mainstream recognition.

"Gachi Boy Wrestling with a Memory," the second feature by 27-year-old Norihiro Koizumi, focuses not on college kids who never got over their schoolboy (or schoolgirl) wrestling obsessions. Fun, frothy, knockabout comedy it's not. Based on a hit play first staged by the Modern Swimmers theater company in 2004, "Gachi Boy" is a story of superhuman persistence in the face of unimaginable loss.

Being a sports movie, it has to end with a big, climatic bout, which is done without wires, CG or stunt doubles, and comes as close as possible to the bruising reality of non-staged ring fighting. Remember the championship bout in "Rocky," when it looked as though the battered hero might end the fight with his pride restored but with permanent brain damage? The "Gachi Boy" finale has the same sort of intensity and suspense.

The hero, Ryoichi Igarashi (Ryuta Sato), is a genius who passed the notoriously tough Japanese bar exam while still an undergraduate. As the film begins, he is working up his courage to enter the headquarters of the once-fabled school pro-wrestling club which has fallen on hard times and is in desperate need of new blood. The members, including the cute manager (Asako Asaoka) and handsome club captain (Chihiro Okudera) — ring name Red Typhoon — welcome Igarashi with open arms.

They notice, though, that he has an odd habit of recording everything they say or do in a notebook or with a camera. Well, geniuses have their eccentricities, don't they? And Igarashi is also enthusiastic, practicing the routines over and over. He gets a ring name, Maririn Kamen, and makes his debut, at an exhibition bout in a shopping mall. He's a hit with the crowd, but forgets it's supposed to be fake and attacks his opponents for real.

His memory, we learn, was short-circuited by a traffic accident a year previously. He can remember everything before the accident, but everything after becomes blank after one day. Every morning he has to reintroduce himself to his teammates, his sport, his entire post-accident life.

He tries to hide this condition from his teammates, but even after he is exposed he refuses to quit. His memories don't linger to the next day, but his wrestling does. The aches and bruises remind him (as do the notebooks he keeps) that he exists in more than the present day. They have become precious to him.

As Igarashi, Sato ("Lorelei") starts in the shallow comic end of the pool, playing up the character's puppy-dog charm. He then moves the deeper dramatic end without sacrificing the qualities that made Igarashi appealing. By the time he steps into the ring, together with Red Typhoon, against his toughest-ever opponents — two blonde brothers with Greek-god bodies and sadistic impulses — he is a fully realized figure who refuses to be defined by his tragedy.

There are gags aplenty, from the obvious to the laugh-out-loud funny. But most of all, "Gachi Boy" has energy, heart — and guts. Sato and the other actors do all their own throws, falls and holds, culminating in the all-stops-out finale. Some stunts look outright dangerous, others must have been brutally exhausting to execute. I half expected to see an outtake reel at the end, as in a Jackie Chan movie, showing their injuries. Their pain, however, is our gain. You'll come out of the theater ready to put a headlock on life.

Still Walking, Aruitemo Aruitemo, rating: ★★★★, runtime: 114 min.

Family drama is the default setting of serious Japanese cinema. No matter what genre first brings Japanese directors fame and fortune, be it yakuza actioners or horror, they often end up making a family drama to establish their auteurist credentials.

Hirokazu Kore'eda had international success with "After Life" (1999), a fantasy set in a way station for the recently dead. He also won kudos for "Nobody Knows" (2004), a harrowing drama about children trying to survive after being abandoned by their mother. A family drama of sorts, but not the type that Yasujiro Ozu — the ultimate master of the form — would have made.

Kore'eda's latest film, "Still Walking," is more Ozuesque, though not in any way a homage. Instead, he has set himself a tough challenge: Depict the inner life of a family while limiting the story to 24 hours and keeping the dialogue and action as naturalistic as possible.

Films or TV dramas with a tight time frame are usually premised on completing a vital task, such as foiling a terrorist plot, before the time is up.

Kore'eda takes quite a different tack in telling the story of a middle-aged brother and sister and their families visiting their aged parents, a situation entirely mundane. Their reason for gathering, however, is not — they are commemorating the death of the couple's oldest son, Junpei, who drowned 15 years earlier when rescuing a boy from the nearby sea.

The story revolves around intergenerational strife. The retired physician father, Shohei (Yoshio Harada), still mourns Junpei, a shining youth and appointed heir to his clinic, while belittling his surviving son, Ryota (Hiroshi Abe), an out-of-work art restorer he considers a second-rater.

Instead of foregroundiing this conflict with the loud confrontations of TV drama, Kore'eda subsumes it into the realistic bustle and chatter of a family gathering. The film begins with Ryota's tart-tongued mother Toshiko (Kirin Kiki), cooking up a storm with her flaky daughter Chinami (You), while Chinami's amiable car-salesman husband (Kazuya Takahashi) plays with their two cute kids.

Then Ryota arrives, reluctantly, with his nervous new wife, Yukari (Yui Natsukawa), and her son from a previous marriage, Atsushi (Shohei Tanaka), a bright, observant boy. This trio fits in awkwardly with the familial goings-on, especially when it becomes obvious that Shohei wants as little as possible to do with Ryota — and the whole scene of chatting, cooking women and noisy, rambunctious children. He poses as the busy medical man, when all he is doing is hiding in his now unused office.

Kore'eda, who wrote an original novel on which the script is based, exploits the comedy in the situation, with veterans Yoshio Harada and Kirin Kiki supplying most of the laughs as the bickering elderly couple. He is more interested, however, in exposing the fault lines in the principal relationships — and how they suddenly crack under the pressure of forced conviviality after long separations.

Ozu did something similar in his masterpiece "Tokyo Story" (1953), in which an elderly couple visiting their adult children in Tokyo encounter coldness and indifference behind the welcoming smiles and solicitous words. Ozu and his collaborators, however, wrote dialogue as stylized as haiku, despite its naturalistic surface.

By contrast Kore'eda, who began his career making TV documentaries, writes dialogue that sounds transcribed from a tape recorder at an ordinary family get-together, while scrupulously avoiding audience cues to pull out the hankies. Instead he produces moments of what might be called heightened awareness — when a key phrase or exchange makes obvious what had been hidden or implied, like firecrackers going off with a flash and a bang.

By the end we see that however long resentments seethe or regrets fester, they soften with time, while their perpetrators — Shohei being the prime one — are not monsters, but fallible, even lovable, human beings.

"Still Walking" was rejected by the Cannes festival, perhaps because it's too much on the quiet side, not enough on the provocative side — which Kore'eda's previous Cannes competition entry, "Nobody Knows," certainly was. For me the film, like all of Kore'eda's better work, sank in deeper on a second viewing, since I was paying less attention to the background noise and more to the hard notes of family discourse (or rather discord) that strangers may downplay or miss but pierce the targets straight through.

The title — and the film — get it right: No matter how much time and space you put between yourself and the past, the ancient family dramas never really end. Until all the players leave the stage.

Ponyo, Gake no Ue no Ponyo, rating: ★★★★, runtime: 100 min.

Hayao Miyazaki's most beloved film in Japan — "My Neighbor Totoro" (1988) — is also among his easiest to understand. Even tots can thrill to the film's epic ride on the Cat Bus — one of the coolest forms of transportation ever invented, as long as you're not allergic to felines.

His latest feature animation, "Ponyo," exceeds even "Totoro" in simplicity, with a core target audience about as old as its hero — 5. This is not to say that those older will be bored, as long as they leave their expectations for the usual Miyazaki film at the door.

In "Ponyo" Miyazaki is not just telling a story to tikes, but imaginatively becoming one. I was reminded of the famous opening of James Joyce's "Portrait of the Artist as a Young Man," with its recital of the hero's earliest memories in the language of infancy ("Once upon a time there was a moocow coming down along the road and . . ."), as if the author were re-inhabiting an earlier self.

He also revisits themes from other, more adult-focused films, such as humanity's destruction of the natural world, and nature's revenge on its human tormentors. The animation is Miyazaki's familiar mix of the realistic and fantastic, with extinct sea creatures swimming contentedly alongside their contemporary — and accurately rendered — descendants. In other words, there is still plenty to engage the mind and eye, as well as keep the small army of Miyazaki explicators busy.

The title character, Ponyo (voice by Yuria Nara), is a girl fish with a human face who decides one day to leave her underwater home — and her school of smaller sisters — to see what lies on the surface. Riding on the back of a jellyfish, she is nearly trapped by a drift net, but escapes — with her head stuck in a glass jar.

Sosuke (Hiroki Doi), a boy who lives on a house on a seaside cliff, spots Ponyo in the shallows and rescues her. He is delighted with his new pet — and Ponyo is delighted to be in the human world at last. She says her first words, to Sosuke's astonishment — and begins a transformation from half-fish to human.

Meanwhile, her human father, Fujimoto (George Tokoro), who lives in an undersea manse with Ponyo's sea-queen mother (Yuki Amami), goes in search of her. With his long hair, beaky nose and tormented, bags-under-the-eyes expression, Fujimoto looks like a decayed aristocrat from a shojo manga (girls' comic), but he possesses magical powers over the waves, which become like living creatures under his command. What can a mere kid, if one with a feisty mom he calls Lisa (Tomoko Yamaguchi), and a good-natured, if mostly absent, ship-captain dad (Kazushige Nagashima), do to stop him?

"Ponyo" is not about a simplistic struggle between good and evil, however. Fujimoto is more of a worried father than a scarily powerful villain. Also, with the aid of her sisters, Ponyo unleashes powers of her own, with awesome, if unintended, consequences.

The film meanders into various byways, such as the day-care center for the elderly that Lisa runs, with a female clientele that ranges from the cute to the cranky — and serves as a Greek chorus to the action.

The focus, though, stays mostly on Sosuke and Ponyo, whose relationship undergoes a change from master/pet to protective older brother/bubbly, if trouble-prone, younger sister. There is something dreamlike about their adventures in both the thrilling wish-fulfillment of them and their spooky shape-shifting. Small children, who naturally live on the borderline between reality and fantasy, will have no trouble following along.

As with most Miyazaki films, I walked out of "Ponyo" thinking less about the rambling story, based loosely on "The Little Mermaid," than certain strangely gripping scenes, such as a grimly determined Lisa zipping along a seaside road in her mini car, with Sosuke at her side, as angry anthropomorphic waves crash and lash around them, or Sosuke and Ponyo puttering idyllically over a submerged town in a toy boat powered by a burning candle, which has magically grown big enough to hold them.

No one but Miyazaki could have created anything like these moments, with anything like his mastery. If "Ponyo" is the start of his artistic second childhood, I say welcome to the sandbox.

Your Friend, Kimi no Tomodachi, rating: ★★★★☆, runtime: 125 min.

Kids often make friends easily — and lose them quickly. The boy who was your best buddy yesterday has today found a new friend, a new crowd, a new world that doesn't include you.

But as Ryuichi Hiroki's new film, "Your Friend," shows, a childhood friendship can also last a lifetime. Based on a novel by Kiyoshi Shigematsu, the film examines various friendships, but its narrative core is a relationship between two girls that begins from conditions neither of them want, but becomes as essential to them as air.

Hiroki, who started his career making "pink" (soft-core porn) films, observes his characters' lives in a small provincial town, from the beauty of the open sky to the casual brutality of school rivalries, with a distanced but perceptive gaze. He has little use for the formulas of the seishun eiga ("youth film") genre, from melodramatic plot turns to a J Pop soundtrack obliterating the dialogue.

Instead he relies on naturalistic dialogue and action that feel like noodling to those used to conventional movie storytelling, but he carefully lays the groundwork for climactic scenes the way a jazz improviser departs from a melody to drill down to its emotional core.

Hiroki also prefers to make his visual points with poetic long shots rather than spell-it-out closeups, so it's no surprise that his central image for the film is clouds, particularly a special cloud that becomes the standard against which the girls measure all others.

This may seem a banal choice. Why not add snow for purity and sunshine for happiness? But in the hands of Hiroki and scriptwriter Hiroshi Saito, the clouds that keep appearing in the heroines' conversation and on the screen are anything but ordinary. Instead they serve interconnecting purposes — as a personal symbol of hope for a sick girl, as a private link between two friends and as metaphors for the presence of death in life and the eternal in the everyday. They are also constants in the film's countryside, where the sky is wider and feels nearer than in the city.

Emi (Anna Ishibashi) and Yuka (Ayu Kitaura) begin the film as elementary school classmates, recruited by a teacher to swing a long jump rope for the other children in a school contest. Emi is selected because she has a degenerative kidney disease that makes hard exercise dangerous, Yuka because she has a permanent limp from a traffic accident — that was inadvertently caused by Emi.

Yuka resents Emi for this — and her anger reduces Emi to tears. Yuka's heart softens, and the two girls become friends, a bond that is strengthened by their disabilities that their healthy classmates can neither understand nor share.

As they become teenagers, Emi spends more time in the hospital and Yuka finds herself alone again, until she is approached by Hanai (Yuriko Yoshitaka), who envies Emi and Yuka's friendship and wants to experience something like it herself. But Yuka cannot forget Emi — or her story about a cloud in the hospital children's playroom (called the "friends' room") that made her feel happy and free. Emi's dream is to become a cloud herself, watching over Yuka everywhere. Yuka begins to photograph clouds — and paints one for a now bedridden Emi that is Yuka's vision of Emi's perfect cloud.

Another plot thread concerns Yuka's socially awkward younger brother, now in the seventh grade, who worships a school soccer star and childhood friend — and is crushed when the star ignores him. Still another deals with a ninth-grade boy who is no longer on the soccer team — all ninth graders quit the club to study for their high-school entrance exams, but still tries to lord it over the younger team members. He, it turns out, has no friends at all.

The film, however, keeps returning to the friendship of Emi and Yuka, framed by Yuka's present as a young woman who is still passionate about photography and teaches at a free school for children with disabilities. A brash college student, Nakahara (Seiji Fukushi), visits the school to photograph and interview the children. He becomes attracted to Yuka — and engrossed in her remembrances of Emi.

Ayu Kitaura glows with a fierce brightness as the prickly Yuka, who has little patience with superficial sympathy, but pours out her grief with a rawness that breaks your heart.

Does Yuka finally find Emi's cloud? The answer is not as obvious as you might think, but the ending hits the note you somehow knew was coming all along: Sad, beautiful, perfect.

Departures, Okuribito, rating: ★★★★, runtime: 130 min.

A culture's attitude toward death is always going to be something of a mystery to outsiders, even ones who try to immerse themselves in the local language and customs. Yojiro Takita's "Departures" focuses on one Japanese death custom that even most locals don't experience: the ministrations of the nokanshi (literally, "encoffining master"), a professional who cleanses and clothes a body. The film's nokanshi hero elevates a simple task to a refined ritual with practiced, elegant movements, while communicating a compassion for the deceased. This, he wordlessly shows the survivors, is no mere lifeless body, but a person worthy of respect and love. With his expert touch, he brings the dead back to a semblance of life.

Takita, together with producers Yasuhiro Mase and Toshiaki Nakazawa, labored nearly a decade to bring "Departures" to the screen, which sounds about right, since the subject does not shout "big box office." More surprisingly, all three are commercial filmmakers, though Takita directed indie black comedies, notably "The Yen Family" in 1988, before going mainstream with films like the period fantasy "The Ying Yang Master" (2001) and teen baseball drama "Battery" (2007).

The film begins with the hero, Daigo Kobayashi (Masahiro Motoki), already a nokanshi, working on a most unusual subject — a young transgender man who has died as a woman, though his relatives have neglected to inform Daigo and his boss, Sasaki (Tsutomu Yamazaki), of the fact. Daigo's discovery of his subject's sex is funny in Takita's old black comic vein — and indicates that "Departures" is going to be hard to describe. But I'll try: It's about finding your bliss, even if the world thinks your bliss is odd, icky and a marriage breaker.

After this intro, we see Daigo in his previous life as a newly out-of-work cellist.

With no prospects for another job, he and his perky wife Mika (Ryoko Hirosue) move to his hometown in rural Yamagata. There he answers an ad for what he thinks is a travel agency and learns from the blowzy receptionist (Yo Kimiko) and later from the gruff president (Tsutomu Yamazaki) that they send clients not to Hawaii but to the next world. Daigo takes the job anyway and discovers that he has an aptitude for it, though his first assignment, an old woman who died alone in her fly-infested house, is stomach-turning.

As a child, Daigo was abandoned by his father and left alone after the death of his beloved mother. As a nokanshi, he finds that by helping others accept their losses, he can better deal with his own. The job is also a natural outlet for his musician's sense of beauty and order. Mika, however, can't get over the yuck factor, as well as the social shame of her husband's profession. She gives him a choice: dead people or her.

Masahiro Motoki had the original idea for "Departures" and, as Daigo, gives the performance of his career — restrained, but fully expressive of his character's many sides. Tsutomu Yamazaki, as the crusty funeral director Sasaki, gets laughs with the scampish shtick he has been perfecting since his breakthrough as the truck-driver/ramen-guru in Juzo Itami's "Tampopo" (1985). But as a pro who thoroughly enjoys the pleasures of life, from the food on his table to the plants he surrounds himself with, Sasaki also serves as a role model for his younger colleague.

The film may idealize the nokanshi's job — Daigo's subjects are often younger and more attractive than the real-life norm — but it also makes a good case for the Japanese way of death. Better to be prepped for the final journey by a nimble-fingered nokanshi creating a human ikebana display than made up, Western-style, like a wax dummy for Madame Tussaud's. Too bad I won't be around to see the show.

Tokyo Sonata, rating: ★★★★★, runtime: 119 min.

Kiyoshi Kurosawa has long been filed under "horror director," though his take on the genre is anything but standard. The villain of "Cure," his creepy 1997 breakout film, is not a maniac with a sharp-edged weapon but a blank-faced drifter who hypnotizes his victims into killing themselves.

Kurosawa sees evil not as an outside force but integral to the strange, menacing nature of our universe. Given the right conditions — a weakening of the psychic immune system in "Cure" or a break in the wall between the living and dead in "Pulse," (2001) — we can all become vulnerable to its invasion. Also, he builds his scares from mundane materials — a flicking light, puddling water or red tape on a door.

Genre cinema, however, is defined by formulas that place limits on even the most creative. Kurosawa danced in his chains better than most, but his recent horror outings have been unfocused and uninspired, even verging on the farcical. In his newest film, "Tokyo Sonata," Kurosawa has abandoned horror for that staple of Japanese cinema — the family drama — and returned to form, brilliantly. Screened in the En Certain Regard section at this year's Cannes Film Festival, "Tokyo Sonata" won the Jury Prize, the only Japanese film to leave the festival with an award this year.

Based on an original screenplay by Australian Max Mannix that Kurosawa and scriptwriter Sachiko Tanaka polished, "Tokyo Sonata" tells a typical story of these economically uncertain times: A middle-age salaryman, Ryuhei Sasaki (Teruyuki Kagawa), loses his job, but doesn't tell his wife, Megumi (Kyoko Koizumi) or two sons — sixth-grader Kenta (Kai Inowaki) and college student Taka (Yu Koyanagi). Instead, he tries to keep up appearances, leaving home each morning dressed in a suit and tie and carrying a briefcase, but spending his days searching fruitlessly for work, killing time in a public library or lining up for a free lunch with the homeless and the other unemployed.

This is similar to the set-up of Toshiaki Toyoda's "Hanging Garden," a 2005 film in which Koizumi also starred. But where Toyoda's film about familial masks had a black comic tone, Kurosawa's is almost entirely straight-faced — and scary.

The scares come not from ghosts but from feelings of grim helplessness and hopelessness that grip Sasaki as his life slowly, inexorably circles the drain. Though he desperately tries to hide the shame of being unemployed, his little poses and ruses are relentlessly stripped bare by a searching glance, a mocking request or a disastrous chance encounter. He is living a nightmare — and since it's largely of his own making, he can't easily escape it.

His one companion in misery is a former high-school classmate, Kurosu (Kanji Tsuda), who has also joined the ranks of the jobless, but has the confident, swaggering air of a survivor. Sasaki clings to him as to a lifeline — but Kurosu is also teetering on the edge.

Megumi sees the change in her husband — she even catches him sneaking home early the day he is fired — but doesn't voice her suspicions. The lines of communication between them are vanishingly thin — about the only time they occupy the same psychic space is the evening meal, which Sasaki chomps down with barely a word. Still, she would rather keep up the illusion of normality than risk a confrontation.

The two boys are less restrained. When Kenta asks his parents if he can study piano and is brusquely refused by his father (for reasons he can't disclose), he takes lessons anyway, paying for them with his lunch money, while telling no one. When Taka tires of his aimless existence, which includes a part-time job handing out tissue packs on street corners — he decides to join the U.S. Army over Sasaki's strenuous objections.

So far so typical: Traditionalist fathers in Japanese family dramas have been watching their authority slip away for decades now. But rather than proceed to the expected denouement — Sasaki sees the error of his ways and reconciles with his family — the film takes unexpected turns, some violent, some deadly, some bizarre, that throw all the principals off their assigned tracks. In short, "Tokyo Sonata" becomes a Kurosawa film, in which everyday reality is upended to better reveal the baseline humanity of the characters.

This is a risky narrative strategy, as Kurosawa has already proved in previous, less successful outings, but the film reaches another, higher level, something like a near-death experience that changes everything, even if a sober explanation of it sounds absurd.

Teruyuki Kagawa, who often plays men at the end of their tethers, does his familiar sweaty, shifty-eyed turn as Sasaki, but with an unusual intensity, as if he is being not just humiliated, but also physically hunted. As Megumi, Koizumi adds layers of dark complexity to that generic character —

the put-upon housewife. Megumi is tough and shrewd — little gets by that appraising glance — but she is also capable of courage, tolerance and passion. She holds the family — as well as Kurosawa's best film in years — triumphantly together.

Achilles and the Tortoise, Achilles to Kame, rating: ★★, runtime: 119 min.

Zeno's paradoxes are ancient mind games that undermine common-sense assumptions about reality. In the most famous, "Achilles and the Tortoise," a fast runner and a tortoise start at the same time toward the same goal, the tortoise with a head start — say it must cover 10 meters while the runner must sprint 100 to the finish line. Can the runner overtake the tortoise and win?

No, says the paradox, since when the runner reaches the tortoise's starting line, the tortoise will have moved to point A. When the runner reaches point A, the tortoise will have moved to point B, and when the runner reaches point C, the tortoise will be at point D, ad infinitum. But would you bet on a tortoise against Usain Bolt?

In Takeshi Kitano's new film, "Achilles and the Tortoise," the runner is a hapless artist named Machisu, the tortoise the art he is seeking to master and, later in life, the success he is trying to win.

In a private joke, all the art on the screen is Kitano's. Also, Kitano plays the artist in late middle-age, whose every attempt to catch the shifting winds of art world fashion ends in ridiculous failure.

This may be a private joke as well, since Kitano's own attempts to win international honors for what might be called the "Kitano trilogy" — "Takeshi's," "Glory to the Filmmaker!" and "Achilles and the Tortoise" — have finished in disappointment, if not outright failure. Festival juries have not exactly showered awards on these films, with their self-referential, self-sabotaging focus on Kitano's public vs. private image ("Takeshi's"), directorial struggles ("Glory to the Filmmaker!") and artistic doubts ("Achilles and the Tortoise"). It's as if, instead of making "City Lights" and "Modern Times," Charlie Chaplin had spent his middle years filming in-joke excursions into the psyche and celebrity of a perfectionist director with a thing for teenage girls.

Not that Kitano is a Chaplinlike genius, but his poison-tipped tongue and unbuttoned mind have rightly made him the king of Japanese TV comedians, while his cheekily unorthodox, thoroughly Kitanoesque approach to filmmaking — every frame being unmistakably his — once made his films, from "Hana-Bi" to "Zatoichi," among the most interesting coming out of Japan.

By comparison, "Achilles" is a schizoid wreck in search of an identity — or at least a coherent story line. The film begins channeling 1950s studio melodramas about family dissolution. Sad-sack young Machisu (Reo Yoshioka) is the pampered son of a wealthy businessman and Western art collector (Akira Nakao) who encourages his boy's budding interest in art. When Daddy's business goes bust, poor little Machisu is cast into the cold, cruel world, like a Dickens orphan, stubbornly clinging to his art as to a lifeline.

Switch to the '60s, when Machisu, now a lugubrious not-so-young man (played by 45-year-old "Takeshi Army" veteran Yurei Yanagi), is still banging away at his art, while working day jobs as a newspaper delivery boy and print shop hand. At the latter job he meets Sachiko (Kumiko Aso), a pretty office worker who is supportive of his artistic ambitions. He is thwarted, however, by a hard-to-please gallery owner (Nao Omori) who urges him to try something more contemporary than the conventionally realistic (and, as it turns out, eminently salable) harbor scene Machisu shows him.

So he slogs off to art school where he meets a wild crowd of conceptual artists whose idea of painting is riding a bicycle hung with paint buckets on the handlebars into a huge white canvas, splatting the paint — and the rider.

So far so fun. But Machisu ages into a middle-age hack (Kitano) who enlists the ever-loyal Sachiko (Kanako Higuchi), now his wife, in ever more hair-brained attempts to make saleable conceptual art, from flinging paint onto a canvas with a small catapult to having Sachiko drown him in the bath so he can paint his near-death visions. But nothing pleases the gallery owner. Then his fed-up teenage daughter (Rei Tokunaga) leaves, followed eventually by Sachiko. Having sacrificed his family and artistic soul on the altar of art-as-business, Machisu is seemingly left with one choice: death.

This third part has next to nothing to do with the first two, being little more than a series of mildly funny sight gags. The banally cynical, boringly downbeat conclusion: The modern art world is a sham, with poseur dealers making fortunes from nonsensical garbage, while scorning and exploiting sad fools like Machisu, who play along but never quite get the hang of the hustle.

In "Achilles," Kitano falls into not only self imitation (much is familiar from the 1995 comedy "Getting Any?" and the 1999 road movie "Kikujiro" especially) but also the tired sentimentalism and rambling incoherence that reliably signal directorial collapse. I had a similar feeling when I saw "Madadayo" (1993), Akira Kurosawa's last and worst film: The game is up. Is it too late for a reset?

2009

Fish Story, rating: ★★★★☆, runtime: 112 min.

Film critics like to be surprised, which comes from being unsurprised too many times. This critic, however, has become tired of "The Sixth Sense" school of script writing, enamored as it is of that 1999 hit's sleight-of-hand ending. But while a good magician can fool the eye in dozens of ways, a scriptwriter can create only one big trick called the plot — and as script-writing teachers never tire of repeating, nearly all can be boiled down to a handful of patterns. The hero wins, the hero loses — the hero turns out to be a ghost.

Yoshihiro Nakamura is a confessed fan of "The Sixth Sense" director M. Night Shymalan. Nearly all his films mess with the minds of the audience on various levels, from the mundane whodunit, as in the medical mystery "The Glorious Team Batista" (2008), to the reality-is-a-big-fat-illusion cosmic, as in the cult hit "The Foreign Duck, the Native Duck and God" (2007).

"Fish Story," Nakamura's 10th film as director, is by far his best. Based on a novel by Kotaro Isaka, who also supplied the story for "The Foreign Duck, the Native Duck and God," "Fish Story" reveals its true message only in its climatic sequence, while carefully preparing us for it from scene one. The big revelation, though, is less a clever plot trick than an eternal verity, presented in a dazzling rush of images. I walked out of the theater feeling more hopeful about humanity and my own luck.

The film skips back and forth between four stories in four main time periods as well as four genres (music, seishun eiga ["youth film"], action and sci-fi). One story follows the fortunes of a pioneering "punk" band from 1973 to its breakup in 1975. Another, set in 1982, focuses on a wimpy college boy (Gaku Hamada) given a chance to prove his courage. A third centers on a ferry-boat waiter (Mirai Moriyama) who dreams of martial arts glory and a teenage passenger (Mikako Tabe) he tries to save from forces of evil.

The film starts in 2012. Only five hours remain, we are told, until a comet will slam into the Earth and obliterate all life. A middle-aged man (Kenjiro Ishimaru) in a wheelchair wanders through an abandoned shopping arcade until he comes across a record store. Inside he finds the goateed manager (Nao Omori) with a nerdy customer, discussing the song "Fish Story" by the aforementioned punk band.

The man thinks they are insane — don't they know humanity is kaput? — but the manager denies it. "A fighter for justice will save the world," he says.

The heroes of all four stories are losers and/or dreamers who struggle against realities around them, to the detriment of their status, career and even survival. It is hard, however, to see how their stories will tie up, as the chronology shifts back and forth and the comet draws ever closer.

Also, at certain points the action grinds to a halt, as when the band members and their harried manager (Omori again) discuss the title of their new song at incredible length. Why "Fish Story?" And what on Earth does it really mean?

This could have become tiresome, but the characters are engaging types who tackle big issues without becoming pompous or ridiculous. Instead, a current of dry humor runs through the film.

Nakamura makes it clear early on that he is after something bigger than easy laughs, however. Bigger fish, you might say, such as five final minutes of pure cinematic satori.

Instant Numa, rating: ★★★★, runtime: 119 min.

Satoshi Miki's latest comedy, "Instant Swamp," is about a cracked journey of self discovery. A dizzying opening montage introduces the heroine and her past at warp speed, but Miki's unique brand of dry obsevatinal comedy is still much in evidence, as is his affection for Japan's odder corners and personalities.

Haname Jinchoge (Kumiko Aso) is a hard-charging magazine editor who considers herself a super-rational type, unlike her flaky, easy-going mother (Keiko Matsuzaka), who tells Haname, with a straight face, that she suspects a kappa (mythical water sprite) is living in their garden.

Then, in quick succession, Haname loses her job when her magazine goes kaput, the pony-tailed photographer she likes dumps her and repo men come to claim nearly everything she owns. She finds herself scraping out a bare, lonely existence, with a pet rabbit her only company. Then, after mom nearly drowns looking for a kappa in a nearby pond and ends up in a coma, Haname decides to find one Noburo Jinchoge, who says in a letter never delivered, but miraculously discovered, that he is her real father.

Haname locates the address in the letter — a tumble-down "antique" (read: "junk") shop run by a brusque man with an electro-shock hairdo — Noburo (Morio Kazama), nicknamed Denkyu (Light Bulb). She refuses to believe that this weirdo is her father, but Gus (Ryo Kase), a punk rocker and a store regular, immediately sees the family resemblance.

A conventional plot would lead to a father-daughter reconciliation and a romance between Haname and Gus, a decent guy despite his no-nonsense persona. But Miki, who also wrote the script, delivers a stranger, more interesting story in which Haname falls victim to what seems to be a cruel scam — and ends up with a pile of mysterious dirt. Then she has a cracked inspiration — make a swamp out of it.

Kumiko Aso has played plenty of oddball characters in a busy career, from the eccentric waitress in "Cafe Isobe" (2008) to the hero's sexually-twisted fiancee in "Then Summer Came" (2008), but her Haname is something special: a woman who takes after her wacky parents but is also her own determined person, as she pursues a vision that the skeptical Gus considers mad.

Her payoff, which also happens to be the film's climax, is neither predictable nor logical, but it made me smile – and gave me the chills. I wouldn't blame you if you thought it a tad silly — and neither, I think, would Miki.

This original, unpretentious comic talent isn't out to convert everyone. But if you've already got a kappa hopping around in your brain, "Instant Swamp" will be your cup of — something a lot like, but not quite, mud.

Bare Essence of Life Ultra Miracle Love Story, rating: ★★★⯪, runtime: 120 min.

Kenichi Matsuyama is one of Japan's Johnny Depps (several actors are vying for that honor), meaning he has legions of female fans, but usually plays off-beat roles with no romantic interest in sight. In Satoko Yokohama's "Bare Essence of Life," Kenichi Matsuyama is Yojin Mizuki, a mentally challenged man living with his grandmother (Misako Watanabe) in rural Aomori Prefecture. Yojin brims with energy that ranges from the playful to the destructive. That is, he is a cross between a full-of-beans kid and a troubled man with all the standard appetites, sex included.

Think a latter-day Japanese version of Boo Radley in "To Kill a Mockingbird": A fleshed-out character who is mythopoetically larger than life.

We first see Yojin shocked awake in his ramshackle house by a cacophony of alarm clocks. After examining the white board where he carefully records his day's schedule, he ventures out into his garden, where he disconsolately examines the cabbages, full of holes made by hungry insects. He then greets his grandmother, who answers curtly, her eyes glued on the television. So far, so mildly comic.

The film soon shifts into a stranger gear with the arrival in town of Machiko (Kumiko Aso), the new teacher at the local kindergarten. She has come all the way from Tokyo to Aomori to not only teach, but also to consult a local medium about the unquiet spirit of her dead husband (Arata), decapitated in a traffic accident.

Yojin and Machiko first meet at the kindergarten, where Yojin has come to sell his vegatables. He takes a liking to this attractive, city-bred woman and, after school, offers to escort her home. When she refuses, he starts to drag her off by main force.

As this scene suggests, where a Hollywood movie with a mentally challenged hero would tiptoe, Yokohama treads boldly, even dangerously. An Aomori native who won many prizes for her early indie work, including her 2006 feature debut "German + Rain," Yokohama films the locals not as an anthropologist studying an exotic tribe, but as an affectionate native daughter who gets both the accents and eccentricities right.

Working from her own script, she has also made more than another feel-good drama about a disabled hero. Yojin is a volatile mix of free-spirited exuberance, romantic fantasies and violent frustration, though he does far more harm to himself than those around him. Finally, after accidentally-on-purpose self poisoning with insecticide, and treatment by the gruff, good-hearted Dr. Misawa (Yoshio Harada), he encounters Machiko's husband, minus his head, on the Other Side.

We are not, we realize, in a typical Japanese commercial drama, easy to classify by genre and target audience. We are also not in one of the many local indie films that proclaim their seriousness with downbeat, wispy naturalism.

Yokohama has instead made an original hybrid that may venture into black comedy and freaky surrealism, but makes emotional sense, however odd. Yojin and Machiko, we see, are two lonely outsiders, one who likes kids, another who happens to think like one. Their unconventional connection has a certain rightness, as does Yojin's apparently mad, self-destructive pursuit of his dream.

The ending shocks — and follows from everything that came before. Is the film itself the "miracle" of the Japanese title? Not quite — it's more a collection of arresting scenes and images than a coherent whole. Is it touched with the magic of a real talent? Most definitely.

Dear Doctor, rating: ★★★★☆, runtime: 127 min.

Movies about impostors and grifters tend to view their roguish heroes with indulgence shading to admiration, but rarely disapproval. Miwa Nishikawa's take on this theme in "Dear Doctor" departs brilliantly from the usual winking and rib poking. Not that she tuts disapprovingly through her story of a fake doctor in a rural middle-of-nowhere, but she takes it seriously. Unlike the grifts that damage only bank balances and egos — phony medicine, she shows us, can kill.

So why does her hero, the elusive Dr. Ino (Tsurube Shofukutei) still have sympathizers, even after the police expose him to his former patients and colleagues as a con artist? This, not the case the cops are trying to close, is the film's central question — and Nishikawa, who also wrote the script, probes the emotional realities behind social masks, while refraining from pat answers.

She does offer plenty of insights, including the one that the right look (white coat and thinning hair) and manner (authoritative and reassuring) make the medico, especially in a village hours from the nearest hospital, where almost any doctor is welcome.

Ino begins the film as an escapee from justice, headed unseen for parts unknown. Our first view of him is in happier days at his clinic, where he greets a young medical school grad awakening from a bump on the head after an accident on a country road. Named Soma (played by the single-named Eita), he has come from the city in his fancy red convertible to work under Dr. Ino for the summer months before returning to civilization.

Soma is inspired by Ino, who spends long hours visiting his mostly elderly patients in their homes, patiently listening to their troubles and cheerfully dispensing advice. Soma, whose own doctor father was an all-business type, marvels at Ino's self-sacrificing attitude — and starts to think of staying on rather than cutting out. But Soma also starts to realize that, while Ino's bedside manner is impeccable, his medical skills are suspect. He is not the only one — a stoic veteran nurse (Kimiko Yo) and a smarmy drug salesman (Teruyuki Kagawa) also know that Ino is living a charade, but for reasons of their own, don't call him on it.

The film's narrative core is Ino's ambiguous relationship with Kazuko (Kaoru Yachigusa), a widow who has been fainting from stomach pains, but has never been to the clinic for an examination. After caring for her invalid husband for years, she has no wish to inflict similar trouble on her own daughters, especially her youngest, who is studying medicine in Tokyo. When Ino finally uncovers her secret — a possible fatal illness — she asks him to lie for her.

His entire life may be a lie, but Ino is torn. He wants her to get proper treatment, even though the truth may emerge — including the truth about him.

Nishikawa also examined the problem of truth and its unintended consequences in the 2006 "Sway," which won domestic prizes and was screened in the Cannes Directors' Fortnight section. But whereas "Sway" was a courtroom drama with a forced whodunit story arc, "Dear Doctor" is a character study that has no false notes whatsoever.

Not that Ino's character is easy to grasp. As played by Shofukutei, he is a riddle wrapped in an enigma who shifts with every tremor of the physic and social wind.

A well-known rakugoka (comic storyteller) and TV personality, Tsurube has been appearing more frequently on the screen in recent years, including a turn as a ne'er-do-well uncle in Yoji Yamada's wartime family drama "Kabee: Our Mother" (2008). Though he can glide by on folksy shtick when it suits him, Tsurube delivers the double-jointed performance of a lifetime as Ino, shifty in his sincerity, genuine in his desire to help and deceive. There is something of the lost boy in this character, who seeks love by lying — even when he knows the lies will destroy the love.

To her credit, Nishikawa does not fall into jokey cynicism, though she does leaven the story with dry humor. She also does not turn it into a cautionary tale, with a strained justice-triumphs-over-evil ending.

Within the flow of the film's naturalistic surface, she has inserted notes that resonate at a metaphorical level. One is Ino's pen, which he inherited from his physician father and carries as a token of promises unfulfilled. Another, is the scene that opens the film — a distraught Soma thrashing through the weeds in the dark, seemingly searching for his disappeared mentor.

Or it is his own illusions that have gone missing?

Zero Focus, Zero no Shoten, rating: ★★★★, runtime: 131 min.

Mystery writer Seicho Matsumoto (1909-1992) was long to the Japanese entertainment industry what Stephen King has been to Hollywood — a one-man fiction factory who supplied material for dozens of films and TV dramas. One of his most popular novels, "Zero Focus," was made into a 1961 film by Yoshitaro Nomura. Now Isshin Inudo has directed a new version set in the 1950s, evidently quite faithful to Matsumoto's novel — unread by me.

Since his feature debut in 1995 with "Two People Talking," Inudo has made a mix of indie and commercial projects with both often featuring strong female characters and a visual richness, even on an indie budget. So Inudo was a natural choice for "Zero Focus," which belongs to its three female leads and unfolds in and around Kanazawa, Ishikawa Prefecture, one of Japan's beauty spots.

The film, which centers on a woman's desperate search for her missing newlywed husband, evokes the work of Alfred Hitchcock in everything from its saturated colors and portentous, dreamy tone ("Vertigo") to a spectacular location where a character takes a long, fatal plunge ("Saboteur" and "North by Northwest").

But there are also echoes of Douglas Sirk, whose 1950s films dramatized the consequences for women who transgressed the era's social and moral codes, such as the upper-middle-class widow's relationship with her younger gardener in "All that Heaven Allows."

Inudo, like Sirk, treats these choices — and the punishments inflicted on the women who make them, both seriously and ripely. His heroines suffer all right — but with costumes, makeup and lightning that accentuate their tragic, noble beauty, as the violins swell. It's melodrama, if you like, but with an undeniable power.

The story begins in 1957 with the arranged marriage of the naive, fresh-faced Teiko (Ryoko Hirosue) to Kenichi (Hidetoshi Nishijima), a pleasant, if guarded, man who works for the Tokyo branch of an ad agency. Seven days after their wedding, he leaves for Kanazawa, his former posting, for what he says will be a brief business trip. But when he doesn't return on the promised day, Teiko becomes worried, then frantic.

She then travels to Kanazawa alone in the dead of winter to find answers, but realizes she knows next to nothing about her husband's background. From one of his former colleagues she learns that Kenichi was close to Gisaku Murota (Takeshi Kaga), the brusque president of a local-building materials company and a major client, and his elegant, regal wife Sachiko (Miki Nakatani), an ardent supporter of a female candidate for mayor who, if elected, will be the nation's first woman in such a post. This pair, however, has little to tell her about Kenichi's possible whereabouts.

Teiko also encounters Hisako (Tae Kimura), a company receptionist whose ability in English — a rare ability in a provincial city then — is offset by her lack of education. She got her coveted job though a connection, Teiko learns — but how and why?

These women, we see, are not what they seem — and have connections with Kenichi that go beyond Kanazawa. But Teiko does not know how her investigation poses a threat to certain people until bodies begin turning up.

One reason the Japanese murder mystery has not made much headway in the West are the lengthy explanations often appended after the killer is unmasked. It's as if Hitchcock had ended "Psycho" with a 10-minute disquisition by the arresting officer.

"Zero Focus" is no exception to the genre rule, but it's also more than a whodunit. Its larger theme is how women in the early postwar period struggled against social and political strictures, while trying to escape poverty and, in some cases, their own pasts. It also illustrates how one breath of scandal could blow away their artificially constructed personas.

The three leads — Ryoko Hirosue, Tae Kimura and Miki Nakatani — were cast for their acting skills as well as their star power, as indicated by their shelves of Best Actress prizes. Nakatani dominates as an upstart provincial aristocrat, her icy, imperious gaze masking a raging ambition — and knawing insecurity. Sirk would have loved her — his Japanese Barbara Stanwyck.

Summer Wars, rating: ★★★★★, runtime: 114 min.

"Revenge," George Orwell once wrote, "is bitter," but it can also be sweet, can't it?

When Studio Ghibli asked Mamoru Hosoda, an up-and-coming animator at Toei Animation, to direct "Howl's Moving Castle" (2004), it was as if the Imperial family had allowed a commoner to marry one of its members. Then Hayao Miyazaki — Ghibli's emperor — decided to take over the film and Hosoda was cast outside of the palace gates. Rather than cry in his futon over the injustice of it all, Hosoda directed the sci-fi anime "The Girl Who Leapt Through Time" (2006) for the Madhouse studio. Featuring a sensitive teenage heroine and a time-traveling storyline, with animation that expressed both emotional nuances and imaginative flights, "Girl" was a surprise hit, as well as a winner of many prizes and festival invitations. Meanwhile, its Ghibli box-office rival, "Tales from Earthsea" (2006), directed by Miyazaki's son Goro, was bashed by critics (this one included) and did, for a Ghibli film, mediocre business.

Hosoda's followup is "Summer Wars," an animation again made with Madhouse and scriptwriter Satoko Okudera, but with a bigger budget and wider distribution by Warner Japan. Focusing on an epic computer game battle, "Summer Wars" is an ambitious step forward for Hosoda — and a sure-footed one it is.

The film also points out the conservatism of so much feature anime, which either endlessly repurpose popular manga, TV anime and game franchises (e.g., the products of Toei Animation) or rework familiar tropes (e.g., Ghibli's spunky young heroines and its evergreen theme of environmental destruction) over and over. "Summer Wars" may contain familiar elements, beginning with its moonstruck hero, but combines them in ways contemporary and dazzlingly imaginative.

Unlike mass audience anime that look back nostalgically to the historical or folkloric past or ahead to various futuristic fantasies, "Summer Wars" is totally of the postmillennial moment. Watching it, I felt like a print-and-ink dinosaur — and more hopeful about the digital culture that has connected nearly everyone in the country. Instead of surrendering their souls to the Internet data stream — the theme of several postapocalyptic anime — the fighters of the title online "wars" retain their individuality and humanity, in every variation from the cute to the obnoxious.

Kenji (Ryunosuke Kamiki) is a teenage math prodigy who, together with his equally nerdy best friend, lives almost completely in an online world called Oz. Then, one summer day, a pretty sempai (senior), Natsuki (Nanami Sakuraba), asks him if he would like to help her with the big birthday celebration being planned for her grandmother (Sumiko Fuji).

Kenji agrees — and finds himself at the grandmother's huge, rambling house in Ueda, Nagano Prefecture, being introduced to Natsuki's large, rowdy family as her "fiance." Kenji is horrified — and secretly thrilled — but he is soon overshadowed by another arrival: the handsome, sardonic Wabisuke (Ayumu Saito), a computer whiz and the deceased grandfather's illegitimate son.

Natsuki flies into Wabisuke's arms — he is her "first love" — and Kenji feels pangs of jealousy.

The plot engine begins to rev when Kenji receives a mysterious e-mail filled with an eye-blurring numeric code. He cracks it, sends his solution to the hacker and, the next day, is shocked to see himself on the news, the prime suspect in a criminal hack that has turned Oz into a wasteland. The real hacker, who has invaded Oz by stealing Kenji's account, starts wreaking real-world havoc as well. Car navigation systems go on the blink, snarling traffic nationwide. Then the hacker seizes control of a weather satellite — and threatens to send it hurling to Earth like a guided missile.

Kenji, together with Wabisuke and Kazuma (Mitsuki Tanimura), a young gamer, challenge the hacker with a rogue AI (artificial intelligence) program. Soon, the aunts, uncles and cousins are also involved, appearing in Oz as a swarm of avatars. Their inhuman opponent, though, is clever, relentless and power-mad.

Despite the dozens of characters — including the 27 members of Natsuki's extended family — a surprisingly large number emerge as individuals. And though plot turns come thick, fast and fantastic, the story focuses more on its human characters than the heroics of its cyberbattle. Some of the developments, such as the revelation of Wabisuke's parentage, are standards, but they are so sharply observed and charged with energy, emotional and physical, that the "cliche" label doesn't apply.

Hosoda and his team have produced scenes of animated spectacle that, in their fluency of motion and brilliance of invention, make the usual sci-fi/fantasy anime look childish and dull. At the same time, the film's universe is grounded in reality, with fantasy confined to the online sphere (though some of the wackier visual gags push the limits of the possible).

This family-friendly entertainment is also an incisive commentary on the ongoing transition from the grandmother's analog world of handwritten cards and letters to her grandkids' realm of digital devices. Will we succumb to our gadgets and machines? The film's "wars" are no fiction — and our victory is not yet certain.

Symbol, rating: ★★★★, runtime: 93 min.

Every once in a while, a distributor will ask audiences not to reveal anything about a film's ending — a gimmick that became popular with "The Crying Game" (1992). But at a press screening of Hitoshi Matsumoto's new comedy "Symbol," I received a personal first — a list from distributor Shochiku of five points not to reveal in my review, including anything that happens in the last act. The proscribed bits are mostly surprise gags and plot turns, which I would not reveal in any case, but following Shochiku's rules to the letter means being vague about what makes "Symbol" special — and special it is.

Anyone familiar with Matsumoto's work — from his countless TV variety shows to his 2007 directorial debut "Big Man Japan" — knows his mind has a comic logic all of its own.

He plays a wise-cracking dimwit in the comedy duo Downtown, but in his film he is capable of brilliant "what if" wackiness that elicits one of two reactions: bemusement or helpless hysterics.

Also, as a comic, Matsumoto seems to have no "front" at all. What you see is what you get, with no pretensions, inhibitions or fear.

"Symbol" begins with a pudgy pro wrestler in a dusty Mexican town silently preparing for a tag-team bout with younger, stronger opponents. Just about the only one who thinks he can win is his equally pudgy young son, who plans to attend the bout with his grandfather. Will the boy be cruelly disappointed? Haven't we seen this movie before?

Meanwhile, in an alternative universe, a man (Matsumoto) wearing polka-dot pajamas and sporting a pudding-bowl haircut wakes up on the floor of a big, white room. He has no idea how he got there — all he knows is he wants out, now. And that is about all Shochiku wants me to tell you about the room, though more than half the story takes place there.

I will say, however, that it reminded me of the situation astronaut Dave Bowman finds himself in after his epic voyage across the stars in Stanley Kubrick's "2001: A Space Odyssey." Totally isolated and dependent on unseen alien beings, he lives (or rather is caged in) what looks to be an apartment in a royal palace, with his every physical need attended to. Meanwhile, he is being prepared for a dramatic — and unexplained — transformation.

Matsumoto's take on his character's similar dilemma is comic, with brilliant running gags. But he also keeps a "2001"-ish cosmic hum in the background, reminding us that his hero's story is more than just a laugh machine — that it has a larger, metaphorical aspect as well.

Meanwhile, Matsumoto keeps us wondering about the Mexican story — we know that somehow the wrestler and the man in the room have to connect, but how? Matsumoto's solution to this problem is obvious enough in hindsight, and gets one of the film's biggest laughs. He also plays it mostly straight in this section, in a grainy, realistic style influenced by Mexican New Wave cinema, from Alejandro Gonzales Inarritu's "Amore Perros" (2003) and on. Even the wrestling scenes are staged for maximum impact, with the full-force body slams making us not only respect the hero's courage — but fear for his life.

The film's focus, however, is the trapped man's desperate interactions with his absurd new world — and how his struggles come to symbolize ours. The ending may strike some as cod-Kubrick — Matsumoto over-reaching for significance — but it impressed me as just right, given the long, careful buildup. Its message is simple enough: Actions have consequences, though our ability to foresee the latter is limited — if not nonexistent. And the Greatest Actor of All? Does He know the consequences, but not care? "Symbol" doesn't say, save symbolically. The interpretation is up to you.

Caterpillar, rating: ★★★★, runtime: 84 min.

Once an enfant terrible, who challenged censors and outraged conservative critics with surreal S&M sex and sympathetic portrayals of Palestinian radicals, Koji Wakamatsu has not mellowed so much as ripened. Wakamatsu still makes films that probe controversial subjects, from the inner and outer journey of a teenage killer ("Cycling Chronicles: Landscapes the Boy Saw," 2004) to the murderous career of the Japanese Red Army in the early 1970s ("United Red Army," 2007).

But he has evolved from the shot-on-the-fly experiments of his early years to stylistically pared-down films that are a form of passionate witnessing from a nuanced viewpoint that reflects his years and experience. Screened in competition at this year's Berlin Film Festival, his new film "Caterpillar" is a case in point. Though based on a story by Edogawa Rampo, Japan's master of the mysterious and bizarre, the film is not Rampo-esque in the least.

Instead it is closer in spirit to the World War II trilogy of the late Kazuo Kuroki — "A Boy's Summer in 1945" (2002), "The Face of Jizo" (2004) and "The Youth of Etsuko Kamiya" (2006)— spare, powerful films that examined home-front realities.

Wakamatsu's hero is Lt. Kurokawa (Shima Onishi), who has returned from China in 1943 minus his arms and legs, his once-handsome face disfigured by burn scars. He is also deaf and able to utter only grunts and croaks. Though decorated with three medals, this "war god" (as his comrades and fellow villagers describe him) is as helpless as an infant — and hates what he has become.

His wife Shigeko (Shinobu Terajima) reacts to his homecoming with undisguised horror, but being a dutiful type, stoically tends to his needs — including his appetite for sex. She soon realizes that being the spouse of a "war god" has raised her status in the village — so she trundles her scowling husband about in a cart, ostensibly to give him fresh air, in reality to lap up praise from all and sundry.

But as the months pass and the war situation worsens, Shigeko begins to hate being enslaved to a man who beat her daily when he was healthy and is now little more than a noisy, unsightly organism that must be constantly fed, cleaned and sexually serviced. Meanwhile, Kurokawa obsessively remembers the Chinese women he raped, killed and left to burn in flames. His visible wounds are only one form of torture; his mental anguish is worse.

Japanese WWII films with an antiwar slant usually portray the folks at home as either nobly pacifistic or mindlessly jingoistic. Shigeko, however, willingly does what is patriotically expected of her, such as proudly displaying her husband's medals and newspaper clippings in a sort of "war god" shrine.But as the reality of her situation sinks in and Japan's loss approaches, she begins to question the propaganda she has been fed. The radio, with its constant stream of faked news and idealistic blather, is no longer a source of comfort. She begins to act out her resentment and hatred. The "war god" is dethroned. She calls him a "caterpillar" — that is, a loathsome bug.

Terajima, whose talents have too often been wasted in formulaic roles in mediocre films, flawlessly registers Shigeko's complex mix of emotions, from the inside out. This career peak performance won her the Berlin Film Festival's Best Actress prize this year.

Onishi plays Kurokawa as both a monster reduced to raw need, and a man trapped inside the monster's ruined shell. He is one of the damned who will live with his crimes for the rest of his life. No metamorphosis for this caterpillar.

Wakamatsu, on the other hand, has evolved in an elder who is the fearless memory and conscience of his tribe. No fragile butterfly he.

Travels with Haru, Haru tono tabi, rating: ★★★★, runtime: 134 min.

Masahiro Kobayashi's knotty, idiosyncratic films, starting with the 1996 "Closing Time," have never found an audience in Japan, though they have become favorites of festival programmers. Four have screened at Cannes, including "Bashing" (2005), a grim drama of alienation and exclusion selected for the competition.

That's four more Cannes invites than most Japanese directors get in a lifetime, stirring up insinuations that Kobayashi, whose long association with France includes study of the language, must have an "in." I'm a Kobayashi fan, though I can't usually describe the experience of watching his films as "enjoyable." But I like his angle of vision, which can illuminate secret corners of the heart with a glare fierce and strange.

In his new film, "Travels with Haru" Kobayashi is attempting something in a more conventionally humanistic vein. One inspiration was the 1999 Zhang Yimou film "Not One Less," while others were such Japanese classics as "Tokyo Story" (1953) and "Ballad of Narayama" (1983). This approach is reflected in his casting of Tatsuya Nakadai, the 77-year-old great whose work with Akira Kurosawa, Mikio Naruse and Kon Ichikawa, among other master directors, is known worldwide.

Nakadai plays Tadao, a retired fisherman living with his granddaughter Haru (Eri Tokunaga) in an isolated Hokkaido fishing village. But Haru has lost her job in an elementary school cafeteria. Since local employment prospects are dim, she decides to go to Tokyo to find work.

Meanwhile, Tadao, disabled by a stroke, has made a decision of his own: Rather than burden Haru as she tries to restart her life, he will go to live with one of his siblings, none of whom he has seen or spoken with in years. One raw spring day, he clumps angrily out of his weathered house with a dubious Haru trailing behind.

This being a Kobayashi film, I could predict what would happen from this point: brutal rejections and bitter disappointments. Tadao's first, quixotic visit is to his rich older brother (Hideji Otaki), who cordially despises him. The brother tells him that he and his wife have been accepted into an expensive private retirement home. The impoverished Tadao need not apply.

Next Tadao and Haru go in search of his scapegrace younger brother Yukio, to whom he feels closest. But Yukio's common-law wife (Yuko Tanaka) tells them he has gone to prison for another man's crime. A soft letdown by Kobayashi standards.

Tadao and Haru continue their rounds, first to Tadao's older sister (Chikage Awashima), now an elegantly kimonoed, sharp-tongued innkeeper at a hot spring bath, then to his youngest brother (Akira Emoto), now a foul-mouthed failed businessman. Their last stop is the home of Haru's slithery father (Teruyuki Kagawa), who left home when she was little and is now the successful proprietor of a horse ranch. His wife (Naho Toda), though a stranger to both Tadao and Haru, is almost angelically decent to them, shades of Setsuko Hara's young widow in "Tokyo Story."

Kobayashi draws an obvious contrast between Tadao and Haru, both misfits with pure spirits, and their mostly conventional relations, who have played by society's rules and become hardhearted as a consequence. At the same time, he has little use for the sentimentality of the usual Japanese family dramas that revel in teary reunions and reconciliations. The hearts of his characters are too damaged for easy repair.

Nakadai's Tadao is a bearish man full of anger and pride who would cut off his nose — or rather his entire family — to spite his face. But his illness, as well as his five years with Haru — starting when her mother committed suicide — have worked a change in him.

Where a lesser actor would have played for audience sympathy, Nakadai refuses to make Tadao pathetic and thus lovable. Instead he keeps us guessing as to his true feelings and motives. Tadao is not posing as something he once was but is rather fumbling to let go of the one person he truly needs.

Eri Tokunaga's Haru is a typical Kobayashi heroine: unsociable and unfashionable, but stubbornly alive in her own person. A former model who has since branched out to TV, films and theater, Tokunaga trots with an odd bow-legged gait and otherwise does all she can to erase her real-life attractiveness. (By contrast, Setsuko Hara always moved with the grace of a dancer, even when playing dutiful daughter types.)

Kobayashi may have intended "Travels with Haru" as a left-handed tribute to Japanese cinema's Golden Age — but it's all Kobayashi, all the way. Or rather it's a lot like Haru herself — ungainly and unforgettable.

Golden Slumber, rating: ★★★★, runtime: 139 min.

Yoshihiro Nakamura has made a mix of indie and commercial films, from the end-of-the-world thriller "Fish Story" (2008) to the hospital mystery "The Triumphant Return of General Rouge" (2009). Whatever the subject, he always injects his personal obsessions, from the shape-shifting nature of truth to the connectedness of human beings, even across decades and generations.

His latest, "Golden Slumber," tells a man-on-the-run story with many Hollywood predecessors (Alfred Hitchcock's "North by Northwest" is one, Doug Liman's "The Bourne Identity," another), but Nakamura uses it, as always, for his own purposes. More than Hollywood thrillers, it's closer in spirit to "The Shawshank Redemption" and "Groundhog Day," with their messages of hope and renewal.

His everyman hero is Aoyagi (Masato Sakai), a delivery-truck driver from Miyagi Prefecture who is reuniting with old college chum Morita (Hidetaka Yoshioka) when something explodes nearby. The new prime minister, riding in an open car, has been assassinated — and Aoyagi becomes the prime suspect. That is, he is the designated patsy of an elaborate plot in which the hapless Morita was involved.

This is a nod to Oliver Stone's conspiracy potboiler "JFK," complete with Morita's observation that Aoyagi is the "new Oswald," but the film's true concern is less with political intrigue — we never learn much about the plot's inner workings — than the issue of trust.

With hundreds of cops on his trail, Aoyagi needs some help from his friends — but which ones? Another college pal, the nervous Gus (Gekidan Hitori), proves to be a bad choice, but encounters with a former flame (Yuko Takeuchi), a scrappy fellow driver (Kiyohiko Shibukawa), a suspected serial killer (Gaku Hamada) and a canny old hospital patient (Akira Emoto) are more fortunate.

Aoyagi became a local hero two years earlier for an act of random heroism. Still, the help he receives is motivated by more than a few news stories. Something has inspired his benefactors to believe in his innocence, despite all the (fake) evidence to the contrary. Are they angels, fools — or something else? And what does the Beatles song that supplies the title have to do with it?

Nakamura, that diligent student of Hollywood, skillfully hurls Aoyagi from one hair-breath escape to another, while semicomically filling in his background, beginning with a college "fast-food circle" where he and other members munched burgers and speculated about the Kennedy assassination. The middle section, in which Aoyagi finds temporary refuge, sags a bit — but lays the groundwork for the big, all-is-revealed climax.

It will be familiar to fans of "Fish Story," in which the myriad plot threads tie together for five minutes of cinematic satori. But if the previous film ended in a cathartic rush of revelation and relief, "Golden Slumber" concludes with a different feeling. All I'll say is I wasn't expecting it — but somehow I knew it was there all along. Just as Paul McCartney knew "a way to get back homeward."

Younger Brother, Ototo, rating: ★★★★, runtime: 126 min.

Selected as the closing film of the upcoming Berlin Film Festival, "Younger Brother" is Yoji Yamada's first contemporary drama in a decade, since "A Class to Remember 4: Fifteen" (2000). In that time Yamada's image has changed from money-spinning maker of the hit "Tora-san" series (48 entries from 1969 to 1996) to internationally celebrated auteur, whose many honors include an Oscar nomination for the period drama "Twilight Samurai" (2002).

"Younger Brother" reunites Sayuri Yoshinaga and Tsurube Shofukutei, who played a long-suffering mother and a scampish uncle, respectively, in Yamada's World War II drama "Kabei: Our Mother"

(2008). This time, Yoshinaga is Ginko, the proprietor of a small drug store in Tokyo and mother to Koharu (Yu Aoi), a sweet-tempered girl who is engaged to be married to a young doctor.

All goes swimmingly until the day of the wedding, when Tetsuro (Shofukutei), Ginko's ne'er-do-well younger brother, appears. A failed actor and an alcoholic, Tetsuro has been cast out of the family for various offenses — and shows why by turning the reception into a rowdy farce.

This should be the end, but it isn't because Ginko has been covering for Tetsuro all his life. When his ex-lover comes begging for money, she has to give and when he falls ill with cancer in Osaka, she has to go.

Good characters in Japanese melodramas are forever making similar sacrifices with noble grimaces and shining eyes, as the violins swell. Ginko, however, is no cardboard saint, but an ordinary woman deeply pained by the waste Tetsuro has made of his life — and who can't forget the hardships they endured together as children.

Yamada strips this story to its essentials, with no showy camera moves, syrupy music or overwrought acting. Instead he keeps the camera at an observant middle distance, steadily building to the moments when pretenses fall away and truth emerges. Some of those moments are sad and even terrifying, but some are beautiful as well.

Many Japanese directors try to jerk tears — it's among the surest routes to box office success here. But Yamada is one of the few who can touch hearts — and he's seldom done it better than in "Younger Brother."

The Accidental Kidnapper, Yukai Rhapsody, rating: ★★★★, runtime: 111 min.

Hollywood constantly remakes and reworks its old hits, but sometimes it falls out of love with stories, even ones once widely popular. The outlaw-on-the-run-with-a-strange-kid story, which Kevin Costner turned into the 1993 hit "A Perfect World," is one example. Perhaps American audiences — long fed horror stories of child abductions by pedophile creeps — cannot bring themselves to see such films any more, even the most innocent. That is not yet the case in Japan. Actor/director Hideo Sakaki's new film "The Accidental Kidnapper" takes inspiration from "A Perfect World" and others like it — but then injects a comic spin.

This could have been a recipe for another cutesy, weepy Japanese dramady, with everyone mugging away. Instead, Sakaki walks the line between comedy and drama with craft and heart. The laughs and tears are all of a piece, while the story tweaks genre formulas in smart ways.

An ex-con, Hideyoshi Date (Katsunori Takahashi), mulls over his life — no job, no wife, no family, no money — and decides to end it all amid the cherry blossoms. But after his half-hearted attempts at suicide end in failure — he notices that a child (Roi Hayashi) has crept into his car. All of 6 years old, he has run away from home, he tells Date, and has no intention of going back.

This gives Date a bad idea: He will fake a kidnapping and extract ¥50 million from the boy's obviously loaded (from the looks of their house) parents. He borrows the runaway's cell phone and, telling him he'll help him with his great escape, makes the fatal call.

At first the boy's spacey mom (the single-named You) doesn't believe that her precious Densuke has been kidnapped, but freaks when she realizes the kidnapper is not kidding. Soon black-suited men are swarming through the house and setting up electronic gear for locating and tracking the kidnapper. Their boss is Densuke's glowering dad (Sho Aikawa) — and the men are not cops, but gangsters. Date has signed his own death warrant.

He doesn't know this yet and, recalling advice about the kidnapping game from an old con (Takashi Sasano) he met in prison, he gets his hands on the ransom without taking a single bullet. There's just one problem: Densuke doesn't want his little adventure to end. In fact, he and Date have become best buddies.

But business is business — or is it?

There is action aplenty, comic and otherwise, supplied by not only the pursuing gangsters, but also a streetwise cop (Eiichiro Funakoshi) and his excitable junior partner (Koji Yamamoto) who wonder what the gang is in a lather about.

The story's focus, though, is the relationship between the ex-con and the boy. Densuke is about what you would expect — a brash, extroverted kid who thinks nothing of bonding with a strange ojisan ("uncle" or middle-age man). Playing him, newcomer Roi Hayashi steals scene after scene without a trace of effort — or the annoying preciousness of the usual acting prodigy.

As the ex-con Date, Takahashi exudes the dark, lonely air of a man who has spent his best years behind bars, but he also plays straight man to his pintsize costar with spot-on comic reactions. Their best scenes together feel unscripted, while being more than the sum of their gags.

Densuke, who has led a sheltered life in his scary father's shadow, learns from this rough-edged ojisan about the basics of being a guy — and being free. Meanwhile, Date starts to regret missing out on fatherhood, while knowing he can only taste its joys fleetingly now.

The feelings these two develop for each other emerge naturally from quarrels, escapades — and quiet moments spent chomping on convenience-store food as they look at the stars. Think of Huck Finn and Jim transposed to Japan and sitting on, not a raft, but the back of an old station wagon. (But forget the films based on Mark Twain's classic, which are all disappointments.)

Sakaki almost didn't get this film released. One of his supporting actors, Manabu Oshio, was arrested on drug charges last August, stirring up a scandal and leading the distributor to indefinitely delay the film's opening.

Sakaki reshot Oshio's scenes, playing his computer-whiz gangster character himself — and now it has finally hit the theaters. Rhapsodic news indeed.

A Piece Of Our Life, Kakera, rating: ★★★★, runtime: 107 min.

Sexual orientation is often defined in black-and-white terms: You're either straight or gay — or kidding yourself. Author Gore Vidal has famously objected to this binary classification, claiming that there's no such thing as homosexuality, only homosexual acts.

In Momoko Ando's debut feature "A Piece of Our Life," the mixed-up heroine, Haru (Hikari Mitsushima), shows that Vidal is right — or does she? More than same-sex bedtime joys, she is searching for connection in the form of a soft warm touch and an understanding heart. She's not so much seduced as gathered into friendly arms, like a lost puppy run away from a bad home.

Ando's approach is unlike that of "Love Juice" (2000), Kaze Shindo's erotic, emotionally explosive portrait of a rocky lesbian relationship. Instead it reminded me of Sofia Coppola's apolitical, but cheeky and original take on the French Revolution in "Marie Antoinette" (2006).

Coppola's film had its enthusiastic supporters and fierce detractors. Ando's, however, has stirred up controversy only for its mildly risque poster, since changed by its distributor. Otherwise, it's more on the inclusive than divisive side. Its hard-to-fault message is delivered with cool intelligence and zero preachiness: Desire is not same-sex or opposite-sex, but human.

It begins with Haru, an indifferent college student, enduring the clumsy embraces and casual disregard of her gun-nut boyfriend (Tasuku Nagaoka). Retreating to a coffee shop to nurse her psychic wounds, she attracts the attention of Riko (Eriko Nakamura), a slightly older woman whose straightforward declaration of sexual interest both intimidates and intrigues her.

The latter feeling wins out — and soon Haru and Riko are going on the standard dates of local romantic dramas: an amusement park, a zoo and, finally, a fireworks display where they exchange their first passionate kiss. Riko even introduces Haru to her dad and mom — warm, good-hearted folks who run a dry-cleaning shop. How sweet. And, if this were an ordinary love story about a straight couple, how cliched.

But Ando, who wrote the script based on Erica Sakurazawa's manga, tells this story at one ironic remove. She doesn't wink at her material so much as take an objective step back from it, while giving it a light comic gloss and sending it on a couple of gently surreal flights of fancy.

Riko, who works as a prosthetist (maker of artificial body parts), is clearly missing something herself. A restless spirit, she wants more than frisky idylls in the bedroom with Haru — she demands unconditional love, absolute possession. Meanwhile, Haru is still agonizing over her break-up with the blatantly unfaithful boyfriend, as well as her sexual identity. Conflict with the all-or-nothing Riko is inevitable.

Mitsushima, whose profile soared with her performance as the kick-ass, Bible-quoting heroine of Sion Sono's indie hit "Love Exposure" (2008), plays Haru as lonely and confused but quietly stubborn, as she sorts out her sexual and emotional life. Mitsushima brings out this last quality well enough to keep the character from sinking into boring passivity — but I couldn't help wanting to see more fire, less fog.

As Riko, Nakamura is something of an enigma — bold and direct with Haru, hesitant and unsure with Toko (Rino Katase), a middle-age client-turned-lover she improbably turns to after she and Haru violently quarrel. Nakamura doesn't quite solve this enigma, but she perfectly expresses Riko's central dilemma: the intensity that wins her lovers prevents her from keeping them.

What first seem like charming quirks, from her wide-eyed, burning gaze to her urgent, tumbling flow of words, reveal themselves as signs of a hunger that knows no bounds, a loneliness that no prosthetic part can heal.

Gay or straight, "Piece of Our Life" tells us, love can burn out as quickly as it flames up. And we're all pieces of kindling for the fire.

Sweet Little Lies, rating: ★★★★, runtime: 117 min.

Marriages are strange creatures. They can die suddenly, when from the outside everything seems fine, or they can linger on for years when it's obvious to everyone, including the two principals, that it's all over.

Hitoshi Yazaki plumbs the mysteries of one such inexplicable (to outsiders) marriage in his aptly titled new film "Sweet Little Lies." Based on Kaori Ekuni's 2004 novel of the same title, it is quite different in style and tone from "Strawberry Shortcakes," Yazaki's quirky 2006 drama about four women looking for love in all the wrong places — and finding common ground at the end.

The pace of this new film is slower, the look is more austere, even chilly, and the emotions are more tamped down, though bubbling away underneath the frozen smiles and averted glances. If "Strawberry Shortcakes" was a series of colorful, revealing Polaroid snaps, "Sweet Little Lies" is a formal portrait, tinged in terminal gray. But Yazaki is still Yazaki, fascinated by the theme of love and death, including the way love can make death easier to bear or embrace; as in two lovers walking hand in hand into the sea — and eternity.

Nothing so dire seems to be in store for the film's couple as the story begins. Ruriko (Miki Nakatani) and Satoshi (Nao Omori) have been married for three years and maintain the rituals of newlyweds. No demanding kids for one thing, no intrusive in-laws for another. They still have a real cooked breakfast together in the morning, a real sit-down dinner when Satoshi comes home from his job at an IT company and, on the weekends, real dates. In the daytime, Ruriko lovingly hand crafts stuffed bears that she exhibits in galleries.

Their marriage, however, is running on empty. Passion has long since given way to strained politeness. Having done his husbandly duty as a dinner conversation partner, Satoshi retreats to a room where he plays video games in blessed isolation. When Ruriko confesses her loneliness, his answer is an embarrassed smirk. She does not press him — and they continue living their little lies.

The lies start to grow. Ruriko meets the young, handsome, burning-eyed Haruo (Juichi Kobayashi) at a gallery show, where he pleads for a bear for his girlfriend. Later, they run into each other at a video shop. He is the passionate spark, she is the dry kindling — and soon an affair is blazing away.

Meanwhile, Satoshi reconnects with Shio (Chizuru Ikewaki), a cute kohai (junior) from his college scuba-diving club. She invites him on dinner dates, then a diving trip to Izu, Shizuoka Prefecture. Not long after, the wet suits come off — and Satoshi's days of isolation are over. Neither Ruriko nor Satoshi breathe a word of these liaisons to anyone, starting with each other.

In the usual Japanese melodrama of martial infidelity the truth will out — followed by shouting matches, stormy exits and floods of tears. Yazaki and scriptwriter Kyoko Inukai (who also worked with him on "Strawberry Shortcakes") more credibly let sleeping dogs — or rather cheating spouses — lie. For one thing, Ruriko and Satoshi find lying rather easy — and show few outward signs of guilt. Instead, they become less tense around each other, as though extramarital sex were a sort of relaxation therapy.

When their lovers become more demanding, they balk. The glue holding this pair together, we realize, is stronger than we thought.

But what is the glue? A subplot involving Ruriko's friendship with a dog belonging to an elderly neighbor (Akiko Kazami) offers one, important answer. Sound strange? But in Yazaki's world, mundane things, such as the title sweets in "Strawberry Shortcakes" or the pooch in "Sweet Little Lies" serve as apt metaphors for something larger, something that has been implied all along.

I won't give that something away. I will only say that Ruriko and Satoshi, now in their mid-30s, feel youth slipping away. Whatever confidence they once had about their future is also crumbling. The lies, we see, are patches for something battered, but still necessary. Their marriage is a lifeboat in a rough sea of uncertainty.

Nakatani has made a specialty of playing women on the verge, such as the luckless heroine of "Memories of Matsuko" (2006) and the doomed provincial aristocrat in "Zero Focus" (2009). As Ruriko she projects a wintery isolation and a steely intensity that can suddenly burst into flames. When she tells Haruo she loves him, her eyes pierce, her words sear.

The ending is no surprise, but Yazaki can't quite decide how to deliver it. It looks as if the credits are about to roll, but another scene begins — then another and another. It's like a band that wears out its welcome with too many encores, but is still too good to hate.

"Sweet Little Lies" tells truths that are not for everyone, especially those who believe that blunt honesty is always the best marital policy. But how do you really know your partner agrees?

Bandage, rating: ★★★★, runtime: 120 min.

Shunji Iwai was once Japan's hottest young director following the smash success of "Love Letter," a 1995 film about a woman who writes a letter to her dead lover — and gets a reply.

No, it wasn't a film about vampires — but it did attract legions of young female fans enraptured by not only the impossibly romantic story, but also by Iwai's knack for capturing every tremor of emotion with his jittery camerawork and offbeat editing rhythms.

Iwai himself, with his pop-star good looks, was of course part of the package.

But since "Hana and Alice," a 2004 drama that focused perceptively and humorously on the friendship of two teenage girls, Iwai has not directed a feature film, though he has produced several — as well as having made a 2006 documentary on director Kon Ichikawa and contributed to the 2009 omnibus, "New York, I Love You."

"Bandage," the latest film Iwai has produced and scripted, is also his creation thematically and stylistically, though music producer Takeshi Kobayashi is credited as both director and composer. This was also the case with "Halfway," a 2008 film about a troubled teen romance that Iwai produced and Eriko Kitagawa directed; it had Iwai's signature touches, from its lyrical shotmaking to its deep identification with its flighty but stubborn heroine, played by Kii Kitano.

Kitano also stars in "Bandage," again as a high school girl, but this time one whose coming-of-age ordeals unfold almost entirely off-campus, in the band scene of the early 1990s.

As hard as it may be to imagine now, when nearly all the pop music acts on television are groomed and packaged by big agencies, back then indie rock bands were commercially hot from televised band talent contests that propelled the winners to instant fame.

The band at the center of "Bandage," called Lands, is on the verge of making it big when two friends — Asako (Kitano) and Miharu (Anne) — see them perform live at a club. The girls are enthralled, especially by moody lead singer Natsu (Jin Akanishi). When they are miraculously invited to a postconcert party, they are giddy with excitement — until the group's no-nonsense manager, Yukari (Ayumi Ito), tells them to beat it after one drink.

As this scene indicates, "Bandage" is a more realistic look at the pop music scene than "Nana," the similarly structured but cartoony 2005 hit based on a best-selling manga about two Nanas — one a glinty-eyed rock singer, the other a glittery-eyed country girl who becomes involved with the former Nana's band.

Asako also becomes involved, but as a hard-working, much put-upon assistant to Yukari, who acknowledges her aptitude for the thankless job of managing a band, while remaining wary of her motives. Asako's only real ally, in fact, is the self-centered, if basically decent, Natsu, who stays friends with her even after failing to make her his latest sexual conquest. But his band mates, especially the acid-tongued keyboardist Arumi (Yuki Shibamoto), regard her with barely disguised contempt.

So why does she do it? Instead of spelling out her reasons in blazing capitals, "Bandage" leaves them as something of a mystery, even to Asako herself.

She keeps Natsu at arm's length — not as a sexual gambit, but because she knows, instinctively, that giving in would short-circuit all her dreams, from the professional to the personal. At the same time, she is an idealist and a fan, who admires Natsu's songwriting talent and hates seeing his work commercialized. But the group, Natsu included, is hungry for a hit, so they rework one of his songs with currently marketable sounds (ironically, Arumi, the "purist" of the group, makes the biggest contribution here) and the result — a catchy J-pop number — soars to the top of the charts.

Fame proves to be fleeting, however, and Asako has more hard lessons to learn about not only the music business but love.

All this may sound bleak — but the film also shows how the band trip can become so addictive, from the adrenaline rush of the shows to the off-duty pleasures. Also, though Asako wears her emotions on her sleeve, she is no frail reed. Instead, she keeps plugging away, even after repeated insults and setbacks, with a tenacity rare in a genre where heroines usually win out because of their pure hearts, not their strong characters.

The various confrontations and reconciliations are a shade on the overwrought side, but the relationships and events remain firmly grounded in the actualities of a music scene that Iwai and Kobayashi, who also collaborated on Iwai's 1996 hit SF drama "Swallowtail," know inside out.

Kobayashi takes Natsu's would-be hit song — a powerful acoustic number we hear only at the end of the film — and deftly turns it into a frothy J-pop tune that, even without the film behind it, could top the chart.

Finally, Akanishi, singer with the pop unit KAT-TUN, is the real rock star deal as Natsu, whose bubble of celebrity and self-regard seems less constructed than naturally grown, like moss on a rock.

The film though, belongs to Kitano, a tiny girl with a big heart and talent, who makes most other teen idols look like grinning air-heads. But you don't need to see "Bandage" to know the latter, do you?

Outrage, rating: ★★, runtime: 109 min.

Takeshi Kitano went to the Cannes Film Festival this year hoping to snag the big prize that had so far eluded him: the Palme d'Or. He left with little more than a stack of negative reviews from the international media for his competition entry, "Outrage." One panel of critics, for the trade magazine "Screen International," gave it the lowest average rating of any competition film: 0.9.

Kitano was feted throughout the 1990s, both at home and abroad, for combining extreme violence with zero cool in his films about cops and gangsters, including his 1993 international breakthrough "Sonatine."

His signature stylistics, from the pawky black humor to the dispassionate recording of tortures and murders, became influential among his fellow directors in Japan, while inspiring critical rhapsodies here and abroad not heard since the heydays of Yasujiro Ozu and Akira Kurosawa.

In the past decade, however, Kitano has ventured away from the underworld themes that made him famous to self-indulgent examinations of his own personal/artistic navel, culminating in the embarrassingly limp "Achilles and the Tortoise" (2008).

"Outrage," an epic about rivalries, betrayals and revenge among contemporary Tokyo gangsters, was heralded as a return to form. The characteristic Kitano violence is certainly present, though the shocks are tamer than some reviewers would have you believe. But on the other hand, the directorial personality that animated the best of his films — fashionably minimalistic, but creatively uninhibited; understanding of his antiheroes but clear-eyed about their fates — has mostly vanished.

It's not that anyone could have made "Outrage," but I wonder why Kitano and his producers thought it could be a major festival winner, as opposed to a hit with his foreign fan base.

The Cannes jury typically honors uncommercial originality (or, if you will, head-scratching artiness), but Kitano's story of all-out gang war has become hackneyed through countless iterations, peaking four decades ago with the "Godfather" duology and Kinji Fukasaku's "Battles without Honor and Humanity" films.

Kitano adds absolutely nothing new to this theme, save his standard black humor, which is at times indistinguishable from schoolyard sadism. He has assembled an outstanding cast to play his hoods and cops, but none of the characters deepen or change.

Instead they only display their tough-guy facades in one verbal or physical confrontation after another, ad infinitum. There is a numbing sameness of narrative inflection and tone. You can walk out for a popcorn break, come back 20 min. later and feel you're still watching the same scene.

Kitano plays Otomo, the hard-pressed captain of a crew belonging to the Ikemoto gang. When the chairman (Soichiro Kitamura) — the boss of all Tokyo bosses — learns that Ikemoto (Jun Kunimura) has become too chummy with Murase (Renji Ishibashi), the boss of a rival gang, he orders a push back — and the canny, craven Ikemoto in turn orders Otomo to handle the rough stuff.

Instead of immediately using muscle, however, Otomo and his boys bait a trap that the greedy Murase gangsters fall for. But Otomo's crew takes things a few beatings, severed fingers and a slashed face too far. The enraged Murase hoods vow revenge.

From here things become very complicated indeed as stratagem follows stratagem, betrayal follows betrayal, leaving a trail of dead and injured. In the process, the traditional yakuza credo of loyalty and obligation is exposed as a hollow sham. All that really matters in the film's gangster world is money in the safe and power to rule over one's fellow thugs. Those who trust anything but a fist, a gun and their own wits are shown to be fools, usually dead ones.

The cynicism on display in "Outrage" is extreme, but it is also by now a genre staple. The classic yakuza film, whose heroes are paragons of gangster virtue, has become vanishingly rare. Kitano, once the outsider thumbing his nose at cinematic convention, has made a film that is a lot like many others, despite a few good jokes and cleverly executed action sequences.

The smell of creative exhaustion evidently carried all the way to the critics and the Cannes competition jury, which left "Outrage" empty-handed. Kitano's career will continue, but his long reign as an international festival darling may be over.

Double review of "Kazura" and "Boys on the Run"

Kazura, rating: ★★★★, runtime: 114 min.

Boys on the Run, rating: ★★★★, runtime: 114 min.

Both "Kazura" and "Boys on the Run" open Saturday and both are good, if in quite different ways. If you're a balding, lonely, middle-aged male, "Kazura" is more likely to hit home; if you're nerdy, clueless and dateless, it should be "Boys on the Run." If you're all of the above, get a life, brother, not a movie ticket.

Directed by Renpei Tsukamoto, from an essay collection by Shinya Kobayashi, "Kazura" could have easily become a one-joke comedy that plays like a stick of gum: Tasty start, flavorless finish. But Tsukamoto, a TV director whose credits include the late-night cult favorite "Statute of Limitations Cop," builds on his slight premise like a standup comic constructing a castle of laughter out of thin air — or rather sharp observations about everyday embarrassments.

His hero is Moriyama (Masakazu Mimura), a salaryman employed by a home builder in the provinces who is transferred to Tokyo to work on a big project. Seeing this as a chance to change his image — particularly his thinning pate — he visits various wig/hair-replacement salons in the big city, where he is quoted outrageous prices for dubious products.

Then he runs across a series of ads (or rather Post-its stuck on telephone poles) leading to a cluttered, eccentrically decorated shop run by one Owada (Kazuki Otake), a mysterious chap wearing huge shades and a wig that crowns his head like a black mushroom on a stalk. But Owada's rock-bottom price and promised delivery date — tomorrow — open Moriyama's wallet. Owada proves to be as good as his word, despite a baffling production process that involves a microwave oven, and Moriyama is soon the satisfied owner of a new rug.

Not for long, though, since he is terrified that he will be unmasked (or rather unwigged) in front of his new coworkers, especially his lovely assistant, Ryoko (Sei Asina). Not to fear — Owada is always there with a helping hand or even a replacement wig. And, of course, a bill.

Mimura and Otake, a comedy team in real life (if you consider Japanese variety shows real life) are in sync as needy customer and all-wise wigmaker, without going over the top in approved variety show fashion. Instead they ground their comedy in real-life anxieties — while taking the occasional bizarre imaginative flight.

The hero of Daisuke Miura's "Boys on the Run" is even more of a sad sack. Rank-and-file salesman Tanishi (Kazunobu Mineta) spends his days filling vending machines with trinkets, masturbating to porn videos and obsessing on Chiharu (Mei Kurokawa), a pretty coworker. A virgin of 29, still living at home with Mom and Dad, Tanishi knows he is a big zero.

But within this google-eyed dweeb beats the heart of a lover and even a fighter. When a rival salesman, the handsome, unprincipled Aoyama (Ryuhei Matsuda), snatches Chiharu away from him (incredibly, she has started to reciprocate his interest), Tanishi is stirred to frustration — and finally rage. But before he can deliver a promised thrashing to Aoyama, he has to train, since he has never thrown a punch in anger in his life. Cue the "Rocky" theme . . .

Based on a comic by Kengo Hanazawa, "Boys on the Run" is in the all-but-exhausted genre of slacker comedy, but Miura, a theater director turned indie filmmaker, has a unique comic mind.

His style is on the dry, understated side (after Tanishi's trainer, an alcoholic, senior salesman, gives him pointers on his boxing stance, he leaves the poor mope standing frozen, like a department store dummy, while he sips his beer), but he also revels in dirty realism, from sleazy sex to brutal punchups, while rejecting any hints of sentimentality.

A punk rocker off-screen (his band Ging Nang Boyz supplies the closing song), Kazunobu Mineta implicitly understands this side of Miura, while keeping the audience on Tanishi's side. We laugh at him and his sorry situation with sympathy. Miura also has his own sense of timing, delivering his punch lines and payoffs at odd moments and angles — and getting bigger laughs as a result.

The ending is no exception. You don't see it coming, but Miura has been setting it up from scene one. It's right, it's satisfying — and it's not "Rocky" in the least. It's "Boys on the Run."

Confessions, Kokuhaku, rating: ★★★☆, runtime: 106 min.

Japanese films featuring school bullying are as common as cherry trees in Ueno Park, and for good reason. When I was teaching at a boys' high school in western Tokyo, I would sometimes see signs of bullying, such as the returnee kid whose natively fluent English inspired titters from his classmates — until he stopped volunteering to speak. Or the quiet, timid boy who explained his bandages and bruises as the results of sports-club practices — until he stopped coming to school altogether.

Yuko Moriguchi (Takako Matsu), the heroine of Tetsuya Nakashima's pitch-black drama "Confessions," teaches a coed class of junior-high freshmen, but has given up trying to contain the chaos. Addressing them on the final day of class, she speaks evenly, slowly and precisely — while her talking, texting and otherwise occupied audience ignores her existence.

She has a reason for her disconnected calm, which is like the numbness of a trauma victim: She is quitting her job — and taking her revenge on those who have destroyed her life. Earlier that year her 3-year-old daughter was found floating face down in the school pool. The police ruled it a death-by-drowning accident, but Moriguchi believed otherwise and, playing detective, unmasked the killers: Two boys in her class.

As she describes the killing she uses pseudonyms for their names, but everyone in the class, by now riveted to her every word, knows who she is talking about.

Why doesn't she turn in the killers to the police? They are too young to be tried and convicted. Instead, she plans to rely on the justice of their peers — which she knows will be stern, but pure.

Best-known abroad for such visually colorful, blackly comic films as "Kamikaze Girls" and "Memories of Matsuko," Nakashima does "Confessions" differently from the usual sort of commercial entertainment. Fans expecting tear-jerking melodrama or brain-teasing mystery will be disappointed. I wasn't, since I was acquainted with Nakashima's earlier, darker work, including "Beautiful Sunday," a 1998 film that coolly dissects the obsessions and perversions of people living in the same Tokyo condo building.

Based on a novel by Kanae Minato, "Confessions" is an orthodox mystery in outline, albeit one that comments on everything from the dire state of Japanese education to the still-lingering prejudice against AIDS victims.

Nakashima's treatment turns genre rules on their heads, however. First, he identifies the two killers early on, draining the film of any whodunit tension. Second, Moriguchi is more like a ghost — dead to every emotion but vengeful rage — than a living being. Her hollow-voiced narration makes the incidents she describes sound as though they are unfolding in another dimension or life.

Lastly, Nakashima films even the most violent and disturbing scenes with stylistics reminiscent of the tonier sort of music video, yet another distancing device. The mother of one of the killers (Yoshino Kimura) is screaming her head off at her son's latest eruption of bizarre behavior — he has become a psychotic recluse since his exposure by Moriguchi — but our eyes are invited to focus on the beauty of the saturated colors, the austere refinement of the composition. Her pain and bewilderment are aestheticized — or rather anaesthetized.

Nakashima's aim may be to probe beyond surface dramatics to inner truths, the way Terrence Mallick filmed the intrusion of the transcendent into jungle combat in "The Thin Red Line." But his story, unlike Mallick's, has a what-if premise that borders on the gimmicky, requiring certain improbabilities to make it work. One example of several: The other killer, a sociopathic science whiz, masochistically remains in school after being outed, allowing Nakashima to stage beautifully horrific scenes of group bullying, but the killer's stubbornness puzzles.

Despite its artiness, "Confessions," has, like much of Nakashima's work, a strange power. There is no catharsis, no redemption, but the chill of seeing into the heart of evil — and grief — remains.

13 Assassins, Jusannin no Shikaku, no rating, runtime: 126 min.

Takashi Miike's rise is complete: This one-time director of cheapo shock pics — which he churned out like sausages and were beloved by foreign fanboys — is now a proven hit-maker and recognized auteur, with his new samurai swashbuckler "13 Assassins" screening in this year's Venice Film Festival competition.

The Miike of old, who trashed formula, while indulging the wilder side of his imagination, is still alive and well in this reworking of Eiichi Kudo's eponymous 1963 film. But there is also a more mature, legacy-conscious Miike present. No longer satisfied with just being the coolest kid in the class, he is matching himself against the Golden Age greats of the samurai genre — not only Kudo, but the greatest of all, Akira Kurosawa; especially his 1954 epic "Seven Samurai."

This oversize ambition, present in every frame, does not result in a self-indulgent genre parody like "Sukiyaki Western Django," Miike's 2007 Eastern-Western. Instead, he has taken his virtuous-few-against-evil-many story line — a genre perennial — to the outer limits of his formidable talent and energy.

There is plenty of splatter action, with black comic touches, in the familiar Miike style. But in the 50-minute climactic battle, the heroes change from cocky, near-superhuman fighters, wasting opponents with everything from massive explosions to sticks and stones, to wounded, desperate men fighting for their lives against overwhelming numbers, filmed in grainy shades that foreshadow doom. There is pathos to their struggle new to Miike's work, but often present in the great samurai epics he is trying to equal or surpass.

"13 Assassins" doesn't strike the deeper chords of "Seven Samurai," with its poignancy about lost lives and its clarity about the limits of heroism. But Miike also shows a new way forward for a genre still struggling to reinvent itself. Rather than try to dazzle with CG wonders like so many of his contemporaries, Miike uses his pixels, together with old-fashioned sweat and smarts, to deliver full-bore action. More than the genre's graying core fans, his target is a younger generation for whom the classic samurai fight scenes, beautifully shot as they are, often look like dance numbers.

The story follows the outlines of the original film, which is in turn loosely based on a real incident. The capriciously cruel Lord Naritsugu (Goro Inagaki) is sowing death and destruction among his hapless subjects when his chief retainer cuts open his own stomach in protest. Lord Doi (Mikijiro Hira), a member of the shogun's Council of Elders, decides that Naritsugu must be stopped before his expected ascension to the council — and possibly even to the shogunate itself.

Doi charges Shimada Shinzaemon (Koji Yakusho), a brave and capable metsuke (a sort of feudal-era intelligence officer) with the task of assassinating Naritsugu. After seeing one victim of his target's sadism — a woman whose legs, arms and tongue have been removed — Shinzaemon needs little persuading.

He gathers a band of 11 like-minded assassins, including the bluff senior metsuke Kuranaga (Hiroki Matsukata), the saturnine ronin (masterless samurai) Hirayama (Tsuyoshi Ihara) and his own dissolute but fearless nephew Shinrouko (Takayuki Yamada). Together they plot to surprise Naritsugu and his minions at a village during his annual journey from Edo (old Tokyo) to his domain.

Enlisting the help of the locals — including a wild-eyed mountain man, Koyata (Yusuke Iseya), who proves his worth as a guide and fighter — they carefully lay their trap. But then they learn that, instead of the smaller force they expected, Naritsugu and his canny lieutenant Hanbei (Masachika Ichimura) have 300 men with them. Knowing that near-certain death awaits them, the 13 assassins (counting Koyata) decide to fight anyway out of pride — and because it's the most fun they know.

Despite the lengthy cast list, the film's stars stand out from the crowd. Playing Shinzaemon, Yakusho brings a dark sense of humor and a hard edge of rage, along with his trademark nice-guy-ness. That is, he makes himself over into the ideal Miike hero. Iseya is also excellent as Koyata, fighting only with guts, instinct and laughing scorn for samurai pretensions.

The surprise is Inagaki as the bad-to-the-bone Naritsugu. A member of mega-pop-group SMAP, Inagaki plays the character with a cold, twisted charisma and force. All those years in show business have evidently taught him well about the many faces of evil.

Could the 50 minutes of bloodshed have been trimmed to 40 or even 30? Yes and yes, but then "13 Assassins" wouldn't be a Miike movie — that is, an entertaining riot of excess. Think Japanese action films have gone flabby? That they can't hold a candle to the masterpieces of the glorious past? Miike may not make you change your mind — but it won't be for lack of trying.

The Borrowers, Kari-Gurashi no Arrietty, rating: ★★★★, runtime: 94 min.

Studio Ghibli is often said to be the animation house that Hayao Miyazaki built, but Miyazaki has directed only nine of its 17 features to date. Four were made by studio cofounder Isao Takahata and four by four other directors. These latter four films, however, are all identifiable as Studio Ghibli products, from their spunky teenage protagonists to their pictorial realism in everything from the play of shadows through the trees to the raising of sticky windows.

Ghibli's latest, "The Borrowers," is directed by veteran Ghibli animator Hiromasa Yonebayashi and scripted by Miyazaki himself. It is a simply told, beautifully animated delight that, like the best Ghibli films, speaks straight to the heart and imagination of the child in all of us.

"The Borrowers" is based on Mary Norton's 1952 novel of the same title but unfolds in a relatively realistic present-day Japan. True, its 14-year-old title heroine (voiced by Mirai Shida), together with her mother Homily (Shinobu Otake) and father Pod (Tomokazu Miura), stand only 10 cm tall, but these "tiny people" are ordinary in every other respect.

Living under the floorboards of a house in the Tokyo suburbs inhabited by the elderly Sadoko (Keiko Takeshita) and her wizened housekeeper Haru (Kirin Kiki), they "borrow" everything they need to live from their human hosts, in amounts so small they are barely noticed.

Pod is a stoic, resourceful sort who carries out his nighttime "borrowing" missions like a veteran mountain climber, methodically scaling the heights of the kitchen with a fishing hook and string. He is also handy with tools, making everything the family needs for its survival and comfort, though the worry-wart Homily is constantly fretting about the threats all around them — the most dangerous being discovery by their human hosts.

The athletic Arrietty is more her father's child than her mother's, fearlessly exploring the house and its lush garden while fending off Sadoko's fat cat, a pesky crow and a variety of insects. Then she is spotted by Sho (Ryunosuke Kamiki), Sadoko's sensitive, sickly 12-year-old nephew, who is resting up for a heart operation at a Tokyo hospital.

Instead of retreating into the shadows, she is drawn to this human, who sympathizes with her situation and understands her isolation. Their unusual friendship leads to potentially disastrous consequences, however. With the loss of their little paradise looming, Pod begins to talk about moving to parts unknown.

Miyazaki reportedly selected Yonebayashi to direct "The Borrowers" for his animation skills. Flights of animated fancy, from the dazzling to the bizarre, that Miyazaki has made his trademark are few. Instead, Yonebayashi and his team (with Miyazaki supervising) have created a world both gorgeously detailed and thrillingly imagined from the perspective of its miniature protagonists.

As Arrietty climbs vines to the roof, plunges on a thread from a kitchen table or performs other feats of derring-do, we have the heart-in-the-throat feeling of not only admiring her pluck, but being in her shoes. Would 3-D enhance this feeling? Possibly, but Ghibli animators creates the illusion of presence and depth without it.

The film has moments that threaten to devolve into the sappy, the preachy and the slapstick, but they are mercifully brief. There are also characters, such as the casually cruel Haru and the high-minded, mature-beyond-his-years Sho, who verge on the cliched, but they also have their virtues. In times of crisis, Sho shows his mettle, while bluntly telling Arrietty that she and her kind will probably disappear. What chance do they have against the billions of humans with whom they uneasily share the planet?

One answer arrives in the form of a tiny "wild boy" (Takuya Fujiwara) Pod encounters in the woods who lives minus the comforts of civilization that Pod has so painstakingly assembled and constructed.

Will this become our answer as well? Like many other Ghibli films, "The Borrowers" comments on the devastation humans have wrought on the environment and speculates on the consequences.

More importantly for this Ghibli fan, however, the film gave me hope that when Miyazaki lays down his pencil for good, the studio will have at least one worthy successor.

2011

Yoyochu in the Land of the Rising Sex. Yoyochu: Sex to Yoyogi Tadashi no Sekai, rating: ★★★★, runtime: 116 min.

Japan's sex industry is huge, diverse and different. One oddity, at least to Western eyes, is the pinku eiga (pink film), a genre of soft porn made according to certain rules (the most important being the inclusion of a simulated sex scene every 10 minutes or so) and shown in specialized theaters. Pink films, which range from black comedies to serious (if porny) dramas, have gained a small but enthusiastic foreign following. Absent from much foreign fan discussion, however, is the career of Tadashi Yoyogi, better known as Yoyochu, a pioneering maker of adult videos (AVs) and the subject of Masato Ishioka's fascinating, instructive documentary "Yoyochu in the Land of the Rising Sex."

This is not surprising, since AVs are often thought of less as cinema than sex aids, while their makers get little respect from the mainstream film world. Some such straight filmmakers, however, such as yakuza-movie maestro Rokuro Mochizuki and Ishioka himself, have AV experience.

My own acquaintance with AV, including Yoyogi's 536 films to date, is slight (insert eye rolls and skeptical smirks here) — and I found Ishioka's brisk, informed explication of Yoyogi's fabled career and the history of the AV industry as a whole enlightening.

Born in 1938 in Kokura, Kyushu as Teruo Watanabe, Yoyogi grew up tough and wild in the chaos of postwar Japan. After running with a local gang and getting into trouble with the police, he tried to go straight, becoming a flower arranger, of all things. But the pull of the mob was strong — and he left Kokura to escape it. Arriving in Tokyo, he finally discovered his métier at a pink-film company.

Then in 1972, while working for a subcontractor for Nikkatsu — a formerly legit studio that was then a porn-industry leader — Yoyogi found himself being prosecuted for obscenity, though he was only a line producer on the busted film. (The director, a family man, asked him to take the rap since Yoyogi already had a criminal record.) Though the trial dragged on until 1980, he was finally declared innocent and kept making films, by now as a director.

The big change in the industry — and Yoyogi's fortunes — came with the start of the video boom in the early 1980s. Quickly grasping the potential of the new medium for more spontaneous and realistic portrayals of sex, in 1981 he directed Kyoko Aizome, bold-eyed beauty who became a hardcore star, in her first adult video, "April of Lust" ("Inyoku no Uzuki"). She melted the brains of men throughout Japan with a performance in the futon that didn't look like a performance at all.

Yoyogi followed up in 1982 with "The Onanie" ("Dokyumento za Onanie"), a documentary-style film that began with the director, off-screen, introducing a woman to her first vibrator and finished with a convincing orgasm. Sales were again explosive — and the industry followed where Yoyogi had led.

Over the next decade Yoyogi continued to push boundaries, but less in the direction of raw exploitation, more in a personal search for the psychological and spiritual realities of the erotic. Think Henry Miller with a camera. One crucial difference is that, where Miller's sex writings were from his priapic male point of view, Yoyogi earnestly tried to understand the needs and fears of his actresses. In his unscripted dialogue with them he often sounds more like a counselor or therapist than a porn director trying to juice the action (though that was undeniably his intent).

At the height of the bubble period, Yoyogi went further into uncharted — and strange — territory, including channeling and hypnotism, while making investments in a Micronesian resort project that, with the bursting of the bubble in the early 1990s, went spectacularly bad. Faced with crushing debt,

Yoyogi fell into depression — but eventually returned to work with enthusiasm. Today he is still at it, still the social rebel, but with the craggy, white-haired look and self-assured manner of a porno sage. Think Hugh Hefner minus the pretension.

Ishioka, whose 2000 fiction feature "Scout Man" is one of the most honest films about the porn business, is obviously a Yoyogi fan and disciple — in fact, he apprenticed under the director. But he probes into the more controversial parts of Yoyogi's career, including a popular series of brutal- looking (if carefully staged) rape videos, with a gentle persistence that makes his old teacher rightfully squirm.

Moralistic this film is not. But it made me want to learn more about Yoyogi — and the art of AV. (Cue final eye roll.)

Cannonball Wedlock, Kigeki Konzen Tokkyu, rating: ★★★★, runtime: 107 min.

Hollywood screwball comedies have long been favorites of Japanese filmmakers, with many listing genre masters Frank Capra, Howard Hawks and Billy Wilder as influences. Screwball comedy heroines, however, are typically self-centered types, while the local feminine ideal is still self-sacrificing and soft-hearted. But Koji Maeda's debut feature, "Cannonball Wedlock" presents one funny exception. Her name is Chie (Yuriko Yoshitaka), a 24-year-old office lady who is not passively waiting for Mr. Right. Instead, she juggles five guys, hanging out with whoever strikes her fancy or fulfills certain needs.

There's the suave 54-year-old beauty-salon owner (Takaaki Enoki) who underwrites her foreign travel plans; the macho motorbike-shop manager (Munetaka Aoki) who takes her on stress-relieving rides; the tousle-haired college kid (Takuya Yoshimura) who's scrumptiously cute; and the once-divorced sales exec (Ryo Kase) who listens to all her troubles.

Finally, there's Takumi (Kenta Hamano), a pudgy, pushy, uncouth guy who works in a bread factory and seems to have no good qualities at all, save an old-shoe familiarity (though she is not thrilled when he takes showers in her apartment as though it were the public gym).

One day, Chie's best friend Toshiko (the singled-named Anne) announces that she is getting hitched — and urges Chie to consider matrimony as well. Chie brushes off this suggestion — freedom is wonderful! — but begins to have second thoughts when she sees the happy glow on Toshiko's face at the ceremony.

Ever practical, she comes up with a plan: Narrow her beaus down one by one and marry the survivor. Obviously, the first to go is Takumi.

Because "Cannonball Wedlock" is a screwball comedy and Chie is so obviously full of herself, we know from the get-go that her splendid plan will blow up in her face. What we don't know is how the script by Maeda and Ryo Takada, adapting his own novel for the screen, will makes its various twists and turns both funny and true.

Bad screwball comedies assume that the mere flouting of convention and common sense is hilarious, when it's merely tiresome. Maeda and Takada know that the genre has its own logic and they scrupulously follow it in building to their comic payoffs — and an ending that makes perfect (or rather, perfectly absurd) sense.

Also, instead of slavishly following Hollywood formula, they add only-in-Japan elements, such as the scene of Kase's sales exec, Takumi and Takumi's date, Mika (Anna Ishibashi), trading lines from the "Manyoshu" — a 1,300-year-old collection of poems that educated Japanese once knew by heart — as a bored and discomfited Chie looks on.

It's as if two guys in a Hollywood "bromance" were to quote Shakespeare to each other as the woman for whom they are competing steams. Wouldn't happen, right? But in "Cannonball Wedlock," this scene makes the characters more comprehensible, if not completely sympathetic. That is, it lights them from different angles, and not always flattering ones.

Yoshitaka, who made her acting debut in Sion Sono's 2006 shocker "Noriko's Dinner Table," plays Chie as a combination of charming ditz and self-centered princess, that is, likable and obnoxious in the same skin and, sometimes, breath. Yoshitaka maintains this difficult balance with little visible strain.

Also excellent is rocker Hamano as the disposable but determined Takumi. Rather than play him as a slob loser who gets lucky, Hamano gives him a winner's confidence verging on arrogance. Still, he's a hard sell as a romantic prospect for Chie, even if he's No. 5 on her list.

The Japanese title, "Kigeki Konzen Tokkyu" (literal translation: "Premarital Express"), may contain a homage to the hit "Ressha" ("Train," 1967-68) and "Ryoko" ("Journey," 1968-72) series by comedy master Masaharu Segawa. The respective heroes of those two series, Kiyoshi Atsumi and Frankie Sakai, were also hardly Clark Gable in the looks department, while their female foils, including queen-of-cute Chieko Baisho ("Ryoko"), would have been far out of their characters' reach in the real world.

Will Maeda also spin his brilliant debut into a series? Unlikely — but screwier things have happened, haven't they?

Hara-kiri: Death of a Samurai, Ichimei, rating: ★★★★, runtime: 126 min.

The samurai movie has a great and glorious tradition, but Japanese directors have long been of two minds about the samurai themselves. For every "Chushingura" remake that celebrates the samurai ethos of loyalty and self-sacrifice, there is a genre masterpiece that questions it.

One is "Harakiri," Masaki Kobayashi's 1962 drama of revenge that exposes the injustice and inhumanity of which the samurai were capable. And yet the samurai hero, played with hollowed-voice gravitas by Tatsuya Nakadai, is noble in his pursuit of righteous vengeance — that eternal samurai movie theme.

Almost half a century after "Harakiri" won the Cannes festival's Jury Special Prize, Takashi Miike's 3-D remake, "Hara-kiri: Death of a Samurai" appeared in the Cannes competition, where it received respectful notices but no awards.

I'm not sure whether Miike was aiming to repeat Kobayashi's festival success, but the fans who know and love his earlier shockers, with their punkish bad attitude and black sense of humor, will probably not have same affection for the subdued, grown-up "Hara-kiri," which favors a classically Japanese sense of the tragic.

As a fan of both Kobayashi's "Harakiri" and Miike's work, the wild stuff included, I'm glad he made the film the way he did, with respect for its serious central story but also with his own flair for violence, from the flamboyantly swashbuckling to the disturbingly self-inflicted. A "real" (i.e., outrageous) Miike film, with 3-D swords jabbing at audience eyes, would have been a travesty.

The story is set in the early 17th century, after the Tokugawa clan consolidated national power and a long era of peace began. Thousands of samurai, their martial skills no longer in demand, found themselves stripped of clan affiliation and stipends. One of these ronin (masterless samurai), the fierce-eyed Hanshiro (Ebizo Ichikawa), comes to the Edo (old Tokyo) compound of the powerful Ii clan with a request: He wants to commit seppuku (ritual suicide) on its grounds.

The clan leader, Kageyu (Koji Yakusho), tells Hanshiro of an earlier visitor, the young ronin Motome (Eita), who asked for the same favor. Unfortunately, he only had a frail bamboo sword to kill himself with, but the clan forced him to use it, resulting in a prolonged, gory and undignified death. They committed this cruelty as an example to other impoverished ronin who were making seppuku requests to extort money from the clans, who would usually pay them to go away rather than deal with the bother and, one imagines, the aftermath.

Hanshiro, however, persists — and the clan reluctantly grants him his wish. Before he cuts his stomach in the courtyard, however, he tells all assembled a story of bitter poverty and unjust loss that reveals him to have a personal reason for his presence. Jaws tighten and hands reach for sword hilts.

Much of the film is devoted to this story, told in an extended flashback, while action scenes are given relatively little screen time. But Miike slowly, surely gathers his narrative strands together, like a vengeful god building storm clouds to terrifying heights. Only then does he hurl his lightning bolts of swords-out violence.

Playing Hanshiro, Kabuki star Ichikawa echoes Nakadai's superlative performance, but with his own inner fires and impeccable technique. As Motome, Eita hits true notes of extreme emotion and pain. Watching him trying to stab himself to death with a sliver of bamboo, I realized again how hard it is to fake physical agony — and how hard it can be to watch when an actor gets it right.

Finally, Hikari Mitsushima is almost too perfectly cast as Miho, Motome's devoted, consumptive wife. She inhabits the role so completely, cavernous eyes and thin frame included, that I worried about her real-life health. Whatever she did to prepare for this role, I thought, couldn't have been good for her.

The 3-D was less of an intrusion than I had feared, but it also makes the compositions look artificial and under-lighted, like old-time stereopticon slides. Or maybe it was just my aging eyes in less-than-perfect screening-room conditions.

"Harakiri," however, rises above technical hurdles and comparisons with the past to achieve a grandeur and pathos of its own. I just hope that next time out, the crazy Miike of old returns — jabs to the eye and all.

Post Card, Ichimai no Hagaki, rating: ★★★★, runtime: 114 min.

Kaneto Shindo is, at 99, the oldest film director in Japan and, after Portugal's centenarian Manoel de Oliveira, the world. As a scriptwriter active since the 1930s, he has worked on many commercial films, but as a director, starting in 1951 with "Story of a Beloved Wife," he has taken a more independent path. The human price of war has been a frequent theme, from his 1952 triumph "Children of Hiroshima" to his latest film, the World War II home-front drama "Post Card," which he also called his last when it won the Special Jury Prize at last year's Tokyo International Film Festival.

Whether or not "Post Card" is indeed the "last," it is by a filmmaker still passionate about his subject, still trying to provoke his audience. While not likely to be mistaken for the work of a young man, it is also not a geriatric shuffle through the attic of memory. In fact, it has a striking relevance to the present moment, with a plucky heroine forced to restart her life after everything collapses around her.

She is Tomoko (Shinobu Otake), whose rough-hewn but loving farmer husband, Sadazo (Naomasa Musaka), is drafted into the army, leaving her to care for his aged parents (Akira Emoto and Mitsuko Baisho). Through a series of disasters I won't detail, she finds herself widowed twice and alone at the end of the war, when she receives a visitor: Sadazo's former comrade, Keita (Etsushi Toyokawa). The night before Sadazo shipped out to the Philippines, never to return, he had asked Keita to take Tomoko a postcard she had sent him, so that she might know he had read it. Sadazo could have written a reply, but was afraid the strict military censors might not pass it. Keita turned out to be a lucky choice as Sadazo's messenger — out of 100 soldiers in their unit, he was one of only six to return home alive.

Though Tomoko resents his good fortune — why did he come back, she rages, and not her husband? — she is also attracted to this tall, handsome straight shooter. She asks him to stay for dinner and then for the night and then… he announces he is going to Brazil. He wants to make a fresh start, he says, especially after discovering that, while he was in the service, his wife had had an affair with his scapegrace father.

This, more than halfway into the film, is where the real drama begins. Will Tomoko and Keita go their separate ways, as have so many Japanese screen lovers, like ships passing in the night?

Sentimentalism is nowhere to be found in "Post Card": Shindo has made a career finale that, in its first half especially, is darkly comic in tone. The patriotic fervor on loud public display — all the marching and singing and shouting — is a front; in private, baser needs and desires bubble up, both the nakedly sexual and the unabashedly selfish.

Tomoko seems the least calculating of the lot, wailing her heart out at the loss of each husband, but she is theatrically performing her grief as well as genuinely feeling it. Otake has been criticized for going over the top in this role, but she aptly expresses the duality that permeates the entire film. She screams both Tomoko's individual pain and a more universal protest against war's cruelty and futility: a cry that falls on deaf ears. Yes, it's stagey, but so is Greek tragedy.

Stylistically, Shindo also plays a double game. His old-fashioned wipes and zooms recall the films of the period, but he also opts for long shots, long takes and frontal compositions that have a distancing, ironic effect. That is, despite his nods toward nostalgia, he rigorously avoids the period's cinematic melodramatics.

His message, to put it simply, is that war (and by extension, life) is a lottery, but having drawn your number, be it the death of a husband or a second chance at life after 94 of your comrades have died, you have to make the best of it. This, for Shindo, is no abstraction: Keita's story is actually his. "I have always had the souls of the 94 with me and have made them the theme of my existence," he said at the aforementioned press conference. "Post Card" is thus among his most personal films, but it is also for those men, dead now more than six decades, and for the generations since who do not know war — or understand its cost.

Household X, Kazoku X, rating: ★★★★, runtime: 90 min.

The recent spate of family dramas by Kiyoshi Kurosawa, Hirokazu Koreeda and other directors has produced much outstanding work, but the on-screen alienation can be depressing, to be honest. The housewives (almost never career women) in these films live joyless lives, expected as they are to sacrifice themselves for family units (hard to call them "members") who barely acknowledge their existence.

So it was with the expectation of another downer that I watched "Household X," a first feature by Koki Yoshida selected for the Forum section of this year's Berlin Film Festival. Influenced by the documentary-like methods of Nobuhiro Suwa (Yoshida was both Suwa's student and assistant director), the film focuses on what mkight be called the ultimate dysfunctional Japanese family. The full-time housewife mother (Kaho Minami), salaryman father (Tomorowo Taguchi) and temp-worker son (Tomohiro Kaku) behave more like stressed strangers in an overcrowded disaster shelter than family members, never exchanging so much as an "Ohayo" ("Good morning").

But the film held my attention to the end, despite its by-now overfamiliar indie techniques, from the barely-there dialogue and extreme closeups with a jittery handheld camera to the absence of background music, back story or any of the other usual devices for building empathy and sustaining interest.

The drama comes instead from Minami's finely calibrated performance as the housewife (we do not learn her name until the film's closing scenes), who is quietly on the verge of madness. Her obsessive-compulsive behavior (washing each dish until it squeaks, arranging the table mats in perfectly squared rows) signals not funny perfectionism but serious illness.

Her mousy husband, who barely speaks to his colleagues, let alone family, and her surly son, who devotes himself with surprising enthusiasm to his manual-labor jobs, react to her odd behavior with avoidance (husband) and disgust (son) — but never understanding.

Her breakdown begins with what might normally be an act of spirited rebellion: buying prepared bento (box meals) for the two ingrates at home instead of slaving in the kitchen for them. But for this fragile personality, such a radical deviation from her ideal (and highly artificial) self-image is the pinprick to the balloon. Once her will to sustain the illusion of a "good housewife and mother" deflates, her entire existence becomes meaningless. All that's needed to complete her collapse is a final, supernova-like explosion.

Yoshida, who also scripted the film, scrupulously excises melodrama and sentiment, so much so that his characters, particularly Taguchi's blank-faced salaryman, seem as capable of strong emotion, positive or negative, as robots. (The shot of a family photo, taken in happier days, is less bitterly ironic than incomprehensible. This, I was thinking, doesn't compute.)

But Yoshida also takes us deep inside his heroine's troubled psyche, as his camera tracks her every move. He does this more by oblique hints than direct statements, as when he follows her on her return from grocery shopping. We never see her face, but we observe, in her defensively hunched back and air of grim fixation, a woman trying desperately to avoid the probing and piercing of human contact. Meanwhile, the voices of her neighbors on the street sound disembodied and somehow threatening, whatever the surface meaning of their words.

In the climax, the film shows us, without overdramatizing or overstating, that family bonds can be stronger than they seem in the more fractious moments of family life.

This lesson, which many of us learned (or relearned) one anxious day six months ago, make "Household X" seem more timely than Yoshida perhaps intended. The disaster the film so starkly describes, though, goes beyond any one event or trend. Words such as "ohayo" may not have prevented it — but they're a start.

My Back Page, Mai Baku Peiji, rating: ★★★★, runtime: 141 min.

The Japanese student-protest movement of the late 1960s and early 1970s had much in common with its American counterpart, from its massive street demonstrations to its taste in music (The Beatles and Bob Dylan) and movies (anything with Dustin Hoffman or Jack Nicholson).

But it was also quite different, as I am reminded nearly every time I see a Japanese film set in the period, from Koji Wakamatsu's stark 2007 docudrama "United Red Army" to Nobuhiro Yamashita's new "My Back Page," a rambling but gripping drama based on autobiographical nonfiction by essayist, translator and film critic Saburo Kawamoto.

For one thing, the influence of the American counterculture was understandably weaker here. Hair was longer among the protestors than the short-cropped male norm, but the concept of politics as theater of the absurd (as seen in the career of jokester-cum-revolutionary Abbie Hoffman) was less in evidence than on the streets of Berkeley. Japanese radicals were serious and, on occasion, murderous.

Instead of the straight-ahead, deep-immersion approach of Wakamatsu's film, Yamashita tells his story from a more oblique angle. His hero is Sawada (Satoshi Tsumabuki), a naive young journalist writing for a weekly magazine and feeling out of place among his harder-headed (if not hard-hearted) seniors. In the opening scenes, we see him getting bloodied at a rally in 1969 while being initiated into the magazine's style of gonzo (and barely legal) journalism. We also see him awkwardly starting a relationship with a disconcertingly doe-eyed but sharply perceptive magazine cover girl (Shiori Kutsuna).

The story proper begins in 1971 as the mass-protest era is ending—and the remaining activists are becoming more extreme. One is Umeyama (Kenichi Matsuyama), a young radical who coolly informs Sawada and an older colleague that his group is planning an action in April with stolen weaponry. The colleague contemptuously dismisses Umeyama as a fake, but Sawada is not so sure, especially after he discovers that Umeyama also likes Kenji Miyazawa (a famed poet and children's literature author) and hears his soulful rendition of Creedence Clearwater Revival's "Have You Ever Seen the Rain" (whose lyrics about "a calm before the storm" make it an appropriate choice).

Most films set in this turbulent era of Japanese history, including Anh Hung Tran's 2010 novel adaptation "Norwegian Wood," in which Matsuyama also starred, miss the queasy ambivalence of the time that "My Back Page" nails precisely—the fiery rage at the establishment versus the dawning realization that real revolution would require real blood on the streets, not just a march or two around the Pentagon or Diet Building.

Even the few who said they were ready to shed it, such as Umeyama, often felt like frauds compared with their revolutionary heroes—Che Guevara, Mao Zedong and Ho Chi Minh among them—who walked the walk even if it meant prison or death.

Yamashita, who is best known abroad for the dryly funny, rousingly energetic teen dramady "Linda Linda Linda" (2005), is not the most obvious director for this material, but from his start as a maker of zero-budget indie comedies (2000's "Hazy Life" and 2003's "No One's Ark" and "Ramblers"), he has been good at capturing not only grubby absurdities but also morally gray complexities. Working from a script by Kosuke Mukai, he exposes fugitive truths of character that another director, trying to make everything simple for a big audience, would either ignore or steamroller.

Both Sawada and Umeyama (who we know from the start is not who he says he is) are, like so many of their generation, making up their identities as they go along—and not always feeling comfortable with the fit. They are also both finally forced to make choices that will permanently change lives, including their own.

Never the most concise of storytellers, Yamashita take his sweet time detailing period atmospherics and building to a climax that is uncharacteristically dramatic in a political/police thriller sort of way. But that was also the reality of the era, whose violent passions and acts now look as distant as the Warring States Period.

Both Tsumabuki and Matsuyama are perfectly cast—not always the case with these two much-in-demand actors. Tsumabuki, who was a bit too clenched as the killer on the run in last year's "Villain" by Lee Sang Il, eloquently expresses both the angst and the tenacity of Sawada, trapped between the demands of his job and his conscience. Matsuyama, who tamped himself down as the wishy-washy, apolitical hero of "Norwegian Wood," is far better as Umeyama, bubbling with dangerous, unstable energy and chilling us with the crystalline hardness of his character's ego.

At the same time, Umeyama can be almost childishly shallow—and blusteringly anxious not to show it. He reminded me again why "bullshit" was the catchword of the era—and why so many of us were guilty of spreading it.

Cold Fish, Tsumetai Nettaigyo, rating: ★★★☆, runtime: 146 min.

Sion Sono is a self-confessed chameleon, who can switch effortlessly from the laugh-a-minute black comedy of 2008's "Love Exposure" to the heartfelt medical melodrama of 2009's "Be Sure to Share" and the splatter shock of his latest, "Cold Fish."

Still, there are connecting threads between these films, including a dark sense of humor, a rather grim view of the human situation and a take on Christianity, from its doctrines to its symbolism, that mixes defiant blasphemy with curiosity and even admiration. ("If there were a Jesus fan club," Sono once told me, "I'd like to join it.")

Sono has a tendency to pile on and run on — and "Cold Fish" is the long-winded rule rather than the pointed exception. Also evident, though, is his talent for strong characterizations and moments that have the force of conviction, however twisted and deviant.

Loosely based on the real-life exploits of a serial killer couple, the story of "Cold Fish" descends into a nightmare of jime (bullying) for the mild-mannered victim/hero, as his worst fears are realized and most shameful weaknesses exposed in an abattoir of blood and gore. It's horror made intimidatingly personal.

Shamoto (Mitsuru Fukikoshi), the hero, embodies the film's English-language title in his own introverted, barely there persona. The owner of a small tropical-fish store in a town near Mount Fuji (whose grandeur silently comments on his insignificance), he is scorned by his rebellious teenage daughter Mitsuko (Hikari Kajiwara) and his slutty second wife Taeko (Megumi Kagurazaka).

One day, in a drenching rain, Shamoto and Taeko are called to a nearby supermarket, where Mitsuko has been caught shoplifting. But a friend of the outraged manager — the bald, aggressively jocular Murata (Denden) — unexpectedly leaps to Mitsuko's defense and even offers her a job at his own tropical-fish store, which is bigger and far more prosperous than Shamoto's.

This benevolence has its price, however, as Shamoto soon discovers. Mitsuko takes to her new job as a shop girl with the enthusiasm of a convert to a (skimpily clothed) cult, never returning home.

Meanwhile, Murata reveals himself as not only a sexual predator with designs on Taeko, but also an ego-mad, homicidal tyrant, with a Lady Macbeth-ish wife (Asuka Kurosawa) who aids him in his murderous schemes. This pair force the hapless Shamoto to help them transport bodies to a ramshackle forest villa where, amid images of Mary and Jesus, they gleefully dismember them as Shamoto vomits his guts out in a sink.

Killing, it turns out, gives Murata and his wife a sexual bang, and humiliating Shamoto a sadistic tingle. Though suspecting he will someday join the long list of victims, Shamoto goes along in the self-sacrificial belief that he is protecting his family from Murata's insane revenge. How little he knows.

Veteran character actor Denden (who is usually cast in avuncular, nice-guy roles) plays Murata as a grinning, raging dynamo who is all extroversion and id; think the noisy playground bully grown unchanged to manhood. But he also has the charisma of the born salesman and seducer. Shamoto, who lives in fear of offending a fly, may be appalled at Murata's audacity (not to mention his crimes), but his success at business and sex makes perfect real-world sense.

In contrast to Denden's Murata, who is all of a sociopathic piece, Fukikoshi's Shamoto is harder to parse. Is he really just a quaking dupe — or is he the tight-lipped worm who will finally turn? It's to Fukikoshi's credit that we don't know — because the character doesn't seem to know, until the last, decisive moment.

Sono slams this climax home with the energy and excess of an over-amped punk band (though the soundtrack drumming that accompanies the dramatic peaks is ironically rhythmic). He also inserts gags amid the gore — but the realistic effects and emotions, including Shamoto's agony over the loss of his soul, make the laughs stick in the throat.

Perhaps Sono should have listened more to his inner Shamoto, less to his inner Murata, who doesn't know the meaning of enough. At the end, I felt like taking a mental shower, while being glad of my empty stomach. But, like Lady Macbeth's damned spot, "Cold Fish" is not so easy to dismiss. And like the Bard, Sono knows his Bible — at least the Devil's best lines.

Love Strikes!, Moteki, no rating, runtime: 118 min.

Based on a popular TV drama that was in turn based on a best-selling comic, "Love Strikes!" begins one year after the story of the drama concluded. The nerdy, bumbling hero, Yukiyo Fujimoto (Mirai Moriyama), is at a turning point in his life at age 31: He is starting a new job, writing for a trendy pop culture website and still looking for a girlfriend after his previous love interests, as detailed in the drama, bid him sayonara.

His cute senior colleague Motoko (Yoko Maki) turns out to be a terror — but Yukiyo finds relief chatting online with a guy who shares his otaku (geeky) interests. When they finally meet in the flesh, however, the guy turns out to be the leggy, gorgeous Miyuki (Masami Nagasawa), who has been hiding her sex to ward off cyber-world creeps. To Yukiyo's amazement and delight, Miyuki is not put off by his geeky looks and style; in fact, she likes the whole package.

Yukiyo has just entered into his moteki (the film's Japanese title), a period when, for whatever mysterious reason, one becomes attractive to the opposite sex. Miyuki, it turns out, has a boyfriend she can't quite bring herself to quit. No matter: Yukiyo bonds with her pal Rumiko (Kumiko Aso), a thirtysomething OL ("office lady" or clerk), in the course of a raucous karaoke session. (They share similar tastes in old J Pop tunes) Then when he accompanies his hipster boss (Lily Franky) to a hostess bar he hooks up with the easy-going, easy-on-the-eyes Ai (Riisa Naka). Incredibly, even the fiery Motoko starts to take a more-than-professional interest in him. But he can't stop longing for Miyuki, the one who started this whole moteki thing.

Unlike like the many manga adaptations that try to please fans by faithfully reproducing as much of the source material as possible, with mugging substituting for acting, "Love Strikes!" is a stand-alone comedy that requires no prior acquaintance with the comic or TV show. Also, despite the fast, even frantic tempo, as seen in a big, goofy musical number beamed in from Broadway, the film takes its characters' quest for love rather seriously, showing the ache of disappointment as well as the giddiness of delight when a sexual fantasy incredibly comes true.

Finally, in a country where critics like to lavish praise and prizes on dull-but-worthy dramas, while dismissing comedies as unworthy of notice, "Love Strikes!" surpassed expectations by being nominated for four Japan Academy Awards, including a Best Actress nomination for Masami

Nagasawa. Was it the excellence of her performance that got her the nod — or certain scenes that made steam pour out of millions of male ears?

The Egoists, Keibetsu, rating: ★★★★, runtime: 136 min.

In his romantic drama "The Egoists," as in all of his films, Ryuichi Hiroki does not trumpet his presence with bold stylistic flourishes; instead his camera seems to float and hover discreetly, so as not to disturb the ambiance of an intimate scene. But this veteran of the pinku (soft porn) film business has none of an earlier era's (often censor-enforced) shyness about sex. Instead, Hiroki is a mix of sensualist and psychologist, who can film a hot bed scene while stripping his characters' souls bare as their skins.

Hiroki draws the best from his actresses especially, while demanding a lot from them. But even in their rawest emotional moments, with tears streaming down their faces, he brings out their inner beauty. Shinobu Terajima in "Vibrator" (2003), Yu Aoi in "The Lightening Tree" (2010) and now Anne Suzuki in "The Egoists" have all never looked — or performed — better on screen. Suzuki plays Machiko, a pole dancer at a Kabukicho club who becomes instantly enamored of Kazu (Kengo Kora), a gaunt, fierce-eyed young gambler who dashes off with her one night when the club is trashed by gangsters. Kazu is in fact one of the trashers, a job forced on him by a gang boss (Jun Murakami) in return for erasing a gambling debt.

This story of young lovers on the run, based on a novel by the late Kenji Nakagami (1946-1992), is a movie staple. As filmed by Hiroki, the Kabukicho scenes have a contemporary, borderless, dangerous feel, but once the action shifts to Nakagami's hometown of Shingu, Wakayama Prefecture, the atmosphere (and accents) change.

We are in the familiar territory of the Japanese family drama, where ancient crimes and animosities fester, but ties are not easily broken. By returning to his home in the countryside, Kazu hopes to escape his old life and start a new one with Machiko. Having accepted Kazu's invitation to flee, while not knowing where or why, Machiko is at a loss at first, especially when Kazu's well-off, short-fused father (Kaoru Kobayashi) all but turns them away at the door.

She and Kazu move to a nearby apartment and Kazu takes a job as a deliveryman for his uncle (Tomorowo Taguchi), the testy owner of a liquor store, while she tries to fit in with Kazu's punk friends. Despite their attempts at normality, Kazu's family sees him as a black sheep and Machiko as Tokyo trash. They get a friendly reception from an elderly, eccentric cafe proprietress (Midori Mako), who was the lover of Kazu's grandfather, but it all starts to go wrong, especially after Kazu foolishly borrows a large sum of money from an implacable loan shark (Nao Omori). His dream is live happily ever after in wedded bliss with Machiko, but his reality becomes a debtor's hell, with Machiko as human collateral.

Kora, who got his big-screen break playing a young killer in Hiroki's "M" (2006), is the ideal choice as the wild, wounded Kazu: he's got the lean, piercing look of a soulful, starving, world-defying wolf. What woman could resist? Suzuki, who starred as a teen in the sci-fi actioner "Returner" (2002) and the Shunji Iwai friendship drama "Hana and Alice" (2004), delivers everything Hiroki asks for and more. Though her Machiko has a sex worker's hard shell, she is intelligently alive to everything around her, from Kazu's burning sincerity to the chill at his big family home.

At the same time, she responds to Kazu's outbursts of passion and anger with fires of her own. Theirs is a match of equals.

I Wish, Kiseki, rating: ★★★✫, runtime: 128 min.

Hirokazu Koreeda has risen to heights of international critical esteem. An American film journal recently devoted nearly an entire issue to his films (with this reviewer contributing). But what foreign critics and fans often think they are getting — a director carrying on the humanistic traditions of Japanese cinema's 1950s and 1960s Golden Age — is not quite what Koreeda is delivering.

Trained as a documentary filmmaker and long a staffer of the TV Man Union production house, he is outside the mainstream of the Japanese film business in which the Golden Age greats and their successors worked. Also, his style of naturalistic filmmaking owes as much to such foreign influences as Hou Hsiao Hsien and Theodoros Angelopoulos as to Mikio Naruse, Koreeda's personal Golden Age hero. Finally, as proven by his latest film, the childhood drama "I Wish," Koreeda is also not quite the indie purist his admirers sometimes imagine. He has long had one eye on the big audience beyond the art house — and "I Wish," with its story of two brothers conspiring to bring their divorced parents back together — targets it squarely.

But if the film does not equal his 2004 masterpiece "Nobody Knows" — one of the best films ever made about children, period — it is still completely Koreeda, meaning a combination of close observation and fine-layered narrative crafting. Also, it may have the look of a promo project for Kyushu, where it is set, and Japan Rail, whose new Kyushu bullet train line plays a big role in the plot, but "I Wish" is the rare Japanese commercial film that comes from the brain and heart of its director, not a production committee exploiting every possible revenue stream.

Two brothers — sixth-grader Koichi (Koki Maeda) and fourth-grader Ryunosuke (Oshiro Maeda) — both live in Kyushu, but are separated by their parent's divorce. Koichi lives grumpily with his working mom (Nene Otsuka), Japanese-sweets-making grandfather (Isao Hashizume) and hula-dance-loving grandmother (Kirin Kiki) in Kagoshima. He doesn't much care for the gritty ash from the nearby volcano or even the bland sweets that granddad turns out. In fact, he wishes the volcano would wipe the whole place off the map — and that Mom and Dad could get back together.

Meanwhile the perpetually chipper Ryunosuke is enjoying life with his laid-back musician father (Joe Odagiri) in Fukuoka. Dad's band-mates are cool (even if their CDs don't sell), and the prettiest girl in Ryunosuke's class, Emi (Kyara Uchida), likes him, though their "romance" consists of hanging out with her and her girlfriends. But he seconds his brother's wish, while remembering little more from family life than constant bickering between his parents.

Then Koichi hears a rumor that when the new bullet trains first pass each other — one coming from Hakata in the north and anther from Kagoshima in the south — the energy they generate will cause wishes to come true. There's just one catch: Wishers have to be there on the spot when the trains pass. Koichi calls up Ryunosuke on his cellphone and proposes a plan: They meet at a midway point and, by combining their wishes, better guarantee a happy outcome — that is, a family reunion.

This may sound like a setup for a saccharine sob-fest, and I'm sure that's what the film would have become if the usual suspects had been in charge. Koreeda doesn't entirely kill the sweetness; his two child leads — real-life brothers who perform as the manzai (comic duo) act Maeda Maeda — are charmers, especially the ball-of-energy younger one, who could give a chipmunk lessons in cuteness. Thankfully, the brothers are also gifted naturals who lend a real-kid credibility to every scene while demonstrating again Koreeda's unsurpassed talent for casting and directing children.

Also, it's hard not to feel good when the brothers, with the aid of school friends and sympathetic adults, make their fantastic plan a reality. At a time when so much has gone so wrong with so many plans in this country, watching Koichi methodically map out the exact point where the two trains will cross — and get it right — is somehow inspiring. (With kids like that around, there's hope for this country yet.)

Instead of a formulaic "innocent kids reunite warring parents" story line, Koreeda complicates his narrative with the sort of selective memories and mixed motivations that are recognizably human, if hardly pure. The kids, we see, are neither angels nor the troubled souls of the usual local "problem" film; they are ordinarily flawed. Finally, Koreeda — much like his idol, Naruse — rejects the tearjerking tactics of the orthodox melodrama. Yes, the tears come (at least to this reviewer), but they are earned, not extracted. That's miracle enough.

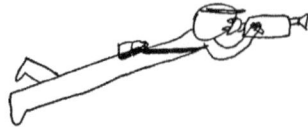

River, rating: ★★★★, runtime: 89 min.

In the year since the March 11, 2011 earthquake, tsunami and nuclear catastrophe in the Tohoku region, dozens of Japanese and foreign filmmakers have taken their cameras north, but not to make mass-audience epics — yet. Instead, they have been documenting or dramatizing the triple disaster and its aftermath more from a sense of mission than the usual career/commercial considerations.

One is Ryuichi Hiroki, whose new film "River," was originally inspired by the random killings on June 7, 2008, by a disturbed man in Tokyo's Akihabara electronics shopping district. After ramming a rented truck into a crowd and killing three, Tomohiro Kato fatally stabbed four more with a knife before being arrested by police. The incident generated an outpouring of commentary on the alienated and despairing state of Japan's marginalized youth.

After March 11, however, Hiroki decided to rewrite the script of "River" to reflect the newer tragedy, whose impact on the national psyche was even greater. He has combined his two story lines into an organic whole that, with poetic insight but no pat answers, addresses such universal dilemmas as how to let go, how to forgive and how to find purpose when all seems futile and arbitrary.

The film begins with a long traveling shot of the heroine, Hikari (Misako Renbutsu), exiting Akihabara Station and walking down the street with a pensive, lonely air that sets her apart from the bustling crowd around her. A photographer (Mami Nakamura) takes an interest in her and, while snapping away, teases out her story: Hikari's boyfriend, Kenji, was one of the killer's victims and, after a long period of depression and solitude, she began revisiting the site of his murder.

Over the course of the day, Hikari encounters a troubled young man (Tokio Emoto) who also has a connection to the killer, a friendly street musician (Michiko Aoki, also known as singer-songwriter Quinka, With a Yawn) whose song touches her heart and a dodgy middle-aged recruiter for a maid cafe (Tomorowo Taguchi) whose blandishments give her ego a lift. But a brief acquaintance with a jaded "maid café" worker (Nahana) makes her realize that faking a cutesy-cute persona to extract money from gullible men is not for her.

Then she finally meets Yuji (Yukichi Kobayashi), a young drifter who may have known Kenji. But he becomes irritated by her obsession with the past. "This is reality," he says pointing to a news program on TV about the recent disaster. But he is escaping from his own past — namely, his estranged parents living in a tsunami-devastated town.

Alternating between handheld camera shots that discreetly observe from a distance and closeups that capture his two leads at their most open and revealing, Hiroki creates an atmosphere at once objective and intimate. At the same time, he likes to push his actresses out of their comfort zones and Renbutsu is no exception. At the film's beginning and end, Hiroki films her in long takes in which she expresses Hikari's changing emotions in a subtle, natural flow rather than with bravura theatrics.

Yuji serves as a catalyst for Hikari, cracking open her shell and opening her to new possibilities. But this street-savvy down-and-outer is as lost and alone in his own way as Hikari is in hers. Kobayashi conveys Yuji's mix of outer cool and inner pain with a feeling of transparency and ease.

"River" is aptly titled, since both Hikari and Yuji appear to be drifting like flotsam on the water, but both are also moving toward something vaster than their individual existences, as they free themselves from past resentments or regrets. What that something might be, the film leaves for us to decide — with "Moon River" playing over the credit crawl. An unusual but appropriate choice — unless you've seen "Breakfast at Tiffany's" too many times and can't get Audrey Hepburn out of your head.

Rent-a-Cat, Rentaneko, rating: ★★★★, runtime: 110 min.

Japanese films, at both ends of the commercial-indie spectrum, are often about extremes. Deadly disease and violence are rampant. Characters sweat bullets and cry rivers.

The films of Naoko Ogigami are not only an answer to the noisy domestic competition, but also an antidote to everyday urban stress. Beginning with her 2006 hit "Kamome Diner," a drama about a middle-aged Japanese woman who finds a second start running the title eatery in Helsinki, she has made one film after another that detox their mainly female audiences with gently comic, enticingly homey visions of a less-hurried way of life.

Meanwhile, members of Ogigami's staff and regular cast have made other films that are similarly woman-centered, life-affirming and blood-pressure-lowering, such as Mika Omori's "Pool" and Kana Matsumoto's "Mother Water." This is not to say Ogigami and her associates are engaged in the cinematic equivalent of aromatherapy: Insights into the vagaries of the heart are served together with images of scrumptious home-cooked meals.

Ogigami's latest, "Rent-a-Cat" is more on the fey and fabulist side than her previous work, beginning with its title occupation, practiced by the 30-something Sayoko (Mikako Ichikawa), who lives alone surrounded by a dozen or so cats. One sunny day we see her trundling six of them along the Tama River in an umbrella-topped cart, calling out to passersby with a small loudspeaker that she is renting the felines to "lonely people."

Her "customers" include an elderly woman (Reiko Kusamura) left alone after her husband's death, a businessman (Ken Mitsuishi) forced to live apart from his family, and a primly proper car-rental shop clerk (Maho Yamada) who never sees a client. The story takes a new turn with the appearance of a former classmate (Kei Tanaka) with a checkered past who is more interested in her than her furry merchandise.

As is usual with Ogigami's films, the simple premise is worked out with great attention to visual detail, from the heroine's charmingly decorated house to her casually ethnic wardrobe. Also, despite its repetitions, the story is told with enough variation, comic and otherwise, to ward off monotony, including periodic appearances by a nosy old neighbor (veteran DJ Katsuya Kobayashi in drag) who always says exactly the one thing that wounds Sayoko, if never fatally.

Outwardly the most stylish, self-assured cat lady ever, Sayoko is inwardly a mess: wanting to marry but without a partner, and still mourning her beloved grandmother years after her death. She is, we see, one of the lonely people and needs her cats more than anyone.

The sudden appearance of the classmate, grown to a good-looking (and still obnoxious) guy, might signal "happy ending" in another film, but Ogigami is not so predictable. She may want to soothe her fans rather than stir them up, but she also respects their intelligence and experience. People, they know, don't change so easily — and that includes Sayoko.

More than a fairy tale for adults, "Rent-a-Cat" is like an illustrated collection of the so-called light essays so popular with female readers here. The style is spare but poetic, the mood is warm but wistful, and the characters are lovable but finally enigmatic.

Somewhat like the cats stretched out on Sayoko's veranda, looking at their owner and us with those watchful, knowing eyes. What do they think of us, really?

Penance, Shokuzaki, rating: ★★★☆, runtime: 270 min. (feature film version)

Kiyoshi Kurosawa, whose 2008 dysfunctional family drama "Tokyo Sonata" won the Jury Prize in the Un Certain Regard section of the Cannes Film Festival, has just received his first major festival invitation in four years.

It is for, not a film, but a five-part drama series Kurosawa made for the Wowow entertainment channel. Broadcast in Japan from January to February this year, "Penance" will screen out of competition at the upcoming Venice Film Festival. Since Venice and other major festivals ignore TV dramas as a rule, the exception made for Kurosawa is a measure of his high international reputation. That is, he's been missed very much indeed.

Based on a novel of the same title by Kanae Minato, "Penance" will not dent that reputation, despite a whodunit story line that, stripped down, wouldn't be out of place in a weekly network "Mystery Theater" program.

The sense of creeping dread familiar to fans of "Cure" (1997) and other of Kurosawa's pioneering J-horror films is still present, however. Also, it is created with his usual artfully minimal means — plastic bags blown eerily by the breeze, a translucent plastic sheet making strange shadows on the wall.

The story of a mother ("Tokyo Sonata" star Kyoko Koizumi) implacably seeking the killer of her young daughter may not please fans hoping for Kurosawa's return to J-horror, though its explorations of the heart of darkness will be familiar to viewers of Tetsuya Nakashima's "Confessions," a 2010 film also based on Minato's fiction.

The story begins with a man dressed in work clothes approaching a group of five girls on a playground and asking one of them to help him with a job. When she fails to return, her friends go looking for her and find her dead in the school gymnasium. They cannot describe the man to the police, despite getting a clear view of his face. After months of fruitless investigation, the victim's mother grimly tells them they will all pay a price for playing dumb, though exactly what their penance will be she leaves up to fate.

The first four episodes focus on the four surviving classmates 15 years on and how they are still linked, willingly or no, to the revenge-bent mother, Asako.

One, Sae (Yu Aoi), has been distrustful of men since the traumatic murder, but marries a sincere-sounding, well-off guy (Mirai Moriyama) who promises her the sheltered life she craves. But her new hubby turns out to be controlling and sexually kinky.

Another, Maki (Eiko Koike), is an elementary school teacher whose strictness is a cover for her insecurities. When she bravely confronts a disturbed school invader, she is feted as a hero — until a smarmy vice principal leads a reaction against her "overuse of force."

Still another, Akiko (Sakura Ando), is a hikikomori (recluse) who feels herself unworthy of human company, until her scampish brother (Ryo Kase) brings his promiscuous new girlfriend and her charming young daughter to visit. Akiko and the daughter hit it off immediately, but her brother's behavior toward the girl awakens memories of an old trauma.

The fourth, Yuka (Chizuru Ikewaki), is running a small flower shop, but still resents her once-sickly older sister (Ayumi Ito) for monopolizing their mother's attention when they were children. While plotting revenge, she comes across a clue to the killer's identity — and contacts Asako.

As for the concluding episode, I'll say nothing, only that throughout the series the minimalist-but-atmospheric Kurosawa style, imparts an eerie, intimate tension to even mundane scenes, while revealing inner lives more by suggestion than the usual TV-drama shouting.

And the penances (including Asako's), have a stern emotional logic, while reminding us that even inactions have consequences and that our demons, creative and destructive, never rest. Thankfully for us, that includes Kurosawa's.

Chips, Potechi, rating: ★★★★, runtime: 68 min.

All of Yoshihiro Nakamura's films as a director, including his 2009 international breakthrough "Fish Story," are intended first and foremost as entertainment, not art. They are also often philosophical investigations into the nature of reality, seemingly inspired by geneticist JBS Haldane's observation that "The universe is not only queerer than we suppose, but queerer than we can suppose."

At the same time, Nakamura is less a sui generis creator than an adaptor of others' work, especially the fiction of Kotaro Isaka, which has inspired some of his best films, "Fish Story" included.

His latest, "Chips," is also based on an Isaka story and shares "Fish Story"'s message: Small, seemingly random acts can have large, meaningful consequences. This may sound trite — "for want of a nail" and all the rest of it — but in Nakamura's telling it takes on a funny, fresh significance.

In contrast to "Fish Story," a sprawling film that ends with a thrilling rush as the various plot threads tie brilliantly together, "Chips" is smaller in scope and less showy in effect, but its climactic epiphany left me in tears. I won't spoil it by saying why, just that this crazy world made more sense as the credits rolled.

The hero is one Tadashi Imamura (Gaku Hamada), a nervous thief who has an advisor in the enigmatic, worldly wise Kurosawa (Nao Omori) and a master in a portly, easily flustered fellow Imamura calls his "CEO" (Nakamura in a cameo). Imamura's level-headed girlfriend, Wakaba (Fumino Kimura), dutifully accompanies him on his jobs, but can't understand his obsession with a baseball player, Ozaki, who is from Imamura's hometown of Sendai and rides the bench of the local pro team. Baseball, in fact, baffles her in general. "A home run is just a ball hit far, right?" she asks him at one point. "What's the big deal?"

The plot begins rolling when Imamura breaks into Ozaki's apartment — and hears a desperate woman on the answering machine calling for help with a stalker. Imamura impulsively decides to go to her rescue, setting into motion an odd chain of events that clarifies his relationship to Ozaki — though making it mean something more than mere chance is finally up to him.

What do the titular potato chips have to do with it? When Imamura mistakenly brings Wakaba salty chips instead of the consomme-flavored ones she requested, she eats them anyway and proclaims them delicious. Imamura is so moved he cries, much to her surprise.

This minor incident holds an important key to Imamura's existential dilemma. He believes himself, we see, to be a "wrong package," beginning with his birth. Wakaba's small act of forgiveness gives him hope that the wrong can become right.

Nearly everyone in the main cast ironically underplays in even extreme situations, giving them a comic veneer of normality. The big exception is Nakamura regular Hamada, whose Imamura is serious about everything — which makes him a funny thief.

As usual with Nakamura, certain characters are not what they seem and their actions do not always make rational sense, but by the end we see that there was a plan, quite an ingenious one, all along.

Unlike previous Nakamura films based on Isaka's fiction, "Chips" plays like a tightly written short story, with a 68-minute running time and no narrative fat whatsoever. Call it minor if you will, but it's also sweet and sure, like the stroke of a hitter who knows, from the crack of his bat, that the ball is out of the park.

Dreams for Sale, Yume Uru Futari, rating: ★★★★, runtime: 137 min.

Ever since her 2003 directorial debut "Wild Berries," a black comedy about a dysfunctional family, Miwa Nishikawa has been exploring the infinite human capacity for duplicity. In "Sway" (2006) two brothers sleep with the same woman and one ends up testifying in court against the other, saying he saw his older sibling push her to her death from a bridge. What really happened, though, is left in doubt. In "Dear Doctor" (2009) a kindly old doctor in a rural village is exposed as a fraud. But his motives remain mysterious.

Similar to these films, her latest, "Dreams for Sale," could have been made as genre entertainment; in this case, a caper comedy. The situation: After seeing their small izakaya (pub) burn to the ground, a couple (Takako Matsu and Sadao Abe) turn to marriage fraud — promising matrimony, borrowing money from one's intended and then absconding — to raise cash for a new eatery.

Nishikawa, who also wrote the script, supplies a scattering of laughs, but she is more interested in examining how the couple's deceptions, beginning with the husband's act of apparent unfaithfulness, eat away at their marriage and souls. The film refuses to either moralize or excuse, leaving the final judgment of the principals up to the audience — or God.

The husband, Kanya (Abe), is impulsive, emotional and boyishly charming, while the wife, Satoko (Matsu), is the smarter, stronger, more mature one.

Soon after the fire an excited Kanya comes home with an envelope full of cash, and a shaky story of how he got it. Satoko soon unearths the truth: He had sex with a middle-aged izakaya regular (Sawa Suzuki), who then gave him the money for reasons of her own. Instead of booting the louse, Satoko decides to exploit his talent for extracting money from vulnerable females.

Soon they are working together at an upscale Japanese-style restaurant, with Satoko assisting Kanya in his wooing of prospective "brides," beginning with an over-30 office lady (Rena Tanaka) unhappy with her job and love life. Among other marks are a sweet, naive weight lifter (Yuka Ebara) with Olympic dreams but no guy; a spunky, if badly abused, prostitute (Tamae Ando) from the provinces; and a hard-working single mom (Tae Kimura) supporting her cute son and sick dad.

But as Kanya and Satoko near their financial goal, cracks begin to appear in the facade of their marriage. Kanya develops inconvenient feelings for his marks, while starting to resent Satoko's superiority.

Movies about crooks and scammers after the big score, from Stanley Kubrick's "The Killing" (1956) on, nearly all share the same story arc, and "Dreams for Sale" is no exception. What sets the film apart is its sharpness about its characters' psychologies, particularly its women. I don't mean that Nishikawa has some special insight by virtue of being a woman herself, but she does see and care about them as individuals, not representative types.

The best example is the weight lifter, Hitomi, who looks and acts like the genuine article (including her lifts of Olympic-class weights) — and would probably be minor comic relief in almost any other film. But while making a joke or two at her expense, Nishikawa shows us the sharp mind and breakable heart beneath the bulging muscles. To his credit, Kanya sees all this as well, and his scheming begins to weigh on his conscience (not that it stops him).

The best performance, however, is that of Matsu as Satoko. Once seen as an ojosama (well-bred young lady) who had her show-business ticket punched from her birth into a distinguished kabuki family, Matsu has proven herself as an actor of depth, range and grit. Her turn as Satoko recalls her similarly excellent performance as the loyal if conflicted wife of an alcoholic, unfaithful writer in Kichitaro Negishi's "Villon's Wife" (2009), right down to her job as an izakaya server. But Satoko has a darker fire in her eyes, a deeper culpability for her own degradation.

Who is she really and what is she after? She gives us clues in her lonely self-pleasuring (a scene Matsu brings off with a forthright naturalness) and her barely suppressed rage at her husband's harsh accusations. Then, after an overly long climatic sequence, we finally get a silently eloquent answer. But how you read it is up to you.

The Drudgery Train, Kueki Ressha, rating: ★★★★, runtime: 112 min.

Nobuhiro Yamashita's early films, such as 1999's "Hazy Life," 2002's "No One's Ark," and 2003's "Ramblers," were exercises in deadpan absurdity featuring loser heroes, with the sly jokes emerging from true-to-life (if inherently ridiculous) situations. Following his international breakout with the high school music film "Linda, Linda, Linda" (2005), Yamashita could have indefinitely repeated its formula of observational humor served up with youthful energy and charm. Instead he tried different genres, such as comic murder mystery ("The Matsugane Potshot Affair," 2006) and 1970s-era political/personal drama ("My Back Page," 2011).

His newest, "The Drudgery Train," is something of a throwback to his black comedy beginnings, but deeper as a character study and more adventurous as a film. Based on an Akutagawa-Prize-winning novel by Kenta Nishimura, "The Drudgery Train" resembles films that have been based on the semi-autobiographical fiction of American writer Charles Bukowski, from "Barfly" (1987) to "Factotum" (2005). The Bukowski character in these films, Henry "Hank" Chinaski, is viewed as a cool loner rebel, despite his marginal existence as a drunk living in rented rooms and working at menial jobs (when he works at all). By contrast, Yamashita's hero, Kanta Kitamachi (Mirai Moriyama), is a loser with absolutely no social skills who blows his warehouse wages on sleazy peep shows and cheap izakaya (pub) booze. He bad-mouths nearly anyone in range once the liquor is in him, while groveling to his disgruntled landlord for another couple days of grace on the rent. Obnoxious and contemptible he is. Cool, he is not. It's hard to imagine Mickey Rourke ("Barfly") or Matt Dillon ("Factotum") clamoring to play him in a Hollywood remake.

In fact, it's a wonder the film got released by major distributor Toei, since in almost every scene, Kitamachi violates the first commandment of a hero in a commercial film: Thou shalt inspire sympathy. But as portrayed by Moriyama, fresh from his success as the similarly socially challenged hero of "Love Strikes!," Kitamachi also happens to be funny and — as a seeming contradiction to everything I've just said, likable in his sheer cussedness.

The story has the ingredients of a typical coming-of-age drama. Kitamachi, a junior high dropout whose father was sent to jail for a sex crime, is toiling as a day laborer in a warehouse when he is befriended by Shoji Kusakabe (Kengo Kora), a new hire who is attending a nearby trade school. A good-natured oddball, Kusakabe soon becomes Kitamachi's boon companion and social facilitator. When Kitamachi reveals that he has been eying a pretty clerk at a used-book store (without adding that he lacks the courage to say hello) Kusakabe smilingly serves as a go-between.

The clerk, Yasuko Sakurai (Atsuko Maeda), turns out to be interested in the same sort of mystery novels as Kitamachi, who is a devoted, if unlikely, bookworm. Miracle of miracles, they become friends and Kitamachi starts to dream the impossible dream: Unpaid sex with a willing partner. To top it all off, he gets promoted to forklift driver. Life, for once in his 19 so-far-pointless years, is wonderful. Of course it can't last.

In an ordinary film, the ensuing crises — mostly caused by Kitamachi's own rock-headed stupidity, would be growth experiences, leading to a wiser, happier hero. But working from a script by pinku eiga (erotic film) maestro Shinji Imaoka, Yamashita turns this formula on its head, with inspired gags that subvert every "learning moment."

"The Drudgery Train" also has a realism not often found in other local films with women-less, prospect-less young male heroes. This goes beyond Kitamachi's many superficial resemblances to creator Kenta Nishimura, from his family background to his tastes in literature: He is not a slacker comedy cartoon, but a fully realized character whose blunders and crimes can be painful to witness, since his victims (including himself) are recognizably human and his actions have unpleasant real-world consequences. But the film is not a downer drama, just as it is not feel-good entertainment.

Instead it's a lot like life — though I hope not like yours.

The Cowards Who Looked to the Sky, Fugainai Boku wa Sora wo Mita,

rating: ★★★☆, runtime: 141 min.

What is your worst nightmare? In this Internet age, public shaming via the Internet has come to rank high. Of course, the sex video that just happens to go viral has propelled more than one "victim" to stardom, but far more reputations have been tarnished by Web notoriety, however temporary or local. Based on Misumi Kubo's award-winning novel, Yuki Tanada's "The Cowards Who Looked to the Sky" examines the fallout from one such shaming, but for all the nowness of its topic, the film is not exploitative. Tanada has portrayed her teenage hero and his housewife lover as real-life combinations of good and bad, strong and weak, admirable and contemptible.

Most of all, they are ordinary people who, whatever happens, get up the next morning and live through the day. Tanada's theme, in fact, is less the depths to which we humans can fall than our tenacity. We just keep coming, disaster after disaster, generation after generation.

Takumi (Kento Nagayama) is the only child of a spunky midwife (Mieko Harada) who runs her clinic together with one no-nonsense assistant, while his improvident father is no longer around. He has been close to the process of birth, in all its pain and glory, since boyhood, as well as being educated by strong women out of typical adolescent male illusions about the opposite sex.

Takumi is also an unusually good-looking guy with the usual adolescent male sex drive. When he meets a vivacious if insecure housewife (Tomoko Tabata) decked out as a cute cartoon heroine at a manga and anime flea market, the sparks begin to fly. And keep flying, even when the housewife, nicknamed Anzu, insists on the proper script and cosplay gear for their sexual encounters.

Which may sound like the makings of a pinku (soft-core porn) comedy, but Tanada films the bed scenes with a hot frankness and intimate tenderness that lifts them above the mechanical genre norm. The dry humor that informed her earlier work, including her 2008 road movie "One Million Yen Girl," surfaces only occasionally, though she observes her characters from a distance, with more sympathy than irony.

Complications quickly multiply. A pretty classmate (Miharu Tanaka) melts Takumi's heart with a brave declaration of love, causing him to dump the middle-aged (by his standards) Anzu. Adding to Anzu's woes, her terror of a mother-in-law (the single-named Ginpuncho) badgers her and her mama's-boy of a husband (Takashi Yamanaka) to produce a grandchild, while unfairly blaming Anzu (whom she calls by her real name, Satomi) for the couple's lack of reproductive success.

Worst of all, a secretly filmed video of Takumi and Anzu in bed ends up online. When it goes viral, all hell breaks loose.

Tanada and scriptwriter Kosuke Mukai have somewhat confusingly structured the film like a three-part omnibus with intersecting, nonlinear storylines. Incidents presented from Takumi's viewpoint are later rewound to show the same scenes from Anzu's perspective. Then, the focus abruptly shifts to Fukuda (Masataka Kubota), Takumi's best pal, who lives a grim existence with his senile grandmother in a rundown danchi (housing development), while fending off bill collectors dunning his mostly absent mother.

With his own bank account melting away, Fukuda works part-time as a convenience-store clerk and newspaper-delivery boy and thinks of quitting school. But what does his sad tale have to do with the putative main story?

Everything, as it turns out, though Tanada goes her own sweet, meandering way in showing us why. Fukuda's struggle, we see, not only links with Takumi's and Anzu's plot-wise, but also illustrates the film's larger themes. Though he flirts with failure and even petty crime, Fukuda has the same strong survival instincts as Takumi and Anzu, as well as the same stubborn capacity for hope.

Cynics may argue that the human capacity for destruction is larger. Tanada's reply is scenes of women giving birth in the clinic, at times in excruciating pain and with worrisome complications. Then the baby arrives and the joyful expressions of everyone in the room say it all: We begin as little miracles deserving life — and a chance.

The Kirishima Thing, Kirishima, Bukatsu Yamerutteyo, rating: ★★★⯨, runtime: 103 min.

High schools are mercilessly hierarchical societies. At mine in rural Pennsylvania varsity basketball players occupied the summit. (Football players didn't because we didn't have a football team.) For a mere honor student to absent-mindedly sit in the "reserved" seat of one of these titans in the cafeteria was to invite an unceremonious dump to the floor by its towering possessor. Resistance was futile.

The same is true, in spades, in the high school of Daihachi Yoshida's engagingly off-kilter, finally poignant "The Kirishima Thing." Based on a novel author Ryo Asai wrote while still a student at Waseda University, the film begins with the sudden, unexplained decision of a star volleyball player, Kirishima, to quit the team.

Here is where things get interesting — and murky. We don't learn of this decision from Kirishima himself: He has vanished from the face of the Earth. Instead we get the news from his flummoxed classmates, in multiple revelation scenes that capture this crucial moment from various perspectives.

Among the hardest hit are Kirishima's best pal Hiroki Kikuchi (Masahiro Higashide), who is angered at being left out of the loop, and Kirishima's cool-as-ice girlfriend Risa (Mizuki Yamamoto), who takes his resignation as a personal affront.

The waves of Kirishima's disappearance pass beyond the outraged volleyball team captain and the luckless second-stringer who has to take the star's place to classmates whose connections to Kirishima range from the indirect to the nonexistent, including Aya (Suzuka Ohgo), a brass-band member with a hopeless crush on Hiroki; Maeda (Ryunosuke Kamiki), the nerdy president of the film club and director-in-embryo; and Kasumi (Ai Hashimoto), a sensitive badminton team player who is a friend of Risa's and a former junior high classmate of Maeda's. Kasumi bridges the status gap between the highest of the high and the lowest of the low.

Fans of Yoshida's previous work, beginning with the manga-esque black comedy "Funuke Show Some Love, You Losers!" that became his international breakout in 2007, may find the more naturalistic acting and mostly serious tone of "Kirishima" surprising, though the one-thing-building-on-another story line will be familiar, as will Yoshida's skill at drawing complex portraits from seemingly generic characters.

After the bravura opening, which promises tension, suspense and big plot reveals, the film gently, firmly upends expectations. The giant hole left by Kirishima's absence continues to echo, but the focus passes to the kids dealing with it, and how it impacts not only their relationships and status, but their view of what — and who — really matters. Hint: It's not necessarily Kirishima.

Yoshida, who also wrote the script, is in no hurry to tie up his various plot threads, which makes for a certain mid-film drift. Also, instead of clearly settling on a hero, he shuttles between the stories of Maeda, Hiroki, Aya and Kasumi to the end, though Hiroki and Kasumi are the more interesting, since they have more potential to change despite having their elite passes punched. That is, they start to question the values of their in group — and see that there is a real world outside it.

"Kirishima" might be called a morality play in the guise of a coming-of-age drama, though what Yoshida admires is less conventional film-hero goodness than qualities such as self-awareness, open mindedness and persistence in the face of indifference, ridicule and the random interruptions that are a daily fact of high school (and, indeed, modern) life. In short, qualities that make for a good film director.

The characters are intended as audience mirrors, though I didn't quite see myself in any of them. Maeda-like, I was a teenage movie nerd; Hiroki-like, I joined a sports team and dated a cheerleader (who dumped me for a better cross-country runner).

But I did see the dilemmas of adolescence brought into sharp focus through the hungry eye of a film-crazy kid with his first 8-mm camera and the perspective of his adult self, who knows that even the most momentous of high school days will have an end — and no sequel.

The Woodsman and the Rain, itsutsuki to Ame, rating: ★★★★, runtime: 129 min.

In movies as in life, first impressions count. Hence all the money lavished on opening credits, all the thought devoted to opening scenes. Quite often though, the flashy beginning comes to feel like a con, as the formulaic story wends its way to its predictable end.

In his new film, "The Woodsman and the Rain," Shuichi Okita persuaded me he knew what he was about from scene one and never disappointed thereafter, making maximum use of his talent with a minimum expenditure of yen. One of my favorites of this year's Tokyo International Film Festival, it was rightly awarded the Special Jury Prize in the competition.

The film opens in a mountain forest, where a 60-year-old lumberjack (Koji Yakusho) is cutting down a large tree. Many another director would have used a series of short cuts or even a stunt double to spare his middle-aged star effort and danger. Instead, Okita shows us Yakusho working hard, sweating profusely and standing by the tree as it comes crashing noisily down.

All this made me think both director and star would go above and beyond the call of duty to make "Woodsman and the Rain" extraordinary. That proved to be the case.

The story is less about elderly derring-do, more about an unusual culture clash and its consequences, from the funny to the teary. Okita, who cowrote the script with Fumio Moriya, tells it with a dry but never cynical eye, together with true-life observations and fine storytelling craft.

Soon after the lumberjack, Katsuhiko, cuts down his tree, he is approached by a nervous assistant director (Kanji Furutachi) who tells him a film is shooting nearby and asks him to quiet down. This request doesn't immediately register in Katsuhiko's puzzled brain, but he is soon drafted into helping the outsiders, who know little more about their location than they can find on Google Maps.

More seriously, the tyro director of this trashy zombie pic within a pic, Koichi (Shun Oguri), has been struck nearly dumb with fear and indecision, as his cast and crew regard him with barely disguised contempt. What can Katsuhiko, who knows nothing about movies but likes playing one of the living-dead extras, do to help? The answer involves several improbabilities that Okita, Yakusho and Oguri seamlessly transform into comic and dramatic gold.

This is not to say that "Woodsman and the Rain" is slick; in fact, like Okita's previous feature, 2010's elightful foodie dramady "The Chef of South Polar," it's on the slow — even gently dreamy — side. But it firmly grounds even its screwiest scenes in the real world (if you consider a film set "real").

The film also exerts an emotional tug not usually found in local zero-to-hero dramadies, with their big, walloping finales. Katsuhiko not only comes to regard Koichi as a surrogate son, but starts to see his real son (Kengo Kora), a slacker nearly the same age as Koichi, with new eyes.

Yakusho once again proves he is the most versatile and adaptable of actors, playing his working-class hero with unforced authority and surprising agility. He strides up mountains as though he has been doing it all his life — or spending months on the StairMaster. Meanwhile, Oguri disguises the ikemen (pretty boy) looks and brash confidence that won him millions of female TV drama fans on such hit shows as "Boys over Flowers."

Most of all, "Woodsman and the Rain" glows with a deep love of the movies, even ones that feature ridiculous zombie holocausts. As Katsuhiko reminds us, his eyes shining as he reads Koichi's script, there's a magic in telling stories for the camera that anyone can understand, even (or rather, especially) if they've spent their lives in forests instead of in front of screens.

Our Homeland, Kazoku no Kuni, ratiing: ★★★★, runtime: 99 min.

Many Japanese directors make family dramas — it's the default setting for serious filmmakers here — but they are usually not telling their own family stories. One who does is Yang Yong Hi. Born and raised in Osaka's zainichi (ethnic Korean) community, she debuted as a director with "Dear Pyongyang," a 2005 documentary that told the story of her father, who emigrated to Japan from the southern Korean island of Cheju but after the partitioning of the country in 1945 became a fervent supporter of North Korea. When she was six her father sent her three teenage brothers to live in North Korea as part of a "repatriation" wave of zainichi who dreamed of a socialist paradise.

The enormity of that error and its lifelong consequences are the themes of Yang's first fiction feature, "Our Homeland," which also draws on her family history and was screened in the Forum section of this year's Berlin Film Festival, winning the CICAE Prize.

The West tends to regard North Korea as either a shadowy hell of extreme poverty and conformity or a bizarre Ruritania run by pudgy dictators with eccentric hairstyles. Yang, by contrast, dramatizes the costs the North's system inflicts on its people without filters and with an abundance of hard-won knowledge.

Her style is TV-drama direct, with every actor in the main cast getting at least one big emotional scene, but also unsentimental and uncompromising. How Yang, so new to directing actors, was able to extract such honesty I don't know, though the raw-seeming, superbly crafted evidence is on the screen.

The story begins with the return of Sung Ho (Arata Iura) to his family in Tokyo after 25 years in North Korea. He is suffering from a brain tumor whose treatment is beyond the abilities of North Korean doctors and has been given three months to find a cure in Japan.

He is welcomed by his anxious mother (Yoshiko Miyazaki), who has prepared the food he loved as a boy; his nervous, defensive father (Masane Tsukayama), who was responsible for sending him away at age 16; and his younger sister Rie (Sakura Ando), a teacher of Japanese who has come to hate her father's "patriotic" ideology and all it has wrought.

Sung Ho is more of an enigma, gazing on the capitalist wonders of his birthplace with shy curiosity, but unwilling — or rather, unable — to open up about his life, feelings and intentions. One reason is the presence of a sullen North Korean handler (Yang Ik June) who watches Sung Ho's every move, but he is also living behind prison bars in his head, resigned to doing his warders' bidding.

Far from being a brainwashed robot, Sung Ho knows exactly what he has lost and fiercely resents it. Attempts by well-meaning friends and family members to reconnect him to his past only stir up thoughts and emotions he has long kept suppressed. Complications arise that hint of medical and political melodrama, but the film stays true to the realities of its characters and their situations to the end. It shades gray what a more commercial film would have painted black and white, but with no diminishment of power.

As Sung Ho, Iura initially seems a weak reed, bending to stronger wills around him. But he also hints at deeper, murkier currents that make Sung Ho hard to read — or to fool. After decades of living with lies, he has little patience with empty assurances and half-truths. They irritate and enrage him.

Miyazaki, a former pinup idol who has become the industry's go-to good-hearted mom, gives the film's strongest performance as Sung Ho's mother. The goodness is still there, since the character is self-sacrificing to a fault, but also starkly apparent is her pain, which as visible as an exposed nerve in every look and gesture.

Yet hope can be seen in her big, startled eyes, even after the worst of shocks. And love too, of course, though to Pyongyang none of it matters. The homeland of this family is finally neither in the North nor the South, but in a past that can never return, in a future that promises more of the same. But promises, even ones by the Dear Leader, are made to be broken.

A Letter to Momo, Momo e no Tegami, rating: ★★★★, runtime: 120 min.

By the time I entered college, my family had moved house seven times. The process of adjusting to a new place grew harder as I became a teenager, though by the time of our last move I was more accepting — or indifferent, take your pick. The difference between 13 and 17, in other words, was huge.

The title heroine of Hiroyuki Okiura's new animation, "A Letter to Momo," is closer to the former, tenderer age than the latter when her mother (voiced by one-name actress Yuka) decides to return to her home island in a remote corner of the Seto Inland Sea. Also, Momo (voiced by Karen Miyama) has just lost her father — and regrets the harsh words that proved to be the last he ever heard from her.

Okiura, a veteran animator and character designer, spent seven years developing "Momo" after the 1999 release of his first feature, the animated sci-fi epic "Jin-Roh: The Wolf Brigade." He presents Momo more as an average girl than the usual spunky anime heroine: When she reluctantly joins the local kids for a swim, she incredulously watches as everyone leaps off a high bridge into the harbor water — and heads for home alone.

Momo also doesn't tough it out when she realizes the old house where she and her mother are staying is also the abode of three yokai (goblins). On spying this trio, who have emerged from a feudal-era picture book and look like ghostly apparitions, she runs for her life, in one of the film's more exhilarating — and funnier — sequences.

But the yokai catch up, and soon become her inseparable companions (whether she likes it or not). The Shrek-like giant Iwa (Toshiyuki Nishida) is the leader, while the lizard-esque Kawa (Koichi Yamadera) is the slyest and therefore most human, and the tiny, round-eyed Mame (Cho) is the most childlike and mysterious. Momo masters her fear by finding a simple way, which I will not describe, to control them. They are hardly her servants, though. She has to constantly keep them from getting into trouble — and dragging her into it.

The early scenes of Momo's adventures with her yokai pals are not just comic relief. For younger viewers, especially, they make the forbidding and strange (i.e., the yokai) more familiar and likeable, while establishing Momo as a girl who can cope and grow, even while being half scared out of her wits. All this sets the stage for later, weightier matters, particularly Momo's response to a letter her father began writing her just before he died: It says only "To Momo" before lapsing into an intolerable silence.

Okiura, who also wrote the script, manages this transition from light to serious with the assurance of a true storyteller, while firmly grounding his characters, human and nonhuman, in their Seto Inland Sea setting, from the narrow portside streets to the expansive view from the island's highest point. Such scenes are hand-drawn with an attention to detail befitting the best of Japanese animation (and produced by the Production I.G studio). Studio Ghibli maestro Hayao Miyazaki is the obvious point of comparison, but unlike many of Miyazaki's more fanciful landscapes, Okiura's port is vividly real — so much so that you can almost smell the salt in the water and feel the warmth of the stones.

He also gives his principal characters fine shadings rarely seen in anime targeted at kids (though "Momo" can certainly be enjoyed by adults as well). A cheerful, energetic sort, Momo's mom is also a bit vain and self-centered, and not above flirting with a local guy out of motives Momo can't quite understand — but that make her see red. Mom also suffers from asthma, not a typical trait for an anime character, though important to the story.

The film's various threads — the realistic and the fantastic, the headlong action and the sensitively rendered human drama — come together in a climax satisfying in ways I wasn't expecting. Those goofy yokai turn out to have a purpose, for one thing — and it's more than just annoying Momo.

Also, the message about the importance of family, though echoed in innumerable saccharine family dramas, has a freshness and urgency that moved this reviewer to tears — if not to move back to the old hometown. I'm here for the duration, I'm afraid — or until I see real-life yokai dancing on my desk.

Outrage Beyond, rating: ★★★☆, runtime: 112 min.

Yakuza movies were once as easy to understand as white-hat-versus-black-hat Hollywood Westerns. A gang that upholds the traditional jingi code of yakuza "chivalry" is being out-fought, out-knifed and outgunned by ruthless, greedy rival hoods. Then a stoic lone outlaw, typically played by Ken Takakura, arrives to save the day with a swift Japanese sword.

In 1973, director Kinji Fukasaku exposed the fiction of gangster virtue in "Battles Without Honor and Humanity," the first installment of a five-part series based on a real postwar gang power struggle in Kure and Hiroshima and full of scheming, double-crossing and violent falls from grace. The characters break every commandment but the first one of gang life: Do unto others before others do unto you.

"Beat" Takeshi Kitano's 2010 gang film "Outrage" was a self-indulgent and bloated "Battles" redux that more than equaled the older film in its body count, if not in originality or contemporary relevance. His followup, "Outrage Beyond," which screened in competition at Venice, is more of the same, if with a stronger, more satisfying story arc. Yes, snarling tough guys are still plotting to kill snarling tough guys, but with a Machiavellian detective in the background pulling — and occasionally tangling — the strings. Think a smart if more convoluted reworking of the 1961 Akira Kurosawa classic "Yojimbo," minus Toshiro Mifune's unshaven charm.

Once again characters and plot turns multiply in confusing profusion in the first hour, but boiled down the story is familiar enough: Ethics-free, power-mad gangsters begin to believe they are invincible — until those they have disrespected and betrayed decide to prove otherwise.

Kato (Tomokazu Miura), the ruthless boss of Tokyo's powerful Sanno group, and Ishihara (Ryo Kase), his razor-sharp, trigger-tempered second-in-command, are plotting to expand the organization's influence into the legit business and political worlds, while pushing the underperforming old guard to the margins.

The smarmy, conniving Kataoka (Fumiyo Kohinata), a cop on an antigang task force, decides to cut the Sannos down to size, first by encouraging disgruntled Sanno gangsters to go to their Kansai (western Japan) rivals, the Hanabishi-kai, led by the puckish, elderly Chairman Fuse (Shigeru Koyama) and his two lieutenants: the shrewd Nishino (Toshiyuki Nishida) and explosive Nakata (Sansei Shiomi).

Kataoka also approaches Otomo (Kitano), a grizzled con who was kicked out of the Sannos five years earlier, and Kimura (Hideo Nakano), a gang boss turned batting-center manager whose face was brutally slashed by Otomo — and who knifed Otomo in prison as payback. Cynically, Kataoka proposes that these two join forces against their common enemies, Kato and Ishihara, but the idea starts to make a kind of sense — and not only to the two principals.

Similar to Kitano's 1997 Venice Golden Lion winner "Hana-Bi" and his other hard-boiled films, "Outrage Beyond" mixes nihilism with macho romanticism and even comedy — though Kitano's idea of a joke may be your idea of abuse, verbal or physical.

The film is repetitive with scene after scene of yakuza shouting and growling at each other in the sort Japanese you will never learn at a language school. But it also builds dramatically, with the pointedness and power missing in its lumpy predecessor. Also, signature Kitano touches are much in evidence, including hyper-short shoot-'em-up scenes, with bodies falling like rag dolls even before the sound of gunfire dies away.

Finally, unlike younger directors who make gang movies the way they make music videos, pounding away from moment to moment, Kitano understands pacing and structure, character and mood. While avoiding the sentimentalism of the old gang actioners, he also gives us heroes to root for and villains to hate — though women hardly exist and absolutely no one is clean.

The most sympathetic of this sorry lot is Nakano's Kimura, he of the close-cropped head and grotesque scars, who cares about others and can smile and laugh like a normal human being. But he also has a burning desire for vengeance, the fuel of nearly every yakuza movie plot engine.

The actors thoroughly enjoy themselves, playing their bad-ass characters to the hilt, mostly without falling into wretched excess. It's as though Kitano gave them a license to be cool, instead of the far more usual (in Japanese films at least) nice: especially Miura, Nishida and Kase, who from their past roles could form a three-man Decency League but who here prove their excellence as unregenerate nasties.

Now that the yakuza genre in its classic forms has almost vanished from the theaters (if not the DVD shelves), this hard-core fan was glad to see a film that understands its disreputable pleasures — and knows how to provide them. Striding out of the screening room, I felt cooler myself, almost as though I'd spent 112 minutes with Ken-chan instead of Kitano.

2013

See You Tomorrow, Everyone, Minasan, Sayonara, rating: ★★★★, runtime: 120 min.
Directors who return to the same theme over and over commonly use the same actor to embody it. Akira Kurosawa cast Toshiro Mifune as the sharp-eyed hero in film after film about masculine, if not always traditionally macho, heroism. Juzo Itami starred wife Nobuko Miyamoto as the tough cookie taking on charming, unreliable guys in comedy after comedy satirizing the excesses of bubble-era Japan.

Simiarly, Gaku Hamada has become the go-to actor for Yoshihiro Nakamura, making five films to date with the director since starring as a naive college student in Nakamura's 2007 "The Foreign Duck, the Native Duck and God." Diminutive and pixie-faced, Hamada looks more likely to be cast in "The Hobbit" than as the hero in a local commercial film.

But as he shows again in the director's latest, "See You Tomorrow, Everyone," Hamada is also perfect, and not only physically, as the "little guy" who turns out to be more feisty in a hostile world than he seems at first glance – that is, the center of many a Nakamura film.

He plays Satoru, who has grown up in a danchi — one of housing projects built in the postwar boom years as self-contained communities. That is, the Japanese version of "workers' paradises" in the West, as a grainy newsreel illustrates with shots of happy housewives shopping and chatting and happy kids learning and playing — all in the danchi!

So when a 12-year-old Satoru (played by an obviously adult Hamada) tells his ever-patient mother (Nene Otsuka) in 1981 that he plans to spend the rest of his life in the danchi and not attend the junior high school outside it, we half understand why she agrees, though a mystery remains since his decision is not fully explained.

When his former classmates traipse off to their new school, Satoru remains; but instead of vegetating in front of the TV, he embarks on a rigorous regime of study, martial-arts training and patrolling the danchi with a clipboard to make sure all his neighbors are safe, month after month, year after year. Yes, Satoru is a bit off, but he is also a nice guy, befriending an effeminate boy (Kento Nagayama) who is being bullied at school. He also has a normal sex drive, as he proves when the no-nonsense girl-next-door (the single-named Haru) invites him over for make-out sessions. At age 20 he even finds a girlfriend in the idol-cute Saki (Kana Kurashina), who shares his desire to stay close to home, and lands his dream job as an apprentice to the gruff master baker (Bengaru) of the danchi cake shop.

But as the years pass and the number of his former classmates dwindle, Satoru's already small world steadily shrinks. Yet every time he tries to go down the steps leading to the bigger world outside, he freezes and panics. Will he end up an urban Robinson Crusoe, marooned on his island of concrete?

Based on a novel by Takehiko Kubodera and scripted by Nakamura and Tamio Hayashi. The film finds an ingenious answer to this question. And as he did in the 2009 "Fish Story," Nakumura ties up all the carefully spun plot threads in a brilliant reveal-all ending. Enough to say that Satoru faces a test that reflects the reality of a present-day "paradise" poorer and more ethnically diverse than anything imagined in that long-ago newsreel.

Nakamura films his boy-to-man story with his characteristic dry humor, though the gags prove to have a serious purpose. And personal quirks that at first seem harmless eccentricities turn to out to have a deeper meaning — and surprisingly practical use.

Finally, this film, which starts out quirky and slow, builds to a climax that started the tears flowing, for reasons I couldn't immediately explain. Danchi nostalgia had nothing to do with it.

The Wind Rises, Kaze Tachinu, rating: ★★★☆, runtime: 126 min.

Hayao Mkiyazaki's new animation "The Wind Rises" is suffused with nostalgia for a vanished time, similar to 1992's "Porco Rosso," Miyazaki's "air pirates" animation set in the inter-war era. Based on a Miyazaki manga that mixes the prewar life of airplane designer Jiro Horikoshi, responsible for the famed Zero fighter, with a 1938 Tatsuo Hori novelette about star-crossed love, the film is made with loving attention to period detail, as well as stirring flights of fantasy, both Miyazaki trademarks.

The story reworks antique formulas such as "determined young man makes good" and "young lovers are parted by cruel fate" that powered many a studio film when Miyazaki himself was younger. In fact, Hori's "The Winds Rises" was made into two live-action films, in 1954 and 1976. Miyazaki, who also wrote the script, does little particularly new with these formulas, save adding dream sequences in which his hero, Jiro Horikoshi (voiced by veteran animator Hideaki Anno), encounters Gianni Caproni (Mansai Nomura), a pioneering Italian aircraft designer and his fabulous (in all senses of the word) planes. Caproni, portrayed as comically portly and blithely fearless, serves as a sort of life guide for the hero, while his planes are sensual delights for not only their grace in the air, but also the carefree, fleshy young women who fill them. After decades of drawing spunky 13-year-olds, Miyazaki has allowed himself a rare moment of erotic freedom.

Jiro is that standard-issue type, the smart, nerdy kid with the big dream. But unlike the many nerds in contemporary movies who are physically weak and socially awkward, Jiro is brave and bold. Coming to Tokyo for college, he selflessly assists a girl he meets on the train in the chaotic and deadly hours following the 1923 Great Kanto Earthquake. Then, after graduating with a degree in aeronautical engineering, he plunges into a new job at Mitsubishi Heavy Industries, a major aircraft maker, with a fresh eye for innovation and a cheerful disregard for naysayers, beginning with a pint-sized, perpetually frowning senior named Kurokawa (Masahiko Nishimura).

In this, Jiro resembles Miyazaki, who as a young animator rose through the corporate ranks of Toei Animation with new ideas backed by a talent for persuasion — and brilliant execution. The path of Jiro and his colleagues is not always onward and upward, however, as planes falling out of the sky prove, but they refuse to be discouraged. Always motivating Jiro is his mission, inspired by Caproni, to "make beautiful airplanes," though his military clients will use them as weapons of war.

Then, a decade after his arrival in the big city, Jiro serendipitously reunites with the girl, Naoko (Miori Takimoto), now a vibrant young woman who loves painting as much as he loves planes. A big-nosed foreigner (Steve Alpert) at the Karuizawa hotel where they are both staying serves as a sort of Cupid, while her well-off father (Morio Kazama) approves of their friendship, which soon blossoms into something more. Their new bliss is symbolized by the balletic flight of a Jiro-designed paper airplane, but Naoko's tuberculosis takes a turn for the worse — and their time together suddenly becomes all the more precious.

So, yes, "The Wind Rises" is an old-fashioned tearjerker, but it is also a visually sumptuous celebration of an unspoiled prewar Japan.

Miyazaki inserts reminders of the era's social and economic turmoil and hints of later environmental calamities, as well as stark visions of the war that would sweep much of the old loveliness away. By the end, the film feels like a summing up of everything he's made and cherished and fought against to date and, perhaps, a swan song. If so, he's crafted a soaring goodbye on the wings of his beloved planes — and paper touched by the hand of genius.

Homesick, rating: ★★★★, runtime: 98 min.

I once had a promising career as a teacher at a city day-care center in Hollywood (yes, that Hollywood). For one thing, I enjoyed interacting (translation: playing) with my charges, mostly African-American kids aged 9 to 12. For another, I liked making stuff with and for them, including a multi-story dollhouse — the product of weeks of break-time labor and scrounging in woodpiles and hardware stores — that was later exhibited at the Los Angeles Board of Education. But late one afternoon, desultorily kicking a ball around with the last boy left, I had an epiphany: I didn't want to be doing this when I was 30. Not long after, I left LA for Japan and the start of what I hoped would be a more adult existence. Good luck with that.

So Satoru Hirohara's film about a jobless 30-year-old man who becomes the summer playmate of three neighborhood boys rang some bells. Made with the production and distribution support of the Pia Film Festival organization, "Homesick" has the setup of a feel-good, up-with-kids movie, but Hirohara, not yet 30 himself, gives his unemployed hero, Kenji (Tomohiro Kaku), no easy outs. Being in tune with your inner child can be a blessing, the film says, but Kenji's Peter Pan existence comes to feel more like a curse.

As the film begins, he is living alone in the family home, which will soon be demolished for a development project. Mom long ago flew the coop, Dad is happily running a B&B out in the boonies and Sis is traveling the world, while regularly sending Kenji letters about her wonderful adventures. Then one day, through no fault of his own, his job as a house painter goes poof. Rather than hustle up a new residence, employer and life, Kenji kills time and sleeps late in what can generously be described as a pigsty.

Smelling an opportunity for mischief, three neighborhood boys ring his doorbell, decorate his brick wall with graffiti and douse his window with water guns until Kenji, tired of being bored, douses them back. In the exhilarating romp that follows, captured up-close and wet by a hand-held camera, Kenji becomes the boys' new playmate. Nicknamed "Suimashin" ("Water Devil") for a character in a card game, he suddenly finds his empty days occupied by hijinks with his new pals, culminating in their joint building of a giant dinosaur out of cardboard boxes in his backyard. What fun!

As played by Kaku, who has been acting in films and on TV since his early teens, Kenji treats the boys as equals, minus the "special" voice so many adults use with kids out of habit or condescension. He also allows them liberties, such as tromping through the house in their muddy shoes, that their mothers, teachers and other responsible adults in their lives would not tolerate. That is, he is more like a gaki taisho (boss of the neighborhood kids) than any sort of authority figure.

Kenji's knack for being one of boys has its downside, though, as he becomes uncomfortably aware when he encounters Nozomi (Erika Okuda), a former classmate now working for the real-estate company that wants to evict him. Smart, attractive and thoroughly grown-up, she smilingly regards him as something of a lost cause. This injures his masculine pride, but doesn't prevent him from lolling in bed until noon — or taking the loneliest of his three small friends, Korosuke (Yuki Kaneda), under his wing.

Hirohara, who also wrote the script, strains out the sentimentality that the usual commercial filmmaker would ladle on, while tossing in welcome dashes of madcap energy and puckish humor. The over-arching mood, however, is one of melancholy — and not only because Kenji is confronting childhood's overdue end. He is also the film's representative of a generation struggling to attain adulthood in an economy that has permanently marginalized many of them.

The film does not regard his plight as a social injustice or a personal tragedy. Kenji's fate, it implies, is finally up to Kenji. He may yet prove Nozomi and the rest of the doubting world wrong, the operative word being "may."

In telling this story, Hirohara makes his points with poignant images as well as words. One is a shadowy medium close-up of Kenji's hands and forearms highlighting their network of prominent, manly veins. Time, it seems to say, makes its mark on everyone, however oblivious they may be to its passing. Another is a long shot of kids playing soccer in an open field, lost in the bliss of childhood's eternal present. Grown-ups can visit that world, but as even the Kenjis learn sooner or later, they can never go back.

The Workhorse and the Bigmouth, Bashauma-san to Bigmouth, rating: ★★★⯨, runtime: 118 min.

Gaman ("perseverance") is the watchword of many a Japanese movie. Just as their heroes gut through to glory in film after film, real-life Japanese endure everything from deadly natural disasters to boring meetings, telling each other to ganbaro ("keep trying"). How admirable, this national stoicism!

But sometimes the smartest, if toughest, thing to do is quit. You know that you are never going to be a major league slugger or concert pianist, even after years of do-or-die effort. You accept being a loser because the alternative is more wasted time, more painful confirmation of your own mediocrity. This sort of turning point, as common in real life as death or taxes, is understandably seldom the theme of commercial films, since the audience is paying for hope, however distant, not unpleasant truth. So Keisuke Yoshida's "The Workhorse and the Bigmouth," which makes quietly powerful drama out its heroine's floundering career as a scriptwriter, is an outlier.

The story, which Yoshida wrote himself, is based on his own decade-long struggle to become a director, as well as his own realization that he was, as he says in a program interview, "not a genius, as I had believed myself to be, but an ordinary person."

The goofy title signals quirky comedy, especially since that is what Yoshida supplied so amusingly in his 2008 "Cafe Isobe." Instead the film is naturalistic to a fault, as though Yoshida had secretly filmed an actual scriptwriting class and transformed the footage into his fictional story with minimal (at times too minimal) changes.

But he also skillfully, unobtrusively shapes his material to his own ends. He makes us understand and like his two principals, even when they are at their most pathetic or obnoxious.

The bashauma (workhorse) of the title is Michiyo Mabuchi (Kumiko Aso), a 34-year-old aspiring scriptwriter who has been plugging away since her school days, but has never sold anything. Then Kiyoko (Maho Yamada), a close friend and fellow scribbler, suggests they try a scriptwriting course for adults. In the class, they encounter Yoshimi Tendo (Shota Yasuda), a 26-year-old with reddish hair and a know-it-all attitude, who confidently proclaims his own talent, though he has yet to write a line. He is, of course, the title's "big mouth."

Michiyo cordially dislikes this upstart and when, out of the blue, he proposes that they date so he can gather material for his first masterpiece, she contemptuously brushes him off.

In a typical romcom, this would be the start of a bumpy but beautiful relationship. Michiyo, however, means what she says: This workaholic scripter not only keeps men at arm's length, but slacks off at her part-time job at a ticket agency and neglects her sweet mom (Yoneko Matsukane) and dad (Jun Inoue) in the countryside, all in single-minded pursuit of her goal.

She is not too proud to grasp at straws, though, as when a casual remark by a visiting director sends her pleading to a former boyfriend and failed actor (Yoshinori Okada) for a volunteer gig at an old-folks' home where he works. Soon after, she starts writing a script based on her own awkward attempts to empathize with her elderly charges, but with a much younger woman as the heroine.

So far, so self-delusive — and nothing improves quickly for these two, which may try the patience of those used to the faster, more predictable rhythms of local zero-to-hero films, with their false dawns before the inevitable triumph. And yet every encounter between this oil-and-water pair, as well as their wounding brushes with the harsh realities of their trade, works changes on their inner chemistry, changes that made me tear up as the credits rolled — and not because Mendelssohn's "Wedding March" was playing over them.

Aso has made a career of playing comically offbeat characters and Michiyo, with her nerd glasses and pixilated earnestness, is yet another. But she is also an actual woman, not a cartoon.

As Tendo, pop star Yasuda (Kanjani8) seems to be reprising his own brash real-life self. But he wisely plays off the more experienced Aso instead of trying to noisily upstage her.

None of this means "The Workhorse and the Bigmouth" will be a hit. The odds, in fact, are against it. But this onetime Little Leaguer who never learned to hit the curve ball can always hope.

Tamako in Moratorium, Moratorium Tamako, rating: ★★★★, runtime: 78 min.

Japanese college students are the nation's leisure class, known more for their partying than studying, but their seemingly carefree minds are often clouded by worries about a post-graduation job. Even serious students — yes, they do exist — have to sweat through arduous and frustrating job searches, starting in their junior year or sooner.

And then there is Tamako (Atsuko Maeda), a recent graduate of a college in Tokyo who has returned to her home in Kofu in rural Yamanashi Prefecture. Instead of beating the bushes for work, she spends her days lolling about her father's sporting-goods store, not bothering to cook or clean or otherwise keep the household wheels turning. That's Dad's job, isn't it?

The unemployed eponymous heroine of Nobuhiro Yamashita's new film "Moratorium Tamako (Tamako in Moratorium)" is a type increasingly common as full-time jobs become harder to find. Neither a rebel nor a depressive, she feels a vague sense of desperation that, as the seasons inexorably change, slowly grows. What in the world is she supposed to do with herself, other than sleep, snack and read manga?

Those familiar with Yamashita's earlier films about post-adolescent slackers and misfits, including the 2003 films "No One's Ark" and "Ramblers" and last year's "The Drudgery Train," may assume

"Tamako" will be more of the same. But Yamashita, working from a script by frequent collaborator Kosuke Mukai, tones down his signature black humor, while showing more sympathy than usual for his do-nothing heroine.

Perhaps this kinder, gentler approach, with its smaller number of cruel-but-funny gags, was motivated by the casting of Maeda as Tamako. In "The Drudgery Train," this former leader of the AKB48 girl pop group played a sweet-tempered book-store clerk who bonds with the loser hero over their mutual love of mysteries. With her smiling tolerance of the hero's eccentricities and perversities, she was every otaku's dream girl — and Tamako is something of a carry-over, with her faults and weaknesses inspiring affection rather than scorn.

And yet just as Maeda is more than another idol-turned-actress, her Tamako is more than a lonely-guy's fantasy date. In her shouting matches with her father (Suon Kan), her awkward encounters with "normal" former classmates and her unusual friendship with a junior high school boy (Seiya Ito) who is a budding photographer, Tamako reveals herself as entitled, isolated and deluded (she wants the boy's portrait pics for a one-chance-in-a-million idol audition). At the same time, there is something admirable in her stubborn determination to steer her own course — or simply let the boat drift.

As the film begins it is fall in Kofu and Tamako, back from Tokyo, is already in full "moratorium" mode, feeding on leftovers and snacks, watching the news on television and complaining about the sad state of Japan. She tells her impatient father, "When the time comes, I'll do something — but not now."

As the weeks stretch to months, signs begin to appear of what that "something" might be. Spurred by her older sister's visit for New Year's, Tamako speaks of contacting their divorced mom and dreams about a trip to Bali. Then, when spring arrives, she starts to prepare for her own version of a job hunt, enlisting the aid of her photographer pal. Enough to say that the job she has in mind has nothing to do with sporting goods — and only a glancing relationship with reality.

That summer, when she hears that Dad has struck up an acquaintance with a pleasant middle-aged woman (Yasuko Tomita) who teaches accessory-making (think beaded bracelets), she decides to investigate, setting off a train of events that upsets her queasy equilibrium — or rather, stasis.

The scenes that follow include some of the film's funniest, while the threatened changes reminded me of the various family dramas of Yasujiro Ozu that ended with the daughter (the angelic Setsuko Hara) sadly leaving the father (the saintly Chishu Ryu). The film subverts this storyline while retaining an Ozu-esque pathos, though it's best not to reveal why.

I will say, though, that "Tamako" struck me as true to the father-daughter dynamic, at least as I know it. Dad can lecture and complain, but he'll miss her when she's gone, even if she leaves her banana peel on the table for him to pick up. And move on she almost certainly will, since moratoriums, by definition, must end.

A Story of Yonosuke, Yokomichi Yonosuke, rating ★★★★, runtime: 160 min.

Plenty of Japanese directors make films about socially awkward or marginal guys: Given all the on-screen examples (as well as their many real-life inspirations), it seems that the onetime country of the samurai has become the land of the otaku and freeter (unemployed or underemployed), clasping to emotional childhood and/or the economic bottom rungs.

Shuichi Okita has also focused on marginal men in his three features to date: the perfectionist Antarctic base-camp cook of 2009's "The Chef of South Polar," the nervous tyro film director of 2011's "The Woodsman and the Rain" and the eponymous hick hero of his latest, "A Story of Yonosuke." Okita may have his gentle if comically pointed fun with them, but he is more interested in their not-immediately-obvious strengths.

Also, despite their feel-good elements, his films are not simplistic crowd-pleasers. Instead Okita avoids obvious messages, while opting for methods that may be indirect but are never obscure.

Based on Shuichi Yoshida's novel, "A Story of Yonosuke" marks a new advance in this line, announcing as it does a major plot point (which I will not detail) well before it occurs. Far from spoiling the film, however, this reveal gives everything that happens after (as well as before) a fresh resonance and poignancy. From a charming fish-out-of-water comedy about a country boy in the big city emerges a smartly made drama that asks — and eloquently answers — one of the biggest questions of all: What do our lives really mean to those around us? How can one person have an impact, especially if he hardly seems to have a clue?

We first meet our hero, Yonosuke (Kengo Kora), as a college freshman in Tokyo in the go-go 1980s, when riches beyond the dreams of avarice seemed less like a fantasy than a national destiny. Fresh from a small town in Nagasaki Prefecture, he comes across as a typical comic naif, but Yonosuke's mix of uncalculating niceness and unshakable self-confidence make him an original, as well as unexpectedly successful at the social game.

Together with two classmates, a puppy-dog-eager guy (Sosuke Ikematsu) he meets at the graduation ceremony and a cute, friendly girl (Aki Asakura) who approaches him in class, he joins the university samba club and quickly finds his niche (if not a sense of rhythm). Flash forward two decades to his new friends, now a married couple, reminiscing about Yonosuke. What is going on here? Rather than fill us in right away, the film soon returns us to the youthful career of our hero. Yonosuke befriends the cool, impeccably fashionable Kato (Go Ayano), who at first rebuffs his advances, but who succumbs to his borderline-obnoxious tenacity. He is also recruited by the sexy, sophisticated Chiharu (Ayumi Ito), a sort of high-class hooker at the hotel where is Yonosuke is working part-time as a bellboy, to help her fend off an importunate client.

His most significant encounter, however, is with Shoko (Yuriko Yoshitaka), a prototypical bubble-era ojosama — that is, the carefully sheltered daughter of a filthy-rich family — who is as blithely unworldly in her way as Yonosuke is in his. She at first treats him as an amusing discovery for the delectation of her wised-up pals, but starts to see him differently when he rescues her from a mishap in the family pool. Love begins to bloom across the cultural/status chasm.

Working from Shiro Maeda's script, Okita makes Yonosuke's leap across this chasm something more than a comic stunt, without doing violence to his innocent essence. He also has the perfect Yonosuke in Kora, who appeared as the slacker son of the lumberjack hero in "The Woodsman and the Rain" as well as an expedition member in "The Chef of South Polar." Often cast in other directors' films as troubled, even violent types, Kora effortlessly makes the stretch to comedy for Okita, without sacrificing his trademark intensity and focus.

Despite his verbal stumbles and social fumbles, his Yonosuke never becomes merely contemptible. Instead, he charms with his sheer brass (as well as his never-commented-upon sharp good looks).

He also takes an unaffected delight in this world and its flawed inhabitants that gives Okita's delightful film a warming glow — and a lingering echo when it ends. Which is about the most, finally, any of us can hope for.

Japan's Tragedy, Nihon no Higeki, rating: ★★★★, runtime: 101 min.

What is a good death? For certain Japanese Buddhist priests it was sokushinbutsu — self-mummification. As practiced by members of the Shingon sect, it was a decade-long process that culminated with the priest's descent into a stone tomb to meditate in darkness, without food or water, until the final breath. After death, the priest's body would naturally mummify as a permanent testimony to his spiritual strength and purity.

This is the unstated backdrop to Masahiro Kobayashi's dark family drama "Japan's Tragedy," whose elderly hero Fujio (Tatsuya Nakadai) attempts his own version of this ancient and painful suicide method. Fujio's motives are not religious but entirely personal, though his dilemma reflects larger events and trends in Japanese society.

The story begins after Fujio's operation for lung cancer in Tokyo on March 11, 2011, and his decision to reject further treatment. Knowing he has only three months to live, he returns to his family home to commemorate the anniversary of his wife's death, accompanied by his unemployed son, Yoshio

(Kazuki Kitamura). The next day, this former carpenter nails himself inside his room and tells Yoshio he intends to die there. "I'll become a mummy," he announces, and adds that he will have no further need of nourishment. Three months, he feels, is too long to wait until he can rejoin his beloved wife in whatever lies beyond. Sitting in front of her funeral photo, he begins to remember past times, both good and bad.

Yoshio, however, is not about to calmly accept his father's sooner-than-expected exit. Instead, he pleads with and rages at the mostly silent man behind the sealed door.

And that, in a nutshell, is the story, since the element of suspense (will Yoshio survive?) never matters to Kobayashi, who also wrote the original script based on a true incident. He has long defied local conventions for commercial filmmaking, preferring to make unflinching studies of people living on the margins as social discards or misfits.

While the two main characters in "Japan's Tragedy" fit that description, the film also focuses on that human universal, the cruelty of death, either natural or self-inflicted, that takes everything, with no chance of recourse.

Filmed almost entirely in black and white in Fujio's Japanese-style house, with long, static takes and straight cuts, "Japan's Tragedy" visually recalls the classics of Japanese cinema's 1950s and '60s Golden Age. But the severity of the film's minimalism, with the camera never moving from the objective middle distance, as well as the extremity of Fujio's actions and the explosiveness of Yoshio's pent-up emotions are less Yasujiro Ozu, more Kobayashi.

So why is the title "Japan's Tragedy" instead of "Humanity's Tragedy"? Fujio's method of ending it all may be unusual, but suicide, as the film notes in an explanatory title, is all too common in Japan, with 27,766 taking their own lives in 2012 alone. Also, Yoshio's situation — depressed and impoverished after losing his job as well as his ever-patient wife (Shinobu Terajima) and child in the 3/11 tsunami — reflects that of millions who struggle to make ends meet with tiny pension and welfare payments or part-time and temporary work.

All this may make "Japan's Tragedy" sounds unremittingly gloomy, but as in much of Kobayashi's work, primal forces bubbling beneath masks or scorn achieve extraordinarily concentrated form. Once a favorite of Akira Kurosawa and the star of Kobayashi's "Haru's Journey" (2010), Nakadai portrays Fujio's meditations on his family's past and his own approaching death with a characteristic gravitas and power, filmed in frontal head-and-shoulder shots that seem to peer directly into Fujio's troubled soul.

In contrast to Nakadai's stillness and centeredness, Kitamura is all raw emotion as Yoshio, a surprise to those who know him only from his many roles as charismatic criminals. When Yoshio's volatile mix of emotions — anger, frustration, love and shame among them — slam against his father's wall of silence, he melts down in dramatic fashion. And yet Kobayashi's discreet camera never milks his agony for audience tears, while Kitamura's energy and intensity never flag.

Truth be told, it is not easy watching this extended breakdown (I started to imagine Fujio cutting through the door with a buzz saw to end it), but it is also the catalyst for an ending that is about as close as a Kobayashi film has ever come to uplifting.

My take away: When you go into that dark, cold night (not, I hope, into a living grave), you'd better have some good memories to keep you warm. And please leave the door open.

It's Me, It's Me, Ore Ore, rating: ★★★★, runtime: 119 min.

Satoshi Miki is best known as a director of comedy, including episodes of the 2006-07 cult hit "Time Limit Investigator" series for TV Asahi and seven feature films. But when I programmed a special Miki section for the Udine Far East Film Festival in 2008, I realized anew how, film by film, his aims had grown beyond extracting laughs with his trademark absurdist gags. In his best film to date, 2007's "Adrift in Tokyo," Miki transformed an oddball road-movie setup — a middle-aged loan shark and his college student client/victim embark on a walk across Tokyo — into an ode to cross-generational friendship and the city itself.

His new film "It's Me, It's Me," which had its world premiere at Udine last month with Miki and star Kazuya Kamenashi in attendance, goes even further beyond cute into territory strange and nightmarish. There are gags aplenty in the dry, quirky style familiar from his earlier films, but there is also a surrealism that undermines a conventional understanding of the story — and reality.

The film starts as a caper comedy. Hitoshi (Kamenashi), a failed photographer turned electronics-store clerk, uses the cellphone an obnoxious fellow customer leaves behind in a fast-food joint to call the customer's mother and, impulsively posing as her son Daiki, persuades her to transfer ¥900,000 to his depleted bank account — an actual, often-used scam in Japan known as "ore ore" ("it's me, it's me").

Soon after, however, Hitoshi not only has a bizarre encounter with his victim, who calls him Daiki and treats him as her flesh-and-blood son, but runs into a stern-faced doppelganger who claims to be Hitoshi and calls him an imposter. Soon, to his bafflement and horror, yet another double, this one on the wild and crazy side and calling himself Nao, pops up, the three "triplets" eventually meet and form a sort of club, which makes bizarre sense since they have a lot in common.

The original Hitoshi (if he is indeed the "original") gamely adapts to his new circumstances and even finds advantages in being one of triplets, but the strangeness escalates with the emergence of "defective" Hitoshi copies and the deterioration of everyday reality (or rather Hitoshi's version of it) into a surreal nightmare. Then the copies begin vanishing and people around the "original," including a sexy, mysterious customer named Sayaka (Yuki Uchida) and Hitoshi's weird, self-involved boss, Tajima (Ryo Kase), become sucked into the mad vortex that is his world.

Based on a prize-winning novel by Tomoyuki Hoshino, "It's Me, It's Me" is reminiscent of "Being John Malkovich," the 1999 Spike Jonze film about an unemployed puppeteer who discovers a portal into actor John Malkovich's brain. When in the course of the story Malkovich himself enters the portal, he emerges into a world populated by other Malkoviches, who can only say "Malkovich." In other words, the ultimate narcissistic hell.

But what is a minor motif in Jonze's film is a major one is Miki's. (The director, in fact, has claimed inspiration from not only Jonze but also the comedy of Monty Python and Charlie Kaufman's 2002 film "Adaptation.") Filmed with a cheerful disregard for grass-is-green logic, "It's Me, It's Me" may send the more emotionally fragile or rigidly rational hurtling toward the exit. There is a lot to process, like gazing into an infinite recession of mirrors in your local fun house.

But Miki, who also wrote the script, maintains the same tight control over his mind-bending material as he did in "Adrift in Tokyo." As in the previous film, he weaves deeper themes, as well as funny sight gags, into his slight story, but with more abandon and ambition, as though he were trying to not only out-Jonze Jonze and out-Kaufman Kaufman, but also to out-Kafka Franz Kafka, who may have transformed salesman Gregor Samsa into a giant bug in his novella "The Metamorphosis," but at least did not clone the poor sod into infinity.

GFP Bunny, Thallium Shojo no Dokusatsu Nikki, rating: ★★★★, runtime: 82 min.

Every once in awhile a movie sees around the corner to where the culture is heading. Stanley Kubrick's "A Clockwork Orange" (1971) was released when baby boomers were still dreaming of communal peace and love, but its dystopian vision of punks with the morals of sharks visiting ultra violence on random strangers by has hardly been proven wrong, though modern-day perpetrators are often wearing hoods rather than the hero's bowler hat.

Yutaka Tsuchiya's docu-drama "GFP Bunny" is likewise clear-sighted about current scientific and cultural trends, though its vision holds out the possibility of hope, even for outsiders with a thing for extreme body modification.

Winner of the Best Picture Award in the 2012 Tokyo International Film Festival's Japanese Eyes section, "GFP Bunny" is ambitious — Tsuchiya says in a program statement that its three themes are "surveillance in a marketing-oriented society, characterization of identity and biotechnology." But it's also smartly edited and consistently engaging, if uncompromisingly disturbing.

Tsuchiya's nameless heroine — a 16-year-old girl (Yuka Kuramochi) who is bullied at school and neglected by her self-involved mom (Makiko Watanabe), is a standard-issue type for Japanese coming-of-age movies, but she is based on a real-life model: a girl who in 2005 tried to poison her own mother with thallium — a deadly tasteless and odorless substance not found in nature.

Also, the girl's responses to her bad situation are anything but ordinary. Fascinated by advances in biology and genetics and well-versed in all things Internet, she analyzes and dissects living things with the methodical thoroughness of a scientist (if one with psychopathic tendencies) and posts the results on her YouTube video diary (thus the film's Japanese title).

Her studies enter a new, dangerous stage when she begins to use her mother as an experimental subject, dripping thallium into Mom's open mouth as she sleeps. Grimly determined to slow the aging process with exercise and cosmetic surgery, Mom is horrified by the changes the poison wreaks on her body, from lethargy to hair loss. To her relentless, inquisitive daughter, they are simply more data, though the cold glint in her eye is not that of an objective researcher.

Along with serving as the girl's off-screen interlocutor (and audience stand-in), Tsuchiya inserts interviews with everyone from university researchers to a New Religion crank to give his story (or rather "meta-fiction," as the program calls it) context and depth. A biologist who has produced transparent frogs as aids to studying biological processes speaks of his ambition to make ones that glow. The girl tries something similar with a fish, while befriending a body-modification artist (played by the single-named Takahashi) who has gone beyond the usual tattoos and piercings and implanted an IC chip in her hand that allows her, as she explains, "to monitor" herself.

The girl also becomes the unwilling subject of her bullies' own video, which is later seen on a porn site by a pervy teacher (Kanji Furutachi). But his shock at recognizing her is mixed with the sexual thrill of seeing her bound-and-gagged, as helpless as a frog in a dissecting tray. This guy's reboot, we see, will require a total replacement of his moral/sexual motherboard.

The film's view of the human condition is thus hardly rosy: "One day you'll get old and die — that's what you're programmed for," the girl bluntly tells her mother. "There's no God, only a program." But it's also not blackly pessimistic. Unlike creatures whose fates are determined by their DNA, we can, the film says, change our programs. "Mom, you should reformat yourself," the girl says — and she is not talking about a new diet-and-exercise regime.

The film's vision of what such a reformatting might entail, as exemplified by Takahashi with her wise-alien-from-another-planet look, will not be for everyone, but its belief in freedom is somehow heartening. There is no guarantee, though, that our freedom to reboot ourselves will result in anything we 21st century mortals would recognize as human.

The Ravine of Goodbye, Sayonara Keikoku, rating: ★★★☆, runtime: 117 min.

What are the limits of forgiveness? Our various gods may forgive our sins, but we humans don't always find it easy to follow suit. Violations of the body are among the crimes hardest to forgive, since the victims are left with not only scars, visible and invisible, but also a cold anger against the perpetrator(s).Tatsushi Omori has been filming the outer limits of human behavior since his 2005 directorial debut "The Whispering of the Gods," whose outlaw hero, sexually abused as a boy, returns to the monastery where he was raised for a confrontation with his now elderly abuser.

Violence is also a frequent motif in Omori's five films to date, including his latest, "The Ravine of Goodbye." Based on a short story by Shuichi Yoshida, whose fiction also inspired the rightly acclaimed "Villain" and "A Story of Yonosuke," the film begins with a media pack besieging the apartment of a woman suspected of murdering her own child. When the police come to make the arrest, the pack's frenzy reaches a peak, though busy with their passionate love-making, the couple next door has been oblivious to the commotion outside.

That night Watanabe (Nao Omori), a jaded magazine reporter who has been desultorily covering the story, meets a reception of quite a different kind from his irritable wife, who rages at him for reasons that go deeper than his late arrival home.

Then the child-killer suspect tells the cops that she has been having an affair with the guy next door, Shunsuke (Shima Onishi), the moody lover of the hot-to-trot Kanako (Yoko Maki). Smelling a big story, Watanabe and his savvy colleague Kobayashi (Anne Suzuki) spring into action.

The above may make "The Ravine of Goodbye" sound like a modern noir — James M. Cain's "The Postman Always Rings Twice" comes to Japan. The film is not lurid or pulpy in the slightest; it is instead an earnest, somber drama about an affair that seems to defy moral sense, but has its own emotional logic.

Watanabe learns that Kanako and Shunsuke's relationship not only goes back 15 years, to when the latter was a star pitcher on his college baseball team, but began with (spoiler alert) the rape of the teenaged Kanako by Shunsuke and his teammates in the course of a drunken party. Shunsuke was expelled from the team as a result, but the damage to Kanako was greater, leading to a train of personal catastrophes that ended with a total breakdown.

How did she move from seething hatred of her defiler to something resembling love? The film's squaring of this psychological circle is probably never going to convince those who feel that the very question is offensive. Also, as Kanako tells Watanabe, who is wrestling with the breakdown of his own marriage, an outsider can't understand their relationship, though judging it may be easy.

What the film attempts, in scenes that show rather than explain, is how Kanako and Shunsuke reunite, years after the incident that ruined their lives: Shunsuke burdened with guilt, Kanako with a past she can't escape, while being harshly punished for trying. To put it simply, they are two lost souls who find each other. But the spark that ignites their passion is a mystery, as is the fuel that keeps it burning, in a remote wooded retreat where they futilely hope to escape the world's prying eyes.

Onishi's Shunsuke is a brooding presence that recalls his drifter hero in Genjiro Arata's "Akame 48 Waterfalls," his breakout role. But this closed-off man, relentlessly hunted by the media and interrogated by the police, gradually opens up to Watanabe, another once-promising athlete, while revealing a more ordinarily human side.

As Kanako, Maki has a harder task in making her character credible. There is a bitter wisdom and simmering rage in her Kanako, but also a fragility and weariness that helps us understand her odd (or, if you will, outrageous) choice of lover.

This woman is no victim who has fallen under the spell of her victimizer. Instead, she has found in Shunsuke a refuge from the world outside. Kanako also has a measure of power over this man who is forever in her moral debt. But this power is not unlimited, as she learns.

Serving as a needed real-world entry-point into the closed universe of this pair is Omori's Watanabe. The brother of the director and the son of famed butoh performer Akaji Maro, Omori has played the hang-dog everyman so often that his Watanabe is more of a revisit than a revelation.

But Watanabe's puzzlement is also ours and his awakening, when it comes, has the force of truth. The "Goodbye" of the English title, we see, is really a farewell to illusion, including the lie that we can make it through this vale (or ravine) of tears alone.

Like Father, Like Son, Soshite Chichi ni Naru, rating: ★★★★, runtime: 121 min.

The English and Japanese titles of Hirokazu Koreeda's dual-family drama "Like Father, Like Son" are quite different in meaning, but both express something important about this extraordinary film, winner of the Jury Prize at this year's Cannes Film Festival.

The English title is one of those commonplaces that rebellious adolescent sons are inclined (programmed?) to reject, but once they have sons themselves, start to see as plain truth.

The Japanese title, which literally translates as "Then to Become a Father," hints at a problem many Japanese men have faced at one time or other. How do you become a father to your kids when, workaholic that you are, you hardly ever see them?

This certainly applies to Ryota Nonomiya (Masaharu Fukuyama), who has devoted himself body and soul to his job at a major construction company, while paying only desultory attention to his 6-year-old son Keita (Keita Ninomiya). He even trains the poor kid to haltingly but successfully lie about a father-son outing in an admissions interview for a prestige school. Soon after, he and his wife Midori (Machiko Ono) get the devastating news, confirmed by a DNA test, that Keita is not really theirs: He and another boy were switched at birth.

This story is as old as the hills (Mark Twain's 1881 novel "The Prince and the Pauper" is a variant on it), while being a common childhood fantasy — or nightmare. But Koreeda referenced true cases in writing his script and his take is correspondingly serious and typically naturalistic, though he does not completely avoid the melodramatics inherent in the material.

Since the two boys are so young, their respective parents begin a gradual transition with brief visits, rather than attempt a straightforward explanation and quick switch. They also initiate legal proceedings against the hospital responsible for the mix-up with the aid of Ryota's lawyer friend (Tetsushi Tanaka).

Everyone's conflicted feelings soon surface. Ryota, a believer in order and protocol, is not pleased by Keita's birth father Yudai Saiki (Lily Franky), the owner of a small electrical-goods store in the suburbs. A let-it-all-hang-out type, Saiki is a playful, indulgent dad to his rowdy brood, including 6-year-old Ryusei (Shogen Hwang). When he suggests that Ryota lighten up and follow his example, the response is chillingly (if politely) negative.

The two mothers — the soft-spoken Midori and the down-to-Earth Yukari (Yoko Maki) — are better than their men at bridging the gap between them, but neither relishes the process of exchanging their son for a stranger. Midori's agony at her slow parting with doe-eyed little Keita is so wrenching to watch — her flowing tears as she packs his things away inspired an outbreak of sobs in the screening room (mine included) — that I began to think the film should have been titled "Haha de Aru" ("To Be a Mother").

Also, Koreeda's direction of the two boys, particularly showbiz pro Ninomiya, is sensitive and unmanipulative. As he did in such child-centered films as "Nobody Knows" and "I Wish," Koreeda captures Keita and Ryusei's doubts, fears and dawning realizations with both the objectivity of a documentary filmmaker (his original profession) and the artistry to elicit and edit exactly the (often heart-wrenching) response the drama calls for.

The film finally, belongs to Ryota and his uncertain progress toward becoming a better father and man. Fukuyama, a popular singer-songwriter and TV drama actor, may seem a strange choice for this difficult role, especially at moments when that famous smile crinkles on that devastatingly handsome (still at 44) face. But he also looks as though he belongs in the dream life Ryota has been striving for since his boyhood in a typical middle-class family: cool job, high salary, spacious high-rise condo, beautiful loving wife and cute (if annoyingly ungifted) son.

When that life begins to crumble before Ryota's eyes his first reaction is to buy his way out — and it's hard to feel sympathy. At the same time, his basic decency and sincerity are hard to ignore. When his own old-school father loudly proclaims the primacy of blood and Ryota argues that time spent together make for stronger father-son ties, we realize that, rather than a plastic Mr. Perfect, he's a human mass of contradictions.

In place of a big third-act awakening, Koreeda takes the less obvious path of small but acute epiphanies for Ryota, as well as reverses that demand more from him than good intentions.

Is his rambunctious birth son really like him? And how about the son he raised for six years? Hardly a universal dilemma, but Ryota has something in common with millions of similarly struggling dads: His sons may not be mirrors, but they reflect back something of himself.

Just try looking.

The Tale of Princess Kaguya, Kaguya-hime no Monogatari, rating: ★★★★☆, runtime: 137 min.

Isao Takahata has long been overshadowed by longtime colleague and Studio Ghibli cofounder Hayao Miyazaki. The younger man (Takahata is 78, Miyazaki 72) has had more and bigger hits, including his latest, the World War II-themed "The Wind Rises," while Takahata's last feature animation, the 1999 family comedy "My Neighbors the Yamadas," was a rare Ghibli box-office disappointment.

And yet Takahata is every bit the anime master that Miyazaki has been widely proclaimed to be, if one with a different style and concerns. His Ghilbi films tend to be more realistic than Miyazaki's, beginning with 1988's "Grave of the Fireflies," a drama about children struggling to survive in the destruction and chaos that enveloped Japan toward the end of WWII. It is the most emotionally devastating film I have ever seen, while being free of the cloying sentimentality that is a prerequisite for commercial tearjerkers here.

Takahata's latest and quite possibly last film, "The Tale of the Princess Kaguya," is based on the oldest-known Japanese folk tale, which dates to the 10th century. Also, its gestation, eight years by the count of producer Yoshiaki Nishimura, was long even by Ghilbi's relaxed standards, with Takahata's reluctance to commit being one factor, production delays another. But far from an uncomfortable fit or a labored effort, "The Tale of the Princess Kaguya" has the feel of a true Takahata film, from its emotional fidelity to its sudden, exhilarating leaps into fantasy.

The animation, with its combination of dynamic strokes and delicate, lightly brushed colors, may look underdone compared with other Ghibli productions, with their lush backdrops and fine detailing, but as the story progressed, I found this more impressionistic style suggestive of the story's origin in the most ancient of tales — and our common desires, fears and dreams.

That tale is known to every Japanese, if not to the outside world, though its motifs are also found in Western fairy tales ("Thumbelina," "King Thrushbeard"). It begins with an old bamboo cutter, Okina (voiced by Takeo Chii), happening upon a strange glowing bamboo in the forest and finding inside a tiny, perfectly formed girl (Aki Asakura). Cradling her in his palms, he takes her to his wife Ouna (Nobuko Miyamoto), but the little creature soon transforms into a baby that the flummoxed couple decides to raise. The strangeness continues as the baby grows far faster than normal (in one spooky sequence she quickly progresses from flailing limbs to a hesitant first step), while taking a laughing delight in the world around her.

Okina finds more treasures in the bamboo, including gold nuggets and kimono meant for a princess — that is, for his pretty adopted daughter, who is called Takenoko (Bamboo), and is obviously destined for better things. But Takenoko is happy with the humble places and common people she knows, especially the rugged, pure-hearted Sutemaru (Kengo Kora), the leader of the neighborhood kids.

Nonetheless, her newly rich parents install her in a mansion, surround her with servants and have her trained in the ways of the aristocracy, from playing the koto to painting her teeth black. (The former she masters, the latter she indignantly rejects). This beautiful, accomplished, fully grown girl, now called Kaguya-hime (Princess Kaguya), attracts five well-born, ridiculously self-important suitors, but she rejects them all, even when they make miraculous efforts to meet her absurd demands. Finally the emperor, who is young, handsome and the most arrogant of all, tries to win her hand, but she spurns him as well — and reveals that she is from the moon and must soon return to the land of her birth.

This is nearly all from the folk tale, which raises the question of what, beyond their way of telling it, Takahata and his collaborators have brought to it. The film's tag line, "A princess' crime and punishment," offers a clue, while Takahata himself has said he wanted to explore what "crime" Princess Kaguya might have committed, since the original story is silent on that point.

His exploration, though, has little to do with plot, everything to do with his heroine's emotional and spiritual journey — and the way it ends. Not to enter spoiler territory, but the climax is a haunting evocation of mono no aware — or as it is literally translated, the pathos of things. The basis of Japanese aesthetics since time immemorial, mono no aware is hard to define, but "The Tale of the Princess Kaguya" gloriously illuminates it with images of life at its transient loveliest, of parting in its terrible finality.

There is a deep wisdom in this film, but a deep sadness too. If it is Takahata's farewell, it's one that will have a long echo, just like his 1,000-year-old source.

2014

Walking With a Friend, Tomodachi to Aruko, rating: ★★★★, runtime: 89 min.

Akira Ogata's "Walking with a Friend," which screened in the Japanese Cinema Splash section of last year's Tokyo International Film Festival, is one of many recent Japanese films about the problems of the elderly in this rapidly graying country. Unlike nearly all these films, its take on its two over-the-hill heroes — friends living disabled and alone in crumbling danchi (housing complex) apartments — is dryly comic, instead of earnestly serious or sentimental.

The true key to the film is its title. There is plenty of real walking in the film by various sets of friends, old and new, but both the title and the story can also be read metaphorically, as in the saying "walk a mile in another man's shoes." The film is about how friendships deepen from not only jointly expended shoe leather, but also shared talk, adventures and pain. Being friends, it says, is not just putting up with another's foibles but feeling his aches — or absence.

Born in 1959, Ogata has extensive experience in everything from indie films to TV documentaries, though his filmography is relatively short, beginning in 2000 with the award-winning coming-of-age drama "Boy's Choir." A project born from a bar chat with scriptwriter Kenji Aoki, "Walking with a Friend" is indie filmmaking at its best, sustained more by its makers' talent and professionalism than by commercial imperatives.

The film is more simply made than the work of many a young auteur, trying to impress with flashy cuts and twisty plots. Some may also find it too slow, though even the pokier scenes are full of sly wit and ingenious visuals. Good walks are not always the briskest.

The film begins with the elderly Tomio (Koichi Ueda) gingerly descending the five flights from his danchi flat, using a cane and dragging a bad leg. Once on level ground he encounters his pal Kunio (Choei Takahashi), who walks in tiny stutter steps, somewhat like a gray-haired toddler.

Together these two make slow progress (at one point they are overtaken by a scurrying insect), until they meet up with a young woman (Hiroko Nozawa) on crutches who joins them on their errand and becomes the object of their lecherous gaze. But Tomio is also genuinely concerned for her welfare, knowing that she injured her leg making a suicidal leap.

The scene shifts to a nearby cafe, where two friends, the porky Mori (Satoru Matsuo) and porkpie-hatted Togashi (Yoichiro Saito) are arguing over that ancient conundrum: If a tree falls in a forest with no one to hear it, does it make a sound? Mori says yay, Togashi nay, and the back-and-forth becomes so heated that another customer — Tomio — tells them to pipe down. But how does their story connect to his?

The film has farther to go — three more parts, in fact but little in the way of a plot. Its episodic nature does not mean it meanders. Instead each part, including Togashi and Mori's awkward encounter with Mori's irascible ex-wife (Kinuo Yamada) and her wimpy new man (Shingo Mizusawa) and a disastrous expedition by Tomio and Kunio to buy a pack of cigarettes, deepens our understanding of the four heroes and brings them — andl the themes they embody — closer together.

Meanwhile, the dry, funny gags keep coming, as does the quirky, perky score, with Ogata adding his own acoustic guitar to the film's catchy East European-flavored theme song.

The ending ties up nicely with the beginning, though the final message is left for us to parse. One is that, now that we can no longer take family ties and support for granted, friends are more important than ever, especially for the live-alone elderly. A dog will keep you company, but will it climb five flights on gimpy legs to make sure you're OK? Yours might, but I'd rather bet on a human.

My Pretend Girlfriend, Momose, Kocchi wo Muite, rating: ★★★☆, runtime: 109min.

First love or 'hatsukoi' is a big theme in Japanese teen films, as well as almost everywhere else in popular culture. It's attractive because of its innocence and purity, as well as the typical fleetingness of the relationship — if indeed, it is one; one party is often far more besotted than the other.

The term "puppy love," which conjures up images of youthful crushes that briefly bloom and inconsequentially fade, is not quite equivalent, since hatsukoi can leave a deep, lasting mark.

That is the case with Noboru Aihara (Osamu Mukai), a 30-year-old author who has returned to his hometown to promote his first novel in Saiji Yakumo's "My Pretend Girlfriend."

Noboru runs into Tetsuko, a former classmate who is now the wife of Miyazaki, one of Noboru's childhood friends. As they talk in a coffee shop, with Tetsuko's young daughter in tow, the conversation turns to their high school days. Back then, Tetsuko and Miyazaki were a popular couple atop the school pecking order, while Noboru was a social zero with one real pal — the porky, equally girlfriendless, Tanabe.

One day Miyazaki calls Noboru into the school library to make an unusual request: Be the pretend boyfriend of Momose (Akari Hayami), a cute girl with bobbed hair (see photos of 1920s star Louise Brooks for reference).

Noboru had glimpsed Miyazaki and Momose having an intimate chat at the town's train station, and Miyazaki fears that gossip about this tryst will reach the ears of Tetsuko (Anna Ishibashi). Not wanting to end his fling with Momose, he asks Noboru to serve as her "beard" – that is, fake romantic partner. Noboru, who has long looked up to the older, cooler Miyazaki, reluctantly agrees. Momose, a bossy type, immediately takes charge of this phony relationship, grabbing Noboru's hand as they walk out the school gates to the curious gaze of classmates — and immediately dropping it with disgust once they are on the street.

Despite this and other comic moments, "My Pretend Girlfriend" takes Noboru's dilemma seriously, especially when it becomes obvious that he has feelings for his imperious tormentor. It's not hard to see why: He is spending much of his free time at school, day after day, in the company of a hot girl who turns on the charm when others are around and talks to him frankly when they aren't. Yes, she scorns his unkempt hair and his lamentable taste in clothes, but she also opens up to him emotionally in ways she can't with others, beginning with Miyazaki.

Though not exactly a friend, he has certain benefits. Even so, he wants to end this awkward farce sooner rather than later — and so does Momose. But she also can't help noticing that Noboru is more honest and decent than his so-called friend, Miyazaki, whom she alternately loves and hates.

Based on a novel by Eiichi Nakata, "My Pretend Girlfriend" may have a farfetched premise but Noboru's hopeless love for a girl who likes the wrong guy is common in any society, country or century. The film, though, is uncommon in its sympathy for both its ostensible hero and the girl who brings him misery. Momose, played by former pop idol singer Akari Hayami in her first starring role, is more than just willfully — and in the end, pathetically — clinging on to a guy who is out of her league; she is capable of feeling and caring for others, beginning with the members of her household, run by her struggling single mother.

She is also not afraid to say what she thinks or to go for what she wants. She has more in common with the famously bold Ms. Brooks than just her hairstyle.

The film's end is implicit in its beginning, but Momose remains an enigma, just as so many first loves are in memory: Frozen in a moment, forever out of reach.

Wood Job!, WOOD JOB! Kamusari Nana Nichijo, rating: ★★★★, runtime: 116min.

Shinobu Yaguchi has become a consistent hit maker by following a simple formula: Generate laughs from the stumbles of ordinary folks learning a new job, art or sport. This formula usually results in audience cheers and tears when triumph finally arrives after many ups and downs. Examples include his 2001 hit "Waterboys" (high school boys try synchronized swimming) and 2004 smash "Swing Girls" (high school girls form a swing band).

Yaguchi is not the first to use this zero-to-hero formula, but he has perfected it.

His latest, "Wood Job!" in which a soft city boy (Shota Sometani) becomes a hard-working apprentice lumberjack, is a return to comic form, with more laugh-out-loud gags than his films have produced in years. One comparison is "The Woodsman and the Rain," Shuichi Okita's 2012 comedy about a neophyte film director's life-changing encounter with a 60-year-old lumberjack played by a spry Koji Yakusho. Okita's film isn't really about the work of being a lumberjack, but Yaguchi's is like a crash course on the subject.

This high information-to-laughs ratio has long been a Yaguchi trademark, but in "Wood Job!" he goes beyond amusing factoids to full-throated appreciation for the rural way of life, which is undervalued in today's wired, alienated-from-nature society.

The hero, Yuki Hirano (Sometani), is the sort of lazy student most teachers are glad to see the back of. But after he fails his college entrance exams and is dumped by his girlfriend, he decides to make a fresh start and joins a one-year trainee program for forestry workers, aka lumberjacks. His motivation is less a love for the great outdoors than a pretty face on a recruiting pamphlet.

When Hirano arrives at his destination — a village so deep in the mountains that he loses his all-important smartphone connection — he immediately tries to make a U-turn, but one absurd circumstance leads to another, and he finds himself in dasai (uncool) work clothes, being schooled in the basics of lumberjacking.

One of his instructors, Yoki Iida (Hideaki Ito), rattles Hirano with his snarling wild-man act, and makes him an object lesson in emergency first aid. This incident once again turns Hirano's thoughts to escape, but he is trapped by lack of transportation — and is assigned as Iida's live-in apprentice.

What keeps him going is not a new-found dedication to forestry — Iida is a daily fount of fresh humiliation and pain — but his infatuation with the aforementioned pamphlet cover girl (Masami Nagasawa), who turns out to be a teacher in the village. She has little but scorn for our wimpy hero, sure that, like so many city-boy apprentices before him, he will turn tail and run.

Often cast as disturbed or dissolute characters, Sometani excels as the chuckleheaded hero, while indirectly kidding his own bad-boy image

He also makes us believe in Hirano's growing admiration for the skills and ethics of Iida and his rough-hewn workmates, despite the agonies they joyfully inflict on him. He also gradually achieves competence in the lumberjack's unforgiving trade.

Often cast in tough-guy roles, such as the steel-jawed hero of the "Umezaru" Coast Guard diver films, Ito comically plays up to his hard-ass image by bellowing a morning wake-up call at his hapless apprentice and knocking his pillow away with a soccer-style kick. He has a warm side, however, as seen in his interactions with his devoted wife (Naomi Nishida).

There's not a lot of subtlety in this oil-and-water pairing, but there is a knotty truth: Human beings, however wrapped in digital cotton wool, thrive on difficulty — especially when it comes with the heady smell of freshly cut wood.

Sad Tea, Sado Tea, rating: ★★★☆, runtime: 120min.

Ensemble dramas about the ups and downs of love, and its various substitutes, are popular now with indie filmmakers. A recent example is Hitoshi One's "Be My Baby," a high-energy romp whose characters are drifting along society's margins. Another is Daisuke Miura's "Love's Whirlpool," which follows a sex party of strangers from its awkward beginning to a bittersweet end. (Miura also scripted the former, quite different-in-tone film.)

Then there is Rikiya Imaizumi's "Sad Tea," which premiered in the Japanese Cinema Splash section of last year's Tokyo International Film Festival, and takes an approach somewhere in the middle. Despite its light comic feel, it is not trying for sitcom-style laughs. It addresses a real-life question with no easy answers — especially for its perplexed principals: What does it mean to properly love someone?

"Sad Tea" is the second film to emerge from the actors' and directors' workshop at Enbu Seminar, a Tokyo-based film school. Comprised of 12 semi-independent sections that tie together at the end, it is a naturalistic, if carefully shaped, examination of how egos, needs and desires can impinge on each other like particles in a super collider of the heart — which can blow apart or bind together when they meet.

Shin Kashiwagi (Seiji Okabe) is an aspiring scriptwriter and director who is living with one woman, Yuko (Chihiro Nagai), while seeing another: the winsome, perceptive Midori (Aya Kunitake). Yuko knows about this situation and seems OK with it, while Midori's feelings are more conflicted. ("Did you ever wish you had never met someone?" she asks Kashiwagi at one point.) Despite a cowlick that gives him the air of a socially challenged nerd, Kashiwagi is adept at rationalizing his own bad behavior, even as he reproves himself for it. ("I know I'm messed up," he says at one point.)

His earnest pal Waseda (Tomohisa Takeda) is his polar opposite. Going into a dress shop to buy a birthday present for his girlfriend Sonoko (Kayo Hoshino), he becomes infatuated with the cute sales clerk and announces to Sonoko that he is dumping her, after she thanks him for his gift.

Convinced he has found true love, Waseda believes his motives are pure. Now he has to win over his new inamorata, who is barely aware of his existence.

Then there is Natsu (Chika Uchida), who puts up with a physically abusive fiancée. (She tells her friends she likes him because they have "honest fights.") A former small-time idol singer, she has also long been basking in the distant attention of a devoted fan. Perhaps unwisely, she decides to finally meet him face-to-face.

As comic relief the film also gives us a middle-aged coffee-shop master, Bon (Takuya Fuji), who is head-over-heels with his only server — the cruelly indifferent Tanako (Fumiko Aoyagi). She in turn has something of a crush on a customer: Kashiwagi. Around and around the merry-go-round goes and where it stops, nobody knows, though the connections between the characters suggest an eventual intertwining of romantic fates.

What we cannot tell so easily is whether the guys (who are mostly self-deluded) will wake up to reality, and whether the women (who are mostly sympathetic types) will stick around for what may be a long wait. This may sound like a typical romantic-comedy setup, with the characters, after many missteps, finally stumbling upon their soulmates. But a realist to the end, Imaizumi knows that we can't always get what we want and don't always know what we need.

The cast is uniformly good, if largely unknown. They seem to improvise their interactions, though Imaizumi made them stick closely to his well-constructed script.

And the meaning of "Sad Tea?" The film doesn't say, though it beats one of Imaizumi's earlier titles, thankfully abandoned: "Nothing to Do and Bored." If hard to imagine on a theater marquee, it certainly describes one of the baser motives for cheating. But are there any noble ones?

Forma, rating: ★★★★, runtime: 145min.

The Japanese film industry used to be like much of the rest of Japanese society: male-centered and male-run. It made plenty of movies about women, but their directors were all men. That began to change when Naomi Kawase won a Cannes Camera d'Or prize in 1997 for her first feature, "Suzaku," but for a long time she headed a very short list of female directors here.

In the past decade or so, that list has expanded dramatically: Directors such as Miwa Nishikawa, Momoko Ando, Yuki Tanada and Yang Yong-hi have made some of the best recent Japanese films, judging by awards, festival invitations and critical praise.

Ayumi Sakamoto now joins their ranks with her first feature "Forma." Stylistically, the film fits the profile of a minimalist Asian festival film: It's 145 min. long, with no close-ups, no music, no narration and several lengthy one-cut scenes, culminating in one that unspools for 24 min.

This may sound like indie aestheticism at the expense of the audience, and I was anticipating a long, hard sit as the film began. But working from her original treatment and a script by Ryo Nishihara, Sakamoto melds style and story with a sure feel for how form expresses meaning, while her view of the film's two protagonists — or rather antagonists — is both distanced and aware.

Not that "Forma" is in any way autobiographical; only that Sakamoto knows and sees her principals in ways that escape the usual male filmmaker, viewing his female characters mostly in relation to their men or their families, less often to each other, be it as friends or enemies.

Ayako (Nagisa Umeno) runs into former high school classmate Yukari (Emiko Matsuoka) on a construction site where Yukari is working as a security guard. Despite the passage of time, Ayako is eager to connect again and even helps Yukari land a job at her company. Yet once Yukari starts work as a copy-making, tea-serving clerk, her higher-ranking colleague Ayako is quick to point out her mistakes and upbraid her for her "informal" language.

Ayako still wants to be pals with Yukari outside the office, but her familiarity — it's hard to call it friendship — takes the form of needling or outright undermining. Hearing that Yukari is engaged to be married, Ayako tells her that "marriage is no guarantee of happiness" and chides her for "just going with the flow." "You haven't changed since high school," she concludes, dismissively. What, we wonder, is going on here?

Yukari, it turns out, was Ayako's senpai (senior) in their high school tennis club and bossed her about. Now the shoe, Ayako notes, is on the other foot. But she wants more than petty payback for ancient slights. Also, it soon becomes clear that Yukari, who changes her mind and plans on flimsy pretexts, is no angel either.

As the story progresses, we see that none of the characters are. All have flaws, even Nagata (Seiji Nozoe), a coffee-shop server who selflessly comes to Yukari's aid and seems be the nicest of nice guys. But when the two frenemies finally take the gloves off that niceness is revealed as a cover for weakness. Also, Ayako's video-editor father (Ken Mitsuishi) seems to be an even-keeled sort, but as his reasons for separating from Ayako's mom surface, we see him in a new, more morally compromised light.

In bald outline, the story may sound like a black comedy: "Mean Girls" in Japan. But "Forma" is serious — and frightening. That aforementioned 24-minute scene may be an experiment in improvisation, but it's also bone-chilling. Instead of conventionally building to this big finale, the film detours for a lengthy flashback that feels like a puzzling distraction, but gives the events in the film a new weight and urgency.

Who is in the right? Who is in the wrong? "Forma" doesn't supply easy answers. Instead it stirs the imagination, while allowing for more than one interpretation. Is that the hand of friendship reaching out — or a fist, gripping a knife?

Ecotherapy Getaway Holiday, Taki o Mi ni Iku, rating: ★★★☆, runtime: 88 min.

Doesn't every kid imagine being lost in the woods? The imagined outcome, of course, is always positive as you follow the first stream you find back to civilization and safety. In reality, a little disorientation can be a scary thing, as I learned in my boyhood explorations of the Western Pennsylvania woods. What if you wander about in a circle, as hunger and thirst do their slow, deadly work? Such is the dilemma faced by the seven heroines of Shuichi Okita's "Ecotherapy Getaway Holiday," all of whom are over 40 and none of whom were expecting anything more than a pleasant hike to a lovely waterfall. Then their pudgy, nervous guide (Daisuke Kuroda) does a disappearing act and they are left to their own devices.

This may sound like a setup for a comedy of middle-aged errors and terrors, but Okita's approach is more character- than gag-driven; more about human possibilities than plot devices. He also knows, more than many of his comedy-making peers, how to time a joke and tell a story. And there's always something sharply observed, if not immediately obvious, bubbling beneath the pleasantly entertaining surface.

Cast from an audition open to amateurs and based on Okita's own script, "Ecotherapy Getaway Holiday" resembles a reality show, with the lost-in-the-woods situation used to bring out each participant's true personality and amusing foibles. But it has the shape and purpose of a real movie, not a shot-on-the-fly stunt.

When the guide doesn't return, the women try to call him on their cellphones, but they have no reception. Finally, four set off in search of him, while the other three wait behind.

The two groups plan to contact each other with a whistle, but Tamaru (Kumiko Kawada), a former opera singer who is one of the searchers, has a better idea: her own big, melodious voice. Another search-party member, the earnest amateur photographer Misumi (Michiko Watanabe), carefully drops corn chip snacks on the trail so they can find their way back.

Meanwhile, the three who have remained behind begin to open up to each other and reveal hitherto hidden talents. The shy Junko (Haruko Negishi) fashions a pretty wreath from the plants at her feet, while the spunky Sekimoto (Yuriko Ogino) practices tai chi, calming her companions with her deft moves. Finally, the youngest of the group, the stylish Yumiko (Chigusa Yasuzawa), comes out as something of a life philosopher, claiming that all women over 40 are essentially the same age.

But the search fails and the day advances. Not only that, Kuwata (Mie Kirihara) — a plain-talking housewife who is friends with Tamaru — injures her back. Also, despite being an enthusiastic mountain hiker, the groups' eldest member, the gritty 79-year-old Hanazawa (Keiko Tokuno), needs to eat, drink and sleep. Minus any supplies beyond the snacks they have in their bags, how can this motley crew do all of the above, and find their way home?

In another, wilder location, the film might have become a harrowing tale of survival. But this is Japan, where daytrips to waterfalls seldom end in anything more disastrous than a sprained ankle. That said, the women have their mettle tested, to predictably inspiring results.

More interesting than their mild adventures are the ways they express themselves as distinct, engaging individuals. Professional actors do this sort of thing as a matter of course, but Okita's cast are unknowns, with little or no acting experience. Even so, they naturally and forcefully embody the truth that women of a certain age, who tend to become invisible to society, have personalities, strengths and importance.

As a film, "Ecotherapy Getaway Holiday" is in a minor key, but as a feminist manifesto, it rings out loud and clear.

My Man, Watashi no Otoko, rating: ★★★☆, runtime: 129 min.

Based on a novel by Kazuki Sakuraba, Kazuyoshi Kumakiri's "My Man" is described as a film about forbidden love, which immediately raises the question of what, if anything, is "forbidden" in this day and age.

Kumakiri's other films — such as last year's "Summer's End," with its classic love-triangle story, and 2010's "Sketches of Kaitan City," with its characters on the edge of ruin, violence or death — examine people on society's margins and at emotional extremes. This time, though, he has found a story that truly lives up to its "taboo" hype: A middle-aged man (Tadanobu Asano) makes a lover of the orphaned girl (Fumi Nikaido) he has been raising as a daughter.

"My Man" shows hot caresses and kisses, and a surreal bed scene in which the lovers are drenched in a rain of blood, expressing their forbidden passion and inseparable connection. This sort of thing was hard to watch — or rather, to stomach. As the taciturn Jungo (Asano) planted his meaty paw on the breast of his schoolgirl ward, Hana (Nikaido), and slowly, possessively fondled it, I felt anger and disgust that admittedly clouded my reading of Kumakiri's intent.

Is there an aim beyond sick exploitation? There is, though Kumakiri and scriptwriter Takashi Ujita confusingly shift the film's focus, while eliding explanations of various mysteries, such as the damage this incestuous bond has wrought on Hana's soul — damage vividly shown in Nikaido's performance, if not verbally expressed.

The film begins with Hana as a child, weaving, in a daze, past bodies and debris — the results of an earthquake and tsunami on an island near Hokkaido. Both her parents have perished in the disaster and a distant relative, Jungo, volunteers to take her in. "You're mine now," he says, grasping her hand.

The scene shifts and Hana is now a bubbly junior high school student with a strange air of secrecy. She also has a rival in Komachi (Aoba Kawai), a clerk at a local bank who is Jungo's lover and the granddaughter of Oshio (Tatsuya Fuji), a town elder. In the normal course of events, Jungo and Komachi would marry and Hana would have the semblance of a family again. But Jungo and Hana's relationship has become abnormal and Hana sees Komachi as a threat to the closed little world she and Jungo share.

In boldly making her claim to this man, who once possessed her and is now possessed by her, she inadvertently makes Komachi and Oshio aware of what is going behind their father-daughter facade. In the resulting uproar, she and Jungo escape to seek new lives, if not peace, in Tokyo. There Jungo declines into alcoholism, as Hana grows into independence and apparent indifference. Then a visitor from their past arrives, upsetting the fragile equilibrium of their existence.

Nikaido's performance as Hana is a tour de force. Her transition from an abused schoolgirl to a poised, emotionally distant woman goes beyond appearances to currents flowing in the depths. Nikaido is always completely and uniquely Hana, beginning with a coolly appraising gaze that speaks volumes about her outer disconnection and inner pain.

Asano plays the latest in a long line of characters both sensitive and explosive behind their stolid masks. He does not try to soften Jungo's perversity, but somehow makes him less than despicable. Whatever his initial motives, Jungo does care for Hana and becomes, in his isolation and dissolution, dependent on her. He is locked in chains he forged himself — or rather with the aid of his demons.

0.5 mm, no rating, runtime: 196 min.

Momoko Ando's second feature, "0.5mm" is a family affair – Ando and star Sakura Ando are sisters, while the film's executive producer, actor and director Eiji Okuda, is their father. Which may make this film about an enigmatic caretaker for the elderly sound like a glorified home movie; it is nothing of the kind. Based on Ando's own novel that she adapted for the screen, the film gambles with audience patience in both its downbeat subject matter, rambling road-movie structure and 196-minute running time.

But Ando, whose previous film was the 2010 lesbian-themed drama "A Piece of Our Life – Kakera," has won her bet in grand fashion, with "0.5mm" being selected as one of the year's 10 best Japanese films by the "Kinema Junpo" magazine's critic's poll and Sakura Ando winning a shelf of Best Actress honors. Along with this critical acclaim, the film also enjoyed a long run since its November 2014 domestic opening. In contrast to the many sober-sided Japanese films about the problems of the aged, "0.5mm" tries to entertain instead of jerk tears or make a statement, with methods anything but predictable.

Some scenes are darkly funny, while others are hard to watch, but the mystery of the heroine's motives intrigue and the strange characters she meets both fascinate and appall. Also, though the story may appear episodic, its narrative and thematic threads tie together powerfully at the end, though the film gives no pat answer to its central question: Who is this woman and what does she want?

She is Sawa (Sakura Ando), who we first see as the caregiver to a bed-ridden elderly man (Junkichi Orimoto). He still craves intimate female companionship but not, says his stressed adult daughter (Midori Kiuchi), sex. Sawa reluctantly agrees to share his futon for one night, but unintended consequences soon have her looking for another job – or any way to financially survive.

Resourcefully, if not ethically, she finagles her way into the lives of one old man after another, including an aged bicycle thief and fetishist (Toshio Sakata) she discovers puncturing tires and a former university professor (Masahiko Tsugawa) she pounces on when he shoplifts a skin book. But as scheming as she may be, Sawa takes a genuine interest in the welfare of her 'clients' – until something happens to send her out in the streets again.

Then she finally meets her match in the wiry, volatile Sasaki (Akira Emoto), the errant father of Makoto (Nozomi Tsuchiya), a sullen teen whose grandfather was briefly Sawa's bed companion. This time it may be Sawa who needs help.

Sakura Ando is hard to read, but always fascinating to watch as Sawa, who smoothly shifts from caring professional to conniving hustler – and back again. She is more than a puzzle to be solved; she is also the face of Japan's social and economic underside, where millions of young people are subsisting on temporary and part-time work rather than building careers.

Meanwhile, a rapidly growing legion of elders is struggling with all the problems of aging, with ever less help as the labor pool shrinks. Better Sawa than nothing.

The Tale of Iya, Iya Monogatari: Oku no Hito, rating: ★★★★, runtime: 169min.

Cycling in the mountains near Tokyo, I often have two thoughts: First, I feel sorry for big-city denizens missing all the natural beauty so near. Second, I wonder how the locals can wrest a living from their tiny fields and orchards, perched precariously on the slopes.

Both thoughts are eloquently amplified and beautifully illustrated in Tetsuichiro Tsuta's "The Tale of Iya," winner of a Special Mention in the Asian Future section at last year's Tokyo International Film Festival. Set in Shikoku's Iya Valley, famed for its grandeur and remoteness, and shot in the now-rare medium of 35 mm film, it focuses on a people whose way of life is disappearing, even as refugees from the city arrive to preserve it. This has long been a theme of Japanese films, fiction and non-fiction, but those expecting the usual sort of social realism had best be warned: TIFF's labeling of the 29-year-old Tsuta's second film as "fantasy/ science fiction" is close enough, though "science" does not come into the equation at all.

Tsuta's sensibility is closer to that of Colombian writer Gabriel Garcia Marquez in his classic "One Hundred Years of Solitude," in which the fantastic and the supernatural not only impinge on the everyday, but poetically coexist with it — and finally supersede it.

This is not an easy trick to bring off, and Tsuta, working from his own script, is at times obscure in his intention and execution, if never incoherent or clumsy. Frame by frame, "The Tale of Iya" is gorgeously photographed, with breathtaking views of the mountains in fog, in the snow and in their verdant summertime glory. Kudos to cinematographer Yutaka Aoki, who also worked with Tsuta on his 2009 "Island of Dreams." While at times not knowing where I was — or why — I was never less than entranced. Magic indeed.

The mind bending begins with the first scene, in which an old man (Min Tanaka) looking like a peasant in a period drama emerges from the woods to discover a wrecked car, a dead woman driver on the hood and, lying on the snow not far away, a baby girl, miraculously alive. Next we see the girl, now a high school student called Haruna (Rina Takeda), living with her rescuer, a silent man she calls "Grandpa," in a dimly lit thatched-roof cottage deep in the mountains.

The focus shifts to Kudo (Shima Ohnishi), a moody 30-something escapee from the city trying to make a new life in Iya. His first stop is a commune run by a friendly, idealistic foreigner (Christopher Pellegrini), but he ends up trying to farm a patch of fallow land near Grandpa's house, with Haruna's support. A testy young construction worker (Hitoshi Murakami) he befriends is openly scornful of his decision to stick it out. "You think life in the country is easy compared to the city," he sneers.

Of course it isn't. Kudo's vegetable patch is invaded by deer, despite the (graphically depicted) efforts by hunters to thin their numbers. The quixotic campaign by the commune members to halt the construction of a tunnel, which they see as a threat to their unspoiled paradise, is strongly opposed by the locals, eager for the economic gains they hope it will bring. Then Grandpa, always a loner, disappears into the woods as a blizzard rages. A frantic Haruna goes in search of him.

Here a transition I won't detail sends the film into another, dreamlike dimension. One comparison is the end of the cosmic journey for the surviving astronaut in Stanley Kubrick's "2001: A Space Odyssey," who finds himself in an eerily elegant apartment provided for him by his unseen alien hosts. That is, Haruna's point of view abruptly shifts — and we are no longer certain that it is the same as ours. Is she in a dream? Bewitched, as local legend would have it, by foxes? Transported into the world beyond? Or trapped in an alternative reality in which scarecrows made by a now-deceased Grandpa come to eerie life?

Similar to Kubrick, Tsuta wants to leave the meaning of his various metaphors open to interpretation, which may leave some viewers feeling lost and abandoned by the end of their 169-minute journey.

For this viewer, Tsuta's puzzling and haunting film soars beyond everyday logic into a world of natural wonder, ruled by gods at once strange and familiar, alien to the waking consciousness, but alive in dreams.

Pale Moon, Kami no Tsuki, rating: ★★★★, runtime: 126 min.

Willie Sutton, who allegedly made more than $2 million over a 40-year criminal career, once told a reporter that he robbed banks because "that's where the money is." But in the usual heist movie the stolen dough soon proves to be a disastrous sort of fairy gold. Instead of rich, the crooks end up arrested or dead. Sutton himself spent more than half his adult life behind bars.

Rika Umezawa (Rie Miyazawa), the heroine of Daihachi Yoshida's ingeniously told immorality tale "Pale Moon," is a different sort of thief. Instead of a hardened criminal, she is a housewife turned bank employee who slips, ever so reluctantly, into embezzlement.

Aged 41 when the story starts in 1994 — after Japan's economic bubble has burst but before the riese of the Internet — she looks to be the soul of propriety as she visits her elderly clients to collect their deposits or advise them on investments. Soon, though, she is using her insider knowledge of forms and procedures to siphon some of that money into her own pocket.

Based on Mitsuyo Kakuta's eponymous novel, the film is close in tone to "The Kirishima Thing," Yoshida's critically acclaimed 2012 high school drama that was more about illuminating inner lives than scoring laughs. "Pale Moon" has its black comic moments, but its view of Rika's choices and crimes is serious — the risks she is taking and the lines she is crossing have life- and character-altering consequences.

The film refuses to sit in judgment of her. Instead it is an unblinking study of how money can shape its human possessors and seekers from the inside out, for good, for bad, or both.

Rika's fall begins the moment she lays eyes on Kota (Sosuke Ikematsu), the louche grandson of a miserly old client (Renji ishibashi). Without even a dog to care for and an often-absent husband offering only token companionship, Rika feels lonely and unloved, so when Kota's insistent wooing lights a spark, it quickly bursts into a full-blown affair, age difference be damned.

Kota, it turns out, is falling behind on his school tuition payments, while his rich grandfather refuses to lend him a single yen. When Rika hears her young lover's sad tale, which just may be true, she decides to run an ingenious scam on Grandpa that may have a noble motive — help a young man complete his education — but is also her first step down the rosy path to disaster.

First, though, the roses. Kota's passionate sexual healing not only awakens Rika as a woman, but makes her realize all she has been missing as a dutiful helpmate to an indifferent corporate warrior. She and Kota begin to live large, courtesy of her unwitting, undeserving clients.

Of course, in the eyes of society, as represented by a stern senior clerk (Satomi Kobayashi) and Rika's smarmy, womanizing boss (Yoshimasa Kondo), she is criminally in the wrong. Meanwhile, a junion employee (former AKB48 star Yuko Oshima) distresses Rika with her winking talk of embezzlment. Has this woman no morals?

Has Rika? In flashbacks to her younger self — an idealistic student at a Catholic girls' school — we see that the answer is not so simple. The road to hell may be paved with good intentions, but to young

Rika, the hypocrisy of those who preach charity while practicing indifference teaches only that their moral/religious game is a con.

Can you blame her for drawing her own conclusions and acting on them? Not if you are caught in the spell of the many-sided, finally mysterious glow of "Pale Moon."

The Light Shines Only There, Soko Nomi Nite Hikari Kagayaku, rating: ★★★★, runtime: 90 min.

Japan's image overseas has a funhouse aspect, but even many foreigners who live here only get a selective view of the place, since their Japanese colleagues and friends mostly come from the educated middle-class and live more or less stable, law-abiding lives. Mipo Oh's third feature, "The Light Shines Only There," focuses on an underclass living close to the edge — or over it. But has Oh gone over the line herself this time? Filmed in the grittier parts of Hokkaido, in shades of pollution-haze brown and dirty-window gray, "The Light Shines Only There" is dorodoro, a hard-to-translate if apt word that signifies a dark, endless swamp of emotional turmoil. From beginning to end, the film is replete with lonely alcoholic binges and loveless, even brutal sex, while family life is portrayed as a pit of grinding poverty, deathly illness and crazy-making despair.

Yasushi Sato, the author of the 1989 novel on which the film is based, committed suicide at age 41 in 1990. Was his "light that shines only there" not of this life, but the next?

The film lives up to its title by justifying the agony of the central couple and giving their pain meaning. But the experience of viewing it is somewhat like enduring a long, illness and, after recovering, seeing things everyone takes for granted — a bird in flight, a walk on the beach — as blissful miracles.

The film's first shot travels slowly up the scarred, sweaty body of the hero, Tatsuo Sato (Go Ayano). He has passed out drunk on the floor and is having a nightmare about discovering a dead body under rocky rubble.

Next we see him in his daily refuge from the reality of a jobless, aimless life — a pachinko parlor. There he meets Takuji (Masaki Suda), a brash kid whose insistent friendliness breaks through his shell. Exiting the parlor, Takuji takes his new pal to the ramshackle house he shares with his bedridden father, careworn mother and wary older sister Chinatsu (Chizuru Ikewaki). While Takuji devours her fried rice like a hungry animal, a current of attraction passes between Tatsuo and Chinatsu.

But Chinatsu's past experiences with men, including her volatile married lover Nakamura (Kazuya Takahashi) and the faceless clients at the bar where she works as a hooker, have destroyed whatever illusions she had about the male species. A romp in the surf dissolves her reserves, though, and soon Tatsuo and Chinatsu are making love in Tatsuo's mess of a room.

This surf-to-sex transition is a big cliche in Japanese films, right up there with soulful talks on school rooftops, but Tatsuo and Chinatsu's relationship has nothing of the standard romantic drama about it. Both bear wounds that defy healing — sexual or otherwise. Tatsuo's searing guilt iprompts his drinking, moodiness and sudden rages. Meanwhile, Chinatsu carries a crushing burden of responsibility for her dysfunctional family, while feeling defective as a woman and a person. She affects a hard shell at work, though Tatsuo — who first encounters her cooking that fried rice — sees her in a softer, more intimate light.

Takuji, with his uncombed blonde hair and unbrushed brown teeth, keeps intruding into the frame like a hyperactive kid. Why, I started to wonder, is this character getting so much screen time?

But Takuji's fizzy energy counterbalances Tatsuo's intense inwardness. And this ticking human time bomb, who craves love but might first explode, gives the gloomy story a needed charge.

With his moody, hangdog air, Ayano's Tatsuo is not always easy to like, though his frank talks with his understanding former boss (Shohei Hino), and flashbacks to his former life as dynamiter at a local quarry, give us glimpses of a better man who once had self-respect.

As Chinatsu, Ikewaki's performance is at once complex and transparent, drilling down into the essence of her character's longing and self-loathing, her capacity for love and her longing for oblivion.

Salvation, as the title implies, is not hers or anyone's for the asking. Sometimes you just have to be with the right person in the right place at the right time to find "the light that shines only there." Just call it grace.

Au Revoir l'Eté, Hotori no Sakuko, rating: ★★★★, runtime: 125 min.

Compared to his French new-wave peers, Eric Rohmer seemed to direct in a lighter, more conventional key: All those casually chic young women photographed in the more attractive parts of France, all those stories about their various love troubles. Also, from a Hollywood perspective, his characters talk too much and his stories ramble too long. But for fans, including me, his films adroitly reveal the complexities and perversities of the human animal. Those long, naturalistic conversations turn out to have a deeper purpose than displaying the charms of the characters.

Rohmer disciple Koji Fukada pays homage to the master in his summer-at-the-beach drama "Au Revoir l'Eté," right down to a French title that references Rohmer's 1996 film "Conte d'Eté (A Summer's Tale)."

And yet the film is hardly a cut-and-paste job. Scripted by Fukada himself, it feels believably Japanese, though its characters are the thin slice of locals who can take longish summer vacations. One is the title heroine, Sakuko (Fumi Nikaido), who has failed her university entrance exams and is girding for another try. Another is her aunt Mikie (Mayu Tsuruta), a university professor who is house-sitting for her sister (Makiko Watanabe) at a seaside town.

The meticulously constructed story feels unmediated, like a day at the beach that unwinds according to whim rather than plan.

The overarching theme, however, is clear enough, being the various stories we construct about ourselves and others — and the consequences when those stories are questioned or revealed to be lies. Sakuko is among the more persistent questioners, though she is also content to listen and observe. She is honest to a fault, while being tolerant of others' obfuscations, as 18-year-old truth-tellers are not always prone to be. The film may be about her coming of age, but she is also its wise-beyond-her-years center of gravity.

Around that center revolve Ukichi (Kanji Furutachi), Mikie's former boyfriend, who manages a business-cum-love hotel in town, as well as his daughter Tatsuko (Kiki Sugino), a cynical college student who waits tables at a beach-side cafe, and his tightly coiled nephew Takashi (Taiga), who evacuated from Fukushima after 3/11 but dropped out of high school and is now working for Ukichi at the hotel.

Then, just as Sakuko is becoming friends with the shy, straight-talking Takashi, he reunites with a willowy former classmate (Ena Koshino) and the attraction between the two is too obvious for Sakuko to ignore. Also, a celebrity professor (Tadashi Otake) visits Mikie, with whom he has been having an affair, but Tatsuko approaches him after one of his lectures. Once they are alone in his car, she brazenly grills him about his love life and one thing, as they say, leads to another.

The comic potential in these and other romantic/erotic situations is certainly there, but Fukada is more interested in the pain the characters feel as their hopes are dashed, masks are removed and bad memories are revived. He is less interested in labeling them as heroes or villains, though he is not averse to making the loathsome look ridiculous.

As we know it must, the story comes down to an adventure Sakuko and Takashi embark on together, as they search for something beyond the structures and strictures imposed by family and society. What they are really looking for, we see, is a clue to their future; especially Takashi, who has come to hate his assigned role as "nuclear victim."

As Sakuko, Nikaido again shows why she is among the best young actors now working. Instead of the standard pouting princess or moody rebel, she creates a more interesting character whose big, inquisitive eyes take in everything but give away little, who pays attention to others but goes her own way.

More troubled, and for good reason, is Taiga's Takashi, who rejects easy sympathy, however well intentioned. Like Sakuko, he is an outsider, though one more dependent on the kindness of the adult world — and more determined to break free from its corrupting embrace.

So who's movie is it, anyway — Sakuko's or Takashi's? The film resists answering this question decisively, while refusing to build to a big, tie-it-all-together climax, romantic or otherwise. This may create an impression of third-act drift, but as revelations are made and confidences are exchanged, we see that Sakuko has learned something that will make this summer more than bike rides and beach walks and a bit of a crush on a younger guy.

This being a Rohmer-esque film, that something can't be summed up in a word. One takeaway: Even lovers of truth need secrets.

Fuku-chan of Fukufuku Flats, Fukufukuso no Fuku-chan, no rating, runtime: 111 min.

Fujita Yosuke is one of the best Japanese comedy directors now working, if not the most prolific. Born in 1963, he did not make his feature debut until 2008 with "Fine, Totally Fine," a comedy about a manual laborer (Arakawa Yoshiyoshi) who longs to build the world's scariest haunted house with the aid of his similarly unevolved pals. The film's out-of-left-field love interest is an oddball artist (Kimura Yoshino) whom we first meet obsessively painting a colorfully kitted-out homeless woman. What begins as another Japanese quirk-fest, if one laugh-out-loud funny, becomes an unexpectedly affecting ode to friendship and love, however unconventional.

"Fine, Totally Fine" and "Encouragement Girls," Fujita's contribution to the 2011 comedy anthology "Quirky Guys and Gals," were widely praised and screened abroad, leading to an unusual production arrangement for his latest, "Fuku-chan of FukuFuku Flats." Instead of the standard consortium of Japanese media companies, the film's backers are from the UK, Germany, Italy and Taiwan, as well as Japan. Rather than put their money on the usual Asian action or horror pic, they are betting that Fujita's talent for comedy, that notoriously hard to export genre, will yield a winner.

They have won their bet. Fujita's dry, warm comic touch is still intact, as is his fondness for stories of misfits who find each other. Also, His sensibility is in tune with Japan's current age of diminished expectations, with the big dream being, not a triumphant walk together into the sunset, but a real human connection, however humble.

The Fuku-chan (Miyuki Oshima) of the title is a tubby, shaven-headed painter who lives in the title apartment building – an old dorm-like place with small rooms and thin walls, but a communal atmosphere. His co-worker Shimacchi (Arakawa again), who resembles Fuku-chan down to the stubble on his skull, is always looking out for the welfare of his lonely buddy, even trying to recruiting a girlfriend for him. But when Fuku-chan brings along two of his strange FukuFuku Flats pals to a double date Shimacchi has set up, what was supposed to be a romantic picnic turns into a disaster.

Meanwhile, Chiho (Asami Mizukawa), a career woman with a high-paying job at a foreign company, wins a photo contest and an offer to study under a famous cameraman.

She chucks the job but the apprenticeship turns sour and, now without employment or prospects, begins to re-evaluate her life. Feeling a lingering guilt for the bullying she and her junior high friends inflicted on a porky classmate, she decides to seek him out and apologize.

Along the way to the fateful reunion between Fuku-chan and a first love who made him permanently female-phobic, Fujita inserts plenty of gently absurd, infectiously funny gags. Even the props and the bit players, such as the goofy Japanese-style kites that Fuku-chan makes and flies and a young painter who sings old kayokyoku (Japanese pop songs) to his rapt co-workers with a starry-eyed sincerity, are used to comic effect.

The story, pre- and post-reunion, is not all laughs, though. Fuku-chan's pain from his past is real enough, as is Chiho's repentance for her youthful sins. But for all the agony, tears and even punches thrown, the film never descends to the bathetic. One reason is the affection Fujita obviously feels for all his creations, even a FukuFuku Flats denizen who is a ticking time bomb, despite his nerdy exterior.

Another is that a comic vibe constantly thrumming in the background, even when the human time bomb finally explodes.

The film is getting media attention in Japan, not for Fujita who is still relatively unknown, but for Miyuki Oshima, a popular TV comic who as Fuku-chan is starring in a film for the first time. This casting is no PR stunt; Oshima makes for a credible middle-aged guy, aided by her character's uncanny resemblance to Arakawa's equally pudgy and close-cropped Shimacchi.

More importantly, Oshima is a gifted physical comedian who knows how to play for the camera – Chiho's as well as Fujita's. Mugging as Fuku-chan while Chiho snaps away, she has a sort of radiance, as well as ridiculousness. The kanji character for "Fuku" means "good fortune" – and Fujita was lucky to have found her. Our luck would be to have another Fujita comedy as good as this one sooner than four more long years.

2015

Antonym, Rasen Ginga, rating: ★★★★, runtime: 73min.

"Opposites attract" is one of those truisms easy to dismiss — until they turn out to be true. Take the sensitive beta-male guy whose sensitive female soulmate ends up with an alpha-male cowboy — or the nearest urban equivalent. Also, the attraction of opposites is not always mutual: Would that famous beauty you ask to pose with average you for a selfie ever ask you to do the same? Maybe not.

The central relationship in Natsuka Kusano's debut feature "Antonym" seems to fit the latter template. Aya (Yuri Ishizaka) is a fashionable woman who exudes arrogance. Her co-worker Sachiko (Asami Shibuya) is a gawky introvert who is perpetually apologizing for her existence. Sachiko admires Aya for her ambition to become a scriptwriter, though she is only attending a night class. Aya, who has yet to sell a script, reacts to Sachiko's praise with barely disguised scorn.

The winner of the Nippon Visions Award at last year's Nippon Connection film festival, the aptly titled "Antonym" is a fresh, incisive take on a common, if little-filmed, type of relationship, especially in hierarchy-loving Japan. Sachiko's attraction to Aya may at first seem sexual, but I was reminded more of the relationship between the otokoyaku (male role) stars of the all-female Takarazuka theater troupe and their devoted female fans, who fantasize about the stars as romantic ideals, not real-life lovers. Similarly, Sachiko is thrilled when Aya asks her for help, but has no discernible longing to jump into bed with her.

Meanwhile, Aya's motivation is purely selfish. Her writing class teacher chose her script "Antonym" for a radio performance, with one condition: She must find a co-writer to help her revise it. Her present script, he tells her in front of the class, is a deeply flawed testimony to her egocentric view of humanity. Offended, but fearing he might be right, Aya asks Sachiko to pose as a manga-artist pal who has volunteered to be her collaborator. Sachiko agrees, but offers apt suggestions instead of the expected silence. This mouse, we see, has a voice, if not a roar. But she has to persuade the proud Aya to listen.

Many films deal with female relationships, but "Antonym" does something I hadn't seen before: show how a relationship between two women that begins as artificial and unequal blossoms into a true partnership, if not quite a friendship. The film accomplishes this unusual transition with a quiet lyricism, shown in its repeated night shots of a colorfully inviting laundromat that Sachiko uses as a kind of retreat. And it concludes with a performance of Aya's script that brilliantly illuminates the bond between its protagonists and the ways each has changed.

As Sachiko, Shibuya has the tougher of the two roles, for reasons hard to detail without giving too much away. But she accomplishes her makeover from socially inept ugly duckling with none of the usual props. Instead of tossing away her glasses, Sachiko begins to glow with a confidence that's

innately attractive. "Smile is the best make-up" goes an old beauty-school slogan. I'd say that talent —
and knowing you have it — runs it a close second.

Round Trip Heart, Romansu, rating: ★★★★, runtime: 97min.

Pushing a food-and-drinks cart on an express train used to be a something of a glamour job for young
Japanese women (or something of a comedown if they aspired to be flight attendants).

The Odakyu Romance Car, which debuted in 1957, is one such express train. It travels between
Tokyo and Hakone, the mountain resort that has been drawing urban visitors for centuries.

In Yuki Tanada's "Round Trip Heart," Hachiko Hojo (Yuko Oshima) is one such cart pusher,
dressed in a spiffy uniform and spreading good cheer. To passengers she may be little more than an
ambulatory convenience store clerk, but to a bumbling junior colleague (Yoshimi Nozaki), Hachiko is
a no-nonsense veteran and a fount of job-survival wisdom.

Her smooth daily routine hits a bump when a goofy-looking passenger pilfers a box of snacks from
her cart. She tries to turn him in to station authorities, but he runs off and an angry Hachiko gives
spirited chase. To shorten a rather incredible story (scripted by Tanada), pursuer and pursued finally
call an exhausted truce and embark on a journey together to find Hachiko's long-lost mom, who has
written her a heartfelt letter suggesting that she might commit suicide.

This plot turn tests audience sympathy, especially since the shoplifter, Sakuraba (Koji Okura), is that
least empathetic of types: a failing movie producer.

Here the film could shift toward either labored opposites-attract rom-com or formula drama about
two lost souls discovering their respective grooves. But "Round Trip Heart" finds a mostly happy
middle ground between these two paths. True, Hachiko tenderly recalls a long-ago family trip to
Hakone, before her flighty, fun-loving mom (Megumi Nishimuta) broke up with her dad. And
Sakuraba, who noisily denies wrong-doing and proclaims himself a big wheel, reveals his more a
pathetic side in the course of their adventure. But rather than milk this material for sighs and tears, the
film stays dry-eyed about its two principals, their chances for romance included. The 26-year-old
Hachiko keeps calling 41-year-old Sakuraba "ossan" ("old man") over his protests. Coming from an
ultra-polite Romance Car attendant this is funny — and indicative of her determination to keep an
assured clear distance from her traveling companion.

Playing Hachiko, Yuko Oshima reveals a talent that may surprise fans who know her only from her
stint with the AKB48 idol group, but not those who saw her as an ethically challenged bank clerk in
Daihachi Yoshida's "Pale Moon" (2014), a performance that won her several best supporting actress
prizes. She more than holds her own with her towering co-star Okura, though he has a far longer
string of film and TV credits — and a habit of stealing scenes.

Also, Tanada's film entertainingly reflects a fundamental truth: Strangers may bond on the road, but
their personalities — and problems — remain the same when they part.

Hachiko nostalgically croons "Ii Hi Tabidachi" ("Departure on a Fine Day"), Momoe Yamaguchi's
1978 hit about a life-changing journey that was her mother's karaoke favorite, but she also longs to
return to the rails — and the Romance Car waits for no one.

Can she get back on track? The answer is worth the ride to the final stop.

Being Good, Kimi wa Iiko, rating: ★★★★, runtime: 121min.

Based on Hatsue Nakawaki's eponymous novel, Mipo Oh's "Being Good" paints a well-orchestrated
group portrait of isolated people, young and old, caught in downward spirals — with some chancing
upon possible ways out.

An elderly woman (Michie Kita) is caught shoplifting at a local supermarket, but it soon becomes
apparent that she is suffering from mild dementia. Then she befriends an autistic boy (Amon Kabe)
whose frazzled mother (Yasuko Tomita) goes through life apologizing for her son's existence.

A single mother, Masami (Machiko Ono), who was physically abused as a child, abuses her own three-year-old daughter and feels guilty as she watches a cheery mom (Chizuru Ikewaki) laugh away the naughty behavior of her rambunctious son at a neighborhood park. The two women become friends, though Masami doesn't see what they have in common beyond their kids.

It's not clear how the lives of these characters will intertwine, but as their stories unfold on parallel tracks the plot begins to matter less than their individual journeys. Some need more help than others. And some may never make it. They are familiar types, but come with a shading and dimensions that makes them distinctive and sympathetic — even the ones who seem to be monsters. In the scenes of Masami abusing her daughter, we see the blows and hear the screams, but the camera stays at an objective distance while the neutral blues and grays suggest a pain shared as well as inflicted.

Meanwhile, a first-year teacher, Okano (Kengo Kora), finds himself embroiled in one classroom crisis after another: From a nervous boy who wets himself rather than ask for permission to use the restroom to a shy girl who becomes the target of cruel teasing. Okano's attempts to solve these crises (and buy himself some peace) backfire spectacularly, however, and he is wallowing in self-pity when the young son of his frank-talking sister (Chika Uchida) comforts him in a way I won't describe — only to say that it warms his heart and switches on a light in his head.

In the midst of his professional troubles, Okano tries to help a boy in his class who is being beaten by his loutish father (Ryota Matsushima), but is afraid to open up — and the school authorities are afraid to act. Solving this problem, Okano realizes, will require not just good intentions, but courage.

This suggests a big feel-good climax, but the film hits its strongest, most moving notes in earlier moments of human connection that seem impossible — until they aren't.

In this film, miracles are everyday acts of simple — not random — kindness. I want to believe.

Kabukicho Love Hotel, Sayonara Kabukicho, rating: ★★★★, runtime: 135min.

Ryuichi Hiroki has become a victim of his own success, though his studio employers probably don't see it that way. This one-time maker of "pink" films (i.e., soft pornography) became internationally celebrated for intimate indie dramas like "Vibrator" (2003) and "It's Only Talk" (2005). He has morphed into the local industry's go-to guy for weepy romantic dramas — a money-making genre here for decades. Hiroki brought his own style and sensibility to commercial films like "April Bride" and "The Lightening Tree" while drawing career-peak performances from his female stars. He couldn't do much about the formula tropes of the stories, however. He has never directed a truly bad film, but compared to his earlier indie work, he hasn't been making what those who celebrated that work — myself included — really wanted to watch.

When his latest, "Kabukicho Love Hotel," was announced, I hoped it would mark a return to form. That hope has been abundantly realized.

Set mostly in a love hotel in the heart of Shinjuku's Kabukicho entertainment district, the film is an ensemble drama revolving around a young hotel manager, Toru (Shota Sometani), who regards the job as a temporary fall from grace. As he is forever reminding everyone, he once worked for a five-star hotel and will again. First, though, he has to get through an eventful shift.

Working from a script by frequent collaborator Haruhiko Arai, Hiroki films this shift with dry humor. He also views the hotel's denizens, staff and guests alike, as individuals, not types, with an affection never forced. His approach is low-key and leisurely compared to the over-heated local norm, but it hit me harder — I cried two tears for every laugh.

Toru begins his shift in a bad mood, since he has quarreled with his musician girlfriend, Saya (Atsuko Maeda), who is on the verge of signing a deal with a record label and leaving her scuffling days behind her. Toru is worried that he will end up on the discard pile as well.

First, duty calls, beginning with a porn film shoot that requires his attention — and renews his once-close acquaintance with the star (Asuka Hinoi).

Meanwhile, Heya (Lee Eun-woo), a Korean call girl, is working her last day at the hotel. She will soon leave Japan for home, a development that upsets her boyfriend Chong-su (Roy from pop group 5tion, aka Son Il-kwon), though her nice-guy manager (Tomorowo Taguchi) is more understanding.

The hardworking hotel cleaning lady (Kaho Minami) also has reason to celebrate. Her live-in boyfriend (Yutaka Matsushige) will soon be free of a crime he committed years ago, since the statute of limitations will expire. A dogged female detective (Aoba Kawai) has taken an interest in the case, though she comes to the hotel as a guest, not a cop.

Finally, a talent scout (Shugo Oshinari) lures a cute runaway teen (Miwako Wagatsuma) to the hotel with the intent of adding her to his stable of underage hookers. She seems an easy a mark, until she tells him her story.

As usual, Hiroki works marvels with his female lead. In her films to date Maeda has mostly played to the cute, likable image she cultivated in AKB48, the all-girl pop group she once headlined. Hiroki takes her out of this comfort zone, in a risky scene that could have been cringe-worthy, but becomes unexpectedly affecting.

Also good in a different way is Lee, who reveals her character's isolation and ordinary humanity with a transparency that charms and sears. No hooker-with-a-heart-of-gold cliches here.

As the lead, Sometani does his familiar tired-of-it-all turn, with comic twists that makes his manager amusingly self-deluded, instead of merely annoying. But the dilemmas and personalities of those around him are more interesting. Check into "Kabukicho Love Hotel" to find out why.

Fires on the Plain, Nobi, rating: ★★★★, runtime: 87 min.

Japanese war films typically frame themselves as anti-war, even when they glorify the sacrifices made by brave Japanese boys in defense of the homeland, as in the 2013 hit "The Eternal Zero."

Kon Ichikawa's 1959 war film "Fires on the Plain" rejected this sort of soft nationalism. Based on Shohei Ooka's semi-autobiographical novel about Japanese soldiers in the Philippines during the desperate last days of World War II, the film spoke the truth as starkly as the era would permit.

So when veteran indie iconoclast Shinya Tsukamoto announced that he was shooting his own version of Ooka's novel, I was skeptical that he could improve on Ichikawa's classic.

He has, by being true to the no-limits, no-concessions Tsukamoto who made "Tetsuo" (1989) and other pioneering cyberpunk sci-fi films. Tsukamoto's "Nobi" is neither punk nor futuristic in the least, though the ominous rumbles and piercing howls of its electronic score — by longtime collaborator Chu Ishikawa — are more 2015 than 1945.

The film's intense, close-up focus on the the hero's present moment and personal experiences — the shock of exploding body parts, the beauty of light shimmering on the long grass — has been compared to the films of Terrence Malick, but this has also long been Tsukamoto's directorial strategy. Whatever his references, every shot is his own.

Tsukamoto is also his own star, as he has frequently been since "Tetsuo" onward, but not as his usual crazed, violent hero. Instead he plays Tamura, an emaciated, tubercular private in the Philippine jungle. Ordered to the field hospital by a brusque superior, he finds there a hellish antechamber to death. Seeing that Tamura can talk and walk, however unsteadily, the medic in charge contemptuously tells him return to his unit and then claims all his food.

While Tamura is being ping-ponged back and forth, an air raid blows his unit to pieces. He survives with only a few raw yams to eat and no matches to light a cooking fire. Searching inside a Catholic church, he dozes off until he is startled awake by a spooning young couple. In a moment of panic (which a shaky camera and rapid crosscuts make chillingly palpable) he pulls the trigger of his rifle — and runs from the now-bloody scene.

Soon after, he encounters other Japanese soldiers on their way to be evacuated from the island. A grizzled corporal (Tatsuya Nakamura) tells him, with a manic grin, that he is immune from bullets, while the others hungrily eye his food sack. Tamura temporarily buys peace by giving them salt, which they devour. Then, traipsing through the jungle past the dead and dying, he reunites with two men from his unit: the half-loony Nagamatsu (Yusaku Mori) and the wily, limping veteran Yasuda (Lily Franky), who induces the younger man to hunt for what they call "monkey meat."

Weakened by hunger, illness and fatigue, Tamura looks ready to be reclassified from human to simian. The film has been criticized for excessive gore, but from the accounts of combat I have read, Tsukamoto is simply portraying the grisly truth. And despite his tiny production budget, he has done a superior job of conveying the incongruous mix of lush natural beauty and disturbing human degradation the film's real-life models experienced in their jungle war.

The widening distance between that war and the present, with its instant amnesia toward anything not trending on social media, has given Tsukamoto a sense of urgency. For him the film represents a last chance to make the reality of war undeniable and unforgettable to a younger generation that has only known peace. More than nearly any other Japanese war film, "Fires on the Plain" is not only a testimony but also a warning.

Three Stories of Love, Koibitotachi, rating: ★★★★☆, runtime: 140min.

Watching recent Japanese films, I often have the feeling that their makers need an imagination injection, or need to get out more. It's not just that few, especially commercial filmmakers, work from original scripts. Plenty of great movies are adapted from other media.

But rather than view their source material through their own lens — that is, make it their own — filmmakers here frequently transfer it more or less whole to the screen, formulas, clichés and all.

Ryosuke Hashiguchi's three-apart omnibus "Three Stories of Love" shows up how derivative much of the local competition is.

This drama about the loves and losses of three vastly different (if loosely connected) people began as a workshop project led by Hashiguchi. In writing the script, a process that took eight months, he tailored each of his stories to the personalities and strengths of his three leads, all unknowns cast from auditions, while drawing on his own life as an "out" gay man who has wrestled with depression.

The film begins with Atsushi (Atsushi Shinohara), a chubby, gloomy, disheveled guy with an unusual gift: A bridge inspector, he checks concrete pilings using only a hammer, his keen hearing and his instincts. But alone in his tiny, trash-strewn apartment, he mourns bitterly for his wife, killed three years earlier by a madman on the street.

Then there is Toko (Toko Narushima), a middle-aged housewife who drudges for her indifferent husband and complaining mother-in-law while obsessively watching an old video of a now-distant, not-close encounter with Princess Masako. Fed up with her treadmill existence, she begins an affair with a scam artist (Ken Mitsuishi) who promises her, not the moon, but a chicken farm.

We also meet Shinomiya (Ryo Ikeda), a gay lawyer with a sardonic grin, an inflated self-regard and a young lover he treats like dirt. Then his life starts to fall apart and he finds refuge with a school friend he once loved, who now has a wife and child.

The stories of Atsushi and Toko begin as exercises in miserabilist cinema, with their central characters mired in seemingly hopeless situations, while Shinoyama's segment initially plays like black comedy (including the "joke" of the smirking hero being pushed down a flight of stone steps by an anonymous hand).

As these stories develop, their central characters reveal unexpected facets that individualize and elevate them. They are, we see, feeling, thinking beings worthy of attention and, yes, love, for all their flaws. They are real and familiar, even if we don't see their exact reflections in our mirrors.

The three leads all create their performances from the inside out, with craft that doesn't call attention to itself. The stand out is Narushima: Her performance as Toko, from her slack-jawed stare at the TV screen to the ungainly herky-jerky dance she performs dressing and undressing, comically exposes an unglamorous private reality. But when Toko finally explains her motives and dreams to her drugged-out lover her complete authenticity gives weight to her words. As strange as it sounds, she achieves a state of grace that illuminates not only her life, but also ours.

100 Yen Love, Hyakuen no Koi, rating: ★★★★, runtime: 113 min.

Boxing films share a similar arc, typically climaxing in a big bout that decides everything relevant to the hero's fate. This does not always means triumph, as fans of the "Rocky" series know, but even in defeat the hero usually inspires respect for surviving a contest of a brutality non-boxers can only imagine. The challenge for a director is to film that big bout — and the ones leading up to it —as part of a story, not just a record of a sporting contest. Some, such as Martin Scorsese with his 1980 classic "Raging Bull," rise to the challenge with blood-splattered realism, while others, such as Fumihiko Sori with the 2011 film "Tomorrow's Joe," evade it with cartoony excess.

Masaharu Take takes the former approach in "100 Yen Love," a film that won the Best Picture Award in the Japanese Cinema Splash section at the 2014 Tokyo International Film Festival. But unlike the many boxing films that are testosterone-driven dramas Take centers his on a woman.

Based on an award-winning script by Shin Adachi, "100 Yen Love" is thus a genre outlier, but its training and boxing scenes are hard-hitting standouts — "Rocky," move over.

Take, who also partnered with Adachi on the low-budget 2013 comedy "Mongolian Baseball," deserves credit, but it is Sakura Ando's all-out performance as the unlikely heroine Ichiko that lifts the film above its shambling story line and pawky gags to moments of greatness.

Ichiko is a 32-year-old slacker who is jobless, boyfriendless and aimless. Home is no haven, with her testy sister (one-name actress Saori) loudly scolding Ichiko for her lazy ways. Her mom and dad are more tolerant, but Ichiko soon gets fed up, moves out and starts working at a local ¥100 shop as a checkout clerk.

The job, however, is hardly a step up. Her middle-age co-worker (Shohei Uno) is a smarmy lech, while her manager (Yuki Okita) is a nagging stickler for the rules. A feisty homeless woman (Toshie Negishi) who raids the store for throwaway food provides some excitement, but Ichiko is more attracted to a regular customer — a moody, silent boxer (Hirofumi Arai) who trains at a neighborhood gym and is nicknamed "Banana Man" for his frequent purchases of said fruit.

The story continues as a slice-of-life comedy when Ichiko and the boxer, Yuji, start dating and living together, though he barely acknowledges her existence at first. Then it takes a turn I won't elaborate on — I'll only say that Yuji abruptly exits the relationship and boxing, which ignites something in Ichiko and she starts training at the gym herself.

The film doesn't explain this change in hackneyed "I'm going to take control of my life" terms. Instead, Ichiko's motives remain somewhat mysterious, but as she transforms from clumsy beginner to laser-focused boxer, we see punching bags and sparring partners take the brunt of a frustration and rage that seem to have been building in her for a lifetime.

Nothing unusual about that, but far from ordinary is Ando's total dedication to the role, striking blows and even jumping rope with fury and skill. Off-screen, Ando reportedly started boxing while still in junior high and her knowledge of the sport shines through, including her close acquaintance with its pain.

That becomes most apparent when she is in the ring, facing off against an actual opponent. The true test of a boxing film is its boxing scenes, and the ones in "100 Yen Love" convey better than almost any other I've seen the sport's ferocity, with blows that would knock the ordinary person flat raining down mercilessly. Yes, two women are in the ring, not Robert De Niro or Sylvester Stallone, but that takes nothing away from the intensity, especially given that one is fighting to defeat her past, and her own label as a "100 yen girl."

But Ando, in the best performance of her already stellar career, comes out as the biggest winner. If she doesn't walk away with a cartload of acting prizes for this role, you know the fix is in.

Bakuman, rating: ★★★★, runtime: 120min.

High school kids dream big dreams, and in Japan one of the biggest is to be a successful manga artist. The financial rewards for a hit manga published in a national magazine and sold in paperback editions are substantial. And the accompanying recognition and power — with adoring fans pleading for autographs and editors begging for your next masterpiece — must seem intoxicating to a would-be mangaka (manga artist) doodling in the margins of his biology textbook.

One of those manga-besotted kids is Mashiro Moritaka aka Saiko (Takeru Sato), the teenage hero of Hitoshi One's buddy comedy "Bakuman," who surreptitiously draws portraits of pretty classmate Azuki (Nana Komatsu). But Saiko knows how tough the manga game is: His uncle (Kankuro Kudo) was a struggling artist who, after making it into the biggest manga magazine, the real-life publication "Weekly Shonen Jump," died of overwork. Though talented, Saiko has no intention of following in his footsteps.

Then that talent is discovered by Akito Takagi, aka Shujin (Ryunosuke Kamiki), a loquacious classmate with a gift for storytelling. Shujin proposes that they team up to assault the citadel of professional mangadom, with Shujin writing and Saiko illustrating. Saiko resists until he receives unexpected encouragement from Azuki. Their inner fires alight, and Saiko and Shujin start the race to manga fame and fortune. Their ultimate goal: "Weekly Shonen Jump."

Based on a manga published in — of course — "Weekly Shonen Jump," "Bakuman" begins as the usual sort of zero-to-hero teen comedy, with frenzied performances from the two male principals. (By contrast, newcomer Komatsu plays Azuki as a cool-eyed teenage goddess who can send Saiko into a dither with a bat of her eyelashes.)

As director of the hit 2011 romantic comedy "Love Strikes!" and the 2013 indie ensemble drama "Be My Baby," One is that rare combination: a perfectionist craftsman with a unbridled imagination. In everything from his script, which departs significantly from the original manga, to the film's meticulous art direction, which includes an exact recreation of the stupendously messy real offices of "Weekly Shonen Jump," One raises "Bakuman" far above the standard for local mainstream entertainment — which, admittedly, is not that high.

He also takes "Bakuman" beyond its predictable story arc of trials and triumph into territory both realistically gritty (or inky, given the usual state of Saiko's drawing hand) and surreally nightmarish.

After making repeated revisions to satisfy a supportive editorial flunky (Takayuki Yamada), the boys triumph in a "Weekly Shonen Jump" contest for newcomers — but this victory is only the beginning. Other winning contestants, including a teen prodigy (Shota Sometani), are fighting for a coveted spot in the magazine. And the god-like senior editor (Lily Franky) who will ultimately decide their fate is, Saiko believes, responsible for his uncle's untimely death.

To satisfy fans, I suppose, "Bakuman" embraces some of the original manga's melodramatic plot tropes. But the film's fantasy sequences, such as the duel Saiko and Shujin fight with the prodigy using gigantic pens and battling manga frames, comment on those tropes with sly humor and dazzling imagery.

Meanwhile, the film's visual phantasmagoria illuminates the inner source of Saiko's creativity in all its fluent beauty and dark terror — starting with his fear of ending up like his uncle.

Is success worth the sacrifice? The film warns that making it as a manga pro is a life-or-death quest, though it celebrates the camaraderie of the artists (all guys, I'm afraid) who survive the editorial baptism of fire. And, as we see in one poignant scene, it's all for kids flipping through comics in a convenience store. But that's how the dream continues.

La La La at Rock Bottom, Misono Yunibasu, rating: ★★★★, runtime: 103min.

Amnesia is one of those medical conditions that might have been invented for the movies. For scriptwriters, it's a godsend — one bump on the hero's head and the story is rolling.

What the movies usually don't get right are the real-life consequences of a massive head trauma wiping out a large chunk of your mental hard drive: a crippling diminishment of self that, if permanent, is tragic.

Nobuhiro Yamashita's new film "La La La at Rock Bottom" gives an affecting spin to the amnesia theme, but one with more hard-driving rock music than heavy-going drama. One reference is Yamashita's 2005 film "Linda Linda Linda," which followed the fortunes of an all-girl amateur band to their big gig at a high school festival. Both their title tune, a catchy 1987 hit by The Blue Hearts, and Korean actress Bae Doona's energetic rendition of it in the film's climax, made "Linda Linda Linda" an international festival favorite.

"La La La At Rock Bottom" is also less of an art film than entertainment (the silly sounding English title is a giveaway), starring Subaru Shibutani of the Kansai-based boy band Kanjani Eight. But instead of a pop confection, the film is a sharp-edged character study set on society's margins, with a comic undertone that at times bubbles into slapstick farce and at other times disappears entirely. It's not hard to see where the film is going, but the emotional payoffs are earned rather than formulaically calculated.

The story begins with a live concert by a group of middle-aged rock/soul musicians (played by members of the real-life Osaka band Akainu) that is rudely interrupted by a skinny, beat-up-looking guy who stumbles onto the stage and grabs the microphone. What ensues is a surprisingly powerful a capella performance, followed by the mysterious singer collapsing like a felled tree. When he comes to, under the ministrations of the band's no-nonsense young manager, Kasumi (Fumi Nikaido), he has no memory of anything — including his name — save the lyrics to the song he had just sung.

Nonetheless, with Kasumi's approval and encouragement, he becomes the group's new lead singer, while acquiring the nickname "Pooch" and a new residence in the house of Kasumi's senile grandfather. But as his past starts to invade his present, we see that Pooch, for all his singing talent, is an unquiet soul — "I might be dangerous," he tells Kasumi.

She discovers just how dangerous when she begins to investigate his identity — and Pooch suddenly recovers his memory. Kasumi finds herself with more on her hands than an unreliable lead singer, while Pooch turns out to be as skilled with his fists as his vocal chords. But how can he fight his way back into what's left of his family, and out of the underworld that nearly claimed his life and mind?

Twenty-year-old Nikaido has earned prizes for her work in such films as "My Man" and "Au Revoir l'Ete." As Kasumi she is all-business, with a furrowed-brow earnestness that comically contrasts with her laid-back ojisan (middle-aged guy) bandmates. But she also radiates an aching emptiness that echoes Pooch's own, if manifested in quite different ways.

Box-office logic calls for the budding of romance between Kasumi and Pooch, but Yamashita is after something harder: a drama about the fraught process of recovering human connection and achieving redemption following traumas that destroy human trust.

He is greatly aided by Shibutani's coiled performance as Pooch, free of pop-idol grandstanding and full of a lived authenticity. He makes the usual gangster movie hero, however swaggeringly cool, look completely fake. And Shibutani can rock, with or without the ojisan backup.

Happy Hour, Happi Awa, rating: ★★★⯪, runtime: 317 min.

'Japanese movies are too long' is a comment I've heard many times over the years. In fact, one Asian film reviewer of my acquaintance writes "(J-film title) could be cut by (number of min.)" so often that he's probably made it into a keyboard shortcut.

Japanese directors have also turned in some excellent long films, however, from Akira Kurosawa's "Seven Samurai" (207 min.) to Sion Sono's "Love Exposure" (237 min.). Even so, I quailed when I saw the running time of "Happy Hour," Ryusuke Hamaguchi's female friendship drama: 317 minutes. That is a long sit by any standard.

But its four female leads, unknowns all, received a collective best actress prize at this year's Locarno International Film Festival, while the script by Hamaguchi and his two co-writers was given a special mention. Deservedly so: "Happy Hour" engages rather than exhausts with its length and complexity.

Despite such standard J-drama tropes as convenient coincidences and stormy exits, the film's story develops organically from its core relationships, not its plot devices. And its four principals grapple realistically with universal questions: How can I love? Who can I trust? When should I leave?

Cast from participants in acting workshops Hamaguchi taught while an artist in residence at Design and Creative Center Kobe (KIITO), the actors, for all their amateurish moments, convey emotional honesty, as though they are living their lines, not just delivering them.

The four friends at the story's center are Akari (Sachie Tanaka), a hardworking nurse who is currently unattached; Fumi (Maiko Mihara), a stressed PR rep married to a sober-sided book editor; Sakurako (Hazuki Kikuchi), a harried housewife with a sullen teenage son, controlling husband and opinionated mother-in-law: and Jun (Rira Kawamura), a self-described "ex-housewife" in the process of divorcing her straight-arrow scientist husband.

One obvious parallel is the HBO hit "Sex and the City," but the resemblance between the American show's quartet of high-living Manhattanites and the film's hard-pressed foursome does not extend much further beyond their enjoyment of each other's company.

Even that is threatened when Akari and Fumi realize that Jun was keeping her divorce a secret between her and Sakurako, a friend since their school days. "If you lie, we can't be friends," Akari tells Sakurako bluntly. Meanwhile, Jun's husband, Yohei, refuses to give her up, even after she tells the divorce court judge that their nearly silent marriage was killing her spirit. Then, with no explanation, Jun disappears.

Other complications arise, most having to do with issues of trust and communication between friends, spouses and family members — issues that fester under the surface of everyday banalities and lies but eventually erupt with consequences unforeseeable.

Hamaguchi, who developed the script in collaboration with his actors and shot the film over a period of eight months, tells this story with a seemingly formless naturalism, while artfully structuring it with simple, powerful metaphors and motifs.

One appears early on at a communications workshop attended by the four friends and taught by a charismatic, if manipulative, artist. He instructs the participants to press an ear against a partner's solar plexus to feel the other person's existential reality.

The ultimate purpose is to break through the isolation of modern life and create bonds beyond social roles and rules. To their credit, the women struggle to keep those bonds alive, even as they are being tested to the limit. That's what friends are for, isn't it?

Obon Brothers, Obon no Ototo, rating: ★★★⯪, runtime: 107min.

"Life imitates art far more than art imitates life," quipped Oscar Wilde, but in the film world mining one's own life for the sake of art — or rather, a script — is an ancient and hallowed practice. Even if the resulting film has only a tenuous relationship with the filmmaker's actual biography.

Director Akira Osaki's bittersweet black-and-white comedy "Obon Brothers" certainly sounds a lot like his own story. The film is about a failing director's struggles to make a new movie while dealing with his cranky older brother and his estranged wife's demand for a divorce.

The film's real and fictional director both hail from Gunma Prefecture, have one previous film to their credit — Osaki's is the 2006 drama "The Catch Man" — and are old friends with the scriptwriter for their new project (in Osaki's case, Shin Adachi).

Other parallels exist, but the point, I think, is obvious: "Obon Brothers" is a darkly humorous alternative take on Osaki's own life and career.

Or is it? His star, Kiyohiko Shibukawa, has been a distinctive presence in dozens of films since his feature debut in Toshiaki Toyoda's 1998 crime drama "Pornostar." Shibukawa's chiseled looks, deep voice and lopsided grin make him instantly recognizable, and though he has played a range of roles, he usually projects the sort of honesty and naivete that makes his characters likable as individuals, even when they are unregenerate slackers. He is no Osaki clone.

Also, the film's woebegone director, Takashi (Shibukawa), faces a perfect storm of fiascoes unlike anything endured by the critically honored Osaki — though the latter may beg to differ. The film frames Takashi's various dilemmas and disasters as both dryly funny and piercingly real. It gets this difficult balance right, without teetering toward obvious caricature on one side or manufactured tears on the other.

When the story begins, Takashi is serving as live-in cook and caregiver to the recovering Wataru (Ken Mitsuishi), an irritable type who is itching for his sponging younger brother to move out. Meanwhile, Takashi's matter-of-fact wife (Makiko Watanabe) wants to make their two-month separation permanent, but is considerate enough to allow him to freely visit their young daughter, Wako. Adding to his woes, a veteran director (Yoji Tanaka) barely glances at a script Takashi has labored on for months with his writing partner and best bud Fujimura (pop singer and actor Koki Okada). Can't a guy catch a break?

Then the excitable Fujimura begs Takashi to join a double date his girlfriend has planned for her single pal Ryoko (Aoba Kawai). Takashi reluctantly agrees — and discovers that Ryoko is not only easy on the eyes, but also takes an unfeigned interest in his work and him. Takashi feels attracted to her as well, but by now certain lies have been told, including a biggie about his marital status.

Osaki and scriptwriter Adachi ignore the screwball comedy potential of this story in favor of slice-of-life realism that borders on the depressing but never plunges in. Also, despite the absurdity of some characters and situations, the film never descends into silliness. Instead, "Obon Brothers" has a spiritual undercurrent that begins as a gag (with Wataru comically peeved about a fortune he receives at a temple) but finally turns serious with an unexpected subtlety.

And the "Obon" in the title becomes more than a cryptic reference to o-Bon, the Japanese Buddhist festival of the dead. I won't say how; just that, after the credits rolled, I felt like throwing a coin in the collection box and praying for the dear departed and suffering humanity — and that Takashi's second masterpiece be green-lit.

2016

Ken and Kazu, Ken to Kazu, rating: ★★★☆, runtime: 96 min.

Most films about the yakuza depict its members as fully formed and distinctly different from the general run of humanity, somewhat like action figures just out of the box. The reality, as Hiroshi Shoji's "Ken and Kazu" shows us with a gritty directness and power, is more quotidian. For Shoji's title heroes, crime is less a way of proving their outlaw manliness than a risky means to an uncertain monetary end as they face a bleak future.

Based on Shoji's own script, "Ken and Kazu" rejects the gangster genre's macho romanticism, while depicting its principals in the round, their dysfunctional families included. In this it resembles "Ryuji," Shoji Kaneko's 1983 indie classic about an ex-con (Kaneko) trying to go straight with his much-put-upon wife's support, a film that was scripted and shot after the director/star apprenticed with an actual gang.

Named Best Picture in the Japanese Cinema Splash section of last year's Tokyo International Film Festival, "Ken and Kazu" reflects a different era to "Ryuji." The lines that once separated the gangs from straight society have since become blurred or erased. In "Ken and Kazu," one guy blurring the line is Ken (Shinsuke Kato), who works at a failing auto repair shop in the Tokyo suburb of Ichikawa.

As the story begins he is also dealing meth with Kazu (Katsuya Maiguma), a punkish pal further down the road to criminality, and Teru (Kisetsu Fujiwara), a dangerously naive young shop hand. Their boss is Todo (Haruki Takano), a shifty senpai (senior) from Ken and Kazu's schooldays, whose enforcer is Tagami (Daisuke Ehara), a silent, watchful yakuza.

Ken helps Kazu beat up rival dealers trying to encroach on their turf, but hesitates when his friend suggests going into business behind Todo's back. The reason: He plans to start a new life with his pregnant girlfriend, Saki (Shuna Iijima), and doesn't want to first end up jailed or dead.

But Kazu needs a big score to rid himself of his dementia-afflicted mother, since permanent care doesn't come cheap. This may seem an unfilial attitude, but as we see in flashbacks, mom brutally abused him as a boy and he can now barely restrain himself from throttling her.

The stage is thus set for melodrama, gangster-movie division, but Shoji instead opts for tight shots and rapid-fire edits that ramp up the tension, while his pointed dialogue brings even formulaic scenes electrically alive. Among exceptions are Ken's interludes with Saki, who expresses her entirely justified discontent in whines instead of roars. The generic action-movie music, an unfortunate distraction throughout the film, also doesn't help.

The film's true focus, though, is on Ken and Kazu's volatile relationship, and here, it is on firmer ground. Though long-time friends, the two are at cross purposes and have quite different personalities. As played by talented character actor Kato, Ken has a dreamy, distracted air (Kazu kiddingly calls him a "dead fish") but can flare into two-fisted violence when the need arises.

As Kazu, Maiguma nails the punk persona perfectly, from the challenging sneer to the rangy physique that looks sculpted from regular street-fighting, not hours in the gym. This type is common enough in action movies, but Maiguma gives us glimpses of the wounded kid within that humanizes the character, if not making him less explosive.

The ending is something of a foregone conclusion, but maybe I've just seen too many films about buddies in deadly peril with everything at stake. And no, I'm not talking about high-body-count Hollywood-style carnage. I hope that's not a spoiler for you. If it is, you've probably never been to Ichikawa.

Creepy, Kuripi, rating: ★★★☆, runtime: 130min.

The title of "Creepy," the new shocker by horror maestro Kiyoshi Kurosawa, sounds like a self-parody. It's like titling a new Adam Sandler comedy "Goofy" (or if you're not feeling charitable, "Crappy"). But "Creepy," which premiered at this year's Berlin Film Festival, is also the title of the Yutaka Maekawa novel on which it's based. And despite his well-deserved reputation for raising goose pimples, Kurosawa has also made well-received straight dramas, including the 2008 "Tokyo Sonata," a film about family disintegration that won the Cannes Un Certain Regard section Jury Prize. That said, "Tokyo Sonata" also had surreal passages that were — creepy, if you will. So does this new film, though it begins as a familiar drama about a cop in crisis.

Takakura (Hidetoshi Nishijima), a detective trained in criminal psychology, resigns from the force after his attempt to talk a dangerous suspect into surrendering goes disastrously wrong. He becomes a university lecturer and, with the aid of his understanding wife, Yasuko (Yuko Takeuchi), starts to get his life back on track. But once a cop, always a cop. When a former colleague (Masahiro Higashide), comes to him with a six-year-old case of a missing family, Takakura can't help but investigate, which leads him to the left-behind daughter Saki (Haruna Kawaguchi), then a child, now a still-traumatized young woman.

Meanwhile, Yasuko is becoming uncomfortably well-acquainted with their odd next-door neighbor Nishino (Teruyuki Kagawa), who swings unpredictably between meek obsequiousness and menacing verbal aggression. What, Takakura wonders, is the problem with this guy, besides his troubled teenage daughter and depressed, never-seen wife?

Working from Chihiro Ikeda's script, Kurosawa takes his sweet time tying these story strands together, until the film starts to feel more like atmospherics than action. But what atmospherics! As he did in his 1997 international breakthrough "The Cure" ("Kua") and many films since, Kurosawa uses everyday phenomena — a breeze through untended bushes, sunlight flickering into a mildewed room — to stir feelings of unease and dread. Also, as an over-wrought Takakura interrogates an uncooperative Saki at his college, Kurosawa's camera shows students silently milling about in the background, behind the blinds of large windows. The effect is at once natural (the students are doing nothing out of the ordinary) and uncanny (their silence and distance and the filtered whitish light make them seem ghostly). This and other scenes unfolding in somehow otherworldly settings intensify the queasy sense that something wrong is going on.

How wrong becomes shockingly clear when Takakura learns the truth about the volatile Nishino and, to put it as vaguely as possible, everything else that he has been taking for granted. Similar transitions to bizarre alternative states have featured in other Kurosawa films, such as in the hero's dream-like near-death experience in "Tokyo Sonata." But in "Creepy," every pretense of normality falls away in the climatic scenes, including the delicate dance of dealing with a weird neighbor. Even the filtered light disappears and we are in the clammy gloom of Horror World.

As Nishino, Kagawa becomes the film's ultimate fright effect with no CGI assists whatsoever. Instead he creates a nuanced portrayal of a borderline case, whose mask of sanity is an ill-fitting cover for a cold psychotic rage that finally consumes him. But Nishino is effective in his own twisted way. Where nice-guy Takakura earnestly plods and desperately pushes, Nishino cuts straight to the quick, bending the weak and defenseless mercilessly to his will. Yes, he goes sailing over the top in the process, but so do the worst nightmares.

Keep telling yourself none of it could really happen, ever. It's too creepy to think about otherwise.

Someone's Xylophone, Dareka no Mokkin, rating: ★★★☆, runtime: 112 min.

Yoichi Higashi has made everything from commercial hits to festival favorites in his five-plus decades as a director, while taking up politically sensitive subjects and unpopular issues. His 1992 smash "The Bridge with No River" ("Hashi no Nai Kawa") depicted the raw prejudice endured by burakumin outcasts in early 20th-century rural Japan. Also, in 2009 he joined the "barrier free" movement, dubbing and subtitling his films for the hearing-impaired, an audience the industry at the time virtually ignored.

Abroad, however, Higashi's profile has never been as high as contemporaries Koji Wakamatsu and Nagisa Oshima who also courted controversy, if with arguably more talent for self-promotion. In Japan he has become known for drawing career-peak performances from his leading ladies, including Kaori Momoi as a drifting college student in "No More Easy Life" (1979) and now, veteran Takako Tokiwa, the queen of TV "trendy dramas" in the 1990s, who has matured into an accomplished, in-demand film actress.

In Higashi's new drama "Someone's Xylophone," Tokiwa plays Sayoko, a seemingly happy middle-aged housewife in a Tokyo suburb, who is blessed with a kindly salaryman husband (Masanobu Katsumura) and a sweet-natured teenage daughter (Mikoto Kimura) — two rarities in the local family drama genre.

Soon after moving to a new neighborhood, Sayoko ventures into a nearby hair salon and has her hair done by the young, curly-headed Kaito (Sosuke Ikematsu), who has a sensitive touch and an understanding professional manner. Suddenly she finds herself in the grip of a hopeless infatuation, emailing Kaito again and again, with ever more personal revelations. This can only end badly.

Scripted by Higashi based on a 2011 novel by Areno Inoue, the film does not turn into the expected story of a May-September affair. Instead, a perplexed Kaito fends off Sayoko's advances while telling all to his amused boss and not-so-amused girlfriend, Yui (Aimi Satsukawa). Sayoko, however, escalates her campaign to insinuate herself into Kaito's life, finally summoning up the courage to push his doorbell.

Instead of an essay on illicit Eros, "Someone's Xylophone" becomes a probing character study of a woman who refuses to fall into any of the expected categories, from deluded stalker to desperate housewife. Her discontent with her life is not hard to see, beginning with her stoic blankness at her husband's caresses, but her true motivations remain unknown. And that keeps the film interesting, since Tokiwa's performance radiates from a core of conflicting emotions that have an interior logic, if not always a clear explanation. Some of the dialogue verges on the overly explicit, but as the action moves back and forth between the real and surreal, with little to divide the two, some of it also pierces, like fragments of a dream that disturb the waking mind.

If Tokiwa is the film's turbulent, mysterious center, Ikematsu, as Kaito, grounds it in the normal and actual. Often cast as sexy, dangerous types, Ikematsu endows Kaito with a libido, temper and sense of humor (none of which he ever displays to his customers). At the same time, Kaito immediately decides that Sayako's cellphone messages (which include a photo of her new mattress) are over the line in a way he doesn't want to follow — or exploit.

There is nothing moralistic in his reaction — or the movie as a whole. Its heroine is neither bad nor mad, but for once, in a life otherwise unexceptional, she feels compelled to follow her heart, however wayward she looks to others. Can we blame her? Higashi certainly doesn't. Or as William Blake once put it, "Sooner strangle an infant in its cradle than nurse unacted desires."

The Mohican Comes Home, Mohikan Kokyo ni Kaeru, rating: ★★★⯪, runtime: 124 min.

Millions of Japanese have come from the countryside to find their fortunes in Tokyo, with most arriving in the postwar boom when jobs were everywhere and the future looked bright. But many, like the punk rocker hero of Shuichi Okita's offbeat, warm-hearted family comedy "The Mohican Comes Home," ended up making a U-turn, however permanent or temporary. This has been a theme of Japanese films for decades, as indicated by the title's reference to the 1951 Keisuke Kinoshita classic "Carmen Comes Home."

The film, based on Okita's original script, has elements in common with these older films, but also with the present-day actualities of rural escapees' lives. The Mohican-sporting hero, Eikichi (Ryuhei Matsuda), who has been trying to make it as a musician in Tokyo for seven years, ends up on a boat headed back to his beautiful home island in the Seto Inland Sea, with his pregnant girlfriend Yuka (Atsuko Maeda) in tow. One reason for his return is that his bandmates are tired of the scuffling musician's life and ready to move on to a more stable existence, health insurance included.

On arrival, Eikichi gets less than a warm welcome from his irascible father (Akira Emoto), who tells him to cut his hair and get a job — demands that Eikichi rejects. Then Dad is diagnosed with terminal cancer and Eikichi, as the oldest son, feels obliged to take over the family liquor store.

Okita, who also depicted a rocky father-son relationship in his 2012 comedy "The Woodsman and the Rain," rejects standard genre tropes, from sentimentalism on. The film views inoperable lung cancer as both comic and tragic, and presents its principal characters, the afflicted father included, as both ridiculous and real.

Also, though a typical Japanese-movie geezer in being good-hearted under his prickly surface, Dad is a rocker himself. Since seeing real-life 1970s pop star Eikichi Yazawa at a Tokyo Budokan concert he has been a super-fan, teaching generations of local junior high brass-band members a Yazawa hit. The latest iteration of the band dutifully slogs through it but secretly thinks it dreadfully old-fashioned. Cue mildly amusing gags about one clueless baby boomer.

Everyone — from Eikichi's devoted Hiroshima Carps fan mom (Masako Motai) to his bubbly bride-to-be — is a bit of an oddball, but no one is a simple cartoon. And though the film takes a serious turn once Dad's illness is discovered, it never loses its comic edge.

Despite his slacker ways, Eikichi is a gentle-spirited soul who wants to do right by his cantankerous father, while stubbornly refusing to give up his dreams. The apple, we see in Matsuda's effortlessly grounded performance, does not fall far from the rebellious parental tree.

As Dad, veteran Akira Emoto does his by-now familiar Crazy Old Man turn — cackling, growling and, in one memorable scene, chasing Eikichi around the family table. There is a rationale for this high-volume performance, but explaining it would mean giving away the film's rousing ending.

Okita is both a miniaturist, carefully shaping the look and mood of every scene, and a storytelling maximalist, taking on big themes with compassion and insight. In "Mohican Comes Home" he tackles two of the biggest themes of all — birth and death — and shows they are not so far apart after all. To quote Bob Dylan, with apologies to Yazawa, "He not busy being born is busy dying."

Your Name., Kimi no Na wa, rating: ★★★★, runtime: 105 min.

Japanese animators have good reason to hate the label "new Miyazaki," meaning successor to animation genius Hayao Miyazaki. First, it saddles them with fan expectations that their films will resemble the master's. Second, their box-office figures are compared to Miyazaki's, which soared to stratospheric heights that few Japanese films, animated or not, have ever approached.

So here's a shout-out to Makoto Shinkai, the most prominent of the "new Miyazakis," whose latest feature "Your Name." is distributed by Toho, the same company that handled all of Miyazaki's biggest hits. Animated with a blend of gorgeous, realistic detail and emotionally grounded fantasy that make comparisons with Miyazaki not absurd, Shinkai's films to date, including his 2007 break-through "5 Centimeters per Second," display a sensibility more romantic than Miyazaki's, with stories about young lovers instead of the maestro's plucky young heroines on a quest.

"Your Name," whose title and story echo a famous postwar radio drama and film trilogy (1953-54) about star-crossed lovers, is the latest in this line. Based on Shinkai's original script, the film focuses on two teenagers: Mitsuha (voiced by Mone Kamishiraishi), a girl living unhappily in the countryside, and Taki (Ryunosuke Kamiki), a Tokyo high school student who is something of an architecture buff.

To the surprise of no one who has ever seen a Japanese *seishun eiga* (youth drama), these two are fated to connect, but the film's way of accomplishing this is unusual, to say the least: They seem to switch bodies in their dreams.

Shinkai's movie also delivers — actually, over-delivers — the comedy of adolescent embarrassment and awkwardness, with Mitsuha, transformed into Taki, finding herself using the feminine "*watashi*" ("I") to his pals' surprise and fumbling for the gender-appropriate "*ore*." These and other gags are cute enough, but so are similar ones in dozens of local TV sitcoms.

The film, however, also regards its gender-crossing pair with a tender seriousness that is uniquely Shinkai's, as they struggle with their odd situations and unfamiliar yearnings. They leave each other notes and even quarrel. Of course, once things reach this stage, we know that love will bloom. But at the heart of the story's mystery is a once-in-a-thousand year comet that appeared in the skies a month before the story begins. Did it portend doom for the budding relationship of our central pair?

The plot takes many twists but stays focused on the respective fates of Taki and Mitsuha. Supporting characters, such as Miki (Masami Nagasawa), Taki's sexy, worldly wise senior at the coffee shop where he works part-time, and Mitsuha's old-school grandmother (Etsuko Ishihara) and no-nonsense kid sister (Kanon Tani), serve primarily to highlight the two principals' personalities and dilemmas (including the dilemma posed by Taki's awkward crush on Miki).

But as climax tops dramatic climax, with the heavens erupting in dazzling displays of color and light, "Your Name." becomes like the dream almost everyone has from time to time, of the lover too perfect, the encounter too short and the ending too abrupt, with bliss dissolving into thin air as waking life takes hold. Yet something remains — a memory, however faint, of paradise. "Your Name." gets that something, a blend of aching pathos and glimmer of unearthly beauty, memorably right. Miyazaki would not have made this film, but Makoto Shinkai did. Just maybe he will lose the "new Miyazaki" tag forever.

Himeanole, Himeanoru, rating: ★★★★, runtime: 99min.

The moral universe of most commercial films is simple: The good guys prevail, the bad guys are punished — and we are seldom in doubt as to who is who. But what if the bad guys deserve sympathy, even the ones who commit horrific crimes? Is that, in a movie world that prefers black and white to gray, even possible?

Keisuke Yoshida unhesitatingly answers "yes" in his new film "Himeanole." This is uncommon indeed in Hollywood, where characters who cross over to the dark side are typically targeted for fatal retribution, not commiseration. But Yoshida, who wrote the script based on Minoru Furuya's alternative manga of the same title, questions whether "choice" exists when the strong crush the weak — and the weak go homicidally mad.

"Himeanole" begins as a smart observational comedy about two loners on society's fringes, similar to Yoshida's criminally under-appreciated 2013 "The Workhorse and the Big Mouth." One is Okada (Gaku Hamada), a wishy-washy, if decent and sensitive, guy working as a building cleaner. The other is his pudgy, wild-haired colleague Ando (Tsuyoshi Muro), who speaks robotically but honestly. He is, he tells Okada, in love with Yuka (Aimi Satsukawa), a cute server at a nearby coffee shop, but has yet to breathe a word of his feelings to her. When Okada goes with Ando to see Yuka for himself, he tells his co-worker upfront that "She's too young and pretty for you." Ando is not to be deterred and, with Okada's reluctant assistance, makes Yuka's acquaintance. But a double date with Yuka and her acid-tongued friend goes sour when the latter promptly sizes up Okada and Ando as losers.

So far, so funny, as scene after crisply directed scene unfolds with a winning combination of warmth and bite. But Ando becomes convinced that a brooding, blonde-haired coffee-shop patron is stalking Yuka. When Okada recognizes him as Morita (J-pop mega-group V-6 member Go Morita), a former high school classmate, at Ando's urging, he timidly approaches him.

Here is where the film makes a sharp, if well-prepared, turn from light comedy to dark psychodrama. Gaunt-faced and scarily intense, Morita is revealed as not just a rival for Yuka's affections but a deranged serial killer. And Okada, who was once Morita's only friend, witnessed the merciless bullying that pushed him over the edge.

Some viewers may feel upset or betrayed by this abrupt turn of events — and I can't entirely blame them, though its aim is not shock. Instead it develops organically, if unconventionally, from the film's central theme: Human beings are capable of both good and evil, and crossing the line from the former to the latter can be more a matter of fate than choice.

This is not to say that Morita is simply to be pitied. His crimes are appalling — and the film thoroughly deserves its R-15 rating for its graphic portrayals of his sexual and homicidal violence. Go Morita also deserves praise for breaking so decisively — and shockingly — with his one-time boy-band singer image. But the film also shows another, more human side to Morita's character — which makes the inhuman treatment he was subjected to at the hands of his classmates all the more unforgivable. In crushing the weak, they created a monster.

And Okada's sin? Silence, in the name of survival. But, as the always excellent Hamada shows in another finely layered performance, he is not entirely contemptible. Instead, Okada finds love and, within himself, unexpected courage and compassion.

That doesn't make him a saint — but, for most of us, it's good enough.

After the Storm, Umi yori no Mada Fukaku, rating: ★★★★, runtime: 117minmin.

Hirokazu Koreeda has a reputation abroad as the one director of his generation carrying on the humanist tradition of Japanese cinema's 1950s and '60s Golden Age. This is not totally off the mark

— he often returns to that favorite Golden Age theme, family dissolution, but his take on it is quite different from that theme's most famous exponent, Yasujiro Ozu.

As Koreeda himself has often said in interviews, his true Golden Age inspiration is Mikio Naruse. Once dismissively labeled a "poor man's Ozu," Naruse has since been recognized as a master with a darker, more unsparing vision of contemporary Japanese society. Where Ozu's characters of the era were typically middle-class, Naruse's were often several rungs down the status and income ladder, with money a cause of worry, discord and rupture.

Ryota (Hiroshi Abe), the hero of Koreeda's new film "After the Storm," is a writer who won a literary prize 15 years ago but has since produced nothing. He has also fallen behind on child-support payments to ex-wife Kyoko (Yoko Maki), who is threatening to withdraw access to their 11-year-old son, Shingo (Taiyo Yoshizawa). Ryota works as a private detective, spying on people having affairs in the name of "research," but his gambling habit keeps him perpetually broke.

To buy Shingo a baseball glove, he extorts hush money from an investigative subject/victim, as an understanding junior colleague (Sosuke Ikematsu) looks on, but he then loses it all at the bike track. The next day, he and his fellow gumshoe stake out Kyoko and her new salaryman boyfriend, and discover that the BF has already bought the boy a glove. Ryota is outraged at the interloper's impudence, and silent about his own responsibility for this state of affairs.

When Shingo appears for his monthly visit, Ryota takes him to see his outspoken elderly mother (Kirin Kiki) in the danchi (housing complex) where she is living alone after the recent death of Ryota's father. His objective: to find the hiding place of Mom's bank book.

This may sound like black comedy, and Koreeda, who also wrote the script, extracts laughs at Ryota's expense. But more than "I Wish," Koreeda's 2011 comedy about two kids trying to bring their divorced parents back together, "After the Storm" is closer in tone and theme to "Still Walking," his 2008 masterpiece about a family torn apart by tragedy but still clinging to appearances, which also starred Abe and Kiki.

Shooting the film in the same Tokyo danchi where he once lived, Koreeda intersperses a wealth of revealing detail, from the shimmering green beauty of the building's grounds after a typhoon (an image that sparked him to make the film) to the cups of frozen Calpis made by Mom, so reminiscent of an earlier, thriftier Japan. But Naruse-like, Koreeda also refuses the pleasures of nostalgia, exposing the poverty and disorder of Ryota's life with a relentless eye.

Is Ryota a figure of pathos — or simply pathetic? As Ryota, Kyoko and Shingo wait out a raging typhoon in the danchi, the film delivers an answer that rings true to anyone who has had moments of close communion with loved ones (or once-loved-ones), free from the background noise of a troubled past. That answer, however, is long in coming and, in the meantime, we have to listen to Ryota's face-saving excuses and self-justifications, which begin to wear as we wait for the expected self-awakening.

Abe's performance is not the problem, save for the sneer that keeps reflexively flitting across his face. In fact, his bedrock seriousness, which under Koreeda's direction never shades to woodenness, gives substance to Ryota's never-healing, if mainly self-inflicted, wounds.

He reminds us that failure, be it as a writer, husband, father or son, hurts even as you deny it — or deserve it. And that when you're having a bad day at the track, it's better to walk away than double down.

Scoop!, rating: ★★★★, runtime: 120 min.

Japanese weekly scandal magazines are pond scum, are they not? Dishing up grainy paparazzi photos of the famous and powerful, accompanied by wink-wink stories about improprieties and crimes — alleged or exposed — they appeal to the lowest common denominator. Wouldn't it be wonderful if they all vanished from the face of the Earth?

But as Hitoshi One shows in "Scoop!," his delightfully scabrous comedy about one such fictional rag, the weeklies can expose truths that their hypocritical subjects — presenting a pure, upright public image that their low-down private words and actions belie — would do anything to hide. These are truths the mainstream media, anxious to avoid offending sources and rocking the institutional boat, too often suppress or ignore.

This is One's third feature, and third set in the media industry, following "Love Strikes!" (2011) and "Bakuman" (2015). In all three films, he uses scuffling heroes as sources of laughs, but never treats them as two-dimensional. Instead, he reveals their flaws for maximum comic and dramatic effect, sometimes in the same perfectly crafted scene.

Based on a 1985 made-for-TV movie by Masato Harada — well-remembered by One, if forgotten by nearly everyone else — "Scoop!" focuses on Shizuka Miyakonojo (Masaharu Fukuyama). Once an up-and-coming news photographer Shizuka has, in middle age, sunk to the paparazzi depths. He works for "Scoop!," a publication whose bread and butter are photos of celebs in flagrante delicto and busty gravure idols (pin-up girls). To help him supply the former, hard-nosed editor Sadako Yokogawa (Yo Yoshida) saddles him with Nobi Namekawa (Fumi Nikaido), a naive new hire.

Unsurprisingly, Shizuka and Nobi are an oil-and-water combo, with the tender-minded Nobi recoiling from her slovenly, profane senior, whose behavior (like that of other male employees of "Scoop!") would have him facing sexual harassment charges at a more enlightened company. But as Shizuka tracks his quarry with the aid of a dissolute tipster pal (Lily Franky), Nobi finds herself, against all her better instincts, enjoying the chase and bagging the game. Even more inexplicably, she starts to feel attracted to this debauched (if still good-looking) guy whose journalistic ideals seemingly died with the last millennium.

A pop star and actor who is a prime paparazzi target himself, Fukuyama is all but unrecognizable as Shizuka, which is to the film's advantage. As Nobi, Nikaido initially plays Shizuka's comic foil in everything from her lip-curling disgust at his latest outrage to her frantic escapes from his infuriated victims. I knew that Nikaido could be funny (see her as a spoiled gangster's daughter in Sion Sono's 2013 "Why Don't You Play in Hell" for proof), but not this funny, throwing herself into gags with a flawlessly executed abandon.

As the film shifts into a more serious groove, with Nobi and Shizuka facing stiffer tests of their professional resolve and personal values, their camaraderie, we see, is built on more than jokes. The surprise climax, for which One has laid the groundwork with ingenuity and precision, hits harder than expected.

One's insistence on realism, from Shizuka's professional tricks to the casting of actual weekly mag staffers in bit roles, is one reason for this. Another is his pairing of Fukuyama and Nikaido, whose comic chemistry stirred up memories of Cary Grant and Rosalind Russell quarreling in "His Girl Friday" (1940). "Scoop!" is the most entertaining film I've seen all year — and yes, you can quote me.

The Long Excuse, Nagai Iiwake, rating: ★★★⯪, runtime: 124 min.

Miwa Nishikawa has made films about various sorts of scapegraces and con artists, but her latest, "The Long Excuse," may be her first about a certifiable jerk. There's no other way to describe Sachio Kinugasa (Masahiro Motoki), a middle-aged celebrity novelist who pontificates on television and lords it over his subordinates, while cheating on his loyal beautician wife Natsuko (Eri Fukatsu) with a pretty young editor (Haru Kuroki).

He is romping with his lover only minutes after Natsuko leaves on a ski trip with an old school friend (Keiko Horiuchi). Then when he gets word that both women have died in a bus accident, he plays the grieving husband at the funeral without shedding a tear (though media cameras capture a few fake sobs).

The film, however, is more about Sachio's redemption than any well-deserved punishment for his many sins, and is based on Nishikawa's eponymous novel. In the course of the story, Sachio tries to transform into a semblance of a human being, similar to the rocky personal journey of Bill Murray's obnoxious weatherman in the 1993 comedy "Groundhog Day."

The film targets the mainstream more directly than Nishikawa's previous work. One sign is her casting of two cute kids as the main agents of Sachio's salvation. But she has lost none of her unblinking insight into the murkier depths of her morally compromised characters, with Sachio being the latest, most contemptible example. As an exercise in feel-good movie-making, "The Long Excuse" is unusual in its telling of unvarnished truths, including the one that a decent gesture or two does not a personality change make.

But at least give Sachio credit for trying. After the funeral, he meets Yoichi (Pistol Takehara), the truck driver husband of his wife's deceased friend, and his children, Shinpei (Kenshin Fujita) and Akari (Tamaki Shiratori). Learning that Shinpei has given up studying for his junior high entrance exams to care for preschooler Akari — Yoichi's long hours on the road force him to be an absent father — Sachio offers to visit two days a week to help out.

Here the film enters a heart-warming sitcom phase. Sachio finds relief from his own guilt by playing a bumbling surrogate parent, with the kids calling him "Sachio." But his budding friendship with the children and their salt-of-the-earth dad does not resolve his unfinished business with his deceased wife.

Masahiro Motoki, who is best known abroad as the tyro funeral-director in the Oscar-winning "Departures" (2008), plays Sachio as a combination of writerly introversion and the kind of preening self-regard commonly associated with showbiz (and, as Motoki confesses in a program interview, reflects aspects of his true self). At a disastrous hanami (cherry-blossom-viewing party) with members of the literary world, Sachio even drunkenly belts out a pop tune with the sort of swagger that thrilled fans of Motoki's 1980s boy band Shibugakitai. That is, Sachio has many facets — and Motoki displays them with a conviction that seems to come from experience.

But as badly as Sachio may behave — and in some scenes he is so insulting as to practically beg for a punch to the face — he never completely forgets how to regret and, yes, love, however mixed with resentment and anger. Whether or not you believe he truly redeems himself — I was of two minds until the end — the film delivers a catharsis that is earned, not tacked onto an obligatory happy ending. It also teaches an object lesson about the mourning process: There's no one right way to do it — and better late than never.

In This Corner of the World, Kono Sekai no Katasumi ni, rating: ★★★☆, runtime: 130 min.

Going into "In This Corner of the World," Sunao Katabuchi's animation about a girl's coming of age in prewar Hiroshima and wartime Kure, I was vaguely expecting an anti-war film like Isao Takahata's classic "Grave of the Fireflies" (1988), with its heart-rending story of a boy struggling to care for his younger sister in the midst of wartime chaos.

Based on Hiroshima native Fumiyo Kono's manga of the same title, "In This Corner of the World" is quite different in attitude and approach. Similar to another film based on a Kono comic, Kiyoshi Sasabe's 2007 live-action "Yunagi Town, Sakura Country," "In This Corner of the World" tells the story of the Hiroshima atomic bombing indirectly, while anchoring it firmly in its period. But whereas the former film views the bombing largely from the perspective of today's younger generation, the latter looks ahead from the standpoint of a prewar Japan idyllically peaceful and a wartime Japan resolutely fighting for victory. Then American bombs rain down — and defeat looms.

Similar to Keisuke Kinoshita's wartime films, "In This Corner of the World" idealizes its characters, who are more self-sacrificing and mutually cooperative than many of their Westernized (and, some would say, corrupted) present-day descendants. But also like Kinoshita, who became one of Japanese cinema's postwar masters, Katabuchi is at heart a humanist, not a propagandist. His characters express guilt, bitterness and other morale-lowering, if true-to-life, feelings that would have a censor of the era reaching for his red pencil.

Our heroine is Suzu (voiced by the single-named Non), who begins the film as a girl living in Hiroshima. Surrounded by a loving extended family and friends, Suzu is a budding artist with a vivid imagination and dreamy temperament. But her time as an innocent girl, in movie terms, is short. Soon she is a teenager being married off to a quiet, kindly guy (Yoshimasa Hosoya) she barely knows and shipped off to the nearby port of Kure, where she is a total stranger. But as befitting a woman of her time, Suzu is soon laboring diligently away at household chores under the indulgent eye of her mother-in-law. She even tries to make nice to her husband's hyper-critical older sister, Keiko (Minori Omi), who seems to find fault with Suzu's very existence. And she makes friends with Keiko's young daughter, Harumi (Natsuki Inaba), who is a mostly sweet contrast to her mean mom.

This family drama unfolds against the ominous backdrop of Japan's war in Asia, which in December 1941 also becomes a war with America. The film depicts this period, from the imposing warships in Kure Harbor to the grinding privations, with a highly detailed realism. But when the agony and pain become too great for Suzu, her world dissolves into a vividly realized surreal nightmare, though she manages to struggle through. And she finally shows she has a temper. But when the biggest shock — the atomic blast at Hiroshima — comes, Suzu experiences it at a remove, not immediately understanding what has happened.

This sort of distancing can be found in many Japanese films, fiction and nonfiction, about the atomic bombings. "In This Corner of the World" uses it to make the horror unleashed on Hiroshima both more humanly comprehensible — and less overwhelming. Instead of being paralyzed by the death and devastation, we see that Suzu and the other good folks of Kure, who once worked so hard and selflessly for victory, will work just as hard and selflessly for recovery.

Takahata gave us young victims of a tragedy as ancient and universal as war itself; Katabuchi offers us inspirational role models for today's Japan.

At the Terrace, Terasu nite, rating: ★★★★, runtime: 95min.

"I know that many film fans have an allergy to films based on plays," writes Kenji Yamauchi on the website for his new film, "At the Terrace." "The never-changing setting and the long conversations bore them." "Boring," however, was not my thought as I watched this ensemble comedy, based on Yamauchi's own award-winning play, at the 29th Tokyo International Film Festival. Similar to "Her Father, My Lover," Yamauchi's 2015 film that also screened in TIFF's Japanese Cinema Splash section, "At the Terrace" wants to be witty and a touch scandalous.

Not often seen in Japanese films, this combination will be familiar to fans of Billy Wilder, Neil Simon and, going back even further than postwar-era Hollywood and Broadway, Oscar Wilde. But while "Her Father, My Lover" struggled under the weight of its own conceits, including the main one of a young woman determined to seduce her best pal's dad, "At the Terrace" remains light on its feet from beginning to end, despite moments when its clever artifices threaten to crumble, like a pastry sculpture left too long in the sun.

The story unfolds in one evening on the title terrace of a company director's luxurious house, whose interior is only glimpsed through the curtains. A party is well underway, with the mustachioed Soejima (Kenji Iwaya) and his buxom wife, Kazumi (Kei Ishibashi), serving as hosts. Their guests are a bearded designer named Saito (Ryuta Furuya) and his wife, Haruko (Kami Hiraiwa); a nervous young man named Tanoura (Hiroaki Morooka) employed by Toyota; and another Saitko (Takashi Okabe), a pasty-faced man recovering from major surgery. The Soejimas' lanky college-age son (Atsushi Hashimoto) is a late arrival.

The catalyst for the ensuing action is Kazumi, who catches Tanoura in the act of admiring Haruko and teases out the admission that he was captivated by her white arms. This inflames the jealousy of Kazumi, who looks quite the temptress in her low-cut gown and sexy-librarian glasses. She takes out her bile on the unsuspecting Haruko, who flares back and tells her husband she wants to leave. But the husband doesn't want to offend Soejima, an important client, so he urges Haruko to be patient. Meanwhile, Saito the Younger struggles to explain away his actions — and manages to offend Saito the Elder. And poor Saito the Younger, trying to be agreeable but failing to handle the stress, passes out flat on the terrace. Surely this soiree will soon come to a merciful (for the participants, at least) end?

In adapting his own play for the screen, Yamauchi finds reasons to keep the party going that expose lies and release inhibitions to funny and erotic effect. Revolving as it does around a battle for social supremacy between two women and explosive sexual secrets between two men, the story may seem old school (thus the Wilder, Simon and Wilde references), but it also depicts an (admittedly thin) slice of local reality with a clever comic spin.

Placed in an unfamiliar environment (i.e., a home party) without clearly defined social roles (e.g., company employee) and lubricated by alcohol, his characters flounder, flail about and otherwise behave in ways recognizably human — and Japanese.

The standout in the excellent cast (who also appeared in the play) is Kami Hiraiwa as Haruko. She turns what could have been a standard movie catfight into an unexpectedly inspiring battle for self-definition. And she performs an uninhibited dance that proves Haruko has more going for her than those white arms. But just as the face of Helen of Troy famously launched 1,000 ships, Hiraiwa's gloriously alabaster wings give flight (with a few dips) to an entertaining film.

Harmonium, Fuchi ni Tatsu, rating: ★★★★☆, runtime: 119 min.

The films of Koji Fukada have long wrapped ambitious themes in deceptively unassuming genre packages. His 2011 international breakout "Hospitalite" begins as a quirky comedy but becomes a perceptive drama of deceptions and secrets. Last year's "Sayonara" starts as an offbeat essay in apocalyptic sci-fi, centering on a terminally ill woman and her robot caregiver, but transitions into a stark examination of death and dissolution.

His latest film, "Harmonium," combines the above elements in a dark family drama that thoroughly deserves the usual adjectives heaped on the better suspense movies — "tense," "gripping," "fingernails-in-the-armrests" — while being insightful about such knotty, never-resolved issues as the vagaries of fate and the nature of evil. Winner of the Jury Prize in the Un Certain Regard section of this year's Cannes film festival, it proclaims the arrival of a major talent in Japanese films.

Scripted by Fukada, "Harmonium" is yet another of his ironic titles, referring as it does to not only the pump organ played by the young daughter of its central couple but also the harmony — or rather the lack of it — in the couple's marriage and lives.

Toshio (Fukada regular Kanji Furutachi) runs a thriving metal-working shop, and his wife Akie (Mariko Tsutsui) serves as his office manager. Their cute 10-year-old daughter, Hotaru (Momone Shinokawa), is reluctantly learning the harmonium — and it sounds it.

The apparently calm, middle-class surface of their lives hides fissures suggested early on — the church-going Akie and Hotaru say grace before meals, while Toshio stays stonily silent — that widen with the arrival of a mysterious visitor. Yasaka (Tadanobu Asano), a just-out-of-prison acquaintance of Toshio's, shows up out of the blue and is soon working in the shop and sitting at the dinner table.

Stiff in manner, polite in language and dressed in dark trousers and a white shirt buttoned at the throat, Yasaka is a queasy combination of the dorky and the menacing. But he tries to ingratiate himself with the suspicious Akie and the shy Hotaru, helping around the house and teaching the girl a new tune on the harmonium. When he makes a stilted, if sincere, confession about his past to Akie and expresses an interest in her church, she begins to see both a tortured soul to save and an attractive man to ... well, do what Toshio no longer does (if he ever did). But Akie also feels a guilt that she cannot shake.

That is as far as I'm taking the plot summary, since the film's story unfolds in ways that surprise, with Fukada's camera tailing his characters as they hesitatingly walk or grimly stride toward whatever lies ahead, with a feeling of heart-in-the-throat suspense.

Unlike the many family dramas here that color even their ostensible bad guys in shades of gray, "Harmonium" goes straight to the heart of evil, which is stronger than Akie's uncertain version of

Christian love. At the same time, the film is no simplistic morality tale. Instead it shows how our crimes and misdemeanors can live on, in forms that forever damage the innocent and brand the perpetrator.

As Yasaka, Asano is working in a familiar groove — he's been playing versions of this unknowable, volatile character for decades by now — but with an undimmed intensity and ferocity. Veteran Tsutsui plays Akie as less contemptibly weak than dangerously vulnerable — she half-understands her danger and half-invites it. As Toshio, Furutachi takes a familiar role — the emotionally distant Japanese male — to unexpected heights in the film's second half, with a power that shocks as much as Asano's by-now patented explosions.

Cannes jurors are not always known for anointing the worthy, but this time, they got it right.

2017

Hamon: Yakuza Boogie, Hamon: Futari no Yakubyogami, rating: ★★★★, runtime: 120 min.

Over the years, acquaintances of mine have boasted of their brushes with local gangsters. But few, I would wager, have become pals with one. Yakuza and katagi (straight citizens) tend to move in separate circles, with the former often viewing the latter as sheep to be fleeced or chickens to be plucked. But in Shotaro Kobayashi's brilliant buddy comedy "Hamon: Yakuza Boogie," the slacker hero (Yu Yokoyama) becomes the unwilling, constantly whining side-kick to a hard-core gangster (Kuranosuke Sasaki) who regards him as unreliable and generally contemptible.

Based on the fifth novel in a best-selling series by Hiroyuki Kurokawa about this unlikely pair, the film is not as contrived as it sounds. The slacker, Ninomiya, works as a "construction consultant" who hires gangsters to resolve (if that is the correct word) labor disputes, while the gangster, Kuwahara, is one of his "contractors," though a new anti-gang law, Ninomiya complains, has reduced his business to nearly nothing.

This pair end up together in a meeting with an elderly, oleaginous film producer, Koshimizu (Isao Hashizume), who wants to pick their brains for an upcoming film set in the gang world. Ninomiya is excited by the idea, as well as by Koshimizu's curvy daughter Reimi (Manami Hashimoto), while Kuwahara is rightly suspicious. To cut a long and financially complicated story short, Koshimizu runs off with the money he has swindled from investors for his nonexistent movie, including that of Kuwahara's urbane boss Shimada (Jun Kunimura). Kuwahara journeys to the boonies of Ibaraki, where he has heard Koshimizu is hiding, with Ninomiya in tow.

There they find their quarry, but also two unruly punks from a bigger, more powerful gang — the Takizawas, who are also looking for recover funds from the producer. Kuwahara's lesson in the finer points of etiquette for this pair leads to not only busted heads but also a major beef with their Takizawa bosses. Meanwhile, Koshimizu and Reimi fly the coop to Macau.

The many ensuing twists elicit more laughs than shocks, though Kobayashi, who also directed a 2015 Wowow drama based on Kurokawa's fiction, stages the gangster dust-ups with wince-inducing stunts, as well as laugh-out-loud gags delivered in flavorsome Osaka dialect.

The film is grounded in realism about not only gang life but also human nature, including its stubborn tendency to surprise. The cowardly, lazy Ninomiya would seem to be useless to a two-fisted type like Kuwahara — until he proves himself useful. Meanwhile, as his no-nonsense cousin Yuki (Keiko Kitagawa) reminds him, he is wasting his time and risking his neck messing with Kuwahara and his yakuza associates. But Ninomiya has his reasons — from family ties to a sneaking admiration for Kuwahara's macho charisma and old-school gangster ethos.

There are, however, no heart-warming revelations or inspiring personal arcs. Kuwahara and Ninomiya face various tests, including the hamon (exile) of the title, but they remain essentially the same, with Ninomiya especially illustrating the age-old maxim "You can't cure stupid."

As Ninomiya, Yokoyama is the latest pop idol (he is a member of the boy band Kanjani Eight) to gamely play a role far removed from idol-dom. (Fellow Johnny's agency talent Go Morita ventured even farther as a psychotic serial killer in last year's "Himeanole.")

But the film's true revelation is Sasaki as Kuwahara. A veteran with a long list of stage, TV and movie credits, Sasaki brings not only the requisite swagger and brio to the role, but also impeccable comic timing and flawless grasp of character. Even the way he sings karaoke in English, with a self-infatuated self-assurance, is Kuwahara through and through.

Obviously, Ninomiya and Kuwahara have to embark on more adventures together — and to date there are five more novels in Kurokawa's series to film. Save for the fact that they hate each other, what's to stop them?

Survival Family, Sabaibaru Famiri, rating: ★★★⯪, runtime: 117min.

To Hollywood, "dystopian future" usually means invading aliens, exotic technology and gigantic explosions. Shinobu Yaguchi's "Survival Family" posits an alternative, more mundane cause of civilizational collapse: Japan's electric grid suddenly freezes up, like a laptop that's been doused with hot coffee. Televisions go blank, smartphones go silent and the internet goes missing. Chaos ensues.

Impossible to imagine, isn't it? Or not so impossible if you were anywhere near Tohoku on March 11, 2011. In Tokyo, we had a brief glimpse of this apocalypse as trains stopped running, gas station lines lengthened and convenience store shelves emptied. Things soon returned to normal, more or less, but doubts were implanted in my mind about the stability of the social order — doubts that Yaguchi brings to funny, scary, plausible life, working from his own original script.

A veteran maker of comedies, including his 2001 box office breakthrough "Waterboys," Yaguchi gets the expected laughs from the plight of the film's title family, the Suzukis. Dad (Fumiyo Kohinata) is a gung-ho salaryman who, sent home from the office after a heroic (in his own mind) effort to do his corporate duty, diligently works by candlelight. Meanwhile, plucky Mom (Eri Fukatsu), a full-time housewife, waits patiently in the long line at the supermarket checkout as overwhelmed cashiers frantically do sums on abacuses seemingly filched from a nearby museum.

The situation soon become more serious, however, as it dawns on the Suzukis and their neighbors that the power isn't coming back on any time soon and supplies are running out. At first, they awkwardly unite to meet this crisis, but soon one family after another makes its silent, shamefaced escape. As Tokyo descends into anarchy the Suzukis — Dad, Mom, their daughter, Yui (Wakana Aoi), and son, Kenji (Yuki Izumisawa) — join the exodus, using their commuter bikes to pedal toward Kagoshima, where Mom's elderly father (Akira Emoto) is a farmer.

Similar to "Robinson Crusoe," "Swiss Family Robinson" and other classics of survival fiction, "Survival Family" illustrates the spiritual and moral benefits of fending off starvation. Kenji and Yui begin the film as typical modern urban teens — Yui glued to her smartphone, Kenji to his headphones — but as the days pass and their choices narrow (cat food for dinner or nothing?) they become more resourceful and, not coincidentally, more likeable. And all four Suzukis, who once barely interacted as a family, become heartwarmingly closer.

This sort of feel-good storytelling has often been Yaguchi's key to box office success, but "Survival Family" is more realistic than much of his past output, at times starkly so, though his sense of humor, which shades to black, never abandons him.

The film's family is well cast, but Kohinata, an in-demand character actor equally adept at comedy and drama, is the stand-out. As Dad, his transformations from insufferable egomaniac to pathetic loser and finally decent human being are both smooth and hilarious.

More than its laughs, though, "Survival Family" is valuable for its object lessons on how to make it alive through the coming debacle. And since this is Japan, these lessons revolve around finding wild edible plants and starting cooking fires, not slaughtering and pillaging a la "Mad Max."

Is the film overly optimistic? Perhaps, but thinking back to the thousands of Tokyo commuters walking stolidly home on the night of the 2011 earthquake, I don't think so. Japan may have its faults, but violent chaos in the wake of disaster isn't usually one of them.

That said, I'm glad my wife and I have decent road bikes and proper riding gear. Kagoshima here we come.

Close-Knit, Karera ga Honki de Amu Toki wa, rating: ★★★☆, runtime: 127 min.

Japan would seem to be a paradise for LGBT people. Transgender "talents" have been appearing regularly on Japanese TV for decades and LGBT folks can walk the streets here with little fear.

But dig below Japan's surface tolerance for sexual minorities, as Naoko Ogigami does in her new film "Close-Knit," and the reality is not so rosy. Known for films about unconventional Japanese women looking for a fresh start, beginning with such as her 2006 break-out hit "Kamome Diner," Ogigami has found her own career's second act in "Close-Knit."

Scripted by Ogigami following her awakening to LGBT issues during a visit to the United States, this new film is more overtly serious than her previous, quirkily comic work. Though not a tear-jerker in the local "women's picture" line, "Close-Knit" flirts with the sort of "social problem" melodrama Ogigami once studiously avoided. And the story slices reality so thin that it borders on only-in-the-movies fantasy.

Nonetheless the film's trans heroine, Rinko (Toma Ikuta), is a fully rounded character, not a flamboyant caricature of the sort found so often in Japan's media. And her dream of becoming a wife and mother, over legal and social opposition, is presented minus false optimism. If Ogigami's previous films were a form of relaxation therapy for her mostly female fans, her latest is closer to tough-love intervention for Japan's still LGBT-unfriendly society.

As the story begins, 11-year-old Tomo (Rinka Kakihara) is living with her negligent mom (single-named Mimura), who feeds her on convenience-store rice balls and vanishes for days at a time. Finally reaching her limit, the plucky girl finds refuge with her uncle Makio (Kenta Kiritani), a nerdy, good-hearted guy who is her mom's younger brother. But Makio now has a live-in girlfriend, Rinko, who Tomo immediately sizes up as different. And Rinko soon tells her why: "I was born a boy," she says. "God made a mistake."

As Tomo is processing this information, Rinko does all she can to make the girl feel at ease, such as preparing delicious bento (box lunches) and teaching her how to knit — Rinko's preferred method of stress relief. And when the girl feels lonely, Rinko takes her in her arms — and begins to dream of becoming her new mom for real.

Meanwhile, Tomo's classmate Kai, who is like a younger version of Rinko, presents her with a moral dilemma: He wants to be her friend, but she can't be seen talking to him at school, where he is a pariah, or she will be tainted by association. But once she sees Rinko as a loving surrogate mother rather than a guy in a dress, she also starts to view Kai differently. Kai's uptight mom, however, spies Rinko and Tomo together in a supermarket and offers to "rescue" Tomo from the "freak."

The whole film rises or falls on Ikuta's performance as Rinko — and he is superb. A versatile actor who recently appear as a goofy undercover-cop-cum-gangster in Takashi Miike's "The Mole Song: Hong Kong Capriccio," Ikuta plays Rinko as a natural woman, if one whose gentle surface can be roiled by injuries and injustices, though she has long since learned to manage her anger. She is, in other words, as far from the stereotypical campy drag queen as can be imagined.

Does this make Rinko an unrealistic ideal, similar to the too-perfect black authority figures (cop, teacher, etc.) once played by Sidney Poitier?

Perhaps, but she is also one of the many Ogigami characters impossible to dislike. And even if you don't buy the film's version of LGBT life in today's Japan, you will definitely want her to cook for you. Prejudice is here demolished one bento at a time.

Alley Cat, Ari Kyato, rating: ★★★★, runtime: 129min.

In Japanese films, a lot of what used to be considered extreme is now routine. Geysers of blood and flying body parts may still thrill fanboys, but to me that sort of play violence has become about as exciting as the spin cycle. Hideo Sakaki's buddy movie "Alley Cat" also deals in violence, but of the kind that has real consequences on actual bodies and psyches. The ex-boxer hero (Yosuke Kubozuka) does not bounce up from brutal punishment, ready for more. Instead he suffers from headaches that nearly kill him — and maybe someday will.

Actor and director Sakaki has had his share of hard knocks as well, including the near-cancellation of his 2010 comedy "The Accidental Kidnapper" when a cast member was arrested for drugs. (Sakaki saved the day by reshooting the busted actor's scenes with himself in the role.) All that and more is reflected in "Alley Cat," whose desperate characters look worn down by life, if not yet defeated by it.

Superb in Martin Scorsese's "Silence," Yosuke Kubozuka plays the boxer, whose cat Maru goes missing as the film begins. Soon after, he finds her in the arms of a blond-haired punk (Kenji Furuya) who calls her Lily and refuses to give her up. Before he can reclaim his cat, the boxer receives a call asking him to serve as a bodyguard. The client, Saeko Tsuchiya (Yui Ichikawa), wants protection when she meets her stalker ex-boyfriend (Hiroshi Shinagawa).

The meeting ends in disaster, but the punk (actually an auto mechanic) helps our hero save Saeko from her crazy ex. Sarcastically calling each other Maru (the boxer) and Lily (the mechanic), these two reluctantly unite to protect Saeko and her small son, Hayato. It's not enough for Saeko, however, and she winds up heading to Tokyo to seek help from a dubious underworld fixer (Masaki Miura) with her protectors. This temp job has turned into a life-or-death mission.

A buddy movie is comic by definition and "Alley Cat" has fun with its central pair, beginning with their mutual fondness for felines. But even the lighter gags have a dark edge, born of Maru and Lily's hardscrabble lives. When they arrive in Tokyo, the film goes full noir but leaves out the typical macho romanticism.

Faced with not only the implacable stalker and the slithery fixer, but also a powerful politician (Yuya Takagawa) with a murderous grudge, Maru and Lily are over their heads — and they know it. When they risk their necks, they behave like ordinary mortals for whom a narrow escape is an adrenaline rush, and a gunshot is a traumatic shock.

Watching the film's action scenes unfold I often felt like I was watching something I had never seen before, specifically the true-to-life depictions of such out-of-the-ordinary events. Familiar thriller tropes eventually appear, but the film stays faithful to the lived humanity of its three principals, flaws and all.

The rail-thin Kubozuka may not have a boxer's physique, but he thoroughly fleshes out Maru's pain, shame, fear and stubborn will to live. As Lily, Dragon Ash frontman Furuya has the look and attitude of a punk who comes from the streets, not a trendy men's magazine. And as Saeko, Ichikawa successfully transcends the cliches of her in-jeopardy, fallen-woman character.

And Maru/Lily? Not to worry — she's an alley cat, the grittiest of them all.

Side Job, Kanojo no Jinsei wa Machigai janai, rating: ★★★★⯨, runtime: 119 min.

The Great East Japan Earthquake of 2011 and its aftermath have been the focus of many films, both fiction and nonfiction. However, most of them have been by filmmakers who've come from outside Fukushima Prefecture, where the disaster hit hardest. Ryuichi Hiroki, a native of Koriyama, Fukushima, reworked his 2011 film "River" to reflect the catastrophic effects of the quake, but he hasn't finished with the subject, as his new film "Side Job." makes clear. Based on his own novel, the film is full of characters and incidents taken from years of research but doesn't turn into a docudrama or a "social issue" weeper, with its pure-hearted heroes and obvious message. Instead, "Side Job." provides a narrative that stays true to the complex and not-always-edifying reality of life in the disaster zone. And that makes it the best film of the dozens I've seen on the topic.

A prolific creator of mainstream romantic dramas, Hiroki has long had a side job of his own directing indie films, including his 2015 ensemble drama "Kabukicho Love Hotel." "Side Job." belongs to the indie category while being a departure from his usual fare.

The filmmaker's signature lyricism is still present — even drone shots of a highway bus entering Tokyo have a floating grace — but there's a shrugging disregard for pieties, official or otherwise: "Recovery" is not a word used by the heroine and many around her; "lasting trauma" may better describe their situation.

Known for pushing famous actresses out of their comfort zones, Hiroki has cast newcomer Kumi Takiuchi in "Side Job." and surrounded her with a great supporting cast that includes Kengo Kora ("M") and Ken Mitsuishi ("Natsumi's Firefly").

Miyuki Kanazawa (Takiuchi) works as a clerk for the city of Iwaki and lives with her father (Mitsuishi) in temporary housing. She lost her mother in the disaster, and her rice farmer father, whose paddies are in the no-go zone, also lost his livelihood. He now spends his days at a pachinko parlor and his nights drinking. On the weekends, Miyuki journeys to Tokyo, ostensibly for English lessons, but actually to work for a deriheru (literally, "delivery health") service. That is, she delivers sex to customers in hotels, as the eagle-eyed Hideaki Miura (Kora) —her driver, guardian and confidant — waits nearby.

Why does Miyuki prostitute herself? She has no mountain of debt or manipulative pimp. One reason may be escape. As Miyuki she faces the prospect of a never-ending sameness, which is not helped by a needy former boyfriend (Atsushi Shinohara) who turns up out of the blue. As Yuki, her deriheru persona, she can find a welcome oblivion, both erotically charged and dangerously degrading. But after two years on the game, she looks jaded — and oblivion of a more permanent sort beckons.

Life for those around her has also become like the seashore near the crippled power plant: quiet and desolate, with the old normality distant or out of sight. One such figure is Miyuki's earnest day job colleague Yuto Nitta (Tokio Emoto). He wants to help the folks who come to his counter, but is still dealing with fallout from the disaster in his own family.

But life, as Miyuki and the others discover, is filled with change — sometimes wrenching, sometimes freeing. In "Side Job.," hope blooms naturally as a kind of benediction from whatever gods are out there. But whether it lasts is another matter.

Dear Etranger, Osanago Warera ni Umare, rating: ★★★☆, runtime: 127 min.

Despite a career spanning nearly three decades, Yukiko Mishima hasn't appeared on many lists of up-and-coming Japanese female directors, mine included. One reason: She had a relatively late start, not releasing her first feature, a drama based on the Junichiro Tanizaki story "The Tatooer," until 2009. Another reason: Her five films to date have not won major festival awards abroad or racked up big box-office numbers at home.

Mishima's sixth and newest film, "Dear Etranger," may not change that. It had its world premiere at the 18th Jeonju International Film Festival last May, but not in the competition. Nonetheless, this film about a middle-aged man's struggles with the consequences of divorce and remarriage, particularly a tween stepdaughter who can't stand the sight of him, represents an advance and, I hope, a breakthrough.

Realism in Japanese family dramas, even the better ones, does not often get this real. But the film is not a two-hour wallow in misery. Change, we see, can bring not only loss and regret, but also relief and even the possibility of happiness, however temporary.

Based on Kiyoshi Shigematsu's 1996 novel of the same Japanese title, Haruhiko Arai's script covers years in the lives of his principals with conventional flashbacks, if with unconventional freshness, as drawing from life in the messy raw, including the sort of interior truths that reveal themselves only rarely — or disastrously.

Makoto Tanaka (Tadanobu Asano) divorced his first wife, Yuka (Shinobu Terajima), four years ago and married the younger Nanae (Rena Tanaka), who is also batsu-ichi ("one strike," or divorced). Nanae left her husband, the alcoholic, dissolute Sawada (Kankuro Kudo), because he beat her and her young daughter. Makoto and Yuka split when they couldn't agree on a second child: He wanted one, she didn't. Makoto continues to see his daughter, Saori (Raiju Kamata), who lives with her mother and new stepfather, while he tries to be a good parent to Nanae's two daughters — cute little Eriko (Miu Arai) and sullen sixth-grader Kaoru (Sara Minami).

When Nanae announces that she is pregnant, however, Makoto wonders out loud whether they need another child, and the fissures in their marriage, already visible, widen. Meanwhile, bad news keeps coming for various characters, career ruin and fatal disease among them.

This is the trajectory of many a family drama here, with personal calamities arriving like clockwork. But Makoto refuses to act like a genre cliche. Similar to the biblical Job, he is subjected to endless trials and torments, though they are more psychological than physical, including humiliation, rejection and adolescent insolence. Nonetheless, he is slow to abandon his ideal: a family in which he is more than the title "etranger" (stranger).

As Makoto, Asano brings his trademark coiled force, if not his usual toe-curling violence, though Makoto's anger boils over when he is sorely provoked. A saint he is not. Neither is anyone else in the film, for that matter.

And yet there is something to like about all of them. The film accomplishes this less by idealizing them than presenting them in the human round. Even the wife-beater, we see, has his decent side — though if I were this movie's God, he'd be my first candidate for Job.

The Third Murder, Sandome no Satsujin, rating: ★★★★, runtime: 124min.

Murder mysteries are popular film and television fodder in Japan, but most revolve around puzzle plots that hold as much real-world probability as the cases of Sherlock Holmes.

Hirokazu Koreeda's "The Third Murder" also presents a puzzle, but it's in the form of twice-convicted killer Takashi Misumi (Koji Yakusho) who, shortly after his release from 30 years in prison, is arrested again on suspicion of committing yet another murder.

The film begins as a noir-ish procedural: Imagine an episode of "Law & Order" transposed to Japan. Working from his own script Koreeda transforms his simple premise into a powerful, intricately constructed meditation on the mysteries of the heart, the elusiveness of truth and the injustices of the Japanese justice system, in which the scales are tipped in favor of the prosecution.

That is the case with Misumi, who early on smilingly admits to murdering his former boss and stealing money from the company safe. As a three-time killer he will almost certainly be sentenced to death.

Assigned to defend this defendant, the cynical Tomoaki Shigemori (Masaharu Fukuyama) and his two legal colleagues brainstorm stratagems for getting the sentence reduced. For them the question of Misumi's actual guilt or innocence is irrelevant and immaterial.

And yet when Shigemori personally delivers a letter of contrition from Misumi to the victim's daughter, Sakie Yamanaka (Suzu Hirose), which she promptly tears to pieces, he notices something that opens a crack in his pat and, as he knows, false defense scenario.

In the course of the film, that crack widens to a chasm with Misumi revealed as an unreliable narrator of his own crimes. That is, his relationship to the truth is as elastic as Shigemori's, though his motives are darker, deeper and finally unfathomable.

More links between lawyer and client emerge: Both have daughters they have managed to alienate, and Shigemori's father (Isao Hashizume) was the judge who sent Misumi to prison (and who now regrets not sending him to the gallows). "If I'd given him the death penalty there would have been no more killing," he says, dismissing Misumi's stated motive for murdering two loan sharks three decades ago. "He didn't have a grudge — he's an empty vessel."

Is this not also true of his defense attorney? The film strikingly underlines this parallelism with eerie shots in the prison visiting room: Shigemori's face reflected in the glass barrier, next to Misumi's impassive visage on the other side. As he gazes into his client's unreadable eyes Shigemori peers, horrified, into a void he fears slipping into himself.

This drama of a flawed man coming reluctantly to terms with his own moral failings and struggling to remedy them is familiar from Koreeda's other films, particularly the 2013 film "Like Father, Like Son," in which Fukuyama played another self-centered and conflicted member of the elite.

But "The Third Murder" also offers the satisfactions of a well-constructed suspense story, with twists that come from the characters of its principals, not plot contrivances. It also relentlessly exposes a judicial system that seems as fixed as a pro-wrestling bout, with defendants assigned predetermined story lines they change at their peril. Misumi, of course, is the heel. Koreeda's film, though, is a masterpiece.

Poolsideman, Purusaidoman, rating: ★★★★, runtime: 117 min.

In his three films to date, Hirobumi Watanabe has created a unique cinematic world. "And the Mud Ship Sails Away" (2013), "7 Days" (2015) and now "Poolsideman" (2016) were all shot in black-and-white in Watanabe's native Tochigi Prefecture, with music by younger brother Yuji and cinematography by Woohyun Bang. All focus on socially marginalized men with lives that range from the aimless to the mundane. And all are tinged with black humor that keeps the proceedings from becoming too brain-numbingly minimalistic.

Echoes of other filmmakers can be heard, notably Jim Jarmusch and Bela Tarr, but Watanabe marches to his own drum, as Yuji's soundtrack provides counterpoint with everything from classical war horses to sinister electronic noise, while becoming more intense — not intrusive — as the story progresses. Bang's tightly composed images, at once gorgeous and stark, add another layer of commentary. This sort of thing is not for everyone: "Poolsideman" won the Japanese Cinema Splash award at last year's Tokyo International Film Festival, but divided critics and fans. I was one of its champions and not only because, like its hero and director, I put in my own time (two summers) as a pool lifeguard.

In its first half the film tests audience patience as a long-limbed, long-haired, long-faced guy named Yusuke Mizuhara (long-time Watanabe friend Gaku Imamura) goes about his rigid daily routine, beginning with a door-banging locker inspection at the pool and concluding after work with a meal at McDonald's, a movie at a local theater and a session with his home PC, none of which we are allowed to see plain and clear. Mizuhara never utters a word to anyone, though he always has his car radio tuned to news about the latest ISIS terrorist outrage or Syrian war atrocity.

There is a truth to this sequence, repeated again and again, that films seldom explore — life for many consists of daily rounds as predictable as the sunrise. Watanabe turns his hero's own round into spare visual poetry that illuminates his unquiet inner life.

But tedium has begun to set in when Watanabe himself makes an appearance as Mizuhara's loquacious colleague Shirasaki, who hitches daily rides to work after they are both temporarily transferred to another pool. Sitting in the passenger's seat, Shirasaki opines on the generational divide between "Dragon Ball" and "One Piece" fans, the trite chatter of his pool colleagues, his memorable teenage encounter with a punk in a game parlor, and anything else that pops into his head. These monologues, scripted by Watanabe himself, are funny enough to suggest a fallback career as a comic. They also reveal Shirasaki's own disconnect from reality as he expatiates on the "friendship" between himself and the anti-social Mizuhara.

Meanwhile, we witness the bizarre result of Mizuhara's obsession with news from the Middle East, as nightmarish montages of war, famine and overpopulation flash on the screen. And yet the film has no obvious message, save perhaps that the craziness of the world can now infect an isolated soul in a rural backwater. And that the solution is not more "communication," since an overload of information has already pushed Mizuhara to the edge.

I suggest swimming laps to reduce the stress and work off the Big Macs. For the rest of us? Try the patience-testing, entertaining and disturbing "Poolsideman."

Outrage Coda, Aoutoreiji Saishusho, rating: ★★★☆, runtime: 104 min.

In his nearly three decades as a director, "Beat" Takeshi Kitano has won many critical plaudits and prizes abroad. But in Japan he is best known as a TV personality and comedian. These two strands of his artistic personality — master director and mass entertainer — have come together in his "Outrage" trilogy about present-day gang wars, with Kitano himself starring as an old-school yakuza, Otomo.

The trilogy ends with the new "Outrage Coda." Similar to "Outrage" (2010) and "Outrage Beyond" (2012), the cast is heavily populated with graying veterans, the characters regularly explode into purple-faced rants and the body count is off the charts.

"Outrage Coda" also features a full complement of gangster types, from the floridly eccentric to the coldly psychotic. If the action isn't especially fresh — Kitano fans will spot references to his earlier films — his talent for spare-but-impactful visuals and mean-but-funny twists is still intact. And this unregenerately macho action flick digs deep into the criminal psyche, exposing its loneliness as well as its unlimited capacity for cruelty.

The story begins with Otomo on the South Korean island of Jeju working for Chang (Tokio Kaneda), a fixer in the local sex industry. One night Otomo is summoned to placate a burly Japanese client dissatisfied with two prostitutes he paid for. He is Hanada (Pierre Taki), part of the Hanabishi-kai, a Kansai-based gang that is the most powerful in Japan. The kinky Hanada physically abused the women, for which an annoyed Otomo demands compensation. In the resulting violent back-and-forth a Chang subordinate ends up dead and Hanada skedaddles back to Japan.

The Hanabishi-kai is headed by Nomura (Ren Osugi), an ex-stock trader who married the former chairman's daughter. This upstart neophyte is thoroughly despised by Nishino (Toshiyuki Nishida), a canny gang elder, who knows that Nomura's blowhard front is a cover for his entirely justified insecurities. Reciprocating this dislike, Nomura schemes to eliminate both Nishino and his grizzled second-in-command Nakata (Sansei Shiomi) by playing one against the other.

Meanwhile, Otomo is steaming over not only Hanada's insult to his Korean boss, but also the still painful fallout from the war between the Hanabishi-kai and his old gang, the now sadly depleted Sanno-kai, detailed in "Outrage Beyond." What happens when his rage boils over?

As in the previous "Outrage" installments, the plot developments are byzantine, while the personalities tend to the grandiose and grotesque. Similar to "Goodfellas," Martin Scorsese's Mafia masterpiece, "Outrage Coda" garishly illuminates the stranger flowers in the criminal weed bed.

One example is Nishino, who obsessively fingers his mouth and jaw like a cross between a chin-stroking wise man and an orally fixated infant. This odd bit of stage business, presumably dreamed up by Nishida, signals not only the character's indifference to social convention, but also his power as a gangster and confidence as a man. All part and parcel of a bravura performance.

And Otomo? Typically for a Kitano tough guy, he expresses himself best with a gun. Not so typically, Kitano gives him the film's most memorable line, as well as a fitting last bow. But what an outrage it would be if I were to tell you what they are.

Hanagatami, rating: ★★★★, runtime: 169 min.

Despite a lengthy filmography that began in the 1960s, Nobuhiko Obayashi is known in the West mainly for his 1977 feature debut "House." This horror-fantasy about a house that devours its inhabitants is a surreal riot of the imagination that tosses local filmmaking conventions out the window. Four decades later the riot continues in Obayashi's new film, "Hanagatami," but the subject, based on Kazuo Dan's 1937 novel, is the lives of teenagers in Karatsu, Saga Prefecture, on the eve of war. Instead of toning down his signature style for this tragic story of youth cut short, Obayashi amplifies it. The result is a phantasmagoria of rapid cutting, perfervid acting and extravagant visuals, with the moon a giant ball bathing the sea and islands near Karatsu in heavenly splendor. It's as though every frame has been Photoshopped out of any relation to reality.

The film is excessive in another sense: The three male leads are all well past 25 and look like cosplayers in their high school uniforms.

Over the film's nearly three-hour running time, this overblown approach ought to amount to a throbbing headache. Instead, Obayashi has captured not only the atmosphere but also the spiritual essence of a strange, febrile moment in time.

Far from being a nostalgic period piece made by an elderly director looking back to the Japan of his childhood, "Hanagatami" is both a timely warning against war's collective insanities and an urgent plea for peace. It's a hallucinatory illustration of the maxim that fiction — in this case, Obayashi's combination of deep memory and delirious visions — can reveal more than fact.

The film's memoirist is Toshihiko Sakakiyama (Shunsuke Kubozuka), who returns from Amsterdam, where his parents are living, to Karatsu. Only 17, he stays with his wealthy aunt Keiko (Takako Tokiwa) and attends the local boys' high school.

There he befriends three classmates: the frenetic, good-natured Aso (Tokio Emoto); the athletic, super-sincere Ukai (Shinnosuke Mitsushima), a god in human form to the impressionable Toshihiko; and the tall, limping Kira (Keishi Nagatsuka), trailing an air of tragic doom.

With his worldly aunt serving as social facilitator, Toshihiko's new home becomes the nexus of a circle that includes not only the above threesome but also his beautiful, tubercular cousin Mina (Honoka Yahagi), the exuberant Akine (Hirona Yamazaki) and the moody, arty Chitose (Mugi Kadowaki), with her camera always at the ready.

Their life of dinner parties in Keiko's elegant home and picnics on Saga's wind-swept coast must have been unimaginable to ordinary Japanese of the era, but these festivities have a hectic atmosphere, with everyone desperately celebrating their youth while knowing their world is rushing headlong over a cliff.

Meanwhile, ghostly soldiers with white-painted faces march off to war to waving flags. Their progress, viewed repeatedly in the course of the film, builds a cumulative power, like a recurring nightmare. At the same time, Toshihiko's wide-eyed infatuation with Ukai has a risibly homoerotic subtext. In one moonlit scene they strip naked, jump on a horse and gallop down the beach, looking like subjects in a Tom of Finland book cover.

At the same time, they burn with a purity that is very much of the period — and is now all but vanished. Almost alone among working Japanese directors, Obayashi not only remembers that time but also revives it — or rather his fever dream of it

Tremble All You Want, Katte ni Furuetero, rating: ★★★★, runtime: 117min.

Hopeless crushes are typically the stuff of teen comedies, not romcoms aimed at grownups. Yet in the corner of many an adult brain exists at least one excruciating memory of that special teenaged someone you never quite worked up the nerve to speak to.

Yoshika (Mayu Matsuoka), the heroine of Akiko Ooku's effervescent comedy "Tremble All You Want," still finds herself in that corner or, in her case, cell. Now a nerdy 24-year-old clerk who crunches numbers for a living, she can't seem to get over her junior high crush, a dreamboat she calls "Ichi"

("No. 1," played by Takumi Kitamura). He spoke maybe 10 unforgettable words to her in her life, but he remains an obsession — and she's never had an actual boyfriend.

All of which may make her sound the pathetic loser, but Matsuoka's star-making turn as Yoshika is a perfect blend of mousy and bubbly, withdrawn and assertive, tongue-tied and talkative. In Japanese she's an uchi benkei, that handy term for types who are extroverted (as in arrogant) with family and close friends, introverted (as in wimpy) with the rest of the world.

At work she unburdens herself to her sympathetic pal Kurumi (Anna Ishibashi), while scorning the attentions of a goofy colleague she calls "Ni" ("No. 2," played by Daichi Watanabe). When she miraculously reunites with Ichi, she haplessly reverts to her bumbling 14-year-old self in his presence. So when Ni, who controls his feelings the way a puppy controls its bladder, blurts out his desire to date her, she can't say no. Second-best is better than nothing, after all — but she still has Ichi on the brain.

Anyone who has seen a romcom knows how this drama will play out, but the Ichi-or-Ni plot is not the only point of the movie. Based on Risa Wataya's novel and scripted by Ooku, "Tremble All You Want" delves into a knottier question: What's in a name? We see Yoshika chatting with various folk: a coffee shop server who looks like a doll, a friendly middle-aged angler who never strays from his favorite fishing spot and an eccentric neighbor lady who plays the ocarina. But she never calls any of them by their proper names and instead just prattles on about herself.

Another of her cute quirks? Perhaps, but as she reveals in a musical number midway through the film, Yoshika is living a lie and is lonelier than she lets on. Her song, which was soon playing on heavy rotation in my head, ends in tears that are far from ironic, providing her with renewed determination to turn her life around.

At last year's Tokyo International Film Festival, where "Tremble All You Want" won the Audience Award, Ooku said that the film reflects experiences she had in her 20s. As such, it's filled with telling details that would never have occurred to the typical male director, such as one close-up of Yoshika slipping on shiny new shoes as she sets off for an encounter with Ichi, and another of the same footwear as she slogs home afterward. The unspoken message: The shoes failed in their mission. Matsuoka, on the other hand, succeeds brilliantly. On camera in nearly every scene, she brings Yoshika to life with originality, charm and never a false note. Applaud all you want.

Going the Distance, Kazoku E, rating: ★★★★, runtime: 117 min.

Marriages in Japan were long between families, with the omiai (arranged marriage) process typically serving to both introduce prospective partners to each other and vet their respective family backgrounds. Have the wrong sort of ancestors? The wedding's off.

As seen in Yujiro Harumoto's drama "Going the Distance," this attitude continues to linger in modern-day Japan. The film is as simple in structure as a folk tale, and ties up as neatly and strongly. Its observations about families are straight and true, and shot with the feel of a fly-on-the-wall documentary. In fact, Harumoto based his script on an incident from the life of his star, Shinichiro Matsuura, who hails from the same Goto Islands chain off Nagasaki as the character he plays, Asahi, and works the same job, boxing trainer.

Unlike Matsuura, Asahi was raised in an orphanage. As the story starts, he's living in Tokyo, working for a gruff-but-kind boxing gym owner and engaged to Kaori (Yumi Endo), the sort of educated middle-class woman who in previous times would have been unattainable for a guy like Asahi. Instead, the couple is happily planning their wedding, though Kaori's mom opposes the marriage and Asahi has only one guest: Hiroto (Masahiro Umeda), his best friend from the orphanage, now a fisherman in the Goto Islands. When Hiroto visits Tokyo, Asahi introduces him to Kita (Nobu Morimoto), a gym client who's opening a restaurant specializing in freshly caught fish. The smooth-talking Kita signs up Hiroto as a supplier.

Then everything goes south. Kita disappears, having never paid Hiroto for his catch. Now in debt, Hiroto gives up fishing and becomes a truck driver, but continues to search for the man who scammed him. Stricken with guilt at Hiroto's change of fortune, Asahi gives his friend the money he had saved for the wedding. When Kaori finds out, she's enraged: Which is more important, she asks him, his friend or their marriage?

Watching the film for the first time at TIFF, I originally saw Kaori as the villain. But watching it again for this review, I could better understand her anger: Asahi lies to her repeatedly about his actions, which threaten to delay their wedding. She had wanted to hold the ceremony before her grandmother slipped too far into senility, but that now seems unlikely. No wonder she looks at Asahi with eyes that, if they shot laser beams, would vaporize him.

But the conscience-stricken Asahi and the heart-of-gold Hiroto are also types seldom seen in mainstream dramas, belonging as they do to a despised, marginalized group. As men without families — save for the "family" they have created together — they are essentially nonpersons. Kaori's mother tries to stop the marriage not because of who Asahi is (they've barely met) but because he is not "qualified" for her daughter's hand. Better that Kaori marry a socially acceptable stranger via an omiai.

The entire film stands on its final scene — and it is perfect, following powerfully as it does from everything that has come before. In its last round "Going the Distance" delivers a knockout.

Yamato (California), rating: ★★★☆, runtime: 119 min.

The American military bases in Okinawa are often in the news, usually because of an accident, protest or crime. The bases elsewhere in Japan, not so much. These reminders of a postwar occupation now seven decades in the past have mostly faded from the public imagination.

Daisuke Miyazaki's true-to-life drama "Yamato (California)" shows, however, that the bases still loom large to those who live near them, including his sullen heroine Sakura (Hanae Kan), a high school dropout and aspiring rapper.

Completed in 2016 and screened at festivals here and abroad, "Yamato (California)" has a lived-in realism — it's set in Yamato, Kanagawa Prefecture, near the Atsugi naval air base, and replicates the deafening aircraft noise the locals in the film have become inured to. At the same time, it is not a docudrama about the problems the base has caused. The film instead focuses more on the personal, with welcome touches of humor, strongly realized characters and none of the stereotyping endemic to local "international" films.

Rapper Sakura wants to tell the world about everything from her feelings of worthlessness to her fear that life is passing her by. Her relationships with local rappers are fractious — she thinks they're pun-spinning poseurs — and her romantic life is nonexistent. But her single mom, Kiko (Reiko Kataoka), is tolerant and big-hearted, while her nerdy brother, Kenzo (Haruka Uchimura), wishes her well, even as he needles her about her pretensions and failings.

The story kicks into gear when Rei (Nina Endo), the daughter of a Japanese mother and Kiko's now-absent American boyfriend, arrives for a visit. Speaking fluent Japanese and looking like a teen fashion model, Rei takes in her new environment with a cool, level gaze. Of course, the hot-tempered and insecure Sakura turns her back on her.

Politely rejecting her hosts' ideas about the Japan foreigners want to see (temples, Harajuku), Rei smilingly cajoles Sakura to "take me where you usually go." Riding Sakura's scooter, the two girls visit a Don Quijote, a hip-hop club, a shopping mall, an eel restaurant and, finally, an abandoned mobile home where Sakura writes lyrics and dreams.

This light-hearted bonding sequence suddenly darkens when a now-intoxicated Rei, a hip-hop fan herself, asks Sakura to rap for her — and Sakura refuses. Rei lashes out: "You're a fake, aren't you?" And even worse: "You're just copying." Their idyll of Japanese-American harmony abruptly ends.

The story, however, continues to defy formula as Sakura, with Rei as a goad, slowly gathers up the courage to confront her demons and fears, from delinquent former pals to the public stage. This narrative arc is hardly new — one point of reference is Nobuhiro Yamashita's much-loved 2005 girl band movie "Linda, Linda, Linda" — but Miyazaki, who also wrote the script, delivers something different from the expected rousing climax, just as Sakura is more than a zero-to-hero plot construct.

As played by the consistently interesting Kan, she is both a pouty, posturing teen —that is, obnoxious — and a genuine rap artist in the making — that is, eloquent and incisive. Kan expresses the various sides of Sakura's personality, as well as her cultural crossings, with fire and precision. Compton, California, meet Yamato, Kanagawa.

Mori, the Artist's Habitat, Mori no Iru Basho, rating: ★★★★, runtime: 99 min.

Fact-checking biopics is an easy game for critics to play since nearly all films about real people fudge facts to tell a story. I've played the game myself, but in the case of Shuichi Okita's delightful "Mori, the Artist's Habitat," it's almost beside the point. Celebrated in Japan for his late-career paintings of flowers, insects and other natural phenomena in a childlike style, Morikazu Kumagai (1880-1977) isn't well-known abroad. So Okita's film, which is based on his own script, is a welcome introduction, though it focuses on only one day in the then-94-year-old artist's life and never shows him actually painting. The story is as simple-seeming as one of Kumagai's cat paintings but goes beyond the surface of his obsessions and quirks, the best known being his reclusion, to pointed, affectionate dissection of his character and world.

In the last decades of his life (the film says 30 years, Wikipedia 20) the painter never left the confines of his house and jungle-like garden, all 60 square meters of it. This looks to be a classic case of agoraphobia, and when Kumagai (Tsutomu Yamazaki) ventures tremulously outside the gates of his house in the film he is soon chased back again by the frown of a neighborhood girl.

The wonders he finds in his garden, however, from ants to goldfish, keep him endlessly occupied. A slow-witted photographer's assistant (Kaito Yoshimura) tells his excitable boss (Ryo Kase) that the sight of Kumagai intently fondling a small stone reminds him of a Chinese sage. "He hates that," the photographer snaps. And in Yamazaki's wry, minimalist performance, Kumagai is less the sage than the eternal small boy, if one who clumps around his paradise on two canes.

Also, far from being a recluse, Kumagai is close to his protective, endlessly patient wife, Hideko (Kirin Kiki), while stoically enduring a daily flock of visitors, from an obsequious innkeeper (Ken Mitsuishi) who wants the master to brush a sign for his business to a thuggish developer (Mitsuru Fukikoshi) whose new multistory apartment building will block most of the sunlight to the garden.

This project has angered Kumagai's fans, who have posted anti-developer signs on his garden wall, but is little more than just another incident in this all-but-plotless film.

Okita, who also directed the similarly true life-based "The Chef of South Polar" (2009), has seeded his script with understated gags that Yamazaki and Kirin — both masters of comedy — bring off flawlessly. But he risks losing his audience — at least ones who aren't Nature Channel fans — with shot after shot of the garden's flora and fauna.

Instead of nodding off, I found myself both laughing at Kumagai, who in close-ups looks like a gray-bearded Gulliver as he inspects his garden's tiny wildlife, and sharing his fascination and joy. When Hideko says she wouldn't want to relive her life (it would, she explains, be "too tiring"), I also understood Kumagai's response: "I'd do it again, I like my life."

Not that, like Kumagai, I've spent years observing the micro as though it were macro, but "Mori" makes his world look both inviting and infinite. Why, I thought, would anyone want to leave it, even when a mysterious visitor offers Kumagai something far bigger and, who knows, better? Heaven can wait.

The Scythian Lamb, Hitsuji no Ki, rating: ★★★☆, runtime 126 min.

Seeing Daihachi Yoshida's "The Scythian Lamb" for the second time at the Foreign Correspondents' Club of Japan, I was reminded of "Black Mirror," the British series with provocative "what if" scenarios set in an alternative present or near future. Yes, I am a binge-watcher.

Not that the film's provincial seaport is a "Black Mirror"-esque dystopia: As young city bureaucrat Hajime Tsukisue (Ryo Nishikido) keeps reminding us, the people are friendly and the seafood is delicious. But his boss tells him that the town's population is declining and fresh blood is needed. His bizarre solution: Secretly bring in six convicted murderers and parole them for a period of 10 years. If they stay clean they will be permanently freed.

Based on a manga by Tatsuhiko Yamagami and Mikio Igarashi, this "what if" is a set-up for black comedy. But Yoshida, whose films seldom obey genre rules, stirs in elements of thriller, social drama and even kaijū (monster) action. Credulity is sometimes strained and the murderers' stories are not equally engaging, but the film goes unblinkingly into the darkness. Also, it squarely addresses the consequences of the ultimate crime for both the perpetrators and the society in which they live. For the paroled six rehabilitation is a possibility, but so is a reversion to violence.

They are the tightly wound Fukumoto (Shingo Mizusawa), so starved for the air of freedom that he sticks his head out the window of Tsukisue's car like a dog, the silent Kurimoto (Mikako Ichikawa), who lovingly and strangely buries dead small animals, the former yakuza Ono (Min Tanaka), who intimidates with his level stare and jagged facial scar, the smirking Sugiyama (Kazuki Kitamura), who can smell out another ex-con a mile away, and the smoldering Ota (the single-named Yuka), who finds the man of her dreams in Tsukisue's stroke-victim dad (Toshiyuki Kitami).

Making the biggest impression, however, is Ichiro Miyakoshi (Ryuhei Matsuda), who is open to his new environment in ways the others are not. Though stiff and distant, like a visitor from another planet, Miyakoshi comes to befriend Tsukisue and date Aya (Fumino Kimura), a recent returnee from Tokyo who plays a fierce lead guitar to Tsukisue's bass in a three-member band. Prickly to Tsukisue, who has had a crush on her since high school, Aya soon warms up to fellow outsider Miyakoshi.

Played by pop idol/actor Nishikido, Tsukisue begins as a nice-guy tour guide to his six charges but reveals a tougher side as their stay in the town lengthens — and they backslide to old ways.

Taking considerable liberties with the manga (the band, for example, is not in it), the film transitions from the gag comedy of the first half to the tense drama of the second through grounded character development, though not all of its six killers gain a third dimension.

Meanwhile, a googly-eyed monster from local folklore appears as a costumed local in an annual festival and looms as a huge statue over the town. Called Nororo, it serves as a metaphor for chthonic forces that doom the weak, the unlucky and the damned.

And the title's "Scythian Lamb?" It refers to the ancient Central Asian myth of a plant whose fruit is living, permanently tethered sheep. Severed from their mother plant, the sheep die. Something like humans cut off from their own humanity.

Oh Lucy!, rating: ★★★☆, runtime: 95 min.

I've seen my share of Japanese movies set partly or wholly in the United States. With a few exceptions, the filmmakers only skim the exotic surface, while the Japanese characters never become more than fish out of water gasping for a breath of the familiar, be it instant noodles or spoken Japanese. Based on her prize-winning MFA thesis short, Atsuko Hirayanagi's "Oh Lucy!" sure-footedly crosses the U.S.-Japan divide. That doesn't mean it's perfect: The gags often play on stereotypes, while the drama sometimes verges on the overwrought. Yet on the whole the film is meticulously crafted; fine detailing is often absent in the usual Japanese "international" movie, whose brush of choice is broad.

Much of this is due to spot-on casting: For her first feature, Hirayanagi snagged some of the best Japanese actors currently working, starting with Shinobu Terajima in the title role. Also, instead of the amateur actors that fill the non-Japanese roles in so many local films, Josh Hartnett plays the love interest. No longer the box-office force that starred in such hits as "Pearl Harbor" and "Black Hawk Down," he is still a recognizable name. That said, Hirayanagi and Boris Frumin's script doesn't always give him and the others a lot to work with. The English dialogue is trimmed to the bone, though it is punchy and pointed enough to get laughs and reveal character.

Our heroine is Setsuko, a 43-year-old OL ("office lady" or female company employee) who hates her dull job and lonely life. So when her feckless niece Mika (Shioli Kutsuna), a maid at a Tokyo maid cafe, asks her aunt to take over her prepaid English conversation lessons — she signed up for a year's worth — Setsuko agrees to give eikaiwa (English conversation) a try as a break from her stultifying routine. The teacher for her trial lesson, John (Hartnett), dubs her "Lucy," makes her don a blonde wig and stuffs a ping-pong ball into her mouth, but he's tall, handsome and gives out hugs as part of his lesson plan. Setsuko is sold. She also makes the acquaintance of another new student, the awkward but enthusiastic "Tom" (Koji Yakusho).

Then John suddenly quits the school and Setsuko learns that Mika has run off with him to California. After drunkenly venting at a company farewell party for a despised colleague, Setsuko decides to fly to Los Angeles together with Ayako (Kaho Minami), her estranged older sister and Mika's worried mom.

This section is mostly East-meets-West comedy, as the sisters, their minimal English notwithstanding, track down a now broke and girlfriend-less John and, with him as a reluctant driver, go in search of Mika in San Diego, trading barbs all the way — some funny, some wounding.

The film's serious undercurrent surfaces as Setsuko's infatuation with John becomes more than a joke. She is, we see, not only a comically desperate 40-something woman, but also a little bad and a little mad. Terajima keeps all these elements under pitch-perfect control, even when the film plunges over the cliff (once literally) into histrionics.

She also keeps the audience on the contrary heroine's side. Flaws and all, you'll love "Lucy."

The Blood of Wolves, Koro no Chi, rating: ★★★★, runtime: 126 min.

The yakuza movie used to bestride the Japanese film industry like a colossus, but now clings to its margins. A well-known director occasionally essays the genre, as Takeshi Kitano did last year with "Outrage Coda," but a true revival has yet to come.

Director Kazuya Shiraishi delivers more of a homage than a revamp in "The Blood of Wolves," a cop thriller based on Yuko Yuzuki's novel of the same Japanese title. But the film's real inspiration, as Shiraishi himself has admitted, is "Battles Without Honor and Humanity," a seminal 1973-74 five-part series directed by Kinji Fukasaku.

Tracing a true-life 20-year gang war in Hiroshima and nearby Kure, "Battles" had a contemporary feel and a shot-on-the-fly propulsion. "The Blood of Wolves" is also set in Hiroshima but its story of a veteran cop (Koji Yakusho) suspected of being in cahoots with the yakuza unfolds in 1988 and has the air of a last hurrah, with its dirty hero being the last of his species. Which doesn't mean the film's many action scenes suffer from middle-aged blahs: The beatings and bloodlettings are staged with visceral realism and old-school punch.

The cop is Shogo Ogami (Yakusho), who's known as "Gami." Rumpled and profane, he bends police rules as casually as shaking out a cigarette from a crumpled pack, but he also gets results. Investigating the disappearance of a gang-connected accountant, he calmly asks new partner Hioka (Tori Matsuzaka), a straight arrow on the elite career track, to pick a fight with a burly gangster in a pachinko parlor. Hioka reluctantly complies and is getting bloodied and bruised when Gami finally comes to the rescue. Gami then smilingly totes up the various crimes he has just witnessed (and incited) that will send the hood, nicknamed Sumo, away for a long stretch. Would Sumo like to spill what he knows?

Witnessing this and other flagrant violations of proper police procedure, Hioka decides that Gami is both a bad role model and a corrupt cop. Gami, however, is more occupied with a brewing gang war. Back in 1974 the Odani-gumi fought a bloody turf battle with the powerful Irako-kai. Now, 14 years later, the Irako-kai's slithery boss (Renji Ishibashi) has joined forces with the Kakomura-gumi to finally take over Odani territory.

Suspecting that the Kakomuras are behind the accountant's disappearance, Gami wants to learn the truth and prevent an Odani-Kakomura war. But he also seems to be supporting the Odanis, while undermining the Kakomuras at every opportunity. What, Hioka wonders, is really going on?

Junya Ikegami's script deftly peels away the plot's layers within layers. Also, despite the many characters, including a canny bar madam (Yoko Maki) and a clownish sound-truck rightwinger (Pierre Taki), the film never feels over-populated. For one thing, violent death thins the herd with maximum impact. For another, both cops and gangsters are more picturesquely flawed individuals than types, while not always being what they seem, Gami first and foremost.

Veteran Yakusho has played similar characters before, including the unhinged cop in Tetsuya Nakashima's "The World of Kanako" (2014), but he brings a fresh energy to the role of Gami, as though tangling with ruthless criminals were a fun game.

But Gami is also a serious professional, if one who hides his true motives behind an un-serious mask. The long wait for it to drop is worth it.

Shoplifters, Manbiki Kazoku, rating: ★★★★★, runtime: 120 min.

When a Japanese director wins the Palme d'Or — the highest award at the Cannes Film Festival, the film world's equivalent of soccer's World Cup — the response of the local media is to celebrate: Our side won. Making the victory sweeter for Hirokazu Koreeda in his sixth Cannes appearance, with the family drama "Shoplifters," was his film's underdog status: Despite ranking high in the critics' poll of Cannes competition films conducted by Screen International magazine, "Shoplifters" was largely ignored in speculation about the probable Palme victor (Japanese media, of course, excepted).

"We were completely bowled over by 'Shoplifters.' How intermeshed the performances were with the directorial vision," jury president Cate Blanchett told the press in explaining the jury's decision. "It was one of the quietest, loveliest and most emotionally enduring films in the competition," she added.

On sitting down to watch this first Japanese Palme d'Or winner since Shohei Imamura's "The Eel" in 1997, I was determined to resist the hype and view it as another of the director's many family dramas, including the underappreciated gem "Still Walking" (2008), the box-office hit "Like Father, Like Son" (2013) and the good-but-flawed "After the Storm" (2016).

But this film about an ersatz family struggling in the shadows in today's Japan rivals Koreeda's best work to date, the thematically similar "Nobody Knows" (2004). The cheers are entirely deserved. Both films are outwardly naturalistic in dialogue and structure: The characters of "Shoplifters" speak in everyday language that sounds less scripted than taped, as one incident of thievery and chicanery leads to the next, with little obvious plotting.

But Koreeda, who trained as a documentary filmmaker and once aspired to be a novelist, inserts lines that illuminate and pierce, while masterfully building to a climax stronger in reflection than the moment. Films centered on a mystery typically go for the big reveal (the hero is really a ghost, for example); with "Shoplifters" the mystery deepens after the credits roll, with no single interpretation being correct.

The film's "family" consists of Osamu (Lily Franky), a day laborer; his wife, Nobuyo (Sakura Ando), who works at a factory-like laundry; her younger half-sister, Aki (Mayu Matsuoka), who strips for unseen clients at a sex shop; and the elderly Hatsue (Kirin Kiki), who illegally draws her late husband's pension and contributes it to the family coffers. Even Shota (Kairi Jyo), a sharp-eyed boy whom Osamu has trained in the finer points of shoplifting, chips in his takings. But they are still living from paycheck to paycheck — and theft to theft.

As the film begins, a lost, abused little girl, Yuri (Miyu Sasaki), wanders into their lives. Rather than report her to the police they take her in — and she soon joins Osamu and Shota in their shoplifting forays. Despite their hardscrabble, larcenous lifestyles, Osamu, Nobuyo and the others are close in ways that belong to an earlier, more naturally human era — no one stares zombie-like at their smartphone. Instead they co-exist mostly peacefully and intimately in Hatsue's ramshackle house and, on a summer trip to the beach, play together with carefree joy.

But we are also aware, from early on, that the family is not what it seems. Shota refuses to call Osamu "Dad" and Nobuyo "Mom," while Shota and Nobuyo drop hints that they are keeping up a front and hiding secrets. Those secrets come out, as they must, but for all its twists, the story is more than about masks dropping. The feelings the family members have for each other are real, as are the kindnesses done and the sacrifices made. The family, for all its lies and crimes, is not completely fake or evil. But the members can also never escape the darkness of their pasts.

"Shoplifters" ends with a last, poignant image that feels captured rather than staged. And yet its sums up everything the film has been saying, with eloquence poetic and plain, about the human condition — midway, as Plotinus once put it, between the gods and the beasts.

One Cut of the Dead, Kamera o Tomeruna!, rating: ★★★★, runtime: 96 min.

Both budgets and box-office prospects for Japanese indie films have been declining for years. As the former approaches the zero mark, so do recognizable actors and other standard indicators of quality. Audiences, smelling amateurism, stay away.

Flying in the face of this dismal trend is Shinichiro Ueda's brilliant zombie comedy "One Cut of the Dead," made for nearly nothing with a no-name cast. An international festival favorite, it has stirred up the sort of pre-release buzz that films with 10 times its ¥2.5 million budget can't buy.

Though he has directed prize-winning shorts, as well as a segment of the 2015 omnibus feature "Cat Quarters," Ueda is a relative newcomer, as is the film's cast, who are all students at Enbu Seminar, a Tokyo film school. "One Cut of the Dead" is a workshop film made under the school's Cinema Project banner. This film differs from the struggling indie hordes in one crucial way: The script, written by Ueda, is a work of pop cinema genius, with a Chinese box of a story whose surprises feel more inspired than contrived. Meanwhile, the film makes laugh-out-loud virtues out of its calculated amateurishness, from helter-skelter staging to slapdash effects.

"One Cut of the Dead" begins as a "making of" video for a zombie movie shoot in an abandoned factory. The director (Takayuki Hamazu), a loudmouthed perfectionist, is driving his cast and crew up the wall and is at a breaking point himself since the producer (Yoshiko Takehara) had the mad idea of shooting the entire story in one long take for TV broadcast — he has flubbed 42 times already. No wonder he's sweating bullets.

While running his exhausted actors through their paces yet again, a real zombie appears on the scene, hungry for human flesh. Instead of telling everyone to run for their lives, the director continues to shoot. After all, this is career-changing footage, but his terrified cast and crew are turning into zombies one by one. His epic may end up being seen only by the zombies themselves, assuming they can work a camera.

Up till this point the film is a knock-about comedy, filmed with a crazed energy and headlong pace, its big joke being the nutty director obsessed with his art in the middle of chaos. Its funniest character, though, is the director's wife (Harumi Shuhama), a retired actress helping out behind the scenes who proves to be a kick-ass zombie fighter.

Thirty-seven minutes in, just as the joke is wearing thin, the story resets, with a fresh perspective that infuses the proceedings with a new energy and meaning. The film becomes even funnier, while making us appreciate the dedication, ingenuity and passion of its on-screen movie folk — and the unknowns who play them.

Then, just as we are waiting for the credits to roll, Ueda tops his topper, taking the film to yet another level. What had begun as a clever, if patchily executed, stunt becomes an even more inspiring ode to filmmaking.

On a personal note, immediately after seeing the film I strongly recommended it to the Udine Far East Film Festival in Italy, where it had its international premiere in April. At the end, the 500-strong audience gave it a five-minute standing ovation. And tossing critical objectivity to the winds, I applauded with them. Another happy victim of the zombie infection.

Dare to Stop Us, Tomerareru ka, Oretachi O, rating: ★★★★, runtime: 119 min.

In the 1960s Koji Wakamatsu was Japanese cinema's enfant terrible: A real-life outlaw — he once joined a yakuza gang and served time in prison — he made pioneering "pink" (softcore porn) films such as "The Embryo Hunts in Secret" (1966) and "Go, Go, Second Time Virgin" (1969), whose extreme sex and violence, filmed with raw energy and wild invention, gave censors and industry guardians conniption fits.

His defenders (including Wakamatsu himself) claimed he was reflecting the era's trends and critiquing its crimes, from the Vietnam War to the Manson family killings.

I interviewed and met Wakamatsu several times prior to his untimely death in a road accident on Oct. 17, 2012. He was feisty and outspoken, but his sense of mission also struck me. He saw himself as a truth-telling guerrilla in a business, society and world dedicated to peddling convenient lies.

All that and more is reflected in "Dare to Stop Us," Kazuya Shiraishi's new film about Wakamatsu, his circle and his era. A former Wakamatsu apprentice who has directed noirish films such as "The Devil's Path" (2013) and "The Blood of Wolves" (2018), Shiraishi has made an affectionate and hard-hitting homage, not a hagiography. Covering the years 1969 to 1972, when Wakamatsu was at the height of his creativity and notoriety, the film shows him as brusque, quick-tempered and self-aggrandizing. But in Arata Iura's inspired performance he is also passionate, dedicated and big-hearted. Not an easy man to work for — or leave.

The story's true focus, however, is Megumi Yoshizumi (Mugi Kadowaki), a 21-year-old newcomer when she joins Wakamatsu Production in 1969 at the urging of a hippy free spirit and Wakamatsu employee known as Ghost. Here she encounters not only the fearsome Wakamatsu, who at first barely acknowledges her existence, but also Masao Adachi (Hiroshi Yamamoto), a radical scriptwriter and director, and Haruhiko Arai (Kisetsu Fujiwara), a caustic film critic and assistant director. These and other members of the Wakamatsu "family" (including Megumi herself) are based on actual people, some still living, but in the film they begin as caricatures, introduced with broad, semi-comic strokes. As the years pass and the story grows more complex, they becomes less cartoonish and more rounded, though they remain subjects in a group portrait.

Meanwhile, Megumi quickly adapts to her testosterone-charged environment, smoking, drinking and even shoplifting records to supplement the company coffers, but she's slow to shake her self-doubts. As she moves up the ladder while catering to Wakamatsu's whims and doing whatever it takes to keep his little movie factory going, she gains competence and confidence.

Then Ghost, her one confidant from her pre-Wakamatsu days, departs the company saying he's used up his "energy deposits." Shaken, Megumi stays on and even makes her first film as director, a 30-minute porno for the love hotel trade, but her old enthusiasm has evaporated. What, if anything, can revive it?

As Megumi, Kadowaki nails the anything-goes vibe of the era's counterculture while thoroughly inhabiting her character's isolation, insecurities and, as Wakamatsu shifts from experimental filmmaking to radical politics, crushing uncertainty. She is by turns funny, likeable, dark and unknowable. More than Wakamatsu himself, she raises the film above the level of a nostalgia piece to a tragic drama of a woman who deserved more than the times — and her own heart — would allow.

458

The Hungry Lion, Ueta Lion, rating: ★★★★, runtime: 78 min.

Teenagers take chances that, to the adults in their lives, are sheer idiocy (as I know first-hand from both sides of the teenager-adult divide). These days anything they do or say can also end up on social media, which can instantly turn an adolescent goof into a mass roasting by thousands of strangers. Short of taking away their smartphones, which would be like exiling them to Siberia, what can be done? Takaomi Ogata's "The Hungry Lion," which premiered at the 2017 Tokyo International Film Festival, does not answer that question with finger-pointing or hand-wringing. Rather, with cool restraint and precision, the film illustrates the process by which the internet destroys, celebrates and forgets a young life touched by scandal.

The entire story plays out in 74 on-screen minutes, with one scene fading starkly into the next — and not a single wasted second. No one comes off particularly well, including the heroine, for reasons best left unexplained. And no one deserves what happens to her.

She is Hitomi (Urara Matsubayashi), a pretty, popular high schooler with a handsome boyfriend, Hiroki (Atomu Mizuishi), as the film begins. Then a male teacher is arrested on an unspecified obscenity charge and a rumor circulates that Hitomi is the girl in the teacher's online sex video. Her friends, beginning with her bestie, Moe (Sakiko Kato), support her, as does Hiroki, initially.

But sooner than you can say "meme," the tide shifts. Her younger sister, Asuka (Miku Uehara), complains that her classmates are teasing her about the now-viral video. Hiroki's rowdy pals make lewd remarks to her face. And her friends find excuses not to walk home with her.

Then, like a dam breaking, the vicious mockery escalates on social media, as does the bullying at school. Getting little understanding from her distracted single mom (Mariko Tsutsui), not to mention the now-unresponsive Hiroki, Hiromi feels isolated and abandoned.

Then suddenly she is gone — and the film widens from its exclusive focus on her personal drama. The media descend like locusts, while teachers who only wanted her out of sight solemnly intone hollow pieties. Strangers laugh about her in the streets, though others leap to her defense. The story plays out, in other words, like hundreds of others that ignite the internet for a day or week and then, like a sparkler, sputter and fade into oblivion.

But as distanced as its treatment of this familiar trajectory may be, the film is not cynical. It also does not overly explain; to the end Hitomi remains an enigma, her motives wrapped in silence. It is clear, though, that whatever her faults and missteps, she is cruelly victimized by her nightmare of shaming, all the more intense since she is without an adult's resources, including a ticket out of town.

If "The Hungry Lion" were a documentary in fact and not just in style, we might expect talking-head experts to use Hitomi's tragedy as an example of a pressing problem, to which they offer up some solutions. But Ogata, who based the film on his own original script, draws no lessons, moralistic or otherwise. Instead he interestingly complicates his story beyond the "innocent victim versus evil SNS and mass media" binary. Yes, he wants us to feel pity — but also to understand the black unknown of the human heart.

Every Day a Good Day, Nichinichi Kore Kojitsu, rating: ★★★☆, runtime: 100 min.

I attended my first tea ceremony decades ago, as part of a company orientation. Kneeling on the floor, I sat in the formal seiza position, stumbled through the motions and sipped the thick green tea. Just as the pain in my legs was reaching a crescendo, I bowed to my host and hobbled out. I had next to no idea what it all meant. A box ticked off in the Japanese cultural experiences list?

Based on a collection of essays by Noriko Morishita, Tatsushi Omori's "Every Day a Good Day" knowledgeably and gorgeously shows how tea ceremony is far more than a feudal-era relic trotted out for bemused observers. For the heroine and her fellow followers of sadō (the way of tea), it is a shining embodiment of mindfulness — the philosophy and practice of living in the moment that is both timeless and trendy. Also, instead of going through the prescribed motions by rote, they use all five senses to experience beauty to the fullest at every seasonal turn. And the matcha that is the end product of their labors looks delicious. (Though as a fan of matcha in just about anything, I may be prejudiced.)

Known for his violent disruptions of conventions both social and cinematic, beginning with his 2005 debut "The Whispering of the Gods," Omori would seem to be out of his element in this decidedly nonviolent story. But he and his staff have created a Japan-esque paradise, where the distractions of the outside world, if not always its tragedies, are subsumed into a regime of beauty, order and, as paradoxical as it may sound, freedom.

His heroine is Noriko (Haru Kuroki), whom we first see as a 20-year-old college student in 1993. At the urging of her mother, Noriko and her cousin Michiko (Mikako Tabe) start tea ceremony classes at the nearby home of the elderly Takeda-sensei (Kirin Kiki). Under her watchful eye and strict, if supportive, instructions, they bumble through the basics, from the proper way to fold a fukusa (small cloth) to the correct way to enter a room. When Noriko, a logical type, questions this ritual, sensei just laughs. "You don't have to understand what it means," she says. First master form, she advises, "then you can pour your heart into it."

As the months and years pass, Noriko faces one crisis after another outside the teahouse — she fails to find a job after graduation and a boyfriend dumps her. Then, when she finally gets to know her way around a tea kettle, a high school girl (Mizuki Yamashita) joins the lessons — and proves to be a prodigy. Feeling outclassed and outcast, Noriko breaks down.

Drawn from Morishita's own life over the course of a quarter century, these incidents are sketched rather than fully developed. But in the course of her practice, Noriko slowly learns the truth of the film's title, taken from an ancient saying on Takeda-sensei's kakejiku (wall hanging): Every day is a good day. Pay attention, the tea ceremony teaches, and the smallest things, such as the sound of water dripping from the tea ladle, come to express the wonder of the present moment.

As Takeda-sensei the late Kirin Kiki, in one of her final performances, embodies that way of life perfectly. A true sage, on screen and off.

Ten Years Japan, rating: ★★★★, runtime: 99 min.

In 2015, a dystopian omnibus film by five young directors from Hong Kong titled "Ten Years" became an indie hit. Envisioning the deteriorating state of the city in a decade's time, the film enraged Chinese authorities — and inspired "Ten Years" versions in Taiwan, Thailand and Japan.

Supervised by acclaimed director Hirokazu Koreeda ("Shoplifters"), "Ten Years Japan" also features five young directors and five versions of this country's near future. Similar to the model on which the project is based, these future Japans are more chillingly possible than thrillingly fantastic — like a Japanese take on the sci-fi series "Black Mirror." The segments are also sharp and to the point, if different in style. Unusual for an omnibus film, the quality level is consistently high.

The first segment is Chie Hayakawa's "Plan 75," which begins with a young bureaucrat (Satoru Kawaguchi) patiently explaining a government euthanasia program to its intended targets: low-income and disabled seniors aged 75, who are deemed disposable. His stressed and pregnant wife (Kinuwo Yamada) then suggests her dementia-afflicted mother for "Plan 75."

Though its ironies are obvious, the segment suggests a likely "Japanese way" of killing off the elderly, with kind gestures, soothing words and subtle pressure to conform. The old folks march obediently to their ends.

In Yusuke Kinoshita's "Mischievous Alliance," a pilot program inculcates approved moral values in kids by wiring their brains to an AI system that monitors their every word and action. But one rebellious boy, with the aid of two classmates, releases an ailing horse from his stable. When he trots into the nearby woods they give chase as an elderly caretaker (Jun Kunimura) cheers them on.

Told with touches of humor, this segment offers hope that kids will keep being kids, even with a "moral adviser" implanted in their heads. But as we are reminded, defective systems can always be upgraded.

In Megumi Tsuno's "Data," a teenage girl (Hana Sugisaki) living with her kindly widowed father (Tetsushi Tanaka) accesses a "digital inheritance" program and learns of a disturbing episode in her mother's past. More a perceptive family drama than doom-laden sci-fi, "Data" nonetheless reaffirms a truth that can only become truer a decade on: In our brave new digital world, your past is both omnipresent and permanent.

In Akiyo Fujimura's "The Air We Can't See," humanity has been driven underground by nuclear disaster. A young girl, Mizuki, falls under the spell of her friend Kaede, who speaks enticingly of the "world above" where the sun shines and skies are blue — both wonders Mizuki has never seen. Despite the cautions of her worried mother (Chizuru Ikewaki), she goes exploring. Told entirely from Mizuki's viewpoint, this segment expresses her childish fears, desires and wonder with lyricism and power.

Last is Kei Ishikawa's "For Our Beautiful Country," in which a young ad agency flack (Taiga) is sent to tell a distinguished artist (Hana Kino) that her design for a new Defense Ministry recruiting poster has been scrapped. Set in a Japan that again drafts its youth to fight in foreign wars, this segment is the most overtly political — and blackly comic. Kino is charming as an unconventional type who likes VR shooting games — and poignant as the daughter of a dead war veteran.

But 10 years from now, how many here will still know or care about that war, especially if a Plan 75 erases the national memory in the name of the common good?

Hard-Core, rating: ★★★☆, runtime: 124 min.

Live-action manga adaptations — from weepy dramas about teenage love to goofy comedies set in fantasy worlds — usually reflect real life only at its extremes, whether it's the melodramatic or the idiotic. Then there is "Hard-Core Heisei Hell's Bros.," a cult manga about two losers — one with an out-of-control temper, the other intellectually challenged — who become inseparable pals in bubble-era Japan. Think of them as a Japanese version of George and Lennie from John Steinbeck's classic 1937 novella "Of Mice and Men."

Written by Marley Caribu and illustrated by Takashi Imashiro, "Hard-Core" ran in Grand Champion magazine from 1991 to 1993 and was published in four paperback volumes. Now it's a film directed by Nobuhiro Yamashita and starring Takayuki Yamada, a "Hard-Core" fan who first brought the manga to Yamashita's attention.

Yamashita has made a specialty of black comedies about men on society's margins, beginning with his 1999 debut "Hazy Life." Yamada has appeared in everything from commercial blockbusters to the "Ushijima the Loan Shark" film and TV series, playing the ice-cool hero. Yamada implicitly understands Yamashita's offbeat humor, as evidenced by the "Cannes Film Festival of Takayuki Yamada," a tongue-in-cheek TV mini-series he and the director made last year about wangling an invitation to the titlular film event.

Their take on the manga (read by me in one marathon session) is faithful to its contrary spirit, if not, thankfully, to its shambling narrative structure. The film's story sounds like a wild-and-crazy grab-bag in which black comedy meets sci-fi meets action-adventure. But Yamashita's default setting is wry detachment, not goofball gags. Also, as odd as they may be, his two main protagonists have deep-rooted traumas that make them more humanly three-dimensional — and the film more than a campy farrago.

Yamada plays Ukon Gondo, a hard-headed, pure-spirited type prone to violent explosions. His salaryman brother, Sakon (Takeru Satoh), is constantly getting him out of scrapes, more with disgust than compassion. Ukon's only friend is Ushiyama (Yoshiyoshi Arakawa), a hulking homeless guy who lives in an abandoned factory and communicates mostly by grunts, though he routinely beats Ukon at shogi. Once a week, Ukon and Ushiyama journey to an abandoned mine in Gunma Prefecture where they labor under the supervision of an eccentric elderly rightist, Kaneshiro (the recently deceased actor and performance artist Takuzo Kubikukuri) and his gruff foreman, Mizunuma (Suon Kan).

Kaneshiro has the crazy idea that the mine contains a trove of long-buried gold, but he pays real wages. Also, Ukon trusts and reveres him, somewhat like a World War II soldier who has volunteered to fight and die for the Emperor.

Then Ushiyama discovers a retro-looking robot in the factory and makes it his friend. Dubbed "Robo," this mechanical man can walk, though not talk, and seems to have a will of its own. Dressed in cast-off clothes, it accompanies Ukon and Ushiyama to town and even saves them from angry gangsters. When Sakon finds out about Robo he has the bright idea of using him to find the gold, assuming it exists.

There is more to the story, including the seduction of Ukon by Mizunuma's daughter Taeko (Kei Ishibashi) and, typically for a manga adaptation, "Hard-Core" sags under the weight of its plot complications. But Robo, after fading into the background for a long stretch, comes flying to the rescue, sending the film into a stranger, more wonderful dimension. Steinbeck can't beat that.

Killing, Zan, rating: ★★★★, runtime: 80 min.

Screening in competition at this year's Venice Film Festival, "Killing" is veteran provocateur Shinya Tsukamoto's first venture into the samurai genre. Made, like most of Tsukamoto's films, on a tiny budget and tight schedule, it does not attempt the scale of classics like "Seven Samurai" (1954) or "Yojimbo" (1961).

Instead, Tsukamoto's camera moves in close to capture the weight of the swords, the lethality of the razor-sharp blades and the swirling chaos of the action. Some of the fight scenes, with their slowly gathering menace and swift death, recall Akira Kurosawa's afore-mentioned masterpieces, but Tsukamoto's overall approach is more intimate and less heroic. As he has said in interviews, the film is the antithesis of the classic samurai movie, in which good battles evil. Much like his 2014 World War II film "Fires on the Plain," with its anti-war message, "Killing" questions the deadly violence that is the genre's bedrock.

How, the young samurai Mokunoshin Tsuzuki (Sosuke Ikematsu) asks himself, can one man bring himself to kill another? Expert with the sword, he hesitates to use it even when his life and honor are at stake. Fans of the genre, eager to see slicing and dicing, may become impatient with Mokunoshin's quest for an answer, but the action, when it comes, is all the more impactful for the hero's struggles with his conscience and courage.

The story is simple: At the end of the Edo Period (1603-1868) samurai rebels are joining forces to overthrow the shogun, while others are rushing to defend him. Meanwhile, Mokunoshin is living quietly in a village not far from the capital. To keep himself in fighting shape, he trains an impetuous young farmer, Ichisuke (Ryusei Maeda), in swordsmanship as the boy's tempestuous older sister Yu (Yu Aoi) looks on. While worried that Ichisuke will get himself into fatal trouble, she is attracted to his teacher, though she and Mokunoshin exchange only the briefest of glances.

Then an older samurai, Sawamura (Tsukamoto), arrives in the village and recruits Mokunoshin and Ichisuke to join a band he is assembling to fight on the shogun's side. But first they have to deal with bandits lurking on the village outskirts, led by the ruthless Genda (Tatsuya Nakamura).

This "samurai defends the peasant village from outlaws" story is familiar from "Seven Samurai." And Sawamura, with his close-shaven head and air of quiet authority, recalls the older film's samurai leader played by Takashi Shimura. But "Killing" soon takes a radically different direction (Tsukamoto says he was inspired by Kon Ichikawa's 1973 nihilistic samurai actioner "The Wanderers"). The attraction between Mokushin and Yu intensifies, as does Yu's anger at the forces of violence gathering around her and those she loves. And Sawamura proves to be a dangerous ally, fanatically devoted to a deadly code. Certain shots, such as a medium close-up of Sawamura's death-mask-like face glowing in the darkness, are starkly evocative, but others, as in the sword-swinging brawl between the samurai and bandits, recall Tsukamoto's origins in cyber-punk cinema, with its disturbing mix of violence and grotesquery. The slashing score of long-time collaborator Chu Ishikawa (who died shortly after filming was completed) adds to the effect.

No, "Killing" is not your father's samurai movie, but it's all Tsukamoto, who has always been about the dark strangeness of the human heart, even when his hero wears a topknot.

Fly Me to the Saitama, Tonde Saitama, rating: ★★★★, runtime: 107 min.

Places considered cool and uncool sometimes exist in uneasy proximity, like New York City and New Jersey — or Tokyo and Saitama. The prefecture adjacent to the Japanese capital has the image of being a land of boring commuter towns with no cultural attractions beyond shopping malls and family restaurants. All this and more is grist for "Fly Me to the Saitama," a comedy by Hideki Takeuchi that takes this city-suburb clash to absurd and fantastic extremes. Based on a manga by Mineo Maya, the film is packed with knowing observations and pointed jabs at the similarly disrespected prefectures of Chiba, Gunma, Tochigi and Ibaraki.

This could have been the definition of an only-for-Japan movie, but Takeuchi, director of the hit time-travel comedy "Thermae Romae" (2012), crosses cultures entertainingly, though his present-day characters journey through the more stupefying bits of the Saitama plain. For this native of Ohio — an American equivalent of Saitama — the gags hit home. The snobberies and status anxieties behind many of them are hardly limited to Japan.

Also, I live uncomfortably close to that benighted prefecture and am secretly glad I have a Tokyo address, though, as the film cruelly reminds me, I can hardly be considered a "real" Tokyoite.

The story begins with the Sugawaras —Mom (Kumiko Aso), Dad (Brother Tom) and adult daughter Aimi (Haruka Shimazaki) — driving from the family home in Kumagaya, Saitama — notorious for being the hottest place in Japan — to a ceremony celebrating Aimi's engagement. Dad, a proud son of Saitama, becomes offended at his daughter's eagerness to leave Kumagaya for Tokyo. To calm troubled waters, Mom tunes to a radio play about the rebellion of Saitama citizens against their Tokyo overlords.

Cut to an alternative Tokyo, where Saitama-ese must have a special visa to enter the capital's hallowed precincts and are regarded by Tokyoites as the lowest of the low. One is Momomi Dannoura (Fumi Nikaido), the cosseted son of the Tokyo governor and student council president at the elite Hakuhodo Academy. However, his primacy there is soon threatened by Rei Asami (the single-named Gackt), a transfer student from America who melts female hearts with his sophistication and long-haired beauty. Enraging Momomi further is Rei's sympathy for scholarship students from Saitama, wretches forced to live in misery apart from the Versailles-like splendors of the Hakuhodo campus.

The governor's butler, Akutsu (Yusuke Iseya), suspects that Rei is not all he seems, but after a sudden kiss, Momomi falls under Rei's spell and becomes his inseparable companion. Then Momomi learns Rei's true identity and background, forcing him to choose between his love or his father, soon to become Rei's sworn enemy?

The guy-meets-guy plot, as Aimi acerbically notes, resembles a "boys love" manga, but Takeuchi and scriptwriter Yuichi Tokunaga expand it with both topical references and action scenes straight from a samurai swashbuckler, complete with feudal-era costumes, if not swords. All this is played with a theatrically straight face — and is funnier for it.

As the sexually conflicted Momomi, Nikaido mixes shōjo manga (girls' comic) seriousness with sly meta humor to hilarious effect. With her playing the lead, "Fly Me to the Saitama" spreads its wings to the world.

Melancholic, Merankorikku, rating: ★★★★, runtime: 114 min.

Almost every year at the Tokyo International Film Festival (TIFF) at least one film by a new Japanese director gets talked up by visiting programmers, journalists and critics as a find.

Last year one such buzz film was Seiji Tanaka's debut feature, "Melancholic." I was among its fans, telling all and sundry that it was the most original film I had seen at the festival. The jury of the Japanese Cinema Splash section, where the film had its world premiere, validated this assessment by awarding Tanaka its best director prize.

Based on his original script, the film had a budget of ¥3 million that Tanaka and his producer and star Yoji Minagawa had scraped together. It had to be shot over the course of several weekends, since Tanaka was working a full-time job at the time.

Given this provenance, "Melancholic" should have been a patchy affair, like so many zero-budget indie films before and since. Instead it is extraordinarily well made, with every performance spot on and every scene taut, without a single wasted moment.

"Melancholic" begins as yet another of the many local films about a lonely misfit guy drifting on the social margins. Instead of the usual exercise in quirky minimalism, however, it becomes a mashup of action, comedy, romance and family drama. Given its family-unfriendly subject matter, this exercise in genre-crossing could have been off-putting, but Tanaka and his cast of accomplished unknowns bring it off engagingly and credibly.

As the story begins, our hero, Kazuhiko (Minagawa), is a recent graduate of the University of Tokyo — Japan's answer to Harvard — but is unemployed and living at home with his (unusual for a Japanese film) supportive parents. Smart, but unworldly and socially awkward, Kazuhiko looks and acts like a typical nerd, right down to his big-framed glasses.

Rather than wander the nerdy mecca of Akihabara, Kazuhiko finds work at a local bathhouse scrubbing the tiles and taking tickets from customers.

By chance, he learns that after hours the bathhouse is used for yakuza-ordered executions and that a hard-faced, shaggy-haired co-worker is the executioner. Outed as a witness to these murders by the co-worker and the cagey bathhouse owner, Kazuhiko is ordered to become the night janitor, with body disposal part of his duties.

Instead of making tracks to the nearest police station, Kazuhiko is drawn into the orbit of those involved in this grim business, including the owner, who is deeply in debt to the yakuza; the hitman, who takes pride in his deadly work; and a friendly, blonde-haired fellow employee (Yoshitomo Isozaki) who is about Kazuhiko's age — and has a past he is not eager to disclose.

Meanwhile, Kazuhiko starts dating Yuri (Mebuki Yoshida), a bubbly former high school classmate who is a bathhouse regular but knows nothing of its deadly sideline.

This story may sound creepy, but "Melancholic" makes it darkly funny, viscerally thrilling and improbably heartwarming, all without departing far from the stark immediacy of its opening scenes. How it accomplishes this alchemy is something of a mystery. One essential ingredient: characters who are baseline likable, even when doing the dirtiest of dirty work. Not that I'd ever be tempted to take up Kazuhiko's broom.

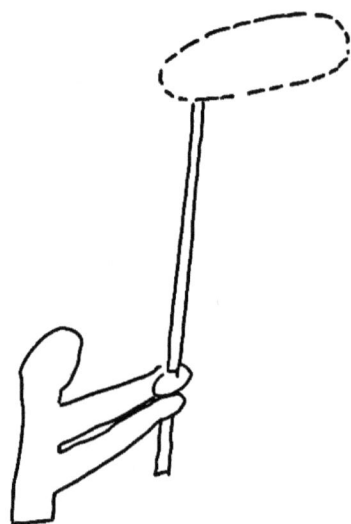

PART 4:
ANNUAL BEST OF LISTS

Best Ten 2000

1. The Face (Kao), Junji Sakamoto
2. Audition, Takashi Miike
3. Monday, Sabu
4. The New God (Atarashii Kamisama), Yutaka Tsuchiya
5. Love/Juice, Kaze Shindo
6. Freeze Me, Takashi Ishii
7. The Dentist (Shikai), Shun Nakahara
8. When the Rain Lifts (Ame Agaru), Takashi Koizumi
9. Zawa-Zawa Shimo-kitazawa, Jun Ichikawa
10. Charisma, Kiyoshi Kurosawa

Best Ten 2002

1. Out, Hideyuki Hirayama
2. The Laughing Frog (Waraeru Kaeru), Hideyoshi Hirayama
3. Shangri-La (Kinyu Hametsu Nippon: Togenkyo no Hitobito), Takashi Miike
4. Doing Time (Keimusho no Naka), Yo'ichi Sai
5. Harmful Insect (Gaichu), Akihito Shiota
6. Suite de Jeudi (Mokuyo Kumikyoku), Tetsuo Shinohara
7. Dog Star, Takehisa Zeze
8. A Woman's Work (Travail), Kentaro Otani
9. Alexei's Spring (Alexei no Izumi), Sei'ichi Motohashi
10. Chicken Heart, Hiroshi Shimizu

Best Ten 2003

1. Vibrator, Ryuichi Hirokix
2. Zatoichi, Takeshi Kitano
3. Karaoke Terror (Showa Kayo Daizenshu), Tetsuo Shinohara
4. G@me, Satoshi Isaka
5. Doppelganger, Kiyoshi Kurosawa
6. Gozu (Gokudo Kyofu Daigekijo Gozu), Takashi Miike
7. Shara (Shara Soju), Naomi Kawase
8. The Grudge (Juon), Takashi Shimizu
9. A Snake of June (Hachigatsu no Hebi), Shin'ya Tsukamoto
10. 9 Souls, Toshiaki Toyoda

Best Ten 2004

1. Blood and Bones (Chi to Hone), Yoichi Sai
2. Nobody Knows (Dare mo Shiranai), Hirokazu Koreeda
3. Howl's Moving Castle (Howl no Ugoku Shiro), Hayao Miyazaki
4. Mind Game, Masaaki Yuasa
5. Survival Style 5+, Gen Sekiguchi
6. Swing Girls, Shinobu Yaguchi
7. Aoi Kuruma (A Blue Automobile), Hiroshi Okuhara
8. Casshern, Kazuaki Kiriya
9. Vital, Shinya Tsukamoto
10. Kamikaze Girls (Shimotsuma Monogatari), Tetsuya Nakashima

Best Ten 2005

1. Whispering of the Gods (Germania no Yoru), Tatsushi Omori
2. Hanging Garden (Kuchu Teien), Toshiaki Toyoda
3. Cycling Chronicles: Landscapes the Boy Saw (17-sai no Fukei: Shonen wa Nani o Mita ka), Koji Wakamatsu
4. Linda, Linda, Linda, Nobuhiro Yamashita
5) Buried Forest (Umoregi), Kohei Oguri
6. A Stranger of Mine (Unmei ja nai Hito), Kenji Uchida
7. World's End/Girl Friend (Sekai no Owari), Shiori Kazama
8. Pacchigi, Kazuyuki Izutsu
9. The Glamorous Life of Sachiko Hanai ("Hanai Sachiko no Karei na Shogai), Mitsuru Meike
10. In the Pool, Satoshi Miki

Best Ten 2006

1. Who's Camus Anyway? (Camus Nante Shiranai), Mitsuo Yanagimachi
2. Bashing, Masahiro Kobayashi
3. Memories of Tomorrow (Ashita no Kioku), Kanako Higuchi
4. Paprika, Satoshi Kon
5. Strawberry Shortcakes, Hitoshi Yazaki
6. Love and Honor (Bushi no Ichibun), Yoji Yamada
7. Hula Girls, Sang-ill Lee
8. Pavilion Salamandre (Pavilion Sansho Uo), Masanori Tominaga
9. Granny Gabai (Saga no Gabai Baachan), Hitoshi Kurauchi
10. Ski Jumping Pairs: The Road to Torino, Riichiro Mashima and Masaki Kobayashi

Best Ten 2007

1. Adrift in Tokyo (Tenten), Satoshi Miki
2. Sakuran, Mika Ninagawa
3. Big Man Japan (Dainipponjin), Hitoshi Matsumoto
4. I Just Didn't Do It (Sore Demo Boku wa Yatteinai), Masayuki Suo
5. The Mourning Forest (Mogari no Mori), Naomi Kawase
6. Last Words (Koi Suru Nichiyobi: Koi Shita), Ryuichi Hiroki
7. The Village Submerged (Mizu ni Natta Mura), Nobuo Onishi
8. 5 Centimeters per Second (Byosoku 5 Centimeters), Makoto Shinkai
9. The Foreign Duck, the Native Duck and God in a Coin Locker (Ahiru to Kamo no Coin Locker), Yoshihiro Nakamura
10. Funuke, Show Some Love, You Losers (Funukedomo Kanashimi no Ai o Misero), Daihaichi Yoshida

Best Ten 2008

1. Tokyo Sonata, Kiyoshi Kurosawa
2. Departures (Okuribito), Yojiro Takita
3. All Around Us (Gururi no Koto), Ryosuke Hashiguchi
4. Still Walking (Aruitemo Aruitemo), Hirokazu Kore'eda
5) United Red Army (Jitsuroku Nihon Sekigun Asama Sanso e no Michi), Koji Wakamatsu
6. Your Friends (Kimi no Tomodachi), Ryuchi Hiroki
7. Fine, Totally Fine (Zen Zen Daijobu), Yosuke Fujita
8. Sex Is No Laughing Matter (Hito no Sex o Warau na), Nami Iguchi
9. Kabee — Our Mother (Kabee), Yoji Yamada
10. Ponyo (Gake no Ue no Ponyo), Hayao Miyazaki

Best Ten 2009

1. Fish Story, Yoshihiro Nakamura
2. Dear Doctor, Miwa Nishikawa
3. Summer Wars, Mamoru Hosoda
4. Villon's Wife (Villon no Tsuma), Kichitaro Negishi
5. Zero Focus (Zero Shoten), Isshin Inudo
6. The Chief of South Polar (Nankyokyu Ryomin), Shuichi Okita
7. Live Tape, Tetsuaki Matsue
8. Instant Swamp (Instant Numa), Satoshi Miki
9. Symbol, Hitoshi Matsumoto
10. Bare Essence of Life (Ultra Miracle Love Story), Satoko Yokoyama

Best Ten 2010

1. Villain (Akunin), Lee Sang-il
2. Caterpillar (Kyatapira), Koji Wakamatsu
3. Confessions (Kokuhaku), Tetsuya Nakashima
4. 13 Assassins (Jusannin no Shikaku), Takashi Miike
5. About Her Brother (Ototo), Yoji Yamada
6. Golden Slumber (Goruden Suranba), Noh Dong-seok
7. Boys on the Run (Boizu on za Ran), Daisuke Miura
8. Sweet Little Lies (Suito Ritoru Raizu), Hitoshi Yazaki
9. The Borrowers (Kari-gurashi no Arietti), Hiromasa Yonebayashi
10. The Accidental Kidnapper (Yukai Rhapsody), Hideo Sakaki

Best Ten 2011

1. Cold Fish (Tsumetai Nettaigyo), Sion Sono
2. Egoist (Keibetsu), Ryuichi Hiroki
3. Love Strikes! (Moteki), Hitoshi One
4. Cannonball Wedlock (Kigeki Konzen Tokkyu), Koji Maeda
5. Household X (Kazoku X), Koki Yoshida
6. Ending Note: Death of a Japanese Salesman (Endingu Noto), Mami Sunada
7. Post Card (Ichimai no Hagaki), Kaneto Shindo
8. I Wish (Kiseki), Hirokazu Koreeda
9. Hara-Kiri: Death of a Samurai (Ichimei), Takashi Miike
10. My Back Page, Nobuhiro Yamashita

Best Ten 2012

1. Our Homeland (Kazoku no Kuni), Yang Yong Hi
2. Dreams for Sale (Yume Uru Futari), Miwa Nishikawa
3. The Woodsman and the Rain (Kitsutsuki to Ame), Shuichi Okita
4. The Cowards Who Looked to the Sky (Fugainai Boku wa Sora wo Mita), Yuki Tanada
5. Outrage Beyond, Takeshi Kitano
6. A Letter to Momo (Momo e no Tegami), Hiroyuki Okiura
7. Key Of Life (Kagi Dorobo no Mesotdo), Kenji Uchida
8. The Land of Hope (Kibo no Kuni), Sion Sono
9. The Drudgery Train (Kueki Ressha), Nobuhiro Yamashita
10. I Have to Buy New Shoes (Atarashii Kutsu o Kawanakucha), Eriko Kitagawa

Best Ten 2013

1. The Tale of the Princess Kaguya (Kaguya-hime no Monogatari), Isao Takahata
2. Like Father, Like Son (Soshite Chichi ni Naru), Hirokazu Koreeda
3. A Story of Yonosuke (Yokomichi Yonosuke), Shuichi Okita
4. The Devil's Path (Kyoaku), Kazuya Shiraishi
5. The Wind Rises (Kaze Tachinu), Hayao Miyazaki
6. The Ravine of Goodbye (Sayonara Keikoku), Tatsushi Omori
7. GFP Bunny (Thallium Shojo no Dokusatsu Nikki), Yutaka Tsuchiya
8. Homesick, Satoru Hirohara
9. It's Me, it's Me (Ore Ore), Satoshi Miki
10. Japan's Tragedy (Nihon no Higeki), Masahiro Kobayashi

Best Ten 2014

1. The Light Shines Only There (Soko nomi nite Hikari Kagayaku), Mipo Oh
2. Pale Moon (Kami no Tsuki), Daihachi Yoshida
3. Tokyo Tribe, Sion Sono
4. The Tale of Iya (Iya Monogatari: Oku no Hiro), Tetsuichiro Tsuta
5. 0.5 mm (0.5 Miri), Momoko Ando
6. My Man (Watashi no Otoko), Kazuyoshi Kumakiri
7. Be My Baby (Koi no Uzu), Hitoshi One
8. Forma, Ayumi Sakamoto
9. Au Revoir L'Ete (Hotori no Sakuko), Koji Fukada
10. Fuku-chan of FukuFuku Flats (Fukufukuso no Fuku-chan), Yosuke Fujita

Best Ten 2015

1. Three Stories of Love (Koibitotachi), Ryosuke Hashiguchi
2. Nobi (Fires on the Plain), Shinya Tsukamoto
3. 100 Yen Love (Hyakuen no Koi), Masaharu Take
4. My Little Sister (Umimachi Diary), Hirokazu Koreeda
5. Kabukicho Love Hotel (Sayonara Kabukicho), Ryuichi Hiroki
6. Being Good (Kimi wa Ii Ko), Mipo Oh
7. Obon Brothers (Obon Kyodai), Akira Osaki
8. Bakuman, Hitoshi One
9. Round Trip Heart (Romance), Yuki Tanada
10. Antonym (Rasen Ginga), Natsuka Kusano

Best Ten 2016

1. Harmonium (Fuchi ni Tatsu), Koji Fukada
2. Creepy (Kuripi: Itsuwari no Rinjin), Kiyoshi Kurosawa
3. Satoshi: A Move for Tomorrow (Satoshi no Seishun), Yoshitaka Mori
4. The Long Excuse (Nagai Iiwake), Miwa Nishikawa
5) A Bride for Rip Van Winkle (Rippu Van Winkuru no Hanayome), Shunji Iwai
6. Scoop!, Hitoshi One
7. Mohican Comes Home (Mohican Kokyo ni Kaeru), Shuichi Okita
8. After the Storm (Umi Yori mo Mada Fukaku), Hirokazu Koreeda
9. Seto Utsumi (Seto to Utsumi), Tatsushi Omori
10. In This Corner of the World (Kono Sekai no Katasumi ni), Sunao Katabuchi

Best Ten 2017

1. The Third Murder (Sandome no Satsujin), Hirokazu Koreeda
2. Foreboding (Yocho), Kiyoshi Kurosawa
3. Side Job (Kanojo no Jinsei wa Machigai Janai), Ryuichi Hiroki
4. Antiporno, Sion Sono
5. Bangkok Nites, Katsuya Tomita
6. Tremble All You Want (Katte ni Furuetero), Akiko Ooku
7. Hanagatami, Nobuhiko Obayashi
8. Alley Cat, Hideo Sakaki
9. Dear Etranger (Osanago Warera ni Umare), Yukiko Mishima
10. Poolsideman, Hirobumi Watanabe

Best Five 2018

1. Shoplifters (Manbiki Kazoku), Hirokazu Koreeda
2. One Cut of the Dead (Kamera wo Tomeru na), Shinichirou Ueda
3. Dare to Stop Us (Tomerareru ka, Oretachi wo), Kazuya Shiraishi
4. Mori, the Artist's Habitat (Mori no iru basho), Shuichi Okita
5. Sennan Asbestos Disaster (Nippon koku vs Sennan ishiwata son), Kazuo Hara

Mark Schilling

Author Mark Schilling set off for Japan in 1975 to immerse himself in the culture, learn the language, and haunt the theaters. He has been there ever since. In 1989 he became a regular film reviewer for "The Japan Times," and has written on Japanese film for publications including "Variety," "Screen International," "Premier," "Newsweek," "Wall Street Journal," "Japan Quarterly," "Winds," "Cinemaya," and "Kinema Jumpo."

Tomoki Watanabe

Cinephile and illustrator Tomoki Watanabe was born in Tokyo in 1980 and is well known in Japan and abroad for his paintings, illustrations and bird sculptures. He also teaches painting, plays piano, and can often be found hitchhiking. You can learn more about recent projects of his by visiting http://suetomii.wix.com/tomoki

Awai Books
Recent Releases

HIM HER THAT
WISUT PONNIMIT
Translated from Japanese by Matthew Chozick

"*It's as if magic coats the pages*"
—
Novelist
Banana Yoshimoto

HIM
HER
THAT

WISUT PONNIMIT

"The English manga book
you simply have to buy"
—*Time Out Tokyo*

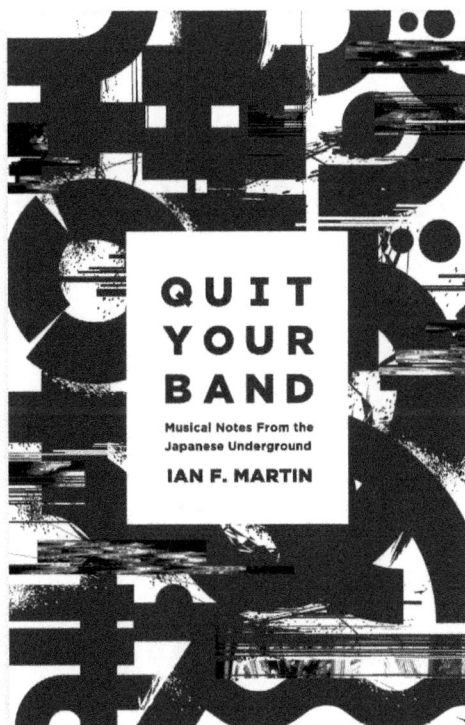

Eiko & Koma

Forrest
Gander

Translated by
Eri Nakagawa
Matthew Chozick

"[Pulitzer Prize awardee Forrest Gander's]
poems are exquisite in their renderings of
corporeal motion and existential curiosity."
—*Metropolis Magazine*

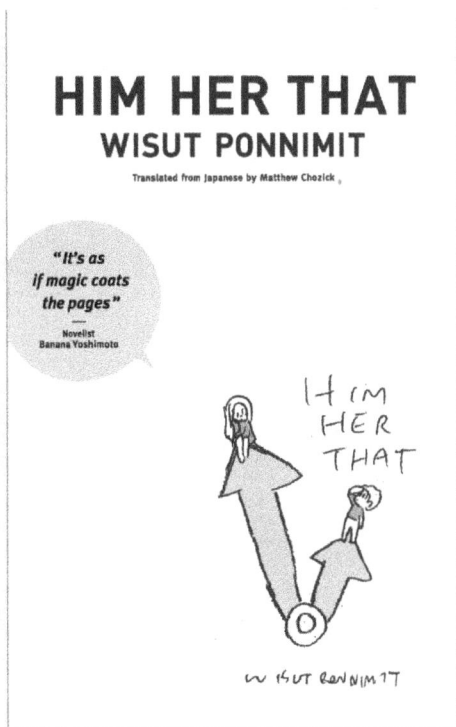

**QUIT
YOUR
BAND**

Musical Notes From the
Japanese Underground
IAN F. MARTIN

"A gateway, a gateway drug even"
—*The Quietus*

www.ingramcontent.com/pod-product-compliance
Lightning Source LLC
Chambersburg PA
CBHW080547270326
41929CB00019B/3220